DECODING CHINESE BILATERAL INVESTMENT TREATIES

This is a major work investigating China's bilateral investment treaties (BITs) regime through various approaches, including textual analysis, case study, comparative study and empirical study. This book tries to unveil some of the puzzles in Chinese BITs. The general consensus is that the evolution of China's BIT regime has its underlying logic, which follows an investment liberalization trend and fits China's changing role from a key capital-importing state to a major capital-exporting state. A similar trend is evident in Chinese BIT-making and BIT policy. This book investigates these theoretical assumptions and looks into some of the loopholes in Chinese BITs.

Shen Wei is KoGuan Distinguished Professor of Law at Shanghai Jiao Tong University Law School, Global Professor of Law at NYU School of Law and L. Bates Lea Professor of Law at Michigan Law School. Professor Shen is an associate member of the International Academy of Comparative Law and sits on various international panels as an advisor. He is an arbitrator for major arbitration centers such as the London Court of International Arbitration, Hong Kong International Arbitration Centre and Singapore International Arbitration Centre. He has been a visiting professor at more than ten law schools in Europe, the USA and Asia. Besides editorial duties for various international journals, he has written and edited over 10 books and published more than 200 articles in both English and Chinese journals.

Decoding Chinese Bilateral Investment Treaties

SHEN WEI
Shanghai Jiao Tong University

CAMBRIDGE
UNIVERSITY PRESS

CAMBRIDGE
UNIVERSITY PRESS

University Printing House, Cambridge CB2 8BS, United Kingdom

One Liberty Plaza, 20th Floor, New York, NY 10006, USA

477 Williamstown Road, Port Melbourne, VIC 3207, Australia

314–321, 3rd Floor, Plot 3, Splendor Forum, Jasola District Centre, New Delhi – 110025, India

103 Penang Road, #05–06/07, Visioncrest Commercial, Singapore 238467

Cambridge University Press is part of the University of Cambridge.

It furthers the University's mission by disseminating knowledge in the pursuit of education, learning, and research at the highest international levels of excellence.

www.cambridge.org
Information on this title: www.cambridge.org/9781108490986
DOI: 10.1017/9781108867146

First published 2021

A catalogue record for this publication is available from the British Library.

Library of Congress Cataloging-in-Publication Data
NAMES: Shen, Wei, 1972– author.
TITLE: Decoding Chinese bilateral investment treaties / Wei Shen, Shanghai Jiao Tong University, China.
DESCRIPTION: New York : Cambridge University Press, 2021. | Includes bibliographical references and index.
IDENTIFIERS: LCCN 2021009245 (print) | LCCN 2021009246 (ebook) | ISBN 9781108490986 (hardback) | ISBN 9781108792059 (paperback) | ISBN 9781108867146 (ebook)
SUBJECTS: LCSH: China – Foreign relations – Treaties. | Investments, Foreign – Law and legislation – China. | Foreign trade regulation – China. | China – Commercial treaties. | International and municipal law – China. | Treaties. | BISAC: LAW / International | LAW / International
CLASSIFICATION: LCC KNQ3202 .S54 2021 (print) | LCC KNQ3202 (ebook) | DDC 346.51/092–dc23
LC record available at https://lccn.loc.gov/2021009245
LC ebook record available at https://lccn.loc.gov/2021009246

ISBN 978-1-108-49098-6 Hardback

In loving memory of my mother Qian Meifang
and
In great honor of my father Shen Guanqun

Contents

Figures

Tables

Acknowledgments

This book is the result of several years of thinking, writing and research.

Throughout the course of writing this book, I greatly benefited from many fruitful discussions and exchanges about various topics and issues with – in alphabetical order – John Armour, Douglas W. Arner, Emilios Avgouleas, Robert P. Bartlett III, Omri Ben-shahar, Sir William Blair, Ross P. Buckley, Congyan Cai, Yun-chien Chang, Julien Chaisse, Lei Chen, Li Chen, Weitseng Chen, Manjiao Chi, Iris H. Y. Chiu, Donald Clarke, Jacques deLisle, David Donald, Ming Du, Eílis Ferran, Hualing Fu, Tom Ginsburg, Say Goo, Andrew Gorwin, Mitu Gulati, Li Guo, Paul H. Haagen, M. Todd Henderson, Liyang Hou, Nicholas C. Howson, Robin Hui Huang, Gloria Xin Jin, Qingjiang Kong, Rainer Kulms, Saul Levmore, Yuwen Li, Feng Lin, Ulla Liukkunen, Dora Neo, Matti Nojonen, Michael Palmer, Eric Posner, Adam Prichard, Tong Qi, Albert Romano, Roberta Romano, Steven J. Saxby, Steven L. Schwarcz, Wenhua Shan, Carrie Shu Shang, Zen Shishido, Mathias Siems, Thomas Stanton, Robert Chang-hsien Tsai, Dicky Tsang, Frank Upham, Matthias Vanhullebusch, Heng Wang, Jiangyu Wang, Casey Watters, Chao Xi, Qingkun Xu, Dali Yang, Simon Young, Kenny Yu, Tao Yu, Sheng Zhang, Wei Zhang, Yun Zhao.

I also want to thank my students taking my courses of international economic law, international financial law, international investment law and international commercial arbitration. They inspire me to think about some issues deeper and further.

I warmly thank all the people at Cambridge University Press including Joe Ng and Gemma Smith who have been supportive of this book from the very beginning and Lori Heaford for her professional editing input. Several autonomous reviewers gave very constructive comments on the book proposal, which helped enhance my thinking on various issues involved in the volume. Research assistance made by Clara Lewis, Shuo Feng, Shuping Li and Kuangran Li are also highly appreciated.

Above all, I am most grateful to my parents for their unconditional support and love throughout my life. My lovely daughter Yixi brings great joy to me. My wife Jin Xin supports my efforts and time on writing and research though she may not support all of my decisions. This book is dedicated to them.

Abbreviations

AIIB	Asian Infrastructure Investment Bank
ASEAN	Association of South East Asian Nations
AUD	Australian dollar
BIT	bilateral investment treaty
BLEU	Belgium–Luxembourg Economic Union
BRI	Belt and Road Initiative
BRICS	Brazil, Russia, India, China and South Africa
BUCG	Beijing Urban Construction Group
CAI	EU-China Comprehensive Agreement on Investment
CAMA	Civil Aviation and Meteorology Authority, Yemen
CCP	Chinese Communist Party
CEPA	closer economic partnership arrangement
CETA	EU–Canada Comprehensive Economic Trade Agreement
CFIUS	Committee on Foreign Investment in the United States
ChAFTA	China–Australia Free Trade Agreement
CIFA	cooperation and investment facilitation agreement
CJV	contractual joint venture (or cooperative joint venture)
CKJ TIT	China–Korea–Japan Trilateral Investment Treaty
CPEC	China–Pakistan Economic Corridor
CPI	Corruption Perceptions Index
CPTPP	Comprehensive and Progressive Trans-Pacific Partnership
DBI	Doing Business Index
DCF	discounted cash flow
DOB	denial of benefits
EFI	Economic Freedom Index
EJV	equity joint venture
EU	European Union
FDI	foreign direct investment
FDII	FDI inward flow
FDIO	FDI outward flow
FDISM	foreign direct investment screening mechanism
FET	fair and equitable treatment
FIE	foreign-invested enterprise
FIL	foreign investment law

fintech	financial technology
FIRRMA	Foreign Investment Risk Review Modernization Act
FTA	free trade agreement
FTZ	free trade zone
G20	Group of Twenty
GATS	General Agreement on Trade in Services
GATT	General Agreement on Tariffs and Trade
GDP	gross domestic product
GE	government effectiveness
ICJ	International Court of Justice
ICS	investment court system
ICSID	International Centre for Settlement of Investment Disputes
IDSM	investment dispute settlement mechanism
IIA	international investment agreement
IIL	international investment law
IMF	International Monetary Fund
IP	intellectual property
IPR	intellectual property rights
IPRI	International Property Rights Index
ISA	investor–state arbitration
ISAT	investor–state arbitration tribunal
ISDS	investor–state dispute settlement
ITA	investment treaty arbitration
JHSF	Ji'nan Hela Schwarz Food Co., Ltd.
KORUS FTA	Republic of Korea–US FTA
LIBOR	London Inter-Bank Offered Rate
MFN	most-favored-nation
MIC	multilateral investment court
MOFCOM	Chinese Ministry of Commerce
MTF	"Moving Treaty Frontier" rule
NAFTA	North American Free Trade Agreement
NGO	nongovernmental organization
NT	national treatment
NVs	notes verbales
OBOR	One Belt One Road Initiative
OECD	Organisation for Economic Co-operation and Development
PCA	Permanent Court of Arbitration
PCIJ	Permanent Court of International Justice
PRC	People's Republic of China, or China, for the purpose of this book, excluding the Special Administrative Region of Hong Kong, the Special Administrative Region of Macau and the territory of Taiwan
PRP	personal remittances: payments
PRR	personal remittances: receipts
PRS	Political Risk Services International Country Risk Guide
RCEP	Regional Comprehensive Economic Partnership
renminbi	the lawful currency of China (RMB or yuan)
REIO	regional economic integration organization

S&D	special and differentiated
SGCA	Singapore's Court of Appeal
SOE	state-owned enterprise
SUNAT	Administramos los tributos del Gobierno Nacional Peruano, Peru
TIP	treaty with investment provisions
TIPP	EU–US Transatlantic Trade and Investment Partnership
TIT	trilateral investment treaty
TPP	Trans-Pacific Partnership, now CPTPP
TRIM	WTO Agreement on Trade-Related Investment Measure
TTIP	Transatlantic Trade and Investment Partnership
UAE	United Arab Emirates
UK	United Kingdom
UNCITRAL	United Nations Commission on International Trade and Law
UNCTAD	United Nations Conference on Trade and Development
US	United States
USD	US dollar, the lawful currency of the United States of America
USMCA	United State–Mexico–Canada Agreement
VCLT	Vienna Convention on the Law of Treaties
WFOE	wholly foreign-owned enterprise
WGI	World Bank's Worldwide Governance Indicators
WGIRL	Worldwide Governance Indicators: Rule of Law
WJPRLI	World Justice Program's Rule of Law Index
WTO	World Trade Organization

1

Current Landscape and Puzzling Issues

This chapter aims to (i) offer a literature review of Chinese investment treaties, mainly bilateral investment treaties (BITs), free trade agreements (FTAs) and other investment agreements that China has signed with other countries or regional organizations; (ii) outline the key themes of this book by listing four interconnected puzzling but underinvestigated issues that this book tries to answer; and (iii) roll out the structure of this book by introducing the key content of each chapter.

1.1 CHINESE BIT LAW SCHOLARSHIP: IN A NUTSHELL

China is the largest emerging market perceived by foreign investors as the sought-after place with great potentialities and attractiveness. In spite of China's economic slowdown in recent years, China has recorded a consistent surge in foreign direct investment inflows (FDII).[1] Some scholars attribute this surge in FDII to the international mode which China chooses to follow in the field of international investment.[2] China's BIT regime is observed with a considerable degree of curiosity, and even suspicion. There has been a large amount of literature touching on China's BIT regime.

This section is devoted to a brief literature review, focusing on research topics explored and methodologies adopted in the field. While international investment law (IIL) has emerged as a complex terrain, a pluralistic set of research themes and methodological tools have been used to study its ongoing development. These tools include comparative study, case law approach (relating to a single body of case law involving investment arbitration cases), historical study,[3] doctrinal study, economic analysis (not only of IIL but also of compensation or evaluation in arbitration cases)[4] and empirical study.

[1] Ajay Sharma, "A Comparative Analysis of the Chinese and Indian FDI Regimes" (2015) 15(1) *Chicago-Kent Journal of International and Comparative Law* 1–31.

[2] Marcia Don Harpaz, "China's Coherence in International Economic Governance" (2016) 21 *Journal of Chinese Political Science* 123–147.

[3] See generally Stephan W. Schill, Christian J. Tams and Rainer Hofmann, *International Investment Law and History* (Edward Elgar 2018).

[4] See generally Marion Jansen, Joost Pauwelyn and Theresa Carpenter, *The Use of Economics in International Trade and Investment Disputes* (Cambridge University Press 2017).

The comparative approach is often undertaken by investment arbitration tribunals[5] to achieve the purpose of "judicial borrowing."[6] Comparative study is a common approach to investigating the uniqueness of the Chinese FDI regime and BIT law. Comparison is made using BITs made by other countries. Usually, two dimensions are approached. One is vertical comparison – comparing new and old BITs made by China to see the evolutionary pattern or trend. The other is horizontal comparison – comparing Chinese BITs with other countries'. For instance, the China–Canada BIT 2012 is selected for comparison to provide a contemporary context for the assessment of the nature, the stages of development and the general state of the China–Africa BIT 1997 regime.[7]

Comparative study can also contextualize BITs in a law and development paradigm. IIL relating to BITs is a legal institution promoting not only economic growth but also the host state's rule of law. While China is compared with other emerging economies such as India, China's consistent surge in FDII is often attributed to its national investment policy-making, though China's marked legal reforms and lack of rule of law are often spotted as being the key deficiencies.[8] Comparative study also shows a sharp contrast between China and Brazil in their BIT strategies even though these two are the emerging markets most sought-after by foreign investors in Asia and South America.[9]

China is also compared with the USA, although on first glance they look like the two extremes of the spectrum: China is the largest host and home country among the emerging states while the USA is the largest host and home developed state. The comparative study indicates the similarity they share in policy-making. As both try to maintain regulatory space, to pursue their own legitimate public policy objectives as a host state and to offer better protections to their outbound investors, there can be a convergence between the two in terms of the objectives of their BITs. The BIT the two countries are negotiating, if reached, could be a template for future investment agreements.[10]

Comparative study serves various purposes. One objective of comparative study is to understand China's BIT-making. For instance, it is appreciated that the BIT between the USA and China is destined to be the most difficult one in history. But Canada managed to enter into a BIT with China, and this BIT may serve, at least in part, as a model for a US BIT with China, for example, to have a pre-establishment national treatment clause.[11]

China is making its own, albeit modest, modifications to the model BITs of the USA and Canada, in which some critical provisions regarding dispute settlement, particularly the

5 Farouk El-Hosseny, *Civil Society in Investment Treaty Arbitration: Status and Prospects* (Brill Nijhoff 2019) 22.

6 Vid Prislan, "Non-investment Obligations in Investment Treaty Arbitration: Towards a Greater Role for States?" in Freya Baetens (ed.), *Investment Law within International Law: Integrationist Perspectives* (Cambridge University Press 2016) 450–451.

7 Won Kidane, "China's Bilateral Investment Treaties with African States in Comparative Context" (2016) 49(1) Cornell International Law Journal 141, 142.

8 Ajay Sharma, *supra* note 1.

9 Dan Wei, "Bilateral Investment Treaties: An Empirical Analysis of the Practices of Brazil and China" (2010) 33(3) *European Journal of Law and Economics* 663–690.

10 Karl P. Sauvant and Huiping Chen, "A China-US Bilateral Investment Treaty: A Template for a Multilateral Framework for Investment?" (2013) 5(1) *Transnational Corporations Review* 1–3.

11 David A. Gantz, "Challenges for the United States in Negotiating a BIT with China: Reconciling Reciprocal Investment Protection with Policy Concerns" (2014) 31(2) *Arizona Journal of International & Comparative Law* 204–250. However, surprisingly, the China–Canada BIT almost imposes no pre-establishment obligations on either party. That means that the China–Canada BIT applies only post-establishment obligations to either party. Matthew Kronby, "Canada-China Investment Treaty: Evidence Doesn't Support Doomsayers" *The Globe and Mail*, October 26, 2012, www.theglobeandmail.com/opinion/canada-china-investment-treaty-evidence-doesnt-support-doomsayers/article4665002/ (accessed September 9, 2020).

abandonment of rights to "consent case by case," to "exhaust local remedies," and to "apply the host country's laws," and the right to invoke the "exception for State essential security," not only deviate from the authorization granted to host states by the relevant international conventions but also harm China's national interests.[12] Therefore, some scholars support the idea that China should insist on protecting its rights as authorized by the international conventions[13] and embracing disciplines commonly found elsewhere[14] throughout the process of negotiating and drafting BITs amid US or Canadian practices that are not widely accepted.[15] Some Chinese scholars claim that protecting the host state's interests could serve as a model for the new international economic order.[16]

In its BIT-making, China is not applying (or copying) Western models mechanically.[17] China is adapting these models in light of different treaty partners. During the negotiation, it is necessary to promote mutual understanding.[18] For example, when Japan joins in negotiating these agreements, it will want to secure nondiscriminatory investment liberation including prohibiting various performance requirements. However, China holds a cautious (or conservative) attitude toward investment liberalization such as national treatment (NT) "as it may crimp industrial policy."[19] More specifically, when negotiating BITs with developed countries, such as the USA, China will take into account the following issues: special and differentiated (S&D) treatment, conduct of investors, and sustainable development.[20] Negotiating a BIT with China presents distinct challenges due to the radical differences that exist between these countries' and China's legal frameworks, their differing values, levels of development, and economy structures.[21]

BIT negotiation situations will be much different between China and developing countries. More details can be analyzed, "taking into account various aspects ranging from environmental concerns to human rights aspects, labor issues, and economic development."[22] What's more, some scholars hold that it is necessary to take into consideration "shifts in Chinese Communist Party (CCP) leadership and the party's perception of what is required to guarantee its stability and continued dominance."[23]

12 An Chen, "Should the Four 'Great Safeguards' in Sino-foreign BITs Be Hastily Dismantled? Comments on Critical Provisions Concerning Dispute Settlement in Model US and Canadian BITs" (2006) 7(6) *Journal of World Investment & Trade* 899, 907.

13 Ibid.

14 Tyler Cohen and David Schneiderman, "The Political Economy of Chinese Bilateral Investment Treaty Policy" (2017) 5(1) *Chinese Journal of Comparative Law* 110–128.

15 Tingliang Wang, "Western Misperceptions and China's Approach to International Investment Law" (2019) 17(1) *Santa Clara Journal of International Law* 1.

16 An Chen, *supra* note 12.

17 This idea is also demonstrated in Xiuli Han, "The China–South Africa Bilateral Investment Treaty: National Rule of Law versus International Rule of Law" (2017) 24(3) *South African Journal of International Affairs* 269–290, where the author holds that China's treaty partner should also take differential policies toward China, considering the future of China.

18 Wei Yin, "Challenges, Issues in China-EU Investment Agreement and the Implication on China's Domestic Reform" (2018) 26(2) *Asia Pacific Law Review* 170–202.

19 Shintaro Hamanaka, "China-Japan-Korea Trilateral Investment Treaty: Implications for Future Investment Negotiations in Asia" in Julien Chaisse, Tomoko Ishikawa and Sufian Jusoh (eds.), *Asia's Changing International Investment Regime: Sustainability, Regionalization, and Arbitration* (Springer 2017) 121–139.

20 Congyan Cai, "China-US BIT Negotiations and the Future of Investment Treaty Regime: A Grand Bilateral Bargain with Multilateral Implications" (2009) 12(2) *Journal of International Economic Law* 457–506.

21 David Hallinan, "The EU-China Bilateral Investment Treaty: A Challenging First Test of the EU's Evolving BIT Model" (2016) 5(1–2) *China-EU Law Journal* 31–53.

22 Catherine Elkemann and Oliver C. Ruppel, "Chinese Foreign Direct Investment into Africa in the Context of BRICS and Sino-African Bilateral Investment Treaties" (2015) 13(4) *Richmond Journal of Global Law & Business* 593–622.

23 Cohen and Schneiderman, *supra* note 14.

The comparative study shows China's dichotomic BIT-making strategy, which makes its BIT laws and practices seem confusing and inconsistent to outsiders. The solution is to make concerted efforts to incorporate higher standards into its BITs and domestic laws.[24]

Country or region study is another branch of study. A focus has been placed on Africa, which is the primary destination of China's outbound investment. In the China–Africa context, apart from FDI, the underlying concerns in relation to BITs include environmental protection, human rights, labor issues and social development. Some other research confirms China's willingness to secure a more favorable environment for Chinese investment by including in its ChAFTA (China–Australia Free Trade Agreement; a memorandum of understanding on an investment facilitation arrangement) related mobility provisions for Chinese workers and an easier threshold (quadrupled from AUD 0.248 billion to AUD 1.078 billion) for non-state-owned-enterprise (non-SOE) investment in Australia.[25] But other research affirms China's loose intention to uphold environmental standards. Its recent FTAs such as the China–Korea FTA 2015 and the China–Korea–Japan Trilateral Investment Treaty (CKJ TIT) 2012 include language imposing obligation on the parties "not [to] waive or otherwise derogate from such environmental measures as an encouragement for the establishment, acquisition or expansion of investments in its territory." Although such language can be interpreted as improving on its previous practice, the improvement is more limited and weaker than the US model BIT.[26] Other purposes such as welfare, development, prosperity[27] or environmental protection[28] are identified in newer BITs (either in treaty preambles or in instrumental terms). In a broader context, the approach with respect to BITs or FTAs relating to environmental protection is part of efforts to promote sustainable development.[29] The right to development, insisted on by a large number of developing countries, covers and relates to the concept of sustainable development in the global economy.[30] In addition, scientific and technological innovation is used as an important explanatory variable in China's investment law and policy. The China–Israel investment relationship is an example of investment diplomacy shaped and dominated by innovation on the bilateral track.[31] China and Israel have a Financial Protocol serving the long-term credit needs of local government-supported projects in China with advanced innovation offered by Israeli manufacturers.[32]

24 Manjiao Chi, "The 'Greenization' of Chinese BITs: An Empirical Study of the Environmental Provisions in Chinese Bits and Its Implications for China's Future BIT-Making" (2015) 18(3) *Journal of International Economic Law* 511–542.

25 Heng Wang, "Paradigm Shift in Investment Rules of China's Free Trade Agreements? The Present and Future" August 14, 2018, https://lki.lk/blog/paradigm-shift-in-investment-rules-of-chinas-free-trade-agreements-the-present-and-future/.

26 Jeffrey J. Schott, Euijin Jung and Cathleen Cimino-Isaacs, "An Assessment of the Korea-China Free Trade Agreement" Peterson Institute for International Economics Policy Brief Number PB15-24, December 2015, 12.

27 Andrew D. Mitchell, David Heaton and Caroline Henckels, *Non-discrimination and the Role of Regulatory Purpose in International Trade and Investment Law* (Edward Elgar 2016) 12.

28 China–Germany BIT 2012, Preambles; China–Panama FTA, Preambles. China and Panama started a joint feasibility study to explore the possibility of negotiating a free trade agreement on January 16, 2018 and have conducted five rounds of negotiations for it since June 12, 2018. www.sice.oas.org/TPD/PAN_CHN/PAN_CHN_e.ASP (accessed April 6, 2021).

29 China–Panama FTA, Article 1.03.

30 See generally Isabella D. Bunn, *The Right to Development and International Economic Law: Legal and Moral Dimensions* (Hart 2012).

31 Hadas Peled and Marcia Don Harpaz, "Innovation as a Catalyst in the China-Israel Investment Relationship: The China-Israel BIT (2009) and the Prospective FTA" in Julie Chaisse, *China's International Investment Strategy: Bilateral, Regional, and Global Law and Policy* (Oxford University Press 2019) 142–143.

32 Ibid., 153.

A textual comparative study is a useful primary approach when comparing Chinese BITs with other countries'. For instance, a comparison indicates that the primary provisions in the China–South Africa BIT 1997 differ in many ways from the BITs that South Africa has signed with Western countries. While this shows the necessity of integrating new elements into BITs so as to make them compliant with the development of IIL,[33] it also suggests China's dominant role in negotiating a BIT with an emerging state, a quite different approach from that it takes when dealing with a developed state as a BIT counterparty.

A textual approach is often taken by scholars to analyze Chinese BIT terms and provisions. The seminal and pioneer book on the subject – *Chinese Investment Treaties: Policies and Practices* – applies textual analysis to provide a detailed account of China's approach to foreign investment.[34] For instance, some scholars try to characterize Chinese BITs and group them into three types in investor–state arbitration (ISA) terms – narrow, broad and special – each providing different admissibility requirements on disputes for ISA.[35] A narrow ISA clause appeared in earlier Chinese BITs, allowing only disputes involving the amount of compensation for expropriation to be submitted to ISA. More recent Chinese BITs adopt broad and special ISA clauses allowing a wider range of disputes for ISA. The shift from narrow to broad and special ISA clauses indicates, as scholars claim, China's BIT policy change from cautious to proactive.

Dispute settlement is the core of BITs, and ISA remains a useful tool for settling investment disputes. China has broadly adopted the investor–state dispute settlement (ISDS) clause in its BITs with trade partners, especially with the One Belt One Road Initiative (OBOR or BRI) countries and regions.[36] It is suggested that China should converge its ISDS clauses. "A more predictable and consistent rule-setting for ISA practice, would contribute to, and be a part of, the development of China's inbound and outbound investment activities under the 'Belt and Road' Initiative."[37]

Scholars have not reached consensus on the application of ISA clauses. The notion of territory is not clearly defined in China's international investment agreement (IIAs), causing doubts with respect to the application of ISA clauses. This problem remains unsolved up to now.[38] Besides, the application of ISA in China may also be hindered by "one country, two systems" because it is argued that BITs could not be directly applied to Hong Kong or Macau. Even though the tribunal in *Tza Yap Shum* v. *Republic of Peru* held that it has jurisdiction on this case, some scholars criticize that this case was wrongly judged and, thus, the decision is "incorrect, unreasonable, and unacceptable."[39] Another unsettled puzzle regarding ISA is whether ISA has jurisdiction on cases relating to SOEs, as ISA is "designed to protect private

33 Xiuli Han, *supra* note 17.

34 Norah Gallagher and Wenhua Shan, *Chinese Investment Treaties: Policies and Practice* (Oxford University Press 2009).

35 Manjiao Chi and Xi Wang, "The Evolution of ISA Clauses in Chinese IIAs and Its Practical Implications: The Admissibility of Disputes for Investor-State Arbitration" (2015) 16(5–6) *Journal of World Investment & Trade* 869–898.

36 Shu Zhang, "Developing China's Investor-State Arbitration Clause Discussions in the Context of the 'Belt and Road' Initiative" in Wenhua Shan, Kimmo Nuotio and Kangle Zhang (eds.), *Normative Readings of the Belt and Road Initiative* (Springer 2018) 147–181. China's "proactive" attitude toward ISAs is illustrated in detail in Manjiao Chi and Xi Wang, *supra* note 35.

37 Shu Zhang, *supra* note 36. The idea of "unification" in different BITs is also supported in Wenlong Zhu, "The National Treatment Clause in Chinese Bilateral Investment Treaties" (2014) 4 *WTO & China* 72, where the author believes that unification will "definitely affects the harmonization and stabilization of domestic legislation."

38 Odysseas G. Repousis, "On Territoriality and International Investment Law: Applying China's Investment Treaties to Hong Kong and Macao" (2015) 37(1) *Michigan Journal of International Law* 113–190.

39 An Chen, "Queries to the Recent ICSID Decision on Jurisdiction *Upon the Case of Tza Yap Shum v. Republic of Peru*: Should China-Peru BIT 1994 Be Applied to Hong Kong SAR under the 'One Country Two Systems' Policy?" (2009) 10 *Journal of World Investment and Trade* 829–864.

investment only." Although there are already two cases involving SOEs, further study on this question is required.[40] Except for ISA, the Multilateral Investment Court (MIC) is put forward by the European Union (EU) as one option for reforming the existing ISDS mechanism and ensuring fair trade and efficient adjudication. In China's view, the MIC should be more reflective of the interests of both developing countries and investors.[41]

Treaty shopping is an effective alternative "by which an investor acquires a convenient nationality in order to enjoy preferable investment protection."[42] The 2012 Cross-Strait Bilateral Investment Protection and Promotion Agreement fails to adopt ISA clauses. Its most-favored-nation (MFN) clause explicitly excludes reference to dispute settlement provisions.[43] Case law demonstrates that the success of treaty shopping depends largely on the standards determining the nationality of an investor, control or ownership by a third person over the investor or investment resulting in denial of benefits, and the time of dispute that has transpired. For example, Taiwanese investors, in order to enjoy the substantive and procedural protections offered by Chinese BITs, may rely on treaty shopping tactics. The proper home state they may shop for depends on a large number of factors including the signatory to the new-generation Chinese BITs as well as Taiwanese IIAs, the economic status of the candidate state, the IIA's standard defining corporate investors, its denial of benefits (DOB) clause, the ISDS clause and the scope of consent to arbitration.[44]

Apart from China's treaty behavior in forming BITs, there are several other issues in the field of Chinese BITs.

Intellectual property rights (IPR) protection is one of the most heatedly debated topics of the past several years given the ongoing US–China trade confrontation. It is undisputed and inevitable that China ought to protect free trade-related IPR, considering that China is endeavoring to transform its economy from a labor-intensive one to an innovation-driven one and to follow the global trend of incorporating higher standards of intellectual property enforcement.[45]

The textual approach is also applied to the study of specific clauses such as IPR provisions in China's FTAs with the purpose of exploring China's position on IPR standards. Despite China's firm stance against the TRIPS-plus standards for IP enforcement, the IP clauses in Chinese FTAs are quite flexible.[46] This flexibility matches China's stage of economic development, innovation capacity and level of IP enforcement. A more flexible stance embracing higher IP standards and stronger IP enforcement serves China's strategy of transforming its economy to an innovation-based one. This flexibility can also be explained as reflecting China's effective approach to engaging in norm-setting activities, its nonreciprocity of BIT terms[47] and its strategic partnership for IP in the region.[48]

40 Anran Zhang, "Letter to the Journal: The Standing of Chinese State-Owned Enterprises in Investor-State Arbitration: The First Two Cases" (2018) 17 *Chinese Journal of International Law* 1147–1153.

41 Ning Hongling and Qi Tong, "A Chinese Perspective on the Investment Court System in the Context of Negotiating EU-China BIT" (2018) 11 *Tsinghua China Law Review* 91–127.

42 Chi-Chung Kao, "Alternative Access to Investor-State Arbitration for Taiwanese Corporate Investors against China via Treaty Shopping" (2015) 23(2) *Asia Pacific Law Review* 121–152.

43 Ibid.

44 Ibid.

45 Guangliang Zhang, "China's Stance on Free Trade-Related Intellectual Property: A View in the Context of the China-Japan-Korea FTA Negotiations" (2016) 24(1) *Asia Pacific Law Review* 36–59.

46 Ibid.

47 Gus Van Harten, "The Canada-China FIPPA: Its Uniqueness and Non-reciprocity" (2014) 51 *Canadian Yearbook of International Law* 3055.

48 Peter K. Yu, "The Incremental Development of the ASEAN-China Strategic Partnership for Intellectual Property" in Christoph Antons and Michael Blakeney (eds.), *Intellectual Property in Southeast Asia* (Edward Elgar 2020).

Human rights present another narrative in which China's outbound FDI is scrutinized. The potential clash between the IIL regime and the human rights regime, a stability vs. flexibility dilemma or an elephant in the room,[49] is inherently in existence in international law.[50] There is a compelling linkage between international human rights law and IIL[51] as states are obliged to adopt regulations aimed at improving social standards and conditions of living for people while being confronted with investment disputes in which investors seek to challenge regulatory interferences through such regulations. The general consensus is that China-led FDI undermines human rights in host states amid a counterargument advocating a mutually affirming relationship between FDI and human rights, meaning that FDI improves the diffusion of human rights norms and correlates with the improved rule of law in host states. Due to the lack of legal and nonlegal measures, there is a chance, as argued, that we will witness a pragmatic approach to insulating human rights from violations that may be associated with Chinese FDIs in some African countries such as Kenya.[52]

Labor protection is another issue well worth considering. Chinese FTAs are criticized for lack of labor protection terms.[53] Currently, the Asia-Pacific region is one of the largest markets in the world, and China has "assumed the mantle of world leader on globalism and global trade, particularly in Asia." It is critical to examine the provisions of Chinese FTAs in the context of Asia-Pacific relating to labor rights.[54] China has just issued a new Social Security Insurance Law. As to the deficiencies in its application and enforcement, the Law adopts broad language, leaving space on specific regulations for local government detail and allowing differences at regional and local levels. Therefore, even though many BITs and FTAs have assumed the role of promoting labor protection standards at the international level, the implementation of these standards largely relies on local laws.[55]

Environment protection should not be ignored given the clash between the host state government's duty to protect the environment and public health and well-being, and its commitment to foreign investments. It is a sideline area with great importance for striking a fine balance between the host state's right to regulate and foreign investor protection.[56] The key to "greenizing" Chinese BITs "depends on how they are applied and how the two seemingly conflicting purposes of BITs, i.e. investment protection and environmental protection, are reconciled in international investment arbitration."[57]

A textual approach is applied to characterize the evolution of Chinese BITs, which are divided into several generations. Western scholars usually prefer to divide Chinese BITs into two generations – conservative and liberal – while Chinese scholars may divide them into three – a first, conservation generation; a second, liberal one; and the third adopting a more

49 Anna de Luca and Angelica Bonfanti, "Investment and Human Rights: Is There an Elephant in the Room?" Columbia FDI Perspectives No. 282, July 23, 2020, http://ccsi.columbia.edu/files/2018/10/No-282-de-Luca-and-Bonfanti-FINAl.pdf (accessed September 18, 2020).

50 See generally Lone Wandahl Mouyal, *International Investment Law and the Right to Regulate* (Routledge 2016).

51 Farouk El-Hosseny, *Civil Society in Investment Treaty Arbitration: Status and Prospects* (Brill Nijhoff 2019) 21.

52 Rosemary Mwanza, "Chinese Foreign Direct Investment and Human Rights in Kenya: A Mutually Affirming Relationship" (2016) 2 *Strathmore Law Journal* 133.

53 Ronald C. Brown, "A New Leader in Asian Free Trade Agreements: Chinese Style Global Trade: New Rules, No Labor Protections" (2017) 35(1) *UCLA Pacific Basin Law Journal* 1–32.

54 Ibid.

55 Ronald C. Brown, "China-U.S. Implementation of ILO Standards by BITs and Pieces (FTAs)" in Ulla Liukkunen and Yifeng Chen (eds.), *Fundamental Labour Rights in China – Legal Implementation and Cultural Logic* (Springer 2016) 169–201.

56 See generally Flavia Marisi, *Environmental Interests in Investment Arbitration: Challenges and Directions* (Wolters Kluwer 2020).

57 Manjiao Chi, *supra* note 24.

balanced approach.[58] This not only draws a larger picture for readers but also indicates the development status of China's BIT law.

An empirical approach to the study of Chinese BITs is rarely used regardless of statistical or quantitative research. Although it is widely claimed that China's success in attracting FDI is partially due to China's efforts to enter into BITs and other international investment instruments,[59] there is no empirical study to support this orthodox proposition. In some research, an empirical approach is applied to the environmental protection clauses incorporated in all 104 Chinese BITs in force. The conclusion is that only a limited number of Chinese BITs contain environmental protection clauses and the generational and regional distribution of such clauses is imbalanced. This suggests a need to "greenize" Chinese BITs.[60]

China is not satisfied with only negotiating and reaching BITs. Through an empirical study of China's BITs and FTAs (i.e., those with investment chapters), China has adopted a "from BIT to FTA" approach, which is a sensible strategy for China given that it wants to enhance its engagement with global trade governance. The pace of FTA-making has been faster in recent years.[61] In general, those BITs and FTAs are helping to promote property rights protection and rule of law in China[62] and improve China's global trade governance.[63] Nor is China content to be just a rule-follower. In the long term, China is likely to become a rule-maker "evolv[ing] from selective adaption to selective innovation."[64]

Policy analysis occupies quite a lot of scholarly effort, attempting to place the current role of investment treaties in China's foreign economic policy.[65] Most academic attention has been paid to China's adoption of a new model of BIT in the past decade, and, more importantly, this new model embraces widely adopted principles and aligns with Western standards, paving the way toward a universal model. From the policy perspective, this movement not only enhances neoliberal norms in IIL but also transforms Chinese domestic policy. A third way of interpreting China's changing BIT policy is to view it as a new product of complex and interacting influences reflected in China's internal debates.[66] The evolution of China's BIT policy is diagnosed as being closely interconnected with policy shifts in the CCP, with a view to maximizing its political benefits. As a result, the pace of BIT negotiations and the scope of the neoliberal norms China has taken in these negotiations largely depend on the CCP's perceptions of what grounds its role in China's political and economic life. This is a typical perspective of the New Haven School of international law.[67] A New Haven reading, as with a political science view, of China's BIT law and practice by and large links the underlying logics to China's political system, geopolitical objectives and ruling party's priority.

58 Tingliang Wang, *supra* note 15.
59 See generally Gallagher and Shan, *supra* note 34.
60 Manjiao Chi, *supra* note 24.
61 Manjiao Chi, "The China-EU BIT as a Stepping Stone towards a China-EU FTA: A Policy Analysis" in Marc Bungenburg et al. (eds.), *European Yearbook of International Economic Law* (Springer 2017) 475.
62 Kate Hadley, "Do China's BITs Matter? Assessing the Effect of China's Investment Agreements on Foreign Direct Investment Flows, Investors Rights, and the Rule of Law" (2013) 45(1) *Georgetown Journal of International Law* 255–321.
63 Chi, *supra* note 61.
64 Heng Wang, "The RCEP and Its Investment Rules: Learning from Past Chinese FTAs" (2017) 3(2) *Chinese Journal of Global Governance* 160–181.
65 See generally Gallagher and Weihua Shan, *supra* note 34.
66 Cohen and Schneiderman, *supra* note 14.
67 Guiguo Wang, "International Investment Law: An Appraisal from the Perspective of the New Haven School of International Law" (2016) 18(1) *Asia Pacific Law Review* 19–44.

Policy study shows the inadequacy of China's BIT regime which, however, is proportionate to the increased pace and volume of Chinese outbound investment.[68] It has been argued, through comparing China's profile vis-à-vis three dimensions of global economic order – trade, investment and development aid – that China has neither sought nor brought about significant changes to IIL. China's engagement with global economic governance is an interactive relationship with the liberal international economic order, a long process of external socialization. This may also explain why Chinese BITs tend to give priority to investor protection.[69]

Since the start of the new millennium, due to the "go globally" strategy and the Belt and Road Initiative (BRI), China has strongly encouraged outbound investment.[70] However, a mere increase in numbers does not mean that other countries also hold a friendly attitude toward China. Rather, "barriers to and protectionism against Chinese investment have been strengthened."[71] Other scholars contend that future Chinese BITs will turn in the opposite direction and be likely to restrict the rights of investors.

Policy study also has a global dimension – looking at China's role in global investment governance. Inherent flaws in the global architecture are hindering China's role and function. China's interest in engaging with global governance is multi-pronged. An effective and China-friendly IIL system would not only help improve China's regulatory regime so as to attract inbound investment but also ensure better protection of its outbound investment. More fundamentally, China prefers to secure international recognition of its unique identity in terms of institutional characteristics and development strategy, which greatly concerns the USA and other Western countries. A mixture of bilateral, regional and multilateral approaches would be a better strategy to achieve China's geopolitical agenda at bilateral, regional and multilateral levels.[72]

North–South is a valid paradigm for contextualizing and theorizing China's BIT law and practice. It is a useful context within which to appreciate the South–South BITs and the much-touched-on new geography of investment. However, other than the discernible differences among the model BITs used by Western countries and the similarity of recalibrating policy space available to states in BITs,[73] the South–South BITs have not indicated or formed emerging norms[74] or patterns. However, the South–South BITs may show some pragmatic value in executing projects in the context of the BRI and the China–Pakistan Economic Corridor (CPEC), and the relevance of IIL in such emerging scenarios.[75] So does the North–South narrative, which also shows some demographical value and suggests that Canada's IPR

68 Huiping Chen, "China's 'One Belt, One Road' Initiative and Its implications for Sino-African Investment Relations" (2016) 8(3) *Journal of Transnational Corporations Review* 178–182.

69 Sauvant and Chen, *supra* note 10.

70 Huiping Chen, *supra* note 68.

71 Fan He and Bijun Wang, "Chinese Interests in the Global Investment Regime" (2014) 7(1) *China Economic Journal* 4–20.

72 Ibid.

73 Andeas Buser, "Recalibrating Policy Space in Bilateral Investment Treaties: Is There a Common B(R)ICS Approach?" in Congyan Cai and Huiping Chen (eds.), *The BRICS in the New International Legal Order on Investment* (Brill 2020) 163–203.

74 Uche Ewelukwa Ofodile, "Africa-China Bilateral Investment Treaties: A Critique" (2013) 35 *Michigan Journal of International Law* 131.

75 Hongdao Qian, Sonia Azam and Hamid Mukhtar, "China Pakistan Economic Corridor: Legal Injunctions and Protection of Chinese Investment in Pakistan under OBOR Initiative" (2018) 6(2) *European Journal Research in Social Sciences* 29–37.

protection standards could be a concern to Chinese investors.[76] Although there have been convergences and mutual influences between the West and the East as well as the North and the South, their interests and approaches stand quite differently, requiring a certain degree of desirable coordination between different systems at bilateral, regional and multilateral levels.[77]

Political science is a useful tool or paradigm for comprehending China's BIT law and practice. China is likely to be challenged by others while it is on the rise as a global superpower. There is a struggle going on between China and other incumbent powers, which are taking protectionist measures aimed at Chinese investments that are also on the rise. China's institutional build-up, including the BRI and the Asian Infrastructure Investment Bank, though addressing the legitimacy crisis in global investment governance, has increased backlash and suspicion.[78]

Case study and cultural perspectives are brought into the analysis of Chinese BITs as differences in political, economic and legal systems and cultures are no longer obstacles to FDI; indeed, the economic growth of all countries is closely linked with its inflow.[79]

Above all, traditional global investment strategy no longer fits in the current world, meaning that older BITs lack breadth, efficiency and dynamics. A clear China-specific investment governance strategy has yet to take shape. China can focus on bilateral, regional and multilateral levels, adapting relatively quickly when facing different treaty partners, and thus contributing to the new architecture governing global investment.[80]

1.2 CONCEPTUALIZING CHINESE BIT LAW AND PRACTICE: PUZZLING ISSUES AND THEORETICAL FRAMEWORK

This section lists four pressing questions that this book tries to figure out in relation to Chinese BITs. The answers to these questions may form a foundation on or framework within which to conceptualize, systemize and theorize China's BIT regime. As the book title suggests, the ideal is to decode the genetic elements and characters of China's BIT law and practice. For this reason, the focus of this book is not purely technical, that is, it does not simply look at the application or systemic analysis of particular substantive or procedural standards in BITs, or at Chinese BIT law through case study or jurisprudential analysis. Rather, this book attempts to reveal whatever patterns exist in Chinese BIT law.

China is a unique player in the global investment governance regime. In the BIT circle, there has been a so-called "China disequilibrium." While China is the second largest country in terms of the BITs it has signed, right next to Germany,[81] the investment arbitration cases involving China, as either a respondent state or a claimant investor, are rare. This is a great puzzle given the weak rights protection that China extends to foreign investors and Chinese

[76] Timothy S. McNamara, "The China-Canada BIT, Its Shortcomings, and the Risks for Chinese Investors" (2019) 10 *Beijing Law Review* 287.

[77] Chang-fa Lo, Nigel Li and Tsai-Yu Lin (eds.), *Legal Thoughts between the East and the West in the Multilevel Legal Order – A Liber Amicorum in Honour of Professor Herbert Han-Pao Ma* (Springer 2016).

[78] Dilini Pathirana, "Rising China and Global Investment Governance: An Overview of Prospects and Challenges" (2018) 4(2) *Chinese Journal of Global Governance* 122–153.

[79] Guiguo Wang, *International Investment Law: A Chinese Perspective* (Routledge 2014).

[80] Ibid.

[81] Leon E. Trakman, "China's Regulation of Foreign Direct Investment" in Julien Chaisse, Tomoko Ishikawa and Sufian Jusoh (eds.), *Asia's Changing International Investment Regime: Sustainability, Regionalization and Arbitration* (Springer 2017).

investors' complaints against their host states, most of which are natural-resource-rich but legal-infrastructure-weak countries.

This small number of cases may be a result of the host state's political position and legal culture.[82] Others argue that the small number of ISA cases between Chinese investors and China's trade partners is related to the widespread doubts that exist at the policy-making level. The argument has also been made to justify the rare involvement of China as a respondent in investment arbitration cases by reference to China's unwillingness to take on more responsibilities in world affairs or to participate in the world's judicial institutions.[83]

From developing states' perspective, the ISDS system sits uncomfortably with capital-receiving states as it requires a great deal of concession from the developing states, granting substantive rights to investors and allowing decision-making by arbitral tribunals outside of their territory. Given the quasi-colonial treatment of extraterritoriality that it has experienced, China has systemically guarded itself from the jurisdictional intrusion embedded in the ISDS.[84]

We need to offer a logical answer to solve this puzzle. Some cultural perspectives have been offered to understand the Chinese cultural values in international arbitration. Both legal and cultural factors are influential in shaping the evolution of international arbitration standards.[85]

The second puzzle is the so-called "return of the state" paradigm. Presently, one of the major concerns among states is the balance between the rights protection offered by BITs to foreign investors and the right to regulate that host states need to preserve while hosting and protecting foreign investment. In the past several decades, in negotiating and signing BITs, more states have been willing to sacrifice their sovereignty by offering better rights protection to foreign investors. Similarly, the ISDS system has also indicated a strong tendency to place more emphasis on rights protection toward foreign investors. This sacrifice of sovereignty by host states has contributed to the emergence of the existing IIL regime and ISDS system. Consequently, host states' right to regulate has been compromised while foreign investment and foreign investors are better protected. This can be described as the "leaving of the state" movement.

In more recent years, there has been a clear shift toward the return of the state, meaning that the states care more about their rights to regulate, or police power, and try to strike a new balance with foreign investment protection. For instance, some of the recently signed BITs allow the host state to possess more police power in regulating FDI activities.

India's latest model BIT underpins preservation of regulatory autonomy, with five methods employed to strengthen it. An investment tribunal is required to give due regard to regulatory autonomy in the preamble. The jurisdiction of arbitral tribunals is narrowed by the definition of investment, investor and the scope of the model BIT so that the possibility of review of regulatory actions is reduced. The scope of treatment of standards is also reduced. Fair and equitable treatment (FET), MFN treatment and the umbrella clause have been removed and the scope of the customary standard full protection and security, indirect expropriation

82 Shu Zhang, *supra* note 36.

83 Guiguo Wang, "Chinese Mechanisms for Resolving Investor-State Disputes" (2011) 1(1) *Jindal Journal of International Affairs* 204–233.

84 Won Kidane, "China and India's Differing Investment Treaty and Dispute Settlement Experiences and Implications for Africa" (2017) 49 *Loyola University Chicago Law Journal* 405–477.

85 Joshua Karton, "Beyond the 'Harmonious Confucian': International Commercial Arbitration and the Impact of Chinese Cultural Values" in Chang-fa Lo et al. (eds.), *Legal Thoughts between the East and the West in the Multilevel Legal Order: Liber Amicorum in Honour of Professor Herbert Han-pao Ma* (Springer 2016) 519–542.

and NT has been reduced. Access to arbitration is limited through the need to first exhaust local remedies. Exceptions applying to general and specific circumstances are introduced.[86]

More recent regulatory movements such as the Committee on Foreign Investment in the United States (CFIUS) reform initiated in the USA and the foreign investment screening mechanism established in the EU can also be viewed as part of this new balancing. Along with this paradigm shift is the uncertainty of the future landscape as host states are retreating from the global international investment arena. China's position in this leaving-and-return-of-the-state paradigm has been neither studied nor clearly understood by insiders or outsiders.

The third issue is how China is making use of its BIT regime to improve its domestic rule of law, which is based on several indicators that measure the extent to which foreign investors have confidence in and abide by the rules of Chinese society. The other way to rephrase the question is how are domestic institutions shaping the success of FDI activities or how are BITs impacting on China's local law reform?

Some research is dedicated to examining China's legal framework for foreign investment and relevant international treaties,[87] but probably not vice versa. There is growing recognition that each state owes certain fundamental obligations to its own and foreign citizens as well as to the wider international society. These responsibilities include an obligation to provide a minimum level of legal and rights protection to foreign investors, which is one of the fundamental purposes of the BIT regime. Yet the effort to make these rule of law norms (such as the effectiveness and predictability of the judiciary and the enforceability of contracts) operational and enforceable remains a Herculean challenge.

The general consensus is that China has not improved its rule of law as much as the rest of the world has expected, especially since China joined the World Trade Organization (WTO), which could have been a great opportunity not only for China but also for the world to witness a rising China in terms of its quality in legal infrastructure and internal governance system. As the US administration has indicated in the ongoing trade war against China, China's accession to the WTO has not changed China's way of internal governance in a substantial manner. Consequently, as the USA has claimed, China has failed to comply with its WTO commitments. The puzzle here is how to assess the interaction between China's BIT regime and its internal rule of law.[88] Do Chinese BITs play only a decorative function in sending signals to the international investment community? In other words, we try to understand the interactive relationship between Chinese BITs and domestic rule of law in China.

Needless to say, BIT negotiations are helping to lift China's investor protection standards, through both outside pressures and internal incentives, and giving China's BIT regime the modernity it may want to have in the new era. However, realization of the objectives that higher-level BITs want to achieve largely depends on China's domestic regulatory regime in the field of foreign investment.[89] China's domestic law, for example, is said to make China's compliance with the International Centre for Settlement of Investment Disputes (ICSID) Convention's recognition and enforcement obligations uncertain. This leads to the need for

86 Aniruddha Rajput, "Safeguarding India's Regulatory Autonomy: Analysis of the New Model Bilateral Investment Treaty" (2017) 14(3) *Manchester Journal of International Economic Law* 279–300.

87 Andrew D. Mitchell and Tania Voon, "Series Editor's Preface" in Julien Chaisse (ed.), *China's International Investment Strategy: Bilateral, Regional, and Global Law and Policy* (Oxford University Press 2019).

88 Cohen and Schneiderman, *supra* note 14 (indicating some academic doubt over any correlation between China's BIT law and practice and the liberalizing movement of China's internal law, in particular economic law).

89 Wei Yin, *supra* note 18.

judicial interpretation by China's Supreme People's Court guaranteeing enforcement of an ICSID award within China's legal system.[90]

A related question is – what is the real driving force shaping China's BIT regime? The general consensus is that China's shifting role from a pure capital-importing state to a capital-importing and exporting state[91] is the key force pushing for the liberalization of the Chinese BIT regime.

It is clear that China's BIT negotiations with other trading partners are shaped by competitive externalities, that is, developments in the negotiation of FTAs or BITs between third parties. Competitive pressures may threaten China with the prospect of disadvantages vis-à-vis key competitors in the others' market for investment.[92] China's domestic reforms are also helping to resolve the issue of reciprocity, which the USA tried to solve through unilateral measures while the EU may take a bilateral approach.

One task of the book is to investigate the correlation between China's liberalization of its BIT regime and all the variables in relation to the evolution of BIT norms, especially among counterparties that have been in BIT negotiations with China. Some empirical studies will be conducted in the book to see how the landscape of China's BIT regime has been shaped in the past four decades. This question is also associated with China's treaty behavior when it comes to negotiating and signing BITs. The conventional consensus is that China has not been an inexperienced rule-maker, particularly in the international law arena. In terms of BITs, China has appeared to follow in the footprints of the EU, the USA and other major trading partners. The other perspective that the book is trying to offer is an investigation of China's treaty behavior and the varying terms in Chinese BITs. There has been evidence indicating China's adherence to its own policy when signing BITs rather than following the uniform approach.[93]

To characterize China's BIT program and to predict its evolution are two interconnected tasks that current scholarship is working on. It is said that the Chinese approach to its BITs used to be an Americanized one but that, for the sake of its own and the world's interests, China should adopt a more balanced, responsive and accountable approach, taking into account multiple elements not limited to the investment regime.[94]

The final issue concerns China's stance in the ongoing, systematic and sustainable development-oriented reform of the global IIA regime,[95] including the ISDS mechanism, and its role in the transformation of global investment governance. The ISDS reform has been heatedly debated with the emergence of a number of reform proposals[96] touching on various dimensions and various investment disputes needing to address social, political and economic concerns.[97] The trade-offs of these reforms are hard to measure or quantify, but improvement of the rule of law, the normative contents of which include justice, fairness,

90 Julian Ku, "The Enforcement of ICSID Awards in the People's Republic of China" (2013) 6 *Contemporary Asia Arbitration Journal* 31–48.

91 Shen Wei, "Expropriation in Transition: Evolving Chinese Investment Treaty Practices in Local and Global Contexts" (2015) 28 *Leiden Journal of International Law* 579 (clarifying China's switching stance of being a pure capital importing state to a capital importing and exporting state).

92 Hallinan, *supra* note 21.

93 Marcia Don Harpaz, *supra* note 2 (arguing that, at least in the sphere of international investment, BITs do not bring any significant changes to China); An Chen, *supra* note 12 (arguing against the idea of China going to copy other countries' model BITs).

94 Congyan Cai, *supra* note 20.

95 UNCTAD, UNCTAD's Reform Package: For the International Investment Regime, 2018, https://investmentpolicy.unctad.org/publications/1190/unctad-s-reform-package-for-the-international-investment-regime-2018-edition (accessed March 6, 2021).

96 Ibid., 80–96.

97 Wenhua Shan and Peng Wang, "A Matrix Analytical Framework for Investment Disputes and Their Settlement" (2018) *Foreign Investment Law – ICSID Review* 1–24.

transparency, efficiency and peace, should be used as a benchmark when making institutional choices in light of the different contexts that the states are facing.[98]

The expanding economic clout of the emerging powers is increasing their political influence well beyond their borders. Moreover, power is shifting from established powers to rising countries and nonstate actors (such as foreign investors in IIL), both of which have become more important in IIL and the ISDS system. While the United States remains at the apex of the international system, the global distribution of power – political, economic, demographic, technological and to some degree military – is shifting toward the developing world, driven by the rise of China, India, Brazil and other nations (and the relative decline of Europe).

A shift in power to the global "South" is a driving force reshaping the global investment governance system. When problems are global, solutions require global collective action including engagement across national borders and levels of decision-making. Suspicions over global governance add to the difficulties of effectively mastering the growing number of challenges. The major economies including the EU, the USA, South Africa and Brazil are all making various proposals to reform the existing defective, if not illegitimate, ISDS mechanism. Some of them have materialized their ideals by codifying some of the ideas and proposals into recently signed BITs or FTAs. The EU has been active in making various proposals to improve the existing ISDS system. The ISDS arrangements provided in Chapter 14 of the United States–Mexico–Canada Agreement (USMCA) represent a new but radical shift from those that have been in force for over a quarter of a century under Chapter 11 of the North American Free Trade Agreement (NAFTA). Canada opted out of ISDS under USMCA with the exception of legacy claims and pending NAFTA claims.[99] The USA and Mexico only consented to highly restricted claims being brought to ISDS.[100]

China's position has yet to become crystal clear,[101] even though it has indicated some interest in an appeal process.[102] Its acceptance or rejection of this new model requires in-depth analysis of the coherences and divergences between the EU and China as well as the effect of core features of the investment court system (ICS) model.[103] Some proposals have been made. For instance, mediation, given its advantages in reducing tension and hostility and creating an amicable atmosphere,[104] may offer solutions to ensure continued operation of the involved investment project and an ongoing cooperative relationship between the foreign

[98] Sergio Puig and Gregory Shaffer, "Imperfect Alternatives: Institutional Choice and the Reform of Investment Law" (2018) 112(3) *American Journal of International Law* 361–409.

[99] USMCA Annex 14-C.

[100] USMCA Annex 14-D. But a wide range of claims can be brought with respect to government contracts according to Annex 14-E.

[101] In its statements on the ISDS reform for UNCITRAL, China said: "We are still making in-depth study on those options and our point of departure is that the Investor-State arbitration regime shall be an effective and efficient one striking the proper balance between investor protection and government's right to regulate. This is one of the guiding principles G20 adopted for global investment policy-making this July, and China welcomes and also keeps an open mind on any option that is conducive to the above-mentioned goal." UNCITRAL, 50th Session, "Settlement of Commercial Disputes, Investor-State Dispute Settlement Framework Compilation of Comments: Addendum" July 3–21, 2017, A/CN/0/918/Add.1, 3.

[102] Anthea Roberts, "Incremental, Systemic and Paradigmatic Reform of Investor-State Arbitration" (2018) 113(2) *American Journal of International Law* 410–432; "G20 Guiding Principles for Global Investment Policymaking?" Hongzhou Summit, July 2016, Part III.

[103] Hongling Ning and Tong Qi, *supra* note 41, 93.

[104] Guiguo Wang and He Xiaoli, "Mediation and International Investment: A Chinese Perspective" (2012) 65(1) *Maine Law Review* 216, 235.

investor and the host state. Therefore, mediation can be used as a step in ISDS.[105] Some mandatory conciliation clauses have appeared in BITs. For instance, the Hong Kong–UAE BIT 2019 makes mandatory conciliation the prerequisite to arbitration, which has been viewed as a breakthrough in BIT law and practice. Accordingly, foreign investors may initiate arbitration only if the host state does not make a request for conciliation in the first place. However, this mandatory conciliation is not an entitlement of foreign investors.[106]

The ultimate decision should rest on China's own interests. Nevertheless, China is still silent and has not indicated its position in ISDS reform, while global investment governance – the collective management of common problems at the international level – is at a critical juncture. On the other hand, China is aggressively executing its BRI and many Chinese companies have been actively investing overseas along the Belt and Road. As such, the stance of Chinese BITs on ISDS reform is important not only to the Chinese BIT scheme but also to China's ongoing BIT negotiations with the EU and the USA, which are likely to be the cornerstone of the new international investment governance regime. The growing number of legitimacy-crisis issues on the IIL agenda, and their complexity and uncertainty, are outpacing the ability of the ICSID and BIT networks to cope. A multipolar world is absolutely complicating the prospects for effective global governance over the next several decades. Mounting global challenges and defects need China to deal not only with its internal problems but also with the global governance deficit issues.

In a broader sense, China, as a global investor, is gaining importance in steering global investment governance, manifested by its forming the G20 Guiding Principles for Global Investment Policymaking and its establishment of the Asian Infrastructure Investment Bank. China's rise as a global superpower in general and a global investor in particular is not only influencing global investment governance but also causing increased backlash against it.[107] Theoretically, China's deeper participation may make the existing global investment governance more complicated.

The issue is to define China's role in international investment governance. Is China a rule-follower, a rule-shaker, a rule-maker or a rule-violator? Some scholars give high praise to China, characterizing it as a rule-shaker in the short and medium term and a rule-maker in the long run through so-called selective adaption and selective innovation.[108] Others may even have positioned China in a leader role in the world economy.[109] This is the best guess or observation without empirical evidence.

1.3 ROADMAP OF THE BOOK: ISSUES, TOPICS AND OUTLINE

This book attempts to tackle these four interconnected China-myth issues which constitute a thematic framework within which to conceptualize and theorize Chinese BIT laws and practices.

[105] Chunlei Zhao, "Investor-State Mediation in a China-EU Bilateral Investment Treaty: Talking about Being in the Right Place at the Right Time" (2018) 17(1) *Chinese Journal of International Law* 111–135.

[106] James Claxton, Luke Nottage and Ana Ubilava, "Pioneering Mandatory Investor-State Conciliation Before Arbitration in Asia-Pacific Treaties: IA-CEPA and HK-UAE BIT" Kluwer Arbitration Blog, September 5, 2020, http://arbitrationblog.kluwerarbitration.com/2020/09/05/pioneering-mandatory-investor-state-conciliation-before-arbitration-in-asia-pacific-treaties-ia-cepa-and-hk-uae-bit/?print=pdf (accessed September 17, 2020).

[107] Dilini Pathirana, *supra* note 78.

[108] Heng Wang, *supra* note 64.

[109] Guiguo Wang, "China's Practice in International Investment Law: From Participation to Leadership in the World Economy" (2009) 34 *Yale Journal of International Law* 575–587.

Chapter 2 offers a landscape of China's foreign investment law (FIL) – its evolution in the past four decades, the key distinctive features of its FDI regime and its recent FIL developments. Chapter 2 lays the foundation for comprehending China's BIT regime, which initially was put in place to attract FDI and boost economic growth and was later to provide better investor protection to China's outbound investment. The evolution of Chinese FIL demonstrates the gradual developments in the Chinese legal system and regulatory framework, and, more importantly, the changing role and function of the government in this process. Apparently, there is a gap in the legal system and governmental function among China, Western countries and other developing or emerging economies. This gap explains the difficulty in converging BIT laws. But the evolutionary path is also clear in the sense that both the legal system and the regulatory structure are more liberal, market-oriented and investor-friendly than they were.

Chapter 3 offers an evolutionary landscape of substantive standards in Chinese BITs by reference to the China–ASEAN investment framework agreement. Both comparative study and a textual approach are adopted. The reason for referring to the China–ASEAN Investment Framework Agreement is that this is the very first regional investment agreement that China has signed in the past decade. Given the deglobalization and anti-multilateralism, regionalism is of particular significance in the current time. The second reason is to investigate the liberty level of substantive standards in Chinese BITs in the South–South context, instead of the South–North context.

The EU and China in January 2014 decided to launch negotiations on a bilateral treaty addressing the promotion and protection of investment between the two parties. Chapter 4 mainly examines the legal positions from which the parties will proceed with their negotiations in terms of the nondiscriminatory standards, that is, the NT and the MFN clauses, which are said to be the cornerstone of foreign investment protection, by focusing on the evolution of nondiscriminatory standards in China's BITs against the same standards in EU BITs, in particular the EU's recently concluded three important treaties regulating, among other things, foreign investment, namely with Canada, Singapore and Vietnam. Domestically, the reference value of BITs signed by China in the 1980s and 1990s has been significantly affected by the dynamic economic reform and market development in the past four decades. Essentially, globalization has fundamentally lifted China's foreign investment standards up to international levels. As a result, while the market anticipates the difficulties in the ongoing negotiations, the gap between EU and China, as argued in this chapter, should be noticeably slight when the EU and China come to negotiate their nondiscriminatory standards.

The doctrine and case law on expropriation in IIL are unsettled due to a variety of factors such as the diversity of interests between capital-importing and exporting states, the divergence in legal, economic and cultural concepts of property rights, and, more importantly, the regulatory role of the state in cross-border investment activities. Although China has been an active "treaty-maker" in the universe of international investment arbitration, evidenced by its nearly 130 BITs, the notion of expropriation in these BITs is in a state of flux. Chapter 5 scrutinizes the expropriation clauses in China's BITs, in particular the Peru–China BIT 1994 and the Peru–China FTA 2009, by reference to the final award of *Tza Yap Shum* v. *The Republic of Peru*, the first Chinese BIT arbitration case. This chapter attempts, in a comparative context, to understand the underlying rationality of China's evolving stance on expropriation in both global and domestic contexts.

Inconsistency has been said to be one of the most severe shortcomings that the existing ISDS system possesses. Inconsistency, if not cured, is likely to affect the legitimacy of ISDS. Partly in response to the claims of inconsistency and illegitimacy of ISDS, the EU has proposed having a permanent investment court to replace the current ISDS mechanism while the USA has proposed having an appellate body for current ISDS and a large camp of undecided states have no firm position on ISDS reform. China, on the other hand, has not issued an official response to the concept of a permanent investment court, partially because of its less active role in the use of the existing ISDS mechanism. More recent years have witnessed China's increasing involvement in ISDS cases. The objective of Chapter 6 is to review these China BIT-related ISDS cases, in particular the awards on jurisdiction and the tribunals' varying techniques in interpreting ISDS clauses in China's BITs with a focus on jurisprudential analysis of these cases and the tribunals' treaty interpretive techniques. Not surprisingly, the interpretative tendency has been quite uniform. In brief, the tribunals have tended to take an expansive approach when called upon to determine jurisdictional issues. Although Chapter 6 is largely jurisprudential, a sense of the tribunals' treaty interpretation techniques may help shape some foundational underpinnings of China's policy response to the proposals to reform the ISDS system made by the EU, the USA and others.

Apart from its overall jurisprudential review, Chapter 6 touches on two unique procedural rules in Chinese BITs. One is related to the legal standing of investors originated from Hong Kong and Macau. Two investment arbitration cases have investigated the legal standing of such investors. Theoretically, two opposite arguments have been made. One is a policy-based treaty interpretation technique, which tries to exclude Hong Kong or Macau-originated investors out of the jurisdiction of Chinese BITs, while the other is to allow such investors to enjoy the benefits of Chinese BITs according to textual interpretation of Chinese BIT terms (e.g., the concepts of investor and investment) even though both Hong Kong[110] and Macau[111] actually have their own BITs.

China believes that treaty interpretation relating to Hong Kong and Macau has been well settled in the context of both international and domestic law (i.e., the Constitution of China, the Basic Law of Hong Kong and the Basic Law of Macau). China's position is clear that those treaties ratified by China may apply to Hong Kong and Macau only when China has expressly so stated. However, this narrow or China-centric treaty interpretation approach has been greatly challenged by the *Tza Yap Shum* v. *Peru* case and the *Sanum Investments Ltd* v. *Laos* case in the context of BITs. There have been clear tensions between China's unilateral declaration and the operation of the "Moving Treaty Frontier" (MTF) doctrine.[112]

The other jurisdictional issue is related to state-owned enterprises (SOEs). Putting aside the importance of SOEs in China's economy and global cross-border investment setting, SOEs are more often involved in public international law as the government instrument

110 Hong Kong has signed twenty BITs to date and nineteen of them are in force. These counterparties are Austria, Belgium-Luxembourg Economic Union, Canada, Chile, Denmark, Finland, France, Germany, Italy, Japan, Republic of Korea, Kuwait, the Netherlands, New Zealand, Sweden, Switzerland, Thailand, the United Kingdom and the United Arab Emirates. The Hong Kong–Australia BIT was terminated. UNCTAD, Investment Policy Hub, https://investmentpolicy.unctad.org/international-investment-agreements/countries/93/hong-kong-china-sar (accessed March 6, 2021).

111 Macao had only two BITs – with the Netherlands (2008) and Portugal (2000), respectively. UNCTAD, Investment Policy Hub, https://investmentpolicy.unctad.org/international-investment-agreements/countries/123/macao-sar-china (accessed March 6, 2021).

112 John Shijian Mo, "The Dilemma of Applying Bilateral Investment Treaties of China to Hong Kong and Macao: Challenge Raised by Sanum Investments to China" (2018) 33(1) *ICSID Review – Foreign Investment Law Journal* 125–155.

triggering state responsibility for breaches of international law due to the rules of state attribution.[113] In one investment arbitration case, the host state tried to defeat the tribunal's jurisdiction on the grounds that China's SOEs are not supposed to enjoy the rights under Chinese BITs as BITs allow only investors, but not the government's arm, to enjoy the legal standing to bring claims to international investment tribunal.

These two China-specific jurisdictional issues are of great legal significance given the large number of investors from China that channel their investment through Hong Kong or Macau, and the fact that foreign investors often do the same thing when investing into China. SOEs are important market players in China. So, too, are they in the global market. A considerable portion of China's outbound investment is made by SOEs. Their legal standing in Chinese BITs needs clarification while developed states, especially the USA and the EU, are trying to exclude SOEs from legal protections offered in BITs and to justify restrictive measures relating to SOE-related investment by applying both the domestic screening schemes[114] and the security exception clause to SOEs.[115] In the China–Canada BIT 2012, China reserves some leniency for its SOEs.[116] The definition of "enterprise" in the China–Australia FTA 2015 (ChAFTA) includes entities that are governmentally owned or controlled, allowing SOEs to enjoy the benefits set out in the investment chapter.[117] The legal battle between China and the USA over SOEs surrounds the legal treatment granted to SOEs. The USA is fighting for legal rules to ensure that SOEs act at arm's length from the state and solely for commercial purposes, while China is fighting for nondiscriminatory treatment of SOEs, especially when they are subject to CFIUS screening rules under national security considerations.[118]

Chapters 7 and 8 continue to focus on procedural rules in Chinese BITs. These procedural rules are vaguely drafted in the BITs, leading to confusion and ambiguity in treaty interpretation.

Classic issues of international commercial arbitration such as parallel proceedings also emerge in international investment arbitration. The parallel existence of international investment arbitration and domestic litigation deserves careful analysis for the sake of international legal certainty and security. Given the small number of international investment arbitration cases involving China and its BITs, the issue of parallel proceedings in Chinese BIT law and practice is underinvestigated. Chapter 7 tries to look into this issue by reference to the case of *Hela Schwarz GmbH* v. *PR China*, an ongoing BIT arbitration case

113 Bernard Hanotiau, "Foreword" in Albert Badia, *Piercing the Veil of State Enterprises in International Arbitration* (Wolters Kluwer 2014) xxi–xix.

114 See Chapter 9. See also European Commission, "Communication from the Commission to the European Parliament, the European Council, the Council, the European Economic and Social Committee and the Committee of the Regions: Welcoming Foreign Direct Investment While Protecting Essential Interests" Brussels, 13.9.2017, COM(2017) 494 final.

115 UNCTAD, *World Investment Report 2015: Reforming International Investment Governance* (UN Publication 2015) 141; Daniel C. K. Chow, "Why China Wants a Bilateral Investment Treaty with the United States" (2015) 33 *Boston University International Law Journal* 101, 120.

116 Hongyu Fu and Meng Wan, "Convergences and Divergences in the China-EU and the China-US BIT Negotiations" in Yuwen Li, Tong Qi and Cheng Bian (eds.), *China, the EU and International Investment Law: Reforming Investor-State Dispute Settlement* (Routledge 2019) ch 3.

117 Vivienne Bath, "Substantive Provisions in ChAFTA's Investment Chapter" in Colin Picker, Heng Wang and Weihuan Zhou (eds.), *The China-Australia Free Trade Agreement: A 21st-Century Model* (Hart 2018) 201.

118 Kyle Dylan Dickson-Smith, "Lessons Learned from the Canada-China FIPA for the US-China BIT and Beyond – Chinese Whispers or Chinese Chequers?" in Julien Chaisse (ed.), *China's International Investment Strategy: Bilateral, Regional, and Global Law and Policy* (Oxford University Press 2019) 138.

registered with the ICSID. Some improvements have been made to relevant jurisdictional clauses in China's more recent FTAs, filling the gap in this gray area.

There has been a shift in Chinese BITs. The transition of China's BITs from the first generation to the second generation is a landmark move for China's more market-oriented economy. However, the discrepancy between the new- and old-generation Chinese BITs, which causes confusion in interpretation and application of BIT terms, has become an obstacle for investors wanting to seek relief through international arbitration under these BITs. With these new-generation BITs that China is renegotiating and re-signing with its counterparties, investors are more likely to encounter difficulty in knowing whether to interpret and apply appropriate treaty terms under either old or new BITs.

Chapter 8, through analyzing the case of *Ping An* v. *Belgium*, addresses the following issues: (a) investment disputes arising prior to the new BIT, which might fall into a "black hole" or "arbitration gap" between the new and the old BITs; (b) the term "dispute" in the transitional clause and its scope of application; and (c) the presumed intention of the contracting parties as to the true meaning of a transitional clause. Chapter 8 makes an in-depth study of how ICSID tribunals interpret and apply transitional clauses (and the rules relating to the interpretation and application of BIT terms) and further examines the retroactivity of transitional clauses. To conclude, Chapter 8 investigates China's current BIT regime, particularly transitional clauses, and suggests an effective way of filling the possible arbitration gap.

China has always been an exceptional case in the IIL arena. The principal purpose of Chapter 9 is to unveil China's evolutionary pattern of BIT practice as well as its underlying logic of BIT policies through statistical and textual analysis of China's BITs. In the analytical paradigm of the return of the state, China was a capital-importing state for a long period of time. Consequently, its BIT policy reflects China's capital-importing status with the aim of attracting foreign investment. Essentially, it is fair to say that China has probably never been in favor of moving away from its position of stressing and protecting its sovereignty while participating in the global BIT network. Seen from this angle, China and most developed states may have been on divergent paths in terms of their approaches toward engaging in the IIL regime. Put differently, while developed countries are now in the trend of returning to state sovereignty by stressing their right to regulate, China has been slightly leaving its position of overly preserving its sovereignty. Being a capital exporter, China may be more conscious of stricter investment protection and less sovereign control.[119] Nevertheless, substantive and procedural standards in Chinese BITs are still quite conservative without granting foreign investors too-liberal rights. Chapter 9, through statistical study, may also confirm that China's economic liberalization is limited, though it claims to advocate globalization, in particular free trade and investment facilitation, by taking on a position of leadership in globalization. This leadership may be symbolic due to its limited neoliberal ideology, as exemplified by the rule of law development, investor rights protection and judicial quality, among others.

Nevertheless, caution must be given to the capital-importing/capital-exporting state dichotomy of interests, which is often used to differentiate states' treaty behaviors, as the boundaries between these two groups of states seem blurred or even delimited. There has been an increase in investment arbitration cases filed against capital-exporting states,[120] giving the USA and EU member states a dual role in the ISDS mechanism, thereby making this capital-

119 M. Sornarajah, *The International Law on Foreign Investment* (3rd edition, Cambridge University Press 2010) 233.

120 UNCTAD World Investment Report 2016: Investor Nationality: Policy Challenges (United Nations 2016) (reporting 40 percent of cases filed against developed countries).

importing/exporting state narrative less useful than before, despite their trajectory shift altering their BIT negotiation position from that of capital-exporting to capital-importing states.[121] This duality narrative, originally used to describe the FDI to and from the USA and now being spread to other countries,[122] complicates the landscape of the IIL regime. There may be some historical dimensions attached to this duality narrative. Historically, ISDS or even IIL is reminiscent of the imperial system of international law[123] with its colonial heritage, given the fact that the current IIL has largely been shaped by conventional developed (capital-exporting) states.[124] Conventional capital-exporting states, as strong drivers of the ISDS mechanism, coordinate their negotiating positions when negotiating BITs with capital-importing states, thereby influencing capital-importing states and even emerging capital-exporting states.[125]

Very little empirical research has been conducted in relation to China's BIT law and practice. Chapter 10 makes a novel attempt to comprehend China's BIT-making by applying an empirical approach. The existing literature has tried to justify and rationalize Chinese BITs' generational evolution by attributing to China a policy shift, transitioning from using BITs to attract foreign investment to using BITs to protect its outbound investment. Because of this policy shift, Chinese BITs are reframed, moving from the old conservative and protectionist approach with its stress on sovereignty to regulate foreign investment to a more liberal approach with more focus on foreign investors' protection. Although the Chinese government has never made it clear to the outside world why and how its BITs have changed, the general wisdom attributes this change to a self-determined government policy move. Through empirical study, Chapter 10 tries to spot the correlation between Chinese BITs and a variety of factors shaping a host state's BIT policy. The finding seems to suggest that China's BIT policy change is due to outside pressures as well as certain endogenous factors.

Chapter 11 concludes the book.

121 David Gantz, "Challenges for the United States in Negotiating a BIT with China: Reconciling Reciprocal Investment Protection with Policy Concerns" (2015) Arizona Legal Studies Discussion Paper No. 14–03, https://papers.ssrn.com/sol3/papers.cfm?abstract_id=238919, 240.

122 José Alvarez, *The Public International Law Regime Governing International Investment* (Martinus Nijhoff 2011) 144.

123 John Linarelli, Margot E. Salomon and M. Sornarajah, *The Misery of International Law: Confrontations with Injustice in the Global Economy* (Oxford University Press 2018) 145.

124 Stephan W. Schill, Christian J. Tams and Rainer Hofmann, *International Investment Law and History* (Edward Elgar 2018) 63.

125 Taylor St John, *The Rise of Investor-State Arbitration: Politics, Law, and Unintended Consequences* (Oxford University Press 2018) 207.

2

China's Foreign Investment Law in the Past Four Decades

The modern IIL regime is primarily an institutional structure in which international investment protection rules and the dispute settlement mechanism distribute and coordinate the interests of concerned subjects at a specific stage.[1] The dynamics among the stakeholders in global FDI activities have impacted the long-term development and evolution of IIL. The pursuit of investment interests by all states in the world has contributed not only to the shaping of a modern IIL regime but also to the development of FDI.[2]

The host state's surrender of sovereignty in the form of less regulatory power over foreign investment, a shorthand being the "leaving of the state," has achieved a balance between state sovereignty and protection of investors' rights and interests and pushed forward the shaping of a modern IIL regime. In recent years, the "return of the state" by retreating from its liberal stance toward foreign investment to a more conservative one has redistributed the balance between state sovereignty and investors in international investment protection rules, thereby calling for the reform of the modern IIL regime.

China's participation in the construction of the international investment legal system has two important dimensions, namely the construction of the domestic legal system and the construction of bilateral investment treaties.[3] China's political, economic, legal and bureaucratic dynamics have pulled its evolutionary engagement with the ISDS system and, more importantly, its possible role in pushing for a restructuring of IIL in the years to come.[4] This chapter traces China's past and present and draws a matrix in which China's legal system and its development of FDI regime are evaluated. While the FDI regulatory landscape has been moving toward systemic efficiency with the aim of promoting economic growth, the complex metrics and underlying logics may change from time to time.

1 See Jonathan Bonnitcha, Lauge N. Skovgaard Poulsen and Michael Waibel, *The Political Economy of the Investment Treaty Regime* (Oxford University Press 2017) 57.

2 Helen V. Milner, "Introduction: The Global Economy, FDI, and the Regime for Investment" (2014) 66 *World Politics* 1, 7.

3 See Richard C. Chen, "Bilateral Investment Treaties and Domestic Institutional Reform" (2017) 55 *Columbia Journal of Transnational Law* 547, 554.

4 Huiping Chen, "China's Innovative ISDS Mechanisms and Their Implications" (2018) 112 *American Journal of International Law* 207, 211.

2.1 CHINA'S FDI LAW IN THE PAST FOUR DECADES

FDI in China is the clearest and most dramatic manifestation of China's open-door and economic reform policy. FDI also exposed China to the outside world.[5] China's success in attracting FDI has made it a great example to other developing states.[6] China's national investment policy-making offers certain learning experiences to others that are about to boost their economy through attracting FDI. There is also a confirmed impact of Chinese BITs on China's inbound FDI.[7]

The history of foreign investment in China is brief indeed. The first three decades after China's founding witnessed the implementation of a self-reliance policy, the failure of which, however, triggered the dramatic and logical change to the open-door and economic reform policy in 1978.[8]

The open-door policy together with the economic reform signaled China's determination to utilize market mechanisms and foreign resources to accelerate economic growth and modernization. The uneasy process of implementing the open-door and economic reform policy went hand in hand with the tension between encouraging foreign investment to achieve favorable economic outcomes and maintaining state control over foreign business activities to mitigate potential risks,[9] which in turn influenced the FIL and the economic structure as a whole.[10]

2.1.1 *Attracting Inbound FDI as the Key Economic Development Strategy*

In the past forty years of reform and opening up, the basic tendency toward liberalization of China's FIL has promoted the development of the country's economy through the continuous introduction of foreign capital, technology and managerial skills. Relevant legislation also revolved around changes in the circumstances of China's attraction of foreign investment. As shown in Figure 2.1, since 1979, the introduction of foreign investment in China has shown a rapid growth in absolute terms. In relative terms, FDI share in total investment peaked at 14.3 percent of gross capital formation and 11.8 percent of fixed asset investment in the 1990s but has now dropped to less than 3 percent or 1 percent depending on the measure, indicating a diminishing role of FDI and an increasing size of China's entire economy.[11] Nevertheless, FDI has a strong spillover effect on the supply chains, research and development, and employment, accounting for between 11 percent and 29 percent of China's employment from 1995 to 2013.[12] From the trend and fluctuation of China's foreign capital inflow in the past forty years, the four decades can be roughly divided into three stages in the 1980s, the 1990s and the new century. China's FIL also has its own characteristics in each of the three stages.

5 Y. Y. Kueh, "Foreign Investment and Economic Change in China" (1992) 131 *China Quarterly* 637–690.

6 Shirley Ayangbah and Liu Sun, "Comparative Study of Foreign Investment Law: The Case of China and Ghana" (2017) 3 *Cogent Social Sciences* 1–22.

7 Kate Hadley, "Do China's BITs Matter? Assessing the Effect of China's Investment Agreements on Foreign Direct Investment Flows, Investors' Rights and the Rule of Law" (2013) 45 *Georgetown Journal of International Law* 255.

8 See Deng Xiaoping, "Emancipating the Mind, Seeking Truth from Facts, Looking Forward Together" in *Selected Works of Deng Xiaoping* (Vol. 2) (Foreign Language Press 1994) 146–147.

9 Michael J. Enright, "China's Inward Investment: Approach and Impact" in Julien Chaisse (ed.), *China's International Investment Strategy: Bilateral, Regional, and Global Law and Policy* (Oxford University Press 2019) 28.

10 Sherif H. Seid, *Global Regulation of Foreign Direct Investment* (Routledge Taylor & Francis Group 2017) 30.

11 Enright, *supra* note 9, at 30.

12 Ibid., at 35.

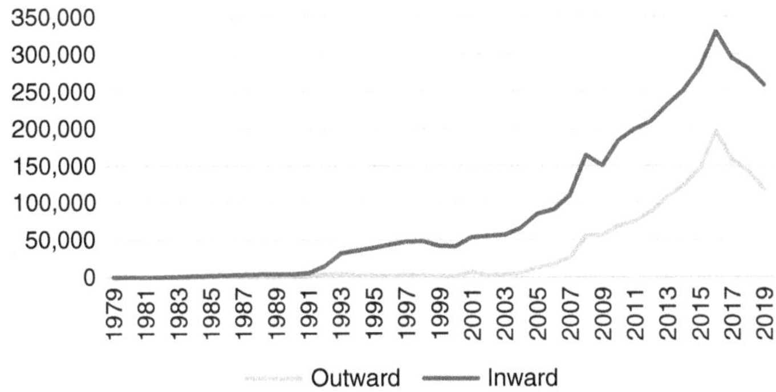

FIGURE 2.1 China's FDI flows, 1979–2019[13] (USD millions)
*Compiled by the author.

Of all the legal institutions that were rebuilt or created in the past four decades, those related to foreign investment have developed the earliest and the fastest. The Sino-foreign Equity Joint Venture Law (the EJV Law) promulgated in 1979 was the first law formulated by China for foreign investment since the reform and opening up. The law for the first time affirmed that foreign investors enjoy rights governed under civil law in China,[14] allowing foreign investors to enter China and to partner with Chinese companies in joint ventures, and through the law to clear the tax, exchange and other issues facing foreign investors who invest in China.[15] At the same time, the law also requires that the relevant contracts must be filed with or approved by the Chinese government, and that production materials should also be purchased in China.[16] The operating mode of the joint venture company should also conform to the economic system of China at that time. Meanwhile, any investment disputes should be settled in principle by the arbitration institution designated by the Chinese government, although the parties may agree that other arbitration institutions may also resolve such matters.[17] In the following year, China followed up with legislation on taxation and contracts, and further refined and guaranteed the implementation of the EJV Law. In 1982, China revised the Constitution in all major aspects to align it with the new situation of reform and opening up. For the first time, it became clear from the language of the Constitution that foreign investors have the right to invest in China and protect their legitimate rights and interests in China.[18] With the continuous enhancement of China's ability to attract foreign investment and the deepening of its economic system reform, the Wholly Foreign-Owned Enterprise Law (the WFOE Law) promulgated in 1986 began to allow foreign investors to set up wholly foreign-owned enterprises (WFOEs) in China.[19]

Similar to the EJV Law, the WFOE Law clearly stipulates tax incentives and exchanges for foreign investors but still emphasizes that investors should conduct investment activities in accordance with Chinese laws and accept the supervision of the Chinese government. The government has the right to seize investor property in the public interest. The promulgation of the Sino-Foreign Cooperative Joint Venture Law (the CJV Law) in 1988 was generally

[13] UNCTAD Data Center, https://unctadstat.unctad.org/EN/ (accessed April 6, 2021).
[14] EJV Law 1979, Art. 1.
[15] EJV Law 1979, Art. 2.
[16] EJV Law 1979, Arts. 3, 6 and 9.
[17] EJV Law 1979, Art. 14.
[18] Constitution of the PRC 1982, Art. 18.
[19] WFOE Law 1982, Art. 1.

consistent with the previous two laws, emphasizing that foreign investors should be subject to the supervision of the Chinese government in terms of finance, taxation and labor when cooperating with Chinese enterprises.[20] Without doubt, the law also shows restrictions on government power. For example, the disputing parties are allowed to choose other arbitration institutions or Chinese courts to resolve their disputes.[21] Although China's investment-related domestic legislation was still rough in the late 1980s and strongly emphasized the government's regulatory power over foreign investment, it is undeniable that it has made tremendous progress in the collection of compensation, national treatment (NT) and MFN status, among others. China has extensively absorbed the legislative experience and international practices of other countries, and outlined the basic framework of China's foreign investment legislation. China's regulatory framework for foreign investment has taken an initial shape.

It is not surprising to see that the first piece of legislation enacted right after the adoption of the open door policy was the EJV Law in 1979. The urgency of attracting foreign investment and satisfying foreign investors' needs to have their investments well protected entailed tremendous efforts to create an FIL regime from scratch. The key purpose of this EJV Law was to encourage foreign investors' participation in China's economic development and modernization program.[22] Other primary legislation and implemented regulations in subsequent years allowed foreign companies to set up representative offices, WFOEs and contractual joint ventures (CJVs) in China. The Constitution revised in 1982 contains a critical provision offering the promise to protect "the lawful rights and interests of foreign investors." The course of China's economic development through foreign investment entails ongoing tensions among the state, the law and market players. The best illustration is that these laws and other regulations centered on the encouragement and protection of foreign investments, with no exception, had Chinese characteristics, mostly in the form of certain compromises among the legal rights protection, the Party-state censorship and parental monitoring.[23] The foreign investment policy at this stage was primitive and inconsistent and often moved back and forth between two extremes of openness and restriction. Although the legal institutions rebuilt after the Cultural Revolution cannot fulfill their supposed role, function and goal of rights protection, they contributed considerably to the economic and societal development in the past four decades.

A unique Chinese characteristic or regulatory feature of the FIL regime in China is the centrality of the state as the primary agent for economic and social development. The regulators are everywhere from collection of taxes, exchange controls, customs regulation, intellectual property, protection from seizure of land, allocation of natural resources and dispatch of employees. The fundamental role of the state in Chinese society and economy was articulated in the Constitution of 1982. The subsequent amendments to the Constitution in 1993, while replacing the state-centered planning economy with the socialist market economy,[24] did not dilute the state-centric function in economic development. In FILs, some commitments were made by the government not to expropriate foreign investment without public interest or compensation. While joint ventures set up by foreign and domestic

20 CJV Law 1988, Arts. 3, 5, 6, 7 and 9.

21 CJV Law 1988, Art. 26.

22 Li Wanqiang, "Chinese Foreign Investment Laws: A Review from the Perspective of Policy-Oriented Jurisprudence" (2011) 19 *Asia Pacific Law Review* 35, 41.

23 Joseph C. H. Chai and Kartik C. Roy, *Economic Reform in China and India: Development Experience in a Comparative Perspective* (Edward Elgar 2006) 51.

24 Constitution of the PRC 1993, Art. 15.

investors were subject to government approval and monitoring,[25] foreign-invested enterprises (FIEs) were given the freedom to submit their disputes with their local partners to arbitration.[26] Nondiscriminatory standards such as NT and MFN treatment,[27] albeit post-establishment only, were codified in FIL, giving foreign investors confidence in China's overall legal system.

In the 1990s, as China's market economy reform continued to deepen, China was in a gradual transition to a market economy system.[28] The entire 1990s witnessed differential liberalization dominance as well as a departure from the conventional state planning system of the old days to a more market-oriented macroeconomic regulation and control.[29] In 1990, China took the lead in opening the amendments to the EJV Law. Compared with the 1979 legislation, the amendments stipulated that the expropriation of joint ventures should be compensated.[30] Meanwhile, the approval items of some joint venture projects were adjusted and the government's approval authority and time limits were further specified. In the late 1990s, China further revised the WFOE Law and the EJV Law. The revision of these two laws is highlighted by the elimination of the restriction that raw materials could be purchased only in China. Now, the production plan of the enterprise does not need to be reported to the government for approval, and the related products are allowed to be sold domestically.

The conceptual approach drove the Chinese government to rely on industrial policies, either sector-based or geography-based ones,[31] in regulating and directing foreign investment. In addition to the legislative amendments to the law, the then state planning authority, the State Planning Commission, the predecessor of the National Reform and Development Commission, issued the *Catalogue of Industries for Guiding Foreign Investment* (the Catalogue) in June 1995. This clarified the segmentation of industrial sectors into the categories of encouraging, permitting, restricting, and prohibiting foreign investment access to different industries, thereby improving the predictability of foreign investment. The "restricted" category limited the equity share that foreign investors could have in certain industries. The Catalogue signaled the state policies' prioritizing of attracting foreign investment.[32]

The State Council approved a revised Catalogue in December 1997 that removed barriers to foreign participation in some restricted sectors, such as distribution, infrastructure, energy, and power generation. The Catalogue also favored those enterprises that were willing and able to bring advanced technology into China or to promote exports, and offered tax exemptions and other benefits to FIEs. In the category of "encouraged" investments, emphasis was placed on high technology, and some industries were moved to the "restricted" category. This differential liberalization policy de facto disfavored SOEs and domestic private enterprises, which effectively gave FIEs a supernational treatment.[33] Against this background, China's openness became a dominant theme. However, the dominance of the state and the

25 EJV Law 1990, Art. 3.

26 EJV Law 1990, Art. 14.

27 EJV Law 1990, Art. 7.

28 In 1993, China further revised the 1982 Constitution, clarifying that China will implement a socialist market economic system.

29 Final Version of the 14th CPC National Congress Report, FBIS Daily Report – China, October 21, 1992.

30 EJV Law 1990, Art. 2.

31 Enright, *supra* note 9, at 26–27.

32 See Meichen Liu, "The New Chinese Foreign Investment Law and Its Implication on Foreign Investors" (2018) 38 *Northwestern Journal of International Law and Business* 285, 288–289.

33 Songling Yang, "China's Administrative Mode for Foreign Investment: From Positive List to Negative List" (2015) 33 *Singapore Law Review* 93, 96–97.

lack of an indigenous private sector also set the uniqueness of China's legal, regulatory and administrative regime in guiding and overseeing FIEs.

Given the changing sector-based industrial policies reflected in the Catalogue, the economic sectors toward which foreign investment has been targeted gradually extended from the labor-intensive manufacturing sectors to technology-based production. The Chinese government made a great effort to steer foreign investment to the export and technology sectors. As a result, particular preferences were given to FIEs denoted as "export-oriented enterprises" and "advanced technology enterprises."[34] The EJV Law and its Implementing Rules specifically encouraged joint ventures to export their products. The acquisition and importation of technology were encouraged by rules allowing IPR and know-how to be contributed as capital by foreign investors. Approval of joint ventures was to be contingent on the satisfaction of the criterion of being either an export-oriented enterprise or an importer of technology.[35]

Preferential treatments in the form of tax holidays were also offered to those foreign investment projects that were able to satisfy these requirements. These more preferential treatments were often labeled supranational treatment, which is not in line with NT under the WTO.[36] Accordingly, joint ventures were to receive tax holidays for the first two profit-making years and reductions in subsequent years.[37] FIEs whose export production value was 70 percent of total production value were to be considered "export-oriented enterprises" eligible for a 50 percent reduction in enterprise income tax, with additional reductions possible.[38] FIEs that were designated as "technologically advanced enterprises" were entitled to extend their initial three-year tax holiday by an additional three years.[39] Similarly, the approval of WFOEs would also be conditional on their use of advanced technology or their exporting of products.[40] Withholding taxes on profits remitted outside China could be exempted for technologically advanced enterprises and export enterprises, which meanwhile were entitled to exemption from the payment of state subsidies for enterprise staff and workers, to priority in obtaining short-term loans, to limits on certain site use fees and to extension of priority status for utility supply and infrastructural requirements.

The legislation, that is, the Provisions on Acquisitions of Domestic Enterprises by Foreign Investors, which blocks foreign purchase of Chinese companies involving "key industries," described as those whose operations influence or might influence "state economic security,"[41] gradually began to reflect concerns about foreign interests acquiring domestic assets below their value,[42] seizing control of strategic industrial sectors[43] and market share in China

34 Provisions of the State Council for the Encouragement of Foreign Investment (1986).

35 EJV Law, Arts. 5 and 9; EJV Law Implementing Rules, Arts. 4, 28 and 62; CJV Law, Art. 8.

36 Wang Wei, "Super-National Treatment: A Misconception or a Creation with Chinese Characteristics?" (2010) 5 *Frontiers of Law in China* 376–396.

37 EJV Law, Art. 7; Joint Venture Income Tax Law, Art. 5.

38 Provisions of the State Council for the Encouragement of Foreign Investment.

39 Provisions of the State Council for the Encouragement of Foreign Investment.

40 WFOE Law, Art. 3.

41 To be more detailed, these industries refer to machinery, automobiles, telecommunications, construction, iron and steel, and non-ferrous metals. See "Control over Key Industries 'Crucial,'" *China Daily*, December 19, 2006, http://english.people.com.cn/200612/19/eng20061219_333839.html (accessed March 18, 2021).

42 For details, see Shen Wei, "Is SAFE Safe Now?: Foreign Exchange Regulatory Control over Chinese Outbound and Inbound Investments and a Political Economy Analysis of Policies" (2010) 11 *Journal of World Investment and Trade* 227, 245–250.

43 Mure Dickie, "Chinese Takeover Fears Grow," *Financial Times*, August 4, 2006, p. 6; Geoff Dyer, Sundeep Tucker and Tom Mitchell, "Forbidden Country? How Foreign Deals in China Are Hitting Renewed Resistance," *Financial Times*, August 8, 2006, p. 11.

without adequate oversight and control.[44] The debate of liberalism versus economic nationalism also mirrors the objective and the direction of economic reform itself in a broader context. Therefore, the foreign investment policy has been an ad hoc and incremental response to continuous changes in the global and domestic economy.

In general, the main direction of China's foreign investment legislation from 1979 to the mid-1990s was to attract foreign investment through continuous opening up and to promote the development of the country's economy. The growth and overall trend of foreign investment in China was positive in the first decade starting from 1979. During this period, the annual average of foreign investment was more than USD 2 billion. There was a decline in 1989–1990, but the volume of foreign investment resumed and was nearly USD 12 billion for 1991. It then climbed very rapidly and contractual foreign investment reached USD 57.2 billion and USD 122.7 billion in 1992 and 1993, respectively. FDI declined again in 1997–1999 due to the Asian financial crisis, but reached a new level in the new millennium. On the one hand, this phase has changed the attitude of vigilance and even hostility toward foreign investment that existed in the past. Through comprehensive legislation from the Constitution to the law, the position of protecting the rights of foreign investors has been clarified and "reassured." On the other hand, China has increasingly attached importance to restrictions on government power. Before the economic reform and opening up, due to China's planned economic system and its imperfect legal system, the government's power was far-reaching. Investment as an economic activity rooted in the host country is closely related to the exercise of government power. Therefore, in order to truly protect the interests of investors, the government must limit its administrative power from both substantive and procedural perspectives. In this phase, China's investment legislation changed its position from its absolute intervention in investment, and showcased the trend of China's intention to restrain its government power.

2.1.2 *Joining the WTO and Conforming to WTO Rules*

China's accession to the WTO in 2002 marked a new chapter of foreign investment. The significance of this event was to outline a roadmap for China to further liberalize and modernize the economy and the foreign investment regime per se. China's entry into the WTO opened up a large-scale revision to legislation on various aspects including investment. The principle of NT was more expansively implemented, and regulation and supervision of foreign investment activities became more subject to legal rather than administrative means. Other significant changes to foreign investment policies included repealing the requirements for nationalization of foreign investment and establishing a legal framework more compatible with the requirements and principles of WTO.

The Catalogue was further amended in 2002 to solidify China's WTO commitments, which reflected an increasingly liberalizing trend.[45] As far as the FIEs are concerned, the approval system, capitalization, market access and financing have been reformed as well. The State Council reformed the investment system, which raised the threshold on local

44 The most high-profile and lasting battle was Carlyle's bid to take a stake in Xugong, China's leading machinery maker, which was finally defeated. Sundeep Tucker, "Carlyle Concedes Defeat in Battle to Take Stake in China's Xugong," *Financial Times*, July 23, 2008.

45 The liberalizing trend was not extended to most publishing activities. Also, genetically modified organisms were also moved to the "prohibited" category.

government approvals of investment projects from USD 30 million to USD 100 million for projects falling within the "encouraged" and "permitted" categories in the Catalogue.[46]

As to foreign capital, relevant research shows that, compared with political factors, a country's economic vitality and potential have a far-reaching impact on the country's ability to attract foreign investment.[47] Therefore, the key to enhancing China's foreign investment attraction is to further improve the market economy system. Since the start of the new century, China's capital import has been increasing, and the call for revision of three FIE laws has become increasingly greater. In 2001, China first revised the EJV Law. In addition to allowing joint ventures to purchase raw materials in the international market and providing foreign investors the right to resolve disputes in Chinese courts, the main emphasis is on the joint ventures having to strictly abide by Chinese laws in terms of labor treatment and insurance.

The Catalogue 2007 demonstrated the new policy switch. For instance, the Catalogue places more emphasis on environmental protection, trade imbalances and high technology. Accordingly, the Catalogue decreases support for export-oriented industries, promotes foreign investment in high-tech and environmentally friendly sectors, and restricts foreign investment in manufacturing and mining industries that once welcomed such investment. These policy changes were viewed as a new round of attempts to disadvantage foreign investors,[48] on the one hand limiting market access by non-Chinese origin goods and on the other hand offering more resources and protections to domestic players that are less competitive in the marketplace.[49] The role of law is ambiguous in balancing control of foreign investment against facilitating the activities of FIEs.

In 2016, the Chinese legislature revised the FIE laws in a unified manner. The main change is that in fields that do not involve the implementation of special management measures for entry into the country, the government will now use a filing system instead of the past approval system, thus relaxing supervision over foreign investment.[50]

In 2017, the legislature once again revised the CJV Law, mainly removing the partial approval power of the government authorities for CJVs. Therefore, judging from the existing legislation, China's foreign investment legislation on FIEs as its main link with the foreign investment community is still in the initial stage of "leaving of the state," and the state government role is still heavy. For example, on the issue of expropriation, both the EJV Law and the WFOE Law stipulate that "the state does not implement nationalization and expropriation of foreign-funded enterprises; in special circumstances, according to the needs of social public interests, foreign-funded enterprises may be expropriated according to legal procedures and compensated accordingly."[51] The provision on the one hand shows the reference to the "Hull formula." On the other hand, it is still essentially a Calvoist provision in the sense that expropriation and compensation are carried on according to domestic laws, and do not involve the intervention of other countries. China's foreign

46 Decision of the State Council on Reforming the Investment System, issued by the State Council on July 16, 2004, https://en.ndrc.gov.cn/policyrelease_8233/200602/t20060207_1193914.html (accessed April 6, 2021).

47 See Pravin Jadhav, "Determinants of Foreign Direct Investment in BRICS Economies: Analysis of Economic, Institutional and Political Factor" (2012) 37 *Procedia-Social and Behavioral Sciences* 5, 12.

48 China Briefing, Guidelines on FDI Released for 2007, www.china-briefing.com/news/guidelines-on-fdi-released-for-2007/ (accessed April 6, 2021).

49 United States Trade Representative, Report to Congress on China's WTO Compliance 6 (2005) https://china.usc.edu/2005-report-congress-china%E2%80%99s-wto-compliance (accessed April 6, 2021).

50 NPC Standing Committee of PRC, Decision of the Standing Committee of the National People's Congress on Amending Four Laws Including the Law of the People' s Republic of China on Foreign-Funded Enterprises, September 3, 2016, www.xinhuanet.com//politics/2016-09/03/c_1119506052.htm (accessed April 6, 2021).

51 EJV Law, Art. 2; WFOE Law, Art. 5.

investment legislation is always on the road to liberalization,[52] by restricting government power and respecting the rights of expropriated people in China's relevant legislation.

The state-centric model of economic growth and development explains the key features of the FIL regime in China that pursues policies of import substitution, export-led growth, technological advancement, and development strategies through specially designed state-driven industrial policies and grand plans.[53] These institutional arrangements have ensured the success of the labor-intensive and export-oriented industries in the past four decades. Heavy reliance on foreign capital in Chinese foreign investment policy also justifies the Chinese government's willingness to offer policy, economic, tax and legal incentives to foreign investors while foreign investors offer capital, managerial skills and technologies to China, shaping a unique bonding relationship between the two. This may explain the Chinese government's efforts to formalize, upgrade and modernize its law, legal infrastructure and legal system, though they are authoritarian in nature. The Foreign Investment Law, together with other laws and norms, has not undermined the state's regulation of foreign investment and recognizes the transnational character of cross-border foreign investment.

China's economic success consistently reminds us of the difficulty and complexity in understanding, justifying and theorizing China's development model. The foreign investment regime in China demonstrates both prospects and dilemmas, which are complexly and paradoxically related to the state or its sovereignty. It appears that there is a retrenchment in China placing a greater emphasis on industrial policy and regulatory regime to review the impact of foreign investment projects on national economic and security interests, which coincided with a notable trend toward rising nationalism, seeking to push back globalization, as well as a switch from fast economic growth to a new harmonious society policy (or sustainable development).

China's policy-making process and legal environment in the arena of foreign investment are complex and dynamic. It is believed that the Chinese foreign investment policy has always been, and continues to be, a product of bargaining dynamics,[54] personalities and clientelism,[55] and bureaucratic processes.[56] This process is now more contested than before among various domestic and foreign interest groups and constituencies as well as champions of global capitalism, notwithstanding the CCP's reliance on continuous growth for legitimacy, a new goal of realizing a harmonious society, and urgent needs to protect socially and economically vulnerable groups. The debate in China, that is, economic nationalism versus liberal treatment toward foreign investment, has been ongoing and zigzagging for decades[57] and that may well explain, if not rationalize, the wavering policy change. In contrast to the growing liberalization, Chinese economic nationalism has appeared in recent years. This may diffuse the difficulty of precisely identifying and predicting China's position in terms of BIT-making.

The great concern often raised by the community of foreign investors has always been and continues to be the lack of laws and regulations and the dysfunction of China's legal institutions and judiciary, which are supposed to offer sufficient protections to foreign

52 See Shen Wei, "Expropriation in Transition: Evolving Chinese Investment Treaty Practices in Local and Global Contexts" (2015) 28 *Leiden Journal of International Law* 579, 600–601.

53 See Xinli Zheng, *China's 40 Years of Economic Reform and Development: How the Miracle Was Created* (Commercial Press/Springer Nature Singapore Pte 2018) 151.

54 Susan L. Shirk, *The Political Logic of Economic Reform in China* (University of California Press 1993) 21.

55 See generally Lucian Pye, *The Mandarin and the Cadre* (University of Michigan Press 1988).

56 See generally Kenneth Lieberthal and Michael Oksenberg, *Policy Making in China: Leaders, Structures, and Processes* (Princeton University Press 1988).

57 Yong Wang, "China's Domestic WTO Debate" (2000) 27 *China Business Review* 54, 56; Zhang Jianhong and He Xinming, "Economic Nationalism and Foreign Acquisition Completion: The Case of China" (2014) 23 *International Business Review* 212, 224–225.

investors and even Chinese citizens. While the levels of predictability, functioning and rights-consciousness cannot be and should not be assessed and measured exclusively in terms of Western ideals,[58] a fair evaluation is that the legal system in China is still in institutional flux and has a long way to go. Although the totalitarian grip of the CCP has weakened since the late 1970s, the bureaucracy, official arbitrariness, spreading corruption, more chaotic social order and crisis of social values all need even more urgently and desperately a rule of law composed of strong legal institutions and a vibrant legal culture.

2.1.3 *Encouraging Outbound FDI as a New Strategy*

With the continuous strengthening of China's economy since the economic reform and open door and the formal establishment of the socialist market-oriented economic system through the Constitution in 1993, China's opening up to the outside world has undergone new rapid changes.

As shown in Figure 2.1, China's inbound FDI since the turn of the millennium has continued to expand. In particular, the outbreak of the Asian financial crisis in 1997 highlighted a potential risk of excessive dependence on foreign investment. Besides, orderly capital outflow is conducive not only to domestic economic development but also to reduction of financial risks and economic stability. Therefore, in light of China's rising strength in investment and other fields, at the National Foreign Investment Conference held in December 1997, then President Jiang Zemin proposed a new strategy of economic reform and opening up that combines "attracting foreign investment" and "going out," emphasizing the need to encourage Chinese enterprises, especially SOEs, to invest in Africa and other overseas markets while promoting the rational use of foreign capital. Investment in other countries and regions, making full use of the market and resources of the relevant countries to promote joint ventures and cooperation projects,[59] can give play to China's comparative advantages and better utilize both domestic and overseas markets and resources in both local and foreign markets.[60] The "go globally" strategy drove China to attach greater importance to outbound investment by unswervingly promoting outbound investment of Chinese enterprises. With the clear push of government policies,[61] the amount of Chinese outbound investment has gradually increased. Until 2014, China's FDI outflow (FDIO) exceeded its inflow (FDII) for the first time, marking China's transition from a traditional capital-importing country to a hybrid country with equal

58 Law is the most overtly culture-bound of all the disciplines. Comparative legal study has not been successful in developing culturally neutral legal concepts. Therefore, the assumption of the universality of Western legal forms and legal ideals or a complete ignorance of cultural bias may not be a good technique for comparative legal study. See Gunter Frankenberg, "Critical Comparisons: Re-thinking Comparative Law" (1985) 26 *Harvard International Law Journal* 411, 434–440.

59 See Jiang Zemin, "Open Strategy for the Implementation of 'Introduction' and 'Going Global'" in *Selected Works of Jiang Zemin* (Vol. 2) (Foreign Language Press 2006) 91–94.

60 Jiang Zemin, "Highly Holding the Great Banner of Deng Xiaoping Theory and Pushing the Construction of Socialism with Chinese Characteristics into the 21st Century" in *Selected Works of Jiang Zemin* (Vol. 2) (Foreign Language Press 2006) 27.

61 Since the 15th National Congress of the Communist Party of China in 1997, "going out" has always been the basic line that the Chinese party and government have adhered to in the field of opening up to the outside world. Until the party's 19th National Congress in 2017, General Secretary Xi Jinping still emphasized the need for "One Belt and One Road": "[With b]uilding as the focus, adhere to the introduction and go out and pay equal attention, follow the principle of joint construction and sharing, strengthen the openness and cooperation of innovation capabilities, and form an open pattern of linkage between the land and the sea, and between the east and the west." See Xi Jinping, "Decisive Victory to Build a Well-Off Society in an All-Round Way to Win a Great Victory in Socialism with Chinese Characteristics in the New Era – Report at the 19th National Congress of the Communist Party of China," *People's Daily*, October 28, 2017.

capital outflow and inflow. At the same time, China started new domestic reforms with the aim of enhancing its economic reform and open door policy.

As early as 2013, President Xi Jinping proposed the BRI for the first time during an overseas visit. After that, the Chinese government further promulgated relevant documents and clarified the development direction of the BRI. As far as investment is concerned, first, China is working to eliminate barriers in investment and trade by promoting measures of investment facilitation and free trade. Second, it plans to expand the scope of foreign investment and the breadth and depth of cooperation in the field of investment along the Belt and Road. Third, China has initiated the establishment of the Asian Infrastructure Investment Bank[62] to focus on investment cooperation in various areas such as infrastructure and construction projects along the Belt and Road.[63] As shown in Figure 2.2, China's investment in countries along the Belt and Road has been on the rise since 2013, especially during the period from 2013 to 2015. Although the investment declined in 2016–2017, it rebounded again in 2018 and has basically recovered to the level of 2016. In 2017, China's outbound investment projects in Belt and Road countries accounted for 12.7 percent of China's total outbound investment.[64] From their characteristics over the past five years,

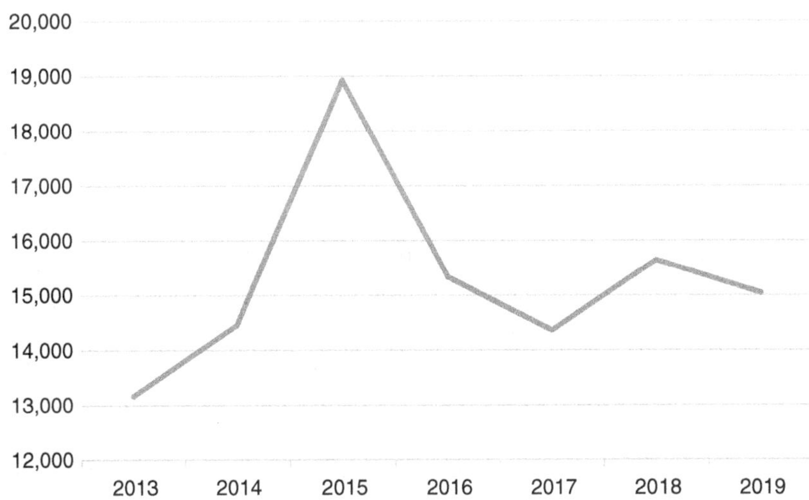

FIGURE 2.2 China's outbound FDI along Belt and Road Initiative countries[65] (USD millions)
*Compiled by the author.

62 On October 24, 2014, the finance ministers and authorized representatives of the first batch of twenty-one intent-initiating member countries, including China, India and Singapore, signed a contract in Beijing to jointly decide to establish an investment bank. On December 25, 2015, the Asian Infrastructure Investment Bank (AIIB) was formally established. From January 16 to 18, 2016, the AIIB opening ceremony and the inaugural meeting of the board of directors were held in Beijing.

63 See National Development and Reform Commission, Ministry of Foreign Affairs, Ministry of Commerce, "Vision and Action to Promote the Construction of the Silk Road Economic Belt and the 21st Century Maritime Silk Road," *People's Daily*, March 29, 2015.

64 Hui Yao Wang and Lu Miao, "China's Outbound Investment: Trends and Challenges in the Globalization of Chinese Enterprises" in Julien Chaisse (ed.), *China's International Investment Strategy: Bilateral, Regional, and Global Law and Policy* (Oxford University Press 2019) 47.

65 See *Ministry of Commerce of the People's Republic of China: China Foreign Investment Cooperation Development Report* (2017), 124. For the relevant data of 2018, see the Department of Foreign Investment and Economic Cooperation of the Ministry of Commerce of the People's Republic of China, *Island Investment and Cooperation in the Countries Along the Belt and Road from January to December* 2018, January 22, 2019, *available at* http://hzs.mofcom.gov.cn/article/date/201901/20190102829086.shtml (lasted visited Feb. 5, 2019).

unlike the traditional rule-oriented investment framework based on IIAs, the cross-border investment activities under the BRI are mainly project-based.

Chinese companies are the key business elites in China's transnational networks, not only presenting China's global posture but also channeling the Chinese government's outbound investment policies to the globalized market. Chinese companies play multiple roles such as enhancing the bond between China and Western capitalism, piggybacking offshore jurisdictions to experiment with transnational rules, adapting to more liberal modes of networking, and integrating Chinese supply and technology chains with the world.

Chinese SOEs occupy a dominant position in China's outbound investment projects, and the investment areas are mainly concentrated in high-speed rail, energy, water conservancy and other industries.[66] Apart from their business functions, SOEs also show a distinctive linkage with Party-state and state-directed capitalism.[67] Although it is not possible to simplify or synergize the BRI completely, it can be seen that China's foreign investment in large-scale infrastructure projects has absorbed China's surplus production capacity to a certain extent, which is conducive to the development of its own economy.[68] At the same time, it has driven the rapid development of infrastructure and construction projects along the Belt and Road. Apparently, the BRI presents great opportunities for win–win investment cooperation between China and its counterparties.[69] Therefore, the foreign investment under the BRI is basically driven by the Chinese government and other countries involved, as a matter of fact with heavy reliance on the economic activities and participation of Chinese SOEs. This type of cross-border investment cooperation, although not inseparable from legal texts such as BITs, is more based on economic complementarity and political mutual trust.

China now has larger FDIO than FDII, which is thanks to China's regulatory framework for outbound FDI, notably government policies, laws and regulations as well as incentive schemes. Consequently, China's outbound investment has even surpassed that of several major developed economies in the past decade.[70] A holistic review of this outbound FDI-friendly framework unveils its two interconnected objectives: to help Chinese firms, in particular SOEs, to be more competitive in the global market and to implement China's development strategy through consorted regulatory and policy efforts. However, China's legal framework is not flawless. While it benefits SOEs the most, it also creates a discriminatory environment and damages other market players.[71]

[66] According to relevant officials of the Chinese government, as of the first half of 2018, more than 80 SOEs in China have undertaken 3,116 investment projects and projects in the countries along the "Belt and Road," involving high-speed rail, water conservancy and energy, which have effectively promoted the local Economic growth. See Wang Wei, "In the second half of the year, SOEs 'anti-risk' five-way progress," *Economic Information Daily*, July 19, 2018, 4th edition.

[67] Nana de Graaff, "China Inc. Goes Global. Transnational and National Networks of China's Globalizing Business Elite" (2020) 27(2) *Review of International Political Economy* 208–233.

[68] Tristan Kohl, "The Belt and Road Initiative's Effect on Supply-chain Trade: Evidence from Structural Gravity Equations" (2019) 12 *Cambridge Journal of Regions, Economy and Society* 77, 90.

[69] Dragana Mitrovic, "The Belt and Road: China's Ambitious Initiative" (2016) 59 *China International Studies* 76, 81–82.

[70] Hui Yao Wang and Lu Miao, 43.

[71] Karl P. Sauvant and Victor Zitian Chen, "China's Regulatory Framework for Outbound Foreign Direct Investment" (2014) 7(1) *China Economic Journal* 141–163.

2.2 FREE TRADE ZONE AND NEW REFORMIST MEASURES

2.2.1 *Free Trade Zone and Negative List*

In recent years, China has begun to actively explore ways to reform its economic governance regime, in particular through the free trade zones (FTZs). This is the typical experimentalist approach toward reform and governance. Before conducting profound reforms of the trade and investment legal framework, China started with reforms on a small scale, in specified geographic zones as testing grounds. FTZs are used as pilot projects to achieve multiple objectives including testing how to upgrade China's trade and investment laws, boosting China's economy in the new normal and preparing China for international law-making and high-standard BIT/FTA negotiations.[72] In this sense, the experimental experiences accumulated in the FTZs provide better approaches or even solutions to challenges faced by China in transforming and upgrading its economic governance model. This domestic–international law interaction or reconciliation is a unique perspective of transnational law process in China's context.

Since the establishment of the Shanghai FTZ in 2013, China has established FTZs in twenty one regions, including Guangdong, Tianjin and Fujian, and has begun to focus on promoting the construction of Hainan Free Trade Port. The FTZ is viewed by the business community and analysts as the Chinese government's most important policy move for economic reform in more than a decade. Both internal and external factors are pushing for deeper reform of China's legal and regulatory regime and a substantial change in China's economic growth model.[73] At home, soaring wages and an aging workforce are forcing China to move toward a "middle-income" trap. Abroad, rivals are rushing into regional free trade deals such as the Trans-Pacific Partnership (TPP, now the CPTPP) and the Transatlantic Trade and Investment Partnership (TTIP) without involving China. Both forces are putting pressure on China. Inefficient and cosseted service sectors must be further opened up in a globally competitive game. For example, compared to Hong Kong, whose service sectors account for 90 percent of the whole economy, Shanghai's services were only 62 percent in 2013.[74] Shanghai therefore needs to use its own economic strength and geographical and political advantages in China to achieve its reform goals.

Thanks to the reform experience of the Shenzhen Special Economic Zone introduced by the Chinese government right after the adoption of the open door and economic reform policy in the late 1970s to encourage local economic experiments,[75] the Chinese government has actively given local governments greater policy freedom in running FTZs, and authorized FTZs to break through the original economic management system. Therefore, in respect of foreign investment, the systemic reform of FTZs is mainly being carried out by breaking the old system and establishing new measures.

Prior to the official launch of the Shanghai FTZ in 2013, the National People's Congress Standing Committee authorized the State Council to operate the China (Shanghai) FTZ

[72] Jie Huang, "Challenges and Solutions for the China-US BIT Negotiations: Insights from the Recent Development of FTZs in China" (2015) 18 *Journal of International Economic Law* 307–339.

[73] Gladie Lui, "Shanghai Pilot Free Trade Zone: Shaping of China's Future Foreign Investment Environment" (2014) 40 *Journal of International Taxation* 31.

[74] People's Government of Shanghai Municipality, "Statistical Bulletin on National Economic and Social Development of Shanghai in 2013," August 26, 2014, www.shanghai.gov.cn/nw2/nw2314/nw2319/nw11494/nw12335/u21aw919456.html (accessed February 26, 2019).

[75] See Deng Xiaoping, "Make a Success of Special Economic Zones and Open More Cities to the Outside World" in *Selected Works of Deng Xiaoping* (Vol. 3) (Foreign Language Press 1994) 61–62.

with some freedom. From October 1, 2013, the EJV Law, the CJV Law and the WFOE Law were temporarily paused to be entirely applied to the setup and operation of FIEs in the FTZ apart from some special measures for the implementation of the national regulations.[76] On December 28, 2014, the Standing Committee of the National People's Congress issued a decision to adjust relevant laws for the FTZs in Guangdong, Tianjin, Fujian and the extended area of the Shanghai FTZ.[77]

In line with the authorization of the Standing Committee of the National People's Congress, the State Council issued two decisions, on December 21, 2013 and September 4, 2014, allowing some regulatory experiments over FIEs in the Shanghai FTZ. On July 1, 2016, the State Council decided to temporarily adjust eighteen administrative regulations such as the Implementing Rules for the Foreign Investment Enterprise Law of the People's Republic of China and the Decision of the State Council on Investment System Reform in the Pilot FTZs, the Catalogue (2004) and other relevant provisions of the ministerial regulations approved by the State Council.[78] Relevant regulations were further amended by the State Council in December 2013, September 2014 and July 2016 to accommodate the special reformist needs in the FTZs. In 2016, the National People's Congress revised the relevant provisions of the FIE Laws: "Where the establishment of a joint venture does not involve the implementation of special admission administration measures as per national regulations, record-filing management shall apply to the approval matters as specified. The special admission administration measures under the national regulations shall be issued by or upon approval of the State Council."[79] Thus, the new practice of the Shanghai FTZ was extended to the whole country.

In terms of local legislation, taking the Shanghai FTZ as an example, at the beginning of the establishment of the Shanghai FTZ in September 2013, the Shanghai Municipal Government simultaneously formulated the Special Management Measures (Negative List) for Access of Foreign Investment to China (Shanghai) Pilot Free Trade Zone (2013),[80] which clarified the scope and content of local regulation. In July 2014, the 14th Shanghai Municipal People's Congress reviewed and approved the Regulation on the China (Shanghai) Pilot Free Trade Zone,[81] which was implemented on August 1 of the same year.

76 NPC Standing Committee of PRC, "Decision of the Standing Committee of the National People's Congress on Authorizing the State Council to Temporarily Adjust the Relevant Administrative Approval Items Prescribed in Laws in China (Shanghai) Pilot Free Trade Zone," August 30, 2013, http://en.pkulaw.cn/display.aspx?cgid=af f2ae6e2040c7a6bdfb&lib=law (accessed June 5, 2019).

77 NPC Standing Committee of PRC, "Decision of the Standing Committee of the National People's Congress on Authorizing the State Council to Temporarily Adjust the Relevant Administrative Approval Items Prescribed in Laws in China (Guangdong) Pilot Free Trade Zone, China (Tianjin) Pilot Free Trade Zone, China (Fujian) Pilot Free Trade Zone, and the Extensions of China (Shanghai) Pilot Free Trade Zone," December 18, 2014, http://lawinfochina.com/display.aspx?id=e1293ff74c8e3a4dbdfb&lib=law (accessed June 5, 2019).

78 PRC State Council, "Decision of the State Council on Temporarily Adjusting the Provisions of Relevant Administrative Regulations, Documents of the State Council, and Departmental Rules Approved by the State Council in Pilot Free Trade Zones," July 1, 2016, http://en.pkulaw.cn/display.aspx?id=4456b97685 822112bdfb&lib=law&SearchKeyword=&SearchCKeyword (accessed June 5, 2019).

79 NPC Standing Committee of PRC, "Decision of the Standing Committee of the National People's Congress on Amending Four Laws Including the Law of the People's Republic of China on Foreign-funded Enterprises," September 3, 2016, www.fdi.gov.cn/1800000121_39_4849_0_7.html (accessed January 26, 2019).

80 Local People's Congresses (incl. Standing Committees) and Governments at Various Levels, Shanghai Municipality, People's Government of Shanghai Municipality, "Measures for the Administration of China (Shanghai) Pilot Free Trade Zone," September 29, 2013, http://en.pkulaw.cn/display.aspx?id=eda25915d2ee977 cbdfb&lib=law&SearchKeyword=&SearchCKeyword (accessed January 26, 2019).

81 Local People's Congresses (incl. Standing Committees) and Governments at Various Levels, Shanghai Municipality, Shanghai Municipality People's Congress (incl. Standing Committee), "Regulation on the China (Shanghai) Pilot Free Trade Zone," July 25, 2014, http://en.pkulaw.cn/Display.aspx?lib=law&Cgid=1765 7380 (accessed January 26, 2019).

This is China's first local regulation concerning the FTZ. The Regulations outline the regulatory system over investment, trade, finance and taxation as well as comprehensive supervision in the FTZ, further condensing the content of institutional innovation with the aim of providing strong institutional support for reform in the FTZ.

After the local legislation clarified the basic framework of the FTZ's economic management system, the central government mainly focused on reforming the negative list in regulating foreign investment. China pledges to provide equal treatment of foreign investment putting foreign investors on equal footing with domestic ones in the Chinese market and giving them equal protections and market access. However, in certain sectors and industries, such treatment and market access can be limited for foreign investors; this is administered by the Chinese government through its negative list, which it revises and publishes from time to time. Under this system, foreign investment is either prohibited or limited in sectors that are on the negative list; foreign investors in sectors not on the list are treated equally with domestic investors, with no additional restrictions on market access.

As a matter of fact, the so-called list (or blacklist) system that is applied in foreign investment regulation can be traced back to the Provisional Regulations on Direction Guide to Foreign Investment in 1995 and the corresponding Catalogue, which were the rudimentary form of the negative list mechanism for market access of foreign investment in China.[82] Since 1995, after more than two decades' development as shown in Table 2.1, the list mechanism related to foreign investment market access has gradually evolved into its current form, as shown in Table 2.2. It reflects the trend of the Chinese government to streamline its regulatory system for foreign investment with less governmental intervention but greater transparency and predictability, indicating the Chinese government's attempt to "leave" (its sovereignty or regulatory power).

Since the first FTZ negative list was issued in the Shanghai FTZ in 2013, experience has gradually spread to other FTZs and even to the whole country. The negative list model of the Shanghai FTZ has been affirmed by the State Council and promotes the "big negative list" of unified market access. On October 2, 2015, the State Council issued the Opinions of the State Council on Implementing the Market Access Negative List Regime, which clarify that the negative list system for market access refers to the list of industries, fields and businesses that the State Council prohibits or restricts foreign investment in the territory of the PRC. The governments at all levels adopt corresponding management measures according to law. All other industries, namely, those not on the list, are opened up for foreign investors. The negative list includes prohibition of access (such as pornography and gambling) and restricted access, which is applicable to investment behaviors of various entities based on voluntary investment, expansion of investment, mergers and acquisitions.[83] From December 1, 2015 to December 31, 2017, the market entry negative list system in some areas (i.e., the provinces where the FTZ is located) was put in place to accumulate experience. The negative list and the corresponding institutional mechanisms formally implemented a unified negative list system for foreign investors' market access in the entire country from 2018. On December 25, 2018, with the approval of the Central Committee of the Communist Party of China and the State Council, the National Development and Reform Commission and the Ministry of Commerce issued the China Negative List 2018. This indicates that China's FDI regulatory

[82] See the relevant discussions subsequent to Table 2.2.

[83] Jiaxiang Hu, "FTZs, Can They Initiate a New Round of Reforms in China?" (2016) 59 *Boletim Ciencias Economicas* 9, 13–14.

TABLE 2.1 *Evolution of the negative list in China*

Title	Effective date	Legal status	Issuing authority(ies)
Provisional Regulations on Direction Guide to Foreign Investment	June 20, 1995	Expired	State Development Planning Commission & State Economic and Trade Commission
Catalogue of Industries for Guiding Foreign Investment	June 28, 1995		
Catalogue of industries prohibited from foreign investment	Dec 31, 1997		
Catalogue of Industries for Guiding Foreign Investment (1997 Revision)	Jan 1, 1998		
Catalogue of Priority Industries for Foreign Investment in Central and Western China	Jun 16, 2000		
Provisions on Guiding the Direction of Foreign Investment	Apr 1, 2002	Effective	State Council
Catalogue of Industries for Guiding Foreign Investment (2002 Revision)	Apr 1, 2002	Expired	National Development and Reform Commission & State Economic and Trade Commission
Catalogue of Priority Industries for Foreign Investment in Central and Western China (2004 Revision)	Sep 1, 2004		National Development and Reform Commission & Ministry of Commerce
Catalogue of Industries for Guiding Foreign Investment (2004 Revision)	Jan 1, 2005		
Catalogue of Industries for Guiding Foreign Investment (2007 Revision)	Jan 12, 2007		
Catalogue of Priority Industries for Foreign Investment in Central and Western China (2008 Revision)	Jan 1, 2009		
Catalogue of Industries for Guiding Foreign Investment (2011 Revision)	Jan 30, 2012		
Catalogue of Priority Industries for Foreign Investment in Central and Western China (2013 Revision)	Jun 10, 2013		
Special Management Measures (Negative List) for Access of Foreign Investment to China (Shanghai) Pilot Free Trade Zone (2013)	Sep 29, 2013		People's Government of Shanghai Municipality
Special Management Measures (Negative List) for Access of Foreign Investment to China (Shanghai) Pilot Free Trade Zone (2014)	Jun 30, 2014		
Catalogue of Industries for Guiding Foreign Investment (2015 Revision)	Oct 4, 2015		National Development and Reform Commission & Ministry of Commerce

(*Continued*)

Opinions of the State Council on Implementing the Market Access Negative List Regime	Jan 12, 2015	Partially Expired	State Council
Draft Negative List for Market Access (Trial Version)	Feb 3, 2016		National Development and Reform Commission & Ministry of Commerce
Catalogue of Priority Industries for Foreign Investment in Central and Western China (2017 Revision)	Mar 20, 2017	Effective	
Special Administrative Measures (Negative List) for the Access of Foreign Investment in Pilot Free Trade Zones (2017)	Oct 7, 2017	Expired	State Council
Catalogue of Industries for Guiding Foreign Investment (2017 Revision)	Jul 28, 2017	Partially Expired	National Development and Reform Commission & Ministry of Commerce
Special Administrative Measures (Negative List) for the Access of Foreign Investment (2018)	Jul 28, 2018	Expired	
Special Administrative Measures (Negative List) for the Access of Foreign Investment in Pilot Free Trade Zones (2018)	Jul 30, 2018		
Special Management Measures (Negative List) for Access of Foreign Investment to China (Shanghai) Pilot Free Trade Zone (2013)	Jan 11, 2018		People's Government of Shanghai Municipality
Market Access Negative List (2018)	Dec 21, 2018	Effective	National Development and Reform Commission & Ministry of Commerce
Special Administrative Measures (Negative List) for the Access of Foreign Investment (2019)	Jul 30, 2019		
Special Administrative Measures (Negative List) for the Access of Foreign Investment in Pilot Free Trade Zones (2019)	Jul 30, 2019		
Catalogue of Industries Encouraging Foreign Investment (2019)	Jul 30, 2019		
Special Administrative Measures (Negative List) for the Access of Foreign Investment (2020)	Jun 23, 2020		
Special Administrative Measures (Negative List) for the Access of Foreign Investment in Pilot Free Trade Zones (2020)	Jun 23, 2020		

*Compiled by the author.

TABLE 2.2 *China's current negative list system*

Title	Key characteristics
Market Access Negative List (the Negative List)	A nationwide negative list for all market players.
Special Administrative Measures (Negative List) for the Access of Foreign Investment (the China Negative List)	A nationwide negative list for all foreign investors.
Special Administrative Measures (Negative List) for the Access of Foreign Investment in Pilot Free Trade Zones (the FTZ Negative List)	An FTZ negative list for all foreign investors.
Catalogue of Industries for Guiding Foreign Investment (the Catalogue)	A positive list for foreign investors in the nation and special regions.

*Compiled by the author.

model has shifted from comprehensive control over FIEs to a negative list system,[84] and it is having a great impact on the liberalization of China's foreign investment supervision model.[85]

On the one hand, the negative list basically changed the government-centered approval regime which was framed by the EJV Law, the CJV Law and the WFOE Law. The extent of state control is best evidenced by the approval regime in the admission of foreign investment. The government authorities are involved in all the stages of foreign investment projects, from formation and operation to termination. Challenges of securing administrative licenses and business approvals and navigating China's licensing and regulatory procedures have been in existence since the inception of foreign investment.[86] The area of law and practice is deeply problematic. Unreasonable delays take place too often. The licensing and approval procedure can take much longer than it should. Confusion very often arises when various authorities interpret and apply laws differently. Discretionary administrative powers and local standards often make it difficult for applicants to do preparation and paperwork and predict the results. Most foreign investors have to devote much more management time and workforce to handling approvals and licensing issues.[87]

As far as the EJV Law, the CJV Law and the WFOE Law are concerned, preliminary approval is required for a feasibility study even before the negotiation and conclusion of the actual foreign investment contract (in the form of either a Sino-foreign joint venture agreement or a foreign investment agreement). Chinese parties to joint ventures may need to obtain approval for their project proposal, so that the project can be listed in the local economic plan. Without project proposal approval, the Chinese party may not even be able to commence formal negotiation with the foreign party for the project.[88] The articles of

84 Baihua Gong, "The Change of the Perspective of Rule of Law from China's Free Trade Pilot Zone to Free Trade Port" (2019) 190 *Journal of Political Science and Law* 109, 113.

85 Louise Watt and Kelvin Chan, "China Pilot Free Trade Zone Opens in Reform Push," September 29, 2013, www.ksl.com/article/27048736/china-pilot-free-trade-zone-opens-in-reform-push (accessed March 26, 2019).

86 Yuwen Li and Cheng Bian, "A New Dimension of Foreign Investment Law in China-Evolution and Impacts of the National Security Review System" (2016) 24 *Asia Pacific Law Review* 149, 161.

87 United States–China Business Council, "Administrative Licensing and Business Approvals, United States CBC 2007 Member Priorities Survey Executive Summary: United States Companies' China Outlook: Continuing Optimism Tempered By Operating Challenges, Protectionist Threats," November 2007, www.uschina.org/public/documents/2007/10/uscbc-member-survey-2007.pdf (accessed June 12, 2019).

88 EJV Law, Art. 3; CJV Law, Art. 5.

association and the joint venture contract (or the foreign investment agreement under the WFOE Law) are also subject to approval by the Ministry of Commerce or its local branch.[89] Until these documents are registered with the State Administration of Industry and Commerce, and the business license is issued by the company registry, the EJV, CJV or WFOE is not formally established. This whole process may take three to six months depending on the size and location of the project.

The actual business activities of the EJV Law, the CJV Law or the WFOE Law are limited by the business scope specified in the articles of association and business license. Unlike some common law jurisdictions, the objects clause in the articles, together with the principle of *ultra vires*, is no longer restricted and the company is basically able to conduct any commercial activities. However, this is not the case in China. The parties to joint ventures or WFOE Law need to specify the business scope explicitly in the project proposal, feasibility study report, joint venture contract and articles of association. The scope of business in the business license will not only affect the scope of business activities that the EJV, the CJV or the WFOE is about to conduct but also influence the treatment that the project may receive from competent government authorities.[90] For instance, the availability of import/export licenses, customs duties, investment incentives, preferential tax rates, market access and other treatments largely depends on the scope of business set out in the business license. The business scope also may affect the way the company operates the business in terms of environmental protection and labor management.[91] Like the operation of objects clause in a common law jurisdiction, the conduct of business activities outside the scope of business does not necessarily become void to a bona fide third party. However, the conduct of legally prohibited or restricted business may be void from the very beginning.

Moreover, the negative list has effectively promoted the liberalization of China's regulatory model for foreign investment. The negative list system is "more demanding in terms of resources" and requires "a sophisticated domestic regulatory regime and sufficient institutional capacity for properly designing and negotiating the scheduling of liberalization commitments."[92] The number of special management items in the FTZ Negative List, from 2013 to 2020, reduced from 190 to 30.[93] The sharp shrinking of the negative list shows the Chinese government's attempt to open wider to foreign investors and promote investment liberalization. This demonstrates a clear trend of China's "leaving" its sovereignty and police power.

In terms of the content, the FTZ Negative List 2019 eliminates investment restrictions in agriculture, mining industry, manufacturing industry and transportation.[94] This demonstrates the Chinese government's firm position of enhancing the freedom and convenience

89 WFOE Law, Arts. 6 and 7.

90 EJV Law, Art. 6; CJV Law, Arts. 7–15; WFOE Law, Arts. 9–13.

91 PRC Environment Protection Law; Joint Venture Labor Regulations; Provisional Regulations on Environmental Control for Economic Zones Open to Foreigners.

92 UNCTAD, Investment Policy Framework for Sustainable Development 2012, 61; UNCTAD, Investment Policy Framework for Sustainable Development 2015, 113.

93 See National Development and Reform Commission & Ministry of Commerce, "Special Administrative Measures (Negative List) for the Access of Foreign Investment in Pilot Free Trade Zones (2019)" http://wzs.mofcom.gov.cn/article/n/202006/20200602976957.shtml (accessed September 3, 2020).

94 Compared with the FTZ Negative List 2018, the FTZ Negative List 2019 has removed investment prohibitions on fishing (Art. 4), printing (Art. 8), production of xuan paper and ink ingots (Art. 12), domestic vessel agencies (Art. 17), development of state-protected wild fauna and flora resources native to China (Art. 34) and construction and operation

of investment, and conforms to its "leaving (of the state)" gesture in the field of investment. Further, the China Negative List 2019 shows the leading role of FTZ in liberalizing restrictions on foreign investment. For example, in the FTZ Negative List 2018, performing brokers, oil and gas exploration and development as well as other opening measures in the China Negative List 2019 were pushed to the whole country in 2019.[95] This gesture shows the Chinese government's willingness to stick less to its sovereignty when it comes to regulating foreign investment.

2.2.2 *Further Leaving of the State under Outside Pressures*

The key reason for China vigorously promoting the reform of its foreign investment regulatory system with its negative list as the core lies in the pressure exerted by developed countries such as the USA and the EU in relevant BITs negotiations. The Chinese authorities have published a keenly awaited negative list of sectors, similar in concept to the USA's mooted TPP, establishing which business lines will be closed to foreign companies in the FTZ, while all others will be open.[96] The move is expected to give foreign investors much more freedom. A short list merely banning a small number of sectors including guns, drugs and pornography to foreign investors is theoretically investor-friendly.

On the other hand, while the Shanghai FTZ legislation incited China's foreign investment legislation, it also had a huge impact on China's negotiation and signing of investment treaties. On the issue of market access, for a long time under the investment approval mode led by administrative examination and approval authorities, Chinese BITs provided only for post-establishment treatment. With this differentiated treatment of domestic and foreign investment, China has never "left" its sovereignty behind. However, as the investment liberalization promoted by developed countries has become the norm in IIL, the gap between China and developed economies in investment policies has become quite prominent. Especially on the issue of market access, due to the Chinese domestic laws, it has also become a major issue in the negotiation of BITs between China and the USA[97] and the EU.[98] With the establishment of the Shanghai FTZ, the National People's Congress authorized the suspension of the FIE Laws and gradually promoted the pre-entry NT plus negative list model, which is a new development in Chinese law thereby impacting China's BIT regime as well. Since 2013, China has changed its consistent attitudes toward foreign investment in its BITs negotiations with the USA and the EU, and has clearly expressed its willingness to engage in substantive negotiations with the USA on the basis of its pre-entry NT and negative list.[99]

of cinemas (Art. 42). Meanwhile, the FTZ Negative List 2019 has simplified investment prohibitions on mining industry (Arts. 5–7) and telecommunications (Art. 23).

95 Chinese Government News Web, "Updating the Negative List for Foreign Investment, What Restrictions Should Be Cancelled? Which Industries Should Be Encouraged?", July 6, 2019, www.gov.cn/fuwu/2019-07/06/content_5406718.htm (accessed July 9, 2019).

96 Heng Wang, "The Differences between China's Recent FTA and the TPP: A Case Study of the China-Korea FTA" in Julien Chaisse, Henry Gao and Chang-fa Lo (eds.), *Paradigm Shift in International Economic Law Rule-Making* (Springer, Singapore 2017) 299.

97 Karl P. Sauvant and Huiping Chen, "A China-US Bilateral Investment Treaty: A Template for a Multilateral Framework for Investment?" (2013) 5 *Transnational Corporations Review* 1, 2.

98 See Wei Yin, "Challenges, Issues in China-EU Investment Agreement and the Implication on China's Domestic Reform" (2018) 26 *Asia Pacific Law Review* 170, 176–179.

99 See Jie Huang, "Challenges and Solutions for the China-US BIT Negotiations: Insights from the Recent Development of FTZs in China" (2015) 18 *Journal of International Economic Law* 307, 316.

In the negotiations of the China-EU CAI, the EU further required the state party not to impose restrictions on technology transfer, investment ratio and investment volume on the basis of pre-entry NT, in an effort to promote China's lifting of its foreign investment protection standards.[100] Through the development of FTZ in recent years and the passing of the new Foreign Investment Law (FIL), to be discussed in Section 2.3, China is indeed showing a more open treaty negotiation posture, a shift to promoting investment liberalization. It appears that the reform carried out in the FTZs in China has been a stepping stone for China's further opening up to foreign investment, showing its commitment to bear a higher level of obligations toward foreign investors.[101] Likely, these reformist measures taken in China's FTZs will become the connecting points between China's domestic law and its BIT regime, as indicated in Figure 2.3.

Just as China is further transforming its investment legislation and policies, the developed economies represented by the USA are questioning China's current trade, investment and economic policy. In the 301 Report published by the Office of the US Trade Representative in 2018, there are many criticisms of China's investment policies. The main problems are the following: First, in view of foreign investment access, the USA believes that China has long imposed legislation and administrative means to require technology transfer by foreign investors in areas such as automobile manufacturing and aviation manufacturing, which has seriously damaged US investors and their rights. This reflects China's problems in the protection of IPR, NT and MFN status.[102] Second, in response to China's foreign investment, the USA believes that the Chinese government has highly controlled the foreign investment activities of Chinese enterprises through foreign investment approval and foreign exchange control measures, and does not meet the requirements of the market economy in terms of policies. At the same time, most of China's outbound investment enterprises are SOEs, and the areas they invest in involve military industry, equipment manufacturing and high-tech

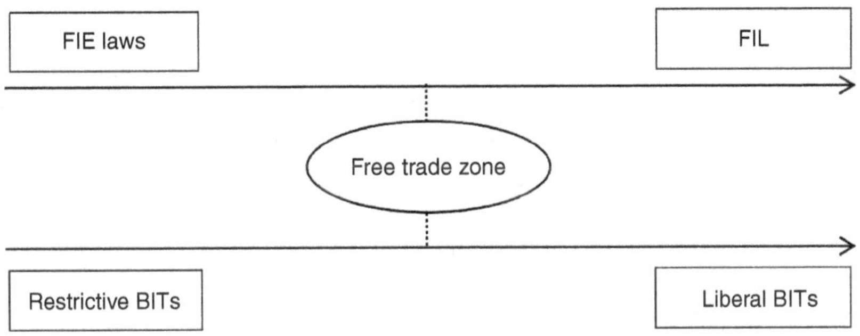

FIGURE 2.3 Moving direction of FIL and BITs
*Compiled by the author.

[100] Jun Xiao, "How Can a Prospective China-EU BIT Contribute to Sustainable Investment: In Light of the UNCTAD Investment Policy Framework for Sustainable Development" (2015) 8 *Journal of World Energy Law and Business* 521,525–528.

[101] See Lin Xiao, *National Test: System Design of China (Shanghai) Pilot Free Trade Zone* (Springer, Singapore 2016) 421–422.

[102] See Office of The United States Trade Representative Executive Office of The President, *Findings of The Investigation into China's Acts, Policies, And Practices Related to Technology Transfer, Intellectual Property, And Innovation Under Section 301 of The Trade Act of 1974*, pp. 29–35, Mar. 22, 2018, *available at* https://ustr.gov/sites/default/files/Section%20301%20FINAL.PDF (last visited Jan. 12, 2019).

industries. Therefore, in the eyes of the USA, China's current foreign investment is an unfair economic act and its abusive market practices against key US interests are threatening the national security and industrial competitiveness of the USA.[103]

Judging from the statistics of relevant international organizations, there is also a big gap between China and the USA in the field of foreign investment supervision. According to the Foreign Investment Restriction Index released by the OECD, among the sixty-eight countries in which it counts, the 2017 China Foreign Investment Restriction Index reached 0.316, ranking fourth, below only the Philippines, Saudi Arabia and Indonesia. The US index is 0.089, which is at the midstream level.[104] From the perspective of specific industries, China currently has clear restrictions on the proportion of foreign equity in automobile manufacturing, telecommunications services, medical care, education, and finance, and the restrictions include prohibiting foreign investment in internet culture businesses and news information services, news broadcasting and other industries, and securities companies. The ratio of foreign shares of securities investment fund management companies is set to not exceed 51 percent. In addition, China currently has many hidden barriers to market access including industry regulation and business licenses in areas such as banking, insurance services, securities fund business, telecommunications network-related services and express delivery services. In contrast, the current US foreign investment regulation does not have special restrictions on these industries. The US restrictions are based on case-review of related transactions according to national security exceptions under the CFIUS regime.

From the perspective of investment policy since 2018, both China and the USA have seen more obvious changes. In recent years, the USA has continuously strengthened its supervision of foreign investment, showing its "return (of the state)" tendency. In contrast, in China in 2018, President Xi Jinping announced to the world at the Boao Forum for Asia and China International Import Expo that China is determined to open up to the outside world. China will relax market access for industries such as finance and automobiles, and will accelerate the opening up of telecommunications, medical care, education and culture. Specifically, the China Negative List 2018 published in June 2018 further narrowed the scope of restrictions and proposed that financial companies such as securities companies and insurance companies cancel the restrictions on foreign shares in 2021.[105] At the beginning of 2019, China had begun to liberalize the market for foreign investors in the fields of finance and telecommunications services, and gradually to promote the opening of relevant industries.[106]

103 See Office of The United States Trade Representative Executive Office of The President, *Findings of The Investigation into China's Acts, Policies, And Practices Related to Technology Transfer, Intellectual Property, And Innovation Under Section 301 of The Trade Act of 1974*, pp. 62–153, Mar. 22, 2018, *available at* https://ustr.gov/sites/default/files/Section%20301%20FINAL.PDF (last visited Jan. 12, 2019).

104 See OECD, *OECD FDI Regulatory Restrictiveness Index, available at* https://stats.oecd.org/Index.aspx?datasetcode=FDIINDEX&_ga=2.141403184.380646240.1547967192-364793636.1547707704# (lasted visited Jan. 8, 2019).

105 The China Negative List 2018, Articles 21 and 22.

106 BT Group announced on January 24, 2019 that it has obtained two value-added telecommunications licenses from China's Ministry of Industry and Information Technology, marking the beginning of China's opening up to the telecommunications services industry. See BT Official Website, *BT First Global Telco to Receive Domestic Telecoms Licences in China*, Jan. 29, 2019, *available at* www.chinadaily.com.cn/a/201901/29/WS5c4fbdfca3106c65c34e70b2.html (lasted visited Jan. 30, 2019). The Business Management Department of the People's Bank of China issued an announcement on January 28, 2019, announcing the completion of the S&P Credit Rating (China) Co., Ltd. completion of the credit rating agency filing, marking the beginning of the overseas financial rating agencies in China. See the Business Management Department of the People's Bank of China (Beijing), Jan. 28, 2019, *available at* http://beijing.pbc.gov.cn/beijing/132024/3753866/index.html (lasted visited Jan. 30, 2019).

China's National Reform and Development Commission and the Ministry of Commerce jointly issued the China Negative List 2019, setting out the sectors where foreign investment is either restricted or prohibited, along with a consolidated encouraged list of sectors for foreign investment, both of which came into effect on July 30, 2019 and further remove restrictions and facilitate foreign investment in China. The China Negative List 2019, like the previous ones, comprises two separate lists that are applicable in the designated pilot FTZs respectively. The China Negative List 2019 specifically eases restrictions on market access in agriculture, mining, infrastructure and manufacturing industries as well as multiple service sectors. The China Negative List 2019 now contains forty items, down from forty-eight in the 2018 version. For FTZs, the FTZ Negative List contains thirty-seven items, down from forty-five. China's National Development and Reform Commission and the Ministry of Commerce also issued in their Joint Order No. 27 a new Catalogue of industries where foreign investment is encouraged. As a replacement for the encouraged industries section of the Catalogue 2017 and the Catalogue of Priority Industries for Foreign Investment in Central and Western China (2017 Revision), the new encouraged list, now containing 1,108 sectors in total with 415 sectors of encouraged industries nationwide and 693 region-specific sectors, not only combines the above two catalogues but also expands the preferential policies for foreign investment to certain new sectors. Being updated on an annual basis, the negative list is gradually easing control on foreign access and streamlining the administrative process with regard to foreign investment. The China Negative List 2019 signals the extent to which China is seeking to loosen its control over foreign access to its markets.

In the automobile manufacturing industry, China will remove the restrictions on foreign-invested shares of special-purpose vehicles and new-energy vehicles. In 2020, the restrictions on foreign-invested shares in commercial vehicles were lifted. In 2022, the restrictions on the foreign-invested shares of passenger vehicles will be eliminated, and the same foreign company will be able to establish no more than two joint ventures that produce similar vehicle products in China.[107] The reforms since 2018 also include drastically reducing tariffs on pharmaceuticals, automobiles, consumer goods and industrial products, accelerating the pilot of FTZs and free trade ports, and promoting a new pattern of high-level reform and opening up.[108] In addition, the rapid advancement of the Foreign Investment Law is also a declaration of policy stance and a response to the US concern. The widening of industrial sectors to foreign investors in the China Negative List 2019 reflects China's positive gesture to cool the economic tension between China and the USA.

By empowering the FTZ with the autonomy to reform, the Chinese government has broken the existing approval-led system and established a new model with a negative list at its core in the field of foreign investment. The negative list system is not only a continuation of the "list system" established by China since the 1990s but also a response to TPP and other models in the negotiation of relevant BITs with developed countries. The negative list model has changed China's foreign investment regulatory model and profoundly affected China's stance on BITs, thus promoting China's liberalization and transformation of domestic law as well as IIL in the form of BITs.

[107] The China Negative List 2018, Article 8.

[108] See Xi Jinping, "Opening, Creating, Prospering, Innovating, Leading the Future – Keynote Speech at the Opening Ceremony of the 2018 Annual Meeting of the Boao Forum for Asia," *People's Daily*, Apr. 11, 2018, 3rd edition; Xi Jinping, "Building Innovation Inclusive Open World Economy-Keynote Speech at the Opening Ceremony of the First China International Import Expo," Nov. 15, 2018, *available at* www.xinhuanet.com/2018-11/05/c_1123664692.htm (lasted visited Jan. 1, 2019).

2.3 CHINA'S NEW FIL

China's National People's Congress approved a new Foreign Investment Law in March 2019 which can be viewed as a great attempt to address key issues raised by the US government as part of the US–China trade war.[109] The new FIL came into effect on January 1, 2020, and is expected to abolish the EJV Law, the CJV Law and the WFOE Law. The purpose of the new FIL is to replace and unify these three FIE Laws.

The existing regulatory regime was established with the promulgation of the EJV Law in 1979. In 1986 and 1988, respectively, the WFOE Law and the CJV Law were promulgated, thereby completing the trio of the so-called "Three FIE Laws," which constitute the three pillars of the foreign investment regulatory regime that has governed foreign investment matters for the past four decades.[110]

Under the three FIE Laws, all foreign investments into China and their subsequent changes require prior, case-by-case approval from MOFCOM (the Ministry of Commerce) or its local branches.[111] In its deliberation of each case submitted for approval, MOFCOM would review not only the background of the foreign investor, the industry and the project that the foreign investor intends to engage in but also the corporate governance terms of the FIEs to be established. Joint venture contracts and articles of associations of FIEs are to become effective only after MOFCOM approval is granted. As a result, FIEs have been subject to a parallel series of regulations in addition to the PRC Company Law, which was promulgated in 1993 and was quite exclusively applied to domestically owned enterprises.

The approval regime, which played a pivotal role in the initial opening up of China to the external world and in bringing foreign capital and technologies into the Chinese market, had long seemed excessive and inefficient.[112] It prolonged the approval process, increased regulatory costs for foreign investors and, to some extent, impeded free competition and liquidity flow.

The new FIL basically transforms the approval system for the setup of FIEs to a record-filing system under which FIEs, like domestically owned enterprises, would come into existence once being registered with the company registrar.[113] This change of the approval system reduces the level of government intervention in the establishment of FIEs and offers equal procedural treatment to foreign investors. In terms of transaction costs, the record-filing system certainly helps save transaction costs for foreign investors which no long need to spend cost and resources on the approval system, which is less predictable due to the discretionary powers exercised by the government authorities. Compared with the FIE Laws, the new FIL has undergone a fundamental change with regard to foreign investment. The new FIL has

109 The Chinese government rushed the legislation through the National People's Congress in an effort to fend off complaints from the US and EU about unfair trade practices. The new law was first introduced as a draft in 2015, but its progress picked up markedly from the middle of last year. Apparently, this was an attempt to address issues identified by the US in the ongoing trade war. If there is pushback against a draft bill and amendments so made, this happens before the NPC sits, at a series of standing committee meetings behind closed doors. The process can take years. This time, the passing of the bill only took three months.

110 See Martin Endicott, *China and International Investment Law: An Evolving Relationship* in *China and International Investment Law Twenty Years of ICSID Membership* 220–221 (Wenhua Shan ed., Brill – Nijhoff 2014).

111 EJV Law, Articles 1, 3; CJV Laws, Article 5; WFOE Law, Article 6.

112 See Jacques Morisset & Olivier Lumenga Neso, "Administrative Barriers to Foreign Investment in Developing Countries," 17–18, May, 2012, *available at* http://documents.worldbank.org/curated/en/556581468766823917/pdf/multiopage.pdf (last visited Jul. 14, 2019).

113 FIL, Articles 29, 30 and 31.

ceased to be a law governing various forms of foreign investment enterprises, leaving the task to the Company Law and the Partnership Enterprise Law.[114]

The new FIL is designed to focus on investment promotion and protection which is supplemented by foreign investment management, and to level the domestic playing field for foreign investors by addressing various concerns raised by the global investment community such as forced technology transfer to Chinese partners, unfair treatment in terms of market access and government procurement, and the theft of commercial secrets from foreign businesses in China.[115] For instance, foreign investors are treated the same as domestic investors not only in the setup period when their business entities are established but also after the establishment of the entities. Foreign investors are assured of equal opportunity as regards government procurement between both domestic enterprises and FIEs.[116] The big ticket item, in terms of foreign companies, is IP theft in the form of the handover of technological secrets as the price of entry to the massive Chinese market – which takes place when multinational firms partner up with a local entity. According to the new FIL, officials are obliged to protect commercially confidential information they obtain from overseas businesses. The new FIL makes it illegal for officials to misuse critical information or to provide it to local firms. The new FIL imposes criminal penalties for sharing sensitive foreign company information, thus adopting a much tougher deterrent against counterfeiting and IP theft, and also offers new avenues for the enforcement of IP protection. There is a clear ban on illegal government interference in the activities of foreign businesses.[117] These changes came after the USA's accusation of Chinese authorities' linking market access to technology transfer from US companies to Chinese partners,[118] and can be viewed as an effort to appease the tension between the USA and China over the issue of protection of foreign IPR.

Unfair subsidies to Chinese companies are also addressed by the new FIL. However, foreign investors may need to be wary of some requirements. For instance, one of the provisions includes a requirement for the local subsidiaries of international firms to report various details of their operations to Chinese officials. These could include performance indicators relating to labor relations, overall staffing numbers, pollution records and the like.[119]

One issue which may be a structural difference between US BITs and Chinese BITs[120] is the pre-establishment NT plus negative list system instead of relying on a case-by-case

114 Bao Zhi, Stanley Jia & Scott Silverman, "China Issues a New Consolidated Law on Foreign Investment," May 9, 2019, *available at* https://globalcompliancenews.com/china-issues-new-consolidated-law-foreign-investment-20190318/ (last visited Jul. 20, 2019).

115 BBC, "China Foreign Investment Law: Bill Aims to Ease Global Concerns," Mar. 15, 2019, *available at* www.bbc.com/news/business-47578883 (last visited Jun. 15, 2019).

116 FIL, Articles 15 and 16.

117 FIL, Articles 22, 23.

118 US companies often license their IP rights to their Chinese subsidiaries formed together with the Chinese partners. In exchange, the Chinese partners and local governments may prefer to see some technology transfer with the aim of fostering economic and technological development by offering some incentives in land, infrastructure, tax and loans on more favorable terms. Although it is true that the Chinese partners may be in a better position to negotiate more favorable terms, it is the US investors that eventually decide to make a deal on a cost-benefit analysis basis. Previously, the US investors may be willing to transfer technology as the Chinese counterparties' ability to adapt and master these transferred technology may be somehow limited. Nevertheless, when the Chinese entities' capability for indigenous innovation has progressed substantially in recent years, the US investors may feel pressured to continue this practice as they see Chinese counterparties as genuine and serious competitors. As a result, the US investors want to change this strategy and accuse this practice of unfair competition or forced technology transfer.

119 FIL, Articles 32, 33, 34.

120 C. Fred Bergsten, Gary Clyde Hufbauer, and Sean Miner, *Bridging the Pacific: Toward Free Trade and Investment Between China and the United States* (Peterson Institute for International Economics 2014).

approval model. In Chinese BITs, the definition of "investment" usually does not cover the "pre-establishment" phase of investment.[121] This means that only "post-establishment" investment can be protected by the BIT, and foreign investors, in order to enjoy BIT benefits, must obtain permission from the Chinese government to invest in an industry or sector on a case-by-case basis according to the industrial policies. Clearly, post-establishment rights dilute the value of investor protections under BITs. Pre-establishment rights instead tend to reduce discretionary requirements and bureaucratic obstacles. Together with the pre-establishment rights is a negative list allowing foreign investors to invest into most industrial sectors as domestic investors on the basis of NT. China's Negative List specifies forty sectors that are not open to foreign investment or, in some cases, not open without conditions or special permission. For instance, there is a complete ban on investing in fishing,[122] gene research,[123] news media and television broadcasting,[124] and religious education.[125] Non-renewable energy automobile production will require partnerships for a few years but then be phased out.[126] The general principle established by the new FIL is that foreign companies will receive and enjoy the same treatment as their Chinese counterparts for the industries that are not listed in the negative list.[127]

Nevertheless, many in the business community in China see this FIL as a kind of sweeping set of intentions rather than a specific, enforceable set of rules. As the wording of the new FIL is still vague and general – which is characteristic of Chinese legislation – many details may have to be addressed in future regulations and rules. It is fair for the international business community to fear that it could be open to different and changing forms of interpretation. Besides, enforcement will be the key metric for evaluating the success of the new FIL. Enforcement, at the end of the day, relies on structural changes and an independent judicial system.[128]

A very important change in the FIL is to strengthen investment promotion and protection by providing more solid legal protection for foreign investors and FIEs.[129] The new FIL includes clauses concerning expropriation, profit remittance, IP protection, non-forced technology transfer, local government compliance and other issues. Foreign investors are also assured of having equal opportunity in regard to government procurement between Chinese enterprises and FIEs.

Following increasing frustration felt by foreign businesses about their inability to compete fairly with Chinese companies, the USA and China became embroiled in trade tensions in 2018. Under then US President Donald Trump, the rhetoric about the spat initially focused on the American trade deficit with China. That resulted in the application of tariffs on USD 250 billion worth of imported goods from China, to which Beijing countered with duties on USD 110 billion worth of goods from the USA. In the last several months, the negotiations between both sides have increasingly centered on issues of IP protection and claims of forced

121 Chapter 3.
122 The China Negative List 2019, Articles 2, 4.
123 The China Negative List 2019, Article 3.
124 The China Negative List 2019, Articles 6, 10, 34–37.
125 The China Negative List 2019, Article 32.
126 The China Negative List 2019, Article 9.
127 FIL, Article 28.
128 "China Issues a New Consolidated Law on Foreign Investment," May 9, 2019, *available at* https://globalcompliancenews.com/china-issues-new-consolidated-law-foreign-investment-20190318/ (last visited Jul. 13, 2019).
129 FIL, Articles 9–21.

technology transfer.[130] The new FIL may not be enough to appease the demands of the USA in ongoing trade negotiations. Passing the law is a clear attempt to translate some of the concerns expressed by the USA and the EU into legislation. It is a step in the right direction. But the trade tensions are wider than that.

The State Council has enhanced the national security review system for foreign investment, under which a security review shall be conducted for any foreign investment affecting or having the possibility to affect state security.[131] The new FIL offers broader retaliation, giving China the right to retaliate against a particular country for restricting Chinese companies there. Such a clause essentially reinforces the unequal footing that foreign and Chinese companies have in accessing each other's countries. US companies have complained that they get less access in China than Chinese companies have in America.

The new FIL can be seen as a strong signal sent by the Chinese government to the global community that it remains an attractive investment destination. The new FIL emphasizes the protection of foreign investors' rights and interests, limits the government's right to intervene in business operations, and clarifies the full implementation of pre-entry NT and the negative list.[132] In terms of foreign investment supervision, on the one hand, the FIL highly emphasizes the importance of administrative agencies in formulating the negative list. However, from the current negative list, there are still many areas that prohibit or restrict foreign investment, and there is a big gap with developed countries. In the ongoing BITs negotiations between China and the USA and the EU, the specific content of the negative list is always the focus of disputes between the parties, especially the clarity of the negative list, the distribution of power between the central government and local governments, and the negative list for specific industries. Some scholars also believe that clarifying the negative list is a difficult point in the BIT negotiations between China and the USA.[133]

On the other hand, although the foreign investment review mechanism established by the FIL clearly defines the position of restricting the administrative power of the government, the provisions still have great ambiguity, and there is also great uncertainty in the specific interpretation and application, which reduces foreign investors' expectations of investment risks and makes them still afraid of investing.[134] Generally speaking, the FIL is not only a summary and effective integration of China's foreign investment legislation over the last forty years of economic reform and opening up but also a recitation of internationally accepted investment standards in the basic position of the CCP's Central Committee to continue to promote economic reform and opening up. In particular, the pre-entry NT, the supervision of the negative list as the core and the legislation of specific measures such as the protection of IPR demonstrate China's basic position as continuing to promote investment liberalization and facilitation. The new FIL is a big step forward in China's investment liberalization.

In short, China's foreign investment legislation over the forty years since the start of economic reform and opening up has experienced a system build-up from scratch, highlighting the basic position of constantly restricting the government's regulatory power and

130 Lee Branstetter, "China's 'Forced' Technology Transfer Problem – And What to Do About It," 2–3, May 31, 2018, *available at* www.uscc.gov/sites/default/files/Branstetter.Forced%20Technology.China%205-24%20US-China%20Commission.pdf (last visited Jul. 11, 2019).

131 FIL, Article 35.

132 FIL, Articles 3 and 4.

133 See Jie Huang, *supra* note 100, at 318–319.

134 FIL Art. 35.

safeguarding the interests of foreign investors,[135] and showing the country's "leaving (of the state)" gesture. However, this "leaving (of the state)" gesture is not sufficient in terms of speed, scope and strength, especially in terms of NT, MFN status and IP protection,[136] and the standards expected by developed economies such as the USA and the EU. From the policy direction of 2018, China has begun to pay attention to reforms in the abovementioned areas, and it continues to highlight the trend of continuously pushing the country's "leaving" (the sovereignty) posture at both the legislative and the administrative levels.

2.4 MIXED IMAGE OF CHINA'S FIL

At the time of the 2008 global financial crisis, China appeared to be on a course of marketization, liberalization and facilitation evidenced by its political will to adhere to its open door policy and the increasing amount of FDIO.[137] However, the global financial crisis also caused a perception among China's policy-makers that the state-driven model is a solution to regulatory and market failure. As a result, China has seemed to rely more on state intervention than market disciplines to manage its macro-economy.

As long as China continues to regulate foreign investment comprehensively and closely, policy may continue to dominate its laws on foreign investment and businesses. Meanwhile, the economic reforms that have significantly transformed China have made necessary development of the legal framework for foreign trade and investment. The evolution of the law, legal institutions and legal infrastructure remains slow and uneven. While the laws and regulations are more available than before, the law enforcement remains a key hurdle to the rule of law in a Western sense. The administrative organs and officials, even if not granted, are used to exercising their discretionary power to interpret and enforce laws, which creates more uncertainty, inconsistency and complexity in enforcement. Recent years may have witnessed China's more authoritarian and paternalist image in terms of its regulation, policy and governance.

China has been heavily criticized for implementing and advocating a state-directed economic model which has distorted fair competition in the global market. This has been one of the heatedly contested issues between China and its Western counterparties. During the trade war negotiations, the US administration demanded reforms of SOEs, but China appears to have reinforced its state-directed economic model by increasing the influence of SOEs as well as CCP intrusions into the boardrooms of private enterprises.[138] Apparently, the USA and China represent two opposing systems for running an economy. The USA adopts a liberal economy model. But China was labeled as a revisionalist state running state capitalism.[139] China's past four decades reveal the close linkage between the state and the market amid its economic miracle. The state plays a triple role in the economy – it is

135 Chunlai Chen, "The Liberalisation of FDI Policies and the Impacts of FDI on China's Economic Development" in Ross Garnaut, Ligang Song and Cai Fang (eds.), *China's 40 Years of Reform and Development* (ANU Press 2018) 612.

136 See Guiguo Wang, "China's Practice in International Investment Law: From Participation to Leadership in the World Economy" (2009) 34 *Yale Journal of International Law* 575, 577.

137 Wangqiang Li, "Chinese Foreign Investment Laws: A Review from the Perspective of Policy-Oriented Jurisprudence" (2011) 19(1) *Asia Pacific Law Review* 35–52.

138 Frank Tang, "China Ignoring US Demand for Trade War Reform by Reinforcing State-Directed Economic Model," *South China Morning Post*, July 13, 2019, www.scmp.com/economy/china-economy/article/3018120/china-ignoring-us-demand-trade-war-reform-reinforcing-state (accessed September 5, 2020).

139 Barry Naughton, *State Capitalism, Institutional Adaption, and the Chinese Miracle* (Cambridge University Press 2015).

a planner, a regulator and a player. In Chinese domestic political terminology, the state has a triple role in the game: it is a soccer player, it is a referee and it is a coach. As a result, the domestic legal system underpins the distinctive market–state relationship. This may work in the Chinese context, but it contradicts the orthodox political economy and the essential norms of international economic law and global economic governance.

Locally, this state–market paradox is hindering China's economic growth and transformation from a labor-intensive one to an innovation-based one. Globally, it is causing controversy between China and its Western counterparts. The Chinese government is highly involved in guiding its economy. In cross-border investment, China's intervention makes it hard to discern whether FDIO is driven by policy or the market.[140] International economic order is also challenged as its inherent market–state dichotomy has a clear boundary which makes it hard to justify China's economic governance model. Policy tools run contrary to the principles of free trade and market competition. Although China is making efforts to convince the rest of the world that it is actually offering the world an alternative model, the world may either need a fresh perspective to comprehend the market–state relationship or take for granted that the market and the state have a mutually exclusive relationship.[141]

140 Joerg Wuttke, "Vetting China's State-Directed Investments," *Wall Street Journal*, March 6, 2017, www.wsj.com/articles/vetting-chinas-state-directed-investments-1488822328 (accessed September 5, 2020).

141 Luyao Che, *China's State-Directed Economy and the International Order* (Springer 2019) (exploring the legal underpinnings of the state-market economic model, and its challenge to the international economic order).

3

Substantive Protection Provisions in Chinese BITs

The USA appears to be taking a route departing from the multilateral approach to global economic governance at the moment and withdrawing from a number of international institutions. In particular, the USA is blocking the appointment of judges to the WTO Appellate Body making the WTO de facto dysfunctional. Meanwhile, the USA is taking a so-called mini-multilateral approach by selecting US allies or strategically important partners with which to form trade alliances. By doing so, the USA is crafting and redefining US-preferred trade and investment rules, and, more tactically, pressurizing the reform of global economic governance, that is, the WTO per se.[1] By including a poison pill clause in the USMCA,[2] the USA is intending to block China from entering into FTAs with US allies, and to replicate this poison pill clause in trade pacts with other trading partners to "legitimize" China's trade, IP and industrial subsidy practices.[3] In this sense, the mini-multilateralism that the USA is implementing is a US-centric trade block in favor of its interests and rule-setting.

China at the same time is becoming an active and loyal proponent of multilateralism, lending strong support to the WTO-centric globalization and multilateral trade system. Because of this trade policy, China has entered into few regional trade agreements, and has been in negotiations with Japan and South Korea to form a trilateral FTA[4] and with the Association of South East Asian Nations (ASEAN)[5] and most of the countries that have FTAs with ASEAN to form the Regional Comprehensive Economic Partnership (RCEP), a

1 Chris Brummer, *Minilateralism: How Trade Alliances, Soft Law, and Financial Engineering Are Redefining Economic Statecraft* (Cambridge University Press 2014).

2 United States–Mexico–Canada Agreement, https://ustr.gov/trade-agreements/free-trade-agreements/united-states-mexico-canada-agreement (accessed September 8, 2020).

3 David Lawder and Karen Freifeld, "Exclusive: U.S. Commerce's Ross Eyes Anti-China 'Poison Pill' for New Trade Deals," Reuters, October 6, 2018, www.reuters.com/article/us-usa-trade-ross-exclusive/exclusive-u-s-commerces-ross-eyes-anti-china-poison-pill-for-new-trade-deals-idUSKCN1MF2HJ (accessed September 8, 2020).

4 Orange Wang, "China, Japan, South Korea Agree to Continue Push for Free-Trade Deal Despite Ongoing Tensions across Region," *South China Morning Post*, December 22, 2019, www.scmp.com/economy/china-economy/article/3043166/china-japan-and-south-korea-agree-continue-push-free-trade (accessed September 8, 2020).

5 ASEAN was founded in 1967 by five states in South East Asia, that is, Indonesia, Malaysia, Singapore, Thailand and the Philippines. Five other states, namely, Brunei Darussalam (1984), Vietnam (1992), Myanmar (1997), Laos (1997) and Cambodia (1999), in the same region became members thereafter. ASEAN's aim is to foster good relations among member states and within the region, especially in the field of economic development.

mega-regional deal.[6] These two trade pacts have been in negotiations for years, and have become more strategically important to China given the USA's mini-multilateralism. These two trade deals not only help boost economic ties with China's neighbors[7] but also mitigate the risk of "decoupling" from Washington and isolation from other trade alliances.[8] Given this backdrop, China's regional investment agreements are of particular relevance and significance.

ASEAN and China entered into an Agreement on Investment of the Framework Agreement on Comprehensive Economic Cooperation (the "ASEAN Treaty") in Bangkok, Thailand on August 15, 2009. The ASEAN Treaty was a product of further collaboration between ASEAN and China in implementing the Framework Agreement on Comprehensive Economic Cooperation reached by ASEAN and China in Phnom Penh, Cambodia on November 4, 2002.[9] The ASEAN Treaty signaled the latest progress made by ASEAN and China in the process of establishing an ASEAN–China Free Trade Area with the aim of promoting investments and creating a liberal, facilitative, transparent and competitive investment regime.[10]

Regardless of its symbolic significance, the ASEAN Treaty, "a carefully crafted and balanced investment agreement,"[11] had tremendous economic, political and legal significance in facilitating investment, improving transparency of investment rules and regulations, providing for the protection of investments, strengthening cooperation in investment, and ultimately liberalizing the investment regime in the whole ASEAN–China area. From a politico-economy perspective, the ASEAN Treaty played a constructive role in promoting regional harmonization in East Asia after the great success of harmonization in the European Union and North America. In terms of investment liberalization, the ASEAN Treaty appeared to be more liberal than the RCEP, the negotiation of which was completed in November 2020. The investment chapter in the RCEP was the result of a rebalancing between the host state's police power and the foreign investors' rights protection. The signing of the ASEAN Treaty and the ASEAN–China Agreement on Trade in Goods heralded the formation of the world's largest free trade and investment region with an estimated market potential of 1.9 billion consumers and a regional gross domestic product (GDP) of USD 2 trillion.[12]

China did not conclude agreements on mutual protection of investment with foreign countries until March 29, 1982 when its first BIT was concluded with the Kingdom of Sweden. Up to 2009, China had already concluded 122 BITs, ranking second only to

6 Shin Kawashima, "Japan's Painful Choice on RCEP," *The Diplomat*, August 3, 2020, https://thediplomat.com/2020/08/japans-painful-choice-on-rcep/ (accessed September 8, 2020).

7 For instance, the China–Japan BIT 1989 still stands but Japan can free-ride on China's other BITs and FTAs by relying upon the MFN provisions in the China–Japan BIT 1989, which does not include a regional economic integration organization exception rule. Shintaro Hamanaka, "Dynamics of Investment Negotiations between China and Japan: The China-Japan-Korea Trilateral Investment Treaty and Beyond," Institute of Developing Economics Discussion Paper No. 613, www.ide.go.jp/library/English/Publish/Download/Dp/pdf/613.pdf (accessed September 9, 2020).

8 Orange Wang, *supra* note 4.

9 The ASEAN Treaty, Recital 2.

10 ASEAN and China also signed the landmark ASEAN–China Agreement on Trade in Goods on November 29, 2004.

11 Vivienne Bath, "'One Belt, One Road' and Chinese Investment" in Lutz-Christian Wolff, Chao Xi and Jenny Chan (eds.), *Legal Dimensions of China's Belt and Road Initiative* (Wolters Kluwer 2016) 8.

12 ASEAN comprises nearly 600 million people and has a combined GDP of some USD 1,500 billion. See Tim Johnson, "A Wider Radius," *Financial Times*, January 28, 2010, p. 7 (analyzing the geostrategic relevance of ASEAN and the complicated economic relations between ASEAN members and China).

Germany (136) in the number of BITs concluded.[13] Nevertheless, also up to 2009, there had not been a single arbitration case brought by any foreign investor against China, and there had been only one case in which a Chinese investor brought a BIT claim against Peru at ICSID.[14] With USD 90.03 billion of FDII in 2009,[15] China was the largest capital importing country in the world. Any severe economic event or any policy change to any aspect of FDI could have triggered a wave of claims against China under these BITs.

ASEAN has its own system of investment protection which was first established by the Agreement for the Promotion and Protection of Investments (the "ASEAN Agreement"), applicable to ASEAN investors.[16] In terms of the content, the ASEAN Agreement largely resembles a BIT, except for its requirement that investments be approved in writing and registered by the host country in order to be protected.[17] The ASEAN Agreement was amended by the Jakarta Protocol in 1996. In 1998, the Framework Agreement on the ASEAN Investment Area was concluded. The aim was to create an ASEAN Investment Area by 2010 when all ASEAN investors would benefit from NT. ASEAN's Framework Agreement on the ASEAN Investment Area is an important regional multilateral investment treaty.

ASEAN member states have entered into various BITs including but not limited to the Malaysia–Belgium–Luxembourg Economic Union (BLEU) BIT 1979, the Singapore–Pakistan BIT 1995, the Belgium–Indonesia BIT 1970, the Netherlands–Philippines BIT 1985, the Germany–Philippines BIT 1997 and the Thailand–UK BIT 1978. Nevertheless, ASEAN is unique too in that there have only been around a half-handful of cases involving ASEAN member states even though ASEAN member states have entered into 240 or so BITs (as indicated in Figure 3.1).[18] In this sense, ASEAN and China share the similarity that few cases were brought by investors against ASEAN members despite huge amounts of FDI

13 UNCTAD, Recent Developments in International Investment Agreements (2006–June 2007), IIA Monitor No. 3 (2007), https://unctad.org/system/files/official-document/webiteiia20076_en.pdf (accessed March 4, 2021); UNCTAD Investment Policy Hub, https://investmentpolicy.unctad.org/international-investment-agreements (accessed April 6, 2021).

14 Fernando Cabrera Diaz, "Chinese Investor Launches BIT Claim against Peru at ICSID," *Investment Treaty News*, March 2, 2007, www.iisd.org/itn/wp-content/uploads/2010/10/itn_mar2_2007.pdf (accessed April 6, 2021); "The First Published ICSID Case in which China was the Respondent," https://leidenlawblog.nl/articles/the-first-published-icsid-case-in-which-china-was-the-respondent (accessed April 6, 2021); *Tza Yap Shum* v. *Republic of Peru*, ICSID Case No. ARB/07/6, www.italaw.com/cases/1126. The ICSID's decision on jurisdiction has been heavily criticized by An Chen, "Queries to the Recent ICSID Decision on Jurisdiction upon the Case of Tza Yap Shum v. Republic of Peru: Should China-Peru BIT 1994 Be Applied to Hong Kong SAR under the 'One Country Two Systems' Policy" (2009) 10(6) *Journal of World Investment & Trade* 829–862.

15 www.mofcom.gov.cn/aarticle/tongjiziliao/v/201002/20100206785656.html (accessed April 6, 2021).

16 Myanmar was not a member of ASEAN at the time of the conclusion of the ASEAN Treaty but applied for ASEAN membership and was admitted in 1997. Pursuant to the Protocol of Admission, Myanmar acceded to a number of Admission on July 23, 1997, including the ASEAN Treaty and the Jakarta Protocol of September 12, 1996. Myanmar also became a party to the Framework Agreement for the ASEAN Investment Area of October 7, 1998, which came into effect to all ASEAN member states on June 21, 1999.

17 Treaty of Amity and Cooperation in Southeast Asia, Article II, February 24, 1976, www.aseansec.org/1217.htm (accessed April 29, 2010).

18 These cases (up to 2010) include *Amco Asia Corporation and others* v. *Republic of Indonesia*, ICSID Case No. ARB/81/1; *Philippe Gruslin* v. *the Government of Malaysia*, ICSID Case No. ARB/94/1, ICSID Report (2005) 483; *Philippe Gruslin* v. *the Government of Malaysia*, ICSID Case No. ARB/99/3; *Malaysia Historical Salvors Sdn Bhd* v. *the Government of Malaysia*, ICSID ARB/05/10; *SGS Societe Generale de Surveillance S.A.* v. *Republic of the Philippines*, ICSID Case No. ARB/02/6; *Cemex Asia Holdings Ltd* v. *Republic of Indonesia*, ICSID Case No. ARB/04/3; *Fraport AG Frankfurt Airport Services Worldwide* v. *Republic of the Philippines*, ICSID Case No. ARB/03/25, http://icsid.worldbank.org/cases (accessed April 6, 2021); also *Yaung Chi Oo Trading* v. *Myanmar* (2003) 43 ILM 540.

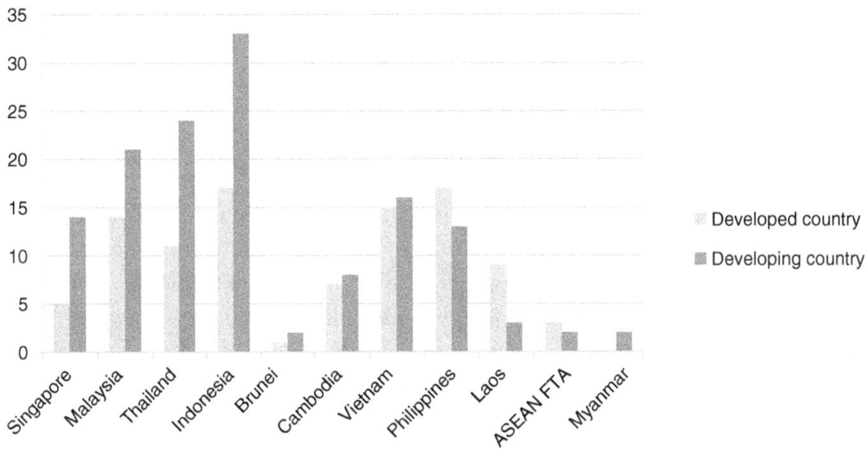

FIGURE 3.1 BITs between ASEAN member states and trading partners[19] (1966–2010)

pouring into the region. Likely, the ASEAN Treaty may pave the way for more ASEAN member state-related investment arbitration cases.

The BIT pattern of ASEAN member states deserves a closer look. Among the ASEAN member states, Singapore and Myanmar occupy two extremes of a spectrum. Singapore stands alone as an advanced economy, which may explain why it has signed more BITs with developing than developed countries. On one hand, Singapore has only been involved in two BIT arbitrations, and only because Singaporean investors were claimants. On the other hand, Myanmar stands alone in ASEAN and is not able to sign any BIT with any developed country simply because it is a completely isolated regime. One of these rare cases was *Yaung Chi Oo Trading Pte Ltd.* v. *Government of the Union of Myanmar* which was brought by a Singaporean company whose investment had been made prior to Myanmar's accession to the ASEAN Treaty.[20] Another case took place in 2004, whereby a Singaporean investor brought a claim for USD 400 million in damages under the ASEAN Agreement against Indonesia for blocking investment in an Indonesian firm.[21]

The rest of the ASEAN members can hardly be uniformly characterized. The Philippines and Laos can be grouped together as the two countries have signed more BITs with developed than developing countries. As a matter of fact, ASEAN, as a whole, can be brought into this group as the region signed three FTAs with Japan, Korea, and Australia and New Zealand but only two FTAs with China and India. The fact of signing more BITs and FTAs with developed than developing countries reflects ASEAN member states' capital FDI importing status.

The remaining members are less developed countries which have capital-importing status, although they have signed more BITs with developing countries than with developed countries. Among these, Cambodia and Vietnam are closer to the Philippines and Laos due to their less developed economy. The BITs are used by these countries as part of their policies to promote and attract FDI. Interestingly, Cambodia is the only state in ASEAN that

[19] The diagram is produced based on BIT data available at UNCTAD Investment Policy Hub, *supra* note 13 (ASEAN entered into five FTAs with Australia and New Zealand, China, India, Japan, and Korea).

[20] *Yaung Chi Oo Trading* Ptd. Ltd. v. Government of the Union of Myanmar, ASEAN I.D. Case No. ARB/01/1, Award, March 31, 2003.

[21] *Cemex Asia Holdings Ltd* v. *Republic of Indonesia*, ICSID Case No. ARB/04/3, Award (embodying the parties' settlement agreement) of February 23, 2007.

signed a Trade and Investment Framework Agreement with the USA in 2006.[22] Indonesia, Brunei, Malaysia and Thailand can be pooled together in a subcategory partly because they are sometimes characterized as mid-income countries and partly due to the gap between the numbers of BITs with developed and developing counties.

Malaysia is probably getting closer to Singapore in its BIT practice pattern. Like Singapore, Malaysia's outbound FDI was impressive, reaching USD 11 billion in 2007 and exceeding inflows.[23] Malaysia's BIT arbitration practice is complicated as it is involved in arbitration not only as a respondent but also as claimants' home state. Malaysian companies have brought two BIT cases against other countries under ICSID and UNCITRAL rules, respectively. MTD Equity, a Malaysian company, won a multimillion-dollar award against Chile for breach of the Chile–Malaysia BIT 1992 in an ICSID arbitration,[24] while Telekom Malaysia Berhad initiated an ad hoc arbitration against Ghana under UNCITRAL rules.[25]

Historically, some ASEAN member states started entering into BITs with Western European countries very early, right after the first BIT between Germany and Pakistan in 1958.[26] Chronologically, Indonesia and Malaysia signed their first BITs in 1968 with Denmark and Germany, respectively.[27] Singapore signed its first BIT with Germany in 1973.[28] Three years later, the Philippines signed its first BIT with France.[29] Malaysia signed its first two BITs with France and BLEU in 1977.[30] Thailand did not sign its first BIT with the UK until 1979.[31] Laos and Cambodia lagged behind and did not sign any BIT until 1993 with China and 1994 with Malaysia, respectively.[32]

As Figure 3.2 illustrates, the 1990s witnessed an explosion of BITs involving ASEAN members. There were several factors causing this "BIT boom." From an economic point of view, the fall of communism and the adoption of free market economies by the former socialist states in the late 1980s made the competition for FDIs more earnest, which may have contributed to the proliferation of BITs in that decade. As the majority of developed countries had already signed BITs with ASEAN members, BITs entered into in the 1990s were mostly with developing states.[33]

22 United States Trade Representative, Cambodia, www.ustr.gov/countries-regions/southeast-asia-pacific/cambodia (accessed July 15, 2010) (describing US–Cambodian trade relations).

23 See World Investment Report: Transnational Corporations and the Infrastructure Challenge (2008), 49 (reporting that for the first time FDI outflows from Malaysia exceeded inflows in 2007), www.unctad.org/en/docs/wir2008_en.pdf (accessed March 23, 2021).

24 *MTD Equity SDN BHD* v. *Rep. of Chile*, ICSID Case No. ARB/01/7, Award (2004) *app. annulment denied*, Ad-Hoc Comm. (2007).

25 See Telekom Malaysia Berhad/Rep. of Ghana, Arrondissementsrechtbank [Rb.] [District Court], den Haag, No. HA/RK 2004.667; see also Telekom Malaysia Berhad/Rep. of Ghana, Arrondissementsrechtbank [Rb.] [District Court], den Haag, Oct. 18, 2004, Nov. 5, 2004, HA/RK 2004.778; BBC, "Ghana Battles with Telekom Malaysia," *BBC News World Edition*, January 6, 2003, http://news.bbc.co.uk/2/hi/business/2632509.stm (accessed March 6, 2021)

26 Treaty between the Federal Republic of Germany and Pakistan for the Promotion and Protection of Investments (November 25, 1959).

27 Denmark–Malaysia BIT 1992; Germany–Malaysia BIT 1960.

28 Germany–Singapore BIT 1973.

29 France–Philippines BIT 1976.

30 France–Malaysia BIT 1975; BLEU–Malaysia BIT 1979.

31 United Kingdom–Thailand BIT 1978.

32 Patricia M. Robin, "The BIT Won't Bite: The American Bilateral Investment Treaty Program" (1984) 33 *American University Law Review* 941–942 (explaining that this treaty signing pattern is consistent with the three-stage BIT progression experienced by Western European countries. Germany and Switzerland came first in the early 1960s. In the 1960s and 1970s, France, the UK, Benelux, Norway and the Netherlands followed in their footsteps. Japan and the USA came last in late 1979 and the early 1980s.).

33 Susan D. Franck, "Foreign Direct Investment, Investment Treaty Arbitration, and the Rule of Law" (2007) 19 *Global Business & Development Law Journal* 348–349 (pointing out that empirical literature on the positive

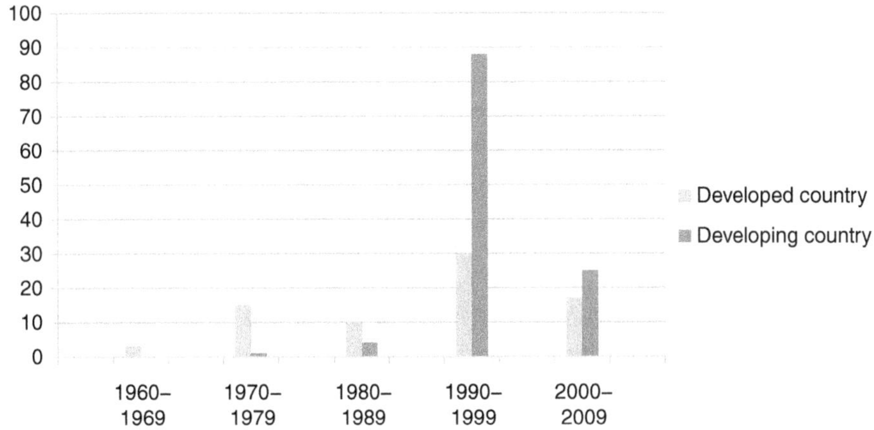

FIGURE 3.2 Growth of BITs between ASEAN member states and trading partners[34] (1966–2010)

It is worth noting that although ASEAN member states are early BIT players, they are not necessarily proactive ones. Good or bad, the global explosion of BIT arbitration cases did not simultaneously affect ASEAN countries, albeit the proliferation of BITs in this area. The Philippines, Indonesia, Malaysia, Myanmar and Thailand were only state parties to around a half-dozen BIT arbitration cases. Unlike Argentina, which has been deeply involved in a large number of cases since the 2001 economic crises and has become the largest respondent state thus far,[35] ASEAN member states survived well the Asian financial crisis. Even though Indonesia suffered massive crises, it has not been involved in billion-dollar BIT claims thereafter. ASEAN's immunity from the BIT arbitration claims may be attributable to two possible factors. First, it did not become a trend to conclude BITs with ASEAN countries until the 1990s, thus the use of investor–state arbitration (ISA) was limited during the Asian financial crisis in 1997. In addition, the role of BITs as the basis for arbitral jurisdiction was not prominent until the award in *AAPL* v. *Sri Lanka* in 1988,[36] and BIT claims did not become mainstream practice until the new millennium.[37]

Another reason may be the restrictive ISA clauses in BITs or the limited consent granted by ASEAN member states to ICSID arbitration. As far as the conclusion of BITs is concerned, ASEAN member states are passively led by their counterparties. For instance, Malaysia signed a BIT with the UK in May 1981 (effective as of October 21, 1988) and with China in November 1988 (effective as of March 31, 1990). The ISA clause in these two BITs, however, was completely different. While the UK–Malaysia BIT adopted a more liberal clause under

relation between investment treaties and FDI is inconclusive, and the impact of investment treaties on the flow of FDI is negligible).

34 This diagram is produced based on BIT data available at UNCTAD Investment Policy Hub, *supra* note 13 (excluding ASEAN and ASEAN members' FTAs).

35 Jude Webber, "Argentina Edges Nearer Debt Deal," *Financial Times*, March 23, 2010, at 23 (reporting that Argentina defaulted USD 100 billion debt in 2001, and has been barred from raising money abroad due to the lawsuits from unpaid creditors who may seek to seize any money raised. Argentina's latest move has been a proposal of a USD 20 billion debt swap offer to the holders of USD 20 billion in still unpaid debt).

36 M. Sornarajah, *The Settlement of Foreign Investment Disputes* (Kluwer Law International 2000), 21.

37 Susan D. Franck, "The Legitimacy Crisis in Investment Arbitration: Privatizing Public International Law Through Inconsistent Decisions" (2005) 73 *Fordham Law Review* 1521.

which Malaysia gave unlimited consent to arbitration,[38] the China–Malaysia BIT contained a very restrictive clause, similar to the one in the Peru–China BIT 1994.

It appears that in the BITs between ASEAN members and European states, the ISA clause is less restrictive. For instance, the Netherlands–Indonesia BIT 1968 requires the host state "to assent to any demand on the part of the national to submit for conciliation or arbitration" any dispute arising from the investment.[39] As a result, refusal to assent may amount to an international wrong. All Chinese BITs signed with Singapore,[40] the Philippines,[41] Laos,[42] Indonesia[43] and Cambodia,[44] however, include a narrow definition of "dispute" and limited consent to arbitration. By contrast, the BIT between Myanmar and China[45] contains a broad formulation and unqualified consent to ICSID or ad hoc arbitration, made possible by China's endorsement of more liberal concepts.

Thailand is another example. Thailand entered into BITs with China and Peru in 1985 and 1991, respectively.[46] The Thailand–China BIT had an identical ISA clause to that in the BIT between Peru–China. However, consent in the Thailand–Peru BIT was without any limitation or qualification.[47]

Overall, this comparison indicates that, in the process of concluding BITs with various counterparties, developed states may have dominated the negotiation process. When China signed BITs with other countries, in particular developing countries, however, it is likely that China took the lead.

Given the trajectory of the globalized economy and the increasing importance of China and ASEAN in absorbing FDI in the post-financial crisis era, disputes involving China or ASEAN member states may inevitably appear. Thus, it is important to focus on a series of substantive rights offered by the ASEAN Treaty from BIT jurisprudential and practical perspectives, in particular the Chinese BIT perspectives. The rest of this chapter will review the definitions of "investor" and "investment" and then look more closely at such core standards as NT, MFN treatment, FET, full protection and security, expropriation, and capital transfer.

It is worth pointing out that the ASEAN Treaty is not necessarily the most "liberal" BIT or IIA that China has signed to date. As a matter of fact, the China–Canada BIT 2012 may have some guiding value for future BITs.[48] For instance, it has been at the forefront of the transparency movement in investment disputes, which may add legitimacy and transparency to ISDS and Chinese BITs.[49] Higher substantive standards such as a broad definition of investment including IPR, nondiscriminatory terms conditioned on extensive exceptions, protection against direct and indirect expropriation and compensation "without

38 UK–Malaysia BIT 1981, Art. 7(1).

39 Netherlands–Indonesia 1961, Art. 9(4).

40 China–Singapore BIT 1995, Art. 13(3).

41 China–Philippines 1992, Art. 10(2).

42 China–Laos BIT 1993, Art. 8(3).

43 China–Indonesia BIT 1994, Art. 9(3).

44 China–Cambodia BIT 1996, Art. 9(3).

45 China–Myanmar BIT 2001, Art. 9.

46 Thailand–Peru BIT 1991; China–Thailand BIT 1985, Art. 10.

47 Thailand–Peru BIT 1991, Art. 10.

48 Jun Xiao, "How Can a Prospective China-EU BIT Contribute to Sustainable Investment: In Light of the UNCTAD Investment Policy Framework for Sustainable Development" (2015) 8(6) *Journal of World Energy Law & Business* 521–541.

49 Matthew Kronby, "Canada-China Investment Treaty: Evidence Doesn't Support Doomsayers," *The Globe and Mail*, October 26, 2012, www.theglobeandmail.com/opinion/canada-china-investment-treaty-evidence-doesnt-support-doomsayers/article4665002/ (accessed September 9, 2020).

unreasonable delay" in the event that it occurs, and capital transfer provisions subject to a balance of payments exception are included in the China–Canada BIT 2012.[50] Given the investment chapter of the EU–Canada Comprehensive Economic and Trade Agreement (CETA), however, a spillover or network effect could lift the BIT standards.

Similarly, the China–Australia Free Trade Agreement (ChAFTA), which came into force on December 20, 2015, is more liberal and is said to be "a 21st-century model."[51] Amid rising populist protectionism in the West, the ChAFTA represents regionalism "of critical importance to world trade law."[52] That said, China signed a dozen BITs after 2009, so some clauses in these "newer" legal instruments will be discussed from time to time.

3.1 SCOPE OF SUBJECT MATTER: THE DEFINITION OF "INVESTMENT"

BITs usually have the scope of application clarified. BITs provide protection only to covered investments, so it is essential to specify the qualifying subject matter. Surrounding the concept of investment are other interconnected terms, such as the admission of investments and the "right of establishment," which impose regulatory requirements on the various stages of investment.[53] While the admission rule regulates the investor's entry into the host state, the right of establishment sets out the requirements about the investor's activity for the duration of the investment.[54] Chinese BITs widely define the term "investment" as encompassing

> every kind of asset invested by investors of one Contracting State in accordance with the laws and regulations of the other Contracting State in the territory of the latter and in particular, though not exclusively, include[ing] (a) moveable and immoveable property as well as any other property rights such as mortgages, liens and pledges; (b) shares, stock, debentures and any other form of participation in a company; (c) claims to money, or to any performance under contract having an economic value associated with an investment . . .; (d) intellectual property rights, including copyrights, patents, industrial designs, trademarks, trade names, technical processes, know-how and goodwill; (e) business concessions conferred by law or under contract permitted by law, including concessions to search for, cultivate, extract or exploit natural resources.[55]

With little differences, a vast majority of Chinese BITs contain this embracing and open-ended definition of assets for "investment," which guarantees that all rights and interests involved in the economic activities in China are covered by the substantive protection supplied by the BIT. The prescription of "in accordance with (or compliance with) the host country laws and regulations"[56] does not specify any narrative or guidelines for interpretation.

[50] For the complete text of the China–Canada BIT 2012, see www.international.gc.ca/trade-commerce/trade-agreements-accords-commerciaux/agr-acc/china-chine/fipa-apie/index.aspx?lang=eng (accessed April 6, 2021).

[51] Colin B. Picker, Heng Wang and Weihuan Zhou (eds.), *The China-Australia Free Trade Agreement: A 21st-Century Model* (Hart 2018).

[52] Pasha L. Hsieh, "The China-Australia Free Trade Agreement: A 21st-Century Model by Colin B. Picker, Heng Wang, and Weihuan Zhou (eds), Oxford: Hart Publishing, 2018. ISBN 978 1 509 91538, 363pp." (2018) 21(4) *Journal of International Economic Law* 923–926.

[53] Ignacio Gómez-Palacio and Peter Muchlinski, "Admission and Establishment" in Peter Muchlinski, Federico Ortino and Christoph Schreuer (eds.), *The Oxford Handbook of International Investment Law* (Oxford University Press 2008) 229.

[54] Ibid., 230.

[55] Trinidad and Tobago–China BIT 2002, Art. 1(1).

[56] China–Israel BIT 1995, Art. 12.

The ASEAN Treaty defines the term "investment" as "every kind of assets which are invested by the investors of a Party in accordance with the relevant laws, regulations and policies of another Party."[57] The "in accordance with its laws, regulations and polices" requirement is a common qualification attached to the definition of investment in Chinese BITs. This qualification sets a jurisdictional limit and has been arbitrated in some cases. For instance, *Inceysa Vallisoletana* v. *El Salvador* indicates that investments that were made fraudulently and therefore not in accordance with the law do not fall under the ICSID jurisdiction embodied in the BIT between El Salvador and Spain 2005.[58] The tribunal in *Fraport* v. *The Philippines* declined its jurisdiction based on the BIT between Germany and the Philippines 1997 due to the fact that the claimant had not made an investment "in accordance with the laws of the Philippines."[59] This qualification, however, has been rarely clarified by Chinese BITs except one amendment to the Cuba–China BIT 1995, which provides that "the expression 'pursuant to the laws and regulations' shall mean that for any kind invested asset to be considered as investment protected in this Agreement, it shall be in accordance with any of the foreign investment modalities defined by the legislation of the Contracting Party receiving the investment and registered as such in the correspondent registry." This amendment is clear in that the investment made by one natural or legal person in a foreign state must take one of the accepted forms of foreign investment in China. The ASEAN Treaty, conforming to the WTO's transparency requirement, makes a further clarification in this regard by providing that "policies shall refer to those affecting investment that are endorsed and announced by the Government of a Party, and made publicly available in a written form."

RCEP, the latest IIA that China signed, clarified that the "characteristics of an investment" include (i) the commitment of capital or other resources; (ii) the expectation of gains or profits; and (iii) assumption of risks.[60] Few Chinese BITs adopt a similar approach to clarifying the meaning of "investment." The clarification is of great use in confining the interpretative power of the tribunal.

The ASEAN Treaty adopts an asset-based definition of "investment,"[61] which is very broad and is supplemented by an illustrative list of particular assets covered by the treaty, ranging from moveable and immoveable property, interests in companies, and IPR, to business concessions and contractual rights.[62] This list is broader than the one in the Netherlands–China and Germany–China BITs, particularly in its references to contract rights. However, this list fails to absorb some positive changes reflected in some other Chinese BITs. For instance, the ASEAN Treaty fails to differentiate debts as an investment and debts from normal trade transactions. The New Zealand–China FTA 2008 is progressive in making a distinction between trade and investment debts in that "bonds, including government issued bonds, debentures, loans and other forms of debts, and rights derived therefrom" is parallel to

57 The ASEAN Treaty, Art. 1(1)(d).

58 *Inceysa Vallisoletana S.L.* v. *Republic of El Salvador*, ICSID Case No. ARB/03/26, Award August 2, 2006.

59 *Fraport AG Frankfurt Airport Services Worldwide* v. *Philippines*, ICSID Case No. ARB/03/25, Award August 16, 2007.

60 RCEP, Art. 10.1(c).

61 There are other ways such as enterprise-based, instrument-based, competence-based and transaction-based approaches to define the "investment."

62 Civil engineering or construction contracts were sometimes accepted by the tribunals as "investments." *Jan de Nul and Dredging International NV* v. *Egypt*, Decision on Jurisdiction, ICSID Case No ARB/04/13, June 16, 2006, paras. 90–106; *Consortium RFCC* v. *Morocco*, Decision on Jurisdiction, ICSID Case No ARB/00/6, July 21, 2001, paras. 37–58.

the category of "investment" which normally covers the forms of shares and stocks.[63] To differentiate the two categories of debts may potentially avoid certain unintended claims being brought under a BIT. This differential approach has won some popularity in BIT practice. For instance, a bank guarantee, being a contingent liability, was not regarded by the tribunal in the *Joy Mining* case as an "investment" within the meaning of the investment treaty.[64] Among others, the US Model BIT has adopted this differential approach.[65]

The list of specific IPR contained in the definition of "investment" is a lengthy one, which is in line with the recent practice that more IPRs will be protected under the BITs.[66] This also reflects China's confidence to provide foreign investors with more IPR protections of international standards. RCEP, however, no longer follows this "list" approach. Instead, RECP defines IPR and goodwill "pursuant to the laws and regulations of the host Party,"[67] giving the host state more say on the scope of IPR protected by the RCEP.

In terms of the category of business concessions, Chinese BITs vary in wording but mainly target business concessions for the exploration of natural resources. The ASEAN Treaty adopts the typical language "including concessions to search for, cultivate, extract or exploit natural resources," as the Netherlands–China BIT 2001, the Germany–China BIT 2003 and the Finland–China BIT 2004 do. There has emerged a new version of the "business concession" term in the Australia–China BIT 1988 which includes "rights to engage in agriculture, forestry, fisheries and animal husbandry" and "rights to manufacture, use and sell products" in addition to "rights to search for, extract or exploit natural resources."[68]

Reinvestment of returns is also covered in the definition of "investment" in the ASEAN Treaty. Most Chinese BITs are silent on this point except several BITs which make clear that reinvestment of returns is well covered. The Finland–China BIT provides that "reinvested returns shall enjoy the same treatment as the original investment."[69] The ASEAN Treaty's wording is slightly different and broader, enough to confirm that "returns that are invested should be treated as investments and any alteration of the form in which assets are invested or reinvested shall not affect their character as investments." The legal significance of adopting such an extensive approach needs to be further observed.

The definition of "investment" in the ASEAN Treaty is pretty standard in the light of China's BIT practice. The ASEAN Treaty does not include "licenses and permits pursuant to law,"[70] "payable services"[71] or "goods that, under a leasing agreement, are placed at the disposal of a lessee in the territory of a Party in conformity with its laws and regulations"[72] in the illustrative list of the "investment."

More notably, the ASEAN Treaty has not absorbed the concept of "indirect investment," which was first introduced into the Gabon–China BIT 1997, under which the "investment"

63 New Zealand–China FTA 2008, Art. 135. Footnote 8 thereof further clarifies that "loans and other forms of debt, which have been registered to the competent authority of a Party, do not mean trade debts where the debts would be non-interest earning if paid on time without penalty."

64 *Joy Mining Machinery Ltd* v. *Egypt*, Award on Jurisdiction, ICSID Case No ARB/03/11, August 6, 2004, paras. 29–30, 41–63.

65 US Model BIT 2004, Art. 1 and footnote 1.

66 Earlier BITs only cover very few IPR such as copyrights, industrial rights, technical process and know-how. Poland–China BIT 1988, Art. 1(1).

67 RCEP, Art. 10.1(c)(iv).

68 Australia–China BIT 1988, Art. 1(1)(v).

69 Finland–China BIT 2004, Art. 1(1).

70 Kuwait–China BIT 1985, Art. 1(1); and New Zealand–China FTA 2008, Art. 135.

71 Turkmenistan–China BIT 1992, Art. 1(1).

72 Portugal–China BIT 2005, Art. 1; Greece–China BIT 1992, Art. 19(1)(f).

includes "every kind of investment invested directly or indirectly by the investors of one Party in the territory of the other Party in accordance with its laws and regulations." The Germany–China BIT 2003 interpreted the term "invested directly" as "invested by an investor of one Contracting Party through a company which is fully or partially owned by the investor and having its seat in the territory of the other Contracting Party."[73] Thus, investments made by an investor in the home country but effectuated via a subsidiary in the other contracting state are also covered by the BIT. The Argentina–China BIT 1992 included the concept of "indirect investment" but through a third-party construction approach as follows: "If natural or juridical persons of a Contracting Party have an interest in a juridical person which was established within the territory of a third State, and this juridical person invests in the other Contracting Party it shall be recognized as a juridical person of the former Contracting Party."[74] The New Zealand–China FTA provides that "investments" extend to investments of legal persons of a third party which are owned or controlled by investors of one party, provided the third country has no, or disclaims its, right to claim compensation for expropriation. As a result, investments made by a New Zealand or Chinese investor may still be covered even if directly made through an offshore vehicle. To be clear, a denial of benefits clause is included in the FTA with respect to investments made by investors of one party, where the investment is made through a legal entity owned or controlled by nationals of the other party or a third party.[75]

The "indirect investment" definition is a useful reference in clarifying the doubt surrounding the *Barcelona Traction* case in which the International Court of Justice (ICJ) decided that the Belgium government was not allowed to exercise diplomatic protection against Spain for its citizens who owned the majority of the shares in a Canadian company, which invested in Spain and allegedly was expropriated by the Spanish government.[76] Without the "indirect investment" concept, the approach must depart from the law of diplomatic protection whereby only the formal location of subject of an infringed legally protected interest is actively legitimated.[77] In international investment case law, in the absence of explicit provisions in BITs, the tribunals may still recognize the protection of indirect investment through either a non-controlling shareholder[78] or an indirect shareholder.[79] The right to claim for alleged infringements of indirect investment is available to the investor within the meaning of a BIT.[80]

The concept of "indirect investment" is important in the Chinese law context in two respects. First, regarding those investors whose home jurisdictions have not signed any BIT with China, they may consider structuring their investments through a subsidiary which is incorporated in a country that does have a BIT with China. Second, the utility of the "indirect investment" concept may clarify the status of holding companies incorporated in Hong Kong or Macau. A Hong Kong or Macau-based investor can secure investment protections under the BIT entered into between China and the investment forum if it invests into that country

73 The Protocol to the Germany–China BIT 2003, Art. 1(b); and the Germany–China BIT 2003, Art. 1(1).

74 Argentina–China BIT 1992, Art. 1(1).

75 Article 149. Cf *Rompetrol Group BV* v. *Romania*, ICSID Case No. ARB/06/3, Decision on Jurisdiction, April 18, 2008.

76 *Barcelona Traction, Light and Power Company Limited (Belgium* v. *Spain)*, 2nd Phase, Judgment of February 5, 1970, ICJ Report 1970 at 3.

77 Also see *Tokios Tokeles* v. *Ukraine*, ICSID Case No. ARB/02/18, Decision on Jurisdiction, April 29, 2004.

78 *CMS Gas Transmission Company* v. *The Republic of Argentina*, ICSID Case No. ARB/01/8, Decision on Objections to Jurisdiction of June 17, 2003, para. 48.

79 *Siemens* A.G. v. *The Republic of Argentina*, ICSID Case No. ARB/02/8, Decision on Jurisdiction of August 3, 2004, para. 137.

80 Germany–China BIT 2003, Art. 1(2); and ICSID Convention, Art. 25(2)(b).

through a China-incorporated subsidiary. Unfortunately, the ASEAN Treaty does not make reference either to the "indirect investment" concept or to third-country construction.

Things can get more complicated when shareholders make a claim for reflective loss on the basis of the definition of "investment" in the BIT including "shares" unless the BIT explicitly limits the right of shareholders to claim remedies involving a direct loss. The CKJ TIT defines "investments" as taking the forms of "shares, stocks or other forms of equity participation in an enterprise, including rights derived therefrom."[81] The ChAFTA provides that:

> 2. In the event that an investment dispute cannot be settled by consultations . . .
>
> (a) the claimant, on its own behalf, may submit to arbitration under this Section a claim:
>
> (ii) that the claimant has incurred loss or damage by reason of, or arising out of, that breach.[82]

This provision is coupled with a footnote saying that:

> For greater certainty, the loss or damage incurred by the claimant that forms that subject matter of a claim under sub-paragraph (a) shall not include loss or damage suffered by the claimant which is a result of loss or damage caused to an enterprise of the respondent that is a juridical person that the claimant owns or controls directly or indirectly by reason of, or arising out of, the alleged breach by the respondent.

This footnote delimits the scope of the BIT right. Otherwise, domestic law may prohibit shareholders' claims for reflective loss on the sole ground that such claims would be prohibited by the municipal corporate law (*lex societatis*).[83] Similar restriction appears in other BITs. For instance, the China–Mexico BIT 2008 provides that "the Contracting Parties recognize that under this Article, minority non-controlling investors have standing to submit only a claim for direct loss or damage to their own legal interest as investors."[84] This provision seems to recognize the difference between two types of case: one is the shareholder's claim for direct loss, and the other is the claim for damage to the shareholder's own legal interests as an investor.

The China–Germany BIT includes the term "share" in the definition of "investment" but allows for the exclusion of some shares from the scope of application on the basis of the shareholder's influence in the management of the company. "For the avoidance of doubt, the Contracting Parties agree that investments as defined in Article 1 are those made for the purpose of establishing lasting economic relations in connection with an enterprise, especially those which allow to exercise effective influence in its management."[85]

3.2 NT AND NONDISCRIMINATION

Early Chinese BITs do not contain an NT provision.[86] This practice was changed by China's later-generation BITs.[87] Fewer than half of Chinese BITs grant an NT standard by merely

81 CKJ TIT 2012, Art. 1(1)(b).
82 ChAFTA 2015, Art. 9.12(2)(a).
83 Lukas Vanhonnaeker, *Shareholders' Claims for Reflective Loss in International Investment Law* (Cambridge University Press 2020) 33.
84 China–Mexico BIT 2008, Art. 13(8).
85 China–Germany BIT 2003, Art. 1(a).
86 China–Israel BIT 1995.
87 Wenhua Shan, Norah Gallagher and Sheng Zhang, "National Treatment for Foreign Investment in China: A Changing Landscape" (2012) 27 *ICSID Review* 120.

adopting the phrase "no less favorable than." China was historically hesitant to apply a full-scale NT doctrine, which explains why Chinese BITs often add various qualifications to the NT standard.

The NT is often qualified by a best effort commitment and is granted "without prejudice to [the host state's] laws and regulations," which was the practice prior to 2008.

China's earlier BITs also contain other types of NT clause. For instance, the China–Ghana BIT 1991 entitles foreign investors to treatment as regards restitution, indemnification, compensation or other settlement "no less favourable" than that accorded to nationals whose investments suffer losses owing to war or other armed conflict, revolution, state of national emergency, revolt, insurrection or riot.[88]

The NT clause is coupled with a grandfather clause, which asymmetrically allows China (but not its counterparty) to maintain existing domestic laws that are incompatible with NT but meanwhile obligates China not to escalate any discriminatory treatment. This grandfather clause appeared in the Cyprus–China BIT 2001[89] and in various Chinese BITs with European states.[90]

The ASEAN Treaty includes a wider NT clause as follows: "Each Party shall, in its territory, accord to investors of another Party and their investments treatment no less favorable than it accords, in like circumstances, to its own investors and their investments with respect to management, conduct, operation, maintenance, use, sale, liquidation, or other forms of disposal of such investments."[91] The inclusion of "full" NT provision in the ASEAN Treaty constitutes a major development. More importantly, this approach is close to the US Model BIT, which applies NT for investors and "covered investments" for the "full life-cycle of investment," including establishment or acquisition, management, operation, expansion and disposition.[92] However, it is worth noting that neither the China–Canada BIT[93] nor the China–New Zealand FTA extends NT to "expansion, management, conduct, operation and sale or other disposition of investment." The China–Korea FTA affords NT only to the "management, conduct, operation, maintenance, use, enjoyment and sale or other disposition of investment," which is largely based on China's old practice. The pre-establishment NT primarily came after China's BIT negotiation with the USA.[94]

The ASEAN Treaty's NT standard is subject to a similar grandfather clause which allows the preservation of existing non-conforming measures, that is, legislation inconsistent with the NT obligation.

1. National Treatment ... shall not apply to:
   (a) any existing or new non-conforming measures maintained or adopted within its territory;
   (b) the continuation or amendment of any non-conforming measures referred to in Sub-paragraph (a).

88 China–Ghana BIT 1991, Art. 4.
89 Cyprus–China BIT 2001, Art. 3(3) and Protocol, Art. 3.
90 BLEU–China BIT 2005, Czech Republic–China BIT 2005, Finland–China BIT 2005 and Netherlands–China BIT 2005.
91 The ASEAN Treaty, Art. 4.
92 Jeffrey J. Schott and Cathleen Cimino, "The China-Japan-Korea Trilateral Investment Agreement: Implications for US Policy and the US-China Bilateral Investment Treaty" in Peterson Institute for International Economics, *Toward a US-China Investment Treaty* (PIIE Briefing 15–1, February 2015) 9.
93 China–Canada FIPA 2012, Art. 6.
94 Jeffrey J. Schott, Euijin Jung and Cathleen Cimino-Isaacs, "An Assessment of the Korea-China Free Trade Agreement," Peterson Institute for International Economics Policy Brief Number PB15-24, December 2015, 11.

2. The Parties will endeavour to progressively remove the non-conforming measures.[95]

There are several significant differences between the ASEAN Treaty and the Germany–China BIT in terms of the grandfather clause. First, the grandfather clause in the Germany–China BIT establishes a one-way right, and only China can enjoy the grandfather clause to maintain non-conforming measures. By contrast, the grandfather clause in the ASEAN Treaty allows both sides to preserve a limited right to discriminate between domestic and foreign investors. This difference makes sense given the fact that China and the majority of ASEAN member states are developing states. Second, the scope of exceptions granted by the grandfather clause in the Germany–China BIT is narrower. The exception only allows the preservation of existing measures and amendments that do not increase the non-conformity level. In other words, the grandfather clause is a "standstill" clause which prohibits new non-conforming measures or changes to the existing non-conforming measures that would increase the degree of discrimination. The ASEAN Treaty's approach to the grandfather clause, however, is a wider one. In addition to grandfathering those non-conforming measures, the clause also waives the NT obligation to the new non-conforming measures. This is so far the only Chinese BIT that adopts this unique wider approach. Third, China made a commitment in the Germany–China BIT to take all appropriate steps in order to progressively remove the non-conforming measures. The language and context indicate a "rollback" commitment in soft law nature, which arguably lacks a binding effect but may be enforced by means at reputational costs. The ASEAN Treaty's language is explicit in that the endeavor to remove the non-conforming measures is a non-binding posture rather than a legally binding obligation. Although the language in the ASEAN Treaty avoids any potential debate on the legal effect and enforceability of "endeavor to remove the non-conforming measures," the legal significance of such commitment to remove the non-conforming measures may unfortunately deteriorate to zero. But China still includes "non-conforming measures" in NT in its FTA with Korea, and the list of exceptions is extensive.[96]

The "in like circumstances" qualification[97] is closely linked to "less favourable treatment," and is bound to affect the determination of "less favourable treatment." The ASEAN Treaty adopts this caveat as follows: "Each Party shall, in its territory, accord to investors of another Party and their investments treatment no less favorable than it accords, in like circumstances, to its own investors and their investments with respect to management, conduct, operation, maintenance, use, sale, liquidation, or other forms of disposal of such investments."[98] The NT standard granted in the ASEAN Treaty is not necessarily a great leap forward as the standard is still subject to both the grandfather clause and the "in like circumstances" qualification. In this sense, the NT standard is of limited symbolic value.

The ASEAN Treaty appears closer to a rather narrow formula by defining, in a non-exhaustive manner, that the NT obligation applies to "the investors and their investments with respect to management, conduct, operation, maintenance, use, sale, liquidation, or other forms of disposal of such investments." Even though the ASEAN Treaty does not explicitly use the wording "associated activities," the non-exhaustive list enables the NT obligation to be extended to "activities associated with investments." The loose language

95 The ASEAN Treaty, Art. 6.
96 Schott, Jung and Cimino-Isaacs, "An Assessment of the Korea-China Free Trade Agreement," 11.
97 NAFTA, Art. 1102.
98 The ASEAN Treaty, Art. 4.

effectively broadens the limited scope of investment and provides a certain level of flexibility. The stance taken by China at that time was to limit the application of BITs to post-establishment measures.

NT is nonreciprocal under the ChAFTA, which means that Australia's obligation applies to a wide range of investment activities from establishment to disposition of investments while China's obligation does not apply to the establishment, acquisition or expansion of investments. The insistence on post-establishment NT can be attributed to China's long-standing foreign investment policy to treat domestic and foreign investment differently. The NT does not apply to non-conforming measures, according to which China is exempted from "any existing non-conforming measures maintained within its territory."[99] Further, the ChAFTA includes few substantive standards including nondiscriminatory provisions, non-conforming measures, and denial of benefits,[100] and defers substantive matters such as minimum standards of treatment, expropriation, transfer, and performance requirements to the future work program.[101] This makes ChAFTA fall short of the commitments that Australia or China has made in other FTAs that cover not only nondiscriminatory requirements but also minimum standards of treatment, conditions on expropriation and compensation, transfer of investment returns and restrictions on performance requirements on foreign investors.[102] These omissions may be made thanks to the China–Australia BIT 1988 which, still being in force,[103] includes a wide coverage of substantive standards making the redundancy in the ChAFTA unnecessary.[104] No matter how the gap occurs, Chinese investors may enjoy less favorable treatment compared to investors from Australia's other partners such as Japan and South Korea.[105]

The ASEAN Treaty's position on the NT standard reflects its recent departure from a conservative to a more liberal stance in offering foreign investment protections.[106] RCEP largely follows China's typical NT clause. In addition, it extends the NT accorded by a party with respect not only to the central government but also to local governments.[107] This appears to enlarge the scope of the NT standard.

99 ChAFTA, Art. 9.5.2.
100 ChAFTA, Arts. 9.1–9.8.
101 ChAFTA, Art. 9.9.
102 China–Korea FTA 2015 (which has a high-quality investment chapter).
103 Vivienne Bath, "Substantive Provisions in ChAFTA's Investment Chapter" in Colin Picker, Heng Wang and Weihuan Zhou, *The China-Australia Free Trade Agreement: A 21st-Century Model* (Hart 2018) 195.
104 ChAFTA, Art. 1.2.2 (stating that "nothing in this Agreement shall derogate from the existing rights and obligations of a Party under ... any other ... bilateral agreement to which both Parties are party") and Art. 1.2.3 (saying that any inconsistency between the ChAFTA and the BIT must be resolved by consultation between the two parties "with a view to finding a mutually satisfactory solution").
105 Australia had FTAs with Japan and South Korea, and these FTAs include more substantive standards than nondiscriminatory treatment. See Korea–Australia FTA 2014, ATS 43, Art. 11; Japan–Australia Economic Partnership Agreement 2015, ATS 2.
106 Locally, the playing field was indeed titled in favor of foreign investors. Prior to the promulgation of the PRC Enterprise Income Tax Law, enacted on March 16, 2007 and effective as of January 1, 2008, the income tax rate for an FIE was 15–25 percent while a much higher tax rate of 33 percent was applicable to a pure domestic entity. In addition, China also offered a "2-year exemption and [a] 3-year half reduction" package to FIEs. Accordingly, an FIE was exempt from corporate income tax in the first two years of making profit and needed to pay only 50 percent of its corporate income tax in the following three years. Under the new PRC Enterprise Income Tax Law, however, unless grandfathered, FIEs are no longer entitled to such preferential tax treatment. FIEs located in national high-tech industrial zones are entitled to a 15 percent preferential tax rate.
107 RCEP, Art. 10.3.

3.3 MFN TREATMENT

All Chinese BITs adopt the MFN standard. Many BITs enumerate the substantive areas to which the MFN clause is limited to apply, such as the "admission, expansion, management, conduct, operation, maintenance, use, enjoyment and disposal" of investments.[108] Several Chinese BITs, however, restrict the application of the MFN treatment obligation to "investments" only.[109]

The MFN treatment clause appears in the ASEAN Treaty as follows: "Each Party shall accord to investors of another Party and their investments treatment no less favourable than that it accords, in like circumstances, to investors of any other Party or third country and/or their respective investments with respect to admission, establishment, acquisition, expansion, management, conduct, operation, maintenance, use, liquidation, sale, and other forms of disposal of investments."[110] RCEP contains a similar clause but adds "in its territory" in the end,[111] which may exclude cross-border transactions with the same effect. Although the ASEAN Treaty does not explicitly use the term "activities associated with such investments," the list of "respective investments" supplements this omission and extends the MFN treatment obligation to a series of investment-related activities. The ASEAN Treaty's MFN provision again uses an "in like circumstances" comparison.

The MFN treatment clauses in most Chinese BITs are not applied to market access (or the "pre-establishment phase") but only to the post-admission stage.

It is obvious that the ASEAN Treaty not only follows this pre-admission route but also makes some new changes. First, it clearly includes "admission" in the list, which is in line with the Japan–China BIT approach. Second, it extends the MFN treatment to "liquidation." Given the fact that "admission," "establishment," "acquisition" and "liquidation" are all included in the NT standard list, it can be reasonably assumed that this is deliberate in order to widen the scope of the MFN and national treatments. The ASEAN Treaty's approach to applying MFN treatment is the widest approach so far and appears in a number of the most recent Chinese BITs such as the New Zealand–China FTA.[112]

There has been significant controversy over the extent to which MFN clauses should apply to substantive rights, to procedural rights or to both. Some Chinese BITs expressly impose the MFN treatment obligation on specific matters such as expropriation and compensation,[113] repatriation of investments and returns,[114] treatment of gains resulted from subrogation,[115] measures taken to deal with losses resulting from war or civil disturbance,[116] and judicial and administrative remedies.[117] Unfortunately, the ASEAN Treaty does not explicitly specify the matters that are subject to the MFN treatment obligation. In this respect, the ASEAN Treaty is clearly restricted and vague in scope as compared with the BITs that provide an express list of specific matters. This vague approach is less instructive for a tribunal trying to resolve a dispute. It is reasonably anticipated that a future protocol may improve this respect by providing a detailed list of activities covered by the MFN treatment obligation.[118]

108 New Zealand–China FTA 2008, Art. 139.
109 Sweden–China BIT 1982, Art. 2(2).
110 The ASEAN Treaty, Art. 5(1).
111 RCEP, Art. 10.4, para. 1.
112 New Zealand–China FTA 2008, Art. 139, para. 1.
113 Germany–China BIT 2003, Art. 4(3).
114 Norway–China BIT 1984, Art. 6(2); Spain–China BIT 1993, Art. 6(6).
115 Singapore–China BIT 1985, Art. 7; Kuwait–China BIT 1985, Art. 7(2).
116 France–China 2007 BIT, Art. 4; Germany–China BIT 2003, Art. 5.
117 Korea–China BIT 2007, Art. 4.
118 Australia–China BIT 1988 is the best example.

All of the Chinese BITs include specific or general exceptions (akin to GATT Article XX)[119] to the application of the MFN clause. These exceptions are generally fairly identical and mostly relate to benefits for the investor that might be found in other international or regional economic treaties entered into by the host states. The typical exceptions are concerned with economic integration organizations such as customs unions and free trade zones, taxation treaties and frontier trade arrangements.[120] The ASEAN Treaty refers to economic integration as the only exception as follows:

> The [MFN] treatment ... shall not include:
>
> (a) any preferential treatment accorded to investors and their investments under any existing bilateral, regional or international agreements, or any form of economic or regional cooperation with any non-Party; and
>
> (b) any existing or future preferential treatment accorded to investors and their investments in any agreement or arrangement between or among ASEAN Member States or between any Party and its separate customs territories.[121]

The regional economic integration units are one of the most commonly found exceptions to the MFN treatment obligation under the BITs. The wording in the ASEAN Treaty on the economic integration exception is relatively broad, covering "bilateral, regional or international agreements, or any form of economic or regional cooperation."

The ASEAN Treaty's economic integration exception has some eye-catching features. First, unlike some Chinese BITs that extend this exception to both existing and future arrangements,[122] subsection (a) above confines the economic integration exception to agreement entered into before the ASEAN Treaty. The ASEAN Treaty seems to imply that any future agreements permitting such favorable treatment would not be permissible. This clears up any doubt about the potentially wide application. Second, the ASEAN Treaty's language seems to have gone beyond "regional" arrangements. As a result, the benefits of the MFN treatment are not extended to those covered by the "existing ... international agreements."

In addition, the ASEAN Treaty attaches to the MFN treatment the same grandfather exception applicable to NT. The ASEAN Treaty's "grandfather" provisions are almost identical to those in the Czech Republic–China BIT 2005[123] and the BLEU–China BIT 2005. The "grandfather" clause in the ASEAN Treaty merely confirms that the MFN treatment does not apply to existing or new non-conforming measures of either contracting party.

Regarding Australia and China, the ChAFTA extends to investors and covered investments "treatment no less favourable than it accords, in like circumstances, to investors and investors in its territory of any non-Party"; it also extends this to the establishment and acquisition of investments. Existing BITs and FTAs are grandfathered.

3.4 FAIR AND EQUITABLE TREATMENT OF INVESTMENT

FET is commonly used but it is the least specific substantive protection standard. This treatment requires the host country to treat foreign investment in a manner that appears, from the

119 China–New Zealand FTA 2008, Art. 200.

120 Austria–China BIT 1985, Art. 3(3) included all three exceptions.

121 The ASEAN Treaty, Art. 5(3).

122 Sweden–China BIT 1982, Kyrgyzstan–China BIT 1992, Ukraine–China BIT 1992, Turkmenistan–China BIT 1992 and Tajikistan–China BIT 1993.

123 Czech Republic–China BIT 2005, Art. 3(3).

perspective of the international community, fair and equitable under the circumstances of each case. Although the exact content and scope of this standard have not been authoritatively determined and are often decided on a case-by-case basis,[124] the standard is often interpreted as an "absolute standard" or "minimum standard," the violation of which may include any "arbitrary, grossly unfair, unjust or idiosyncratic, discriminatory" conduct or conduct that "exposes the claimant to sectional or racial prejudice, or involves a lack of due process leading to an outcome which offends judicial propriety."[125] Nevertheless, the level of fairness and equity is not supposed to be a baseline for foreign investment protections as the application of the standard also involves the claimant's reasonable reliance on the representations made by the host state.[126] Hence, the standard should be at a level generally acceptable to the international commercial community. In other words, a pure local concept of fairness and equity under domestic law may be likely to be rejected by the international commercial community.[127] Due to its less specific content and vague scope, this treatment has been emerged as a "catch-all" ground of investment treaty claims and become more often associated with the concept of legitimate expectations.

The prevailing interpretation of the required standard of FET is relatively stringent on the host country given its wide coverage. It has been interpreted to protect foreign investors against unjustified or unpredictable adverse changes in regulatory rules,[128] nontransparent or inconsistent decision-making in administrative procedures, the government's failure to negotiate in good faith, or gross deficiencies in the host country's judicial system.[129] These misconducts may violate the standard even if not motivated by a specific discriminatory or otherwise malevolent intent. From a conceptual perspective, the standard is overarching for all legislative, administrative and judiciary branches of the host state. Thus, the possibility of invoking protections under FET will be more substantial, not only for the protection of foreign investors in the economic and commercial activities but also for shaping the host state's rule of law, judicial due process, and domestic administrative law, which are often regarded as subcomponents under the umbrella of rule of law.

In the Chinese law context, to invoke the FET standard in ISA is likely to touch upon these systematic deficiencies in law enforcement by the administrative agencies and courts, which enjoy wide discretion and arbitrariness.[130] Although China is making progress in improving its legal institutions and governance quality, progress appears slower than often anticipated especially given China's accession to the WTO. According to the World Bank's Worldwide Governance Indicators (WGI), as indicated in Figure 3.3, China's governance rankings were all lower in 2008 than in 1996 except the indicator of voice and accountability.[131]

124 See, e.g., Rudolf Dolzer, "Fair and Equitable Treatment: A Key Standard in Investment Treaties" (2005) 39 *International Law* 87; Barnali Choudhury, "Evolution or Devolution? Defining Fair and Equitable Treatment in International Investment Law" (2005) 6 *Journal of World Investment & Trade* 297; Christoph Schreuer, "Fair and Equitable Treatment in Arbitral Practice" (2005) 6 *Journal of World Investment & Trade* 357.

125 *Waste Management, Inc.* v. *The United Mexican States*, ICSID Case No. ARB(AF)/00/3, Award of April 30, 2004, para. 98.

126 Ibid.

127 *Saluka* v. *The Czech Republic*, Partial Award of March 17, 2006, para. 291 et seq.

128 *CMS* v. *Argentina*, para. 29; *LG&E* v. *Argentina*, para. 100.

129 *Compania de Aguas del Aconquija, S.A. & Compagnie Generale des Eaux (Vivendi)* v. *Argentina*, ICSID Case No. ARB/97/3, Award of November 21, 2000, para. 80; *Loewen Group, Inc. and Raymond L. Loewen* v. *United States*, ICSID Case No. ARB(AF)/98/3, Final Award of June 26, 2003, para. 132.

130 Randall Peerenboom, *China's Long March Toward Rule of Law* (Cambridge University Press 2002) 394.

131 The World Bank's Worldwide Governance Indicators (WGI) measure six dimensions of governance between 1996 and 2008: voice and accountability, political stability and absence of violence/terrorism, government effectiveness, regulatory quality, rule of law, and control of corruption. See Daniel Kaufmann, Aart Kraay and Massimo Mastruzzi, "Governance Matters VIII: Aggregate and Individual Governance Indicators 1996–2008,"

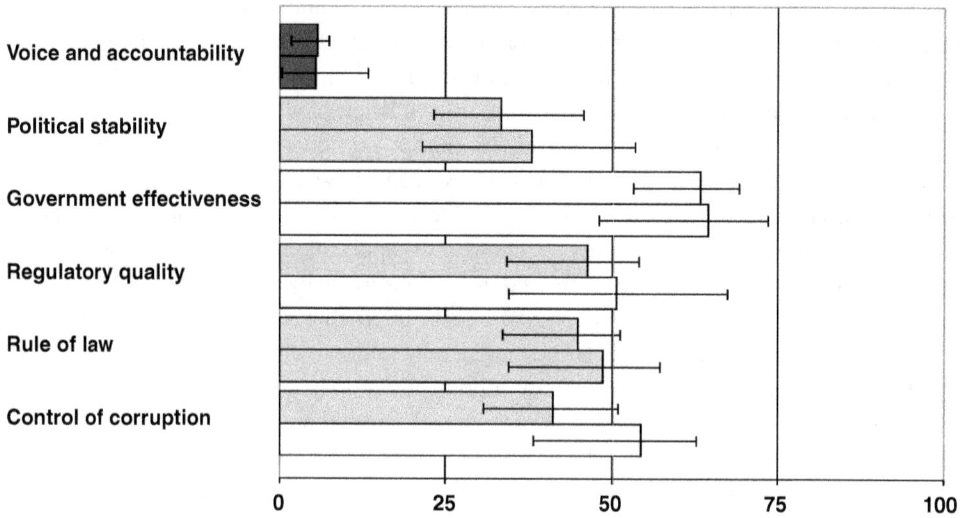

FIGURE 3.3 Comparison of China's governance quality[132] (2008–1996 in top–bottom order)

Most Chinese BITs include a FET provision, accompanied by a "full protection and security" clause. The standard often appears in the section of "treatment of investment" which creates a concrete legal obligation on the contracting parties. However, these Chinese BITs, through broad and general phrasing, do not make express reference to a particular body of law or other standards. Nor does the typical FET provision provide for any qualifications or elements (in an exhaustive or indicative list) or refer to international law in general. As such, the treatment may trigger wide claims and be assessed against other provisions in the BIT, and then against general international law and the domestic law of the host state. In a number of Chinese BITs, references are made to such criteria as domestic law,[133] the present BIT,[134] international treaties to which both parties are contracting parties,[135] generally recognized principles of international law accepted by both parties, and universally accepted principles of international law.[136] The qualifications of domestic law and international treaties are not China's mainstream BIT practices. More recent Chinese BITs tend to abolish the qualifications of domestic law[137] and accept international law as a qualification. These qualifications generally are still vague in determining and applying FET. The ASEAN Treaty makes an attempt to define and substantiate the standard by providing for the following:

World Bank Policy Research Working Paper WPS 4978 (June 2009). However, it should be pointed out that Kaufmann et al. concede the difficulties of assessing trends in a particular country indicator given the large margins of error. The decrease indicated in Figure 3.3 may be attributable to the addition of new data sets and more margins of error. Besides, WGI aggregates result from some other data sources that rely on subjective judgments made by public organizations, private institutions and nongovernmental organizations (NGOs), which may be out of line with objective circumstances and may not necessarily be expert assessments. Also, according to WGI, China outperforms or at least performs as well as the average country in the same income class on these core indicators.

132 Kaufmann et al. ibid.; http://info.worldbank.org/governance/wgi/ (accessed April 6, 2021).

133 Finland–China BIT 2004, Art. 3.

134 Sri Lanka–China BIT 1985, Art. 3(2); Mauritius–China BIT 1996, Art. 3(2).

135 Singapore–China BIT 1985, Art. 3(2).

136 Costa Rica–China BIT 2007, Art. 3; Seychelles–China BIT 2007, Art. 4(1).

137 For instance, Finland–China BIT 2004, Art. 3(1) removed the domestic law qualification.

For greater certainty:

(a) fair and equitable treatment refers to the obligation of each Party not to deny justice in any legal or administrative proceedings; . . ..[138]

This is a seemingly new and sharp variation to the existing practice but is of great help in boiling down the scope of FET, which is conventionally treated as a broad concept covering the requirement of stability, predictability and consistency of the legal framework, the principle of legality, the protection of investor confidence or legitimate expectations, procedural due process and denial of justice, substantive due process or protection against discrimination and arbitrariness, the requirement of transparency, and the requirement of reasonableness and proportionality.[139] The thrust of Article 7(1) suggests that FET merely refers to access to justice in legal or administrative proceedings, and arguably extends to procedural due process if it is interpreted in a wider sense. It is hard to explain why this provision is crafted to define FET. The only sensible reason may be that the contracting parties to the ASEAN Treaty are not able to unanimously accept other qualifications such as references to the principles of international law but are able to reach consensus by following the general investment treaty jurisprudence.

The New Zealand–China FTA takes a similar approach by defining FET as including "the obligation to ensure that, having regard to general principles of law, investors are not denied justice or treated unfairly or inequitably in any legal or administrative proceeding affecting the investments of the investor."[140] Under the China–Canada BIT, both countries are obliged to treat investors in accordance with international law including minimum standards addressing a wider range of interests, and including expectations related to transparency, performance requirements, transfers and expropriation.[141] Provisions on performance requirements affirm the preexisting terms of the WTO Agreement on Trade-Related Investment Measures (TRIMs), which have a gap with those in the Republic of Korea–US FTA 2007 (KORUS FTA), TRIM-plus, covering explicit and extensive policies such as technology transfer and indigenous innovation policies.[142] The US–Uruguay BIT 2005, for instance, defines treatment, based on customary international law, to include the obligation not to deny justice in criminal, civil or administrative adjudicatory proceedings in accordance with the principle of due process.[143] In any event, the ASEAN Treaty's approach reduces the "catch-all" nature of FET by providing that "a breach of another provision in the [Treaty], or of a separate international agreement" does not "establish that there has been a breach of [FET and full protection and security provision]."[144]

The ASEAN Treaty's way of bringing the prohibition against "denial of justice" in the ambit of FET may be treated as a new attempt to clarify the scope of the term by setting a "floor." This approach approximates the FET standard to the international minimum standard, which has the merit of relative clarity as there is a substantial body of jurisprudence

138 The ASEAN Treaty, Art. 7(1).

139 Stephan W. Schill, "Fair and Equitable Treatment under Investment Treaties as an Embodiment of the Rule of Law," IILJ Working Paper 06 (2006).

140 New Zealand–China FTA 2008, Art. 143(1).

141 Megan Seto, "Making the Most of the New China," McInnes Cooper, November 6, 2014, www.mcinnescooper.com/publications/legal-update-making-the-most-of-the-new-china-canada-bilateral-investment-treaty/ (accessed September 8, 2020).

142 Schott, Jung and Cimino-Isaacs, "An Assessment of the Korea-China Free Trade Agreement," 10–12.

143 US–Uruguay BIT 2005, Arts. 5(1)–(3).

144 The ASEAN Treaty, Art. 7(3).

concerning the elements of the international minimum standard including due process and access to justice in administrative or legal proceedings.[145] The advantages of this provision are twofold. First, it prevents the possibility of an interpretation of FET to allow a standard that is lower than the "access to justice in legal or administrative proceedings." Second, it closes the door for an expansive interpretation of the standard covering obligations beyond the "access to justice in legal or administrative proceedings." In applying this test, the right to access to justice in any legal or administrative proceedings should be sufficient to meet the investor's "legitimate expectations," which is generally regarded as the central or "dominant" element in FET.[146] In some arbitration cases, the tribunals have tried to limit the application of FET to a "reasonable and legitimate" level.[147]

The "no denial of justice" doctrine does not refer to any established body of international law or legal principles. This omission, however, may constitute an advantage as it will clearly avoid any potential confusion. The application of principles of international law or domestic law, on the contrary, still relies on the tribunal judging what is "fair and equitable." The case law has indicated that an express reference to any body of law is of little help and may well require the tribunal to resort to other elements in the case or sources of law. The *Middle East Cement* v. *Egypt* case is a good example, in which the tribunal ruled that the FET provision "must be given particular relevance in view of the special protection granted by Article 4 against measures 'tantamount to expropriation,' and in the requirement for 'due process of law' in Article 4.a."[148] In the absence of any reference to a body of law or principles in the BIT, the tribunal is able to apply international law in arbitration cases. As the case *Siemens* v. *Argentina* demonstrated, the tribunal was still "bound to find the meaning of these terms under the international law" even if the governing BIT did not refer to "international law."[149]

As regards other elements or sources, some Chinese BITs try to establish a linkage between the BIT and other international agreements. The United Arab Emirates–China BIT 1993 is the one that makes reference not only to the present treaty but also to other treaties to which both contracting parties are members, providing in relevant part: "Once the investment is established, it shall at all times enjoy the full protection and security that is in conformity with relevant international agreements to which both Contracting Parties are members." This provision effectively extends the reference from the current BIT to all other relevant treaties such as regional or multilateral investment agreements to which both parties are members. The ASEAN Treaty takes a clear-cut approach against this by providing that "a breach of another provision of this Agreement, or of a separate international agreement does not establish that there has been a breach of this 'fair and equitable treatment.'"[150] This clause basically strikes out the possibility of relying on the ASEAN Treaty itself or any other international treaties in determining breach of the FET obligation. RCEP offers a greater certainty to the FET provision. First, FET is accorded in accordance with the customary

145 UNCTAD, Key Issue I, at 213; *Compania de Aguas del Aconquija, S.A. & Compagnie Generale des Eaux (Vivendi)* v. *Argentina*, ICSID Case No. ARB/97/3, Award of November 21, 2000, para. 80; *Loewen Group, Inc. and Raymond L. Loewen* v. *United States*, ICSID Case No. ARB(AF)98/3, Final Award of June 26, 2003, para. 132.

146 *Saluka Investments BV (The Netherlands)* v. *The Czech Republic*, UNCITRAL Arbitration, Partial Award March 17, 2006, para. 302.

147 *National Grid* v. *Argentina*, 1(17) IAI Reports, December 17, 2008, www.iareporter.com/arbitration-cases/national-grid-v-argentina/ (accessed April 6, 2021).

148 *Middle East Cement Shipping and Handling Co. SA* v. *Egypt*, ICSID Case No. ARB/99/6, Award April 12, 2002, para. 143.

149 *Siemens A.G.* v. *Argentina Republic*, ICSID Case No. ARB/02/08, Award February 6, 2007.

150 The ASEAN Treaty, Art. 7(3).

international law minimum standard of treatment of aliens.[151] Second, FET requires each party not to deny justice in any legal or administrative proceedings. Third, FET does not require treatment to be accorded to covered investments in addition to or beyond that which is required under the customary international law minimum standard of treatment of aliens, and does not create additional substantive rights.[152]

3.5 FULL PROTECTION AND SECURITY STANDARD

The full protection and security standard is often combined with the FET standard in BITs,[153] and it appears in virtually all Chinese BITs. As a result, the standard is sometimes treated as part of FET. The doctrine underscores FET by obliging the host country to commit to protect the investment against civil unrest, public disturbance, threats and attacks targeted at it by reason of its foreign nature.[154] In essence, the standard is a "police protection" obligation on the part of the host state to make good-faith efforts to protect the foreign-invested properties.[155] The case law in this respect is more expansive, requiring the host country not only to provide physical protection, saving the foreign-owned commercial property from being destroyed by the host state's armed forces,[156] but also to ensure "the stability afforded by a secure investment environment."[157]

The ASEAN Treaty tries to substantiate the standard by providing:

> For greater certainty:
>
> (b) full protection and security requires each Party to take such measures as may be reasonably necessary to ensure the protection and security of the investment of investors of another Party.[158]

The thrust of this provision is to suggest that police protection or taking reasonably necessary measures would satisfy the "full protection and security" standard under the ASEAN Treaty. In this sense, the approach has the merit of relative clarity. Arguably, this approach is in line with case law which clarifies that the "protection and full security" obligation is applicable not only to "physical interferences" but also to "any act or measure which deprives an investor's investment of protection and full security."[159] The uncertainty in this provision is that the ASEAN Treaty does not clarify the level or magnitude of police protection required under customary international law. RCEP also combines full protection and security together with FET.[160] According to the RCEP, full protection and security

[151] RCEP, Art. 10.5, s. 1.

[152] RCEP, Art. 10.5, s. 2.

[153] This is also endorsed by case law, i.e., *Occidental Exploration and Production Company* v. *Ecuador*, London Court of International Arbitration, Case No. UN 346, Award July 1, 2004 (holding that a breach of the FET obligation amounted to a breach of the protection and security standard also).

[154] Helge Elisabeth Zeitler, "The Guarantee of 'Full Protection and Security' in Investment Treaties Regarding Harm Caused by Private Actors" (2005) 3 *Stockholm International Arbitration Review* 1–34.

[155] Ibid.

[156] *American Manufacturing & Trading, Inc. (AMT)* v. *Republic of Zaire*, ICSID Case No. ARB/93/1, Award of February 21, 1997, para. 6.04; *Asian Agricultural Products Ltd. (AAPL)* v. *Republic of Sri Lanka*, ICSID Case No. ARB/87/3, Final Award of June 27, 1990, para. 45.

[157] *Azurix* v. *Argentina*, ICSID Case No. ARB/01/12, Final Award July 14, 2006.

[158] The ASEAN Treaty, Art. 7(2).

[159] *Compania de Aguas del Aconquija SA and Vivendi Universal* v. *Argentine Republic*, ICSID Case No. ARB/97/3, Award August 20, 2007.

[160] RCEP, Art. 10.5, s. 1.

requires each Party to take such measures as may be reasonably necessary to ensure the physical protection and security of the covered investment.[161]

3.6 EXPROPRIATION

The origin of expropriation can be traced back to the international law standards for the protection of aliens. In modern international investment protection law, expropriation is permitted only if it is carried out on a nondiscriminatory basis, for a public purpose, in compliance with due process and the principle of payment of compensation. BITs regulate the exercise of the state's power to expropriate investments. However, the elaboration of these key elements may somehow provide useful clarification and guidance to tribunals but indeed add little to international expropriation law. In fact, the investor's chance of succeeding in a claim against a state for expropriation is rather slim, in particular in such cases where the disputed expropriation is a regulatory one. Tribunals always find it difficult to conclude either that the state's action amounts to an actual taking or that the accumulative effect of the state's act can be evidenced as reaching the threshold of expropriation. In some cases, tribunals may look into the technical side of the dispute, for example whether there is "a sufficient causal link between an actual breach of the BIT and the loss sustained," to determine the grant of compensation.[162]

Expropriation is a critically important BIT issue considering China's history of nationalizing foreign investment soon after the founding of the PRC[163] and China's "new state order" and "creeping renationalization" to "attack private enterprises" by grabbing state land from privately owned coal mines.[164] In line with the general BIT practice,[165] most Chinese BITs contain a generic expropriation clause covering "nationalization," "expropriation" and any other "similar measures" without providing any detailed definitions of these terms. The ASEAN Treaty basically adopts this structure in outlining the expropriation term as follows: "A Party shall not expropriate, nationalize or take other similar measures ('expropriation') against investments of investors of another Party, ..."[166] Like other Chinese BITs, the ASEAN Treaty covers "investments of investors," which is broad enough to cover both tangible and intangible assets. Likely, this provision can to a great extent be applied to the contract rights in the concession agreement[167] and other nondiscriminatory regulatory actions taken by the state government. While this provision is able to provide full-scale protection to investors, the disadvantage is also obvious in that the catch-all expropriation clause effectively prohibits all measures that have an effect equivalent to expropriation and does not include special carve-outs for the right of states to regulate.

161 RCEP, Art. 10.5, s. 2(b).
162 *Biwater Gauff (Tanzania) Ltd* v. *Tanzania*, ICSID Case No. ARB/05/22, para. 779.
163 Laurie A. Pinard, "United States Policy Regarding Nationalization of American Investments: The People's Republic of China's Nationalization Decree of 1950" (1984) 14 *California Western International Law Journal* 148.
164 Jamil Anderlini and Geoff Dyer, "Beijing Accused of Attacking Private Enterprise" and Geoff Dyer, "Crackdown on Coal Mines Ignites Fears of State Land Grab," *Financial Times*, November 26, 2009, p. 3.
165 Andrew Newcombe, "The Boundaries of Regulatory Expropriation in International Law" (2005) *ICSID Review – Foreign Investment Law Journal* 8–9.
166 The ASEAN Treaty, Art. 8(1).
167 *Compania de Aguas del Aconquija SA and Vivendi Universal* v. *Argentina*, ICSID Case No. ARB/97/3, para 7.5.4; *Waste Management, Inc.* v. *Mexico*, ICSID Case No. ARB(AF)/00/3 Final Award April 30, 2004, paras. 163–167; *Parkerings-Compagniet AS* v. *Lithuania*, ICSID Case No. ARB/05/8.

3.6.1 *"Indirect Expropriation"*

Under investment treaty jurisprudence, it is almost settled that, subject always to the precise words of the BIT, expropriation extends to both direct and indirect measures as well as to "creeping expropriation."[168] Some Chinese BITs such as the Germany–China BIT touch on "indirect expropriation" by stipulating that "investments by investors of either Contracting Party shall not directly or indirectly be expropriated, nationalized or subjected to any other measure the effects of which would be tantamount to expropriation or nationalization in the territory of the other Contracting Party."[169] The Mexico–China BIT expressly refers to expropriation being made directly or "indirectly through measures tantamount to expropriation or nationalization."[170] The Mauritius–China BIT 1996 provides that the parties shall not "take any measures depriving, directly or indirectly, nationals and/or companies ... of their investments ...."[171] A large number of Chinese BITs have other variations to similar effect. Examples are the Czech Republic–China BIT 2005, the Denmark–China BIT 1985, the Indonesia–China BIT 1994 and the Iceland–China BIT 1994 with the phrase "having an effect equivalent to ...,"[172] the Greece–China BIT 1992 with the caveat of "tantamount to"[173] and the France–China BIT 2007 with the phrase "same effect." Based on the extensive jurisprudence, any of these formulations may be held by the tribunals to have the effect of bringing indirect expropriations into the ambit of a treaty[174] as the state's actions or measures effectively "neutralize the benefit of the property of the foreign owner."[175] The most sophisticated definition of "indirect expropriation," drawing on recent BIT case law, appears in the New Zealand–China FTA, under which it is confined to measures which are (a) equivalent to direct expropriation, "in that [they] deprive ... the investor in substance of the use of the investor's property ..."; (b) either severe or indefinite; and (c) disproportionate to the public purpose.[176]

In comparison with other Chinese BITs, the ASEAN Treaty is silent on "indirect expropriation." This silence adds to the uncertainty that investors face when considering whether to bring an ISA claim. The phrase "other similar measures" in the ASEAN Treaty may be interpreted by the tribunal to cover "indirect expropriation" simply because the term "expropriation" alone can be interpreted to cover both direct and indirect expropriation. Alternatively, the tribunal could take a more expansive approach to interpreting the ASEAN Treaty's wording. Due to the lack of guidance in the ASEAN Treaty about how the treaty standard should be applied to specific circumstances, the application of international law to relevant disputes seems to be an option. This is legitimate when the investor

168 For a general account of the concept of indirect expropriation, see Andrew Newcombe, "The Boundaries of Regulatory Expropriation" (2005) 20 *ICSID Review – Foreign Investment Law Journal* 1; Rudolf Dolzer, "Indirect Expropriation of Alien Property" (1986) 1 *ICSID Review – Foreign Investment Law Journal* 41; George C. Christie, "What Constitutes a Taking of Property under International Law?" (1962) 28 *British Yearbook of International Law* 207.

169 Germany–China BIT 2003, Art. 4(2); Jordan–China BIT 2001, Art. 5(1); Uganda–China BIT 2004, Art. 4(1).

170 Mexico–China BIT 2008, Art. 7(1).

171 Mauritius–China BIT 1996, Art. 6.

172 Indonesia–China BIT 1994, Art. 6(1).

173 Germany–China BIT 2003, Art. 4(2).

174 *ADC Affiliate Limited and ADC & ADMC Management Limited* v. *Hungary*, ICSID Case No. ARB/03/16, para. 426; *Waste Management, Inc.* v. *Mexico* (Number II), ICSID Case No. ARB(AF)/00/3, Final Award April 20, 2004, para. 143 (making a distinction between indirect expropriation and measures tantamount to expropriation).

175 *CME Czech Republic BV* v. *Czech Republic*, UNCITRAL Partial Award September 13, 2001, para. 6-4.

176 Annex 13 to the New Zealand–China FTA 2008 (providing clear interpretative guidelines on what actions constitute expropriation).

brings the claim to ICSID arbitration according to the investment disputes clause under the ASEAN Treaty.[177] The ICSID Convention allows the tribunal to apply the law of the host state "and such rules of international law as may be applicable."[178] Therefore, the ICSID Convention's reference to international law provides an illustrative context bringing into play the supplementary and corrective effects of international law. Investment arbitration jurisprudence has already indicated that tribunals usually "look to international law in determining the relevant criteria for evaluating the claim of expropriation,"[179] and hold the general view that "no distinctions have been attempted between the general concept of dispossession and the specific forms thereof."[180]

3.6.2 *Compulsory License: The Case of Indirect Expropriation*

IPRs have long been recognized as a form of "investment" entitled to protection under BITs. The ASEAN Treaty, like most Chinese BITs, in the definition of "investment," provides a detailed list of the types of IP that may be considered a form of investment asset, for example "copyrights, patents and utility models, industrial designs, trademarks and service marks, geographical indications, layout designs of integrated circuits, trade names, trade secrets, technical processes, know-how and goodwill."[181] The inclusion of IPRs in the definition of "investment" reflects that IP has drawn sufficient attention in the investment protection field.

In authorizing a compulsory license, the government authority, in response to some emergent need, may interfere directly with an IPR privately owned by the foreign investor by compelling the owner, on an *ex post* basis, to grant use of an IPR to the state or to other third parties in exchange for a licensee's payment.[182] Thus, compulsory license, a case of indirect expropriation, may cause a direct impact on FDI involving IPRs, that is, constituting a potential threat to security in private property and the innovative economy,[183] and triggering an alleged violation of the terms of the BIT.[184] Despite the standard inclusion of IPRs in the definition of "investment" and the increasing importance of IPRs in a more science-oriented globalized economy, there have been surprisingly few publicly reported cases concerning an IPR-centered investment dispute.[185]

177 The ASEAN Treaty, Art. 14(1)(4)(b).

178 ICSID Convention, Article 42 (providing that "the Tribunal shall decide a dispute in accordance with such rules of law as may be agreed by the parties. In the absence of such agreement, the Tribunal shall apply the law of the Contracting State party to the dispute (including its rules on the conflicts of laws) and such rules of international law as may be applicable.").

179 *LG&E* v. *Argentina*, ICSID Case No. ARB/02/1, para 185; *Metalpar SA and Buen Aire SA* v. *Argentina*, ICSID Case No. ARB/03/5, para 173; *Continental Casualty Company* v. *Argentina*, ICSID Case No. ARB/03/9, para 284.

180 *Lauder* v. *Czech Republic*, UNCITRAL Award, para 200.

181 The ASEAN Treaty, Art. 1(1)(d)(iii).

182 Robert Bird and Daniel R. Cohay, "The Impact of Compulsory Licensing on Foreign Direct Investment: A Collective Bargaining Approach" (2008) 45 *American Business Law Journal* 283 n. 1; Carlos M. Correa, "Investment Protection in Bilateral and Free Trade Agreements: Implications for the Granting of Compulsory Licenses" (2004) 26 *Michigan Journal of International Law* 346.

183 Ronald A. Cass, "Compulsory Licensing of Intellectual Property: The Exception that Ate the Rule?," Washington Legal Foundation Working Paper Series No. 150 (2007).

184 *Shell Brands International AG and Shell Nicaragua S.A.* v. *Republic of Nicaragua*, ICSID Case No. ARB/06/14.

185 Tsai-Yu Lin, "Compulsory Licenses for Access to Medicines, Expropriation and Investor-State Arbitration under Bilateral Investment Agreements – Are There Issues Beyond the TRIPS Agreement?" (2009) 40 *International Review of Intellectual Property Law* 152 (noting that no claim regarding compulsory licenses has been brought before investor–state arbitration and led to an arbitral award).

Under international law, some form of compulsory licensing has been recognized. The Paris Convention, for example, recognizes compulsory licensing as a means to address the abusive exercise of patent rights on "failure to work" grounds, thereby justifying issuance in limited cases.[186] Within the WTO framework, the Agreement on Trade-Related Aspects of Intellectual Property Rights (the "TRIPS Agreement") also addresses compulsory license, in the phrase of "use without authorization of the right holder," with an array of conditions. Article 31 of the TRIPS Agreement, together with Articles 7, 8, 40 and 42, permits the grant of a compulsory license by WTO member states, so long as an overriding public interest is served,[187] certain procedures are followed, and certain terms are fulfilled.[188] The Doha Declaration on the TRIPS Agreement and Public Health, adopted by the WTO in 2001, confirms that member states have the right to grant compulsory licenses to protect public health.[189] In any event, issuing a compulsory license may involve contentious, facts-specific and case-by-case decisions,[190] placing the IPR owner at odds with the host state authorizing the compulsory license. The foreign investor may consider claiming its rights under the international standards either under the WTO system or through investment arbitration.

By definition, a compulsory license does not deprive the IPR owner of ownership over the protected IP. Thus, the government's authorization of a compulsory license does not fall within the scope of direct expropriation. Albeit a lack of a "mechanical formula" in determining whether a compulsory license amounts to an indirect expropriation, the fact that the compulsory license has a potential impact on an investor's rights in its investment may allow it to be viewed as a form of government interference in the wider context of indirect or regulatory expropriation. The expropriation term in the ASEAN Treaty, as in other Chinese BITs such as the new Germany–China BIT 2003, illustrates a common approach to confirming protection in cases of indirect expropriation as follows:

> Investments by investors of either Contracting Party shall not directly or indirectly be expropriated, nationalized or subjected to any other measure the effects of which would be tantamount to expropriation or nationalization in the territory of the other Contracting Party ("expropriation") except for the public benefit and against compensation. Such compensation shall be equivalent to the value of the investment immediately before the expropriation is taken or the threatening expropriation has become publicly known, whichever is earlier . . . .

This provision is wide enough to cover indirect expropriation and "any other measure the effects of which would be tantamount to expropriation or nationalization." However, there is

186 Paris Convention on the Protection of Industrial Property, Art. 5A, paras. (2), (3) and (4).

187 In terms of "a public purpose," there is recognition in Article 31(b) of the TRIPS Agreement that a national emergency or circumstances of extreme urgency, i.e., dictated by national security or public health concerns, could justify a compulsory license. Article 31(1) or Article 31(k) of the TRIPS Agreement, on a broader anticompetitive rationale, respectively recognizes a more indirect public purpose that compulsory license may be needed to permit the exploitation of an important "second" ("dependency") patent or to remedy anticompetitive practices.

188 The most important terms include: (i) each compulsory license is considered on its individual merits; (ii) the effort must have been made to obtain authorization from the right holder on reasonable commercial terms and conditions but failed; (iii) the license is granted on a non-exclusive and non-assignable basis, with a scope and duration limited to the purpose for which the license is issued, and it must cease if and when the conditions change to eliminate that purpose; (iv) the license must be used predominantly for the supply of the domestic market of the authorizing state; (v) the right holder must be paid adequate remuneration in the circumstances of each case, taking into account the economic value of the authorization. See Article 31(a)–(h) of the TRIPS Agreement.

189 WTO, The Doha Declaration on the TRIPS Agreement and Public Health, adopted on November 14, 2001, WT/MIN(01)/DEC/2, November 20, 2001.

190 Calos M. Correa, *supra* note 182, 348.

no guidance on how this treaty standard should be applied in relation to a compulsory license. The case law jurisprudence in this respect is relatively restrictive. The "sole effect doctrine" adopted by the tribunal for the case of *Starrett Housing Corporation* set a high threshold that a compulsory license constitutes an indirect expropriation if "measures ... can interfere with property rights to such an extent that these rights are rendered so useless that they must be deemed to have been expropriated ...."[191]

The ASEAN Treaty contains a more important provision that directly addresses compulsory licenses but complicates the matter as follows: "The [expropriation clause] shall not apply to the issuance of compulsory licenses granted to intellectual property rights in accordance with the TRIPS in Annex 1C to the WTO Agreement."[192] The ASEAN Treaty's provision brings the WTO disciplines directly into play in the investment dispute context. To the extent that a compulsory license is TRIPS Agreement compliant, the expropriation provision will not apply at all.

This "cross-reference" approach bears some significance. First, it manifests the linkage between compulsory license and investment arbitration. Second, it ties the question of the validity of a host state's issuance of the license to compliance with the TRIPS Agreement. Third, the wording is clear enough that the tribunal should "apply" the TRIPS Agreement rather than simply rely on it for "interpreting" the regulatory treatment standard in this respect. In other words, the WTO Agreement here does not just provide an interpretive context or suggestive guidance for considering detailed aspects of a compulsory license; it requires an ISA tribunal to rule on the basis of WTO substantive and procedural rules. Yet, this does not end the argument. This provision excludes only TRIPS-compliant compulsory licenses, which may imply that TRIPS-incompatible compulsory licenses may still be subject to expropriation rules. Meanwhile, even compliance with the TRIPS Agreement does not necessarily yield immunity. In this respect, the ASEAN Treaty is of little help in guiding tribunals in issuing awards. In any event, the possible reference to the TRIPS Agreement shows the complex interplay between two different treaty-based regimes providing different levels of protection and different types of remedies. Furthermore, the ASEAN Treaty may complicate the situation since the ICSID Convention, as one *lex arbitri*, calls for application of domestic and international law which may apply as a relevant basis for bringing in international law in the case of a dispute under the ASEAN Treaty. "International law" here, on the other hand, is unclear and may include customary international law[193] or even FET.[194] Hence, this particular issue is still half-open to challenge.

This provision is closely parallel, if not identical, to the wording of a clause in the US–Uruguay BIT 2005: "This Article does not apply to the issuance of compulsory licenses granted in relation to intellectual property rights in accordance with the TRIPS Agreement, or to the revocation, limitation, or creation of intellectual property rights, to the extent that such issuance, revocation, limitation, or creation is consistent with the TRIPS Agreement."[195] The US–Uruguay BIT language not only provides some leeway for governments in their regulation with respect to the compulsory license but also makes an attempt to define the scope of "compulsory license." Nevertheless, as discussed, it does not explain how to deal with TRIPS-incompatible compulsory licenses under the BIT framework. Again, the

191 *Starrett Housing Corporation* v. *Islamic Republic of Iran*, 4 Iran-US CTR 122, 154 (1983).

192 The ASEAN Treaty, Art. 8(6).

193 *Mondev* v. *United States*, Final Award, ICSID Case No. ARB(AF)/99/2, para. 121 (October 11, 2002).

194 NAFTA, Art. 1105(1).

195 US–Uruguay BIT 2005, Art. 6(5).

ASEAN Treaty, like the US–Uruguay BIT, has the effect of importing WTO rules, as applicable law, into the context of investment disputes regarding a compulsory license.

3.7 CAPITAL TRANSFER AND REPATRIATION

Capital transfer and repatriation provisions guarantee the free flow of funds, which is the most fundamental right that foreign investors want to secure under a BIT. The capital importing states like China and some ASEAN member states, nevertheless, in many instances enact foreign exchange control laws for their need to retain foreign exchange to pay for essential goods and services.[196] Therefore, the capital transfer provisions in BITs often attempt to balance the conflicting interests between investors and host states.[197] This is the main reason why old-generation Chinese BITs explicitly ensured China's right to implement its foreign exchange control measures.[198]

3.7.1 *Free Transfer Provision*

The host state's obligation to ensure the free transfer of funds into and out of the host state is a common feature in BITs, which usually set out a non-exhaustive list of the types of payment. The host state's obligation is materialized in a relatively standard manner: those specified types of payment can be transferred without delay in the convertible currency of the original investment and at the rate of exchange fixed on the transfer date. The ASEAN Treaty contains a detailed free transfer of payments provision with an illustrative list of the types of payments, which should be especially welcome, given China's and some ASEAN member states' foreign exchange control. This list operates in the same way as the illustrative list used in the definition of "investment."[199] The ASEAN Treaty covers the flows of funds both "into and out of its territory,"[200] which signals a move away from the old-generation BITs which exclusively addressed outward transfers.[201] Free inward transfers are covered by the transfer provisions in more new-generation Chinese BITs such as those with Finland, Mexico and Turkey.[202]

The ASEAN Treaty's free transfer provision includes a wide range of payments.[203] It is clear that the profits from the investment or the proceeds generated on a sale of investment are payments relating to the "investment" and returns.[204] The ASEAN Treaty also explicitly refers to "the initial capital" as well as "any additional capital" used to maintain or expand the investment.[205] This reference combines features in both the Mexico–China BIT 2008, which clarifies that the free transfer of payments covers those payments relating to "establishing, maintaining or expanding the investment," and the Portugal–China BIT 2005, under which both the initial capital and any additional capital are freely transferable.[206] In addition, payments under loan agreements, as royalties and for technical assistance all relate to an

196 Rudolf Dolzer and Margrete Stevens, *Bilateral Investment Treaties* (Martinus Nijhoff 1995) 85.
197 Kenneth J. Vandevelde, *United States Investment Treaties: Policy and Practice* (Kluwer 1992) 143.
198 UK–China BIT 1986, Art. 6(4).
199 See Section 3.1.
200 The ASEAN Treaty, Art. 10(1).
201 E.g., Korea–China BIT 1992.
202 Finland–China BIT 2004, Art. 6(1); Turkey–China BIT 2015, Art. IV.
203 The ASEAN Treaty, Art. 10(1).
204 The ASEAN Treaty, Arts. 10(1)(b) and 10(1)(c).
205 The ASEAN Treaty, Art. 10(1)(a).
206 Mexico–China BIT 2008, Art. 8(1)(a); Portugal–China BIT 2005.

investment as well.[207] Net earnings and other compensations of natural persons are also payments relating to the "investment."[208] While returns, loan payments, liquidation proceeds, and payments from licenses and royalties are guaranteed free transfer, the transfer of salaries is a qualified right.[209] The usual qualification is that the natural person who is employed and allowed to work in connection with an investment in the territory is entitled to this right.[210] This qualification appears in other Chinese BITs such as the Indonesia–China BIT[211] and the Malaysia–China BIT.[212] Some Chinese BITs are intended to be wide enough to cover other income earned by the employees. For instance, the Finland–China BIT covers "earning and other remuneration" while the Cyprus–China BIT and the Norway–China BIT make reference to "unspent earnings" or "legitimate incomes."[213] The ASEAN Treaty is broader in scope covering not only net earnings but also "other compensations," which is likely to be interpreted to cover bonus payments and other benefits earned by the employees. The list in the ASEAN Treaty also makes reference to free transfers of compensation awarded under the expropriation provisions and compensation for damages and losses provisions.[214] The transfer provisions in Chinese BITs including the ASEAN Treaty reflect the general treaty practice, with little deviation.

In order to make the transfer obligations more meaningful to foreign investors, BITs impose other substantive criteria on transfer. First, transfer is carried out in a freely convertible currency. Most commonly, BITs use a "freely convertible currency"[215] or "freely usable currency" as the ASEAN Treaty does.[216] Although these terms are rarely defined in BITs,[217] the general consensus is that any "hard" currency can be regarded as a "freely convertible currency."[218] Second, the exchange rate between the local currency and the "freely usable currency" must be made at an acceptable rate, namely, an "official rate of exchange"[219] or "the prevailing market rate of exchange."[220] Chinese BITs use the "official"[221] or "market"[222] rate of exchange. References to "Special Drawing Rights"[223] and "an official exchange rate determined by the Central Bank of the Contracting State"[224] also appear in some Chinese BITs. Certainly, the "prevailing market rate of exchange" is the most popular option. The

207 The ASEAN Treaty, Arts. 10(1)(f), 10(1)(d) and 10(1)(b).
208 The ASEAN Treaty, Art. 10(1)(e).
209 Rudolf Dolzer and Christoph Schreuer, *Principles of International Investment Law* (2nd edition, Oxford University Press 2012) 193.
210 The ASEAN Treaty, Art. 10(1)(e).
211 Indonesia–China BIT 1994, Art. VII(1)(h).
212 Malaysia–China BIT 1988, Art. 6(1)(e).
213 Cyprus–China BIT 2001, Art. 6(1)(h); Norway–China BIT 1984, Art. 6(1)(d).
214 The ASEAN Treaty, Art. 10(a)(g).
215 Energy Charter Treaty, Art. 14(2).
216 The ASEAN Treaty, Art. 10(1).
217 The Energy Charter Treaty defines a "freely convertible currency" as "a currency that is widely traded in international foreign exchange markets and widely used in international transactions." However, the ECT does not specify any "freely convertible currency." Article 1.1(e) of the Egypt–Malaysia BIT 1997 defines "freely usable currency" as the "US dollars, pound sterling, Deutschemark, French Franc, Japanese yen and any other currency that is widely used to make payments for international transactions."
218 The Article of Agreement of the International Monetary Fund, Art. XXX(f).
219 China-Philippines BIT 1992, Art. 6.
220 Portugal–China BIT 2005, Art. 6(2).
221 Philippines–China BIT 1992, Malaysia–China BIT 1988, Denmark–China BIT 1985 (without any reference to host state).
222 Czech Republic–China 2005 BIT.
223 Benin–China BIT 2004, Art. 6(4); Finland–China BIT 2004, Art. 6(4); New Zealand-China FTA 2008, Art. 142(2).
224 Ghana-China BIT 1989, Art. 6(1).

ASEAN Treaty follows this formulation. Third, the transfer must be carried out without delay. Some Chinese BITs set a cap on the time frame in order to clarify the term "without delay." For instance, the time limits set out in the Protocols to the Portugal–China BIT, the Brunei–China BIT and the Korea–China BIT are two, four and six months, respectively.[225] The France–China BIT does not impose a time limit; rather, it interprets the term "without delay" to be "a period normally required for the completion of transfer formalities according to the international financial practice."[226] The Italy–China BIT 1985 not only defines the meaning of "without delay" but also sets a time limit. The Protocol defines "undue delay" as meaning "within such period as is normally required according to international financial practice and not later, than six months." In this respect, the ASEAN Treaty does not clarify its position.

3.7.2 *Limitations on Free Transfer Obligations*

It is not uncommon to see some limitations imposed on the freedom of transfer of funds, for example compliance with bankruptcy measures. These limitations often appear in the form of a list of exclusions to free transfer in BITs. Accordingly, the host state may take some currency control restrictions or other measures. Usual limitations include the fiscal,[227] financial,[228] "due"[229] or tax obligation on an investor seeking to make a transfer. Other exceptions include balance of payment restrictions or any other specific exception such as protection of lawful creditors.[230] The ASEAN Treaty includes specific exclusions in Article 10 (3), which states:

> … a Party may prevent or delay a transfer through the equitable, non-discriminatory and good faith application of its law and regulations relating to:
>
> (a) bankruptcy, loss of ability or capacity to make payments, or protection of the right of creditors;
> (b) non-fulfilment of the host Party's transfer requirements in respect of trading or dealing in securities, futures, options or derivatives;
> (c) non-fulfilment of tax obligations;
> (d) criminal or penal offences and the recovery of the proceeds of crime;
> (e) social security, public retirement or compulsory saving schemes;
> (f) compliance with judgments in judicial or administrative proceedings;
> (g) workers' retrenchment benefits in relation to labor compensation relating to, amongst others, foreign investment projects that are closed down; and
> (h) financial reporting or record keeping of transfers when necessary to assist law enforcement or financial regulatory authorities.

The ASEAN Treaty's exclusion list is extensive, not only covering the investor's fiscal, tax and financial obligations but also including other "social" obligations such as the recovery of the proceeds of crime, settlement of social security and compliance with judgments. The advantage of having this extensive list is to make the non-transfer provision more operative, which increases the investor's predictability in bringing a claim

225 Protocol to the Brunei–China BIT 2000, Art. 6; Protocol to the Korea–China BIT 2007, Art. 6.
226 Protocol to the France–China BIT 2007, para. 3.
227 Bulgaria–China BIT 1989, Oman–China BIT 1995, Ukraine–China BIT 1992 and Yemen–China BIT 1998.
228 Slovenia–China BIT 1993, Art. 5.
229 Yugoslavia–China BIT 1997.
230 China–Israel BIT 1995, Art. 5.

against the host state's non-transfer decision, action or measure. China is still implementing an exchange control policy and Chinese currency, renminbi, is not freely convertible. Some Chinese BITs confirm such practice. The Protocol to the Syria–China BIT 1996, for example, confirms that particular types of payments, liquidation amounts, and royalties will be subject to the approval of the appropriate foreign exchange authority for China. In the process of slowly but systematically liberalizing its laws and regulations on capital transfers and foreign exchange control, China has also demonstrated its flexibility in BIT negotiations by lifting the "subject to its laws and regulations" limitation on transfers, which often appeared in old-generation Chinese BITs.[231]

The utility of the free transfer of payments provision is somehow set off by the "domestic laws and regulations" carve-out. Unlike the old-generation BITs under which the freedom of capital transfer is often subject to the "domestic laws and regulations,"[232] the ASEAN Treaty does not directly include this carve-out. Instead, the ASEAN Treaty attaches the "domestic laws and regulations" qualification to the host state's prevention or delay of capital transfer.[233] As a result, when the host state prevents or delays a transfer, "the transfers … shall comply with relevant formalities stipulated by the host Party's domestic laws and regulations relating to exchange administration, insofar as such laws and regulations are not to be used as a means of avoiding a Party's obligations … ."[234] The application of the host state's "laws and regulations" then must satisfy the qualifications of "equitable, non-discriminatory and good faith."[235] This signals a substantial move toward transparency and rule of law in restricting the transfer of funds by investors.[236] These two provisions clarify how the local law requirement should be interpreted and operated in practice. The local law requirement must be satisfied by the investor in transferring funds but cannot be intentionally created and used to circumvent the host state's commitments under the BIT. In other words, the local law requirement cannot be applied in such a way as to frustrate the guarantee of free transfers. Yet, it is unclear to what extent this can be relied on to assist investors in practice. The ASEAN Treaty's "domestic law" approach is different from the "grandfather" approach adopted in the Germany–China BIT 2003, which envisages an abandonment of existing foreign exchange restrictions.[237] Accordingly, the introduction of new foreign exchange control restrictions is not permissible. From the foreign investment protection perspective, the ASEAN Treaty's provisions are less protective than those in the Germany–China BIT. In addition, the Germany–China BIT obliges China's foreign exchange authority to handle the request for capital transfers within two months,[238] which does not appear in the ASEAN Treaty either. The CKJ TIT 2012 includes a balance of payments exception, allowing the state discretion to institute temporary safeguard measures,[239] which may undercut the parties' commitments to free transfers.[240]

231 E.g., Finland–China BIT 2004, Art. 6.
232 Djibouti–China BIT 2003, Art. 6.
233 The ASEAN Treaty, Arts. 10(3) and 10(4).
234 The ASEAN Treaty, Art. 10(4).
235 The ASEAN Treaty, Art. 10(3).
236 China has removed all restrictions on current account transactions according to Article VIII of the IMF Agreement. For the accounts of Chinese foreign exchange control on outbound and inbound investments, see Shen Wei, "Is SAFE Safe Now? Foreign Exchange Regulatory Control over Chinese Outbound and Inbound Investments and a Political Economy Interpretation of Policies" (2010) 11(2) *Journal of World Investment and* Trade, DOI: 10.2139/ssrn.2332830.
237 Protocol to the Germany–China BIT 2003, Art. 6(a).
238 Germany–China BIT 2003, Arts. 6(3) and Ad Article 6(b).
239 Art. 19.
240 Art. 13.

It is worth noting that the ASEAN Treaty explicitly confirms that the transfer provisions should be applied in accordance with MFN requirements. This allows the investors to avail themselves of the best treatment with regard to transfers. Under some Chinese BITs such as the Oman–China BIT 1995, "without restricting the generality of the [MFN clause]," the parties agree to accord to any transfer "treatment as favorable as that accorded to transfer originating from investments made by investors of any third state."[241] The ASEAN Treaty's wording is largely the same except it has an "in like circumstances" caveat, which also appears in the MFN clause in the ASEAN Treaty. Accordingly, "each Party undertakes to accord to the transfer . . . treatment as favorable as that accorded, in like circumstances, to the transfer originating from investments made by investors of any other Party or third country."[242]

Exceptions to the freedom of transfer are allowed in times of financial crisis. For example, the host state is permitted to temporarily restrict transfers out of the state when there is a "serious balance of payments difficulties and external financial difficulties or the threat thereof. . . ."[243] The ASEAN Treaty includes this exception allowing the host state to "impose restrictions on any capital transactions inconsistent with its specific commitments [under the ASEAN Treaty]."[244] This leaves some discretion for the host state to determine when the financial crisis comes or there is a threat of such financial difficulties. However, recourse to the financial crisis exception is subject to several restrictions. First, the financial crisis exception exists only "in exceptional circumstances."[245] This restriction suggests that the host state may not rely on the financial crisis exception very often or too easily. In terms of what constitutes an "exceptional circumstance," the ASEAN Treaty does not provide a definition or an exhaustive list of events. Nevertheless, the ASEAN Treaty gives two examples: "movements of capital cause, or threaten to cause, serious economic or financial disturbance in the Party concerned"[246] and "the event of serious balance of payments and external financial difficulties or threat thereof."[247] Second, the financial difficulties must reach the threshold of severity. The ASEAN Treaty states that "movements of capital cause, or threaten to cause, serious economic or financial disturbance in the Party concerned." This qualification can be satisfied only if the "movements of capital" are causing or are likely to cause a serious consequence. Third, restrictions "do not affect the rights and obligations of the Parties as members of the WTO under Paragraph 1 of Article XI of GATS, and the measures are taken in accordance with paragraph 2 of Article 11 of this Agreement, *mutatis mutandis*."[248]

Under the ASEAN Treaty, the balance of payments exceptions are also allowed at the request of the IMF[249] or under the article of Measures to Safeguard the Balance of Payments.[250] Where the host state relies on the article of Measures to Safeguard the Balance of Payments to restrict the free transfer of funds, prompt notification must be served to the other party,[251] and restrictions are limited to the following:

241 Oman–China BIT 1995, Art. 6(2); Norway–China BIT 1984.
242 The ASEAN Treaty, Art. 10(2).
243 Uganda–China BIT 2004.
244 The ASEAN Treaty, Art. 10(5).
245 The ASEAN Treaty, Art. 10(5)(c).
246 The ASEAN Treaty, Art. 10(5)(c).
247 The ASEAN Treaty, Art. 11(1).
248 The ASEAN Treaty, Art. 10(5)(c).
249 The ASEAN Treaty, Art. 10(5)(b).
250 The ASEAN Treaty, Art. 10(5)(a).
251 The ASEAN Treaty, Art. 11(3).

(a) be consistence with the Articles of Agreement of the IMF;
(b) not discriminate among the Parties;
(c) avoid unnecessary damage to the commercial, economic and financial interests of any other Party;
(d) not exceed those necessary to deal with the circumstances [of serious balance of payments and external financial difficulties or threat thereof];
(e) be temporary and be phased out progressively as the situation the situation [of serious balance of payments and external financial difficulties or threat thereof] improves; and
(f) be applied such that any other Party is treated no less favorable than any third country.[252]

It appears that the temporary restrictions on transfer must be imposed on an "equitable, non-discriminatory, and in good faith basis." In addition, the restrictions should reach the necessity threshold in order to deal with severe financial times.[253] These criteria effectively require the host state to impose restrictions if not to the least extent then proportionate to the aims sought to be achieved. The ASEAN Treaty's balance of payments exceptions are onerous in a practical sense with the aim of not too easily sacrificing protections to foreign investors in transferring funds. As the ASEAN Treaty stresses, the balance of payments exceptions should not "affect the rights and obligations of the Parties as members of the IMF under the Articles of Agreement of the IMF."[254]

3.8 CONCLUSION

A comparative review of substantive rights offered by the ASEAN Treaty and other Chinese BITs demonstrates that Chinese BITs have gradually evolved toward a more "liberal" stance of foreign investment protections that prevail in international practice. Unlike the old-generation Chinese BITs prior to 1998, which were marked by a reluctance to apply strong investment protection standards and adopt a comprehensive ISDS mechanism,[255] a new generation of Chinese BITs starting with the Barbados–China BIT 1998 indeed departed from a pure capital importing state's traditional position in that they are more liberal in providing foreign investors with stronger and more comprehensive substantive and procedural protections largely comparable to those of capital-exporting states.[256] In this sense, China's stance in BIT practice is evolving from a restrictive stance to a liberal one. The most important groundbreaking feature of the ASEAN Treaty, consistent with recent Chinese BIT jurisprudence, is the investor–state dispute resolution procedure under which the foreign investor is entitled to initiate arbitration and to claim damages against the host state in an international arbitration. China's BITs are developing in terms of substantive protection standards offered to foreign investors. Unlike its previous practice, China is now more willing

252 The ASEAN Treaty, Art. 11(2).

253 The ASEAN Treaty, Art. 11(1).

254 The ASEAN Treaty, Art. 10(5).

255 Congyan Cai, "Outward Foreign Direct Investment Protection and the Effectiveness of Chinese BIT Practice" (2006) 7(5) *Journal of World Investment & Trade* 621 (listing a limited scope of national treatment to treatment based on domestic laws and regulations, transfer rights and recourse to investor–state arbitration to the determination of compensation for expropriation).

256 Stephan W. Schill, "Tearing Down the Great Wall: The New Generation Investment Treaties of the People's Republic of China" (2007) 15(1) *Cardozo Journal of International and Comparative Law* 73–118 (revealing that it was China that took initiatives in proposing to have a comprehensive dispute settlement provision in the new Germany–China BIT 2003); Yuqing Zhang, "The Case of China" in Michael Moser (ed.), *Investor-State Arbitration – Lessons for Asia* (Juris Publishing 2008) 156 (remarking that it was Western countries that wanted China to adopt the modern dispute resolution clause when updating their old BITs with China).

to offer NT protection to foreign investors, which increasingly conforms to international standards. While other substantive protection standards remain largely unchanged, they are slowly evolving toward some "hybrid" forms combining both Chinese and capital-exporting states' characteristics. The ASEAN Treaty is the latest product in this movement. However, the ASEAN Treaty does not represent any breakthrough in offering more substantive protections. For instance, it does not clarify the nature of the umbrella clause. In any event, the substantive rights incorporated in the ASEAN Treaty are more readily enforceable by foreign investors due to the comprehensive ISDS provisions.

It is no coincidence that the change in Chinese BIT policy and practice actually overlapped in time with the launch of the "go globally" strategy in 1998.[257] In contrast to the long-pursued policy of encouraging FDII, China's long-term firm stance was not to encourage, if not to discourage or restrict, FDIO. Starting from 2001, China shifted its policy and has been steadily promoting FDI overseas in order to lessen the external surplus and secure access to natural resources in other developing countries. In embarking on its well-known "go globally" strategy, the Chinese government set a clear objective of nurturing up to fifty globally competitive "national champions" by 2010, and plays a guiding role in promoting overseas expansion by Chinese companies.[258] Presently, China is proactively negotiating BITs with countries that do not have BITs with China, such as the United States.[259] The conclusion of a large number of modern BITs including the ASEAN Treaty with other countries and regional economic organizations reveals China's growing acceptance of modern BIT jurisprudence and IIL as well as its great efforts and confidence in providing sufficient protections to foreign investors.

There has been growing "policy coherence" concern over the core standards offered by the BITs for various reasons. First, the precise meaning of certain core protective standards is a "matter of some debate" and is still being developed.[260] Second, the core standards implicate public international law and may be less amenable to clear definition than is the case for certain rights in private law.[261] Third, the universe of BITs is evolving toward a more complicated and atomized system[262] due to the lack of a central authority to coordinate, regulate or provide a framework for the structure or content of BITs. In reality, BITs are somewhat formulaic instruments and all tend to provide similar, if not exactly identical,

257 The "Go globally," or "Going abroad," strategy was first put forward by the Central Committee of the Communist Party of China (CPC) in 1998. The strategy was for the first time included in the 10th Five-Year Plan for National Economy and Social Development in 2001. The Central Committee of the CPC repeated its commitment to implementing this strategy in its decision on some issues concerning the improvement of the social economy market, http://news.xinhuanet.com/newscenter/2003-10/21/content_1135402.htm.

258 Florencia Jubany and Daniel Poon, "Recent Chinese Engagement in Latin America and the Caribbean: A Canadian Perspective," Canadian Foundation for the Americas Research Report (March 2006), www.focal.ca/pdf/china_latam.pdf (accessed March 6, 2021)

259 China and the United States were in intense negotiations to enter into a BIT in the 1980s. However, the efforts failed partly due to the Tiananmen Square accident and partly because of the USA's staunch position on its domestic law requirements for the timely, adequate and sufficient compensation for expropriation and nationalization. The two countries recently resumed their negotiations and included this in the Strategic Economic Dialogue launched in September 2006. See, e.g., Pat K. Chew, "Political Risk and U.S. Investment in China: Chimera of Protection and Predictability" (1994) 34 *Virginia Journal of International Law* 615, 661; Yuqing Zhang, *supra* note 256, 155–156.

260 R. Doak Bishop, James Crawford and W. Michael Reisman, *Foreign Investment Disputes: Cases, Materials and Commentary* (Kluwer International Law 2005) 10.

261 Matthew Saunders, "Bilateral Investment Treaties Oil the Wheels of Commerce: An Increase in BITs Is Helping to Encourage and Protect International Business," IBA in the News, June 23, 2004.

262 UNCTAD, *Development Implications of International Investment Agreements*, IIA Monitor No. 2 International Investment Agreements, at 2, UNCTAD/WEB/IIA/2007/1 (2007).

packages of investment protections with minor or major variations, exceptions and nuances. Due to the gradually more uniform institutional mechanisms, IIL principles will be implemented in a more consistent manner albeit with abundant conflicting and inconsistent decisions generated by numerous investment tribunals, multiplicity of sources and multiplicity of proceedings.[263]

In the realm of IIL, the potential for and existence of inconsistencies in investment treaty arbitration (ITA) is a natural result of bilateralism but will be diminished by multilateralism. Given the uniform principles adopted by BITs such as NT, MFN treatment, FET, prohibitions on direct and indirect expropriation, and the investor's rights to initiate proceedings against the host state for violation of treaty obligations, and the joint efforts being made by capital-exporting states in pushing forward a more favorable investor protection regime, the consistency, uniformity and convergence are about to outweigh the inconsistency, diversity and divergence. The ASEAN Treaty presents a good case study to demonstrate that, given the increasing array of case law, "the international investment law and policy regime is evolving, and is likely to continue to do so in the future."[264]

[263] Susan D. Franck, *supra* note 37, at 1521.

[264] Karl P. Sauvant, "Introduction, International Investment Law and Policy 2008–2009: Overview" in Karl P. Sauvant (ed.), *Yearbook on International Investment Law & Policy 2008–2009* (Oxford University Press 2009) 6.

4

Nondiscriminatory Standards in China's BITs

The willingness of the EU and China to strengthen their trade and investment relationship has been evident for more than two decades,[1] and has been boosted since China's accession to the WTO.[2] The decision to start bilateral negotiations toward an EU–China BIT, premised on China's first policy paper on the EU[3] and the EU's release of "Building a Comprehensive Partnership with China,"[4] was announced at the end of the EU–China Summit held in Beijing on November 21, 2013.[5]

[1] China and the EU are very important trading partners to each other, with a total trading volume of USD 560 billion in 2013. Ying Ding, "A Seamless Joint by Cementing a Strategic Policy of Cooperation, China and Europe Forge a More Practical Partnership," *Beijing Review* (April 10, 2014, No. 15 ed.) www.bjreview.com.cn/quotes/txt/2014-04/08/content_612036.htm (accessed April 11, 2016). To put this into perspective, China is the second largest trading partner to the EU and the EU constitutes China's number one trading partner. In 2020, China overtook the USA as the EU's largest trading partner. Trade between China and the EU was worth USD 709 billion in 2020, compared with USD 671 billion worth of imports and exports from the USA. "China Overtakes US as EU's Biggest Trading Partner," *BBC News*, February 17, 2021, www.bbc.com/news/business-56093378 (accessed March 23, 2021). However, in terms of FDI flow, neither side can be considered a more important destination than the other. Statistics show that the EU's FDI into China amounts to EUR 11 billion and China's investment into the EU is USD 10 billion. Thilo Hanemann and Daniel H. Rosen, "China Invests in Europe: Patterns, Impacts and Policy Implications" (2012) 25, http://rhg.com/wp-content/uploads/2012/06/RHG_ChinaInvestsInEurope_June2012.pdf (accessed April 12, 2016). The amount of Chinese FDI in the EU rose to EUR 37.2 billion in 2016. In 2019, 9.5 percent of companies had their ownership based in China, Hong Kong and Macau, up from 2.5 percent in 2007. "How Much of Europe Does China Own?," *BBC News*, April 20, 2019, www.bbc.com/news/world-47886902 (accessed March 24, 2021). The total M&A value of EU companies into China amounted to USD 71 billion for the past three decades, which is lower than the USD 117 billion recorded in the same period from US investors. Kane Wu, "Investment Deal Expected to Bolster European Dealmaking in China," Reuters, January 7, 2021, www.reuters.com/article/us-china-eu-investments/investment-deal-expected-to-bolster-european-dealmaking-in-china-idUSKBN29C0LE (accessed March 24, 2021).

[2] UNCTAD: "China: WTO Accession and Growing FDI Flows" (press information notes) (2002) Genève United Nations.

[3] "China's Policy Paper on the EU: Deepen the China–EU Comprehensive Strategic Partnership for Mutual Benefit and Win–Win Cooperation," April 2, 2014, www.fmprc.gov.cn/mfa_eng/wjdt_665385/wjzcs/t1143406.shtml (accessed March 6, 2021).

[4] EC: "Communication from the Commission – Building a Comprehensive Partnership with China," COM 181 Final, Brussels, March 25, 1998.

[5] Hong Yan, "China–EU Investment Treaty: Can It Be Achieved?" (Commentaries) (December 6, 2013) S. Rajaratnam School of International Studies No. 224/2013. Signing an EU–China BIT in which all twenty-eight EU member states would be represented together by the EU could become possible only after the signing of the Lisbon Treaty, which came into force on December 1, 2009. The Lisbon Treaty provides the EU with full and exclusive competency to craft and implement FDI policy on behalf of member states.

Since its accession to the WTO, China has been proactively improving its own BIT program, making BITs more user-friendly to foreign investors. More recently, China has been making great efforts to enter into a number of major BITs with key trading partners such as the EU and the USA while the USA until recently took a leading role in negotiating two major multilateral investment agreements, that is, the TPP (now CPTPP) and the TTIP.

The ongoing negotiation of the EU–China BIT, together with the US–China BIT negotiation, becomes even more important after the US withdrawal from the TPP, given the fragmentation of IIL and the emergence of megaregional investment treaties. The future EU–China BIT, that is, the EU–China Comprehensive Agreement on Investment (CAI), is likely to introduce economic, political and legal significance into the global international investment arena, and together with other major megaregional investment treaties, for instance the potential US–China BIT, eventually deepen and reshape IIL.

The CAI is a critically important legal instrument with geopolitical significance in the international investment sphere for both the EU and China. China's BIT negotiations with the EU and the USA could further open up China's domestic market to greater competition and deepen China's economic ties with the rest of the world. From a legal perspective, BITs between China and its major economic partners such as the EU and the USA could create a rule-based international economy and strengthen international rule of law in the economic sphere. These BITs, as liberalizing devices, will help transplant international standards into the domestic legal system. Domestically, China could utilize its upgraded BITs to improve its economic governance by fighting favoritism and local protectionism which unfairly differentiate investors based on their nationalities, shrinking the advantages enjoyed by the SOEs, removing onerous regulations and effecting fair law enforcement. More liberalizing BIT terms including but not limited to nondiscriminatory standards, acting as a process of economic rationalism, effectively facilitate shaping more market-oriented economic policies and a more pro-competitive investment environment and free market economy in China. As far as China is concerned, through negotiating these major BITs, it will have a greater stake not only in global trade and investment but also in global economic governance and international rule-making processes. Economically, Chinese companies are more likely to have easier access to the EU and US markets.

Against this backdrop, the purpose of this chapter is to review the possibility of aligning China's nondiscriminatory standards, that is, NT and MFN treatment standards, with those in some of the latest EU BITs as the benchmark by looking into the evolution of nondiscriminatory standards in Chinese BITs. The CAI needs to address the concern of discriminatory treatment of foreign investors in the Chinese market. In Chinese FDI law, there are various limitations or restrictions applicable to foreign investors: among others, foreign ownership limitation, approval procedures (exclusively applicable to FIEs), favorable policies toward SOEs, inconsistent implementation of national laws at the local level, and lack of transparency and consistency in the application of laws and regulations. These raise real concerns among international investors that their rights are inadequately protected, and, relevant to what is discussed here, justify a CAI, which will help create an even playing field for European investors. Despite its legal significance, the negotiation process of the CAI has been slow (in the sense of significant progress)[6] and nontransparent (in terms

[6] Yong Wang, "China's BIT Progress and Implications for China–Canada FTA Talks" (2017) Center for International Governance Innovation Policy Brief No. 104, www.cigionline.org/sites/default/files/documents/PB%20no.104web.pdf (accessed March 6, 2021).

of the availability of a draft BIT text or its details),[7] leaving sufficient discussion on the progress and difficulties of the CAI negotiation since the end of 2013 less feasible and fruitful. Amid the coronavirus pandemic, the EU and China completed the seven-year negotiation over a comprehensive investment agreement on December 30, 2020.[8] Both sides are committed to further opening up their markets with the focus on level-playing-field disciplines (SOEs, transparency rules for subsidies and rules tackling forced technology transfers)[9] as well as investment liberalization (market access offers). Progress has been made with regard to the entry and temporary stay of intracorporate transferees and business visitors for establishment purposes,[10] corporate social responsibility, sustainable development and state-to-state dispute settlement.[11]

An evolutionary review of Chinese BITs with some EU member states compared with the EU's latest BITs explicitly demonstrates a narrowing gap between the EU and China in terms of their treaty behavior and strategy. The rest of this chapter proceeds as follows. Sections 4.1 and 4.2 investigate NT and MFN respectively and try to understand the logic behind these two nondiscriminatory standards moving from restrictive to liberal ones. Section 4.3 outlines the exceptions and limitations attached to nondiscriminatory standards. The scope of these exceptions and limitations shows exactly the negotiating stance and treaty objectives that a particular state may possess. Section 4.4 ends the chapter and makes an attempt to position China's BIT strategy in a (anti-)globalization context.

4.1 NT AND NONDISCRIMINATION

NT is the core standard that underpins the principle of nondiscrimination and requires the host state to accord equal treatment under BITs. The purpose of this standard is to promote equal treatment between foreign and domestic investors while avoiding arbitrary or discriminatory measures. A typical clause requires host states to grant foreign investors treatment that is "no less favourable than"[12] or "as favourable as" that accorded to the host state's own citizens.[13] The difficulty in applying this treatment in reliance upon the "no less favourable than" criterion is to properly determine when foreign and domestic investors are in a comparable situation so as to judge whether the foreign investor has been unjustifiably discriminated against. The other way of describing this standard is to use the phrase "same treatment," which does not prevent foreign investors from enjoying more favorable treatment.

4.1.1 *Qualified National Treatment Provisions*

Up until now, China has signed thirty-four BITs (including Protocols) with EU member states. Nineteen earlier Chinese BITs (that were signed in the 1980s and 1990s) with EU

7 The EU and China negotiators reached conclusions on the comprehensive scope of the EU–China IBT and moved into a phase of specific text–based negotiations in early 2016. "EU and China Agree on Scope of the Future Investment Deal," January 15, 2016, http://trade.ec.europa.eu/doclib/press/index.cfm?id=1435 (accessed March 6, 2021).

8 Wu, *supra* note 1.

9 European Commission Directorate–General for Trade, Directorate B – Services and Investment, Intellectual Property and Public Procurement, Brussels, July 28, 2020, Trade.B2/4592206.

10 European Commission Directorate–General for Trade, Directorate B – Services and Investment, Intellectual Property and Public Procurement, Brussels, July 6, 2020, Trade.B2.

11 European Commission Directorate–General for Trade, Directorate B – Services and Investment, Intellectual Property and Public Procurement, Brussels, May 29, 2020, Trade.B2.

12 Multilateral Agreement on Investment, Art. 1(1).

13 GATT, Art. 3.

member states did not mention the NT doctrine at all. Only three Chinese BITs signed with the UK, the Czech Republic and Slovakia, and Slovenia during the same period unusually included the NT provisions. China's earlier BITs with other countries largely adopted the same practice. For instance, the Singapore–China BIT 1985 and the Philippines–China BIT 1992 followed China's policy of not including NT provisions. Investors under these BITs are only allowed to rely upon international investment arbitration to adjudicate disputes concerning the amount of compensation for expropriation. China gradually departed from its past practice by including the protections of NT for foreign investors, though in many instances with limitations. China's second model BIT (1989) includes NT provisions, but the scope is limited. China's third model BIT (1997) contains a comprehensive NT clause. This may explain why China, starting from the beginning of the new century, was due to enter into or amend its BITs with EU member states (except with Romania in their Protocol) with NT clauses. When China amended its BITs with Germany and the Netherlands, an NT clause was added. Details of NT provisions in Chinese BITs with EU member states can be found in Table 4.1.

Less than half of Chinese BITs grant an NT standard by merely adopting the phrase "no less favourable than." The treatment accorded is supposed to be "no less favourable" provided that the investors and investments being compared are "in like situations."[14] The provisions do not require "most favourable" treatment.

China was historically hesitant to apply a full-scale NT doctrine, which explains why Chinese BITs often add various qualifications to the NT standard. The restrictive approach to granting NT to foreign investors provides government authorities with deference to discriminate against foreign investors under domestic laws.[15] The first Chinese BIT which incorporated the NT standard was the UK–China BIT 1986, which is, however, subject to substantial qualifications: a soft "best-effort" obligation and a local law caveat. The UK–China BIT 1986 states: "... either Contracting Party shall to the extent possible, accord treatment in accordance with the stipulations of its laws and regulations to the investment of nationals or companies of the other Contracting Party the same treatment as that accorded to its own nationals or companies."[16] This heavily qualified provision bringing "domestic law" into play fails to bind the host country to eliminate existing discriminatory measures or not to take new discriminatory actions, provided that these actions are in the form of local "laws and regulations." Moreover, the limitation "to the extent possible" reduces the effect and goodwill of the host state's undertakings to guarantee equal competition among foreign and domestic investors. As a result, NT granted by the BIT as such remains symbolic and provides insufficient guarantees to foreign investors.

The NT was rarely included or was heavily qualified in the early Chinese BITs. The rationale of offering such ineffective protection to foreign investment was twofold: (i) to protect infant industries, in particular the SOE sector; and (ii) to leave some flexibility for the government to discriminate against foreign investors in favor of domestic ones. Early Chinese BITs, by contrast, guaranteed MFN treatment. China's refusal to include unqualified NT clauses in its early BITs matches China's role as a major capital-importing state which often imposes local content and performance requirements on foreign investment.

14 Article X.7(1) and X.8(1) of CETA's investment chapter.

15 Alex Berger, "Investment Rules in Chinese Preferential Trade and Investment Agreements: Is China Following the Global Trend towards Comprehensive Agreements?" (2003) German Development Institute Discussion Paper 10.

16 UK–China BIT 1986, Art. 3(3).

TABLE 4.1 *NT provisions in Chinese BITs with EU member states (1982–2009)*

No.	BIT	Signing and effective dates	NT	Remarks
Old-generation BITs				
1	China–Sweden BIT	Signed on March 29, 1982 Effective as of March 29, 1982	No NT	
2	China–Germany BIT	Signed on October 7, 1983 Effective as of March 18, 1985	No NT	Replaced by the new BIT. Invalid now.
3	China–France BIT	Signed on May 30, 1984 Effective as of March 19, 1985	No NT	Replaced by the new BIT. Invalid now.
4	China–BLEU BIT	Signed on June 4, 1984 Effective as of October 5, 1986	No NT	Replaced by the new BIT. Invalid now.
5	China–Finland BIT	Signed on September 4, 1984 Effective as of January 26, 1986	No NT	Replaced by the new BIT. Invalid now.
6	China–Italy BIT	Signed on January 28, 1985 Effective as of August 28, 1987	No NT	
7	China–Denmark BIT	Signed on April 29, 1985 Effective as of April 29, 1985	No NT	
8	China–Netherlands BIT	Signed on June 17, 1985 Effective as of February 1, 1987	No NT	Replaced by the new BIT. Invalid now.
9	China–Austria BIT	Signed on September 12, 1985 Effective as of October 11, 1986	No NT	
10	China–UK BIT	Signed on May 15, 1986 Effective as of May 15, 1986	*NT (Art. 3(3))*	
11	China–Poland BIT	Signed on June 7,1988 Effective as of January 8, 1989	No NT	
12	China–Bulgaria BIT	Signed on June 27, 1989 Effective as of August 21, 1994	No NT	
13	China–Hungary BIT	Signed on May 29, 1991 Effective as of April 1, 1993	No NT	
14	China–Czech Republic and Slovakia BIT	Signed on December 4, 1991 Effective as of December 1, 1992	*NT*	
15	China–Portugal BIT	Signed on February 3, 1992 Effective as of December 1, 1992	No NT	Replaced by the new BIT. Invalid now.
16	China–Spain BIT	Signed on February 6, 1992 Effective as of May 1, 1993	No NT	Replaced by the new BIT. Invalid now.
17	China–Greece BIT	Signed on June 25, 1992 Effective as of December 21, 1993	No NT	
18	China–Croatia BIT	Signed on June 7, 1993 Effective as of July 1, 1994	No NT	
19	China–Estonia BIT	Signed on September 2, 1993 Effective as of June 1, 1994	No NT	
20	China–Slovenia BIT	Signed on September 13, 1993 Effective as of January 1, 1995	*NT*	

(Continued)

TABLE 4.1 (Continued)

No.	BIT	Signing and effective dates	NT	Remarks
21	China–Lithuania BIT	Signed on November 8, 1993 Effective as of June 1, 1994	No NT	
22	China–Romania BIT	Signed on July 12, 1994 Effective as of September 1, 1995	No NT	
New-generation BITs				
23	China–Cyprus BIT	Signed on January 17, 2001 Effective as of April 29, 2002	NT	
24	China–Netherlands BIT	Signed on November 26, 2001 Effective as of August 1, 2004	NT	Re-signed
25	China–Germany BIT	Signed on December 1, 2003 Effective as of November 11, 2005	NT	Re-signed
26	China–Finland BIT	Signed on November 15, 2004 Effective as of November 15, 2006	NT	Re-signed
27	China–BLEU BIT	Signed on June 6, 2005 Effective as of December 1, 2009	NT	Re-signed
28	China–Spain BIT	Signed on November 24, 2005 Effective as of July 1, 2008	NT	Re-signed
29	China–Slovak Republic	Protocol: Signed on December 7, 2005 Effective as of May 25, 2007	NT	
30	China–Portugal BIT	Signed on December 9, 2005 Effective as of July 26, 2008	NT	Re-signed
31	China–Romania BIT	Protocol: Signed on April 16, 2007 Effective as of September 1, 2008	No NT	
32	China–Bulgaria BIT	Protocol: Signed on June 26, 2007 Effective as of November 10, 2007	NT	
33	China–France BIT	Signed on November 26, 2007 Effective as of August 20, 2010	NT	Re-signed
34	China–Malta BIT	Signed on February 22, 2009 Effective as of April 1, 2009	NT	
	China–Ireland China–Latvia	No BIT No BIT		

4.1.2 *Full-Scale NT Provisions*

Very few Chinese BITs include a full-scale NT provision. The typical example is the provision in the Japan–China BIT 1988 as follows: "[T]he treatment accorded by either Contracting Party within its territory to nationals and companies of the other Contracting

Party with respect to investments, returns and business activities in connection with the investment shall not be less favorable than that accorded to nationals and companies of the former Contracting Party."[17] This provision applies not only to the "business activity," inter alia, "the maintenance of branches and other establishment necessary for the business activity, the control and management of companies, the employment and discharge of personnel and the making and performance of contracts"[18] but also to "the purchase of raw materials, power and fuel, marketing of products, obtaining loans, etc."[19]

However, the significance of this provision cannot be overexaggerated as its efficacy was substantially reduced by the BIT's Additional Protocol, which provides: "[I]t shall not be deemed treatment less favourable for either Contracting Party to accord discriminatory treatment, in accordance with its laws and regulations, to nationals and companies of the other Contracting Party, in case it is really necessary for the reason of public order, national security or sound development of national economy."[20] This caveat included in the Protocol and other Chinese BITs, such as the Czech and Slovak Republic–China BIT 1991, is in broad terms since such concepts as "public order" and "sound development of national economy" are not explicitly defined. Besides, the application of these terms is completely subject to the tribunal's interpretation and discretion. The tribunal may have to rely on the host state in interpreting whether a discriminatory measure upholds "public order" or furthers "sound development of national economy" because these terms cannot be "self-judged" by the tribunal.[21] Even worse, these catch-all terms give China considerable leeway to implement existing discriminatory measures against foreign investors, or even adopt new ones.

Moving away from the UK–China BIT 1986 type of restrictions with the best-effort character,[22] China has been gradually more willing to accept general NT since late 2001.

The grandfathered NT clause in the China–Mexico BIT 2012 states:

1. Without prejudice to its laws and regulations at the time the investment is made, each Contracting Party shall accord to investors of the other Contracting Party treatment no less favorable than that it accords, in like circumstances, to its own investors with respect to the operation, management, maintenance, use, enjoyment or disposal of investments.
2. Without prejudice to its laws and regulations at the time the investment is made, each Contracting Party shall accord to investments of investors of the other Contracting Party treatment no less favorable than that it accords, in like circumstances, to investments of its own investors with respect to the operation, management, maintenance, use, enjoyment or disposal of investments.[23]

17 Japan–China BIT 1988, Art. 3(2).

18 Ibid., Art. 3(3).

19 Agreed Minutes to the Japan–China BIT 1988.

20 Japan–China BIT 1988, Additional Protocol, Art. 3.

21 *CMS Gas Transmission Co.* v. *Republic of Argentina*, ICSID Case No. ARB/01/8, Award of May 12, 2005, para. 353 et seq. The tribunal in that case needed to consider the exceptions from BIT obligations under Article XI of the US–Argentina BIT 1991. Article XI provides that "this Treaty shall not preclude the application by either Party of measures necessary for the maintenance of public order, the fulfilment of its obligations with respect to the maintenance or restoration of international peace or security, or the Protection of its own essential security interests." The tribunal was of the opinion that the decision on that issue was not "self-judging."

22 UK–China BIT 1986, Art. 3(3) (stating that "each Contracting Party shall to the extent possible, accord treatment . . . to the investments of national or companies of the other Contracting Party the same as that accorded to its own nationals or companies").

23 Mexico–China BIT 2008, Art. 3.

The caveat "without prejudice to its laws and regulations" reduces the effectiveness of the NT provision to a best-effort clause. A literal interpretation of this qualification means that the host state does not grant foreign investors NT protection unless the host state's laws and regulations grant foreign investors treatment not less favorable than that accorded to domestic investors.

In the new Germany–China BIT 2003, a more general NT provision is offered. Accordingly, China "shall accord to investments and activities associated with such investments by the investors of the other Contracting Party treatment not less favourable than that accorded to the investments and associated activities by its own investors."[24] Nevertheless, this "full" NT standard is still subject to a "grandfather" clause, under which the NT standard does not apply to:

(a) any existing non-conforming measures maintained within its territory;
(b) the continuation of any such non-conforming measure;
(c) any amendment to any such non-conforming measure to the extent that the amendment does not increase the non-conformity of these measures.

The People's Republic of China will take all appropriate steps in order to progressively remove the non-conforming measures.[25]

This amendment allows China to maintain laws and regulations toward foreign investors that are incompatible with NT. Progress has been made in the form of a standstill commitment toward non-conforming measures, that is, there would be no increase in discriminatory treatment toward foreign investors, plus a promise to gradually remove non-conforming measures. Of more interest is a differential treatment secured by China in such NT clauses to the effect that Chinese investors can rely on NT in the respective partner country while the Chinese government is still allowed to discriminate against foreign investors. This differential NT treatment, common to trade law, has rarely been adopted in investment treaties which are reciprocal in nature. As a result, this NT provision is stronger than the best-effort provision. This "grandfather" clause also appears in the Cyprus–China BIT 2001[26] and various Chinese BITs with European states.[27]

The New Zealand–China FTA 2008 includes a grandfathered NT clause that is combined together with more details as follows:

1. Article 138 does not apply to:
   (a) any existing non-conforming measures maintained within its territory;
   (b) the continuation of any non-conforming measure referred to in subparagraph (a);
   (c) an amendment to any non-conforming measure referred to in subparagraph (a) to the extent that the amendment does not increase the non-conformity of the measure, as it existed immediately before the amendment, with those obligations.
2. The Parties will endeavour to progressively remove the non-conforming measures.[28]

This NT clause is a hybrid form mixing the features of both a grandfathered hard NT and a "best efforts" soft NT (to remove non-conforming measures instead of according treatment to the extent possible). The significant deviation in relation to this clause is a reciprocal promise to gradually remove non-conforming measures.

24 Germany–China BIT 2003, Art. 3(2).
25 Germany–China BIT 2003, Additional Protocol, Art. 3(2).
26 Cyprus–China BIT 2001, Art. 3(3) and Protocol, Art. 3.
27 BLEU–China BIT 2005; Czech Republic–China BIT 2005; Finland–China BIT 2005; Netherlands–China BIT 2005.
28 New Zealand–China FTA 2008, Art. 141.

China's practice of restrictive NT provisions was characteristic of its development strategy in a transitional process. The uniqueness of China's BIT practice is to apply differentiated NT protections to investors from developed and developing countries in order to attract FDI from European and other developed countries. China uses the respective provision of its BITs with developing countries to restrictively grant NT without prejudice to the host states' laws and regulations. Meanwhile, in its BITs with developed countries, NT treatment is granted provided that the continuation of existing non-conforming measures is guaranteed. This qualified NT provision exclusively applies to the Chinese market while a no less favorable NT standard than that afforded to domestic investors is applied to Chinese investments in the respective developed country. China has indicated a gradual yet decisive policy change toward stronger and more comprehensive NT protections. This gradualist approach not only matches China's change from a pure FDI-importing country to a more important FDI-exporting country; it also shows China's increasing desire and capability to adhere to international standards of legal protections to foreign investors.

The EU's routine approach is to rely on a GATS type of "positive list" – a list of types and volume of investment that should be admitted, which is similar to the trade-like aspects of access to foreign markets. In the pre-Lisbon era, the EU adopted this GATS-inspired market access approach to make specific commitments in specified areas.[29] The EU way of formulating the NT clause is to limit it to the post-establishment phase.[30]

The traditional purpose of signing BITs is to offer better legal protection to foreign investors. BITs usually do not deal with the host state's policy to admit foreign investors, leaving this with the host state, which may use its own discretion. The US and Canada BITs took the lead by providing for market access through expanded NT clauses covering the pre-establishment or establishment phase.[31]

Most EU member states' BITs provide for "unqualified" NT and MFN, applicable only to post-establishment. The scope of these clauses is determined by reference to the "operation, management, maintenance, use, enjoyment or disposal of the investment." BITs signed by Germany, the UK, France and Austria follow the traditional approach of providing only investment protection and leave the regulation of market access to the host states. This traditional approach, also termed the "investment control model" by UNCTAD,[32] does not grant a right of admission to foreign investors or investment. Other EU member states such as Bulgaria, the Czech Republic, Estonia, Latvia, Lithuania, Poland, Romania and Slovenia,

[29] See, e.g., the provisions on "commercial presence" of Article 65 et seq. Economic Partnership Agreement between the CARIFORUM states, of the one part, and the European Community and its Member States, of the other part, signed October 15, 2008 (entry into force: provisional application: December 29, 2008), Official Journal L 289/I, November 30, 2008, 3, as well as section C of chapter 7 of the EU–Korea FTA, signed October 15, 2009 (entry into force July 1, 2011), Official Journal L 127, May 14, 2006, which provides for MFN treatment and specific market access commitments and NT in separate schedules. See Angelos Dimopoulos, *EU Foreign Investment Law* (Oxford University Press 2011) 52–53.

[30] Freya Baetens, "Discrimination on the Basis of Nationality: Determining Likeness in Human Rights and Investment Law" in Stephen Schill (ed.), *International Investment Law and Comparative Public Law* (Oxford University Press 2010) 279–315.

[31] See, e.g., Article 3(1) Canadian Model FIPA 2004 ("Each Party shall accord to investors of the other Party treatment no less favourable than that it accords, in like circumstances, to its own investors with respect to the establishment, acquisition, expansion, management, conduct, operation and sale or other disposition of investments in its territory."), https://investmentpolicy.unctad.org/international-investment-agreements/treaty-files/2820/download (accessed March 24, 2021).

[32] UNCTAD, International Investment Agreements: Key Issues – Volume, UNCTAD/ITE/IIT/2004/10, 2004, 148–153, https://unctad.org/system/files/official-document/iteiit200410v3_en.pdf (accessed March 24, 2021).

however, granted NT at the pre-establishment stage accompanied by a negative list of sectoral reservations and exceptions in their BITs with the USA.

The EU–South Korea FTA 2011 requires that NT be accorded to "establishment and investors" of the other party.[33] A "positive list" approach is followed to secure binding market access and NT commitments on the economic activities specified in the list of commitments contained in Annex 7-A and subject to any reservations specified therein. The EU–Colombia–Peru FTA and the EU–Singapore FTA adopt the GATS-type "positive list" approach with respect to market access provisions and NT.

The EU–Canada CETA marks a breakthrough, however, by adopting a "negative list" approach with respect to the "establishment, acquisition (and possibly expansion) of investment."[34] A "negative list" approach extending NT to the pre-establishment stage concerns market access and investment liberalization and could become a benchmark for future EU investment treaty negotiations.[35]

The EU presents a mixed picture. At the EU level, there is a switch from the extension of MFN and NT obligations from the post-establishment stage to the pre-establishment phase with a negative list from a positive list. Member States are, however, still divided in the sense that some continue with their traditional approach while others switch to a pre-establishment admission plus a negative list approach. It appears that the EU's BIT negotiation strategy is to switch from its Member States' practice to a more NAFTA-type investment treaty practice.

Including a pre-establishment NT provision in the BIT tends to lift the market entry barrier to foreign investment. The policy of accepting pre-establishment NT commitments is often made on the basis of the balance of outbound and inbound FDI of the economy. Contrary to the admission model according to which legal protection is offered to foreign investors only after the admission of the investment project, the pre-establishment model effectively restricts the screening powers of host states in the pre-establishment stage and the sovereignty in regulating the market entry of foreign investors, leading to a more transparent and liberalized FDI regulatory regime in the host states.

Market access provisions, being the critical component of the CAI negotiation,[36] could improve and guarantee transparency and stability. More importantly, the provisions could help EU-based investors remove some restrictions they may otherwise face when they enter into restrictive sectors in the host states. Relevant to China, according to the Business Confidence Survey 2013, published by the EU Chamber of Commerce in China, 45 percent of EU companies lost business opportunities due to market access and regulatory barriers.[37] OECD's FDI Regulatory Restrictiveness Index measures statutory restrictions on FDI in sixty-two countries and points to China's regulatory requirements as being particularly burdensome to foreign investors.[38] On the other hand, the pre-establishment NT represents a new trend in investment agreement negotiations worldwide. More countries have adopted the pre-establishment obligation plus a negative list approach. Both the positive list

33 Article 7.11 of the EU–South Korea FTA 2011.

34 Article X.7 National Treatment, Draft CETA Investment Text, November 21, 2013.

35 Wenhua Shan and Sheng Zhang, "Market Access Provisions in the Potential EU Model BIT: Towards a 'Global Bit 2.0'" (2014) 15(3–4) *Journal of World Investment & Trade* 422–453.

36 Frank Bickenbach, Wan-Hsin Liu and Guoxue Li, "The EU–China Bilateral Investment Agreement in Negotiation: Motivation, Conflicts and Perspectives" (2015) Kiel Policy Brief No. 20, 20.

37 European Union Chamber of Commerce in China, European Business in China: Business Confidence Survey 2073, 2013, www.europeanchamber.com.cn/en/publications–business–confidence–survey (accessed March 6, 2021).

38 OECD FDI Regulatory Restrictiveness Index 2017, www.oecd.org/investment/fdiindex.htm (accessed March 6, 2021).

approach and the negative list approach may reach the same results. Nevertheless, the negative list approach is more transparent, predictable and ultimately more liberalizing. A negative list may be more likely to impose obligations with respect to new investment sectors (i.e., FinTech).

China's positive list approach has long been the target of complaints and criticism from the international business community. The positive list approach confines foreign investment to a narrow list of authorized sectors. In other words, the list of exclusions is too long to be used together with this positive list. China has agreed to negotiate a BIT with the USA on the basis of a negative list approach concerning NT.[39] To this end, China and the USA exchanged their proposed negative list in early 2015.[40] This approach suggests that any sector that does not appear in the negative list should be presumed to be open to foreign investment. By having a negative list, China is bound to remove behind-the-border barriers to market access, and deal with all stages of foreign investment on the basis of a negative list.

In the negotiation of a BIT with China, the EU insisted on the inclusion of pre-establishment NT on the basis of a negative list.[41] China, on the other hand, has submitted a negative list offer of sectors that would remain off-limits to US investors in the course of China–US BIT negotiation in 2016.[42] China also committed to considering "pre-establishment rights" which would ensure NT at the preliminary phase of an investment project.[43] Technically, there is a possibility that two BIT parties may commit to a negative list and a positive list simultaneously. For instance, in the chapter on cross-border trade in services under the ChAFTA 2015, China takes a positive list approach to the core obligations of MFN treatment, market access and NT, whereas Australia takes a negative list approach. This means that these obligations apply to China only in service sectors specified by China, while for Australia, the obligations apply with respect to all service sectors except those expressly excluded by Australia. The application of negative and positive lists to different parties as under ChAFTA is unusual.

4.1.3 *"In Like Circumstances" Qualifier*

Unlike the European BITs, the North American BITs normally incorporate an "in like circumstances" qualification.[44] NAFTA and the 2004 US Model BIT attach a likeness test to NT and MFN standards. International investment tribunals often refer to such clauses as

39 MOFCOM, "MOFCOM'S Spokesman Shen Danyang Comments on China and US to Promote Energetically Negotiations on Bilateral Investment Agreement," July 16, 2013, http://english.mofcom.gov.cn/article/newsrelease/policyreleasing/201307/20130700200566.shtml (accessed April 5, 2021).

40 Francois Godement and Angela Stanzel, "The European Interest in an Investment Treaty with China" (2015) European Council on Foreign Relations Policy Brief, https://ecfr.eu/publication/the_european_interest_in_an_investment_treaty_with_china332/ (accessed April 5, 2021).

41 Li Jiabao, "China, EU Talking Investment," *China Daily* USA, January 22, 2014, http://usa.chinadaily.com.cn/epaper/2014-01/22/content_17251011.htm (accessed April 5, 2021).

42 Reuters, "China to Submit 'Negative List' for US Investment Treaty Talks Next Week," June 6, 2016, www.reuters.com/article/us–china–usa–trade–idUSKCN0YS024 (accessed March 6, 2021). As early as in 2013, the USA and China agreed to BIT talks on the basis of pre–establishment national treatment with a negative list approach. Xinhua, "China, US to Start Negative List BIT Negotiations," *China Daily*, July 10, 2014, www.chinadaily.com.cn/business/2014–07/10/content_17700488.htm (accessed March 6, 2021).

43 Peterson Institute for International Economics, "Toward a US–China Investment Treaty," February 2015, PIIE Briefing 15–1, 11.

44 NAFTA, Art. 1102. Canadian Model FIPA 2004, Art. 3(1).

"similar situations," "like circumstances," or "similarly situated" comparators or "likeness."[45] The "likeness" test, in the form of "in like circumstance" or "in like situations," is to provide a comparator so that investors or investment can be compared.

In assessing whether an NT standard has been breached or not, the tribunals often apply a three-step approach: to identify the subject of comparison (a "comparator" or "like investor"); to compare the treatment received by the foreign and the "comparator" investors with a view to establishing any discrimination; and to ascertain whether there is any justification for such differential treatment.[46] First, the tribunal must identify a "like investor" and compare the treatment this "like investor" receives with that received by the foreign investor. Under NAFTA, tribunals will resort to the phrase "in like circumstances" in determining the scope of the subject of comparison. For instance, the tribunal in *SD Myers* v. *Canada* ruled that the term "like circumstances" invited an examination of whether a non-national investor complaining of less favorable treatment was in the same "sector" as the national investor.[47] The tribunal in *Methanex* v. *United States*, in applying a narrower approach, decided to choose only entities that were in the most closely "like circumstances" rather than comparators that were in less similar circumstances to the comparator.[48] Although the inclusion of the "in like circumstances" caveat can be used by the tribunal to determine the breach of NT standard, there is no uniform approach to the comparator in arbitration practice. The "in like circumstances" caveat may justify differences in treatment. Tribunals in several NAFTA cases left host states significant flexibility in applying different treatments to domestic and foreign investors as long as the policy considerations were rational. In *SD Myers* v. *Canada*, the tribunal confirmed that the assessment of "like circumstances" needed to take into account circumstances that would justify governmental regulations that treated investors differently in order to protect the public interest.[49]

Chinese BITs usually follow the European approach and tend not to include a "like circumstance" qualification (except in the case of a few BITs).[50] The New Zealand–China FTA, however, contains a similar caveat, requiring "treatment no less favourable than that accorded, in like circumstances, to the investments ... by its own investors."[51] The adoption of this caveat seems to be a new trend in recent years. The utility of this better-crafted language may avoid potential confusion. In the absence of this phrase, the textual interpretation may suggest that the comparison may be made to a broader group of domestic investors.[52] With the "like circumstances" caveat, the tribunal may interpret the NT standard to imply the requirement of "comparability" between two investors.

In IIL, there is no context-independent meaning of likeness,[53] which is, however, an inherent limitation at the level of text. WTO law, on the other hand, offers contextual guidance to an adjudicator faced with understanding the scope and elements of GATT

45 An investment liberalization objective will guide an investment tribunal established to resolve disputes under the Model BIT to require a competitive relationship between investors and their investments in determining that the two are in "like situations." Under the NAFTA, for instance, the analysis on likeness focuses on the establishment of a competitive relationship criterion for "likeness."

46 UNCTAD, Investor–State Dispute Settlement and Impact on Investment Rulemaking (United Nations 2008) 48.

47 *SD Myers, Inc.* v. *Canada*, UNCITRAL, First Partial Award of November 13, 2000.

48 *Methanex* v. *United States*, UNCITRAL, Final Award of August 3, 2005, Part IV, Chapter B, para. 19.

49 *SD Myers* v. *Canada*, First Partial Award of November 13, 2000, para. 250.

50 Mexico–China BIT 2008, Art. 3; and New Zealand–China FTA 2008, Art. 138.

51 New Zealand–China FTA 2008, Art. 138.

52 *Cf.* Netherlands–China BIT 2001, Art. 3(3); Germany–China BIT 2003, Art. 3(2).

53 *Pope & Talbot* v. *Canada*, at para. 75 ("By their very nature, 'circumstances' are context dependent and have no unalterable meaning across the spectrum of fact situations.").

Article III, which explicitly states that the purpose of the NT guarantee is to prevent the application of measures so as to afford protection to domestic production. This technique is often borrowed by an arbitral tribunal into investment law to determine the "likeness" of foreign and domestic investments to the extent that both produce the identical goods or services in the host state. In essence, the likeness in BITs is in place to constrain the purposeful protectionism. A simple formula for a breach of NT is that a less favorable treatment to a foreign investor is not based on any legitimate reason other than the nationality of the foreign investor.[54] The operationality of this formula relies on a comparison between the treatments afforded to foreign vis-à-vis domestic competing investors in the host state. In providing some contextual guidance, a direct link between the NT obligation and the core objective of promoting fair competition has been structured in some FTAs. For instance, the recitals of the US–Singapore FTA 2003 confirm its role in protecting the competitive opportunities of foreign investors in the host state.[55] The BIT, though less manifest, also discerns a need to manage competitive opportunities in the host state. The first recital of the 1994 US Model BIT expresses a desire by the parties "to promote greater economic cooperation between them, with respect to investment by nationals and companies of one Party in the territory of the other."[56] The Chinese Model BIT also "desir[es] to intensify the co–operation of both States on the basis of equality and mutual benefit."[57]

4.1.4 *Scope of Application*

In terms of the scope of application, some Chinese BITs adopt a wider formula by applying the NT obligation not only to "investments of investors" but also to "investments and activities associated with investments"[58] and to other issues such as legal remedies and compensation for losses due to war.[59]

When defining the term "investment," most Chinese BITs require that investment be made "in accordance with national law." This is in line with the international law principle that the admission of foreign investment is a matter of domestic law, meaning that a state may choose not to admit aliens or may impose conditions on their admission.[60] Nevertheless, this caveat limits the effect of the extension of NT to the pre-establishment phase.

More recent Chinese BITs appear closer to the rather narrower formula by defining, in a non-exhaustive manner, that the NT obligation applies to "the investors and their investments with respect to the management, conduct, operation, maintenance, use, sale, liquidation, or other forms of disposal of such investments."[61] The list indicates that the NT

54 Article 17(2) of the 2007 Investment Agreement of the Common Market for Eastern and Southern Africa; the OECD National Treatment Instrument.

55 The preambular recitals of the 2003 US–Singapore FTA recognize that "open and competitive markets are key drivers of economic efficiency innovation and wealth creation" as well as the explicit desire to use the commitments in the FTA to promote competition.

56 Campbell McLachlan, Laurence Shore and Matthew Weiniger, *International Investment Arbitration: Substantive Principles* (Oxford University Press 2007) 201, 386.

57 Rudolf Dolzer and Christoph Schreuer, *Principles of International Investment Law* (Oxford University Press 2008) 352.

58 BLEU–China BIT 2005; Cyprus–China BIT 2001; Latvia–China BIT 2004.

59 Korea–China BIT 2005, Arts. 3(4) and 5(1); Japan–China BIT 1988, Art. 4.

60 James Crawford, *Brownlie's Principles of Public International Law* (Oxford University Press 2012) 608.

61 The Agreement of Investment of the Framework Agreement on Comprehensive Economic Cooperation Between the Association of Southeast Asian Nations and the People's Republic of China (ASEAN Treaty).

obligation may apply at the pre-establishment phase as the term "other forms of disposal of such investments," plus a no-inclusion of "establishment" or "acquisition" in the list, can arguably be broad enough to cover the pre-establishment phase if the tribunal tries to be more aggressive on this point. Yet, it has to be pointed out that the stance taken by China so far is to limit the application of BITs to post-establishment measures, which is in contrast to the US approach of applying BITs to both pre-establishment and post-establishment measures.[62] Therefore, an investor is not able to bring a claim against China for any measures restricting the establishment of an investment in China. The investment can only be "admitted subject to its right to exercise power conferred by its laws"[63] or "in accordance with [the Contracting State's] laws and regulations."[64] Based on these provisions, the admission of foreign investment, or, in Chinese terminology, the approval of foreign investment, is at the discretion of the Chinese government. This is also the arrangement under the WTO framework, where the Chinese government is permitted to exclude foreign investors from a limited number of specific sectors.

The position taken by more recent Chinese BITs on the NT standard reflects its recent departure from a conservative to a more liberal stance in offering foreign investment protections. This move makes sense as China is now expanding its FDI activities overseas while remaining the largest capital-importing state. China's outbound FDI increased from USD 68.811 million in 2010 to USD 127.560 million in 2015, close to inbound FDI of USD 135.610 million in 2015.[65]

Along with more and more Chinese nationals and companies going abroad to invest in other natural-resource-rich countries, mainly in Africa, Latin America and the Middle East, China is gradually taking on dual roles and becoming both the home state of outbound investment and a major host state for foreign investment. This is leading to a change in China's motives for signing BITs[66] – not only sending a signal to the international investment community for better rights protection but also having a strong desire to protect Chinese investors for their outbound investments. The Chinese government is, therefore, eager to enter into BITs with other countries and bargain for a full NT clause in BITs, along with other substantive protection standards. China more recently has in fact signed more BITs with developing than developed countries. Africa along with Latin America have replaced Europe as the most important partner regions for China to sign new BITs with.[67] This changing pattern, as shown in Figure 4.1,[68] is attributable to the growing importance of developing countries, in particular in Africa and South America, as the key destinations absorbing Chinese outbound FDI. Other factors which have contributed to the appearance of a full-scale NT provision in recent Chinese BITs include (but are not limited to) China's accession

62 Kenneth J. Vandevelde, "US Bilateral Investment Treaties: The Second Wave" (1993) 14 *Michigan Journal of International Law* 621; Kenneth J. Vandevelde, "A Brief History of International Investment Agreements" (2005) 12 *UC Davis Journal of International Law and Policy* 157.

63 UK–China BIT 1986, Art. 2(1).

64 Uruguay–China BIT 1993, Art. 2.

65 UNCTAD, World Investment Report 2016 – Investor Nationality: Policy Challenges (2016) 197.

66 Ryan Suda, "The Effect of Bilateral Investment Treaties on Human Rights Enforcement and Realization" in Oliver De Schutter, *Transnational Corporations and Human Rights* (Hart 2006) 80–81.

67 China signed BITs with major Western European countries in the 1980s and China is in the process of updating BITs with these countries.

68 BITs here include both old and new BITs concluded with developed countries, the Pakistan–China FTA of November 24, 2006 (ch. 9), the New Zealand–China FTA of April 7, 2008 (ch. 11).

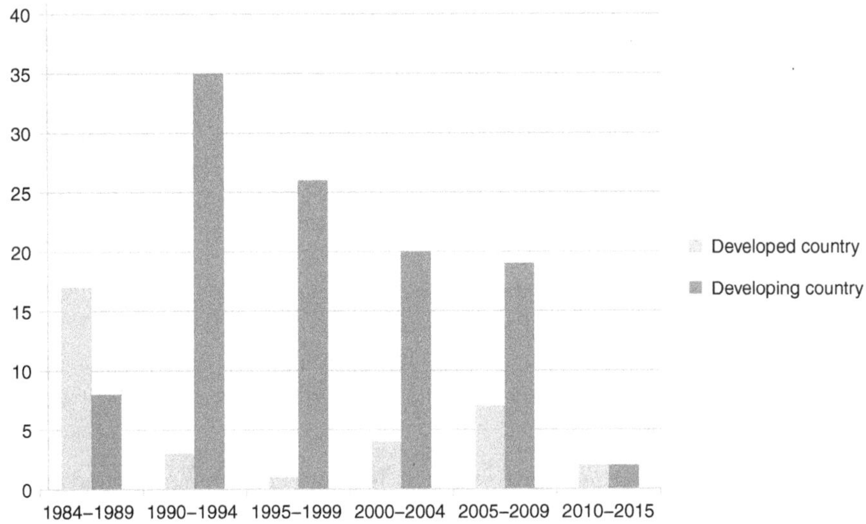

FIGURE 4.1 Growth of Chinese BITs with trading partners* (1984–2015)
*Compiled by the author based on information available at UNCTAD's Online Database of International Investment Instruments: www.unctad.org/templates/page.asp.

to the WTO,[69] its rapid economic growth and the positive development of a "socialist market economy"[70] and the rule of law.[71]

4.2 MFN TREATMENT

MFN treatment is the most commonly adopted standard in international investment treaties.[72] The purpose of this standard is to create a level playing field among foreign investors from different states regardless of their nationalities as the relevant parties undertake to treat each other in a manner that is at least "as favourable as" or "not less favourable than"[73] the way in which they treat a third-party national under this standard. At the substantial level, due to the availability of the commitments made by the host state under one BIT to others, MFN treatment creates the economic effect of leveling the playing field so that foreign investors are able to compete more fairly against one another in a given host country.[74] Procedurally, a foreign investor is able to invoke the benefit of initiating ISA on the basis of an MFN clause applicable to the investment dispute settlement mechanism under which the host state offers more favorable procedural treatments to the investors from a third-party state. The procedural dispute settlement benefits centered on an MFN clause have been partially but indecisively confirmed by case law.[75]

69 Qingjiang Kong, "Towards WTO Compliance: China's Foreign Investment Regime in Transition" (2002) 3 *Journal of World Investment* 859–878.

70 PRC Constitution, Art. 15.

71 Randall Peerenboom, *China's Long March Toward Rule of Law* (Cambridge University Press 2002).

72 Dolzer and Schreuer, *supra* note 57, at 186 (noting that the MFN standard is in "virtually all investment treaties").

73 Laos–China BIT 1993, Art. 3(2); Indonesia–China BIT 1994, Art. IV(2).

74 Gus Van Harten, *Investment Treaty Arbitration and Public Law* (Oxford University Press 2007) 43.

75 *Plama Consortium* v. *Bulg.*, ICSID Case No. ARB/03/24, Decision on Jurisdiction, 44 ILM 721 (2005); *Maffezini* v. *Spain*, ICSID Case No. ARB/97/7, Decision on Jurisdiction, 5 ICSID (World Bank) 396 (2000); *Siemens A. G.* v. *Arg.*, ICSID Case No. ARB/02/8, Decision on Jurisdiction (2004); *Salini Costruttori S.p.A.* v. *Jordan*, ARB/

4.2.1 *MFN's Scope*

All Chinese BITs adopt the MFN standard. In some Chinese BITs, the MFN treatment is offered alongside other standards such as NT and fair and equitable treatment standards. In these BITs, the MFN standard is linked with the fair and equitable treatment standard and used as a reference point of the latter. These limited MFN provisions appear in some Chinese BITs with some EU member states. The Slovenia–China BIT 1993 includes the following:

1. Investments and activities associated with investments of investors of either Contracting State shall be accorded fair and equitable treatment and shall enjoy protection in the territory of the other Contracting Party.
2. The treatment and protection referred to in Paragraph 1 of this Article shall not be less favourable than that accorded to investments and activities associated with such investments of investors of a third State.[76]

Other Chinese BITs such as the Denmark–China BIT 1985 contain more "standard" MFN provisions as follows:

1. Neither Contracting Party shall subject investments made by nationals or companies of the other Contracting Party or returns of such investments to treatment less favourable than that which it accords to investments or returns of nationals or companies of any third State.
2. Neither Contracting Party shall in its territory subject nationals or companies of the other Contracting Party, as regards their management, maintenance, use, enjoyment or disposal of their investments or returns, to treatment less favourable than that which it accords to nationals or companies of any third State.[77]

Many BITs enumerate the substantive areas to which the application of the MFN clause is limited. Several Chinese BITs, for instance, restrict the application of the MFN treatment obligation to "investments" only.[78] Other Chinese BITs extend the MFN treatment to the "admission, expansion, management, conduct, operation, maintenance, use, enjoyment and disposal" of investments.[79] The MFN treatment in these Chinese BITs covers both "investment" and "investment-related activities" (or "any activity connected with these investments").[80] While some BITs tend to stipulate them in two separate sections,[81] other BITs merge the two sections and confirm that the host state shall not "subject investments and activities associated with such investments by the investors of the other Contracting Party to treatment less favourable than that accorded to the investments and associated activities by the investors of any third State."[82]

A number of Chinese BITs expressly impose the MFN treatment obligation on specific matters such as expropriation and compensation,[83] repatriation of investments and returns,[84]

02/13, Decision on Jurisdiction, 44 ILM 573 (2004); *Gas Natural SDG* v. *Arg.*, ICSID Case No. ARB/03/10, Decision of the Tribunal on Preliminary Questions on Jurisdiction (2005).

76 Slovenia–China BIT 1993, Art. 3.

77 Denmark–China BIT 1985, Art. 3.

78 Sweden–China BIT 1982, Art. 2(2).

79 New Zealand–China FTA 2008, Art. 139.

80 Indonesia–China BIT 1994, Art. IV(2).

81 The typical example is Austria–China BIT 1988, Art. 3, which has two subsections: one relates to treatment no less favorable for "investments" and the other covers "investment-related activities."

82 BLEU–China BIT 2005; Australia–China BIT 1988, Art. 3(c).

83 Germany–China BIT 2003, Art. 4(3).

84 Norway–China BIT 1984, Art. 6(2); Spain–China BIT 1992, Art. 6(6).

treatment of gains resulting from subrogation,[85] measures taken to deal with losses resulting from war or civil disturbance,[86] and judicial and administrative remedies.[87]

China's new BITs, such as the Germany–China BIT 2003, cover "indirect" investment. This MFN clause has considerable weight in the Chinese context. The MFN clause in the old-generation Chinese BITs, given the uncertainty and narrower scope, is not a reliable means for foreign investors to enjoy the favorable benefits available under other BITs. China's new-generation BITs with their full range of substantive protections give the protected investor a significant competitive advantage. Therefore, foreign investors in China may prefer to seek protection under one of such new-generation BITs by channeling the investment through a country that is a signatory to a new-generation BIT. Such restructuring, however, must be made before any investment dispute arises.

Such investors would need to claim that the MFN clause entitles the investors protected under an old-generation BIT to rely on the more advantageous provisions of the new-generation BITs, including the full scope ISA clause, for example, concerning not only the amount of compensation for expropriation but also the violation of other substantive rights. Careful corporate structuring with a special purpose vehicle incorporated in a jurisdiction which enters into a "modern" BIT with China may lend some benefits to investors who are based in such jurisdictions that enter into less favorable BITs with China.[88] In other words, investors covered by old-generation BITs may have recourse to the more comprehensive protection under new-generation BITs. However, the validity of this option technically depends on the definitions of "investor" and "investment" in the concerned BIT. Chinese BITs often cite "substantial business rules" meaning that incorporation (without substantial operations) in a partner country is insufficient to fall under the scope of a BIT. In addition, recent Chinese BITs require that companies have a registered office, seat or other genuine link[89] to the country in order to be considered an investor for the purpose of the treaty, which forms a barrier preventing European investors from gaining treaty protections by setting up "shell" (intermediary or subsidiary) companies in third-country jurisdictions. The corporate nationality test must be satisfied before the occurrence of any dispute if the European investor intends to channel its investment through the other EU member state for the purpose of enjoying greater treaty protections.

These options, however, are not necessarily reliable as the BIT jurisprudence is not entirely coherent. While arbitrators advocating the broad interpretation of the MFN clause might be supportive,[90] it would be squarely rejected by other arbitrators advocating a more restrictive or conservative jurisprudence on binding non-signatories to an arbitration clause in a BIT even

85 Singapore–China BIT 1985, Art. 7; Kuwait–China BIT 1985, Art. 7(2).

86 France–China BIT 2007, Art. 4; Germany–China BIT 2003, Art. 5.

87 Korea–China BIT 2007, Art. 4.

88 Stephan W. Schill, "Tearing Down the Great Wall: The New Generation Investment Treaties of the People's Republic of China" (2007) 15 *Cardozo Journal of International and Comparative Law* 73, 85.

89 The Chinese BITs with Cyprus, Czech Republic, France, Germany, the Netherlands, Portugal and Spain rely on the corporate seat as the corporate nationality test while the Chinese BITs with BLEU, Finland and Latvia use registered office as the test. The China–Malta BIT adopts either seat or registered office. The China–Sweden BIT uses seat or predominant Swedish interest as the corporate nationality test.

90 The tribunal in the case of *Tza Yap Shum* v. *Peru*, the first ever case involving an old–generation Chinese BIT, adopted an expansive approach by broadly interpreting the access to international arbitration provision in the China–Peru BIT 1994, a typical old–generation Chinese BIT, as follows – "[the dispute involving the amount of compensation for expropriation] includes not only the mere determination of the amount but also any other issues normally inherent to an expropriation, including whether the property was actually expropriated in accordance with the BIT provisions and requirements." *Tza Yap Shum* v. *The Republic of Peru*, ICSID Case No. ARB/07/6, Award on Jurisdiction, June 19, 2009, para. 188.

if the BIT's MFN clause did not explicitly encompass an ISDS clause.[91] As a result, investors may need to look for other alternatives because the outcome of an arbitration based on the relevant line of argument is not predictable or sustainable.[92]

Like other developing states' BITs,[93] China's earlier BITs include post-establishment MFN status. The MFN treatment clauses in earlier Chinese BITs are not applied to market access but only to the post-admission stage. The first Chinese BIT that extended this standard to investment admission was the Japan–China BIT 1988, which included the following provision: "Nationals and companies of either Contracting Party shall within the Territory of the other Contracting Party be accorded treatment no less favourable than nationals and companies of any third country in respect of the admission of investment and matters in connection therewith."[94] This could be counted as the starting point when pre-establishment MFN began to be covered by Chinese BITs while the MFN clauses extended to both pre- and post-establishment more often appear in post-2007 Chinese BITs. The Finland–China BIT 2003 has extended the MFN treatment to "establishment."[95] According to the MFN provision applicable to the pre-establishment stage, better market access under the provisions of other BITs such as provisions on investment liberalization and prohibition of performance requirement can be imported into the concerned BIT. Provisions on judicial access as well as administrative tribunals and agencies (local remedies) can also be imported.

More recent BITs also extend the MFN treatment standard to the investment admission stage but in a different form. The Finland–China BIT 2004 provides that investors from the other contracting party shall receive no less favorable treatment than that accorded to investments of investors from any third state relating to the "establishment, acquisition, operation, management, maintenance, use, enjoyment, expansion, sale or other disposal of investments." The distinction between the terms "establishment" and "expansion" may be expansively interpreted to include pre-admission treatment within the ambit of MFN treatment.

4.2.2 *MFN's Exceptions*

The standard systemic exceptions refer to, first, regional economic integration. This exception precludes the application of MFN to treatment granted as a process of economic integration.[96] The second exception refers to taxation, and removes from the scope of MFN treatment any treaty for the avoidance of double taxation and any "other international agreement or arrangement relating wholly or mainly to taxation."[97]

All of the Chinese BITs include express exceptions to the application of the MFN clause. These exceptions are generally fairly identical and mostly relate to benefits for the investor that might be found in other international economic treaties entered into by the host states.

[91] Cf. *Emilio Augustin Maffezini* v. *Spain*, ICSID Case No. ARB/97/17, Decision on Objections to Jurisdiction of January 25, 2000; *Plama Consortium Ltd* v. *Bulgaria*, ICSID Case No. ARB/03/24, Decision on Jurisdiction of February 8, 2005, paras. 183, 200 and 205 (claiming that "the reference must be such that the parties' intention to import the arbitration provision of the other agreement is clear and unambiguous").

[92] *Telenor Mobile Communications AS* v. *Republic of Hungary*, ICSID Case No. ARB/04/15, Award of September 13, 2006, para. 81 et seq.

[93] India–Singapore Comprehensive Economic Cooperation Agreement (2005), Art. 6.22.1 excludes market access disputes from the ambit of investor–state dispute settlement.

[94] Japan–China BIT 1988, Art. 2(2).

[95] Article 3(3) of the Finland–China BIT 2004 (entry into force on November 15, 2006).

[96] EU-Canada CETA 2016, Article X.8(3)(a).

[97] EU-Canada CETA 2016, Article X.8(3)(b).

The typical exceptions are concerned with economic integration organizations such as customs unions and free trade zones, taxation treaties and frontier trade arrangements.[98] Some treaties also brought "common market," "economic multilateral or international agreement"[99] and "regional or sub-regional arrangement"[100] into the exceptions list. However, not all Chinese BITs include all of the three common exceptions. For instance, the France–China BIT 1984 and the Sweden–China BIT 1982 included only one exception of economic integration; the Korea–China BIT 1992 and the Iceland–China BIT 1994 do not have the exception for frontier trade arrangements; and the Turkey–China BIT 2015 does not cover taxation exceptions.

Regional economic integration units such as customs unions and free trade zones are one of the most commonly found exceptions to the MFN treatment obligation under BITs.[101] The WTO does not prohibit such regional economic integration agreements as long as they are compatible with the multilateral trading system.[102] The wording in the Czech Republic–China BIT 2005[103] on the economic integration exception is a relatively broad one covering "bilateral, regional or international agreements, or any form of economic or regional cooperation." Apparently, this expression can be widely interpreted to cover "economic and monetary union, regional economic cooperation or other similar agreements,"[104] "economic union, organisation of mutual economic assistance"[105] or "any arrangement with a third State or States in the same geographical region designed to promote regional cooperation in the economic, social, labour, industrial or monetary fields within the framework of specific projects."[106] Some Chinese BITs extend the economic integration exception to both existing and future arrangements.[107]

Apart from the economic integration exception, some Chinese BITs attach to the MFN treatment the same "grandfather" exception applicable to NT.[108] The grandfather clause relates to "any existing or new non-conforming measures or continuation or amendment of any non-conforming measures."[109] Similarly, there is no obligation imposed on both contracting parties to eliminate any such measures, even though both have promised to progressively remove these non-conforming measures, which would be beneficial to all investors.

Despite Article 5(3)(b) allowing for preferential treatment between a contracting party and its separate customs territories, it is still a conventional economic integration exception. A typical taxation treaty exception generally refers only to any "international agreement or arrangement relating to taxation."[110] Arguably, this exception may be interpreted as a tax

98 Ibid. Art. 3(3) included all three exceptions.
99 Indonesia–China BIT 1994, Art. IV(3).
100 Philippines–China BIT 1992, Art. 3(3).
101 Sayantan Gupta, "Changing Faces of International Trade: Multilateralism to Regionalism" (2008) 3(4) *Journal of International Commercial Law and Technology* 260–273; Rudolf Adlung and Martin Molinuevo, "Bilateralism in Services Trade: Is There Fire Behind the (BIT)–Smoke?" (2008) WTO Staff Working Papers ERSD-2008-01, World Trade Organization (WTO), Economic Research and Statistics Division.
102 GATT 1994, Art. 24; GATS, Art. 5; and WTO Understanding on Article 24 of GATT 1994.
103 Czech Republic–China BIT (2005), Art. 3(3).
104 Finland–China BIT 2004.
105 Poland–China BIT 1988.
106 Singapore–China BIT 1985, Art. 3(3); Philippines–China BIT 1992, Art. 3(3); and Mauritius–China BIT 1996, Art. 5.
107 Sweden–China BIT 1982; Kyrgyzstan–China BIT 1992; Ukraine–China BIT 1992; Turkmenistan–China BIT 1992; and Tajikistan–China BIT 1993.
108 Czech Republic–China BIT 2005, Art. 3(3).
109 The China–ASEAN Treaty, Art. 6(1) and (2).
110 Korea–China BIT 1992, Art. 3(4); Greece–China BIT 1992, Art. 3(3).

treaty exception as the arrangement between a contracting party and its separate customs territory may address issues such as the customs concession or avoidance of double taxation. Judging from the language, this subsection is intended to exclude any arrangement between China and its separate customs territories such as Hong Kong and Macau from the coverage of the MFN treatment. This is important as mainland China concluded a Closer Economic Partnership Arrangement (CEPA) with Hong Kong and with Macau, both in 2003, both of which are designed to be permissible regional FTAs under the WTO rules.[111]

4.2.3 *MFN and Procedural Rights*

There has been significant controversy over the extent to which MFN clauses should apply to substantive rights or procedural rights, or both. As the MFN treatment clauses in the BITs usually grant investors, as regards "management, maintenance, use, enjoyment or disposal of their investment," no less favorable treatment, it is always controversial whether the investor can invoke the MFN obligation to invoke the more favorable dispute resolution provisions in other BITs, which may include consent to ICSID arbitration as an option for all disputes. Arbitration practice indicates that the broader the language used, the more likely it is that the tribunal will extend the MFN standard to cover procedural rights. For instance, the investors may make use of the MFN treatment in some cases to bypass procedural impediments, namely the requirement to resolve the dispute in the local courts first.[112] It has been confirmed in other cases that the MFN treatment may be relied on to broaden the tribunal's jurisdiction,[113] from disputes relating to the amount or payment of compensation as under the basic treaty, to all disputes including the existence of expropriation under a third-party BIT.[114] The case law in this respect, however, is divergent.[115]

Unlike other earlier cases[116] which have seen substantial contradiction in the reasoning of the tribunals adjudicating the extension of the MFN treatment to procedural rights in BIT cases, the tribunals in China-BIT-related cases indicate some consistency not only in rejections but also in interpretative techniques. In *Tza Yap Shum* v. *Peru*, the tribunal was faced with the claimant's concerned attempts to extend the scope of jurisdiction to issues not covered by the arbitration clauses in the disputed China–Peru BIT 1994 according to the

[111] The main text of CEPA covers three broad areas: trade in goods, trade in services, and trade and investment facilitation. CEPA is relevant to multinational investors with significant subsidiaries already established in Hong Kong or Macau. Foreign investors can leverage on the CEPA benefits through a Hong Kong or Macau holding company to explore the vast opportunities of the mainland China market. Similar to CEPA, mainland China and Taiwan also signed an Economic Cooperation Framework Agreement on June 29, 2010, http://en.wikipedia.org/wiki/Economic_Cooperation_Framework_Agreement (accessed March 6, 2021).

[112] *Emilio Agustin Maffezini* v. *Kingdom of Spain*, ICSID Case No. ARB/97/7, Decision on Objections to Jurisdiction of January 25, 2000.

[113] The case law evinces a growing inclination on the part of tribunals to formulate the exhaustion of local remedies clauses as conditions to be satisfied before jurisdiction can be established. In some cases, the tribunals apply a more deferential arbitral treatment of local remedy first provisions. Matthew C. Porterfield, "Exhaustion of Local Remedies in Investor–State Dispute Settlement: An Idea Whose Time Has Come?" (2015) 41 (Fall) *Yale Journal of International Law Online*, https://ssrn.com/abstract=2735036 (accessed March 9, 2021).

[114] *RosInvestCo. UK Ltd* v. *Russian Federation*, SCC Case No. Arb. V079/2005.

[115] *Kilic Insaat Ithalat Ihracat Sanayi ve Ticaret Anonim Sirketi* v. *Turkmenistan*, ICSID Case No. ARB/10/1; *Joseph C. Lemire* v. *Ukraine*, ICSID Case No. ARB/06/18; *Amboiente Ufficio S.p.A. and others* v. *Argentine Republic*, ICSID Case No. ARB/08/9.

[116] *Plama* v. *Bulgaria*, ICSID Case No. ARB/03/24, Decision on Jurisdiction February 8, 2005; *Maffezini* v. *Spain*, ICSID Case No. ARB/97/7, Award on Jurisdiction January 25, 2000; *Salini et al.* v. *Morocco*, ICSID Case No. ARB/00/4, Decision on Jurisdiction July 23, 2001, 42 ILM 609 (2003).

Peru–Columbia BIT 2007.[117] The tribunal was self-disciplined, largely sticking to the "best indicator" of the "intention of the parties expressed in the text,"[118] not to overexaggeratedly broaden its discretion without having any clear indications in the disputed BIT.

In the case of *Beijing Urban Construction Group Co Ltd.* v. *Republic of Yemen*, one defense raised by the respondent was that the 1998 Yemen–China BIT's MFN clause could not be used to circumvent the limits of its dispute resolution clause. The tribunal dismissed most of the respondent's jurisdictional objections but agreed that the wording of the MFN clause tied it to activities that took place "in the territory" associated geographically with the investment. Thus, the MFN clause could not be used by the tribunal to import a broader dispute resolution clause from the Yemen–UK BIT to expand the scope of jurisdiction (which itself is not an activity inherently linked to the respondent's territory) over non-expropriation BIT claims, which are beyond Article 10 of the Yemen–China BIT 1998.[119] The tribunal's approach demonstrates its tendency to interpret BIT clauses in line with the object, context and purpose of the dispute resolution clauses and the BIT as a whole.

In *Ansung Housing Co., Ltd.* v. *China*, the claimant invoked the MFN clause to save its claim from being time-barred as other Chinese BITs do not prescribe a three-year limitation period within which an investor is required to initiate an arbitration claim. Relying on a plain reading of the MFN clause,[120] the tribunal held that the MFN clause did not extend to a state's consent to arbitrate with investors or to the temporal limitation period for ISA. Further, the tribunal pointed out that the BIT offers specific MFN protection in relation to an investor's "access to courts of justice, administrative tribunals and authorities," without making any reference to international dispute resolution such as arbitration under the BIT.[121] Accordingly, the tribunal dismissed the case for lack of jurisdiction.[122]

In response to the debate on MFN clauses and procedural rights, recent Chinese BITs have tried to eliminate all potential controversies by making clear that the MFN treatment does not cover procedural rights. The relevant provision in the New Zealand–China FTA 2008 reads: "For greater certainty, the obligation in this Article does not encompass a requirement to extend to investors of the other Party dispute resolution procedures other than those set out in this Chapter."[123] There is a clarification, too, in the EU–Canada CETA 2016 that MFN treatment not be extended to dispute settlement provisions,[124] which effectively avoids any *Maffezini*-like interpretations of the MFN clause.[125]

117 *Tza Yap Shum* v. *Republic of Peru*, ICSID Case No. ARB/07/6, Decision on Jurisdiction and Competence of June 19, 2009, paras. 189–190.

118 Ibid., para. 206.

119 *Beijing Urban Construction Group Co Ltd.* v. *Republic of Yemen*, ICSID Case No. ARB/14/30, Decision on Jurisdiction, para. 120, www.italaw.com/sites/default/files/case-documents/italaw8968.pdf (accessed March 9, 2021).

120 China–Korea BIT 2007, Art. 3(3).

121 China–Korea BIT 2007, Art. 3(5).

122 *Ansung Housing Co. Ltd.* v. *People's Republic of China*, ICSID Case No. ARB/14/25, Award, paras. 136–141.

123 New Zealand–China FTA 2008, Art. 139(2).

124 EU-Canada CETA 2016, Article X.8(4).

125 *Maffezini* v. *Spain*, ICSID Case No. ARB/97/7, Decision on Jurisdiction January 25, 2000, paras. 38–64. See, among others, Martins Paparinskis, "MFN Clauses and International Dispute Settlement: Moving Beyond Maffezini and Plama?" (2011) *ICSID Review–Foreign Investment Law Journal* 14–58; Yannick Radi, "The Application of the Most-Favoured-Nation Clause to the Dispute Settlement Provisions of Bilateral Investment Treaties: Domesticating the 'Trojan Horse'" (2007) 18 *European Journal of International Law* 757–774.

Disputes concerning market access are not supposed to be solved through the ISDS mechanism. In other words, such disputes are subject to state-to-state dispute settlement.[126] Under the EU–Canada CETA, disputes with respect to pre-establishment commitments are not subject to ISDS.

4.2.4 *MFN and Ratchet Clause*

The latest innovation in relation to MFN treatment appears in the ChAFTA 2015. A special ratchet clause is added to ensure that future benefits conferred on other countries such as those in the EU and the USA will flow automatically to Australia.[127] This MFN deal will keep Australia on a level playing field with key competitors for valuable trade and investment with China.

The investment chapter in the ChAFTA is also unique in its tentative nature. Both parties are under obligations to conduct a review to determine whether negotiations of a comprehensive investment chapter could be envisaged.[128] The ChAFTA anticipates a long list of foreseen topics for further negotiations,[129] including minimum standard of treatment, expropriation, performance requirements, senior management and board of directors, investment-specific state-to-state dispute settlement, the application of investment protections and ISDS to services supplied through commercial presence, and scheduling of investment commitments by China on a negative list basis.[130]

4.3 EXCEPTIONS TO NT AND MFN

The EU adopts significant limitations and exceptions to NT and MFN with the purpose of balancing investment protection and regulation.[131] Well-recognized exceptions include the regional economic integration organization (REIO) exception, the taxation exception, and country-specific exceptions (which may restrict access to specific sectors of the economy or grandfather non-conforming measures).[132] Most exceptions conform to those of the Canada Model BIT 2004,[133] and are similar to those in NAFTA[134] or the US Model BIT 2012.[135] Article X.14 "Reservations and Exceptions" of the EU–Canada CETA provides that both the EU and the Member States should maintain one Schedule in Annex II with respect to sectors, subsectors or activities. The advantage of this list of exceptions is its exhaustive nature,

[126] Council of the European Union, Meeting Document from the European Commission to the Trade Policy Committee Concerning the EU Canada Comprehensive Economic and Trade Agreement – Landing Zones, Brussels, November 6, 2012, lapresse.ca/html/1633/Document_UE_2.pdf (accessed March 9, 2021).

[127] John Garnaut, "Australia Scores 'Most Favoured Nation' Provisions in FTA with China," *Sydney Morning Herald*, March 13, 2015.

[128] China–Australia FTA 2015, ch. 9.

[129] China–Australia FTA 2015, Art. 9.9.3.

[130] China–Australia FTA 2015, Art. 9.9.3(c).

[131] Specific exceptions to national treatment and/or MFN obligations are listed in Article X.14 entitled "Reservations and Exceptions," as well as in Article X.16 on "Formal Requirements." These appear in section 5 of CETA on "Reservations and Exceptions."

[132] These exceptions refer to non–conforming measures and excluded sectors/subsectors of the economy, which are negotiated on an ad hoc basis with each counterparty and are included in Schedules attached to Annexes to the BIT or IIA.

[133] Article 9 of Canada Model BIT 2004.

[134] Article 1108 of NAFTA.

[135] Article 14 of the US Model BIT 2012.

meaning that any measure that pursued a purpose not on the list and caused disparate impact on a foreign investor would be invalidated.

These general exceptions that apply to norms of nondiscrimination and incorporate a balancing test are similar to Article XX ("General Exceptions") of GATT.[136] Nevertheless, there is an inconsistency between the substantive obligation and the balancing test when it comes to the nondiscriminatory standards.[137]

A small number of Chinese BITs do not include an REIO exception for the MFN clause. The absence of an REIO exception in the Japan–China BIT 1989 was caused by the fact that neither China nor Japan had signed any FTA or REIO by that time. While provisions in other BITs can be imported where the MFN clause in a BIT includes an RIEO exception, provisions in other FTAs cannot be relied on.

The latest innovation is the incorporation of a "right to regulate" provision in TTIP[138] and the EU–Canada CETA. Given the cumulative effect of wide categories of policies and the open-ended list of policies, the states may be granted an unfettered right to regulate regardless of substantive investment protection standards. Effectively, this broad right to regulate,[139] a modern version of the public policy objective,[140] may negate any effect that investment protection standards are supposed to achieve in attracting inbound investment or encouraging outbound investment. It is technically difficult to reconcile goals of investment protection and policy justifications simultaneously. The right to regulate exception also seems at odds with both the investment protection and the investment liberalization purposes of the EU–Canada CETA, as the basic function of this exception is to give the signing party of the BIT more regulatory space, which effectively defeats the purpose of restricting the regulatory power the regulators may possess in monitoring and regulating foreign investment activities. The EU's objective of adopting a right to regulate provision is to strike a balance between incentivizing investment and maintaining regulatory space. This is a sensible move in the aftermath of the latest global financial crisis which justifies more regulatory discretion and processes.

As far as Chinese BITs are concerned, the closest equivalent to the right to regulate provision may be the public moral or public order exception, which gives China plenty of regulatory space to regulate FDI. China is a developing country. It makes more sense that, from an EU standpoint, ample policy space is accorded to China. But from China's perspective, it may be more desirable not to accord more regulatory space to the EU, whose investors are more likely to be actively involved in arbitration claims against China even though for the time being not many cases have been filed by European investors with

136 European Commission, "TTIP: Trade in Services, Investment and E-commerce: chapter II – Investment" (Proposal) (November 2015) s. 3, subs.–4. GATT Art. XX is to achieve an effective balance between the obligation and the policy justification.

137 GATT Art. XX requires a WTO member invoking an exception to first show that its law or regulation is justified under one of the substantive heads of exemption. The adjudicator would further consider whether any application of the otherwise permitted measure meets the conditions of the chapeau of Art. XX, which disallows the measure being applied in an arbitrary or unjustifiable way.

138 TTIP, s. 2, Art. 2(1) (stating that the Parties reaffirm their right to regulate).

139 European Commission, "Investment in TTIP and Beyond – The Path for Reform," May 6, 2015, http://trade.ec.europa.eu/doclib/docs/2015/may/tradoc_153408.PDF (accessed March 9, 2021).

140 Finland–China BIT 2004, Art. 6(6) ("nothing in this Agreement shall be construed as preventing the Contracting Parties from taking any measure necessary for the maintenance of public order"); EFTA–Singapore FTA (2002), Art. 43 ("Nothing in this Chapter shall be construed to prevent a Party from adopting, maintaining or enforcing any measure consistent with this Chapter that in the public interest"); Consolidated EU–Canada CETA text, Preamble ("Recognizing that the provisions of this Agreement preserve the right to regulate within their territories and resolving to preserve their flexibility to achieve legitimate policy objectives").

ICSID or other arbitration institutions. In other words, more favorable provisions of the more "liberal" investment treaties of the EU may be less beneficial to China as a whole.

China's BITs often contain REIO and taxation exceptions. REIO exceptions appear in the China–Sweden BIT 1982,[141] the China–France BIT 2007[142] and other BITs between China and EU member states. China's BITs with Germany 2003[143] and Belgium–Luxembourg 2005[144] contain a typical exception in relation to taxation. The China–Canada BIT 2012 lacks this typical taxation exception but nevertheless contains more exceptions in respect of cultural industries, environmental measures, reasonable measures for prudential reasons, monetary and related credit policies or exchange rate policies, information protection and compliance with WTO case decisions.[145]

The exceptions and limitations employed in BITs affect the scope and application of NT and MFN standards, which in turn determine the scope of the host state's regulatory space.[146] The EU tends to strike a fine balance between promoting FDI and maintaining regulatory space in devising and implementing EU policies in areas of regulation which may be affected by investment protection obligations. The inclusion of general exceptions clauses is a clear manifestation of states parties' engagement in a concerted push to pare back the extensive protections offered by the classic model BITs.[147]

The EU–Canada CETA contains a provision on market access in the form of prohibition of specific limitations to foreign investors[148] coupled with a prohibition of performance requirements.[149] More recent Chinese BITs such as the China–Germany BIT, also contain a prohibition of "local content or export performance requirements."[150] What is interesting is that the CETA does not contain the most controversial feature of the *Salini* criteria – the "contribution to the development of the host state."[151]

The longer the list of performance requirements, the more discriminatory the host state's FDI law may be toward foreign investors. Therefore, the effort to shorten the list of performance requirements is also one way of securing nondiscriminatory investment liberalization

141 Article 2 of China–Sweden BIT 1982.
142 Article 4 of China–France BIT 2007.
143 Article 3 of China–Germany BIT 2003.
144 Article 3 of China–BLEU BIT 2015.
145 China–Canada BIT 2012, Art. 33.
146 Andrew Newcombe, "The Use of General Exceptions in IIAs: Increasing Legitimacy or Uncertainty" in Armand De Mestral and C. Lévesque (eds.), *Improving International Investment Agreements* (Routledge 2012) ch. 15. *Pope & Talbot* v. *Canada*, Award April 10, 2001, paras. 78, 79, 88 and 93; *GAMI Investments, Inc.* v. *Mexico*, Final Award November 15, 2004, para. 114.
147 José E. Alvarez, "The Once and Future Foreign Investment Regime" in Mahnoush H. Arsanjani, Jacob Katz Cogan, Robert D. Sloane and Siegfried Wiessner (eds.), *Looking to the Future: Essays on International Law in Honor of W. Michael Reisman* (Brill 2010) 607–648; José E. Alvarez, "The Return of the State" (2011) 20(2) *Minnesota Journal of International Law* 223–264.
148 EU-Canada CETA 2016, Article X.4: "Market Access."
149 EU-Canada CETA 2016, Article X.5: "Performance Requirements," section 2: "Establishment of Investment," chapter 10: "Investment," EU–China Trade Agreement. The EU–Canada CETA includes performance requirements in Article X.5, modeled after Article 7 "Performance Requirements" of the 2004 Canadian Model BIT. Performance requirements are important policy tools used by the developing countries for the economic development of the host states. Nevertheless, a fine balance must be maintained between the need for regulatory space and the need to promote foreign investment.
150 China–Germany BIT 2004, Article 3(3).
151 *Salini Costruttori S.p.A. and Italstrade S.p.A.* v. *Kingdom of Morocco*, ICSID Case No. ARB/00/4, Decision on Jurisdiction July 23, 2001, para. 52: "The doctrine generally considers that investment infers: contributions, a certain duration of performance of the contract and a participation in the risks of the transaction (cf. commentary by E. Gaillard, cited below, p. 292). In reading the Convention's preamble, one may add the contribution to the economic development of the host State of the investment as an additional condition."

for foreign investors. China has been attempting to shorten the list of performance requirements in its BITs. However, little progress has been made. For instance, performance requirements prohibited under the China–Korea–Japan Trilateral Investment Treaty 2012 (CKJ TIT) remain limited. Prohibition of performance requirements beyond the measures listed in the Agreement on Trade-Related Investment Measures (TRIMs) is only extended to export and technology transfer. Prohibition is limited to imposing unreasonable or discriminatory measures concerning the two. Thus, a reasonable technical transfer request imposed in a nondiscriminatory manner is acceptable as far as the CJK TIT is concerned. The trend that China is moving toward is to have performance requirements compliant with TRIMs, meaning that performance requirements for trade in goods concerning export and technology transfer are abolished. Local content and localization are still permissible as long as the measures conform with TRIMs, which is incorporated into the BIT or the investment chapter of the FTA. There is a lack of a clear pattern of performance requirements clauses in China's FTAs. The commitment concerning performance requirements appears half-hearted in the China–South Korea FTA while they are completely missing in the ChAFTA.

4.4 CONCLUDING REMARKS

After the Trump administration's decision to pull out of the TPP, the EU and China have been in the spotlight and turned out to be the driving force of globalization. The world anticipates that the EU–China BIT, a model to be followed by other states, will be a major milestone of foreign investment protection and liberalization law with the pivotal effect of reducing the fragmentation and reinforcing the consistency of IIL and policy going forward.

The EU is making a departure from the general practice of short BITs with broad protection provisions and few limitations or qualifications preponderant in most of its member states. Rather, it will follow the US Model BIT by opting for a longer BIT with more complicated and more tightly circumscribed provisions.[152] This may explain why EU member states' BITs are short but the EU–Canada CETA is long with more clearly formulated standards of protection and specific exceptions.

China has been in a transitional process from being a pure capital-importing state to a hybrid major capital-importing and capital-exporting state, which is triggering China's desire to upgrade the substantive and procedural standards in BITs by ushering in various innovations.

Previously, China has been quite conservative in negotiating BITs. For instance, China was less willing to delegate explicitly to the ICSID for arbitration and made no reference to pre-consent in its old-generation BITs. These BIT preferences appear to be closer to those of a capital-importing country than a capital-exporting one. The updated China–Germany and China–Dutch BITs, departing from China's past BIT practice, represent a breakthrough and constitute a fundamental shift toward making more favorable protections available to foreign investors.[153] While China is making a sacrifice of a portion of its sovereignty by agreeing to more liberal substantive protection standards, the trade-off that China may have is the aggregate gain to the public good (not only in the economic sense but also in the form of rule of law and rights protection standards) through the broad cross-border investment protected and fostered by arbitration.[154]

152 US Model BIT 2004 and 2012.
153 Schill, *supra* note 88, at 73, 76.
154 Guillermo Aguilar Alvarez, "The New Face of Investment Arbitration: NAFTA Chapter 11" (2003) 28 *Yale Journal of International Law* 365, 399.

Given the complications added into the NT and MFN clauses, EU-initiated BITs may head in the direction of aligning IIL with international trade law.[155] China appears to be following this trend by incorporating TRIMs, inter alia, Article 2 and the Annex of TRIMs, into the "performance requirements" provision of the latest China–Canada BIT.[156] Investment negotiations are generally concerned with investor rights protection standards while trade negotiations are more relevant to bargaining over market access concessions. A convergence of international trade law and IIL may confuse the chief purposes of these two parallel pillars of international economic law and secure unnecessary trade-offs between high (post-)investment protection standards and enhanced market access commitments.

While China is also making progresses in crafting its BITs, a gap is still in existence between the two when it comes to the NT and MFN standards. The gap lies in the fact that the EU is moving closer to the NAFTA type of nondiscriminatory standards being extended to the pre-investment stage with more carefully and heavily negotiated exceptions and limitations. Although these exceptions and limitations, inter alia, the right to regulate exception, may be more acceptable to China given its tradition in regulating foreign investments,[157] the pre-investment protection may be the most challenging clause for the negotiators from China and the EU. More recent Chinese BITs are evidence of China's conscious efforts to grant more favorable protections to foreign investors. In the aftermath of the China–Canada BIT, the MFN treatment raises the level of substantive protection guaranteed by each of China's BITs to the level guaranteed by its more investor-friendly BIT. A quick comparison among the EU's and China's latest BITs can be found in Table 4.2. The comparison demonstrates a high level of terminological, formalistic and typological similarity between the EU–Canada CETA and the China–Canada BIT, indicating a surprisingly small difference between Chinese and EU BITs in terms of nondiscriminatory clauses. The network effect[158] created by the China–Canada BIT may ultimately help fill in the gap between the EU's and China's BITs on key substantive protection standards, in particular the nondiscriminatory standards. Given the higher investor protection standards in the EU–Canada CETA, being praised as the new gold standard,[159] there is a chance to lift the protection standards in Chinese BITs through piggybacking on the EU–Canada CETA.

155 Rainer Hofmann, Stephan W. Schill and Christian J. Tams (eds.), *Preferential Trade and Investment Agreements: From Recalibration to Reintegration* (Nomos 2013); Donald McRae, "The World Trade Organization and International Investment Law: Converging Systems – Can the Case for Convergence Be Made?" (2014) 9 *Jerusalem Review of Legal Studies* 13–23.

156 China–Canada BIT 2012, Art. 9.

157 In terms of safeguarding regulatory autonomy, the ChAFTA 2015 contains a novel mechanism regarding public welfare measures with respect to the ISDS. When faced with an ISDS claim against such a measure, the respondent host state may issue a notice to this effect, triggering a consultation process with the home state. If the states parties agree that the measure is "non–discriminatory and for the legitimate public welfare objectives of public health, safety, the environment, public morals or public order," that determination is binding on the ISDS tribunal and the claim against that measure cannot proceed. This is a significant protection for policy space that may be followed in future China BITs.

158 A network effect, a term of art mostly used in economics and business, refers to the positive effect that Canada may have created over the EU–China BIT due to the fact that Canada, being the point of connection, brings the value of the EU–Canada CETA to the EU–China BIT. Here, the network effect can create a bandwagon effect, resulting in a positive feedback loop when more parties are involved. It has been pointed out that the MFN clauses, as a matter of doctrine, multilateralize international investment treaties. Stephan W. Schill, "Multilateralizing Investment Treaties through Most–Favored–Nation Clauses" (2009) 27(2) *Berkeley Journal of International Law* 496, 568.

159 Giorgio Sacerdoti, "Is USMCA Really 'the New Gold Standard' of Investment Protection?" Columbia FDI Perspectives No. 281, June 29, 2020, http://ccsi.columbia.edu/files/2018/No–281–FINAL–Sacerdoti.pdf (accessed September 18, 2020).

TABLE 4.2 *Comparison of nondiscriminatory standards in selected EU and China BITs*

	TTIP (EU Proposal) (2015)	CETA (2016)	EU–Singapore (2015)	CKJ TIT (2012)	China–Canada (2014)
NT/MFN	Scope conditioned on investors/ investment in "like situations"; MFN not applicable to dispute resolution procedures	Scope conditioned on investors/ investment in "like situations"; MFN not applicable to dispute resolution procedures	No MFN clause	Scope conditioned on investors/ investment in "like" situations' with respect to investment activities; MFN not applicable to dispute resolution procedures; MFN extended to admission of investment	Scope conditioned on investors/ investment in "like situations"; MFN not applicable to dispute resolution mechanisms; MFN extended to establishment only
Express right to regulate exception	Yes	Yes	No	No[160]	No
General exceptions	GATT XX-like (applicable to NT, MFN, performance requirement but not FET/FPS and expropriation) Includes a GATT XX-chapeau-like feature (Chapter VII, Art. 7-1)	GATT XX-like (applies to NT, MFN, performance requirements but not FET/ EPS and expropriation). Includes a GATT XX-chapeau-like feature (Art. 28.3(2))	GATT XX-like chapeau that applies to NT only (Art. 9.3(3))	Security exceptions	GATT XX-like (applies to NT, MFN, performance requirements but not FET/EPS and expropriation). Includes a GATT XX-chapeau-like feature (Art. 28.3(2))

160 Art. 5(1)(a) of the China–ASEAN Treaty, however, includes a wide "public order" exception allowing the party's adoption or enforcement of "measures necessary to protect public morals or to maintain public order."

The traditional purpose of BITs is to provide better legal protection to investments originating from capital-exporting countries into capital-importing countries. It is desirable to have a pre-investment clause in the EU–China CAI,[161] given the fact that market access remains the largest impediment and the most salient barrier to the EU's investment in China.[162] A pre-investment clause would be beneficial to European investors' wider and easier entry into the Chinese market. Nevertheless, the question arises as to whether China would benefit from this investment liberalization clause as China's outbound investment is more focused on energy, oil and mineral sectors in capital-importing states. In addition, as argued, market access may be less urgent for China as the EU has been already open to foreign investments.[163] China's dual role in being both a capital-importing and a capital-exporting state casts doubt on the proactive stance that China may take when it comes to the negotiation table with the EU for a BIT (CAI) deal.

As a host state, China seems more willing to provide economic incentives and policy support to foreign investors. On the other hand, in order to protect its outbound investment, China, being a home (investor) state, seeks to attain a high level of legal and institutional protection for its national investors abroad. As a general rule, the reduction of investment barriers increases productivity and secures better protection of investments against discrimination. In this sense, any further investment liberalization effort should benefit China's outbound FDI even though it is yet uncertain whether the length of China's negative list will be meaningfully short. This remains one of the key concerns of China's counterparties.[164] The finding that international investment policy and treaties may have a very limited impact on business operations, profits and welfare[165] may somehow cast doubts on China's possible stance to either liberalize its market entry rules for foreign investors or lift substantive standards in protecting national investors investing overseas. The interests of a host state and a home state may be in severe conflict in most circumstances, which may in turn complicate China's policy strategy in negotiating BITs and FTAs.[166]

Largely for its own economic and political interest, China has been undergoing a remarkable transition from its restrictive BIT policy toward a more liberal stance, which is in line with China's growth of outbound investment and internal economic reform.[167] Abandoning its long-term hostile stance on NT, introducing a negative list nationwide to guide foreign investment[168] and implementing more market-oriented economic reforms in

161 EU and China reached the agreement on investment in principle in December 2020, https://trade.ec.europa.eu/doclib/press/index.cfm?id=2115 (accessed April 5, 2021).

162 Insa Ewert, "The EU–China Bilateral Investment Agreement: Between High Hopes and Real Challenges" (2016) Security Policy Brief No. 68, Egmont Royal Institute of International Relations.

163 Ibid.

164 Peterson Institute for International Economics, "Toward a US–China Investment Treaty," February 2015, PIIE Briefing 15–1, 25, 33.

165 Robert Basedow, "A Legal History of the EU's Investment Policy" (2016) 17(5) *Journal of World Investment & Trade* 743, 769; Jennifer Tobin and Marc L. Busch, "A BIT Is Better Than a Lot: Bilateral Investment Treaties and Preferential Trade Agreements" (2010) 62(1) *World Politics* 1–42.

166 Qingjiang Kong and Yilin Wang, "Transparency Standards in International Investment Agreement Negotiations: A Chinese Lawyer's Perspective on the UNCITRAL Rules" (2015) 1(1) *China and WTO Review* 7, 25.

167 UNCTAD, Investment Policy Monitor (2016) No. 15, https://investmentpolicy.unctad.org/publications/143/investment-policy-monitor-no-15 (accessed April 5, 2021).

168 China's National Development and Reform Commission and Ministry of Commerce released the 2017 version of the Catalogue for the Guidance on Foreign Investment Industries (the Catalogue) on June 28, 2017. The 2017 version Catalogue introduces a negative list nationwide specifying the industries in which foreign investment is restricted or prohibited and opens a variety of new industrial sectors to foreign investment, creating appealing new opportunities for investment. Alexander Chipman Koty and Zhou Qian, "China's 2017 Foreign Investment

newly established free trade zones[169] are great examples of this switching stance. Regardless of the fact that China has not incorporated the Canadian type of pre-investment protection into the recent China–Canada BIT,[170] a US or Canadian type of pre-investment provision, if it were finally to appear in the EU–China CAI, may be of more symbolic value to China in the sense that such an investment liberalization device may help streamline China's foreign investment law regime and transform its investment-driven economic growth model to a consumption-based one, unless China simultaneously and significantly reforms its entrenched SOEs, which are dominating its key economic sectors for the time being.[171]

By looking closely at the key components of the nondiscriminatory clauses, the conclusion of this chapter is that the gap between the EU and China may be a minor one. This narrowing gap suggests that China's BITs are up to international standards. Further, there are clear indicators of China's evolving stance in international law – its willingness to follow international law rules, its seriousness about its treaty obligations and its readiness to be a rule-maker in the international law sphere. Nevertheless, the real difficulty, as far as China is concerned, is to shorten the negative list it is currently negotiating with the EU and the USA. The length of this negative list, which is relevant to China's determination to truly reform its market entry regime to be more user-friendly to foreign investors, is not only the real hurdle of China's BIT negotiations with the EU and the USA but also the obstacle China has to overcome in order to deepen its economic reform in a more globalized economic system.

The US withdrawal from the TPP, the centerpiece of the Obama administration's pivot to Asia with the aim of strengthening the USA's ties with the region, has created political and economic uncertainty in Asia and beyond. The sword of protectionism is now hanging over global trade and investment even though the global economy is gaining momentum.[172] As national policies have spillover effects across borders in the hyperconnected world, any policy shift to protectionism and any move to dismantle the international architecture and institutions that have underpinned the world economy would threaten global growth.

While the USA has set about pursuing a protectionist goal in trade and investment, it also risks leaving the door open for China to dominate trade in Asia.[173] China's role in the context of international economic law may be enhanced, given the potential for the RCEP to step in and fill the gap where the TPP has failed. The ongoing negotiating difficulties at the WTO and a stronger anti-globalization tendency may offer China more space in reshaping its

Catalogue Opens Access to New Industries," China Briefing, July 11, 2017, www.china-briefing.com/news/2017/07/11/ (accessed March 9, 2021).

169 Shen Wei and Matthias Vanhullebusch, "Where Is the Alchemy? The Experiment of the Shanghai Free Trade Zone in Freeing the Foreign Investment Regime in China" (2015) 16(2) *European Business Organization Law Review* 321–352; Shen Wei, "'A Tale of Three Zones' – Promises and Pitfalls of Three Financial Experimental Zones in China" (2014) *Banking Law Journal* 399–435.

170 China–Canada BIT 2012, Art. 3, which states: "Each Contracting Party shall encourage investors of the other Contracting Party to make investments in its territory and admit such investments in accordance with its laws, regulations and rules." The NT and MFN protections are only extended to "the establishment, acquisition, expansion, management, conduct, operation and sale or other disposition of investments." China–Canada BIT, Arts. 5 and 6. The China–Canada BIT further clarifies: "The concept of 'expansion' in this Article applies only with respect to sectors not subject to a prior approval process under the relevant sectoral guidelines and applicable laws, regulations and rules in force at the time of expansion. The expansion may be subject to prescribed formalities and other information requirements" (China–Canada BIT 2012, Art. 6(3)).

171 Shen Wei, "Expropriation in Transition: Evolving Chinese Investment Treaty Practices in Local and Global Contexts" (2015) 28(3) *Leiden Journal of International Law* 579–604.

172 "Watching and Waiting for Donald Trump's Protectionism," *Financial Times*, March 20, 2017 (online).

173 Freddie Kleiner, "Trump Leaves Asia Door Open for China to Dominate Trade," *Financial Times*, March 2, 2017 (online).

negotiating and rule-making stance in the remolding of international economic law, particularly in the context of trade and investment.[174] Against this backdrop, China's growing economic influence in Asia and its efforts to finalize RCEP negotiations could leave it gaining the upper hand in an increasingly important economic region. The forthcoming EU–China CAI thus may serve as a template not only for future EU investment agreements with other developing and emerging countries[175] but also for future Chinese BITs with other developed countries, in particular the USA. From an evolutionary viewpoint, the EU–China CAI may emerge as (part of) a global BIT 2.0 leading the direction of international investment rules.[176]

[174] The EU plans to cover all operations accompanying investment in the forthcoming EU–China CAI, including payments, transfer of profits, and protection of intangible assets such as IPR. Likely, the EU will also ensure consistency between the norms and rules in the EU–China CAI and the EU's own long-term policies on the protection of the environment, health and safety at work, consumer protection, cultural diversity, development and competition. EC: Towards a Comprehensive European International Investment Policy, COM (2010) 343, p. 7. As a result, the EU–China BIT will substantially bring China's FDI law up to international standards, leading to a better and more effective rule of law regime for FDI activities in China. This would eventually benefit China's own economic and legal infrastructure.

[175] Artur Gradziuk and Damian Wnukowski, "Rocky Road to a Level Playing Field in EU–China Investment and Trade Relations" (2014) 8(91) Polish Institute of International Affairs Policy Paper.

[176] Wenhua Shan and Lu Wang, 'The China–EU BIT: The Emerging 'Global BIT 2.0'" (2014) Columbia FDI Perspectives No. 128.

5

Expropriation in Local and Global Contexts

International law scholarship appears to overlook, if not ignore, the interconnection between international law and domestic law. In the field of international investment, the impact of BITs on domestic law has been appreciated due to the "new constitutionalism" which removes key aspects of economic life from the influence of domestic politics within sovereign states. This orthodoxy is premised on the network of BITs which protects foreign investors from discrimination and expropriation and confers on foreign investors the right to sue the host states when their investments are impaired.[1] The increasing importance of domestic law in international investment law is reflected in both BITs and investment arbitration awards, as well as the states' attempts to curtail the jurisdiction and power of investment arbitration tribunals with respect to domestic law. The role of domestic law, either as a question of "fact" or as a source of "law,"[2] is also confusingly placed in international investment law jurisprudence.[3]

It is contended that foreign investors' rights under Chinese law have expanded and become more enforceable due to changes in the BITs (evidenced by the general perception of the international investment community that China is being ranked as one of the safest emerging markets for FDI projects),[4] and these changes promoted rule of law developments in China.[5] In the same vein, China's BITs serve as a credible commitment by the Chinese government to

[1] David Schneiderman, "Investment Rules and the New Constitutionalism" (2000) 25(3) *Law & Social Inquiry* 757–787. The South African government changed the constitution to mention that land expropriation without compensation could enhance the property rights on which investment depends. The underlying rationale is that the measure is essential to end racial land ownership patterns that favor whites, after the end of apartheid. Steven Friedman, "Changes to the Constitution May Boost, Not Weaken, South African Property Rights," The Conversation, August 3, 2018, https://theconversation.com/changes-to-the-constitution-may-boost-not-weaken-south-african-property-rights-100979 (accessed September 8, 2020).

[2] See generally Daniel Peat, *Comparative Reasoning in International Courts and Tribunals* (Cambridge University Press 2019).

[3] Andrew D. Mitchell and Tania Voon, "Senior Editor's Preface" in Jarrod Hepburn (ed.), *Domestic Law in International Investment Arbitration* (Oxford University Press 2017) vii.

[4] Robert Ginsburg, "Legitimizing Expectations in Arbitration through Political Risk Analysis" in Andrea K. Bjorklund (ed.), *Yearbook on International Investment Law & Policy 2014–2015* (Oxford University Press 2016) 224.

[5] Kate Hadley, "Do China's BITs Matter? Assessing the Effect of China's Investment Agreements on Foreign Direct Investment Flows, Investors' Rights and the Rule of Law" (2013) 45 *Georgetown Journal of International Law* 255.

property protection and liberal investment policies.[6] Many norms such as transparency, fairness and rights protection in the BITs can diffuse into local laws and lift rights protection standards in the domestic legal system. This chapter tries to theorize the interconnection between Chinese BITs and domestic law through the lens of expropriation rules in Chinese BITs.

The origins of expropriation can be traced back to the international law standards for the protection of aliens. In modern international investment protection law, expropriation is permitted only if it is carried out on a nondiscriminatory basis, for a public purpose, in compliance with due process and the principle of payment of compensation. BITs regulate the exercise of the state's power to expropriate investments. In fact, investors' chances of succeeding in a claim against a state for expropriation are rather slim, in particular in such cases where the disputed expropriation is a regulatory one. Tribunals have always found it difficult to conclude either that the state's actions amount to an actual taking or that the accumulative effect of the state's act reaches the threshold of expropriation.

Expropriation is a critically important issue in Chinese BITs,[7] considering China's enormous amount of foreign capital, its history of nationalizing foreign investment soon after the founding of the PRC,[8] and the tendency of its emerging "new renationalisation" by grabbing state land (or taking back shares) from privately owned coal mines and residents (or previously privatized firms).[9] However, the utility of expropriation clauses in China's 129 BITs and dozen FTAs including the Peru–China Free Trade Agreement entered into between China and Peru on April 28, 2009, is a mysterious arena given the fact that extremely few BIT arbitration cases brought to ICSID involved Chinese BITs.

Up to today, *Tza Yap Shum* v. *The Republic of Peru* is one of few cases that touch on the expropriation clause in a Chinese BIT,[10] that is, the Agreement between the Government of the Republic of Peru and the Government of the People's Republic of China Concerning the Encouragement and Reciprocal Protection of Investments, dated June 9, 1994. Tza Yap Shum, the claimant, a Chinese national resident in Hong Kong, brought a claim before the ICSID on September 29, 2006 against the Republic of Peru, the respondent. The claim involved an alleged tax debt of 12 million Peruvian nuevos soles (S/.) and a tax lien charged and imposed by the Superintendencia Nacional de Administración Tributaria (SUNAT), Peru's tax authority, on bank accounts belonging to TSG Peru S.A.C. (TSG), a Peruvian company in the business of manufacturing fish-based food products and distribution and export thereof to Asian markets, which was indirectly owned by Tza with a 90 percent stake. Tza claimed that the freezing of TSG's bank accounts amounted to an expropriation without compensation, which is prohibited under the Peru–China BIT. The Final Award on the

6 Ibid.

7 All the BITs cited herein are available at ita.law.uvic.ca/investmenttreaties.htm; www.unctadxi.org/templates/DocSearch_779.aspx; or www.kluwerarbitration.com/BITs-countries.aspx.

8 Laurie A. Pinard, "United States Policy Regarding Nationalization of American Investments: The People's Republic of China's Nationalization Decree of 1950" (1984) 14 *California Western International Law Journal* 148.

9 Zhangkai Huang et al, "Limites of Autocracy: An Analysis of China's Renationalization" June 23, 2017, available at ckgsb.edu.cn/uploads/201408/26/papers%20170623-Zhangkai%20Huang.pdf (accessed May 7, 2021); Joe Zhang, "How China Renationalized Its Economy" July 7, 2015, available at asia.nikkei.com/NAR/Articles/How-China-renationalized-its-economy (accessed May 7, 2021).

10 The other case that is related to the Chinese BIT and its expropriation clause is *Ping An Life Insurance Company, Limited and Ping An Insurance (Group) Company of China, Limited* v. *Kingdom of Belgium*, ICSID Case No. ARB/12/29. Ping An, China's insurance giant, filed a claim with the ICSID against the Belgian government for the loss of about 15.7 billion yuan on its investment in Fortis NV, a bank that was nationalized and sold off by the Belgian government in the aftermath of the 2008 global financial crisis. Ping An claimed that the Belgian government's role in dismantling Fortis was tantamount to confiscation. The case is still ongoing. Details are available at http://italaw.com/node/2042 (accessed December 31, 2014).

Merits rendered by the arbitral tribunal on July 7, 2011 (ICSID Case No. ARB/07/6)[11] is of great value for understanding how a large number of expropriation clauses in Chinese BITs can be interpreted, applied and eventually utilized for foreign investment protection.

Apart from its 129 BITs, China has been an active player in negotiating and concluding FTAs with various countries, including, relevant to our analysis here, Peru (Peru–China FTA 2009). Further, China has been proactive in promoting multilateral efforts in regional integration by entering into regional or multilateral FTAs and economic cooperation agreements with regional organizations. As of January 2013, China has signed FTAs with eighteen countries and regions and is in negotiations with numerous other countries including Australia, the Gulf Cooperation Council, Norway and the Southern African Customs Union.[12] According to the figures of the Chinese Ministry of Commerce, a quarter of the Chinese mainland's foreign trade is with its FTA partners.[13] The latest products include an Agreement on Investment of the Framework Agreement on Comprehensive Economic Cooperation[14] concluded with the Association of South East Asian Nations (ASEAN) in Bangkok, Thailand on August 15, 2009 (China–ASEAN Treaty) and the Agreement among the Government of the Republic of Korea, the Government of the People's Republic of China and the Government of Japan for the Promotion, Facilitation and Protection of Investment (CKJ TIT), signed by China, Korea and Japan on May 13, 2012 in Beijing. China's FTAs and multilateral investment treaties such as the China–ASEAN Treaty and CKJ TIT often include a chapter providing for investment protections. The expropriation clauses in these FTAs are more detailed, if not more advanced, than those in China's BITs.

This chapter makes an attempt to understand the expropriation clauses in the Peru–China BIT (one of the old-generation Chinese BITs) and the Peru–China FTA (an equivalent of the new-generation Chinese BITs) by reference to the award. The focus of this chapter is to understand how and why the notion of expropriation evolved in Chinese BITs and the rationale behind such evolution against a wider legal/economic background. The chapter is structured as follows. Section 5.1 looks into the scope and content of an "indirect expropriation" under various Chinese BITs. Section 5.2 investigates those key conditions that validate a justifiable expropriation. Compensation and its key components are explicated in Section 5.3. Section 5.4 tries, from both local and global perspectives, to rationalize China's move from a restrictive to a liberal stance on its expropriation clauses in BITs. A short conclusion finishes up.

5.1 CONCEPT OF "INDIRECT EXPROPRIATION": SCOPE AND CONTENT

Under investment treaty jurisprudence, it is almost settled that, subject to the precise words of the BIT, expropriation extends to both direct and indirect measures as well as to "creeping expropriation."[15] However, investment treaties do not define expropriation, in particular indirect expropriation, and leave the specific contours of the concept to customary

[11] The Award was issued in Spanish only, and is available at http://opil.ouplaw.com/view/10.1093/law:iic/382-2009.case.1/IIC382(2009)DF.pdf (accessed October 15, 2013).

[12] PRC Ministry of Commerce, China FTA Network, China's Free Trade Agreements, http://fta.mofcom.gov.cn/english/fta_qianshu.shtml (accessed March 6, 2021).

[13] *China Daily*, "Deal Sealed with a Handshake and Fish," May 3, 2013 (accessed May 20, 2014).

[14] Agreement on Investment of the Framework Agreement on Comprehensive Economic Cooperation Between the Association of Southeast Asian Nations and the People's Republic of China, https://asean.org/storage/images/archive/22974.pdf (accessed April 6, 2021).

[15] International investment jurisprudence often equates direct expropriation to a forcible taking by the government of tangible or intangible property owned by individuals or companies through administrative or legislative actions while placing an emphasis on the effect of the measures taken by the host governments on the investment in

international law.[16] This approach has also been recognized in BIT jurisprudence,[17] recent US BITs[18] and Chinese FTAs.[19] The lack of a uniform definition of "indirect expropriation" has become the greatest source of trouble not only for host governments but also for investment arbitration tribunals.

Some Chinese BITs, such as the Germany–China BIT 1983, touch on "indirect expropriation" by stipulating that "investments by investors of either Contracting Party shall not directly or indirectly be expropriated, nationalised or subjected to any other measure the effects of which would be tantamount to expropriation or nationalization in the territory of the other Contracting Party."[20] The Mexico–China BIT 2008 expressly refers to expropriation being made directly or "indirectly through measures tantamount to expropriation or nationalization."[21] The term "tantamount to . . . expropriation"[22] allows a number of tribunals to provide the broadest protection for the investments of foreign investors who may suffer harm by being deprived of their fundamental investment rights.[23] For instance, in *Eureko* v. *Republic of Poland*, the tribunal concluded that "tantamount to deprivation" extends to the frustration of the benefits of an investor's contractual rights.[24]

A large number of Chinese BITs have other variations to similar effect. Examples are the Czech Republic–China BIT 1991, the Denmark–China BIT 1985, the Indonesia–China BIT 1994 and the Iceland–China BIT 1994 with the phrase "having an effect equivalent to . . .,"[25] the Greece–China BIT 1992 with the caveat of "tantamount to,"[26] and the France–China BIT 1984 with the phrase "same effect." Based on the extensive jurisprudence, any of these formulations may be held by the tribunals to have the effect of bringing indirect expropriations into the ambit of a treaty[27] as the state's actions or measures effectively "neutralise the benefit of the property of the foreign owner."[28] In line with general BIT practice,[29] the Peru–China BIT 1994, like most Chinese BITs, contains a generic expropriation clause as follows:

adjudicating "indirect expropriation" even in the absence of formal transfer of title or outright seizure. The situation in which an investment may be affected by measures gradually but eventually resulting in expropriation is known as creeping expropriation. Campbell McLachlan, Laurence Shore and Matthew Weiniger, *International Investment Arbitration: Substantive Principles* (Oxford University Press 2007) ch. 8.

16 Jack Coe Jr. and Noah Rubins, "Regulatory Expropriations and the TECMED Case: Context and Contributions" in Todd Weiler (ed.), *International Investment Law and Arbitration: Leading Cases from the ICSID, NAFTA, Bilateral Investment Treaties and Customary International Law* (Cameron May 2005) 601.

17 *Saluka Investments BV* v. *Czech Republic*, UNCITRAL Ad Hoc Arbitration, Partial Award, March 17, 2006, para. 261.

18 US Model BIT 2004, "Annex B Expropriations," at 38.

19 New Zealand–China FTA 2012, Article 143; Peru–China FTA 2009, Article 132(2)(c).

20 Germany–China BIT 1983, Article 4(2); Jordan–China BIT 2001, Article 5(1); Uganda–China BIT 2004, Article 4(1).

21 Mexico–China BIT 2008, Article 7(1).

22 Greece–China BIT 1992, Article 4(1).

23 *Pope & Talbot Inc.* v. *Government of Canada* (Merits, Phase 1) (June 26, 2000), para. 99; *Waste Management Inc.* v. *United Mexican States* (Merits), paras. 143–145; *GAMI Investments, Inc.* v. *Government of the United Mexican States* (Merits), para. 131; *Tecnicas Medioambientales Tecmed, SA* v. *United Mexican States* (Merits), paras. 113–115 and 121; *Compania del Desarrollo de Santa Elena, SA* v. *Republic of Costa Rica* (Merits), paras. 71–72 and 76.

24 *Eureko B.V.* v. *Republic of Poland*, Ad Hoc Arbitration, Partial Award, paras. 240–242 (involving the Netherlands–Poland BIT 1992).

25 Indonesia–China BIT 1994, Article 6(1).

26 Greece–China BIT 1992, Article 4(2).

27 *ADC Affiliate Limited and ADC & ADMC Management Limited* v. *Hungary*, ICSID Case No. ARB/03/16, para. 426; *Waste Management, Inc.* v. *Mexico* (Number II), ICSID Case No. ARB(AF)/00/3, Final Award, April 20, 2004, para. 143.

28 *CME Czech Republic BV* v. *Czech Republic*, UNCITRAL Partial Award September 13, 2001, para. 6-4.

29 Andrew Newcombe, "The Boundaries of Regulatory Expropriation in International Law" (2005) *ICSID Review – Foreign Investment Law Journal* 8–9.

> Neither Contracting Party shall expropriate, nationalize or take similar measure (hereinafter referred to as "expropriation") against investments of investors of the other Contracting Party in its territory, unless the following conditions are met:
>
> (a) for the public interest;
> (b) under domestic legal procedure;
> (c) without discrimination;
> (d) against compensation.[30]

A similar provision appears in the Peru–China FTA 2009.[31] However, subtle differences exist between these two documents as indicated in Table 5.1.

In comparison with other Chinese BITs and the Peru–China FTA 2009, the Peru–China BIT 1994 contains no rules on indirect expropriation through reference to "other measures having

TABLE 5.1 *Definition of expropriation under the Peru–China BIT and the Peru–China FTA*

Perspective	Peru–China BIT	Peru–China FTA
Nationalization	√	√
Expropriation	√	√ "An action or a series of actions by a Party cannot constitute an expropriation unless it interferes with a tangible or intangible property right or property interest in an investment."[32]
Direct expropriation	No mention	"direct expropriation occurs when a state takes an investor's property outright, including by nationalisation, compulsion of law or seizure."[33]
Indirect expropriation	No mention	"indirect expropriation occurs when a state takes an action or series of actions that have an effect equivalent to direct expropriation in that it deprives the investor in substance of the use of the investor's property, although the means used fall short of those specified in [the direct expropriation clause above]."[34] "In order to constitute indirect expropriation, the action or series of actions must be: (a) either severe or for an indefinite period; and (b) disproportionate to the public interest."[35]
Measures having equivalent effects	"similar measures"[36]	"measures equivalent to expropriation or nationalisation against investments of investors of the other Party in its territory."[37]

*Compiled by the author.

[30] Peru–China BIT 1994, Article 4(1).
[31] Peru–China FTA 2009, Article 133.
[32] Peru–China FTA 2009, Annex 9, Article 1.
[33] Peru–China FTA 2009, Annex 9, Article 2(a).
[34] Peru–China FTA 2009, Annex 9, Article 2(b).
[35] Peru–China FTA 2009, Annex 9, Article 3.
[36] Peru–China BIT 1994, Article 4.
[37] Peru–China FTA 2009, Article 133.

similar effects,"[38] which resembles the wording in NAFTA.[39] The Peru–China BIT's silence on "indirect expropriation" adds uncertainty to be faced by an investor when considering whether to bring a claim to ISA. Nor does the Peru–China BIT, apart from the phrase of "other similar measures," contain a more functionalist definition of "indirect expropriation," which consequently may allow the tribunals to adopt a more expansive approach to cover "indirect expropriation."[40] Due to the lack of guidance in the Peru–China BIT in applying the treaty standard to specific circumstances, the application of international law to relevant disputes seems to be an option.

What is noteworthy is the completeness contributed by the Peru–China FTA 2009 to the definition of "indirect expropriation," which not only covers an "equivalent effect" scenario but also provides a two-pronged test of determining the existence of "indirect expropriation," that is, the severity or an indefinite period of the expropriatory act and proportionality to the public interest. In determining the legal nature of SUNAT's measures, the tribunal looked into two critical elements: first, the effects of the measures; and second, the severity of the effects.[41] As discussed, this two-pronged test does not appear in the Peru–China BIT but it does appear in the Peru–China FTA. The Peru–China BIT does not specify the evidentiary requirement of a causal link between a measure of expropriation and subsequent damages. Apart from the severity of impact, the tribunal placed an emphasis on the duration of the impact.[42] The theoretical consensus is that "the intensity and duration of the economic deprivation is the crucial factor in identifying an indirect expropriation or equivalent measure."[43] The deprivation needs to be permanent or for a substantial period of time. The length of an administrative action, that is, "an indefinite period" has been included in the Peru–China FTA as one of three elements in considering whether the action constitutes indirect expropriation.[44] The tribunal eventually determined that SUNAT's measures created a "direct, close or permanent" other than an "indirect, remote or temporary" effect. Therefore, SUNAT's preliminary measures constituted indirect expropriation without compensation.[45]

International investment treaty jurisprudence makes a structural distinction between full or substantial deprivations and "regulatory takings," the latter referring to measures taken in the context of the modern regulatory state including strangulating taxation.[46] This distinction is not easily sustained[47] but has been recognized as one of the most contentious issues in international investment law[48] by both international legislative documents[49] and case law.

[38] China–Finland BIT 2006, Article 4(1); China–Germany BIT 2003, Article 4(2); China–Portugal BIT 1992, Article 4(1). China recognized the concept of indirect expropriation in its Model BIT adopted as early as the 1980s. See "Chinese Model BIT," reprinted in Wenhua Shan and Nora Gallagher, *Chinese Investment Treaties, Policies and Practice* (Oxford University Press 2009) appendix 4.

[39] NAFTA 1992, Article 1110, 107 Stat. 2057, 32 ILM 289.

[40] The Protocol to the TIT, Article 2a(ii), includes an identical definition of "indirect expropriation," which details key perspectives of "indirect expropriation."

[41] Award, para. 159.

[42] Award, para. 156.

[43] Christoph H. Schreuer, "The Concept of Expropriation under the ETC and Other Investment Protection Treaties" (2005) 5(2) *Transnational Dispute Management* 28.

[44] Peru–China FTA 2009, Annex 9, Article 3(a).

[45] Award, para. 170.

[46] Stephan W. Schill, *The Multilateralization of International Investment Law* (Cambridge University Press 2009) 82.

[47] Rosalyn Higgins, "The Taking of Property by the State: Recent Developments in International Law" (1982) 176 *Recueil des Cours* 331.

[48] Thomas Walde and Abba Kolo, "Environmental Regulation, Investment Protection and 'Regulatory Taking' in International Law" (2001) 50 *International and Comparative Law Quarterly* 811, 814.

[49] The official commentary to the OECD Draft Convention of 1967 states that "the taking of property, within the meaning of the Article [3], must result in a loss of title or substance – otherwise a claim will not lie." OECD Draft

The general rule is that a diminution in value remains uncompensated, so long as rights of use, exclusion and alienation remain untouched.[50] Most tribunals follow this legal approach while others integrate some economic elements. In the latter approach, economic elements are taken into account to assess questions of causation and damage. Some tribunals have favored the economic approach. The tribunal in *Telenor* required "a major adverse impact on the economic value of the investment,"[51] and in *Parkerings* "a substantial decrease of the value of the investment."[52] In *Tecmed,* the tribunal held that the deprivation analysis is focused on "economic use and enjoyment of its investments" as the rights related thereto – such as "the income or benefits related to the expropriation – ha[d] ceased to exist."[53]

The Peru–China FTA 2009 sides with a more legalistic approach by providing that "the fact that an action or series of actions by a Party has an adverse effect on the economic value of an investment, standing alone, does not establish that an indirect expropriation has occurred."[54] The tribunal in this case took both approaches into account but leaned toward a more legalistic stance.[55] One thing the tribunal decided was whether Tza was substantially deprived of the economic use and enjoyment of his investment. This was regarded by the tribunal as one of the main elements distinguishing "regulation" from "expropriation."[56] However, the tribunal made no reservations in deciding that a total destruction of value would be considered an expropriation, a position adopted by other tribunals.[57] Therefore, the tribunal pragmatically avoided the technical difficulty of contemplating the concept of "expropriation" by merely looking into the destructive harm the exercise of taxation policing power had brought to Tza. The award ruled that SUNAT's imposition of interim measures had constituted an indirect expropriation of Tza's investment. In sum, a taking does not have to be complete or full but must "have the effect of depriving the owner, in whole or in significant part, of the use or reasonably-to-be-expected economic benefits of property even if not necessarily to the obvious benefit of the host State."[58]

There has been some doubt over the question of whether the "sole effect" doctrine should be the only factor in determining whether a regulatory measure in the field of tax, environment,

Convention on the Protection of Property, Adopted by the Council in Its 150th Meeting on October 12, 1967 (1968) 7 ILM 117, 126.

50 Higgins, *supra* note 47, at 271.

51 *Telenor Mobile Communications AS* v. *Republic of Hungary*, ICSID Case No. ARB/04/15, Award, para. 64.

52 *Parkerings-Compagniet AS* v. *Lithuania*, ICSID Case No ARB/05/8, Award, September 11, 2007, para. 455.

53 *Tecnicas Medioambientales Tecmed S.A.* v. *United Mexican States*, ICSID Case No. ARB(AF)/00/2, Award, May 29, 2003, para. 115.

54 Peru–China FTA 2009, Annex 9, Article 4.

55 The tribunal in Lauder held that a "formal" expropriation is a measure aimed at a "transfer of property" while a "de facto" expropriation occurs when a state deprives the owner of his or her "right to use, let or sell [his or her] property" (*Ronald S. Lauder* v. *The Czech Republic* 2001, para. 200). The tribunal in the case of Nykomb Synergetics went even further. Even if the investment became worthless, the tribunal still held that "the decisive factor for drawing the border line towards expropriation must primarily be the degree of possession taking or control over the enterprise the disputed measures entail" (*Nykomb Synergetics Technology Holding AB* v. *Latvia*, SCC Case No. 118/2001, Award, December 16, 2003, para. 4.3.1). This more stringent "control" test was adopted in a number of arbitration cases in which the tribunals did not recognize expropriation where the investor retained control over the investment and the government did not have day-to-day management over the investment. CMS *Gas Transmission Co.* v. *The Republic of Argentina* (Merits), ICSID Case Arb/01/8, Award (May 11, 2005).

56 *Tecnicas Medioambientales Tecmed S.A.* v. *United Mexican States*, ICSID Case No. ARB(AF)/00/2, Award, May 29, 2003, para. 115.

57 *CME Czech Republic BV* v. *Czech Republic* (Partial Award 2001), para. 575 (suggesting that a destruction of the legal basis of the investment constituted sufficient expropriatory deprivation).

58 *Metalclad Corporation* v. *Mexico*, ICSID Case No Arb (AF)/97/1, Award August 30, 2000, para. 103.

health, human rights and other welfare interests of the state affects a taking.[59] It has been argued that the purpose and context of the governmental measure should be taken into account. Peru's argument is reflective of a greatly narrow, restrictive and obsolete approach which required Tza to prove an expropriatory "purpose." This is a purpose-oriented approach focusing on the host state's intention or motivation to expropriate.[60]

Further clarity has been brought to China's newer BITs and FTAs. Both the Finland–China BIT 2004 and the Netherlands–China BIT 2001 are even closer to the US approach[61] to expropriation.[62] The most sophisticated definition of "indirect expropriation," drawing on recent BIT case law, appears in the New Zealand–China FTA 2008, under which it is confined to measures which are (a) equivalent to direct expropriation, in that "[they] deprive ... the investor in substance of the use of the investor's property ..."; (b) either severe or indefinite; and (c) disproportionate to the public purpose.[63] Clear interpretative guidelines are provided on what actions constitute expropriation.

In the Protocol of the India–China BIT 2006, the criteria for indirect expropriation were stipulated in detail as follows:

> (2) The determination of whether a measure or a series of measures of a Party in a specific situation, constitute measures as outlined in paragraph 1 above requires a case by case, fact based inquiry that considers, among other factors:
>
> (i) the economic impact of the measure or a series of measures, although the fact that a measure or series of measures by a Party has an adverse effect on the economic value of an investment, standing alone, does not establish that expropriation or nationalization, has occurred;
>
> (ii) the extent to which the measures are discriminatory either in scope or in application with respect to a Party or an investor or an enterprise;
>
> (iii) the extent to which the measures or series of measures interfere with distinct, reasonable, investment-backed expectations;
>
> (iv) the character and intent of the measures or series of measures, whether they are bona fide public interest purposes or not and whether there is a reasonable nexus between them and the intention to expropriate.
>
> (3) Except in rare circumstances, non-discriminatory regulatory measures adopted by a Contracting Party in pursuit of public interest, including measures pursuant to awards of general application rendered by judicial bodies, do not constitute indirect expropriation or nationalization.[64]

59 Rudolf Dolzer, "Indirect Expropriations: New Developments?" (2002) 11 *New York University Environmental Law Journal* 79–80.

60 Anne K. Hoffmann, "Indirect Expropriation" in August Reinisch (ed.), *Standards of Investment Protection* (Oxford University Press 2008) 156–158.

61 The approach taken by the USA in negotiating its BITs is to ensure that the standards created by the takings clause of the Fifth Amendment to the US Constitution are also applied to the protection of investment. To this end, the term "expropriation" explicitly covers both direct and indirect expropriation. Accordingly, any expropriation is required to be consistent with the general absolute treatment standards such as fair and equitable treatment, full protection and security, and treatment in accordance with customary international law. Kenneth J. Vandevelde, *U.S. International Investment Agreements* (Oxford University Press 2009) ch. 7.

62 Finland–China BIT 2004, Article 4; Netherlands–China BIT 2001, Article 5.

63 New Zealand–China FTA 2008, Annex 13.

64 Protocol to India–China BIT 2006, Article III, Ad Article 5.

These largely copy the provisions from the US Model BIT 2004[65] and indicate China's intention to emulate the US approach on the subject of expropriation. Few BITs specify the treaty interpretative methodology. The Peru–China FTA 2009 calls for "a case-by-case, fact-based inquiry."[66] This common-law type of case-by-case method is also codified into other BITs including the Canadian Model BIT 2004.[67] This pragmatic and realist approach was adopted by the tribunal in this instant case. The tribunal echoed that the constitution of expropriation "cannot be answered in the abstract but only on the basis of particular circumstances and in the context of particular purposes."[68]

5.2 DEFENSES TO UNLAWFUL EXPROPRIATION

Expropriation is not unlawful under international law as long as certain conditions are complied with by the state. This is a highly formalistic area of law. Under customary international law,[69] the well-recognized conditions include four elements, namely, the expropriation must be for the public interests, pursuant to domestic legal procedure, non-discriminatory, and with compensation. These four elements consistently appear in almost all Chinese BITs except a few such as the UK–China BIT 1986[70] and the Italy–China BIT 1985.[71] Both the Peru–China BIT 1994 and the Peru–China FTA 2009, in a fairly traditional term, clone the Chinese investment treaty practice by imitating these four elements. The Peru–China BIT, like most BITs to which China is a party, allows expropriation only upon the satisfaction of certain conditions. However, the Peru–China BIT offers little guidance since the key terms such as "public purpose" and "discrimination" are not defined.

5.2.1 *"Public Purpose"*

In international law, the existence and validity of public interests have traditionally been accepted. A "public purpose" is germane to expropriation as the regulatory measure can be authorized by the government for diverse reasons. The requirement of public purpose for an act of expropriation is a widely accepted principle in customary international law as well as investment treaties.[72] However, the term "for a public purpose" has not been well defined. Nor has it been explained in the form of illustrative grounds. Thus, the application of this criterion in expropriation analysis leaves the tribunal with some discretion. Variations to the phrase "for a public purpose" include "for the public interests" adopted by a large number of Chinese BITs such as the Cyprus–China BIT 2001 and the Benin–China BIT 2004 and "for public benefits," which appears in the Germany–China BIT 2003. These terminologies do not indicate substantial differences. The formulae of "public purpose, security or national interests" adopted by the BLEU–China BIT 2005 makes this criterion more operative even though the host state may be in a more advantageous position as such an operative criterion is

65 US Model BIT 2004, Annex B, Article 4.

66 Peru–China FTA 2009, Annex 9, Article 4. An identical terminology also appears in the Protocol to the TIT, Article 2b, para. 1.

67 Canadian Model BIT 2004, Annex B 13(1)(b).

68 Robert Jennings and Arthur Watts (eds.), *Oppenheim's International Law* (9th edition, Longman 1992) 916–917.

69 Rudolf Dolzer and Christoph Schreuer, *Principles of International Investment Law* (Oxford University Press 2008) 91.

70 UK–China BIT 1986, Article 5(1).

71 Italy–China BIT 1985, Article 4(2).

72 Energy Charter Treaty, Article 13(1)(a); NAFTA, Article 1110(1).

easier satisfied. Other variations such as "the need of social and public interest" and "national security and public interest" appearing in the Argentina–China BIT 1992[73] and the Philippines–China BIT 1992[74] respectively are less operative due to their wide or vague coverage. But these varied terms indicate the scope and nature of the "for a public purpose" criterion, and would entail consideration of detailed facts in the specific case.

Some Chinese BITs[75] contain a carve-out for the reasonable exercise of a state's "police powers," which is intended to offer a safe harbor for regulation that is reasonably justified in the public interest. Given the lack of a "police powers" carve-out in some BITs, the "for a public purpose" condition may function as a safe harbor for expropriation regulations. "Public power" that refers to the authority of state governments to enact measures to protect public health, welfare and morals serves the "public purpose." As it may serve a local protectionist purpose, it is difficult to discern from an international perspective. The tribunals may then weigh heavily such elements as bad faith, arbitrariness or discrimination in determining whether a "public" but more domestic "purpose" is acceptable or not.

Peru's defense[76] was based on a "presumable legitimacy" doctrine.[77] Promoting a public interest, that is, the maintenance of order, health or public morals, as the Peruvian government argued, justified the confiscation of property. This is similar to the "pre-eminent public interest" theory that some tribunals have adopted to justify expropriation even in the absence of express treaty provisions. In *Saluka*, for example, the tribunal made a similarly categorical statement: "[I]t is established in international law that States are not liable to pay compensation to a foreign investor when, in the normal exercise of their regulatory powers, they adopt in a non-discriminatory manner bona fide regulations that are aimed at the general welfare."[78] In adjudicating this "pre-eminent public interest" doctrine, the tribunal resorted to some arbitral awards and acknowledged the "considerable consensus" reached by these tribunals.[79] In weighing the deferential treatment of the state's regulatory power against the exercise of such power vis-à-vis the investor,[80] the tribunal rejected Peru's argument.

BIT jurisprudence recognizes that the invocation of pre-eminent public interests and the termination of rights according to laws are acceptable deprivations that do not require payment of compensation. This suggests that bona fide and nondiscriminatory regulation, even when fully destroying the value of an investment, may not constitute expropriation. Some tribunals may have simplified the formula by looking into the investor's ability to carry out its business. If the investor still possesses the ability to continue its business, interferences then do not justify the investor's claim for compensations even if profits are diminished.[81] Still, partial destruction of the value or temporary deprivation may be tantamount to an expropriation "in some contexts and circumstances."[82] Other tribunals have refused to accept a blanket exception for regulatory measures on the grounds that this would "create a gaping loophole in international protection against expropriation."[83] The tribunal in *Pope and*

73 Argentina–China BIT 1992, Article 4(1).
74 Philippines–China BIT 1992, Article 4(1).
75 New Zealand–China FTA 2008, Annex 13.
76 Award, para. 171.
77 CMD, paras. 256–265.
78 Saluka, para. 255.
79 Award, para. 181.
80 Award, para. 179.
81 LG&E, para. 191.
82 GAMI, para. 131; SD Myers I, para. 283.
83 *Pope & Talbot Inc* v. *Canada*, UNCITRAL Ad Hoc Arbitration, Interim Award, June 26, 2000, para. 99.

Talbot explicitly rejected Canada's argument that regulation cannot amount to expropriation and pointed out that "much creeping expropriation could be conducted by regulation."

A claimant's counterargument toward the respondent state's public interest defense can be that the depriving measure was illegally or arbitrarily imposed. Even if the government's police power has a legitimate objective, it remains possible that officials may act with arbitrariness and disproportionality. This possibility requires the tribunal to review "whether the measure was proportionate or necessary for a legitimate purpose; whether it discriminated in law or in practice; whether it was not adopted in accordance with due process of law; or whether it interfered with the investor's legitimate expectations when the investment was made."[84] This counterargument is based on illegality and lack of due process. Arbitrariness is also grounded on a lack of proportionality. The rationale is that the state can take any action in pursuit of the public interest but that action is lawful only when taken in a manner that is legal, procedurally appropriate and proportionate. Public interest comes in all types and varieties, covering the full spectrum from the most weak and ordinary to the most serious. The pervasive uncertainty surrounding any effort to determine the public interest justifies a straightforward approach by which compensation should be paid as long as property is fully or substantially destroyed.

5.2.2 *"Due Process"*

Due process is a required element to satisfy the public interest exception. Some Chinese BITs prescribe that the expropriation must be effected according to notions of due process. Different from the Western terminology, a large number of Chinese BITs often use the term "under domestic legal procedure"[85] or "applicable domestic law"[86] instead of "in accordance with due process." Only in the CKJ TIT[87] is the condition "in accordance with international standard of due process of law" adopted.[88] In a few Chinese BITs, the phrase "due process" is used but with some Chinese characteristics. For instance, the expropriation may need to be carried out in accordance with the "due process of national laws"[89] or "due process of law."[90] For instance, the China–Poland BIT 1988 requires "due process of national law" to conduct expropriations.[91] However, the meaning of "due process of national laws" or "due process of law" has never been clarified. The distinction between these two similar terms seems clear that "due process of law" is closer to "due process" whereas "due process of national laws" leans more toward "national laws." The China–Poland BIT 1988 provides: "If an investor considers the expropriation ... incompatible with [host state] laws ... the competent court ... may, upon the request of the investor[,] review the said expropriation."[92] The investor can be protected in a better way if "due process of law" is adopted as the investor may rely on customary international law for protection while "due

84 *Archer Daniels Midland Co et al.* v. *Mexico*, ICSID Case No ARB(AF)/04/05, Award, November 21, 2007, para. 250.
85 Pakistan–China FTA 2006, Article 49.
86 New Zealand–China FTA 2008, Article 145.
87 CKJ TIT here refers to the Agreement among the Government of the Republic of Korea, the Government of the People's Republic of China and the Government of Japan for the Promotion, Facilitation and Protection of Investment, signed by China, Japan and South Korea in 2012.
88 CKJ TIT, Article 11.
89 Czech Republic–China BIT 2005.
90 Austria–China BIT 1985; Mexico–China BIT 2008; Sweden–China BIT 1982.
91 China–Poland BIT 1988, Article 4(1).
92 China–Poland BIT 1988, Article 4(3).

process of national laws" may give the investor less leeway. Therefore, it is easy to understand why some Chinese BITs used the term "in accordance with its laws"[93] or "relevant domestic laws"[94] instead. The most advanced version may be the "laws and international standard of due process of law" adopted by the TIT.[95]

Both the Peru–China BIT and the Peru–China FTA adopt the term "under domestic legal procedure."[96] The reference to "domestic" law provides the state with more flexibility and control over the process as the expropriation process will be subject to the domestic laws of the expropriating state. The Peru–China BIT's "under domestic legal procedure" is different from "due process of law."[97] Legally speaking, "domestic legal procedure" can be narrower than "due process," thereby bringing more local law elements into international investment arbitration.

Under some Chinese BITs, the norm "due process of national laws" or "in accordance with its laws" is more operative as the investor is granted the right to a judicial review of a completed expropriation and of the amount of compensation due. The UK–China BIT 1986, for example, provides that "the national or company affected have a right, under the law of the Contracting Party making the expropriation, to prompt review, by a judicial or other independent authority of that Party, of his or its case and of the valuation of his or its investment in accordance with the principles set out in this paragraph."[98] Similar rights are granted under other Chinese BITs such as the Germany–China BIT 2003, according to which the investor may request "the legality of any such expropriation and the amount of compensation shall be subject to review by national courts . . .."[99] The China–ASEAN Treaty 2009 does not follow this route of providing investors with the right to review. Accordingly, the investor may have to rely on ISA for claims against expropriation.

Since the Peru–China BIT does not offer a functional definition of "under the domestic legal procedure," the tribunal made a reference to both international and domestic law. This again confirms the hybrid nature of the international investment arbitration jurisprudence which is composed of both international and municipal law.[100] The tribunal assessed the legitimacy of Peru's regulatory measures by focusing on two conditions. First, the proceedings must be reasonable. Second, the said measures must not be deployed in a confiscatory, abusive or discriminatory manner.[101] The tribunal determined that SUNAT failed to comply with its own internal guidelines and procedures which required, inter alia, (i) a more precise identification of the assets to be seized via interim measures; (ii) a reasoned basis for the imposition of the "exceptional" remedy of interim measures accompanied by detailed evidentiary support; and (iii) efforts to avoid interfering with the debtor's business operations. The tribunal was of the opinion that SUNAT could have seized TSG's accounts receivables instead of imposing preliminary measures such as seizure of TSG's funds in the bank

93 New Zealand–China BIT 1988, Article 6(1); Singapore–China BIT 1985, Article 6(1).

94 United Arab Emirates–China BIT 1993, Article 6(1)(b); Guyana–China BIT 2003, Article 4(1)(b); Kuwait–China BIT 1985, Article 5(2).

95 CKJ TIT, Article 11.

96 See Table 5.1.

97 Most BITs that China signed with European countries adopt "due process of law" instead of "under domestic legal procedure." China–France BIT 1984, Article 4(3); China–Denmark BIT 1985, Article 4(1).

98 UK–China BIT 1986, Article 5(1).

99 Germany–China BIT 2003.

100 Andrew Newcombe and Lluís Paradell, *Law and Practice of Investment Treaties* (Wolters Kluwer 2009) section 2.7.

101 Award, para. 95.

accounts.[102] Arbitrariness was also evidenced by SUNAT's failure to make relevant inquiries or requests for additional information from the auditor before imposing interim measures.

States are under an obligation to provide a fair and effective system of justice to correct the challenged action.[103] This problem of "denial of justice" has been often tested in international investment law. The state is held liable only if the system as a whole has been tested and the initial delict remained uncorrected.[104] Violation of international law lies in the inadequacy or misadministration of civil or criminal procedure, denial of access to courts, or unjust decisions.[105] Other judicial failures such as unconscionable delay, manifest discrimination, corruption, or subservience to executive pressure may also amount to a breach of international law.[106] The tribunal's characterization of SUNAT's failure as a denial of justice fits well in the international investment law jurisprudence.

5.2.3 *"Without Discrimination"*

Nondiscrimination in regard to the status and treatment of aliens and alien property is a well-established principle of customary international law,[107] treaty law[108] and case law.[109] Breach of the nondiscrimination principle gives rise to international responsibility.[110] The nondiscrimination requirement appears in many Chinese BITs and is absent in only a small number of BITs between China and Austria, Germany, Indonesia, Italy, Oman and the UK. This requirement adds more value to the investor protection if the BIT does not offer NT protection. In practice, discrimination complaints are more likely to be raised with regard to due process and payment of compensation. However, the discriminatory factor, due to the lack of guidance and specificity, is "extremely difficult to prove in concrete cases."[111] Thus, the blanket exception for nondiscriminatory measures may create more complexity or a "gaping loophole in international protections against expropriation."[112]

It is worth noting that the tribunal was mindful that, despite the fact that the Peru–China BIT makes no mention of any exclusion clause, the Peru–China FTA provides a legitimate ground for indirect expropriation, that is, a deprivation of property shall not be "discriminatory in its effect, either as against the particular investor or against a class of which the investors forms part"; or in breach of the state's prior binding written commitment to the investor, whether by contract, license, or other legal document.[113] Under the Peru–China FTA, an indirect expropriation may be "reasonably justified in the protection of the public welfare, including public health, safety and the environment."[114]

102 Award, para. 209.
103 Jan Paulsson, *Denial of Justice in International Law* (Cambridge University Press 2005) 100.
104 *Jan de Nul NV Dredging International NV* v. *Arab Republic of Egypt*, ICSID Case No. Arb/04/13, Award, November 6, 2008, para. 258.
105 A. O. Adede, "A Fresh Look at the Meaning of the Doctrine of Denial of Justice under International Law" (1976) 14 *Canadian Yearbook of International Law* 72, 91.
106 Paulsson, *supra* note 103, at 204.
107 *Alex Genin and others* v. *Republic of Estonia*, ICSID Case No. Arb/99/2, Award June 25, 2001, para. 368.
108 Energy Charter Treaty, Article 13(1)(b); NAFTA, Article 1110(1)(b).
109 *BP* v. *Libya* (1979) 53 ILR 297, 329; *Libya* v. *Libyan Am. Oil Co.* (1981) 20 ILM 20, 58.
110 Ian Brownlie, *System of the Law of Nations: State Responsibility, Part I* (Clarendon Press 1983) 81.
111 Malcolm N. Shaw, *International Law* (5th edition, Cambridge University Press 2003) 751.
112 *Pope & Talbot Inc.* v. *Canada*, Interim Award June 26, 2000, para. 99.
113 Peru–China FTA 2009, Annex 9, Article 5.
114 Peru–China FTA 2009, Annex 9, Article 6.

The tribunal did review the legitimacy of SUNAT's actions against the difficulty of conferring deferential treatment on the public authority's regulatory power, and chose to make reference to other relevant BIT cases in which the legitimacy of tax authorities' measures and actions was the key issue. It was noticed by the tribunal that arguments in favor of indirect expropriation in these cases had often been rejected. In addition, considerable consensus had been formed in the BIT jurisprudence that the imposition and application of tax measures could attain an expropriatory character if they were of a confiscatory, arbitrary, abusive or discriminatory nature,[115] or were applied unfairly and inequitably. The tribunal recognized the deference given to a state's regulatory and administrative powers and noted the general rule that a state is not liable for any losses resulting from the good faith application of general taxes and regulations. However, such a defense was also bound by the principle of reasonableness and non-arbitrariness reflected in public international law, Peruvian law and treaty practice. The approach taken by the tribunal in examining the procedural side of the governmental action represents its concern over the quantum threshold of the interferences as well as the proportionality, which is identified by the Peru–China FTA as one of the three elements for the assessment of "indirect expropriation."[116]

Table 5.2 summarizes key differences in the defenses in the Peru–China BIT, the Peru–China FTA and the award.

5.3 COMPENSATION AND KEY COMPONENTS

Payment of compensation is required to validate expropriation. In some of the most recent cases, the "lawfulness" of the expropriation depends on satisfaction of the requirement of compensation.[117] Tribunals have increasingly focused on the adequacy of compensation for expropriation instead of the legality of expropriation. It is difficult to reach consensus on an acceptable standard of compensation for lawful expropriation. The great majority of BITs adopt customary international law on lawful expropriation including the Hull formula,[118] with the exception of some variations in language.[119] Under old-generation Chinese BITs, the standard of compensation is usually not clarified. The relevant provision in the Norway–China BIT 1984 was a typical example: "Compensation shall be made without under delay and shall be realizable and freely transferable. It shall amount to the value of the investment immediately before the expropriation, and shall include interest until the date of payment."[120] This apparently was far away from the Hull formula, which was viewed by China as a typical standard demanded by developed countries.

Chinese BITs prefer to endorse "reasonable" or "appropriate" compensation. For instance, the UK–China BIT 1986 defines the "reasonable standard" by providing that "such compensation shall amount to the real value of the investment expropriated immediately before the

115 Award, para. 181.

116 Peru–China FTA 2009, Annex 5, Article 3(b).

117 *Marion Unglaube and Reinhard Unglaube* v. *Republic of Costa Rica*, ICSID Consolidated Cases Nos. Arb/08/1 and Arb/09/20, Award May 16, 2012.

118 The Hull Formula or Hull Rule refers to the formula of "adequate" or "just" compensation as a prerequisite of expropriation required by customary international law. The formula also requires that compensation be "effective" and "prompt." It is named after the US Secretary of State Cordell Hull who put forward these standards in his note to the Mexican government in 1938 on the expropriation of assets of US nationals by the Mexican government. Green H. Hackworth, US Department of State, Pub. No. 1708 (1942) 3 *Digest of International Law* 655–661.

119 UNCTAD, Bilateral Investment Treaties 1995–2006: Trends in Investment Rulemaking (2007) 52.

120 Norway–China BIT 1984, Article 5(2).

TABLE 5.2 *Conditions to lawful expropriation in the Peru–China BIT, the Peru–China FTA and the award*

Perspective	Peru–China BIT	Peru–China FTA	Award
Public interest	No further detail	Public interest "disproportionate to the public interest";[121] "the exercise of a state's regulatory powers as may be reasonably justified in the protection of the public welfare, including public health, safety and the environment, . . ."[122]	• Narrowly defined "public interest"; • Rejected the "presumable legitimacy" or "pre-eminent public interest" doctrine • Relied more on the legalistic approach weighing the proportionality (of expropriation) to public interest
Without discrimination	"without discrimination"		• availability of effective remedy • compliance with domestic rules by government authority • measures are routine, non-abusive and nondiscriminatory
	No further detail	"discriminatory in its effect, either as against the particular investor or against a class of which the investor forms part"[123]	
Due process	"under domestic legal procedure"		• "tax proceeding must be reasonable" • regulatory act must not "be deployed in a confiscatory, abusive or discriminatory manner"

*Compiled by the author.

expropriation or impending expropriation became public knowledge, shall include interest at the normal rate until the date of payment, shall be made without undue delay, be effectively realizable and be freely transferable."[124] This may be seen as a de facto Hull formula. The China–Australia BIT 1988 contains a prompt, adequate and effective formula for compensation.[125] Other BITs like the China–New Zealand BIT 1988 make reference only to "compensation which shall be effectively realisable."[126] Later BITs made in the 1990s, albeit with the Hull standard, indicated no pattern of general principles or rules.[127]

121 Peru–China FTA 2009, Annex 9, Article 3(b).
122 Peru–China FTA 2009, Annex 9, Article 6.
123 Peru–China FTA 2009, Annex 9, Article 5(a).
124 UK–China BIT 1986, Article 5(1).
125 M. Sornarajah, *The International Law on Foreign Investment* (3rd edition, Cambridge University Press 2010) 210.
126 Ibid.
127 Ibid., at 416.

5.3.1 "Value"

Investment treaty jurisprudence has shown an increasing level of convergence in that compensation needs to be equivalent to the "market value"[128] or the "fair market value."[129] On a few occasions, variations such as "real value"[130] and "genuine value"[131] are used instead. These formulae refer to the price voluntarily reached by the seller and the buyer in an arm's-length transaction. As such, modern BIT jurisprudence appears to support full or "adequate" compensation[132] even though the degree of specificity and sophistication concerning the calculation of compensation differs from one to another.[133] A number of Chinese BITs link compensation to the "value of the expropriated investment."[134] Some BITs clarify the "value" by reference to "genuine,"[135] "actual,"[136] "market"[137] or "fair market"[138] value. The reliance on the "value of the expropriated investment" demonstrates the host state's willingness to provide the investors with "just compensation." At the technical level, a tribunal is more capable of achieving "just compensation" as the "value" formulation reflects the genuine value of the property affected.[139]

The Peru–China BIT 1994 adopts the following "compensation" clause: "The compensation mentioned in Paragraph 1, (d) of this Article shall be equivalent to the value of the expropriated investment at the time when the expropriation is proclaimed, be convertible and freely transferrable. The compensation shall be paid without unreasonable delay."[140]

Among others, the investment chapters of some recent FTAs such as the New Zealand–China FTA 2008[141] and the new-generation Chinese BITs including the Germany–China BIT 2003 have the most detailed provisions on awarding compensation for lawful expropriation. These provisions not only adopt the Hull formula but also spell out the details of the compensation terms.

The Peru–China FTA 2009 adopts a similar "compensation" clause as follows: "The compensation mentioned in subparagraph 1(d) of this Article shall be equivalent to the fair market value of the expropriated investment immediately before the expropriation took place ('the date of expropriation'), convertible and freely transferrable. The compensation shall be paid without unreasonable delay."[142] This provision reflects the characteristics "adequate" and "prompt," respectively. The first sentence in the quoted clause connects the financial concept of fair market value to the abstract concept of adequate compensation as the market value of the taken property is supposed to be adequate to compensate the investor. BITs usually do not explicitly define the term "fair market value." Given the fact that China has

128 China–ASEAN Treaty 2009, Article VI(1).
129 NAFTA, Article 1110(2); ECT, Article 13(1).
130 UK–USSR BIT 1989; France Model BIT 2006, Article 6(2).
131 Czech Republic–Netherlands BIT 1991, Article 5.
132 World Bank, Report to the Development Committee and Guidelines on the Treatment of Foreign Direct Investment (1992) 31 ILM 1366, Article IV.3.
133 UNCTAD, Bilateral Investment Treaties 1995–2006: Trends in Investment Rulemaking (2007) 52.
134 Austria–China BIT 1985, Article 4(1).
135 Mauritius–China BIT 1996, Article 6(1)(c); Zimbabwe–China BIT 1996, Article 4(2); Brunei–China BIT 2000, Article 4(2).
136 BLEU–China BIT 2005.
137 Australia–China BIT 1988, Barbados–China BIT 1998, Spain–China BIT 2005.
138 Netherlands–China BIT 2001, Article 5(1)(c); Finland–China BIT 2004, Article 4(2); Mexico–China BIT 2008, Article 7(2)(a).
139 *CME Czech Republic BV* v. *Czech Republic*, UNCITRAL Final Award March 14, 2003, para 493.
140 Peru–China BIT 1994, Article 4(2).
141 New Zealand–China FTA 2008, Article 145.
142 Peru–China FTA 2009, Article 133(2).

insisted on "appropriate compensation" in the past few decades,[143] accepting the "fair market value" requirement highlights China's willingness to align with the Hull formula and to be more liberalized on these expropriation-related terms. As a result, the provisions of expropriation in Chinese and American BITs are strikingly similar.

These two legal instruments are in line with the general "value" formulae, but the differences are also obvious. The Peru–China FTA moves one step further by stipulating that compensation shall "be equivalent to the fair market value of the expropriated investment." However, neither of these two "value" formulae is operative in a practical sense. First, neither formulae provides for the standard of fair market value and the method for its calculation. By contrast, NAFTA, for instance, states that compensation must be "equivalent to the fair market value of the expropriated investment immediately before the expropriation took place," and the valuation criteria for calculating the fair market value shall include "going concern value, asset value including declared tax value of tangible property, and other criteria, as appropriate."[144] Second, the distinction is not made in these two instruments between lawful and unlawful expropriation; compensation can be awarded in either case. However, when property is unlawfully expropriated, compensation covers the lost future profits (*lucrum cercans*) in addition to the loss actually suffered (*damnum energens*).[145] Third, it is not clarified in these two instruments whether and how interest should be calculated. The Energy Charter Treaty explicitly states that compensation shall include "interest at a commercial rate established on a market basis"[146] while NAFTA requires interest to be included in compensation, calculated at a commercially reasonable rate and transferred freely.[147]

Peru and Tza were in agreement that the compensation amount should be calculated on the basis of the value of TSG. Nevertheless, there was a stark difference between Peru and Tza in terms of the value of the expropriated company. Tza based his requested damages on the discounted cash flow (DCF) of TSG while Peru argued that the appropriate standard was the company's adjusted book value. Tza claimed that his company was worth PEN 56,497,500, but Peru (which engaged a damage expert) only agreed a price ranging from USD 0 to USD 771,856.[148] Tza's claim took into account his damage, expert's projected cash flow between 2005 and 2008 (using DCF) as well as the estimated liquidation value of the assets of the company in 2009.[149] Peru, having disagreed with Tza's use of DCF,[150] used the adjusted book value and estimated value of TSG as of December 31, 2004, the date right before the expropriation was carried out.[151] The tribunal noted that using the DCF methodology would allow TSG to benefit from the substantial increases in the fishmeal market from 2005. Given the fact that TSG operated for only three years up to January 2005 when the administrative measures were imposed, the tribunal agreed that it was not appropriate to use the DCF methodology as TSG did not have a long record of favorable and certain results to

143 Congyan Cai, "China-US BIT Negotiations and the Future of Investment Treaty Regime: A Grand Bilateral Bargain with Multilateral Implications" (2009) 12 *Journal of International Economic Law* 457, 476.
144 NAFTA, Article 1110(2).
145 H. Van Houtte, *The Law of International Trade* (2nd edition, Sweet & Maxwell 2002) 252.
146 Energy Charter Treaty, Article 13(1).
147 NAFTA, Article 1110(3)–(6).
148 Award, para. 256.
149 Award, para. 258.
150 Award, para. 259.
151 Award, para. 260.

justify the assumption that the company would have continued making profits between 2005 and 2008.[152] As a result, the positive projected results of TSG lacked certainty.[153]

The tribunal rejected Tza's requested DCF-based damages, noting that TSG had been in operation for only two years during which its cash flow was negative. When SUNAT imposed its interim measures, TSG had begun to lose market share in the industry. Further, TSG was highly leveraged. The tribunal also considered the argument made by Peru that TSG had no value by reference to a number of BIT cases such as *ELSI*, *Genin*, *MTD* and *Biwater*. The tribunal did not find equivalent circumstances in this case to confirm that the value of the company was zero. The tribunal took into account some other factors such as the market change and the reduction of the competitive advantages of TSG.[154]

The tribunal also made some analysis of the distinction between direct and indirect expropriation while determining the compensation.[155] The tribunal discussed the addition of residual value to the total compensation package. In the current case (different from the cases of *Metalclad* and *Tecmed*), the tribunal found no reason to reduce the amount of compensation by the residual value retained.[156] As to compensation, the Tribunal's approach of measuring damages was to place Tza in the same position he would have not encountered the expropriatory act. As the tribunal finally decided, compensation in this case must be the market value of the company.[157]

In terms of damages, the tribunal sided with Peru and preferred to accept the adjusted book value method which, as the tribunal said, would be more proportional and certain, and would be more reflective of Tza's original capital investment and the company's net worth.[158] Based on the adjusted book value of TSG (not its adjusted future cash flow), Tza was awarded USD 786,306.24 in compensation, plus interest at the biannual average of the US Treasury Bond rates for ten years.[159] Interest would be compounded semiannually, according to the well-established practice.[160] No moral damages were awarded. In this case, the tribunal applied the generally accepted principle of splitting arbitration costs equally between the parties.[161]

As to compensation, the tribunal's approach of measuring damages was to place Tza in the same position as if there had been no expropriation. Some Chinese BITs, for example the China–Sweden BIT 1982, have expressly codified this methodology to "place the investor in the same financial position as that in which the investor would have been if the expropriation or nationalisation had not taken place."[162] The China–Greece BIT 1992 further clarified this approach by adding the wording "... and on the basis of generally accepted methods"[163] even though there have been no uniform international standards in this regard.

Neither the Peru–China BIT nor the Peru–China FTA explicitly adopted this approach. The tribunal confirmed that the Draft Articles on Responsibilities of States for International

152 Award, para. 262.
153 Award, para. 263.
154 Award, para. 270.
155 Award, para. 271.
156 Award, para. 273.
157 Award, para. 255.
158 Award, para. 264.
159 Award, para. 290.
160 Award, para. 291.
161 Award, para. 296–301.
162 China–Sweden BIT 1982, Article 3(1).
163 China–Greece BIT 1992, Article 4(2).

Wrongful Acts, adopted by the International Law Commission (ILC) in 2001,[164] are the key source of customary international law, according to which the state is under a legal obligation to make full reparation for the injury caused by the international wrongful act. Reparation here is meant to wipe off all the consequences of the illegal act and re-establish the status that would have existed if the act had not been committed.[165] In practice, however, the principle of full reparation is still a vague doctrine; it can determine the exact amount of compensation for damages only if other disciplines including valuation and calculation are taken into consideration.

Some Chinese BITs took a lead by incorporating practical valuation methods or introducing valuation-related terms. For instance, under the Zimbabwe–China BIT 1996, the calculation shall be made taking "as may be appropriate, the net asset value as certified by an independent firm of auditors as well as the market value."[166] The valuation under the Guyana–China BIT 2003 shall be determined as "if the investments were to be sold as an ongoing concern on the open market."[167] To adopt more operative valuation methods and principles is the approach recommended by the World Bank, incorporated in NAFTA and endorsed by some tribunals in order to increase the transparency of the valuation method.[168] Another concern about the Peru–China FTA's compensation formulae is that it is still not clear if the wording actually refers to the full market value. In this sense, the Peru–China FTA makes little progress in clarifying how to evaluate the expropriated investment. Certainly, it may be arguable that the Peru–China FTA's approach gets closer to the Hull formula since the wording has absorbed some market-oriented factors.

5.3.2 *Moral Damages*

Tza requested compensation for the moral damages he suffered from the expropriation in the value of S/. 15 million, which, as Tza argued, would restore the investor's status to where the wrongful act had not occurred.[169] Tza's claim for moral damages was based on the grounds of (i) the Ministry of Production's defamatory and biased report accusing him of avoiding his tax liability; (ii) seizure of all of TSG's fish products; (iii) personal discredit against Tza; and (iv) ill effects of Tza's health.[170] Tza's claim of moral damages was largely related to his reputation and image in the social and business contexts after the event.[171]

Peru, however, argued that Tza's claim was not up to "exceptional circumstances," which were the precondition to the grant of compensation for moral damages.[172] In addition, Peru argued that Tza had failed to demonstrate the causal link between the adoption of the preliminary measures and his alleged health problem. Nor did Tza prove the reputational

[164] International Law Commission, Draft Articles on Responsibilities of States for Internationally Wrongful Acts, in Report of the International Law Commission to the General Assembly, 56 UN GAOR Supp. (No. 10) at 43, UN Doc. A/56/10 (2001), reprinted in [2001] YB Int'L Comm'n pt. 2 at 20, 47–49, 52–54, UN Doc. A/CN.4/SER.A/2001/Add.1.

[165] Award, para. 254.

[166] Zimbabwe–China BIT 1996, Article 4(2).

[167] Guyana–China BIT 2003.

[168] World Bank Guidelines on the Treatment of Foreign Direct Investment (1992) 31 ILM 1366, Article IV.5; NAFTA, Article 1110(2); CME *Czech Republic BV* v. *Czech Republic*, UNCITRAL Final Award March 14, 2003, para. 103.

[169] Award, para. 274.

[170] Award, para. 275.

[171] Award, para. 276.

[172] Award, paras. 277 and 278.

damage.[173] According to Peruvian law such as the General Administrative Procedure Law, it is TGS that was entitled to moral damages. Tza, as the shareholder, does not have the status to make this claim.[174]

The tribunal made reference to the "exceptional circumstance" principle and the recent case of *Lemire* v. *Ukraine*,[175] as the international standard, in considering that the circumstances in which moral damage can be granted include:

a. The acts of the State must involve a physical harm or threat to the investor, the standards of behavior foreseeable in civilized nations;
b. The acts of the State must have caused a deterioration in health, stress, anxiety or other mental distress such as humiliation, embarrassment or loss of reputation, credibility and status; and
c. Both the causes and the effects of expropriation must be serious and substantial.[176]

The tribunal opined that the above three elements all failed. There was no severity of harm to the mental health of Tza. Nor was there causality between the alleged damages and Peru's conduct.[177] The evidence presented by Tza to confirm his mental suffering (hypertension) and involvement in bankruptcy proceedings failed to prove the necessary gravity for the purpose of establishing moral damages.[178] In conclusion, the tribunal rejected Tza's wholesale request for moral damages since none of these elements were satisfied.

5.3.3 *Valuation Date*

The appropriate date of expropriation is important in calculating interest,[179] which is an integral part of the total compensation awarded by the tribunal for expropriation, and can be the most keenly contested issue. Chinese BITs usually fix the valuation date by relying on one or two cut-off points, for example "immediately prior to the time when the expropriation became public"[180] or "immediately before the expropriation measures were taken."[181] Few Chinese BITs designate the date of the taking as the valuation date. The Greece–China BIT 1992 adopts both and states that "such compensation shall amount to the value of the investments affected immediately before the measures ... occurred or became public knowledge."[182] This level of clarity helps guarantee that the "value of the expropriated investment" will not depreciate once expropriation is known to the public. It may also guarantee the investor full and adequate recovery in cases of "creeping" expropriation.

The Peru–China FTA uses "the date immediately before the expropriation took place" as the date of expropriation. While this may be beneficial to the aggrieved investor, it does not

173 Award, para. 279.
174 Award, para. 280.
175 ICSID Case No. ARB/06/18.
176 Award, para. 281.
177 Award, para. 282.
178 Award, paras. 283, 284 and 285.
179 However, it has also been suggested to distinguish the "moment of expropriation" from the "moment of valuation" as the former is related to the question of liability while the latter goes to the question of damages. W. Michael Reisman and Robert D. Sloane, "Indirect Expropriation and Its Valuation in the BIT Generation" (2004) 74 *British Year Book of International Law* 115.
180 Austria–China BIT 1985, Article 4(1).
181 Netherlands–China BIT 2001, Article 5(1)(c); New Zealand–China FTA 2008, Article 145(2); Mexico–China BIT 2008, Article 7(2)(a).
182 Greece–China BIT 1992, Article 4(2).

offer much clarity or practicality. In this regard, the China–ASEAN Treaty's wording that "at the time when expropriation was publicly announced or when expropriation occurred, whichever is earlier"[183] may be a useful reference. The cut-off point for the valuation purpose is clearer as the caveat of "whichever is earlier" allows the choice of an earlier time between the occurrence of expropriation and the announcement of expropriation. The purpose of having such a caveat, as the China–ASEAN Treaty provides, is that "the fair market value shall not reflect any change in market value occurring because the expropriation had become publicly known earlier."[184] This seems to avoid potential upward or downward effects on the value of the expropriated property. The standard of compensation is therefore equated with the genuine value of the property affected,[185] thereby ensuring just compensation.

The general practice is that the accrual of interest should begin at the time when the expropriation occurs and end on the date when the payment is made. The full compensation principle led the tribunal to determine the interest due from the date of expropriation to the actual payment of compensation.[186] As the expropriation took place during the period in which the preliminary measures were taken by SUNAT, the tribunal determined to use the date of adoption of the measures as *dies a quo*, meaning that interest began to accrue on January 28, 2005. This ruling was consistent with the case law principle that the date of expropriation is the time when the first actual interference by the host government occurs.[187] The *dies ad quem* in this case is the time the actual payment occurs.[188]

5.3.4 *Interest*

Old-generation Chinese BITs such as the Peru–China BIT usually do not provide for interest to be payable on compensation,[189] which is consistent with the earlier investment treaty practice of not being specific on the payment of interest.[190] Starting from the late 1990s, interest provision appears in some Chinese BITs with a reference to the "normal,"[191] "commercial,"[192] "appropriate,"[193] "fair and just,"[194] "usual bank"[195] or "LIBOR [London Inter-Bank Offered Rate]"[196] rate of interest. More recent Chinese BITs attempts to standardize the practice by incorporating more specific terms.

As one example, the interest provision in the China–ASEAN Treaty reads as follows: "The compensation shall be settled and paid without unreasonable delay. In the event of delay, the compensation shall include interest at the prevailing commercial interest rate from the date

183 China–ASEAN Treaty 2009, Article 8(2).
184 China–ASEAN Treaty 2009, Article 8(2).
185 *CME Czech Republic B.V. v. The Czech Republic*, UNCITRAL Final Award and Separate Opinion March 14, 2003, paras. 490–495.
186 Award, para. 286.
187 Vance R. Koven, "Expropriation and the 'Jurisprudence' of OPIC" (1981) 22 *Harvard International Law Journal* 269, 277, 311–320.
188 Award, para. 291.
189 Bulgaria–China BIT 1989, Algeria–China BIT 1996, Syria–China BIT 1996.
190 Rudolf Dolzer and Margrete Stevens, *Bilateral Investment Treaties* (Martinus Nijhoff 1995) 112–114.
191 Chile–China BIT 1994, Iceland–China BIT 1994, UK–China BIT 1986.
192 Jordan–China BIT 2001, New Zealand–China FTA 2008.
193 Denmark–China BIT 1985, Greece–China BIT 1992.
194 India–China BIT 2006.
195 Lebanon–China BIT 1996.
196 Oman–China BIT 1995, Russia–China BIT 2006.

of expropriation until the date of payment."[197] The first sentence in the cited paragraph is not that meaningful as the term "delay" is not well defined. The sentence immediately following seems to suggest that it constitutes a delay when compensation is not made at the date of expropriation. This interpretation, however, does not seem sensible as the investor and the state may be in dispute on the existence of expropriation. The Iceland–China BIT 1994 prescribes the exact meaning of a delay in payment by providing that "the delay starts by the submission of a relevant application and must not exceed six months."[198] It seems that waiting until a tribunal finds expropriation would incentivize states' refusal to admit expropriation and delay payment without the state needing to pay interest. The Iceland–China BIT seems to largely address this problem.

The phrase "prevailing commercial rate" also appears in other Chinese BITs such as the Germany–China BIT 2003 and the Netherlands–China BIT 2001. The reference to the "prevailing commercial rate" of interest is practically specific so as to avoid the interest rate being determined by the tribunal in an overly subjective manner due to lack of restriction. The China–ASEAN Treaty continues to follow this general practice by specifying that the interest is payable between the "date of expropriation" and the "date of payment." This may result in a fairer scenario whereby the arbitral tribunal awards interest from the date of the arbitral award, which may be earlier than the date of payment. Neither the Peru–China BIT nor the Peru–China FTA makes reference to any specific interest rate. Both, however, require compensation to "be paid without unreasonable delay." This ambiguity provides a prospective tribunal with some flexibility.

Tza asked for an 11 percent interest rate to be used to calculate the interest for the period from the issuance of the award to the actual payment of compensation due. This 11 percent rate was actually the interest rate paid by TSG for the foreign credit line, and thus incorporated a risk factor that the tribunal determined was no longer applicable post-expropriation.[199] Peru, however, tried to use the US Treasury Bonds rate, which was lower.

The tribunal rejected Tza's requested interest rate of 11 percent. Instead, it sided with Peru that the appropriate interest rate should approximate the rate of return had the damages awarded been reinvested for a favorable return. The tribunal seemed to prefer a more balanced approach to determining a suitable interest rate. In its opinion, the most appropriate interest to be paid to Tza was the same amount as could have been earned if the compensatory amount had been favorably reinvested.[200] Therefore, the tribunal used a more conservative interest rate such as that would result from a low-risk financial investment. The other justification for using this interest rate was that the US Treasury Bonds rate is more stable and less sensitive to market changes such as unexpected changes in inflation.[201] In addition, the US Treasury Bonds rate has a lower liquidity premium rate and is the rate best suited to the period covered by this case.[202]

Interest gets compounded semiannually in line with well-established practice, which considers it the most desirable method for recognizing the realities of trade and fully compensating the investor. Compounding also somewhat counteracts the risk assumed by the investor against the accrual arising from the award and ideally is an incentive for its timely

197 China–ASEAN Treaty 2009, Article 8(3).
198 Iceland–China BIT 1994, Article 4.
199 Award, para. 287.
200 Award, para. 289.
201 Award, para. 288.
202 Award, para. 288.

payment.[203] The final ruling on this point was that the interest rate on damages would be tied to the average monthly rate on ten-year US Treasury bonds. At the date of the award, the interest awarded was USD 227,201.30.[204]

5.3.5 *Exchange Rate*

Compensation should be made in a form that is usable by the investor. The currency of payment must be freely usable or convertible into a freely usable currency.[205] The China–ASEAN Treaty, for instance, states that "the compensation, including any accrued interest, shall be payable either in the currency in which the investment was originally made or, if requested by the investor, in a freely usable currency." Thus, if the "currency in which the investment was originally made" is not satisfactory to the investor, perhaps because it is not freely convertible, the China–ASEAN Treaty provides leeway for the investor to choose a freely usable currency, defined by the China–ASEAN Treaty as "any currency designated as such by the IMF under its Articles of Agreement and any amendments thereto."[206] Under this standard, "freely usable currency" is limited to the US dollar, the euro, the pound sterling and the Japanese yen.[207] As such, the China–ASEAN Treaty makes compensation effective. Nevertheless, it has to be pointed out that this clause in the China–ASEAN Treaty is not the most satisfactory arrangement for the investor. Some Chinese BITs confirm that "compensation will be convertible and realizable and freely transferable without delay,"[208] which effectively gives investors more protection from the risk of currency depreciation.

Some Chinese BITs adopted formulae such as the "average of the daily exchange rates,"[209] the "official exchange rate" on the day of transfer,[210] or the "exchange rate applicable for the payment of the compensation … on the date used to determine the value of the investment,"[211] all of which are helpful in avoiding a potential dispute. Neither the Peru–China BIT nor the Peru–China FTA specifies a way to determine the exchange rate between the local currency and the freely usable currency. However, both require compensation to "be convertible and freely transferrable."[212] Tza made his monetary claim in Peruvian nuevos soles but the tribunal granted damages in US dollars. Likely, the tribunal took into consideration the required elements of convertibility and free transferability.

5.3.6 *Arbitration Costs*

The tribunal was aware of the different perspectives of certain arbitral tribunals with respect to awards on costs, including the principle that the losing party pays arbitration costs[213] and

203 Award, para. 291.
204 Award, paras. 286–292.
205 World Bank Guidelines, Article IV.7.
206 China–ASEAN Treaty 2009, Article 1(1)(b).
207 The Article of Agreement of the International Monetary Fund, Article XXX(f).
208 Israel–China BIT 1995, Article 4(1); Laos–China BIT 1993, Article 4(2); Mongolia–China BIT 1991, Article 4(2); Spain–China BIT 2005.
209 Australia–China BIT 1988.
210 Korea–China BIT 2005.
211 Greece–China BIT 1992, Article 4(2).
212 Peru–China BIT 1994, Article 4(2); Peru–China FTA 2009, Article 133(2).
213 *Methanex* and *EDF*.

the more generally accepted public international law principle that costs should be borne equally by the parties, absent egregious conduct by one of the parties in arbitration.[214] The tribunal applied this generally accepted principle in this case by splitting arbitration costs equally between the parties.[215]

A simple comparison of key elements in the two compensation provisions of the Peru–China BIT and the Peru–China FTA and the tribunal's interpretations is set out in Table 5.3.

TABLE 5.3 *"Compensation" under the Peru–China BIT, the Peru–China FTA and the award*

	Peru–China BIT	Peru–China FTA	Award
Value of the expropriated investment	"value of the expropriated investment"	"fair market value of the expropriated investment"	"adjusted book value," "market value"
Interest	No mention		US Treasury Bond rates, "should approximate the rate of return had the damages awarded been re-invested for a favourable return"
Adequate, effective and prompt	No mention[216]		No mention
Without delay, realizable and transferrable	"without unreadable delay," "convertible" and "freely transferrable"		Awarding compensation in US dollars even though Tza made his monetary claim in Peruvian nuevos soles
Evaluation of value	No mention		"To place Tza in the same position as if there were no expropriation"
Date of calculation	"at the time when the expropriation is proclaimed"	"immediately before the expropriation took place"	Date of expropriation
Exchange rate	"the prevailing exchange rate"[217]	"the prevailing market rate of exchange"[218]	No mention
Moral damages	No mention		Not granted
Arbitration costs	No mention		Equal splitting

*Compiled by the author.

214 *Waste Management II*.

215 Award, paras. 296–301.

216 It appears that China indirectly practiced the customary international law of the Hull formula after it adopted the reform and opening door policy in 1978. For instance, China signed a lump sum agreement with the USA to pay the USD 80.5 million for 41 percent of the US assets that were nationalized by the Chinese government after the founding of the PRC in 1949. China reached similar agreements with Canada in 1981 and with the UK in 1987 for similar purposes. Richard B. Lillich and Burns H. Weston, "Lump Sum Agreements: Their Contribution to the Law of International Claims" (1988) 82 *American Journal of International Law* 69, 78.

217 Peru–China BIT 1994, Article 6(2).

218 Peru–China FTA 2009, Article 135(2).

5.4 RATIONALIZING CHINA'S EVOLVING STANCE IN LOCAL AND GLOBAL CONTEXTS: WHERE ARE WE AND WHERE ARE WE GOING?

Both the Peru–China FTA and the award offer more jurisprudential value to understanding China's BIT practice and guiding prospective tribunals in assessing the existence of expropriation. A review of the expropriation clauses in the Peru–China BIT and the Peru–China FTA indicates that China has made liberalizing progress in its BIT practice. In terms of the BIT rules and compensation standards, China's BITs are already closer to Western practice. Recent China BITs and FTAs have afforded "full protection and security" to investments, and otherwise are remarkably compatible with the American approach. There are both internal and external reasons for recent dynamic changes.

China's internal stress on the rule of law[219] has led to its continuous expansion of the limited protection to investors[220] and to liberalization of previously restrictive rules on expropriation. China's progressive liberalization approach is deeply rooted in its social, economic and geopolitical contexts. China's Property Rights Law has been in a changing process in the past decade. In 2004, China amended its constitution to enshrine private property rights. But the symbolic constitutional amendment did not bring any substantial changes until the passing of the Property Rights Law in 2007. The Property Rights Law is a landmark law in the sense that it offers the same legal protection for individuals' property as for the state's. The passage of the Property Rights Law indicates the ruling party's determination to move away from Chinese egalitarianism and toward a market-oriented economy.

Expropriation of land for piffling or no compensation has been the main cause of thousands of protests across the country.[221] The Property Rights Law does not necessarily bring full property rights protection, which is what China's economic and democratic developments need. The Property Rights Law, however, is a necessary step in building up a more sophisticated legal system. The Property Rights Law, if fully implemented, may secure legal foundation for private entrepreneurship and enhance social stability, the lack of which may shake the legitimacy of the Chinese government's ruling. The government is in the process of amending the land expropriation law to improve the legal regime and the associated takings practices. Some regulatory reforms have indicated promising improvements in laws on compulsory land seizures. The regulations of the State Council, China's cabinet, promulgated in January 2011 and concerning the compulsory expropriation of urban properties allow government seizures of urban land rights and real estate only for truly "public interest projects," thereby eliminating the possibility of exercising unconstrained public power to serve private and for-profit projects. The regulations also require a court order before evictions can occur, which is a significant improvement that will prevent procedural abuses by local governments.[222]

Still, China's eminent domain law is imperfect compared to its Western counterparts. For example, the "public interest" prerequisite is vaguely defined. The current laws and regulations do not set detailed compensation standards to allow farmers to capture more of the value generated from converting land to non-agricultural use. The process lacks transparency and

[219] The Communist Party of China held its Fourth Plenum of the 18th Central Committee from October 20 to 23, 2014 and assigned the latest gravity to advance the rule of law and the overarching role of the Constitution in China's legal system. "Party's Leadership 'Most Fundamental Guarantee' for Rule of Law in China: Communique," http://news.xinhuanet.com/english/china/2014-10/23/c_133738127.htm (accessed December 30, 2014).

[220] Spencer S. Griffith, "US-China BIT Negotiations March On: The Road Ahead Is Challenging but Worthwhile" (2009) *China Brief* 13.

[221] Zhu Keliang and Roy Prosterman, "Land Reform Efforts in China," *China Business Review*, October 1, 2012, www.chinabusinessreview.com/land-reform-efforts-in-china/ (accessed March 22, 2021).

[222] State Council's Regulations Regarding the Expropriation and Compensation of Housing on State-Owned Land.

public participation. Nevertheless, China's changing eminent domain law allows China to take a more liberal stance in its BIT negotiations.

China is not only a major capital importer but also a significant capital exporter. China became the third largest investor in 2012 and 2013, right after the United States and Japan.[223] In terms of its FDI stock, China is one of the largest developing country investors in Africa.[224] It is the top investing country in some least developed countries such as Sudan, Nigeria, Zambia and Algeria.[225] Starting in 2001, China shifted its policy and has been steadily promoting outbound FDI in order to lessen the external surplus and secure access to natural resources in other developing countries. The Chinese Communist Party (CCP), China's ruling party, took the initiative in crafting the well-known "go global" strategy in 1998.[226] In embarking on this strategy, the State Council not only included it in the 10th Five-Year Plan for National Economy and Social Development of 2001 but also set a clear objective of promoting up to fifty globally competitive "national champions" by 2010.[227] In playing a guiding role in the promotion of overseas expansion,[228] the State Council in 2004 formulated regulations replacing the substantial approval regime with the registration regime.[229] This regulatory and policy change may adequately explain why, after 2004, China's outbound FDI saw a sharp surge,[230] as indicated in Figure 9.1 of Chapter 9.

Given China's massive foreign currency reserves and its continuous efforts to liberalize its foreign exchange controls,[231] Chinese companies desire to grow globally. Likely, this wave of outbound investment from China will continue to increase.[232] Since the global financial crisis, Chinese players have yet to slow their expanding pace. Rather, more Chinese companies are finding their way to a heightened profile in a growing number of industries.[233] It appears inevitable that Chinese companies will become a major force in FDI in the global sphere.

Naturally, China has placed more emphasis on using BITs as legal instruments for the protection of Chinese investments overseas by signing new BITs with developing countries

[223] UNCTAD, World Investment Report 2013: Global Value Chains: Investment and Trade for Development, xiii; UNCTAD, World Investment Report 2014: Investing in the SDGs: An Action Plan, p. 7.

[224] UNCTAD, World Investment Report 2013: Global Value Chains: Investment and Trade for Development, xvi.

[225] Ibid., 5.

[226] See People.com.cn, http://finance.people.com.cn/GB/8215/126457/8313172.html (accessed April 29, 2010); see also Ministry of Commerce of the P.R.C.-MOFCOM, http://njtb.mofcom.gov.cn/subject/zcq/index.shtml (in Chinese) (accessed March 22, 2021).; see also Communist Party of China's Central Committee, Improvement of the Social Economy Market, http://news.xinhuanet.com/newscenter/2003-10/21/content_1135402.htm (accessed March 22, 2021).

[227] See Usha C. V. Haley, Hearing on China's World Trade Compliance: Industrial Subsidies and the Impact on U.S. and World Markets Statement before the U.S.-China Economic and Security Review Commission on April 4, 2006, www.uscc.gov/hearings/2006hearings/written_testimonies/06_04_04wrts/06_04_04_haley.php (accessed March 22, 2021).

[228] Florencia Jubany and Daniel Poon, "Recent Chinese Engagement in Latin America and the Caribbean: A Canadian Perspective," FOCAL (March 2006), www.focal.ca/pdf/China-Latin%20America_Jubany-Poon-FOCAL_Chinese%20Engagement%20Latin%20America%20Caribbean%20Canadian%20Perspective_March%202006.pdf (accessed March 22, 2021).

[229] China's State Council, Decision on Reforming the Investment System, Parts II and III, http://news.xinhuanet.com/zhengfu/2004-07/26/content_1648074.htm (in Chinese) (accessed March 22, 2021).

[230] See Editorial, "China's Forex Reserve Overtakes the Total Amount of G7 Countries," http://news.163.com/08/0603/02/4DFRH5E00001234J.html (in Chinese) (accessed March 22, 2021).

[231] Shen Hong, "Beijing Steps In to Tame Currency," *Wall Street Journal*, October 16, 2013, C2.

[232] Daniel H. Rosen and Thilo Hanemann, "The Rise in Chinese Overseas Investment and What It Means for American Businesses," www.chinabusinessreview.com/the-rise-in-chinese-overseas-investment-and-what-it-means-for-american-businesses/ (accessed March 22, 2021).

[233] Julie Jiang and Jonathan Sinton, "Overseas Investments by Chinese National Oil Companies," Information Paper (February 2011).

and updating old BITs with developed countries. China massively signed over 100 BITs right after its adoption of the open door policy.[234] Against this background, China's stance in BIT practice was evolving from a restrictive to a balanced or even a liberal stance. Starting with the Barbados–China BIT 1998, China began to provide foreign investors with stronger and more comprehensive substantive and procedural protections, largely comparable to those of traditional capital-exporting states.[235] It is no coincidence that the change in Chinese BIT policy overlapped in time with the launch of the "go globally" strategy. China's increased confidence in providing sufficient protections to foreign investors, its increasing outbound FDI and its more sophisticated legal system well explain China's growing acceptance of modern BIT jurisprudence and related international investment law. Owing to more disputes being raised on the ground of indirect expropriation, recent BITs concluded by the USA and Canada have included more detailed provisions, and China appears to be taking on this trend in BIT jurisprudence and practice.

China's growing outbound FDI, the USA's promotion of the Trans-Pacific Partnership (TPP) without the involvement of China and the TPP's having more preference margins than the BITs[236] have affected and even reshaped China's strategy for negotiating and entering into BITs with its trading partners. The key goal of the USA's expansion of BITs, and particularly the TPP, was to entrench some protections of customary law so as to assure full protection and security, to dismantle public law regulations inimical to the market,[237] and to protect the rights of the TPP countries to regulate in the public interest.[238] Apart from its economic, political and ideological importance, the TPP was designed to help the USA reshape a newer FTA standard worldwide in the twenty-first century and a better investment environment for its trading partners.[239] After the Trump administration decided to withdraw from the TPP in January 2017, the remaining eleven TPP countries renamed it the Comprehensive and Progressive Trans-Pacific Partnership (CPTPP) in late 2018.

Without tying itself to the CPTPP or a new wave of FTA standards influenced by the CPTPP, China may not maintain its competitiveness and avoid marginalization in the global market. China's attitude toward the CPTPP may imply its geopolitical concerns. However, it would be in China's great interest to upgrade its BIT standards and expand its FTA network to offset any impacts that the CPTPP may exert upon the Asia-Pacific region. The CPTPP covers a wide range of fields and includes investment,[240] which provides China with a new tool for serving its internal structural reform and external institutional objectives. For instance, a negative list approach is being transplanted into China, in particular in Shanghai's free trade zone. China is now considering joining the CPTPP as its priority, as a strategic step to deepen its engagement with the Asia-Pacific countries in trade liberalization

234 Sornarajah, *supra* note 125, at 185.

235 Stephan W. Schill, "Tearing Down the Great Wall: The New Generation Investment Treaties of the People's Republic of China" (2007) 15 *Cardozo Journal of International & Comparative Law* 73, 73–118; Yuqing Zhang, "The Case of China" in Michael Moser (ed.), *Investor-State Arbitration – Lessons for Asia* (Juris 2008) 156.

236 It is usually the case that the bilateral trade agreements offer more preference margins than the multilateral ones. Donald Barry and Ronald Keith (eds.), *Regionalism, Multilateralism and the Politics of Global Trade* (UBC Press 1999).

237 Akira Kotera, "Regulatory Transparency" in Peter Muchlinski, Federico Ortino, and Christoph Schreuer (eds.), *The Oxford Handbook of International Investment Law* (Oxford University Press 2008) 617, 623.

238 Congyan Cai, "Trans-Pacific Partnership and the Multilateralization of International Investment Law" (2013) 6 *Journal of East Asia and International Law* 385, 400.

239 Zhongwei Liu and Jiewen Shen, "The Review of Research Frontier and Frameworks of Trans-Pacific Partnership Agreement (TPP)" (2012) 36 *Journal of Contemporary Asia-Pacific Studies* (in Chinese) 44–45.

240 See ch. 12, p. 4, www.fta.gov.sg/fta_tpfta.asp?hl=12 (accessed September 24, 2020).

and investment facilitation.[241] China's accession to the CPTPP, depending on the terms of entry, could solidify its position as a dominant economic player in Asia especially when the USA is on the CPTPP sidelines.[242]

Meanwhile, China is actively exploring the possibility of reaching a regional trade and investment pact through the framework of the Regional Comprehensive Economic Partnership (RCEP), involving the ten ASEAN member states and their FTA partners such as India, Australia, Japan, Korea and New Zealand.[243] In a larger context, China needs to reconsider and re-engineer its policies and strategies in foreign investment protection by being more active in negotiating FTAs with pro-investment terms. The wider FTA network gives China a new opportunity to participate in shaping multilateral rules and global administrative law order.[244] One strategy that China may take is to upgrade its standards of review, and one core standard is compensation for expropriation. It may be fair and safe to predict that China may be likely to move toward a more pro-investment protection stance in its further BIT/FTA/RCEP negotiations.

5.5 CONCLUSION

This chapter, with reference to the first China-BIT-related ICSID case, explores the evolvement of expropriation clauses in Chinese BITs across two generations, namely the Peru–China BIT 1994 and the Peru–China FTA 2009. The survey of Chinese BIT practice in relation to the issue of expropriation appears to demonstrate a commitment on the part of China to embracing a principled and internationally accepted standard on the subject matter. However, why, one might ask, would China ever enter into a BIT the subject matter of which would be questioned by or in a tribunal who would cast doubt on the legality of the Chinese government's approach to promulgating laws and regulations and to regulating foreign investment activities? It is the theme of this chapter that China's seemingly not static stance on the expropriation issue in the context of BIT practice is indeed reflective of its internal improvements on the rule of law and its increasing external FDI in other countries. China is in a two-way street of attunement where international norms and domestic rules are being worked to a nexus. In the arena of investment law, China's model of norm dynamics[245] includes norm internalization through the adoption of international rules being filtered into local discourse[246] and norm anti-internalization distancing the application of international rules from the domestic political discourse.[247] As China plays a larger and more active role in global cross-border transactions, it will likely be compelled to adopt a more market-oriented

[241] Lu Zhenhua, "Premier Sends 'Powerful' Signal for China to Join Asia-Pacific's Largest Trade Pact," May 29, 2020, www.caixinglobal.com/2020-05-29/premier-sends-powerful-signal-for-china-to-join-asia-pacifics-largest-trade-pact-101560855.html (accessed September 24, 2020).

[242] Gary Clyde Hufauer, Jeffrey J. Schott, and Zhiyao Lu, "China and the Trans-Pacific Partnership: In or Out?," www.piie.com/blogs/trade-and-investment-policy-watch/china-and-trans-pacific-partnership-or-out (accessed September 24, 2020).

[243] UNCTAD, World Investment Report 2014: Investing in the SDGs: An Action Plan, xix.

[244] Gus Van Harten and Martin Loughlin, "Investment Treaty Arbitration as a Species of Global Administrative Law" (2006) 17(1) *European Journal of International Law* 121–150 (claiming the emergence of global administrative law based on international investment arbitration).

[245] Martha Finnemore and Kathryn Sikkink, "International Norm Dynamics and Political Change" (1998) 52 *International Organization* 887.

[246] Harold Hongju Koh, "Internationalization through Socialization" (2005) 54 *Duke Law Journal* 975.

[247] Judith Kelley, "Assessing the Complex Evolution of Norms: The Rise of International Election Monitoring" (2008) 62 *International Organization* 221.

approach and create a level playing field consistent with international standards so as to remain competitive in the global market, especially in the face of the mounting pressure from the USA (now the trade war and previously the TPP negotiations). Meanwhile, in the face of external pressures or lawfare inspiration, China is in a process of social learning and adaptation,[248] and its domestic policy process is more entrepreneurial in combining political pluralization with fragmented authoritarianism.[249]

[248] Nigel Barber, *Evolution in the Here and Now: How Adaptation and Social Learning Explain Humanity* (Prometheus Books 2020) (arguing that social learning and adaptation explain the idiosyncrasies of human behavior in a more complete and nuanced way).

[249] Andrew Mertha, "'Fragmented Authoritarianism 2.0': Political Pluralization in the Chinese Policy Process" (2009) 200 *China Quarterly* 995.

6

How Are Chinese BITs Interpreted? Jurisprudential Review of Treaty Interpretative Tools in Chinese BIT-based Arbitration Cases

There is an apparent so-called "China disequilibrium" in the international investment arbitration arena.[1] While China is the second largest signatory state, having signed 139 BITs[2] and 21 treaties with investment provisions (TIPs) such as FTAs that include investment chapters, and has robust outbound investment flows, the number of ISA cases involving China or Chinese BITs, as listed in Table 6.1, is remarkably low no matter whether as a respondent state or as an investor claimant.

There are two opposite schools of thought explaining this "China disequilibrium." One is to argue that the Chinese government has already been offering sufficient investment protection to foreign investors.[3] As a result, there are few cases involving the Chinese government as a respondent. This explanation, however, could not justify the very low number of ISA cases in which Chinese investors are claimants especially in the context that China has become the second capital-exporting state while Chinese outbound investment often encounters legal, political and economic difficulties in host states. The other school of thought attributes the low utility rate of Chinese BITs to the restrictive nature of the BIT terms such terms as investor, investment, dispute and fork-in-the-road, among others.[4] The argument is based on the fact that the early-generation Chinese BITs often incorporated narrowly defined terms of investor, investment and dispute, which basically disallow foreign investors from easily initiating ISA against the Chinese government even if the Chinese government or its local governments did harm foreign investors' interests. An interconnected argument on this side is China's preference for settling disputes informally

[1] Shen Wei, "The Good, The Bad, or The Ugly? A Critique of the Decision on Jurisdiction and Competence in Tza Yap Shum v. The Republic of Peru" (2011) 10(1) *Chinese Journal of International Law* 55, 55.

[2] According to UNCTAD, China signed 128 BITs and 109 BITs are effective. Taking into other international investment treaties (IIAs) such as FTAs which incorporate a chapter on foreign investment protection, China signed 150 IIAs in total and 128 IIAs are effective. UNCTAD, Investment Policy Hub, http://investmentpolicyhub.unctad.org/IIAA (accessed September 18, 2020).

[3] Yuqing Zhang, "The Case of China" in Michael Moser (ed.), *Investor-State Arbitration – Lessons for Asia* (Juris 2008) 159.

[4] Stephan W. Schill, "Tearing Down the Great Wall: The New Generation Investment Treaties of the People's Republic of China" (2007) 15(1) *Cardozo Journal of International and Comparative Law* 73–118.

TABLE 6.1 *Investment arbitration cases involving Chinese BITs*[5]

Case no.	Claimant	Respondent	BIT
Respondent: China			
ARB/20/34	Goh Chin Soon	China	China–Singapore BIT 1985
ARB/20/22	Macro Trading Co., Ltd.	China	China–Japan BIT 1988
UNCITRAL	AsiaPhos Limited	China	China–Singapore BIT 1985
ARB/17/19	Hela Schwarz GmbH	China	China–Germany BIT 2003
ARB/14/25	Ansung Housing Co., Ltd.	China	China–Korea BIT 2007
ARB/11/15	Ekran Berhad	China	China–Israel BIT 1995, China–Malaysia BIT 1988
PCA 2019-39	Jason Yu Song	China	China–UK BIT 1985
Claimant(s) nationality(ies): China			
CONC/20/1	Barrick (Niugini) Limited[6]	Independent State of Papua New Guinea	Contract, ICSID Convention, ICSID Conciliation Rules
ADHOC/17/1	Sanum Investments Limited	Laos	China–Laos BIT 1993
ARB/15/41	Standard Chartered Bank (Hong Kong) Limited	Tanzania	Contract
ARB/14/30	Beijing Urban Construction Group Co. Ltd.	Yamen	China–Yamen BIT 1998
ARB/12/29	Ping An Life Insurance Company of China, Limited and Ping An Insurance (Group) Company of China, Limited	Belgium	China–Belgium BIT 2005
ARB/10/20	Standard Chartered Bank (Hong Kong) Limited	Tanzania Electric Supply Company Limited	Contract
ARB/07/6	Tza Yap Shum	Peru	China–Peru BIT 1994

through diplomatic consultations[7] and foreign investors' possibility of gaining more benefits through negotiations.[8] While the accuracy of these two opposite schools of thought is beyond the scope of this chapter, it does bring out a closely interconnected question: How can foreign investors better protect themselves under the restrictive Chinese BIT regime? It

[5] Based on data available at https://icsid.worldbank.org/en (accessed September 18, 2020).

[6] Barrick (Niugini) Limited is a 50%–50% joint venture between Barrick Gold Corporation, a local entity of the Independent State of Papua New Guinea (ISPNG), and Zijin Mining Group Co., Ltd. The joint venture has 95 percent equity in Porgera, a gold mine in ISPNG. This is the first mediation case filed with the ICSID in 2020, and the 13th mediation case in ICSID history.

[7] Axel Berger, "China's New Bilateral Investment Treaty Programme: Substance, Rational and Implications for International Investment Law Making" [*sic*] (2008), Retrieved from www.die-gdi.de/uploads/media/Berger_ChineseBITs.pdf (accessed March 9, 2021); Qingjiang Kong, "Bilateral Investment Treaties: The Chinese Approach and Practice" in K. Sik, Miyoshi Masahiro, M. Pinto and S. Subedi (eds.), *Asian Yearbook of International Law 1998/1999* (Martinus Nijhoff 2003); Wenhua Shan and Jinyuan Su (eds.), *China and International Investment Law: Twenty Years of ICSID Membership* (Brill Nijhoff 2015).

[8] Leon Trackman, "Geopolitics, China and Investor–State Arbitration" in Lisa Toohey, Colin B. Picker and Jonathan Greenacre (eds.), *China in the International Economic Order: New Directions and Changing Paradigms* (Cambridge University Press 2015).

was then argued that the home states of foreign investors, especially those major capital-exporting states, should bargain for better substantive and procedural terms and sign new-generation BITs with the Chinese government thereby upgrading the rights protection standards and offering more favorable rights to foreign investors.[9] In his seminal article, Stephen Schill therefore made a call for tearing down the Great Wall by more rigorous negotiations between Western European countries, in the interest of their outbound investment, and the Chinese government for a more liberal and investor-oriented BIT.[10]

Almost a decade thereafter, there have been fewer than a dozen Chinese BITs-related ISA cases, a sharp contrast to the increasingly growing number of ISA cases worldwide. Figure 6.1 indicates this sharp contrast. Surprisingly, most of these Chinese BITs were old-generation BITs with restrictive terms of investor, investment, dispute and fork-in-the road. The general consensus is that capital-exporting states such as Western European countries may need to tear down the Great Wall through treaty negotiations with China by bargaining for more preferential treatments in favor of their investors. Nevertheless, as far as foreign investors or home states are concerned, a more effective way, as this chapter indicates, is to rely on sophisticated treaty interpretative methodologies adopted by the investor–state arbitral tribunals to achieve an expansive scope of jurisdiction for investor rights protection. The purpose of this chapter therefore is to focus on the treaty interpretative methodologies applied by various tribunals in these Chinese BIT-related cases. There are at least two points of significance related to the key theme of this chapter.

First, it is important to see how vaguely worded terms in Chinese BITs have been interpreted and what treaty interpretative devices have been deployed by tribunals. This is relevant to the efficacy and sustainability of investor rights protection when foreign investors have to rely upon these treaty terms as well as their persuasive (though non-binding) authority (through treaty interpretation) to initiate arbitration claims. The interpretative approaches, one essential function in investment law-making, employed by tribunals have a constraining effect not only on future tribunals in resolving gaps and ambiguities in existing BITs but also on China as well as its counterparties in formulating future treaties through internalization of the pros and cons of different treaty interpretations.

Second, inconsistency and incoherence have been argued to be the major defects of the current BIT regime and ISA system[11] notwithstanding the counterargument that current international investment law represents a coherent and consistent body of law.[12] Given the severity of these defects, the EU, the USA, Australia and other states have put forward various proposals calling for a larger and deeper scale of reforms so that the efficiency and legitimacy of the ISA system can be improved or restored.[13] For the time being, China is silent on these proposals and has not formed its official policy toward these various reformative movements.[14]

9 Ibid.

10 Ibid.

11 Giovanni Zarra, "The Issue of Incoherence in Investment Arbitration: Is There Need for a Systemic Reform?" (2018) 17(2) *Chinese Journal of International Law* 127–185.

12 Moshe Hirsch, "International Tribunals as Agents of Harmonization" in Zdenek Drabek and Petros C. Mavroidis (eds.), *Regulations of Foreign Investment: Challenges to International Harmonization* (World Scientific 2013) 342.

13 The EU switched from the traditional mode to an Investment Court System (ICS) in its FTAs with Canada, Singapore and Vietnam. The ultimate goal of the EU is to establish a Multilateral Investment Court. The USA insists on taking an incrementalist approach and favors retaining the existing system with modest reforms. Australia does not trust the ISDS at all. See UNCITRAL Working Group III Investor-State Dispute Settlement Reform documents.

14 Anthea Roberts, "The Shifting Landscape of Investor-State Arbitration: Loyalists, Reformists, Revolutionaries and Undecideds," June 15, 2017, www.ejiltalk.org/the-shifting-landscape-of-investor-state-arbitration-loyalists-reformists-revolutionaries-and-undecideds/ (accessed March 9, 2021).

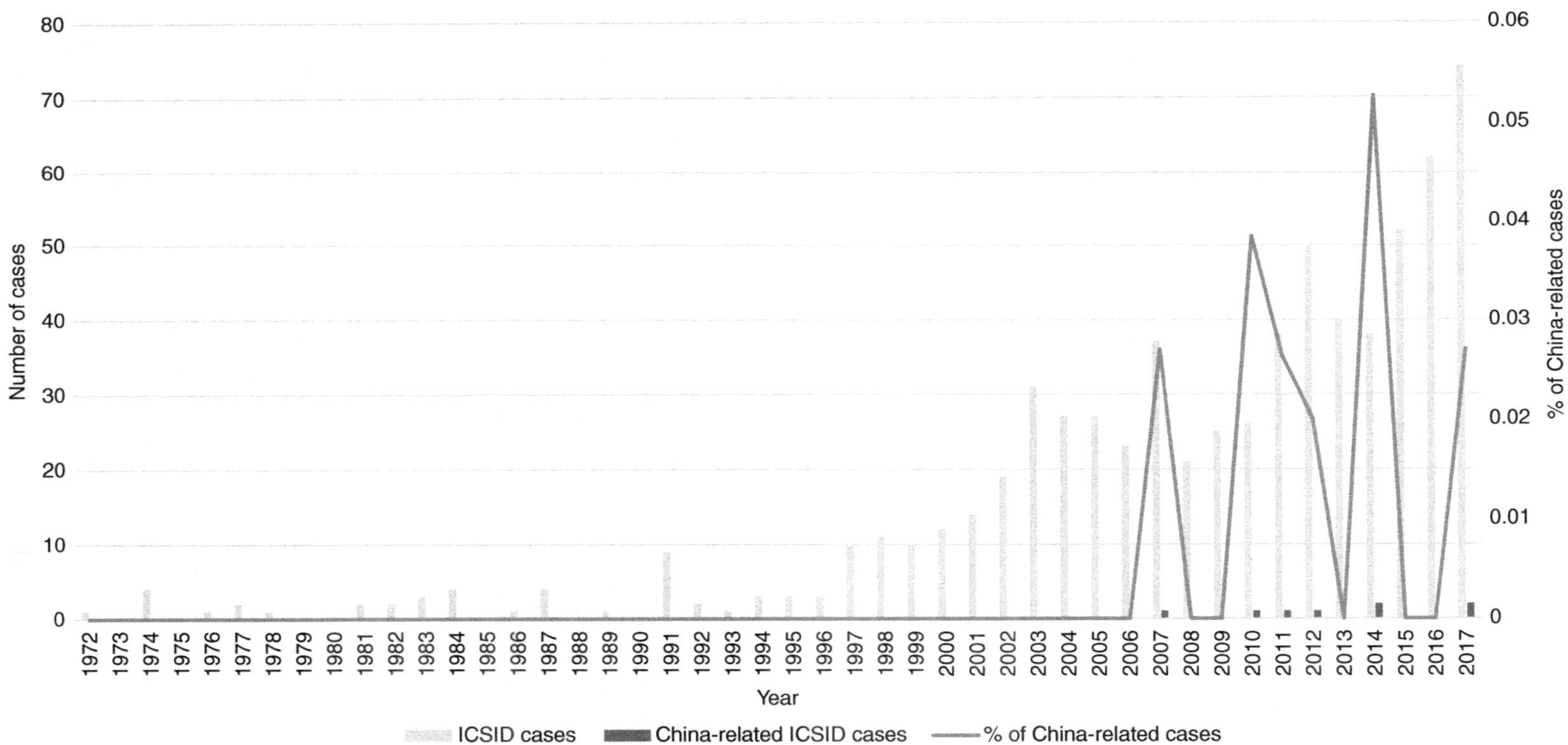

FIGURE 6.1 ICSID cases generally and China-related ICSID cases

Part of China's policy is supposed to be built on the fact of whether China has suffered from any inconsistency and incoherence of the current BIT regime and ISA system or any unbearable imbalance of power between itself as a treaty party (that creates the law) and tribunals (that apply the law in relevant cases).

Against these backdrops, a review of treaty interpretative approaches and their consistency and coherence is of importance not only to investment protection but also to the continuity, coherence and legitimacy of the ISA system. Treaty interpretation is the major but controversial adjudicative device that tribunals have relied on to enhance their legitimacy and authoritativeness. The way that tribunals interpret Chinese BITs is supposed to be aligned with the objective that China, being a treaty party, tries to achieve through its BITs. Otherwise, there is a gap between the rule-maker and the rule-appliers; the gap of interpretative imbalance needs to be filled by instruments such as treaty terms with explicitly defined limits, extent and specificity that leave little space to tribunals for expansive interpretation and choices of analogies borrowing concepts, doctrines and principles from other legal fields for greater certainty.[15]

The rest of this chapter proceeds as follows. Section 6.1 briefly lists major Chinese BIT cases. A review of the treaty interpretative tools outlined in the Vienna Convention on the Law of Treaties (VCLT) and the use of these interpretative tools is contained in Section 6.2. The usual jurisdictional objections are raised on the issues of "investor," "investment," "dispute," "fork-in-the-road" provision, limitation period and MFN treatment of procedural rights, which often appear in Chinese BIT cases.[16] These issues will be discussed in Sections 6.3 to 6.8 in the context of China-related BIT cases with a focus on treaty interpretative devices applied by tribunals. As far as China is concerned, a unique question in investment arbitration jurisprudence is the application of Chinese BITs to investors from Hong Kong or Macau. To date, two cases have touched on this territorial issue and Section 6.3 explores the uncertainty surrounding it. The conclusion follows in Section 6.9 summarizing the application of key treaty interpretative approaches deployed by various tribunals in Chinese BIT cases. The conclusion we may draw from this jurisprudential review of treaty interpretation approaches, like others observed elsewhere, conforms to the general view that the tribunals are likely to lean toward expansive treaty interpretation approaches with a preset purpose of expanding their jurisdictional scope in order to move arbitration cases ahead especially at the jurisdictional stage[17] where the tribunals need to confirm their jurisdiction first.

6.1 OVERVIEW OF CHINESE BIT CASES

Investor–state dispute settlement (ISDS) is a common feature in the 129 BITs concluded by China. According to current records, Chinese companies are claimants in four cases before

15 See generally Valentina Vadi, *Analogies in International Investment Law and Arbitration* (Cambridge University Press 2016).

16 Some uncommon issues did appear in Chinese BIT cases. For instance, the case of Ping An was about the black hole or a gap created by two successive BITs which deprived valid claims of a jurisdictional basis. Sebastian Green Martinez, "Case Comment: Ping An Life Insurance Company of China, Limited and Ping An Insurance (Group) Company of China, Limited v. Kingdom of Belgium – A Jurisdictional Black Hole between Two BITs?" (2015) *Transnational Dispute Management*. As the applicability and potential effects of the intertemporal rule of international law was a unique legal issue in the Ping An case, this article does not specifically analyze this issue and the Ping An case.

17 Susan D. Franck, "Development and Outcomes of Investment Treaty Arbitration" (2009) 50(2) *Harvard International Law Journal* 435–489.

the ICSID: *Beijing Urban Construction Group Co., Ltd.* v. *Republic of Yemen*; *Ping An Life Insurance Company of China, Limited and Ping An Insurance (Group) Company of China, Limited* v. *Kingdom of Belgium*; *Standard Chartered Bank (Hong Kong) Limited* v. *Tanzania Electric Supply Company Limited*; and *Tza Yap Shum* v. *Republic of Peru*. China is the respondent in only three cases, that is, *Ansung Housing Co., Ltd.* v. *China*; *Ekran Berhad* v. *People's Republic of China*; and *Hela Schwarz GmbH* v. *China* (which is still pending).[18]

Chinese investors have been more proactive in outbound investment while taking advantage of China's extensive network of investment treaties in protecting their investment in the host states. The claims raised by Chinese investors are a tangible reminder of the fact that Chinese investors have become a significant source of foreign direct investment in the world. This economic reality not only explains why China has entered into a large number of BITs in the past several decades but also rationalizes China's switching position in optimizing its BITs in its interest.

The first ICSID arbitration under a China BIT was *Tza Yap Shum* v. *Republic of Peru*,[19] which concerned Tza Yap Shum, a Hong Kong resident and PRC national, and his dispute arising out of taxes imposed by the Peruvian authorities on a fish flour manufacturing and export company owned by Tza. The award on merits supported Tza's claim and granted Tza compensation in the amount of USD 786,000 in July 2011. A hearing on Peru's application for annulment of the award was held in March 2014 and the Committee's decision was not to reverse the award on merits.

The second ICSID arbitration under a China BIT was *Ping An Life Insurance Company of China* v. *Kingdom of Belgium*.[20] Ping An, a major Chinese insurance and financial services company, sought compensation in relation to a USD 2.3 billion write-off on its investment in Fortis, a Belgian–Dutch financial institution that was bailed out by Belgium in 2008. The tribunal rejected Ping An's claim due to a lack of jurisdiction.

China Heilongjiang International Economic & Technical Cooperative Corp., Beijing Shougang Mining Investment Company Ltd., Qinhuangdaoshi Qinlong International Industrial Co. Ltd. v. *Mongolia* is also an international investment arbitration case in which Chinese investors brought investment claims into ad hoc proceedings administered by the Permanent Court of Arbitration (PCA). The dispute concerned the Mongolian government's cancellation of licenses held by PRC investors in the Tumurtei iron ore mine in 2012. This claim was also rejected by the tribunal due to lack of jurisdiction; the PCA tribunal declined to exercise jurisdiction over the investors' claims that Mongolia had expropriated their investments without compensation in violation of the China–Mongolia BIT 1991. The claimants later filed a petition to the US District Court Southern District of New York in order to vacate the arbitral award.

In the most recent case, *Sanum Investments Limited* v. *Lao People's Democratic Republic*,[21] an ad hoc UNCITRAL tribunal held that it had jurisdiction to hear claims by a Macau entity under the China–Laos BIT 1993. The award was set aside by the High Court in Singapore but was then reversed by the Appellate Court of Singapore.

Although the PRC is a signatory to 129 BITs and more than a dozen FTAs incorporating investment chapters, compared to those cases in which Chinese investors brought claims against host state governments, international investment arbitration cases brought by foreign

18 See Table 6.2.

19 *Tza Yap Shum* v. *Republic of Peru*, ICSID Case No. ARB/07/6.

20 *Ping An Life Insurance Company of China* v. *Kingdom of Belgium*, ICSID Case No. ARB/12/29.

21 *Sanum Investments Limited* v. *Lao People's Democratic Republic*, PCA Case No. 2013–13.

investors against the Chinese government are still rare. China was the respondent in only three BIT arbitration cases under the ICSID Convention.

The first publicly known investment claim against China was brought by a Malaysian construction and development company in May 2011. In the case of *Ekran Berhad* v. *People's Republic of China*, the dispute concerned the revocation of Ekran Berhad's Chinese subsidiary's 70-year lease of 900 hectares of land in China's Hainan province.[22] The arbitration was suspended by agreement a month after being registered and discontinued on unknown terms.

In the case of *Ansung Housing Co., Ltd.* v. *People's Republic of China*, Ansung, a South Korean property developer, became the second ever investor to request ICSID arbitration against China.[23] The case was about a development project for a golf country club and condominiums in Sheyang County, Jiangsu Province. Ansung made investments in late 2006. However, due to the various arbitrary and illegal actions and omissions of the Sheyang County government, Ansung has been deprived of the use and enjoyment of its investment as its investment plan has been impeded. As a result, in October 2011, Ansung was forced to dispose of its entire investment to a Chinese purchaser at a price significantly lower than the amount Ansung had invested. Ansung suffered losses of more than renminbi 100 million and sought an award for damages.

The third case, that is, *Hela Schwarz GmbH* v. *China*, is discussed in Chapter 7.

6.2 TREATY INTERPRETATION APPROACHES: AN OVERVIEW

There has been an improvement in the frequency and systematic use of the VCLT[24] in treaty interpretation by investor–state arbitration tribunals (ISATs),[25] the majority of which primarily rely on Article 31(1) of the VCLT.[26] The four main criteria contained in Article 31(1) of the VCLT are good faith, ordinary meaning, context, and object and purpose.[27] Studies of investor-state arbitral tribunal (ISAT) awards reveal how ISATs refer to certain norms and terms from the VCLT to support their reasoning and conclusions in a systematic manner.[28]

The starting point of interpretation is to establish the ordinary meaning of an investment treaty provision,[29] since the signed text is presumed to be the written record and authentic

22 *Ekran Berhad* v. *People's Republic of China*, ICSID Case No. ARB/11/15.

23 *Ansung Housing Co., Ltd.* v. *People's Republic of China*, ICSID Case No. ARB/14/25.

24 VCLT, May 23, 1969, 1155 UNTS 331; (1969) 8 ILM 679.

25 Ole Kristian Fauchald, "The Legal Reasoning of ICSID Tribunals—An Empirical Analysis" (2008) 19(2) *European Journal of International Law* 301, para. 314.

26 J. Romesh Weeramenatry, *Treaty Interpretation in Investment Arbitration* (Oxford University Press 2012), para. 3.07.

27 YILC (1966-II), at 221, para. 12. This section of the ILC's commentary is quoted with approval in *Methanex* v. *US*, UNCITRAL, Partial Award, para. 98.

28 Thomas W. Wälde, "Interpreting Investment Treaties: Experiences and Examples" in Christina Binder, Ursula Kriebaum, August Reinisch and Stephan Wittich (eds.), *International Investment Law for the 21st Century: Essays in Honour of Christoph Schreuer* (Oxford University Press 2009), p. 724, para. 746.

29 *Wintershall Aktiengesellschaft* v. *Argentine Republic*, ICSID Case No. ARB/04/14, paras. 79–80; *Czech Republic* v. *European Media Ventures SA* [2007] EWHC 2851 (Comm), para. 16. See also Elihu Lauterpacht and Daniel Bethlehem, "The Scope and Content of the Principle of Non-refoulement: Opinion" in Erika Feller, Volker Türk and Frances Nicholson (eds.), *Refugee Protection in International Law: UNHCR's Global Consultations on International Protection* (Cambridge University Press 2003), p. 104; Ian Robertson Sinclair, *The Vienna Convention on the Law of Treaties* (Manchester University Press 1984), para. 115; Andrew Newcombe and Lluis Paradell, *Law and Practice of Investment Treaties* (Kluwer Law International 2009), p. 111, para. 2.28.

expression of the common consent of the parties.[30] To accomplish this, ISATs frequently refer to the dictionary to search out the ordinary meaning of legal terms.[31]

More often, an inquiry into the ordinary meaning of a treaty term may not yield conclusive results,[32] either because of the generality and vagueness of the term used in nature,[33] or because there is more than one "ordinary meaning" attached to the term.[34] In such cases, the context or the object and purpose criterion, though subsidiary to the ordinary meaning criterion,[35] may have a decisive impact on an interpretation.[36]

The contextual criterion assists the concerned tribunal in qualifying the meaning of terms in a treaty to prevent a random literal interpretation or selecting an ordinary meaning where more than one such meaning exists.[37] It is common practice for ISATs to conflate the criteria of ordinary meaning and context into one interpretative step in search of the "ordinary contextual meaning" of a treaty term.[38]

Reliance on the object and purpose of the treaty arises where the asserted interpretation is incompatible with the object and purpose of the treaty or its provisions,[39] or justifies a broader or more expansive rather than restrictive interpretation of the tribunal's jurisdiction.[40] The

[30] *Salini Costruttori S.p.A. and Italstrade S.p.A.* v. *The Hashemite Kingdom of Jordan*, ICSID Case No. ARB/02/13, Decision on Jurisdiction, para. 79; *Methanex Corporation* v. *US*, UNCITRAL, Final Award, Part IV, ch. B, para. 37, Part II, ch. B, para. 5, and Part IV, ch. B, para 35; citing *Yearbook of the International Law Commission*, 1966, Vol. II, p. 223, para. 18; *Wintershall* v. *Argentine Republic*, ICSID Case No. ARB/04/14, Award, para. 78, 86–88; *Czech Republic* v. *European Media Ventures* SA [2007] EWHC 2851 (Comm) (Eng. High Crt), para. 16. See also John P. Gaffney and James L. Loftis, "The 'Effective Ordinary Meaning' of BITs and the Jurisdiction of Treaty-Based Tribunals to Hear Contract Claims" (2007) 8(1) *Journal of World Investment & Trade* 5, para. 20; Max Huber (1952) 45 *Annuaire de l'Institut du Droit international* 199.

[31] *Alasdair Ross Anderson et al* v. *Republic of Costa Rica*, ICSID Case No. ARB(AF)/07/3, paras. 48 and 57 (Oxford English Dictionary, Webster's Deluxe Unabridged Dictionary (2nd edition), and Webster's Third New International Dictionary); American Manufacturing, Arbitrator Golsong's separate opinion, at 40, para. 12; *Marvin Roy Feldman Karpa* v. *United Mexican States*, ICSID Case No. ARB(AF)/99/1, Award, para. 96; *Methanex Corporation* v. *US*, UNCITRAL, Partial Award, paras. 135–136; *MTD Equity Sdn. Bhd and MTD Chile S.A.* v. *Republic of Chile*, ICSID Case No. ARB/01/7, para. 113; *Ronald S. Lauder* v. *The Czech Republic*, UNCITRAL, para. 221.

[32] For example, in interpreting the words "fair and equitable treatment" in a BIT, the tribunal in *Saluka* v. *Czech* observed that the ordinary meaning can only be defined by terms of equal vagueness, referring to the international approaches of previous tribunals.

[33] For example, "fair and equitable treatment," "full protection and security" and "expropriation and measures tantamount to expropriation," which are rarely defined in the treaty text and which reasonable persons may interpret differently. Jeswald W. Salacuse, *The Law of Investment Treaties* (Oxford University Press 2010) 139.

[34] Weeramenatry, *supra* note 26, para. 3.36.

[35] Fauchald, *supra note* 25, para. 314.

[36] *Asian Agricultural Products Ltd.* v. *Republic of Sri Lanka*, ICSID Case No. ARB/87/3, Final Award, para. 51; *Ceskoslovenska Obchodni Banka, A.S.* v. *The Slovak Republic*, ICSID Case No. ARB/97/4, Decision on Jurisdiction, para. 57; Salacuse, *supra* note 33, at 146; *Saluka Invs.* v. *Czech Republic*, Partial Award, UNCITRAL, para. 255; *S.D. Myers, Inc.* v. *Government of Canada*, UNCITRAL, Partial Award, para. 229; *Wena Hotels Ltd.* v. *Arab Republic of Egypt*, ICSID Case No. ARB/98/4, Decision on Jurisdiction, paras. 81 and 84.

[37] Richard K. Gardiner, *Treaty Interpretation* (Oxford University Press 2008) 177.

[38] *Plama Consortium Limited* v. *Republic of Bulgaria*, ICSID Case No. ARB/03/24, Decision on Jurisdiction, para. 147.

[39] *Compañia del Desarrollo de Santa Elena S.A.* v. *Republic of Costa Rica*, ICSID Case No. ARB/96/1, Award, para. 64; *Mondev International Ltd.* v. *USA*, ICSID Case No. ARB(AF)/99/2, Award, para. 91; *Aguas del Tunari, S.A.* v. *Republic of Bolivia*, ICSID Case No. ARB/02/3, Decision on Jurisdiction, para. 153; *Emilio Agustín Maffezini* v. *The Kingdom of Spain*, ICSID Case No. ARB/97/7, Decision on Jurisdiction, para. 31; *Tokios Tokelés* v. *Ukraine*, ICSID Case No. ARB/02/18, Dissenting Opinion (Chairman Prosper Weil), paras. 2 and 19; *Vacuum Salt Products Ltd.* v. *Republic of Ghana*, ICSID Case No. ARB/92/1, Award, paras. 32, 46, 77 and 86.

[40] *Tokios Tokelés* v. *Ukraine*, ICSID Case No. ARB/02/18, Opinion, paras. 2 and 19; *Vacuum Salt Products Ltd.* v. *Republic of Ghana*, ICSID Case No. ARB/92/1, Award, para. 46 (in this case the object and purpose of a specific

treaty's preamble has on a number of occasions assisted ISATs to elucidate a treaty's object and purpose.[41] The object and purpose of an investment treaty referred to by ISATs includes but is not limited to the protection of foreign investment,[42] the promotion of economic cooperation and the flow of capital and technology between states,[43] all of which often call for a balanced approach to the interpretation.[44]

ISATs' references to the good faith criterion when carrying out treaty interpretation are scarce,[45] largely due to the broad and undefined nature of good faith giving considerable discretion to arbitrators.[46] The term good faith, as an overly subjective interpreting notion, is likely to be used to justify a certain predetermined desired result.[47]

In summary, the four main criteria of treaty interpretation contained in Article 31(1) of the VCLT, that is, good faith, ordinary meaning, context, and object and purpose, should be read and utilized as a whole, though they are often applied in sequence, with emphasis placed on certain criteria depending on the circumstances of each individual case. It is also important to note that the ordinary meaning, the context, and the object and purpose should by and large come from the text of the treaty[48] instead of from an investigation into the intention of the parties,[49] so that the interpretation can remain a rather objective one based on the text of the treaty.

6.3 DEFINITION OF "INVESTOR"

In the ISDS cases involving China, the tribunals kept an expansive approach to determining the scope of "investor" under Chinese BITs. One focal issue is whether and when SOEs from mainland China can be protected under BITs in ISDS cases, which now appears quite

provision (Article 25(2)(b) of the ICSID Convention) was utilized); *Marvin Roy Feldman Karpa* v. *United Mexican States*, ICSID Case No. ARB(AF)/99/1, Award, para. 35.

41 *Amco Asia Corporation and others* v. *Republic of Indonesia*, ICSID Case No. ARB/81/1, Decision on Jurisdiction, paras. 23–24; *LG&E Energy Corporation and ors.* v. *the Republic of Argentina*, Decision on Liability, ICSID Case No. ARB/02/1, para. 124; *Metalclad Corporation* v. *The United Mexican States*, ICSID Case No. ARB(AF)/97/1, Award, para. 71; *Philippe Gruslin* v. *Malaysia*, ICSID Case No. ARB/99/3, ICSID Case No. ARB/99/3, para. 13.8; *Saluka Invs.* v. *Czech Republic*, Partial Award, UNCITRAL, para 299; *Vacuum Salt Products Ltd.* v. *Republic of Ghana*, ICSID Case No. ARB/92/1, para. 39. See also Rudolf Dolzer and Margrete Stevens, *Bilateral Investment Treaties* (Martinus Nijhoff 1995), para. 20.

42 *Compañia del Desarrollo de Santa Elena S.A.* v. *Costa Rica*, ICSID Case No. ARB/96/1, Award, para. 64; *Tokios Tokelés* v. *Ukraine*, ICSID Case No. ARB/02/18, Opinion, paras. 2 and 19; *Vacuum Salt* v. *Republic of Ghana*, ICSID Case No. ARB/92/1, para. 32; *Loewen Group, Inc. and Raymond L. Loewen* v. *US*, ICSID Case No. ARB(AF)/98/3, Decision on Jurisdiction, para. 53. *Amco Asia Corporation and others* v. *Republic of Indonesia*, ICSID Case No. ARB/81/1, Decision on Jurisdiction, para. 18; *Kaiser Bauxite Company* v. *Jamaica*, ICSID Case No. ARB/74/3, Decision on Jurisdiction, para. 17.

43 *Aguas del Tunari, S.A.* v. *Republic of Bolivia*, ICSID Case No. ARB/02/3, Decision on Respondent's Objections to Jurisdiction, paras. 153 and 241; *Tokios Tokelés* v. *Ukraine*, ICSID Case No. ARB/02/18, Opinion, paras. 2 and 19; *Vacuum Salt Products Ltd.* v. *Republic of Ghana*, ICSID Case No. ARB/92/1, Award, para. 31.

44 *Saluka Invs.* v. *Czech Republic*, Award, UNCITRAL, para. 300. On this issue, see generally Omar E. García-Bolivar, "The Teleology of International Investment Law: The Role of Purpose in the Interpretation of International Investment Agreements" (2005) 6(5) *Journal of World Investment and Trade* 751.

45 Weeramenatry, *supra* note 26, para. 3.22.

46 *Wintershall Aktiengesellschaft* v. *Argentine Republic*, ICSID Case No. ARB/04/14, para. 88.

47 *Hrvatska Elektroprivreda d.d.* v. *Republic of Slovenia*, ICSID Case No. ARB/05/24, Jan Paulsson Individual Opinion, para. 51.

48 *Asian Agricultural* v. *Sri Lanka*, ICSID Case No. ARB/87/3, paras. 51 and 61; *Ronald S. Lauder* v. *The Czech Republic*, UNCITRAL, para. 219; *Tradex Hellas S.A.* v. *Republic of Albania*, ICSID Case No. ARB/94/2, Award, para. 59; *Yukos Universal Limited (Isle of Man)* v. *The Russian Federation*, UNCITRAL, PCA Case No. AA 227, Interim Award, para. 411.

49 *Wintershall Aktiengesellschaft* v. *Argentine Republic*, ICSID Case No. ARB/04/14, Award, paras. 88.

relevant to Chinese investors and their host states given the ongoing trade war between China and the USA. The role of SOEs in Chinese outbound investment is likely to draw more attention.[50] Some Chinese BITs and FTAs such as the China–New Zealand FTA 2008 explicitly include SOEs in the scope of investors covered.[51] Given the importance of SOEs in BIT practice, some Chinese BIT cases are particularly relevant and deserve careful analysis.

In the case of *BUCG* v. *Yemen*,[52] defining the scope of "investor" was the main issue. Beijing Urban Construction Group (BUCG), an SOE in China, won a tender process for the selection of a construction contractor for a new international terminal at Sana's International Airport in Yemen, and entered into a construction contract with the Yemen Civil Aviation and Meteorology Authority (CAMA) in 2006. The claimant commenced ICSID arbitration proceedings alleging that Yemen had unlawfully deprived its investment by employing military forces and security apparatus to assault and detain the claimant's employees and to forcibly deny its access to the construction site, thereby rendering the claimant incapable of performing its contractual obligations. Yemen, claimed by BUCG, used this incident as an excuse for CAMA to terminate BUCG's contract. In its request for arbitration and subsequent submissions, BUCG claimed that it was expropriated, and Yemen was in violation of Article 4 of the China–Yemen BIT 1998.

One of the jurisdictional objections raised by Yemen was that BUCG, being an SOE, should not be regarded as a "national of another Contracting State" as required by Article 25(1) of the ICSID Convention[53] for the reasons that (i) BUCG was under the direction and control of the Chinese government in carrying out its activities, and (ii) BUCG was empowered to exercise elements of governmental authority in China.

BUCG contended that the question of whether or not it qualified under Article 25(1) must be considered in the specific context of the investment that had given rise to the dispute. It argued that its investment in Yemen was made while acting as a commercial enterprise, after participating in a competitive tender, and did not involve the exercise of governmental or public powers. According to BUCG, its structural links to the Chinese government and public functions inside China were irrelevant to its standing as an investor under the ICSID Convention.

The tribunal held that, notwithstanding the fact that BUCG was an SOE, the evidence demonstrated that the claimant was, in carrying out this work, acting as a commercial contractor and was neither an agent of the Chinese government nor fulfilling governmental functions in the fact-specific context.[54] In this regard, the tribunal found it particularly noteworthy that "BUCG participated in the airport project as a general contractor following

50 Hui Yao Wang and Lu Miao, "China's Outbound Investment: Trends and Challenges in the Globalization of Chinese Enterprises" in Julien Chaisse (ed.), *China's International Investment Strategy: Bilateral, Regional, and Global Law and Policy* (Oxford University Press 2019) 44.

51 Sheng Zhang, "The Status of State-Owned Enterprises in ISDS from a Chinese Perspective" in Yuwen Li et al. (eds.), *China, the EU and International Investment Law: Reforming Investor-State Dispute Settlement* (Routledge 2019) 198–210.

52 *Beijing Urban Construction Group Co., Ltd.* v. *Republic of Yemen*, ICSID Case No. ARB/14/30. The Decision on Jurisdiction, May 31, 2017, www.italaw.com/sites/default/files/case-documents/italaw8968.pdf (accessed March 12, 2021).

53 The ICSID Convention provides a forum for the settlement of investment disputes brought by foreign investors against host states but excludes state-to-state disputes. The ICSID Convention, however, does not specifically address the standing of SOEs.

54 *Beijing Urban Construction Group Co., Ltd.* v. *Republic of Yemen*, ICSID Case No. ARB/14/30. The Decision on Jurisdiction, para. 39.

an open tender in competition with other contractors. Its bid was selected on its commercial merits. Its contract was terminated, Yemen contends, not for any reason associated with the PRC's decisions or policies but because of BUCG's failure to perform its commercial services on the airport site to a commercially acceptable standard."[55]

In the case of *Beijing Shougang Mining Investment Company Ltd. et al.* v. *Mongolia*, both sides submitted arguments over the term "investor" related to SOEs. The claimants asserted that they are "qualifying investors" under Article 1(2) of the BIT because they are "economic entities" that are "established and domiciled in the territory of the PRC in accordance with the PRC's laws."[56] In denying that Beijing Shougang and China Heilongjiang are "agencies" of the Chinese government or exercise "any element of governmental authority,"[57] the claimants emphasized the fact that the BIT does not exclude SOEs from qualifying as investors.[58] Mongolia, however, claimed that Beijing Shougang and China Heilongjiang are not investors as they cannot be classified as "economic entities" under Article 1(2) of the BIT.[59] Mongolia suggested applying a narrow formulation of "economic entities." As the tribunal focused on the "involving" formulation and the fork-in-the-road provision to deny jurisdiction, it did not elaborate on the standing of SOEs in the BIT.

Another key issue is who qualifies for protection as a "Chinese investor." The wording of PRC investment treaties typically protects PRC nationals and PRC-incorporated companies, without elaborating on the criteria for establishing such nationality. The main controversy is whether individuals or companies from "special administrative regions" (SARs) of China, that is, Hong Kong and Macau, can be covered by this definition.

Two arbitral tribunals have answered this in the affirmative. In *Tza Yap Shum* v. *Peru*, an ICSID tribunal held that a Hong Kong resident was entitled to claim damages under the China–Peru BIT 1994.

More recently, in the case of *Sanum* v. *Lao Republic*, an UNCITRAL tribunal held in 2013 that a Macau-incorporated company could take advantage of the China–Laos BIT 1993. *Sanum* was the subject of a main challenge by the Laos government in the courts of Singapore where the arbitration was based. In 2015, a single judge of the Singapore High Court annulled the jurisdictional ruling, holding that Macau investors could not avail themselves of the BIT because "the China-Laos BIT does not apply to Macau." But in September 2016, the Singapore Court of Appeal (SGCA), Singapore's highest court, restored the award, holding, on its own independent review of the China–Laos BIT 1993, that its terms covered Macau investors. The SGCA's ruling does not quell the controversy over this issue. In October 2016, the PRC's Ministry of Foreign Affairs reacted by stating that it disagreed with this decision and considered that only mainland Chinese investors should be entitled to treaty protection; Hong Kong and Macau investors should not be allowed to take advantage of Chinese nationality for such purposes.

The issue is complicated by the fact that Macau and Hong Kong still have their own independent investment treaties with some countries – as highlighted recently by *Philip Morris* v. *Australia*, in which Philip Morris Asia Limited, the claimant, attempted to use the Hong Kong–Australia BIT 1993 and, more specifically, its UNCITRAL arbitration clause as a basis for challenging Australia's Tobacco Plain Packaging Act, which, as the claimant

55 Ibid., para. 40.
56 *Beijing Shougang Mining* v. *Mongolia*, PCA Case No. 2010–20, para. 228.
57 Ibid., para. 276.
58 Ibid., para. 274.
59 Ibid., para. 269.

argued, amounted to an expropriation of its IPR. The case was dismissed by a tribunal established under the auspices of the PCA on non-jurisdictional grounds,[60] without any discussion of the status of Hong Kong.

Peru argued in *Tza Yap Shum* v. *Peru* that, by virtue of Tza's residency in Hong Kong, he lacked standing to assert a claim under the Peru–China BIT 1994. Peru made two objections to Tza's nationality. First, the claimant failed to prove his Chinese nationality. Procedurally, the claimant bore the burden of proof to produce a certified copy of his birth certificate as documentary evidence of his Chinese nationality and such a failure during the stage of production of documents led to a failed establishment of such nationality. Second, a copy of the passport issued by the government of the Hong Kong SAR, as Peru claimed, was not sufficient evidence of the claimant's nationality.[61] The claimant produced his Hong Kong passport and identification card indicating that Fujian province was his place of birth even though he was not able to produce a birth certificate as requested by the tribunal due to the succession of sovereignty by the Communist Party of China in 1949.[62] More importantly, an investment, as the claimant argued, made by a Hong Kong resident was not excluded from the investment protected under the Peru–China BIT because China did not file a notice with the ICSID according to Article 70 of the ICSID Convention to limit the territorial application to China.[63] Similarly, the definition of "investor" in the Peru–China BIT does not attach any domicile or residence qualifier.[64]

The tribunal ruled that the claimant *prima facie* validly holds Chinese nationality[65] on the grounds that: (i) the PRC Nationality Law confers Chinese nationality on natural persons of Chinese descent born in the Chinese territory[66] and forbids Chinese nationals from having any nationality other than the Chinese one; and (ii) Tza's residency does not change the fact that Hong Kong residents of Chinese descent and born in the Chinese territories (including Hong Kong) are Chinese nationals as the PRC Nationality Law applies equally in Hong Kong.[67] The tribunal accepted Tza's Hong Kong passport as sufficient evidence to demonstrate Tza's Chinese nationality.

The tribunal technically relied on both Article 25 of the ICSID Convention and the Peru–China BIT 1994 to establish its jurisdiction for "disputes arising out of an investment between a Contracting State and a national of another Contracting State, which the parties to the dispute consent in writing to submit to the ICSID."[68] As Article 25 does not explicitly exclude Chinese nationals resident in Hong Kong, and "China has not excluded Hong Kong by written notice from the application of the ICSID Convention" in accordance with Article 70 therein,[69] all Chinese nationals including Hong Kong residents are therefore included in the scope of Article 25 of the ICSID Convention. In connection with the Peru-China BIT 1994, the definition of "investor" in respect to China refers to "natural persons who have nationality

60 The decisive objection was that the claimant's claim configured an abuse of right as the claimant changed its corporate structure to obtain BIT protection for an existing or foreseeable dispute, and therefore constituted abuse of rights and was inadmissible. The award is available at www.italaw.com/sites/default/files/case-documents/italaw7303_0.pdf (accessed March 12, 2021).

61 *Tza Yap Shum* v. *Peru*, Award, para. 44.

62 Ibid., para. 49.

63 Ibid., para. 50.

64 Ibid., para. 51.

65 Ibid., para. 61.

66 Ibid., paras. 58, 61.

67 Ibid., paras. 54, 60.

68 Ibid., para. 70.

69 Ibid., n. 29.

of the PRC in accordance with its laws. . . ." Neither this definition nor any other provisions exclude Hong Kong residents from the scope of application thereof. In applying Article 31 of the VCLT, the tribunal is bound to interpret the Peru–China BIT "in good faith and in accordance with the ordinary meaning to be given to the terms of the treaty in its context and in the light of its object and purpose." In other words, the tribunal underscores the explicit intention expressed by China and Peru in the BIT, which did not impose any additional requirements on the term "investor." The tribunal's position is clear that nationality is fundamentally a question of domestic law and the tribunal must strictly apply domestic laws. Thus, the tribunal took an expansive approach of interpreting the term "investor" in the BIT and stayed clear of the nationality problem.

Similarly, in response to the respondent's analysis of the legislation governing any other particular in Hong Kong, the tribunal stuck to the BIT language and concluded that the legislation other than those strictly determining the nationality of its residents is of little relevance to the jurisdiction.[70] This was also the approach taken by the tribunal in considering the fact that Hong Kong itself entered into BITs with some countries. The tribunal's approach to interpreting the BIT term is consistent: strictly confining itself to the BIT term without considering any other elements raised by the respondent to narrow the scope of "investors" under the BIT so as to strike out the tribunal's jurisdiction.

The tribunal's ultimate dismissal of Peru's objections to the claimant's Chinese nationality effectively established the jurisprudence that a Hong Kong resident holding Chinese nationality, depending on the language of the BIT in question, is able to bring an investment treaty claim not only under a Hong Kong BIT but also under a Chinese BIT. By contrast, a Hong Kong resident who is not a Chinese national would not be able to invoke Chinese BITs, while a Chinese national who is not a resident of Hong Kong could not invoke Hong Kong BITs. This is confirmed by the Hong Kong BIT which usually protects "physical persons who have the right of abode in its area."[71] However, the *Tza Yap Shum* case addressed only the nationality of a natural person, not all issues surrounding legal persons, corporate ownership or nationality. It is not clear whether a Hong Kong-incorporated entity is entitled to treaty protections under a Chinese BIT. Different from the Chinese nationality which is conferred by Chinese law on natural persons, the incorporation of a Hong Kong company is based on Hong Kong law, which is fundamentally and conceptually different from Chinese law. In theory, a Hong Kong-incorporated company should not be regarded as the same company incorporated in China and then should not have standing to pursue claims under Chinese BITs.[72] This line of distinction between a Hong Kong resident and a Hong Kong company (unless it is effectively controlled by a Chinese national or entity[73]) may lead to a dramatically different treatment. Some Chinese BITs clearly exclude Hong Kong from their coverage. Therefore, investors from Hong Kong should carefully review any such BITs to ensure that they include sufficiently broad language before relying on them for investment protections.

70 Ibid., para. 75.

71 Thailand-Hong Kong BIT 2005, Article 1(4)(b)(i).

72 E.g., Article 126 of the Peru–China FTA 2009 provides that "investor" for China means "economic entities established in accordance with the laws of the PRC and domiciled in the territory of the PRC."

73 E.g., Article 126 of the Peru–China FTA 2009 provides that "investor" for China means ". . .; or legal entities not established under the law of the PRC but effectively controlled, by natural persons [who have nationality of the PRC in accordance with its law] or by economic entities [established in accordance with the laws of the PRC and domiciled in the territory of the PRC]."

The *Sanum* v. *Laos* award arose from an international arbitration brought by Macau-based Sanum Investments Limited ("Sanum") against the government of the Lao People's Democratic Republic (the "Lao government") in 2012 under a 1993 China–Laos BIT for claims of expropriation of gaming investments. One of the main issues centered on the scope of "Chinese investor" under the China-Laos BIT 1993. This is particularly relevant and special to China as Macau and Hong Kong have their own BITs and investors from Macau and Hong Kong are supposed to be protected by the BITs signed by Macau and Hong Kong with their counterparties. In Sanum, not only the ICSID tribunal but also courts in Singapore dealt with this troubling issue from various legal perspectives. Thus, Sanum is a landmark case on the legal issue of applying Chinese BITs to investors from Macau and Hong Kong, and will have a great impact on future Chinese BIT cases dealing with similar issues.

In essence, the arbitral tribunal seated in Singapore found that the China–Laos BIT 1993 applied to Macau SAR, and ruled that it had jurisdiction to determine Sanum's expropriation claims. The Lao government filed a jurisdictional challenge to the Singapore High Court, which overturned the tribunal's ruling and halted the arbitration.

On September 29, 2016, Sanum prevailed in its appeal against the High Court's decision before a five-judge Court of Appeal. The SGCA also appointed two *amicus curiae*, Mr. Christopher Thomas QC and Professor Locknie Hsu, to opine on various novel and complex issues concerning public international law and international investment law. In a seventy-four-page judgment delivered by Chief Justice Sundaresh Menon, the SGCA held that the High Court "was wrong to conclude that the Tribunal lacked the jurisdiction to hear the claims," finding that the China–Laos BIT 1993 did apply to Macau and that the tribunal had subject-matter jurisdiction over Sanum's expropriation claims.

The question the SGCA had to struggle with was whether the China–Laos BIT, which had been signed and entered into force in 1993, became applicable to Macau following the handover from Portugal to PRC in 1999. According to the Vienna Convention on the Succession of States in respect of Treaties, the SGCA held that "the PRC–Laos BIT will be presumed to automatically apply to the territory of Macau upon restoration of Chinese sovereignty with effect from 20 December 1999."

The SGCA found that there was "nothing in the text, the objects and the purposes of the PRC–Laos BIT, or in the circumstances of its conclusion that points to an intention to displace the [moving treaty frontier] rule such that it would lead to the conclusion that the BIT does not apply to Macau." This followed from an extensive review of the evidence, including the 1987 China–Portugal Joint Declaration on the question of Macau, the PRC's dealings with the UK in relation to Hong Kong, and various publications from the UN and the WTO. Notably, even though the Lao government produced formal diplomatic correspondence between itself and China in 2014 and 2015 expressing both governments' views that the China–Laos BIT 1993 was not applicable to Macau, the Court declined to place any weight on such evidence, which was only adduced after Sanum's commencement of the arbitration proceedings.

Also, the SGCA addressed a number of international law concepts in this case, including the interpretation of treaties, rules of evidence in international law and the critical date doctrine. Dealing with the justiciability of the jurisdictional issue, the SGCA observed that the Singapore courts are not only competent but also obliged to interpret and apply treaties, as the parties had designated Singapore as the seat of arbitration.[74] The Court laid down that it

[74] *Sanum* v. *Laos*, para. 38.

would undertake a *de novo* review of the tribunal's award on jurisdiction, and added that "there is no basis for deference to be awarded to the Tribunal's findings."[75] The *de novo* review standard for deciding the jurisdictional question has been a consistent view taken by the Singapore courts.[76]

The issue of jurisdiction in this case was not only limited to interpreting the scope and application of the China–Laos BIT 1993 but also involved the fundamental question of whether the China–Laos BIT extended to the territory in question. The inquiry into the applicability of the China–Laos BIT 1993 to a particular territory necessitated the application of principles of treaty interpretation and other customary international law rules. Of particular importance is the emphasis by the Court on Article 31 of the VCLT,[77] which encapsulates the principles relating to the interpretation of treaties in international law.

In deciding whether the China–Laos BIT 1993 applied to Macau, the Court examined the rule on state succession under Article 29 of the VCLT[78] and Article 15 of the Vienna Convention on Succession of States in respect of Treaties.[79] The Court further noted that the aforementioned provisions represent the "Moving Treaty Frontier" Rule (MTF Rule) in customary international law.[80] The Court of Appeal relied on the opinions of experts in international law while assessing the relevance and effect of the MTF Rule and observed that the MTF Rule, being a presumptive one, would automatically apply to Macau, upon restoration of Chinese sovereignty.[81] The Court next went on to examine the exceptions to the MTF Rule[82] and held that none of the exceptions to the MTF Rule applied in this case as extension of the China–Laos BIT 1993 to Macau (i) could not be said to be incompatible with the object and purpose of the BIT; (ii) would not radically change the conditions of its operation; and (iii) there was nothing in the text, objects or purpose of the China–Laos BIT that pointed to an intention that the BIT was *not* intended to apply to Macau.[83]

A significant issue that arose for consideration regarding the relevance of evidence was the "critical date doctrine"[84] in public international law. The SGCA affirmed that the critical

75 Ibid., para. 41.

76 *PT First Media TBK* v. *Astro Nusantara International BV and others and another appeal* [2014] 1 SLR 372, *PT Tugu Pratama Indonesia* v. *Magma Nusantara Ltd.* [2003] 4 SLR (R) 257, *AQZ* v. *ARA* [2015] 2 SLR 972.

77 VCLT, Article 31.

78 Article 29 – Territorial scope of treaties. Unless a different intention appears from the treaty or is otherwise established, a treaty is binding upon each party in respect of its entire territory.

79 When part of the territory of a State, or when any territory for the international relations of which a State is responsible, not being part of the territory of that State, becomes part of the territory of another State:
(a) treaties of the predecessor State cease to be in force in respect of the territory to which the succession of States relates from the date of the succession of States; and
(b) treaties of the successor State are in force in respect of the territory to which the succession of States relates from the date of the succession of States, unless it appears from the treaty or is otherwise established that the application of the treaty to that territory would be incompatible with the object and purpose of the treaty or would radically change the conditions for its operation.

80 *Sanum* v. *Laos*, para. 47.

81 Ibid., para. 49.

82 Ibid. The exceptions are as follows: "(a) It appears from the PRC-Laos BIT, or is otherwise established, that the application of the PRC-Laos BIT would be incompatible with the object and purpose of the BIT (Art 15(b) of the VCST) (b) It appears from the PRC-Laos BIT, or is otherwise established, that the application of the BIT to Macau would radically change the conditions of its operation (Art 15(b) of the VCST) (c) An intention appears from the PRC-Laos BIT, or is otherwise established, that the BIT does not apply in respect of the entire territory of the PRC (Art 29 of the VCLT)" (*Sanum* v. *Laos*, para. 50).

83 Ibid., *Sanum* v. *Laos*, paras. 50–55.

84 "In all cases, there is a point in time in the factual chronology of the dispute beyond which the conduct of the parties and other events can no longer affect the decision of the case. This time is called the critical date"

date was "the date on which the dispute was crystallized (14 August 2012), when the arbitration proceedings were initiated."[85] Laos sought to admit new evidence before the High Court in the form of two notes verbales (NVs) and two further NVs before the SGCA. The SGCA noted that while the broad principles of *Ladd* v. *Marshall*[86] *and Lassiter*[87] would be helpful in determining the admissibility of new evidence, when the dispute engages questions of public international law, the Court must consider the evidence within the framework of applicable principles of international law, like the critical date doctrine. The SGCA held that the burden of proof was on Laos to prove its assertion that it had otherwise established that the MTF Rule was displaced by the evidence arising before the critical date[88] as the new evidence could be adduced only to confirm the pre-existing position. However, the SGCA found that the pre-critical date evidence did not establish that the MTF Rule had been displaced, and hence the NVs were ultimately not relevant to the issues before it.[89]

The SGCA adopted a finely nuanced line of reasoning that relied upon the critical date doctrine to discount the weight to be applied to the 2014 NVs. The overall reasoning and result were correct, given the particular facts of the case, including a complete absence of any evidence to show that China and Laos ever addressed the territorial scope of application of the BIT in any of their bilateral engagements prior to the 2014 NVs.

Although the SGCA was placed in the difficult position of having to deal with an exchange of diplomatic correspondence by the contracting state parties to a BIT that purported to agree on the territorial scope of their BIT, the exchange of diplomatic correspondence was made after the arbitral award was rendered but before the filing of the court challenge.

The implications for future determinations of the applicability of Chinese BITs to China's SAR remain clear. In both of the aforementioned cases, the tribunals held that investors from China's SAR(s) should still be protected by Chinese BITs. While clarifying that post hoc documents that retroactively alter the scope of those treaties will be not be given effect, the Court also confined its findings to the features of the particular China–Laos BIT. The Court appeared to accept *obiter* that, had the China–Laos BIT, like NAFTA, permitted the states to issue binding interpretive statements, the 2014 NVs might have resulted in a different outcome. The effect of binding interpretive statements is far from noncontroversial, having on occasion sparked rebuke from tribunals that have seen it as a way for contracting states to avoid liability.[90] Commentators have also noted that some interpretative statements are tantamount to retroactive amendments, which may undermine the rule of law.[91] Given the increasing number of newer generation investment treaties that permit contracting states to issue binding interpretive statements, this will continue to be a fertile topic for debate.

Notably, the PRC Ministry of Foreign Affairs issued a statement criticizing the judgment and repeating its position that Chinese treaties do not apply to Macau and Hong Kong. Given

(Robert Pietrowski, "Evidence in International Arbitration" (2006) 22(3) *Arbitration International* 373–410, at 399); *Sanum* v. *Laos*, para. 65.

85 *Sanum* v. *Laos*, para. 67.

86 [1954] 1 WLR 1489 – "(1) The evidence could not have been admitted with reasonable diligence for use in the lower court (2) the evidence would probably have an important influence on the result of the case (3) the evidence must be apparently credible" (*Sanum* v. *Laos*, para. 27).

87 *Lassiter Ann Masters* v. *To Keng Lam* [2004] 2 SLR(R) 392.

88 *Sanum* v. *Laos*, ibid., para. 103.

89 Ibid., para. 112.

90 *Pope & Talbot* v. *Canada*, Award in Respect of Damages, May 31, 2002.

91 Gabriella Kaufmann-Kohler, "Interpretive Powers of the Free Trade Commission and the Rule of Law" in Emmanuel Gaillard and Frédéric Bachand, *Fifteen Years of NAFTA Chapter 11 Arbitration* (JurisNet LLC 2011) 190–192.

how much of the *Sanum* judgment was focused on the particular facts of the case, it remains unclear how future tribunals or courts will approach the territorial scope of different Chinese BITs in different contexts, in light of the state practice of China, and the conduct of other states in response even though the Court's careful forensic analysis of the various pieces of extrinsic evidence will no doubt be of considerable influence.

6.4 DEFINITION OF "INVESTMENT"

Another major issue in international investment arbitration cases is the definition of "investment." It must be pointed out that Article 25 of the ICSID Convention does not provide for any specific definition of investment, which technically leaves certain room to develop this generic notion.[92] Naturally, this flexibility may lead to an expansive jurisdiction that tribunals may exert in cases. In China-related investor–state disputes, three cases touch on this critical term.

In respect of Chinese SOEs, their overseas investment is attracting mounting regulatory scrutiny. The host state government may rely on national security review or other regulatory schemes to block SOE investments. When the SOE resorts to ISDS for protection of its legal rights, the host state government then invokes security exceptions under the applicable investment treaty to justify its actions. Even Chinese BITs allow contracting states to apply prohibitions or restrictions (in the form of a security exception clause) in respect of essential security interests. More recent BITs typically include a WTO-like security exception clause to clarify essential security interests with an exhaustive list.[93] Therefore, the host state government is justified in taking restrictive measures to protect its national security interests under certain circumstances and is further exempted from the obligation for compensation. Without a security exception clause, the host state government is subject to investment commitments on nondiscriminatory treatment, fair and equitable treatment, and expropriation, but can invoke the necessity defense under customary international law[94] and bear the obligation for compensation.[95]

However, invoking a self-judging security exception clause does not guarantee the host state government's absolute regulatory discretion and is subject to the tribunal's treaty interpretation. The SOE may not be able to challenge the state's action by resorting to ISDS under a BIT[96] that provides only post-establishment protections to foreign investors. Nevertheless, the dispute over admission[97] may be challenged under a BIT[98] recognizing nondiscriminatory treatments to the pre-establishment phase. Under these BITs, the host state government is obliged not to impose such restrictions as market access, performance

92 *Abaclat and Others* v. *Argentina*, ICSID ARB/07/05, Jurisdiction and Admissibility, October 28, 2011, para. 347(ii).

93 China–Canada BIT 2012, Art. 33.

94 Different from the security exception clause, the invocation of necessity is much more restricted due to strict conditions that may be hard to satisfy. For instance, the customary international law may not, and it is uncertain to what extent, provide an excuse for protecting strategic industries unless a severe crisis resulting in social upheavals takes place or no other means are available to achieve the intended policy objective. UNCTAD, The Protection of National Security in IIAs, UCTAD Series on International Investment Policies for Development (UN Publishing 2009) 36–37.

95 Sergey Ripinsky, "Global Economic Crisis and the Danger of Protectionism: Does International Law Help?" (2009) 1 *Amsterdam Law Forum* 3, 11.

96 China–UK BIT 1986.

97 The CFIUS review decision; see Chapter 9 of this book.

98 The US Model BIT 2012.

requirements, and NT on the establishment of investment unless these matters are explicitly excluded in the negative list. Even under these BITs, the host state government may argue that the security exception clause may be wide enough to cover the CFIUS review. The instance is the CETA, under which Canada explicitly reserves its sovereignty over reviewing an acquisition under the Investment Canada Act.[99] This line of arguments has not been tested in real cases.

In *BUCG* v. *Yemen*, Yemen argued in arbitration that BUCG was purely a paid contractor that had to provide a performance guarantee, and this did not qualify as an "investment."[100] BUCG contended that its investment consisted of rights acquired under the contract which falls under the definition of "investment" under Article 1(1) of the BIT.[101] As a result, its claim arose out of a qualifying investment in Yemen.

As claimed by Yemen, investment needs to be registered in order to gain protection under the BIT. However, BUCG had failed to register its investment "in accordance with the laws and regulations of Yemen," which rendered BUCG's investment unqualified for the purposes of the BIT.[102] BUCG discounted the registration requirement under Yemeni law, given the irrelevance of Yemeni law to BUCG's claim and the lack of illegality attached to the failure to register the investment.[103] The tribunal held that the registration requirement could not expressly be inferred from the BIT.

The tribunal seemed to keep a distance from the widely held but not uniform view that a qualified investment does not have to satisfy the required element of investment under both the BIT and the ICSID Convention.[104] Nevertheless, it did hold that there was "no difficulty" in concluding that there was an "investment" under both the ICSID Convention and the BIT[105] in circumstances where BUCG had made a contribution (in a contract for works extending over a substantial time period and, therefore, involving a risk) to Yemen's economic development[106] that clearly exposed it to risks posed by the sovereign power.[107] Relying on the definition of "investment" in Article 1 of the BIT,[108] the tribunal clearly saw that BUCG's commitment under a contract being performed in Yemen explicitly qualified as an investment[109] as it constitutes "claims to any performance having an economic value" not only satisfying the Salini test but also within the meaning of Article 1 of the BIT.[110]

In the case of *Beijing Shougang Mining Investment Company Ltd. et al.* v. *Mongolia*, three claimant companies incorporated under the laws of China invested in a joint venture called Tumturei Ltd. with BLT LLC, a Mongolian company holding a license to exploit certain iron ore deposits, to commercially develop an iron ore mine in Mongolia. This license was duly transferred from BLT LLC to Tumturei in 2005 and iron ore production commenced in early 2006. Largely due to the then-higher price of iron ore, the new Mongolian government began efforts in 2006 to find a way to take back its now-valuable mining concession. The license was later revoked and claimed by Mongolia to belong to a domestic SOE. Three

99 CETA, Annex I.
100 *BUCG* v. *Yemen*, The Decision on Jurisdiction, para. 122.
101 Ibid., para. 123.
102 Ibid., para. 122.
103 Ibid., para. 123.
104 Ibid., para. 128.
105 Ibid., para. 138.
106 Ibid., para. 137.
107 Ibid., para. 136.
108 *Salini* v. *Morocco*, ICSID Case No. ARB/00/4, Decision on Jurisdiction, July 23, 2001, para. 52.
109 *BUCG* v. *Yemen*, The Decision on Jurisdiction, para. 135.
110 Ibid., para. 136.

Chinese companies served their request for arbitration on February 12, 2010, claiming that Mongolia unlawfully expropriated their investment and seeking recourse through arbitration pursuant to the 1991 China–Mongolia BIT. An ad hoc tribunal was duly constituted and the PCA was selected to administer the proceedings. A 153-page-long award declining to exercise jurisdiction over the essential question was rendered on June 30, 2017. The award was not made public. Three Chinese companies later brought the case to the District Court of Southern New York petitioning for an order to vacate the award.

Mongolia objected to the jurisdiction on a series of grounds. One objection was that the Chinese companies had not made a qualifying investment, insofar as they had not incurred investment risk, which, as Mongolia argued, is a "situation in which an investor cannot be sure of a return on his investment, and may not know the amount he will end up spending."[111] Mongolia also made a distinction between investment risk and policy risk – the investment risk concerns a likelihood of profitability while policy risk refers to a likelihood of accruing benefit to the state.[112] In Mongolia's view, the Chinese claimants in this case faced "state policy risk" instead of "investment risk."[113] In addition, Mongolia submitted that the Chinese claimants did not make any contribution to Mongolia's economic development.[114]

The Chinese claimants submitted that their investment comprised their shares in the joint venture and their indirect interest in the license. These interests fell within the definition of "investment" in Article 1(1) of the BIT. The claimants argued for an ordinary meaning of Article 1(1) as any recourse to supplementary means of interpretation is not supported by the VCLT.[115] The Chinese claimants were also of the opinion that they undertook investment risk as "shareholdings in a mining company and concessions over natural resources carry with them the inherent risk that no return (or no sufficient return) be received on the investment made."[116] The tribunal did not elaborate on the concept of "investment" in the award while completely relying on the narrow interpretation of "dispute" in declining its jurisdiction.

6.5 DEFINITION OF "DISPUTE"

The phrase "involving the amount of compensation for expropriation" was a heavily contentious issue in the case of *Tza Yap Shum* v. *Peru*. The objection concerned the tribunal's jurisdiction over Tza's claims other than those substantive issues relating to expropriation, fair and equitable treatment, and full protection and security. According to Article 8(3) of the Peru–China BIT 1994, "a dispute involving the amount of compensation for expropriation may be submitted at the request of either party to the international arbitration of the ICSID." Peru interpreted "involving" as meaning "limited to" or "exclusively." Based on such a restrictive interpretation, disputes that could be arbitrated merely covered "disputes related to the determination of the value of the investment" but excluded such "potentially important matters" as "whether expropriation has taken place" and "whether any compensation must be paid."[117] Therefore, Peru made the most significant challenge to jurisdiction: Tza's claims fell outside the scope of Article 8(3) of the BIT; and the tribunal did not have jurisdiction over liability of expropriation to determine if the Peruvian tax authority's actions constituted an

111 *Beijing Shougang Mining Investment Company Ltd. et al.* v. *Mongolia*, PCA Case No. 2010–20 Award, para. 278.
112 Ibid., para. 279.
113 Ibid., para. 280.
114 Ibid., para. 281.
115 Ibid., para. 281.
116 Ibid., para. 284.
117 *Tza Yap Shum* v. *Republic of Peru*, Award, para. 150.

expropriation of Tza's investment in TSG. The claimant, on the contrary, expanded to "the other end of the interpretation spectrum" so that "a determination of other important matters related to the alleged expropriation" would also be allowed.[118] While acknowledging that "such wording seemed to seek certain limitations," the tribunal tried to ascertain the "exact scope of such limitations."[119]

In resolving such a "core interpretation issue,"[120] the tribunal followed the guidance outlined in Article 31 of the VCLT.[121] Instead of viewing the phrase as imposing some "limitations," the tribunal agreed that the phrase "may have a great variety of possible meanings."[122] The tribunal, in applying its "ordinary meaning" approach, relied on the Oxford Dictionary, which defines the word "involving" as meaning "to enfold, envelope, entangle, include."[123] This led the tribunal to endorse the claimant's "broadest interpretation" as the "most appropriate" approach.[124] The tribunal found that a narrow interpretation of "involving the amount of compensation" would "invalidate" the arbitration clause. This narrow interpretation, the tribunal contended, would make the host state's consent to arbitration illusory since the investor could not actually have access to arbitration unless the host state agreed to allow it.[125] As a result, given the sub-elements (of expropriation) listed in Article 4 of the BIT[126] and the inclusive nature of the phrase "involving," the tribunal drew the broadest spectrum and permitted arbitration of claims concerning all aspects of expropriation "such as whether (i) an instance of expropriation, nationalization, or similar measure has taken place; (ii) the same has met the requirement of public interest; (iii) the same has followed an appropriate domestic legal procedure; (iv) there has been discrimination; (v) compensation will be paid; (iv) such compensation has been equivalent to the value of investments expropriated, paid in a convertible and freely transferable currency and without unreasonable delay."[127]

The tribunal further resorted to "the wording of the Preamble of the BIT" as the supplementary means of interpretation, partly to lay down more supportive grounds for its "broadest interpretation" approach. The tribunal was well aware that the "purpose of including the entitlement to submit certain disputes to ICSID arbitration is that of conferring certain benefits to promote investments."[128] Considering the surrounding context, that is, inter alia, the importance of granting the investor the benefits of submitting an expropriation-related dispute to ICSID arbitration, the tribunal felt satisfied that the right of submission to arbitration should not be excluded by the phrase "involving the amount of compensation for expropriation." Otherwise, the tribunal would be skeptical about the real purpose of the Article 8 mechanism in "attracting foreign investors."[129] This interpretative methodology is applied from time to time in shaping the tribunal's textual analysis in rendering the award.

In the case of *Sanum* v. *Laos*, one of Laos's major jurisdictional objections was that Sanum's claims fell outside the scope of the dispute resolution clause in Article 8(3) of the

118 Award, para. 150.
119 Award, para. 145.
120 Award, para. 149.
121 Award, para. 146.
122 Award, para. 150.
123 Award, para. 151.
124 Award, para. 150.
125 Award, para. 148.
126 Article 4 of the Peru–China BIT 1994.
127 Award, para. 152.
128 Award, para. 153.
129 Award, para. 153.

China–Laos BIT 1993 on the ground that the clause permits arbitration only where the issue in dispute is the amount of compensation payable on expropriation but not the liability itself. Sanum argued for a broader reading of Article 8(3) so as to allow arbitration as long as the claims include a dispute over the amount of compensation. As to jurisdiction *ratione materiae*, the Lao government contended that a narrow interpretation of Article 8(3) of the China–Laos BIT 1993 should be adopted such that recourse to arbitration may be had where the only issue in dispute is the amount of compensation for expropriation. The tribunal concluded that the arbitration clause made the existence of an expropriation arbitrable.[130] The first instance court in Singapore disagreed.

The SGCA accepted the broad reading approach. In line with Article 31 of the VCLT, the SGCA considered the interpretation of Article 8(3) in light of its ordinary meaning, context, object and purpose. The ordinary meaning approach is capable of supporting both interpretations. SGCA then considered the context, object and purpose of Article 8(3).

The Court held that "the Lao Government's interpretation of Art 8(3) of the China–Laos BIT is not tenable" in the context of the China–Laos BIT 1993, which contained a "fork-in-the -road" provision to the effect that once an expropriation claim is referred to the national court, no aspect of that claim can then be brought to arbitration. In this regard, the Court was mindful that cases of direct expropriation were becoming increasingly rare, and, even in those rare cases with only amounts of compensation being in dispute, host states could effectively avoid arbitration by simply denying that they had engaged in expropriatory acts. Echoing the arbitral tribunal's sentiments in the highly published decision of *Tza Yap Shum* v. *Peru*, the Court observed that this "would lead to an untenable conclusion – namely that the investor could never actually have access to arbitration." In addition, the Court agreed with Sanum that the broad interpretation of Article 8(3) "is also consistent with the BIT's objective of protecting investments."

The SGCA found that issues of quantum and liability for expropriation were incapable of segregation and it is not possible for a tribunal to arbitrate the question of quantum without looking into the issue of liability. The SGCA found that the fork-in-the-road provision in Article 8(3) meant that the investor cannot bring any aspect of the same dispute to arbitration if "any dispute" is brought to national courts. The SGCA also held that, if the narrow interpretation approach is taken, it would be open to the host state to avoid arbitration by not submitting the liability dispute to its courts, which would render investor protection under Article 8(3) illusory and run counter to the principle of effective interpretation under international law. The SGCA ruled that taking a narrow interpretation would lead to "an untenable conclusion – namely that the investor would never actually have access to arbitration." The SGCA found that the specific context surrounding Article 8(3) of the BIT supported a broad interpretation. The SGCA held that the primary object and purpose of the BIT was to promote investment and protect investors albeit subject to "the principles of mutual respect for sovereignty," which was consistent with a broad interpretation of Article 8(3).[131]

130 *Sanum* v. *Laos*, Award, paras. 3 and 42.

131 SGCA distinguished a number of arbitral awards relied upon by the Lao government, where arbitral tribunals had arrived at narrow interpretations of dispute resolution clauses that also referred to "the amount of compensation." SGCA paid particular attention to the differences in language and architecture of the various BITs under consideration, as well as the interpretative context, placing particular emphasis on whether the BITs under consideration expressly demarcated the determination of the legitimacy of the expropriation from the amount of compensation, and whether there was a fork-in-the-road provision.

With respect to the "amount of compensation" clause, the SGCA read Article 8(3) purposively in light of the principle of effective interpretation, and was careful to give Article 8(3) a meaning that would not render nugatory the investor protections under the BIT. The Court did not find the ordinary meaning of the words in the BIT to be dispositive, as the China–Laos BIT 1993 was at best ambiguous. This approach may be contrasted with the decision of the Svea Court of Appeal in *Juan Ignacio and others* v. *Russia*, Case No T 9128-14, January 18, 2016, which, in setting aside the award in the *Renta 4* case, took a highly textual approach to interpreting a similar clause in the Russia–Spain BIT 1991. In contrast, the SGCA focused more comprehensively on the object, purposes and other provisions of the BIT (in particular its fork-in-the-road clause) while being careful to limit its conclusions to the China–Laos BIT 1993.

The tribunal in the case of *BUCG* v. *Yemen* followed suit with *Tza Yap Shum* v. *Peru* and *Sanum* v. *Laos*. In the *BUCG* v. *Yemen* award handed down on May 31, 2017, the tribunal held that it had jurisdiction on the basis that a clause in the China–Yemen BIT 1998 granting jurisdiction over "any dispute relating to the amount of compensation for expropriation" covered both quantum and liability issues arising out of alleged expropriation.[132] Similar to other treaties negotiated by China prior to 1998, the China–Yemen BIT 1998 in its Article 10 contemplates ICSID arbitration for "any dispute relating to the amount of compensation for expropriation."

Yemen argued that the tribunal's jurisdiction was limited to disputes concerning the calculation of "the amount of compensation" where there is admitted liability by the host state. Yemen's narrow reading of Article 10 would lead to the tribunal's lack of jurisdiction were liability not conceded by the host state or were the investor to complain about anything other than the host state's monetary assessment of its alleged loss. In contrast, BUCG advocated for a broad interpretation to extend the jurisdiction to both the liability of a claim for expropriation and an assessment of compensation. BUCG argued that without determining the issue of liability there could be no consideration of quantum.

The tribunal accepted BUCG's position and found that Article 10 allows an investor to bring expropriation claims relating to issues of both liability and quantum. In this regard, the tribunal found that the ordinary meaning of the words "amount of compensation" was not conclusively in favor of either party's position. As the ordinary meaning of the BIT was not conclusive in favor of either the broad interpretation or the narrow interpretation, the tribunal's task of interpretation moved to consider the context, object and purpose of the BIT.

For the tribunal in the case of *Beijing Shougang Mining Investment Company Ltd., et al* v. *Mongolia*, the question was whether Article 8(3) of the China–Mongolia BIT 1991 applies to a particular type of controversy, that is, a dispute over whether an expropriation has occurred. The tribunal in this case adopted an extremely narrow construction. In its view, the only matter that is arbitrable is "disputes which involve the amount of compensation for expropriation." Further, the tribunal held that it is the allegedly offending state that can determine whether it expropriated property.[133] As a result, the tribunal dismissed the case on jurisdictional grounds.

The claimants then submitted a petition to the District Court of New York South District in order to vacate the arbitral award. The Court disagreed with the tribunal's interpretation as it would leave an investor in the perverse position that only if the state's executive or legislature admitted that it had expropriated the investment, or if the state's own courts could be persuaded

132 Para. 87.

133 *Beijing Shougang et al.* v. *Mongolia*, Award, paras. 435–454.

so to declare, could that investor then proceed to international arbitration.[134] The Court held that the arbitration clause in the China–Mongolia BIT 1991, based on the conclusions of other tribunals and courts, is to give tribunals jurisdiction to determine, inter alia, whether an expropriation has occurred and whether it was effected legally. Therefore, the Court vacated the award and held that Article 8(3) supports the arbitrability of questions of whether expropriation occurred.

6.6 FORK-IN-THE-ROAD PROVISION

The tribunal in *Beijing Shougang Mining Investment Company Ltd. et al.* v. *Mongolia* analyzed the specific wording and overall structure of Article 10. The tribunal noted that Article 10.2 "clearly indicates a fork in the road," which means that when confronted with an unresolved "legal dispute," the concerned BIT grants investors "the choice between taking its dispute to a competent court of the Contracting Party, in this case Yemen, or to ICSID arbitration, but not both." In the tribunal's view, "an interpretation that nullifies either of the choices granted to the investor is to be avoided."

The interconnected heavily contentious procedural issue in *Tza Yap Shum* is related to the "fork-in-the-road" (*electa una via*) provision in the Peru–China BIT 1994. More specifically, the contention was how the tribunal should adjudicate multiple proceedings before national and international fora, that is, the domestic court and ICSID arbitration, both of which are available to the investor under Article 8 of the BIT.

A simple reading of Article 8 does create an impression that the domestic court and ICSID arbitration are organized in chronological order and on a "first come, first exhausted" basis. The Peru–China FTA 2009 confirms this sequence by stipulating that "... if the disputing investor has not submitted the dispute for resolution to the competent court or any other binding dispute settlement mechanism of the Party receiving the investment, it may be submitted to ICSID ...."[135] Simply based on the plain meaning of Articles 8(2) and 8(3), as a matter of treaty interpretation, where the investor chooses to submit the dispute to the courts in the host state, the investor's right to international arbitration will be lost.[136]

The tribunal looked into the "ordinary meaning" of Articles 8(2) and 8(3) but reached an opposite conclusion on two grounds. Effectively, the tribunal characterized the jurisdictional relation of the domestic court and the international arbitral tribunal as a "horizontal configuration." Thus, as the award spells out, the claimant is entitled to institute arbitration directly without first exhausting the remedies offered by local courts. This mode of interaction between the local court and ICSID arbitration was confirmed by both ICSID[137] and non-ICSID tribunals[138] in various cases.

[134] *Beijing Shougang Mining Investment Company, Ltd.* v. *Mongolia* (1:17-cv-07436-ER), paras. 424–436.

[135] Peru–China FTA 2009, Art. 139(2).

[136] Christina Binder, Ursula Kriebaum, August Reinisch and Stephan Wittich (eds.), *International Investment Law for the 21st Century: Essays in Honour of Christoph Schreuer* (Oxford: Oxford University Press 2009) 724, paras. 102, 364; Pamela B. Gann, "The US Bilateral Investment Treaty Program" (1985) 21 *Stanford Journal of International Law* 373, 437–438; Antonio R. Parra, "Provisions on the Settlement of Investment Disputes in Modern Investment Laws, Bilateral Investment Treaties and Multilateral Instruments on Investment" (1997) 12 *ICSID Review – Foreign Investment Law Journal* 334–335, 351–352.

[137] *Amco Asia* v. *Indonesia*, ICSID Case No ARB/81/1, Decision on Annulment of May 16, 1986, para. 63; *Lanco International* v. *Argentina*, ICSID Case No ARB/97/6, Decision on Jurisdiction of December 8, 1998, para. 39; *Generation Ukraine, Inc.* v. *Ukraine*, ICSID Case No ARB/00/9, Award of September 16, 2003, paras. 13.1–13.6.

[138] *CME* v. *Czech Republic*, Final Award, March 14, 2003, 9 ICSID Reports 264, para. 412; *Yaung Chi Oo* v. *Myanmar*, ICSID Case No ARB/01/1, Award of March 31, 2003, 42 ILM 540 (2003), para. 40; *Nycomb*

A similar fork-in-the-road provision appears in the China–Laos BIT 1993. Article 8(2) of the China–Laos BIT gives an option to the investor for submission of the dispute to a competent court of the contracting state accepting the investment, while Article 8(3) provides for a dispute involving the amount of compensation for expropriation to be submitted to an ad hoc arbitral tribunal, and further provides that Article 8(3) is inapplicable if the investor resorted to the procedure in Article 8(2).

As noted by the SGCA, a fork-in-the-road provision requires a party to make a selection, and once the selection is made, the other remedy is no longer available. As contended by Sanum and as accepted by the SGCA, a narrow interpretation of Article 8(3) would have meant that an investor would first have to have approached a court to determine whether an impermissible expropriation had occurred. Once the investor had approached a court under Article 8(2), the remedy of arbitration in Article 8(3) would no longer be available, thus rendering Article 8(3) otiose. The SGCA agreed with the tribunal that a narrow interpretation would be against the principle of *effet futile* (effective interpretation).[139]

The SGCA noted that a similar conclusion was reached in the ICSID decision in *Tza Yap Shum* v. *Republic of Peru*[140] while interpreting a similarly worded BIT between China and Peru. The Court distinguished the cases cited by Laos, favoring a narrow interpretation,[141] inter alia, on the language and structure of the BITs in question, and concluded that they did not involve similar fork-in-the-road provisions. The Court concluded in favor of a broad interpretation to Article 8(3). Singapore courts have consistently ruled in favor of broad, effective interpretation of arbitration clauses. This re-emphasizes the pro-arbitration stance of the judiciary in Singapore.

6.7 LIMITATION PERIOD

Ansung Housing Co., Ltd. v. *China* is the second registered case and the first published ICSID case in which China is the respondent. It is the first case at the ICSID involving China as a respondent state that has proceeded to a substantive hearing that has led to an award. This is also the first case to be brought at the ICSID by a South Korean investor.

The claimant, Ansung Housing Co., Ltd., was a privately owned company incorporated under the laws of South Korea. It invested in a golf course and condominium development project in Sheyang County, Jiangsu Province, China. On December 12, 2006, Ansung entered into an investment agreement with the Sheyang Harbor Industrial Zone Administration Committee (the Committee). Ansung was unable to start its construction work due to the failure to transfer all the land needed for the construction of the project under the investment agreement. Ansung had no alternative option but to dispose of all its assets in the golf business in October 2011 and finally made an agreement on transferring the shares on December 17, 2011. On October 7, 2014 Ansung filed a claim against China for serious financial losses and damages on the basis of the China–Korea BIT 2007.

Synergetics Technology Holding AB v. *Latvia*, SCC Case No 118/2001, Award of December 16, 2003, sec. 2.4, (2005) 1 Stockholm International Arbitration Review, p. 53.

139 *Sanum* v. *Laos*, para. 128.

140 *Tza* v. *Peru*, ICSID Case No ARB/07/06, Decision on Jurisdiction and Competence, June 19, 2009.

141 *Plama Consortium* v. *Bulgaria*, ICSID Case No ARB/03/24, Decision on Jurisdiction, February 8, 2005, *Austrian Airlines* v. *Slovakia*, UNCITRAL Final Award, October 9, 2009, *ST-AD GmbH* v. *The Republic of Bulgaria*, PCA Case No 2011–06, Award on Jurisdiction, July 18, 2013; *Vladimir Berschader and Moise Berschader* v. *The Russian Federation*, SCC Case No 080/2004, Award, April 21, 2006; *RoInvest Co UK Ltd* v. *The Russian Federation*, SCC Case No V079/2005, Award on Jurisdiction, October 1, 2007.

China, as the respondent, raised several objections concerning jurisdiction, the most debated of which was the limitation period. The respondent submitted that Ansung's claim was time-barred under Article 9(7) of the BIT as it instituted the proceedings more than three years after the date on which it had acquired the knowledge that it had incurred loss or damage. Ansung countered that its claim was timely on the grounds that (i) it first acquired the knowledge that it had incurred loss or damage only around December 17, 2011, more than one year after the government had failed to provide the additional land promised for a second phase of the project; (ii) it had made a claim through submission of its notice of intent on May 17, 2014 or on filing its request for arbitration on October 7, 2014.

The respondent asserted that the claimant "necessarily knew of the fact that it had incurred loss or damage on the same date prior to the disposal of its investment in October 2011," the date on which the claimant sold its investment "in order to avoid further losses." This should be the start date for such a temporal limitation period, known as *dies a quo*. The respondent stated that the three-year period commenced when the claimant knew "of the fact that some loss has occurred, not upon its full realization."[142] Turning to the *dies ad quem*, the end date for the three-year limitation period, the respondent argued that the end date must be November 4, 2014, the date on which the ICSID registered the claimant's request for arbitration.

The claimant argued that it could not ascertain its loss or damage until after its expectations and plan for the construction had been completely frustrated. The claimant stated that the continuing loss was a consequence of government inaction and that it had tried to resolve the problem with the government.[143] Therefore, the claimant explained that the *dies a quo* must be December 17, 2011,[144] when the deal to sell its entire investment in the project was closed and the losses became unavoidable for the purposes of Article 9(7).

The tribunal agreed with China's request and could not accept the claimant's arguments. From the perspective of the tribunal, the claimant ignored the plain meaning of the determinative words "first" and "loss or damage" in Article 9(7). The limitation period began with the investor's first knowledge of the fact that it had incurred loss or damage, not on the date on which it gained knowledge of the quantum of that loss or damage. The claimant's actual sale of its shares on December 17, 2011, marked the date on which it could finalize or liquidate its damage, not the first date on which it had to know it was incurring damage.[145] The tribunal did acknowledge the claimant's legal argument that a continuing omission by a host state and damages for such a continuing breach may be measured from different times after the first incident of that omission. But this could not change the date, which was before October 2011, when the claimant first knew it had incurred damage. In the tribunal's view, the claimant was neither required nor permitted to wait and observe the complete extent of the damage for purposes of Article 9(7). Accordingly, the tribunal determined the *dies a quo*, that is, the start date for the limitation period to be October 2011 or earlier.[146] Here, the tribunal emphasized that the limitation period started on the first date on which the investor knew there was loss or damage, even if there was a continuing breach. This technical emphasis meant that the investor needed only to be

[142] *Ansung Housing Co., Ltd.* v. *China*, para. 76.
[143] Ibid., para. 93.
[144] Ibid., para. 94.
[145] Ibid., para. 110.
[146] Ibid., paras. 107–114.

aware that loss or damage had or may have occurred; full knowledge of the loss or damage was not required in order to bring a claim.

As a result, the tribunal found that it lacked jurisdiction *ratione temporis* and dismissed the case.[147] The instant case suggests that the scope of the time-bar provisions often turns on its precise wording, and the clear wording of the time-bar provisions will often be given full effect and can form the basis of any early dismissal where the relevant arbitration rules permit this for claims that are manifestly without merit.[148]

6.8 MFN TREATMENT OF PROCEDURAL RIGHTS

There has been significant controversy over the extent to which MFN clauses should apply to substantive rights or procedural rights, or both. Arbitration practice indicates that the broader the language used, the more likely it is that the tribunal will extend the MFN standard to cover procedural rights. It has been confirmed in other cases that the MFN treatment may be relied on to broaden the tribunal's jurisdiction,[149] from disputes relating to the amount or payment of compensation as under the basic treaty, to all disputes including the existence of expropriation under a third party BIT.[150] The case law in this respect, however, is divergent.[151]

Unlike other earlier cases[152] which have seen a substantial contradiction in the reasoning of the tribunals adjudicating the extension of the MFN treatment to procedural rights in BIT cases, the tribunals in China–BIT-related cases indicate some consistency not only in rejections but also in interpretative techniques.

In *Tza Yap Shum* v. *Peru*, the tribunal was faced with the claimant's concerned attempts to extend the scope of jurisdiction to issues not covered by the arbitration clauses in the disputed China–Peru BIT 1994 according to the Peru–Columbia BIT 2007[153] without limited jurisdiction *ratione materiae*. The MFN clause in the China–Peru BIT provides: "The treatment and protection referred to in Paragraph 1 of this Article [fair and equitable treatment] shall not be less favourable than that accorded to investments and activities associated with such investments of investors of a third State." It is clear from the language that the MFN clause merely applies to fair and equitable treatment and constant protection but not to all matters under the BIT. Further, the MFN clause in Article 3 of the BIT applies only to investment but not to dispute settlement rights accruing to investors as arbitration is a procedural right of an

147 Ibid., paras. 73 and 92.

148 In other investment arbitration cases, the guidance on early dismissal of claims which are manifestly without merit may also extend beyond the interpretation of the ICSID rules. The SCC commercial arbitration and SIAC commercial arbitration and investment arbitration rules contain similar provisions allowing for the early dismissal of unmeritorious claims.

149 The case law evinces a growing inclination on the part of tribunals to formulate the exhaustion of local remedies clauses as conditions to be satisfied before jurisdiction can be established. In some cases the tribunals applied a more deferential arbitral treatment of local remedy first provisions. Matthew C. Porterfield, "Exhaustion of Local Remedies in Investor-State Dispute Settlement: An Idea Whose Time Has Come?" (2015) 41 (Fall) *Yale Journal of International Law Online*, https://ssrn.com/abstract=2735036 (accessed March 12, 2021).

150 *RosInvestCo. UK Ltd* v. *Russian Federation*, SCC Case No. Arb. V079/2005.

151 *Kilic Insaat Ithalat Ihracat Sanayi ve Ticaret Anonim Sirketi* v. *Turkmenistan*, ICSID Case No. ARB/10/1; *Joseph C. Lemire* v. *Ukraine*, ICSID Case No. ARB/06/18; *Amboiente Ufficio S.p.A. and others* v. *Argentine Republic*, ICSID Case No. ARB/08/9.

152 *Plama* v. *Bulgaria*, ICSID Case No. ARB/03/24, Decision on Jurisdiction, February 8, 2005; *Maffezini* v. *Spain*, ICSID Case No. ARB/97/7, Award on Jurisdiction, January 25, 2000; *Salini et al.* v. *Morocco*, ICSID Case No. ARB/00/4, Decision on Jurisdiction, July 23, 2001 (2003) 42 ILM 609.

153 *Tza* v. *Peru*, ICSID Case No. ARB/07/6, Decision on Jurisdiction and Competence of June 19, 2009, paras. 189–190.

investor and a right to invoke arbitration is a personal right that must be held by an investor but not an investment.

The tribunal found that the submission to ISA in Article 8(3) reflected the parties' agreement on two fundamental issues – that expropriation disputes should be submitted to ICSID arbitration and that specific agreement would be needed to submit other types of dispute to ICSID arbitration.[154] The tribunal therefore determined that the "specific wording of Article 8(3) should prevail over the general wording of the MFN clause in Article 3."[155] The tribunal was self-disciplined, largely by sticking to the "best indicator" of the "intention of the parties expressed in the text,"[156] not to overexaggeratedly broaden its discretion without having any clear indications in the disputed BIT.[157]

In the case of *BUCG* v. *Yemen*, one defense raised by the respondent was that the 1998 Yemen–China BIT's MFN clause could not be used to circumvent the limited jurisdiction of its dispute resolution clause.[158] The tribunal dismissed the respondent's most jurisdictional objections but agreed that the wording of the MFN clause tied it to activities that took place "in the territory" associated geographically with the investment. Thus, the MFN clause could not be used by the tribunal to import a broader dispute resolution clause from the Yemen–UK BIT 1982 to expand the scope of jurisdiction (which itself is not an activity inherently linked to the respondent's territory) over non-expropriation BIT claims, which are beyond Article 10 of the Yemen–China BIT.[159] The tribunal's focus was unique when it came to the issue of applying the MFN provisions to dispute resolution provisions. Instead of addressing this jurisprudential issue in the abstract or relying on other investment tribunal decisions extending the terms of access to international arbitration based on MFN provision, the tribunal focused on the issue of whether the text of the BIT lends itself to such an application.[160] More precisely, the territorial limits imposed on the treatment in Article 3.1 of the Yemen–China BIT 1998 restrained the tribunal from extending more favorable procedural rights (in the form of international arbitration) to the claimant.[161] The tribunal's approach demonstrates its tendency to interpret BIT clauses in line with the object, context and purpose of the dispute resolution clauses and the BIT as a whole.

In *Ansung Housing Co., Ltd.* v. *China*, Ansung sought to invoke the MFN clause in Article 3(3) of the China–South Korea BIT 2007 to save its claim from being time-barred as other Chinese BITs do not prescribe a three-year limitation period within which an investor is required to initiate an arbitration claim against the host state.[162] Relying on a plain reading of the MFN clause,[163] the tribunal held that the MFN clause did not extend to a state's consent

[154] Under Article 8(3) of the BIT, the tribunal's jurisdiction is limited to expropriation. Jurisdiction over all other matters is subject to specific agreement. Those "other matters" include the interpretation of the MFN clause in the first place. This means that the tribunal actually lacks the subject-matter jurisdiction to consider whether MFN can be applied to expand subject-matter jurisdiction.

[155] *Tza* v. *Peru*, para. 216.

[156] Ibid., para. 206.

[157] However, the tribunal appeared to be mistaken in its reasoning. The tribunal took an effect utile approach by differentiating between the applications of the MFN clause based on an a priori categorization of general and specific provisions. This is unsound as the purpose of the MFN clause is to establish and maintain at all times fundamental equality without discrimination among all the countries concerned.

[158] Para. 110.

[159] *BUCG* v. *Yemen*, ICSID Case No. ARB/14/30, Decision on Jurisdiction, para. 120, www.italaw.com/sites/default/files/case-documents/italaw8968.pdf (accessed March 12, 2021).

[160] Ibid., para. 114.

[161] Ibid., para. 117.

[162] *Ansung Housing Co., Ltd.* v. *China*, Award, paras. 125–126.

[163] China–Korea BIT 2007, Art. 3(3).

to arbitrate with investors or to the temporal limitation period for ISA in Article 9(7).[164] Further, the tribunal pointed out that the BIT offers specific MFN protection in relation to an investor's "access to courts of justice, administrative tribunals and authorities," without making any reference to international dispute resolution such as arbitration under the BIT.[165] Accordingly, the tribunal dismissed the case due to the application of the limitation period in Article 9(7).[166] The instant case appears to suggest that MFN provisions are not to provide a way to escape limitation periods even though this may turn on the precise wording of the MFN provisions in question.

In response to the debate on MFN clauses and procedural rights, recent Chinese BITs have tried to eliminate all potential controversies by making clear that the MFN treatment does not cover procedural rights. There is a clarification in the EU–Canada CETA 2017 that MFN treatment cannot be extended to dispute settlement provisions,[167] which effectively avoids any *Maffezini*-like interpretations of the MFN clause.[168]

6.9 RATIONALIZING THE INTERPRETATION OF CHINESE BIT TERMS

Chinese BITs have been characterized by relatively high bars to access, which are intentionally made so by the Chinese treaty drafters. Many procedural terms and issues discussed in this chapter such as the juristic way of applying the fork-in-the-road provision, the limitation period and the MFN clauses indicate conflicting features of Chinese BITs that have barred foreign investors' access to ISDS in the past. On the one hand, narrow interpretations such as the one adopted in *Heilongjiang* could limit access to arbitration in cases in which the occurrence of expropriation has been already declared or determined. On the other hand, the broad interpretation adopted in *Tza Yap Shum*, followed in *Sanum* and *Beijing Urban Construction*, rebuffed the view that the restrictive dispute resolution clause found in China's earlier BITs limits arbitration to disputes regarding the amount of compensation in case of expropriation, providing Chinese or foreign investors with more room to arbitrate expropriation claims. A number of tribunals have shown a tendency to rely on a more expansive treaty interpretation approach that, though despised by the Chinese government, is technically in line with the international norms aimed at promoting and protecting cross-border investments. Reliance on broader arbitration clauses and more expansive interpretation approaches is in the interest of Chinese investors who need a more vibrant ISDS regime to protect their rights while investing overseas.

The abstractly and vaguely worded text of the Chinese BITs left the question of how to adopt an appropriate treaty interpretation method explaining vague treaty terms. Almost all ISDS cases already establish the hurdle that Chinese or foreign investors must overcome when bringing claims under first-generation BITs that provide for limited consent to international arbitration.

164 *Ansung Housing Co., Ltd.* v. *China*, Award, paras. 140–141.
165 China–Korea BIT 2007, Art. 3(5).
166 *Ansung Housing Co. Ltd.* v. *China*, Award, paras. 136–141.
167 EU-Canada CETA, Article X.8(4).
168 *Maffezini* v. *Spain*, ICSID Case No. ARB/97/7, Decision on Jurisdiction, January 25, 2000, paras. 38–64. See, among others, Martins Paparinskis, "MFN Clauses and International Dispute Settlement: Moving Beyond Maffezini and Plama?" (2011) *ICSID Review – Foreign Investment Law Journal* 14–58; Yannick Radi, "The Application of the Most-Favoured-Nation Clause to the Dispute Settlement Provisions of Bilateral Investment Treaties: Domesticating the 'Trojan Horse'" (2007) 18 *European Journal of International Law* 757–774.

Most ISA is treaty-based. The rules of treaty interpretation in the VCLT therefore play a guiding role in determining the meaning of applicable provisions in BITs. Section 3 of Part III of the VCLT governs the interpretation of treaties and comprises Articles 31, 32 and 33.

Looking at the ordinary meaning of the terms to be interpreted is the starting point of treaty interpretation usually by way of referring to the dictionary and comparing the meaning with other similar words for distinction.[169] Some tribunals took the view that the terms to be interpreted were clear by reference to the meanings or criteria set out in the precedents, and therefore there was no need for further interpretation.[170] Notwithstanding the initial search for the ordinary meaning of the text, a narrow but purely linguistic exercise is often not appropriate for the interpretation of an international treaty[171] and thus the task of interpretation moves to the context, and, if necessary, the object and purpose of the treaty.[172]

It is widely acknowledged by tribunals that the interpretation of a term shall also take into account its context because the terms and provisions of a treaty cannot be read in isolation.[173] A wide variety of contextual factors needs to be considered by tribunals, such as the sentence that follows the provision,[174] other articles in the treaty,[175] and the context of the treaty generally.[176] While the immediate context of a term may help determine or distinguish its meaning accordingly,[177] it is the broad context of the whole BIT that leads the tribunals to an interpretation. A primary example is whether the expression "any dispute relating to the amount of compensation for expropriation" in Chinese BITs'[178] grants to the ICSID tribunal full jurisdiction over the issue of liability as well as quantum in connection with the expropriation.[179] Many cases supported a wider interpretation which is more consistent with the disputed provisions of the BITs.[180] Likely, a narrower interpretation would compel

169 See *Tza Yap Shum* v. *The Republic of Peru*, ICSID Case No. ARB/07/6, Award (original in Spanish), para. 151. See also *Sanum* v. *Laos*, UNCITRAL, PCA Case No. 2013–13, Award on Jurisdiction, para. 329; *Ping An* v. *Belgium*, ICSID Case No. ARB/12/29, Award, paras. 214–218.

170 *Ansung Housing Co., Ltd.* v. *China*, ICSID Case No. ARB/14/25, Award, para. 111.

171 *Ping An* v. *Belgium*, ICSID Case No. ARB/12/29, Award, para. 218.

172 *BUCG* v. *Yemen*, ICSID Case No. ARB/14/30, Decision on Jurisdiction, para. 77. See also *Sanum* v. *Laos*, UNCITRAL, PCA Case No. 2013–13, SGCA, para. 126.

173 *Sanum* v. *Laos*, UNCITRAL, PCA Case No. 2013–13, Award on Jurisdiction, para. 330; *Beijing Shougang et al.* v. *Mongolia*, UNCITRAL, PCA, Award, para. 425.

174 *BUCG* v. *Yemen*, ICSID Case No. ARB/14/30, Decision on Jurisdiction, para. 78.

175 *Ping An* v. *Belgium*, ICSID Case No. ARB/12/29, Award, para. 212; *Sanum* v. *Laos*, UNCITRAL, PCA Case No. 2013–13, Award on Jurisdiction, para. 330.

176 In the case *Beijing Shougang et al.* v. *Mongolia*, to interpret the dispute provision of the BIT, the tribunal considered the context of the evolution of the Chinese treaty practice since 1998, which shows that the PRC's more recent desire to expand the level of protection accorded both to foreign investors investing in the PRC and to Chinese investors investing in other countries.

177 *BUCG* v. *Yemen*, ICSID Case No. ARB/14/30, Decision on Jurisdiction, paras. 118–120.

178 China–Yemen BIT 1998, Art. 10.2; China–Peru BIT 1998, Art. 8(3); China–Laos BIT 1993, Art. 8(3); China–Mongolia BIT 1993, Art. 8(3).

179 *Beijing Shougang et al.* v. *Mongolia*, UNCITRAL, PCA, Award; *Sanum* v. *Laos*, UNCITRAL, PCA Case No. 2013–13, Award on Jurisdiction; *BUCG* v. *Yemen*, ICSID Case No. ARB/14/30, Decision on Jurisdiction; *Tza* v. *Peru*, ICSID Case No. ARB/07/6, Award (original in Spanish).

180 *Sanum* v. *Laos*, UNCITRAL, PCA Case No. 2013–13, Hearing Transcript (Day 1, September 14, 2015) 47:18 to 48:13. Also see *Tokios Tokelés* v. *Ukraine*, ICSID Case No. ARB/02/18, Decision on Jurisdiction (April 29, 2004), paras. 21–70; *Saluka Investments* v. *Czech Republic*, UNCITRAL Partial Award (March 17, 2006), at 46–50; *Noble Ventures, Inc.* v. *Romania*, ICSID Case No. ARB/01/11, Award (October 12, 2005), paras. 46–62; *Pope & Talbot* v. *Canada*, Award on the Merits of Phase 2 (UNCITRAL April 10, 2001) and *Metalclad* v. *Mexico*, ICSID Case No. ARB(AF)/97/1, Award (August 30, 2000).

the investors to national courts and preclude a claim in arbitration due to a fork-in-the-road clause,[181] which often creates an internal contradiction of the treaty.[182]

A number of arbitral awards have made explicit reference to the "object and purpose" of a treaty or a particular provision in the treaty, and such a criterion often plays a dominant role in the treaty interpretation process.[183] Due to the need for a dynamic balance between the protection of foreign investments and the development of economic cooperation between the sovereign states,[184] it does not mean that one aspect of the object and purpose should be given preponderance over the meaning of a particular clause or justify leaving without effect a clause of the treaty.[185] At this juncture, the principle of *effet utile* or "effective interpretation"[186] is relied on to give a treaty its fullest weight and effect consistent with the normal sense of the words of the text and in such a way that a reason and meaning can be attributed to every part of the text.[187]

The treaty interpretation matrix is quite flexible, allowing arbitrators to structure different configurations of interpretative tools on a case-by-case basis. As the general rule of treaty interpretation comprises several subnorms and there is no uniform way of applying these subnorms, the flexibility of the interpretative matrix leads to conflicting trends in arbitral jurisprudence concerning a variety of procedural and substantive provisions in BITs. Consequently, the lack of coherence of the system is an inherent defect in treaty interpretation thereby affecting the legitimacy of the BIT regime and ISA as a whole.

The VCLT also leaves space for evolutionary treaty interpretation, meaning that certain norms have to be interpreted in a dynamic and changing context so as to reflect the changes in formulating BITs over time.[188] The evolutionary approach makes sense in interpreting Chinese BITs as BIT terms are evolving while China is changing its role from a capital-importing state to a capital-exporting state. As the statistics have indicated, the tribunals have tended to expansively interpret BIT terms while they were called upon to determine the scope of jurisdiction. This also seems to be the case, at least evidenced by the majority of Chinese BIT cases, when the tribunals are asked to interpret Chinese BIT terms. A brief summary can be found in Table 6.2.

It has been argued that an MFN clause has a multilateralizing effect[189] as it is operated in such a way as to extend the greatest protection offered by a state in a single BIT to the beneficiaries of all of its BITs. As a matter of fact, treaty interpretation devices deployed in

181 *BUCG* v. *Yemen*, ICSID Case No. ARB/14/30, Decision on Jurisdiction, para. 84. *Tza* v. *Peru*, ICSID Case No. ARB/07/6, Award (original in Spanish), para. 188. See also *Beijing Shougang et al.* v. *Mongolia*, UNCITRAL, PCA, Award, para. 340.

182 *Renta 4 S.V.S.A. et al* v. *Russian Federation*, SCC Case No. V 024/2007, Award on Preliminary Objections, para. 56, cited in *Tza* v. *Peru*, ICSID Case No. ARB/07/6, Award (original in Spanish), para. 188.

183 *Ping An* v. *Belgium*, ICSID Case No. ARB/12/29, Award, para. 149; *BUCG* v. *Yemen*, ICSID Case No. ARB/14/30, Decision on Jurisdiction, para. 78; *Sanum* v. *Laos*, UNCITRAL, PCA Case No. 2013–13, Award on Jurisdiction, para. 86; *Tza* v. *Peru*, ICSID Case No. ARB/07/6, Decision on Jurisdiction, para. 128; *Beijing Shougang Mining Investment Company Ltd., et al.* v. *Mongolia*, UNCITRAL, PCA, Award, para. 425.

184 *BUCG* v. *Yemen*, ICSID Case No. ARB/14/30, Decision on Jurisdiction, paras. 90–91. See also *RosInvestCo UK Ltd.* v. *Russian Federation*, SCC Case No. V 079/2005, Award on Jurisdiction, October 5, 2007, para. 83.

185 *Sanum* v. *Laos*, UNCITRAL, PCA Case No. 2013–13, Award on Jurisdiction, para. 338; *BUCG* v. *Yemen*, ICSID Case No. ARB/14/30, Decision on Jurisdiction, paras. 338–339.

186 *BUCG* v. *Yemen*, ICSID Case No. ARB/14/30, Decision on Jurisdiction, para. 72; *Sanum* v. *Laos*, UNCITRAL, PCA Case No. 2013–13, para. 128.

187 *Sanum* v. *Laos*, [2016] SGCA 57, Judgment, September 29, 2016, para. 128.

188 VCTL, Art. 31(1)(c).

189 Stephen Schill, *The Multilateralization of International Investment Law* (Cambridge University Press 2009) 65–106, 121–196.

TABLE 6.2 *Comparison of interpretating techniques in China-related investment arbitration cases*

Case	Significance	Key jurisdictional issue	Relevant BIT and clauses	Interpretative approach	Jurisdiction
Tza Yap Shum v. *Republic of Peru*	The first known ISDS case involving China as home state.	"Investor"	China–Peru BIT, Article 12(a)	Is a Hong Kong resident qualified as an investor for the BIT purpose? The tribunal viewed it as beyond the dispute at issue. The tribunal relied on Article 25 of the ICSID Convention to grant jurisdiction.	Yes
		"Investment"	Article 1(1)	Peru claimed that Tza's investment was "indirect investment" made through a BVI holding company. The tribunal extended its jurisdiction via Article 25(1) of the ICSID Convention which does not impose any restriction on the jurisdiction of ICSID tribunals. The definition of "investment" is very broad.	
		"Dispute"	Article 8(3)	The tribunal followed Article 31 of the VCLT and interpreted it in "good faith in accordance with the ordinary meaning to be given to the terms of the treaty in their context and in the light of its object and purpose." The broadest interpretation is the most appropriate approach to recognize the inclusive nature of the phrase "involving." Besides, the "wording of the Preamble of the BIT" is the supplementary means of interpretation.	

(*Continued*)

	Fork-in-the-road	Article 8	The tribunal looked into the "ordinary meaning" to conduct textual analysis and characterized the jurisdictional relation of the domestic court and the international arbitral tribunal as a horizontal configuration. Thus, the claimant was entitled to institute arbitration directly without first exhausting the remedies offered by local courts.	
BUCG v. *Yemen*	Is BUCG, an SOE, a qualified investor?	China–Yemen BIT, Art. 10 ("any dispute relating to the amount of compensation for expropriation")	Beyond the ordinary meaning – moving to consider the context (fact-specific context), object and purpose of the BIT.	Jurisdiction was established over expropriation claims regarding both liability and compensation, based on a broad interpretation of the dispute settlement clause of the BIT as it promotes the BIT's overall purpose and objective. Structural links to the Chinese government and public functions inside China were irrelevant to BUCG's standing as an investor at ICSID.
	Subject-matter jurisdiction (*ratione materiae*)	ICSID Convention, Art. 25(1)	"Contextual approach"	

(*Continued*)

TABLE 6.2 *(Continued)*

Case	Significance	Key jurisdictional issue	Relevant BIT and clauses	Interpretative approach	Jurisdiction
Sanum v. *Laos*	The first investor–state tribunal asked to determine the application of Chinese IIAs to legal entities incorporated and established in Macao. The first judgment by Singapore's highest court involving the curial review of an investment award. The first time the SGCA issued a decision on a jurisdictional challenge concerning an ISA.	"[T]erritorial scope of the China-Laos BIT" Qualification of an investor Subject-matter jurisdiction: scope of "dispute"	Customary international law + the fulfillment of the goals of the BIT (para. 295). PRC–Laos BIT, Art. 1(2)(b) PRC–Laos BIT, Art. 8(3): "a dispute involving the amount of compensation for expropriation" to be submitted to international arbitration	China–Laos BIT applies to Macau: a broad approach. SGHC adopted a restrictive approach. The SGCA did not find a different intention – the MTF Rule presumptively applied. The balance of probabilities as the relevant standard of proof – the critical date doctrine. The SGCA accepted a broader reading of Art. 8(3) proposed by the claimant. The SGCA considered the interpretation of Art. 8(3) in light of its ordinary meaning, context, object and purpose – ordinary meaning was equivocal and capable of supporting both interpretations – and then focused on the context, object and purpose of Art. 8(3). Adopted a broader approach (purposively in light of the principle of effective interpretation instead of a highly textual approach to interpreting a similar clause).	Jurisdiction was confirmed by the tribunal. No jurisdiction: rejected the applicability of the BIT to Macau and the tribunal's broad interpretation of the treaty's dispute settlement clause. Jurisdiction, but the implications for future determinations of the applicability of PRC BITs to Chinese SAR remain unclear. Singapore courts have consistently ruled in favor of broad interpretation of arbitration clauses. This is a pro-arbitration stance of the judiciary in Singapore.

(Continued)

			Fork-in-the-road provision	A narrow interpretation of Art. 8(3) would have meant that an investor first had to approach a court to determine whether an impermissible expropriation had occurred. Once the investor had approached the court under Art. 8(2), the remedy of arbitration in Art. 8(3) would no longer be available, thus rendering Art. 8(3) otiose. The Court of Appeal agreed with the tribunal that a narrow interpretation would be against the principle of *effet utile* (effective interpretation). The broad interpretation of Art. 8(3) "is also consistent with the BIT's objective of protection investment."	
Beijing Shougang Mining Investment Co., Ltd., China Heilongjiang International Economic & Technical Cooperative Corp., and Qinhuangdao Qinlong International Industrial Co., Ltd. v. *Mongolia*	First ad hoc BIT case administered by the PCA.		Art. 8, China–Mongolia BIT 1991	The tribunal interpreted the BIT, the purpose of which was to provide incentives for investment from the PRC into Mongolia, to require that the national courts of Mongolia first declare that other arms of the government of Mongolia had expropriated the assets of the Chinese investors; only then could there be arbitration, and the only arbitrable question would be the amount of compensation for the taking.	Tribunal – narrow interpretation. Court – taking into account the object and purpose of the BIT – wide interpretation.

(Continued)

TABLE 6.2 *(Continued)*

Case	Significance	Key jurisdictional issue	Relevant BIT and clauses	Interpretative approach	Jurisdiction
				The tribunal – it could have jurisdiction only if Mongolia admitted that it had expropriated the investment, and the tribunal would have jurisdiction only to resolve any controversy over the amount of compensation that Mongolia should pay. The District Court of New York: "Indeed, every other tribunal to address this question under PRC BITs has rejected the narrow interpretation adopted by this Tribunal."	
			Art. 8(3): subject matter of the claim (*ratione materiae*)	The question is whether the arbitration clause in Art. 8(3) of the BIT applies to a particular type of controversy – namely a dispute over whether an expropriation has occurred – a question of arbitrability.	
			Fork-in-the-road clause	The Mongolia–China BIT 1991 is distinguishable from many other BITs which do commit the question of arbitrability to the arbitrators; the disputed BIT does not commit the question of arbitrability to the arbitrators.	

(Continued)

		Art. 4(1)	The tribunal in this case adopted an extremely narrow construction in which the only matter that was arbitrable was the amount of compensation for expropriation. According to the tribunal, only the alleged offending state itself can determine whether it expropriated property. If it denies having done so, the independent tribunal established by the BIT can never come into existence. Thus, an investor is left in the perverse position that only if the state's executive or legislature admits that it has expropriated the investment, or if the state's own courts can be persuaded so to declare, can that investor then proceed to international arbitration. The interpretation defeats the purpose of ISA and deprives the investor of much of the benefit of the treaty. Citing *Tza Yap Shum* v. *Peru*.
		Art. 1(2)(b), "Investor" Art. 1(1), "Investment"	

(Continued)

TABLE 6.2 *(Continued)*

Case	Significance	Key jurisdictional issue	Relevant BIT and clauses	Interpretative approach	Jurisdiction
Ansung Housing Co., Ltd. v. PRC	The first published ICSID case in which China was the respondent. The first claim to be brought to the ICSID by a South Korean investor and the first claim at the ICSID to involve China as a respondent state that has proceeded to a substantive hearing that led to an award.	Limitation period	Art. 9(7) China–South Korea BIT 2007	Plain meaning; interpretation on the basis of the plain language – the tribunal emphasized that the "limitation period begins with an investor's first knowledge of the fact that it has incurred loss or damage, not with the date on which it gains knowledge of the quantum of that loss or damage" (para. 110).	No jurisdiction; time-barred as the investor initiated arbitration more than three years after acquiring knowledge of the loss or damage
		Whether an MFN clause applies to dispute settlement provisions (in this case, to a limitation period in the dispute resolution provision of the BIT).	Art. 3(3)	The possibility of invoking the MFN clause to apply more favorable dispute settlement depends on the precise wording of the MFN clause.	

ISDS cases also have a similar but quite weak multilateralizing effect as the tribunals usually pay a certain level of attention to previously rendered arbitral awards, and treaty interpretations made in these previous awards have persuasive authority, arguably binding later tribunals facing similar factual scenarios and/or interpretation tasks. In this sense, the awards and their interpretation methodologies analyzed here are of relevance to our understanding and application of broadly or vaguely worded Chinese BIT terms. The treaty interpretative approaches can be the major means the treaty parties rely on to defend the treaty purposes they are meant to realize in the first place. In other words, by borrowing the metaphor used by Schill, treaty interpretive devices are the means to guarding (or tearing down) the Great Wall.

7

Parallel Proceedings under Chinese BITs

In international arbitration, the basic norm is that arbitration and litigation are two separate dispute resolution methods that are independent from and mutually exclusive to each other. The two proceedings in theory cannot be carried out at the same time, which otherwise constitutes parallel proceedings. This principle is embodied in the 1958 Convention on the Recognition and Enforcement of Foreign Arbitral Awards (the "New York Convention"). Since the New York Convention has been ratified by over 160 countries in the world,[1] there is technically no concurrency issue in the field of international commercial arbitration.

Under special circumstances, parallel proceedings or dual–track proceedings may occur between arbitration and litigation in the field of international investment arbitration. The concurrency issue may result in conflicting rulings (awards) between the arbitral tribunal and the court, which is not conducive to the timely and effective resolution of disputes in the BIT context, and may even undermine the legitimacy of the ISDS mechanism.

Hela Schwarz GmbH (Hela), a German manufacturing entity, brought a claim at the ICSID against the PRC in 2017, claiming expropriation of assets by the Chinese government over its investment. Ji'nan Hela Schwarz Food Co., Ltd. ("JHSF"), Hela's local subsidiary in China, filed the same claim with the Chinese courts before the arbitration claim was filed with the ICSID and tried to invalidate the government's administrative decision to expropriate the assets. This is the third investment arbitration case based on the Chinese BIT.[2] This is also the first China–related investment arbitration case which involves the parallel proceedings issue.

This chapter investigates the parallel proceedings issue in the contexts of *Hela Schwarz GmbH* v. *PR China* and Chinese BITs. The significance of this investigation lies in the fact that Hela is the only case touching on the parallel proceedings issue among fewer than a dozen Chinese BIT–related investment arbitration cases filed with the ICSID. A close look at the Hela case may reveal a black hole in Chinese BIT law and practice, which may lead to potential uncertainty in determining the jurisdiction of the tribunal while foreign investors make their claims against the Chinese government in order to protect their rights.

[1] www.newyorkconvention.org/list+of+contracting+states (accessed March 17, 2021).

[2] The first two cases were *Ansung Housing Co., Ltd.* v. *China*, ICSID Case No. ARB/14/25; and *Ekran Berhad* v. *People's Republic of China*, ICSID Case No. ARB/11/15.

This chapter is structured as follows. Section 7.1 outlines the key factual setting of *Hela Schwarz GmbH* v. *PR China* and brings out the issue of parallel proceedings. Section 7.2 then discusses the so–called parallel proceedings in (or concurrency of) domestic litigation and investment arbitration, their defects and impacts as well as some general solutions. By way of background, this section discusses a number of BIT norms such as the exhaustion of local remedies clause, the umbrella clause and the MFN clause, all of which may lead to the issue of parallel proceedings. The focus of Section 7.3 is to investigate the dispute resolution clauses in the China–Germany BIT 2003 and its Protocol 2003 surrounding the parallel proceedings issue. Possible outcomes of the Hela case will also be analyzed in this section. Section 7.4 moves beyond the China–Germany BIT 2003 and categorizes the dispute settlement clauses in China's BITs with 104 states according to the different ways of addressing parallel proceedings between domestic litigation and international arbitration. This categorization indicates the complexity of the parallel proceedings issue in BIT law. Section 7.5 discusses the possibility of relying on the MFN treatment clause to solve the issue of parallel proceedings. The real challenge to and difficulty in the conflicts is a need for a broader thinking of parallel proceedings, which will be discussed in Section 7.6.

7.1 *HELA SCHWARZ GMBH* V. *PR CHINA* AND DOMESTIC COURT PROCEEDINGS

On May 2, 2017, Hela Schwarz GmbH, a German manufacturer of compound spices and food additives, filed a Request for Arbitration against China with the ICSID according to the Agreement between the People's Republic of China and the Federal Republic of Germany on the Encouragement and Reciprocal Protection of Investments dated December 1, 2003 (hereinafter referred to as the China–Germany BIT 2003) and the Protocol (the Protocol 2003) as well as the ICSID Convention. The ICSID Secretary–General registered the Request for Arbitration and notified the parties.

A tribunal was constituted for the Hela case on January 8, 2018, and the first telephone hearing was held in February 2018. The Chinese government, as the respondent, filed an objection against the jurisdiction on December 17, 2018. To date, the details of the Hela case have not been fully published on the ICSID website except for two Procedural Orders.[3] However, we may have a glimpse of the case through the rulings made by the Chinese courts.

The predecessor of JHSF was a joint venture established in 1999 by Hermann Laue Condiment Co., Ltd. and Ji'nan Meat Factory in China. Thereafter, JHSF was restructured to be an entity wholly owned by Hela. JHSF was granted the legal right to use a parcel of state–owned industrial land (the Land) in Ji'nan City, the capital of Shandong Province, China for fifty years until July 29, 2051. JHSF built some factory buildings (the Buildings) on 4,821.18 square meters of the Land, which was located in the Huashan Area, Licheng District, Ji'nan City. In June 2004, JHSF moved to the Buildings, and later became a well–known manufacturer of compound spices, food additives and condiments in China.

On September 11, 2014, the Ji'nan Municipal People's Government issued a Housing Expropriation Decision, the Notice Ji Zheng Gao No. 9 (2014), to expropriate the Land and the Buildings, as part of the renovation project in the Huashan Area being carried out by the Ji'nan Municipal People's Government. The whole area for this renovation project is east of Jiangjun Road, north of Xiaoqing River, west of Qinghe River and south of Jiqing

[3] Procedural Order No. 1 and Procedure Order No. 2, *Hela Schwarz GmbH* v. *People's Republic of China*, ICSID Case No. ARB/17/19.

Expressway (North Line). The Housing Expropriation Decision merely targeted the state–owned land within the set boundaries. The compensation was to be made in accordance with the Compensation Plan for the Housing Expropriation in the Renovation Project in Huashan Area. According to the media reports, the Huashan Area's renovation project is the largest land development project in Ji'nan City's history covering 14.69 square kilometers in total and affecting twenty–three villages. In July 2013, the demolition officially started, but many households still have not signed the demolition contracts.[4]

JHSF's factory buildings are located within the scope of demolition in the Huashan Area and are directly affected by this renovation project. Against the Housing Expropriation Decision, JHSF filed an administrative case against the local government's expropriation with the Ji'nan Intermediate People's Court on May 3, 2016 requesting the court to rule against the Notice Ji Zheng Gao No. 9 (2014).

On July 19, 2016, the Ji'nan Intermediate People's Court made an administrative ruling (2016) Lu 01 Xing Chu, No. 296, and rejected the claim made by JHSF, which then appealed to the Shandong High People's Court challenging the administrative review decision. The Shandong High People's Court further rejected the appeal and upheld the original ruling on December 6, 2016. Hela, the parent company of JHSF, was so dissatisfied with the Chinese courts' decisions that it filed the arbitration case with the ICSID.

While the administrative litigation was ongoing, the Ji'nan Municipal People's Government issued a Housing Expropriation Compensation Decision which offered to pay JHSF the amount of renminbi 32,954,380 as compensation for the expropriation of the Land and the Buildings. Nevertheless, Hela viewed this amount as inadequate.

Prior to the filing of the arbitration claim with the ICSID, the JHSF made a complaint to the Ji'nan Municipal People's Government, which turned down the JHSF's request. After Hela filed the Request for Arbitration with the ICSID, the Ji'nan Municipal People's Government applied for enforcement of the Compensation Decision at the Licheng People's Court of Ji'nan City, which issued an Enforcement Decision on June 12, 2017, granting the enforcement application and ordering JHSF to vacate the Buildings within ten days of service. However, the local government did not undertake any enforcement action and JHSF did not vacate the Buildings in the following five months. JHSF was informed by an administrative ruling on November 17, 2017 that compensation in the amount stated in the Compensation Decision had been placed in escrow at the Licheng District Court.

The JHSF remained in operation in the Buildings up to November 30, 2017 when the Ji'nan Municipal People's Government issued a public announcement ordering JHSF to evacuate the Buildings within five days, failing which would lead the local government to initiate forced evacuation. At that point, most of the buildings in the same area surrounding JHSF's premises had already been demolished, and the construction of new buildings had begun. As of February 1, 2018, JHSF's premises had been fully evacuated and all the Buildings had been demolished.

Hela submitted an Urgent Request for Provisional Measures with the ICSID tribunal on December 4, 2017 based on its concern about the possibility of aggravation of the dispute in the future. The tribunal denied Hela's request for provisional measures on the grounds that the demolition of the Buildings had been largely completed by the time of December 2017, but the tribunal was constituted on January 8, 2018.[5]

4 For details of Chinese court proceedings, Ji'nan Intermediate People's Court Administrative Ruling (2016) Lu No. Xing Chu No. 296 and Shandong High People's Court Administrative Ruling (2016) Lu Xing Zhong No. 1491.

5 Procedure Order No. 2, *Hela Schwarz GmbH* v. *People's Republic of China*, ICSID Case No. ARB/17/19, paras. 110–112.

The Hela case raises a matter of concern, that is, if a foreign investor submits a case to the court in the host state and the court makes a final judgment, can the investor still submit the dispute to the ICSID for arbitration or vice versa? This is a so-called concurrency issue between international arbitration and domestic court proceedings in international dispute settlement as the obligations (or rights) concurrently imposed (or granted) by two parallel treaty provisions on the disputing parties are coexisting in nature. The practical difficulty is that the disputing parties are to fulfill (or enjoy) dual, or even conflicting, obligations (or rights) under these coexisting treaty provisions.

7.2 PARALLEL PROCEEDINGS IN LITIGATION AND ARBITRATION

Parallel proceedings are where the same parties are litigating substantially the same issues based on the same facts in two different forums, that is, arbitration[6] applying of different rules or principles.[7] The principle of *res judicata* prevents continued litigation of identical disputes, which requires three elements: *personae* (same parties), *petitum* (same object of claims) and *causa petendi* (same legal basis of claims), three aspects of the so-called triple identity test. If the other forum is another court, it is duplicative or parallel litigation.[8] Dual-track or parallel proceedings in arbitration and litigation would bring some side effects or "double jeopardy" on both the arbitration and the litigation.[9] Apart from delays, financial burden and waste of judicial resources, the key risk for the disputing parties is contradictory decisions on the same dispute. As the parties have reached an arbitration agreement, parallel proceedings in arbitration and litigation certainly damage the parties' party autonomy and contractual freedom, eventually undermining the effectiveness of arbitration. Involving the same parties for the same dispute in the other forum violates the arbitration agreement. As the Institut de Droit International stated: "[P]arallel litigation in more than one country between the same, or related, parties in relation to the same, or related, issues may lead to injustice, delay, increased expense, and inconsistent decisions."[10]

The concept of *lis abili pendens* (literally meaning dispute elsewhere pending) is a norm that operates with a first-in-time rule, meaning that priority is given to the arbitration first-seized, and the court second-seized has no right to decide whether it has jurisdiction or not and has to decline jurisdiction.[11] Although the doctrine of *lis pendens* as a tool to avoid parallel proceedings is a general principle of international law,[12] there is no uniform standard for dealing with parallel proceedings globally.[13] In common law jurisdictions, the court may

6 The parallel proceedings may also occur in different courts, i.e., ICJ and ECHR, at the same time. *Banro v. Congo*, Award on Jurisdiction of September 1, 2000, ICSID Case No. ARB/98/7, para. 25.

7 Norbert Horn, "Arbitration and the Protection of Foreign Investment: Concepts and Means" in Norbert Horn and Stefan Kroll (eds.), *Arbitrating Foreign Disputes* (Kluwer Law International 2004) 1–2.

8 James P. George, "Parallel Litigation" (1999) 51(4) *Baylor Law Review* 774–776.

9 Philip I. Bruner, "Dual Track Proceedings in Arbitration and Litigation: Reducing the Peril of 'Double Jeopardy' by Consolidation, Joinder and Appellate Arbitration" (2014) 31(4) *International Construction Law Review* 537, 557.

10 Institut de Droit International, Resolution on the principles for determining when the use of the doctrine of forum non conveniens and anti-suit injunctions is appropriate, Session de Bruges, 2003.

11 The doctrine of *forum non conveniens* and the doctrine of *abus de droit* serve the similar function to curtail the abuse that the parallel proceeding might entail with the purpose of frustrating the legitimate rights of another party. Yuval Shany, *The Competing Jurisdictions of International Courts and Tribunals* (Oxford University Press 2003) 157.

12 Norah Gallagher, "Parallel Proceedings, Res Judicata and Lis Pendens, Problems and Possible Solutions" in Loukas A. Mistelis and Julian D. M. Lew (eds.), *Pervasive Problems in International Arbitration* (Kluwer Law International 2006) 334.

13 Nadine Balkanyi-Nordmann, "The Perils of Parallel Proceedings: Is an Arbitration Award Enforceable If the Same Case Is Pending Elsewhere?" in Thomas E. Carbonneau and Jeanette A. Jaeggi (eds.), *Handbook on International Arbitration and ADR* (Juris 2006) 185.

issue an anti-suit injunction to safeguard the sanctity of agreements between parties in case of dispute. Once the anti-suit injunction is issued, the party has to forfeit the foreign proceedings so that the counterparty's interest is protected. The doctrine of *lis pendens* is to some extent supplemented by the rule of *forum non conveniens*, according to which a court or tribunal may refuse to exercise jurisdiction when the other court or tribunal may be in a more appropriate position to decide the dispute. When multiple states are involved, the courts and tribunals may have to take into account principles of comity, judicial deference and sovereignty.

The use of arbitration in the international investment field to resolve investment disputes between host countries and foreign investors started in the 1960s. The ICSID, established under the Washington Convention, introduced arbitration for the first time to resolve investment disputes between the host state and foreign nationals investing into the host state. The Washington Convention states: "The jurisdiction of the Centre shall extend to any legal dispute arising directly out of an investment, between a Contracting State (or any constituent subdivision or agency of a Contracting State designated to the Centre by that State) and a national of another Contracting State, which the parties to the dispute consent in writing to submit to the Centre. When the parties have given their consent, no party may withdraw its consent unilaterally."[14] This "consent in writing" provision is equivalent to an arbitration agreement, being a direct agreement, a treaty provision or a unilateral offer to arbitrate under domestic law[15] that requires the contracting state to agree to arbitrate the investment dispute between itself and the nationals of another contracting state under the auspice of the ICSID. If the contracting parties ratify the ICSID Convention and consent to submit a specific dispute to arbitration, investment disputes will be settled through arbitration in the ICSID. As a result, there should be no concurrency issue between international arbitration and domestic courts.

Nevertheless, the jurisdiction of the ICSID tribunal under the Washington Convention is somehow limited. The Washington Convention retains the principle of "exhaustion of local remedies" in customary international law by stating: "Consent of the parties to arbitration under this Convention shall, unless otherwise stated, be deemed consent to such arbitration to the exclusion of any other remedy. A Contracting State may require the exhaustion of local administrative or judicial remedies as a condition of its consent to arbitration under this Convention."[16] Although the functionality of this conditional access to ICSID tribunals (or the exclusive remedy rule) was debated in some BIT cases,[17] it is generally recognized that local remedies are no longer the hurdles or preconditions to international arbitration[18] unless the exhaustion of local remedies is explicitly required by the host state in the BIT.[19]

"Exhaustion of local remedy" is the principle under the customary international law.[20] It means that after a foreigner is damaged in the host state, they must first seek local remedies

14 Washington Convention, Art. 25, para. 1.

15 Georges Delaume, "ICSID Arbitration in Practice" (1984) 2 *International Tax and Business Lawyer* 58, 60.

16 Washington Convention, Art. 26.

17 *Southern Pacific Properties (Middle East) Limited* v. *Arab Republic of Egypt*, ICSID Case No. ARB/84/3, Decision on Jurisdiction (November 27, 1985) 3 ICSID Rep. 125 (1995).

18 To date, Guatemala is the only state that made a reservation to the exhaustion of local remedies when joining the ICSID Convention. Katia Yannaca-Small, "Practical Proceedings" in Peter Muchlinski, Federico Ortino and Christoph Schreuer (eds.), *The Oxford Handbook of International Investment Law* (Oxford University Press 2008) 1026.

19 Chittharanjan Felix Amerasinghe, *Local Remedies in International Law* (2nd edition, Cambridge University Press 2004) 269–270; *Hochtief Aktiengesellchaft* v. *Argentina Republic*, ICSID Case No. ARB/07/31, Decision on Jurisdiction (October 24, 2011), Dissenting Opinion of JC Thomas, para. 7.

20 International Court of Justice Reports of Judgements, Advisory Opinions and Orders Case Concerning Elettronica Sicula S.P.A (ELEI) (*United States of America* v. *Italy*), p. 42.

before they can rely on international recourse such as an international court or arbitration tribunal to hold the host state liable for such damages. The Washington Convention allows a state party to exhaust local remedies as long as the host state makes it clear in the BIT, which means that the ICSID can exert its jurisdiction in addition to the domestic judicial remedies in each state party.[21] This raises the possibility of a concurrency issue between the ICSID's arbitration jurisdiction and the state party's domestic judicial process.

The decentralized structure of the ISDS system facilitates or even worsens parallel or multiple proceedings between domestic litigation and international investment arbitration.[22] In practice, some investment arbitration cases added more confusion instead of solutions. In the case *Attorney General* v. *Mobil Oil NZ Ltd.*, the High Court of New Zealand stayed proceedings conducted in parallel under ICSID arbitration based on the discretion under Article 26 of the ICSID Convention.[23] There has been a massive practice evidencing that ICSID tribunals insisting on their exclusive jurisdiction to this effect and domestic courts observe this requirement.[24] In the case of *SPP* v. *Egypt*, the ICSID tribunal relied on comity instead of the doctrine of *lis pendens* to suspend proceedings while the parallel litigation was pursued before the Cour de Cassation in France.[25]

There has been continuing debate in the context of ICSID cases and parallel proceedings before other arbitration fora or domestic courts on these issues since the case of *Klöckner*.[26] The debate over parallel proceedings may even become more complicated when the legal issue can touch on both contract-based and treaty-based claims. An ICSID tribunal may favor its exclusive jurisdiction viewing the claim to be a treaty-based one according to the umbrella clause in the concerned BIT[27] while the contract-based choice of forum has a different view.[28] As a result, the same dispute may be arbitrated simultaneously by an ICSID tribunal which characterizes the dispute as a treaty claim and bases its jurisdiction on the BIT and by an international commercial arbitration tribunal viewing the dispute as a contractual claim.[29]

The real damage that parallel proceedings may bring to BIT arbitration cases is in the inconsistency of various awards (or court rulings), which could effectively lead to a legitimacy crisis across the entire ISDS system. Given the lack of uniformity in treaty interpretation and the unlikelihood of possible consolidation, parallel proceedings may end up with inconsistent or even contradictory outcomes, as evidenced by the cases of *CME*[30] and *Lauder*.[31] Apparently, the decentralizing nature of arbitration may ultimately lead to greater parallelism and less cooperation.

21 Washington Convention, Art. 26.

22 August Reinisch, "The Issues Raised by Parallel Proceedings and Possible Solution" in Michael Waibel, Asha Kaushal, Kyo-Liz Chung and Claire Balchin (eds.), *The Backlash Against Investment Arbitration: Perceptions and Reality* (Kluwer Law International 2010) 115.

23 *Attorney General* v. *Mobil Oil NZ Ltd.*, ICSID Reports, Vol. 4, 1987, 117.

24 *Holiday Inns* v. *Morocco*, ICSID Case No. ARB/72/1; *AMCO* v. *Indonesia*, ICSID Reports, Vol. 1, 1993, p. 410, at 412; *MINE* v. *Guinea*, Decision of December 4, 1985.

25 *SPP* v. *Egypt*, ICSID Reports, Vol. 3, 1985, at 129.

26 *Klöckner* v. *Cameroon*, 1983 ICSID Reports, Vol. 2, 1983, 3.

27 Campbell McLachlan, Laurence Shore and Matthew Weiniger, *International Investment Arbitration: Substantive Principles* (Oxford University Press 2007) 292.

28 *Compania de Aguas del Aconquija S.A. and Vivendi Universal* v. *Argentine Republic*, Decision on Application for Annulment, July 3, 2002, International Legal Materials, Vol. 41, 2002, 1135, para. 98; *Joy Mining Machinery Ltd.* v. *Arab Republic of Egypt*, Award on Jurisdiction, August 6, 2004, para. 89.

29 *Compania de Aguas del Aconquija S.A. and Vivendi Universal S.A.* v. *Argentine Republic*, ICSID Case No. ARB/97/3; *CMS Gas Transmission Company* v. *The Republic of Argentine*, ICSID Case No. ARB/01/8.

30 *CME* v. *Czech Republic*, Partial Award of September 13, 2001.

31 *Ronald S. Lauder* v. *The Czech Republic*, UNCITRAL, Final Award, September 3, 2001.

Still, many host states retain local remedies in BITs, which is one of the primary causes of parallel proceedings between international arbitration and domestic courts. Foreign investors can either seek another decision after recourse to the national courts or pursue an international legal claim simultaneously together with a domestic legal claim. Take China as an example. Most BITs signed by China with other countries in the early days of China's reform and opening up, such as the China–France BIT 1984,[32] have retained local remedies clauses. According to the local remedies clause in the China–France BIT 1984, if a foreign investor has a dispute with China, the investor should first file a complaint with an administrative organ or a judicial action with a court in China. The investor can resort to international arbitration or a local court for the dispute over the amount of compensation resulting from expropriation which cannot be settled through amicable settlement within six months. Procedurally speaking, the amicable settlement of the dispute between the state and the foreign investor during a specified period of time is a jurisdictional precondition to access to ICSID arbitration.[33] An arbitral tribunal is not only an additional forum but also an alternative to the state courts. This means that the proceedings of the local Chinese court may coincide with the international arbitration proceedings. In IIL, exhaustion of local remedies may not be a procedural requirement for having access to ITA.[34] Rather, it may be precluded by the fork-in-the-road provision.

Judicial jurisdiction is an important manifestation of a host state's sovereignty. Any country has absolute jurisdiction over investment disputes that occur within its own territory. If a foreign investor has already resorted to a domestic court for the resolution of an investment dispute, and the domestic court is hearing or has already made a judgment, allowing international arbitration for the same dispute obviously disrespects or even damages the host state's sovereignty.

Since international investment arbitration is a special hybrid procedure involving a foreign national on one hand and a host state on the other, in theory, it is neither a domestic legal process (a procedure between individuals and individuals) nor a customary international law procedure (between countries).

Due to this hybridity, there has been considerable debate as to whether the principle of *res judicata* is applicable to cases involving both international investment arbitration and domestic civil procedure. In both international law and the domestic legal system, a valid and final judgment extinguishes the whole claim and precludes a second discussion of the same claim.[35] In the well-known case of *Loewen Group, Inc. and Raymond L. Loewen* v. *United States of America*,[36] Loewen was punished by a US court for punitive damages. Loewen then requested arbitration at ICSID, claiming that it had been unfairly treated by the US courts and that the United States had violated its obligations under the NAFTA. Despite the fact that the arbitral tribunal dismissed Loewen's request on the grounds of the nationality continuation principle, the arbitral tribunal still held that the US court's judgment did violate the principle of due process. The Loewen case and its ruling triggered a

[32] China–France BIT 1984, Art. 8.

[33] *Wintershall Aktiengesellschaft* v. *Argentine Republic*, ICSID Case No. ARB/04/14, Award of December 8, 2008, para. 142.

[34] In BIT law, the exhaustion of local remedies is required only with regard to denial of justice claims. *Loewen Group, Inc. and Raymond L. Loewen* v. *United States of America*, ICSID Case No. ARB(AF)/98/3, Award June 26, 2003, para. 50.

[35] Charles N. Brower and Paula F. Henin, "Res Judicata" in Meg N. Kinnear, Geraldine R. Fischer et al. (eds.), *Building International Investment Law: The First 50 Years of ICSID* (Kluwer Law International 2015) 55.

[36] *Loewen Group, Inc. and Raymond L. Loewen* v. *United States of America*, ICSID Case No. ARB(AF)/98/3.

fierce backlash to the NAFTA which, as criticized by some scholars,[37] subjects US domestic courts to the reexamination of the international arbitration institution, thus sacrificing the USA's sovereignty. The United States thereafter changed its policy in its subsequent BIT negotiations, and began to reemphasize the importance of domestic law and domestic court procedures, while limiting the right of investors to directly arbitrate disputes against the state in international fora. While the *Lauder* and *CME* cases triggered a certain level of suspicion over the legitimacy of investment arbitration as a whole,[38] a formalist application of *res judicata* to the two competing decisions stemming from the same legal order is not only justified by the principle of due process but also supportive of the decisions rendered in these cases.[39]

One of the key functions that BITs are supposed to fulfill is to grant NT to foreign investors, emphasizing that foreign investors enjoy equal legal protection with the host state's own nationals. When a foreign investor has a dispute in the host state, the foreign investor can seek local legal protection like the host state's own nationals, including administrative relief and judicial relief. This supranational treatment granted by BITs to foreign investors has long attracted the attention of the United States. After the Loewen case, the US government repeatedly emphasized in the subsequent BIT negotiations "to ensure that foreign investors are not allowed to obtain more substantive rights than domestic investors in the United States."[40]

7.3 DISPUTE SETTLEMENT CLAUSES IN THE CHINA–GERMANY BIT AND PROTOCOL

Hale's claim was filed with the ICSID on the basis of the China–Germany BIT 2003 and its Protocol signed in 2003. The relevant provision in the China–Germany BIT 2003 reads:

(1) Any dispute concerning investments between a Contracting Party and an investor of the other Contracting Party should as far as possible be settled amicably between the parties in dispute.
(2) If the dispute cannot be settled within six months of the date when it has been raised by one of the parties in dispute, it shall, at the request of the investor of the other Contracting State, be submitted for arbitration.
(3) The dispute shall be submitted for arbitration under the Convention of 18 March 1965 on the Settlement of Investment Disputes between States and Nationals of Other States (ICSID), unless the parties in dispute agree on an ad-hoc arbitral tribunal to be established under the Arbitration Rules of the United Nations Commission on the International Trade Law (UNCITRAL) or other arbitration rules.
(4) Any award by an ad-hoc tribunal shall be final and binding. Any award under the procedures of the said Convention shall be binding and subject only to those appeals

37 Jeremy Carver, "How to Avoid Conflicting Awards: The Lauder and CME Cases" (2004) 5 *Journal of World Investment and Trade* 23.

38 Gus Van Harten and Pavel Malysheuski, "Who Has Benefited Financially from Investment Treaty Arbitration? An Evaluation of the Size and Wealth of Claimants" (2016) 12 Osgoode Legal Studies Research Paper No. 14.

39 Matti Kurkela, "Due Process in Arbitration: A Finnish Perspective" (2004) 21(2) *Journal of International Arbitration* 221; Kai Hobér, "Res Judicata and Lis Pendens in International Arbitration" (2013) 366 *Recueil de courses* 311.

40 Charles N. Brower, Micael Ottolenghi and Peter Prows, "The Saga of CMS: Res Judicata, Precedent and the Legitimacy of ICSID Arbitration" in Christina Binder et al. (eds.), *International Investment Law for the 21st Century: Essays in Honour of Christoph Schreuer* (Oxford University Press 2009) 846.

> or remedies provided for in this Convention. The awards shall be enforced in accordance with domestic law.[41]

The China–Germany BIT 2003 can be considered representative of the new generation of Chinese BITs, which, as widely agreed, started with the China–Barbados BIT 1998, removing some jurisdictional hurdles to international investment arbitration.[42] The earlier generation of Chinese BITs was relatively more conservative in terms of the dispute settlement clauses, which often imposed restrictions on the use of international arbitration for investment dispute settlement. Even if the investors were allowed to submit their disputes to arbitration, they would be subject to review on a case-by-case basis, or they should submit to arbitration only a "controversy over the amount of compensation arising out of expropriation." Since China joined the WTO, it has begun to adopt a more open attitude toward the ISDS mechanism. The China–Germany BIT 2003 allows foreign investors to submit any disputes arising from their investment within China to ICSID or other ad hoc arbitral tribunal for arbitration. In terms of international arbitration and court proceedings in the host country, the provisions of the China–Germany BIT 2003 basically adopt a so-called prior recourse model (Model A discussed later in this section). As long as the investment dispute cannot be resolved within a certain period of time, the investor can submit it to international arbitration. This model also appears in other Chinese BITs (i.e., the China–Uruguay BIT 1993) as well as some other BITs signed by Latin American countries.[43] As mentioned, this model greatly expands the jurisdictional scope of arbitration institutions such as the ICSID on investment disputes, and is prone to parallel proceedings between local litigation and international arbitration. Even if the investor has already submitted the dispute to a Chinese court, as long as the Chinese court fails to resolve the dispute within a certain period of time (e.g., six months), the investor can still resort to arbitration. According to this model, the ICSID will undoubtedly have jurisdiction over the dispute in the Hale case.

The China–Germany BIT 2003 is also accompanied by its Protocol, which makes the following supplementary provision to Article 9 of the China–Germany BIT:

> With respect to investments in the People's Republic of China, an investor in the Federal Republic of Germany may submit a dispute to arbitration under the following circumstances only: (a) the investor has referred the issue to an administrative review procedure according to Chinese law, (b) the dispute still exists three months after he has brought the issue to the review procedure, and (c) in case the issue has been brought to a Chinese court, it can be withdrawn by the investor according to Chinese law.[44]

These provisions are closer to a waiver approach (Model B summarized later). Some conditions may need to be satisfied if the investor prefers to withdraw the lawsuit from the local court prior to the submission of the dispute to international arbitration. When a German investor has a dispute with the Chinese government, the dispute should be submitted to

[41] China–Germany BIT 2003, Art. 9.

[42] Won Kidane, "China's Bilateral Investment Treaties with African States in Comparative Context" (2016) 49(1) *Cornell International Law Journal* 141–177; Yu-Ting Ye, "Towards a Balanced and Liberal Chinese Bilateral Investment Treaty Regime in the Context of One Belt One Road" (2018) 41 *Houston Journal of International Law* 107; Tingliang Wang, "Western Misperceptions and China's Approach to International Investment Law" (2019) 17 *Santa Clara Journal of International Law* 1.

[43] Pierre-Marie Dupuy, "Preconditions to Arbitration and Consent of States to ICSID Jurisdiction" in Meg Kinnear, Geraldine R. Fisher et al. (eds.), *Building International Investment Law: The First 50 Years of ICSID* (Kluwer Law International 2016) 220.

[44] China–Germany Protocol 2003, Art. 6.

China's administrative review procedure in the first place. If the dispute persists after three months, the investor may submit it to arbitration. Where the investor submits the dispute to a Chinese court after the administrative review procedure, as long as "it can be withdrawn by the investor according to Chinese law," the investor may resort to international arbitration. Conversely, if the investor has submitted the dispute to a Chinese court after the administrative review procedure but the proceedings cannot be withdrawn under Chinese law, the investor can no longer submit the dispute to arbitration but can only continue litigation in Chinese courts.

Compared with the prior recourse model (Model A), the wording of Article 6 of the Protocol is more conducive to the Chinese side. In effect, these rules constitute a restriction posed on German investors' right to arbitration, a hurdle they have to overcome. Under Model A, filing a lawsuit in a Chinese court is not an end to international investment arbitration. The investor may still submit the dispute to arbitration if the dispute is not resolved within a certain period of time.

However, the Protocol is still significantly different from the waiver approach (Model B), under which the investment dispute "can only be submitted to international arbitration after the investor has withdrawn it from the domestic court." According to Article 6 of the Protocol, as long as "investors can withdraw according to Chinese law," the dispute can be submitted to arbitration. This involves a legal construction of the wording "investors can withdraw under Chinese law," which could be a challenge facing the Hela case.

In the specific context of the Hela case, how should we understand the meaning of the above provisions, in particular the wording "investors can withdraw according to Chinese law"?

7.3.1 *When the Dispute Is Settled in the Second Instance*

According to the judgment made by the Shandong People's High Court, JHSF filed an administrative lawsuit against the Ji'nan Municipal People's Government's Expropriation Decision to expropriate JHSF's Land and Buildings. The claim was rejected by the Ji'nan Intermediate People's Court and the Shandong People's High Court respectively. Hela then continued to submit the dispute for arbitration to ICSID. According to the traditional principle of "exhaustion of local remedies," Hela's request for arbitration seems reasonable because it has exhausted local remedies in China. However, according to Article 6 of the Protocol 2003, after the investor has filed a lawsuit in a Chinese court, the dispute can be submitted to arbitration only if it can be withdrawn under Chinese law. The question that needs to be settled is thus whether JHSF may withdraw the lawsuit after the final trial of the second instance.

The PRC Administrative Litigation Law stipulates: "If the plaintiff applies for withdrawal of an appeal before the judgment or ruling of an administrative case is pronounced, or the defendant changes its administrative actions, if the plaintiff agrees and applies for withdrawal of the lawsuit, it is the court that makes a decision over the withdrawal."[45] It appears that the parties in the administrative litigation in China can apply for withdrawal of the lawsuit only before the court pronounces its ruling. After the court has made a second-instance judgment, which is the final ruling in China's legal system, the plaintiff may not apply for withdrawal of the case. Therefore, according to Article 6(3) of the Protocol 2003, Hela is no longer able to

45 PRC Administrative Litigation Law, Art. 62.

submit the dispute to arbitration after the ruling is rendered by the court in the second-instance proceeding. In other words, in this scenario, the ICSID tribunal does not possess jurisdiction over the dispute.

7.3.2 *When the Case Is under Retrial*

The Administrative Litigation Law also sets out a trial supervision procedure to safeguard due process, justice and fairness in administrative proceedings. The relevant clause reads: "If the parties believe that there is a mistake in the judgment or ruling that has already taken legal effect, they may apply to the people's court at the next higher level for retrial, but the judgment or ruling shall continue to be executed or enforced."[46] According to this clause, Hela seems to be entitled to a remedy, that is, first to bring a trial supervision procedure to the Chinese court, and then to apply for withdrawal, and then to submit the dispute to the ICSID for arbitration. By doing it this way, the conditions of Article 6(3) of the Protocol 2003 can be satisfied.

According to the Administrative Litigation Law, where the application of the party meets one of the following circumstances, the people's court shall retry the case where: (1) failing to file the case or rejecting the lawsuit is indeed wrong; (2) there is new evidence sufficient to overturn the original judgment or ruling; (3) the main evidence on which the original judgment or ruling relies to determine the facts is insufficient, without cross-examination or forgery; (4) the law that the original judgment or ruling applies is wrong; (5) the violation of the law may affect the fair trial; (6) the original judgment or ruling may have omitted the claim; (7) the legal document based on which the original judgment or ruling was made is revoked or changed; (8) the judge in the trial of the case has committed corruption, bribery, malpractice and/or defamation.[47]

It is hard to presume or predict whether JHSF may bring the case to a Chinese court in the trial supervision procedure based on any particular ground(s) listed above. Assuming that the higher court accepts JHSF's application for retrial, the next question is whether JHSF may withdraw the case according to Chinese law so as to satisfy the conditions listed in Article 6(3) of the Protocol.

According to the Administrative Litigation Law, before the people's court declares a judgment or ruling in an administrative case, the plaintiff applies for withdrawal of the lawsuit, or the defendant changes its administrative action and the plaintiff agrees and applies for withdrawal of the lawsuit, it is the people's court that makes a decision.[48] Therefore, in the retrial procedure, the application for withdrawal of the case must be approved by the court. The key here is – does the wording "can withdraw under Chinese law" in Article 6(3) of the Protocol 2003 really require the court to allow it to withdraw its application? In other words, is the word "can" here a legally "can" or a de facto "may"? This involves an interpretation of the legal phrase. As the dispute has been submitted to the ICSID, the right to interpret the phrase is in the hands of the ICSID tribunal.

Judging from past ICSID jurisprudence, until the case of *AAPL* v. *Sri Lanka* in 1990, the ICSID established the general principle of treaty interpretation for BIT terms, and clearly stipulated that it should be "in accordance with the generally accepted treaty interpretation rules established in practice, and formed by the Institute of International Law in 1956 and

46 PRC Administrative Litigation Law, Art. 90.
47 PRC Administrative Litigation Law, Art. 91.
48 PRC Administrative Litigation Law, Art. 62.

codified by Articles 31–33 of the Vienna Convention on the Law of Treaties." Most ICSID decisions involving the interpretation of BITs in recent years have also followed the treaty interpretation rules formulated in the VCLT. According to Article 31 of the VCLT, a treaty shall be interpreted in good faith in accordance with its usual meaning, its context and with reference to the object and purpose of the treaty. Therefore, the meaning of the word "can" (in the sentence – it can be withdrawn by the investor according to Chinese law) in the Protocol 2003 should be interpreted by means of textual interpretation, purpose interpretation, common meaning interpretation and good faith interpretation.

Since both the China–Germany BIT 2003 and its Protocol are written in Chinese, German and English, the meanings of the three languages should be considered together. Whether it is "can" in Chinese, "can" in English or "kann" in German, there are several ways of interpreting the basic meaning, which can be used to refer to legal authority granted by the court or possible result of the party's own action. Therefore, the sentence "it can be withdrawn by the investor according to Chinese law" can be understood either as "Chinese law allows investors to withdraw their complaints" or as "investors can withdraw [their complaints] under Chinese law." If the former is the correct understanding, Article 62 of the Administrative Litigation Law, which allows the plaintiff to apply for withdrawal of the lawsuit, works well with the provisions of Article 6(3) in the Protocol 2003. On the other hand, the latter understanding would have trouble fitting with Article 6(3) of the Protocol as Article 62 of the Administrative Litigation Law requires the plaintiff's withdrawal to be approved by the court. Thus, Hela must present the evidence to the ICSID tribunal showing that it has obtained the Chinese court's approval to withdraw its case.

Which of the above two interpretations stands depends on the ICSID tribunal's interpretation of the treaty terms. Given the fact that ICSID has tended to expand its jurisdiction over the past years, the ICSID tribunal is likely to rely on the former to interpret that "can" constitutes legal authority granted to the claimant. This interpretation has some merits especially if Article 6(3) of the China–Germany Protocol is compared with the dispute settlement clauses in China's other BITs. For instance, the China–Netherlands BIT 2001 states:

> An investor may decide to submit a dispute to a competent domestic court. In case a legal dispute concerning an investment in the territory of the People's Republic of China has been submitted to a competent domestic court, this dispute may be submitted to international dispute settlement, on the condition that the investor concerned has withdrawn its case from the domestic court. If a dispute concerns an investment in the territory of the Kingdom of the Netherlands an investor may choose to submit a dispute to international dispute settlement at any time.[49]

According to this clause, if a Dutch investor wants to submit a dispute to arbitration after its submission of the same dispute to a Chinese court, the investor must first withdraw the case from the Chinese court. This is obviously different from "[the case] can be withdrawn according to Chinese law" as stipulated in Article 6(3) of the China–Germany Protocol. The former requires that the lawsuit has been withdrawn whereas the latter requires only that the lawsuit may be withdrawn under the domestic law.

From the Chinese government's perspective, in order to prevent the ICSID tribunal from making an interpretation that is unfavorable to the Chinese side, the Chinese court may refuse to accept the case that Hale may file through the administrative supervision procedure, thereby making Hela's arbitration request fail to satisfy the precondition set out in the China–Germany Protocol.

49 China–Netherlands BIT 2001, Art. 10, para. 2.

It is worth noting that Hela may have already failed to satisfy the conditions outlined in the China–Germany BIT 2003 by filing the arbitration claim with the ICSID before the Chinese court made the second-instance ruling. The ICSID would have accepted the case if Hela had filed the claim earlier as Article 6(3) of the Protocol merely says that "it can be withdrawn by the investor according to Chinese law." As discussed, when a dispute is being adjudicated by a Chinese court, the plaintiff is able to make an application to withdraw the case according to Article 62 of the Chinese Administrative Litigation Law.

The contextual interpretation of "can" would give preference to a Chinese perspective where the court would have to authorize the submission for withdrawal of the case; however, the literal meaning of "can" would from the German perspective give more autonomy to the litigant party. Both could be perfectly good faith interpretations. Yet, the German perspective must further contextualize its reading and thus give weight to the final authorization of the Chinese court. "Can be" may be seen as a combination of the autonomy of the litigant party and the authority of the Chinese court. Yet, due to the lack of judicial independence, the latter reading, from the investor's perspective, would probably avoid any cause for arbitrariness on behalf of the judge.

7.4 THREE MODELS UNDER CHINESE BITS DEALING WITH PARALLEL PROCEEDINGS

7.4.1 *Three Models in Chinese BITs*

According to the official website of China's Ministry of Commerce, China has already signed more than 120 BITs with 104 countries in the world.[50] Most of these BITs provide for dispute resolution clauses between foreign investors and the host state. There are several different ways of configuring the relationship between domestic litigation and international arbitration. This subsection tries to categorize Chinese BITs by outlining three models dealing with the interaction between domestic litigation and international investment arbitration on the basis of the dispute resolution clauses in the Chinese BITs. This categorization indicates the complexity and uncertainty of the parallel proceedings issue in Chinese BIT law.

7.4.1.1 Model A: Litigation Followed by Arbitration

Many BITs signed by China in the 1980s stipulate that if a dispute over the amount of compensation as a result of expropriation cannot be settled through amicable settlement by the investor and the host state within a certain period of time, it can be submitted directly to arbitration. For example, the China–Switzerland BIT 1986 states:

> 1. En cas de contestations entre une Partie Contractante et un investisseur de l'autre Partie Contractante et si un règlement amiable n'a pas pu être trouvé dans un délai de six mois, l'investisseur pourra soumettre à l'arbitrage international: a) les différends portant sur le montant de l'indemnité due au titre de l'Article 7 du présent Accord; b) les différends portant sur d'autres questions en relation avec le présent Accord, pour autant que les parties concernées en conviennent.[51]

[50] China Ministry of Commerce's website.
[51] China–Switzerland BIT 1985, Art. 12, para. 1.

These BITs usually provide that the arbitral award is final and binding, and that both parties shall enforce the award in accordance with their respective laws.

This model also appears in Chinese BITs with the UK (1986), Bulgaria (1989), Pakistan (1989), Ghana (1989), Hungary (1991), Spain (1992), Ukraine (1992), Kazakhstan (1992), Armenia (1992), Uzbekistan (1992), Kyrgyzstan (1992), Belarus (1993) and Tajikistan (1993).

Some Chinese BITs have more detailed dispute resolution clauses. They first allow investors to rely on local remedies, including court litigation. It is further stipulated that if the local remedies are not successful within a requisite time frame, the dispute can be submitted to arbitration. The limitation period attached here is designed to preclude claimants from making stale claims. Accordingly, a foreign investor's recourse to the domestic courts for a certain period of time is a precondition to the right to refer the matter to international arbitration under the BIT. This is often called a prior recourse clause.[52]

Article 8 of the China–France BIT 1984 is a good example. Investors may file the case with a domestic court when the dispute concerns the amount of compensation as a result of expropriation. However, if the court does not make a final judgment within one year, the investor can resort to arbitration. This means that international arbitration can be in parallel with domestic court proceedings.

Other BITs are rather vague in the wording. For example, the China–Poland BIT 1988 stipulates:

> [I]f an investor challenges the amount of compensation for the expropriated investment assets, he may file complaint with the competent authority of the Contracting Party taking the expropriatory measures. If the claim is still unresolved within one year after the complaint is filed, at the request of the investor, the court with competent jurisdiction or the ad hoc international arbitral tribunal shall review the amount of compensation.[53]

Literally speaking, domestic administrative proceedings and international arbitration proceedings can run in parallel, and investors can make a choice. If the investor first chooses arbitration, the arbitral award is final. However, the BIT is not clear about the finality of the domestic administrative proceedings if the investor first chooses that route. This may suggest that after the parties choose domestic proceedings, they can theoretically still submit the dispute to international arbitration.

Chinese BITs with Kuwait (1985), the Netherlands (1985), Malaysia (1988), Australia (1988), Pakistan (1989), Turkey (1990), Czechoslovakia (1991), Greece (1992), the Philippines (1992), Israel (1995) and Yemen (1998) largely adopt this model.

Although a few BITs signed by China have adopted the "fork-in-the-road" clauses, they are silent on whether domestic litigation can exclude international arbitration. In theory, investors can still submit the dispute to arbitration after they have chosen to file a domestic lawsuit in the first place. Chinese BITs signed with Lithuania (1993), Morocco (1995), Saudi Arabia (1996), Gabon (1997), Qatar (1999) and Madagascar (2005) adopt this model. The China–

Author's translation: In the event of disputes between a Contracting Party and an investor of the other Contracting Party and if an amicable settlement has not been reached within six months, the investor may submit to international arbitration: (a) disputes relating to the amount of compensation due under Article 7 of this Agreement; (b) disputes relating to other matters in connection with this Agreement, provided that the parties concerned so agree.

52 Marco Adda, "Consolidation of Arbitral and Court Proceedings in Investment Disputes" in Bernardo M. Cremades Sanz-Pastor and Julian D. M. Lew (eds.), *Parallel State and Arbitral Procedures in International Arbitration* (Kluwer Law International 2005) 100.

53 China–Poland BIT 1988, Art. 10.

United Arab Emirates BIT 1994 even allows investors to choose one or two among three options – domestic administrative procedure, domestic litigation and international arbitration.

7.4.1.2 Model B: Arbitration after Withdrawal of Domestic Litigation

Since the start of the twenty-first century, China has begun to pay attention to the parallel proceedings issue in BIT law and practice. Article 10 of the China–Netherlands BIT 2001 is one example.

Investment disputes of Dutch investors in China can be directly submitted to international arbitration. The arbitral awards are final and binding, meaning that investors can no longer sue in Chinese courts. Dutch investors can also file a lawsuit in a domestic court first. However, once the dispute is filed with a Chinese court, the investor cannot file the claim for international arbitration unless the investor first withdraws the case from the Chinese court. This model is also adopted in the Chinese BITs with Finland (2004), Cuba (2007) and Switzerland (2009).

This model is quite close to a waiver clause requiring the waiver of recourse to any other forum as a condition for referring the dispute to arbitration. Both attempt to avoid duplicative proceedings. A good illustration of the "classic" waiver clause is in the NAFTA, which has been considered in some investment arbitration cases such as *Waste Management* v. *Mexico*[54] and reads as follows:

> A disputing investor may submit a claim under Art. 1116 to arbitration only if: … (b) the investor … waive[s its] right to initiate or continue before any administrative tribunal or court under the law of any Party, or other dispute settlement procedures, any proceedings with respect to the measure … that is alleged to be a breach … except for proceedings for injunctive, declaratory or other extraordinary relief ….[55]

The approach taken by Chinese BITs, nevertheless, is slightly different from a pure waiver clause in the sense that Chinese BITs allow a halfway waiver and a foreign investor can resort to international arbitration as long as a withdrawal from the domestic court is made. This is closer to Model A. The difference between Models A and B is that the former is conditional on a lapse of time but the latter's condition is the foreign investor's own withdrawal. Model A also differs from Model B in that Model A does not exhaust local remedies while local remedies must end in Model B.

7.4.1.3 Model C: Fork-in-the-Road Clause

The solution to avoid a duplication of proceedings is a fork-in-the-road clause, under which a claimant must select between pursuing a claim in a domestic court or international arbitration, or alternatively must waive claims in any other forum as a precondition to international arbitration. These two techniques, that is, selection and waiver, are often codified in the fork-in-the-road clause.

The France–Argentina BIT 1991 is a good illustration of the fork-in-the-road clause as follows:

[54] *Waste Management, Inc.* v. *United Mexican States*, ICSID Case No. ARB(AF)98/2, Award (June 2, 2000).
[55] NAFTA, Art. 1121(1).

1. Any dispute relating to investment, within the meaning of this agreement, between one of the Contracting Parties and an investor of the other Contracting Party, shall, as far as possible, be resolved through amicable consultations between both parties to the dispute.
2. If such dispute could not be solved within six months from the time it was stated by any of the parties concerned, it shall be submitted, at the request of the investor:
   - either to the national jurisdictions of the Contracting Party involved in the dispute;
   - or to international arbitration.[56]

Once an investor has submitted the dispute either to the jurisdictions of the contracting party involved or to international arbitration, the choice of one or other of these procedures shall be final.

An example of the waiver technique can be seen in Article 1121 of the NAFTA. However, it must be pointed out that these techniques may not necessarily be clear-cut, especially when the dispute may be categorized as either a contract-based claim or a treaty-based claim.

As far as China is concerned, the China–France BIT 2007 stipulates:

> Tout différend relatif aux investissements entre l'une des Parties contractantes et un investisseur de l'autre Partie contractante est réglé à l'amiable entre les deux parties concernées. Si un tel différend ne peut être réglé dans un délai de six mois à compter de la date a laquelle il a été soulevé par l'une ou l'autre des parties au différend, il est soumis ou la demande de l'investisseur:
>
> a) au tribunal compétent de la Partie contractante partie au différend; ou
> b) à l'arbitrage d'un tribunal arbitral ad hoc établi conformément aux règles d'arbitrage de la Commission des Nations Voies pour le droit commercial international (CNUDCI), sous réserve de la faculté pour la Partie contractante qui est partie au différend de demander a l'investisseur concerné de recourir aux procédures administratives internes d'examen prévues par les dispositions législatives et règlementaires en vigueur dans cette Partie contractante avant que le différend soit soumis à cet arbitrage; ou
> c) à l'arbitrage du Centre international pour le règlement des différends relatifs aux investissements (CIRDI), crée par la Convention pour le règlement des différends relatifs aux investissements entre États et ressortissants d'autres États, signée è Washington le 18 mars 1965, sous réserve de la faculté pour La Partie contractante qui est partie au différend de demander à l'investisseur concerné de recourir aux procédures administratives internes d'examen prévues par les dispositions législatives et règlementaires en vigueur dans cette Partie contractante avant que le différend soit soumis au CIRDI.
>
> Lorsque l'investisseur a soumis le différend au tribunal compétent de la Partie contractante concernée, à l'arbitrage du tribunal arbitral ad hoc constitué conformément aux règles de la CNUDCI ou à l'arbitrage du CIRDI, le choix de l'une de ces procédures est définitif.
>
> La sentence arbitrale est définitive et contraignante pour les deux parties au différend. Les deux Parties contractantes s'engagent ou en assurer l'exécution.[57]

56 France–Argentina BIT 1991, Art. 8(2).

57 China–France BIT 2007, Art. 8(2).

Author's translation: Any investment dispute between one of the Contracting Parties and an investor of the other Contracting Party shall be settled amicably between the two parties concerned. If such a dispute cannot be settled within six months from the date on which it was raised by either party to the dispute, it shall be submitted or under the request of the investor be submitted:

This is a typical fork-in-the-road clause, according to which investors can choose only between domestic litigation and international arbitration, and can choose only one of them. The choice of one option is exclusive to the other option. This model appears in Chinese BITs with Singapore (1985), Denmark (1985), Sri Lanka (1985), New Zealand (1988), Japan (1988), Papua New Guinea (1991), Mongolia (1991), Portugal (1992 and 2005), Bolivia (1992), Argentina (1992), Moldova (1992), Vietnam (1992), Georgia (1993), Laos (1993), Estonia (1993), Croatia (1993), Albania (1993), Slovenia (1993), Uruguay (1993), Azerbaijan (1994), Egypt (1994), Romania (1994), Jamaica (1994), Peru (1994), Chile (1994), Ecuador (1994), Indonesia (1994), Iceland (1994), Oman (1995), Cuba (1995), Algeria (1996), Cambodia (1996), Zimbabwe (1996), Mauritius (1996), Lebanon (1996), Sudan (1997), South Africa (1997), Macedonia (1997), Ethiopia (1998), Barbados (1998), Cape Verde (1998), Syria (1998), Bahrain (1999), Congo (2000), Iran (2000), Myanmar (2001), Cyprus (2001), Nigeria (2001), Trinidad and Tobago (2002), Guyana (2003), Tunisia (2004), Belgium and Luxembourg (2005), Equatorial Guinea (2005), Spain (2005), Portugal (2005), North Korea (2005), France (2007), Korea (1992 and 2007), Mali (2009), Malta (2009), Uzbekistan (2011), Japan and Korea (2012) and Tanzania (2013).

7.4.2 *Analysis of the Three Models*

This subsection further analyzes three models of occurrence of parallel proceedings in Chinese BIT law.

7.4.2.1 Model A

Under Model A, foreign investors should first seek local remedies, including local court proceedings, after a dispute with the host state occurs. If the dispute cannot be resolved within a reasonable period of time, the investor can seek international arbitration. Thus, prior recourse to the local court and no resolution by the local court are two preconditions to accessing international arbitration. The BIT case law has made it clear that these preconditions are mandatory.[58] Under such circumstances, it is most likely to see concurrent proceedings in a domestic court (which is still ongoing after the lapse of the fixed period of time) and international arbitration.

(a) to the competent court of the contracting party to the dispute; or
(b) to arbitration by an ad hoc arbitral tribunal established in accordance with the Arbitration Rules of the United Nations Commission on International Trade Law (UNCITRAL), subject to the right of the Contracting Party which is a party to the dispute to request the investor concerned to have recourse to the internal administrative review procedures provided for by the laws and regulations in force in that Contracting Party before the dispute is submitted to such arbitration; or
(c) arbitration by the International Centre for Settlement of Investment Disputes (ICSID), established by the Convention on the Settlement of Investment Disputes between States and Nationals of Other States, signed in Washington on March 18, 1965, subject to the right of the Contracting Party which is a party to the dispute to require the investor concerned to have recourse to the domestic administrative review procedures provided by the laws and regulations in force in that Contracting Party before the dispute is submitted to ICSID.

Where the investor has submitted the dispute to the competent court of the Contracting Party concerned, to arbitration by the ad hoc arbitral tribunal constituted in accordance with the rules of UNCITRAL or to ICSID arbitration, the choice of one of these procedures shall be final.

The arbitral award shall be final and binding on both parties to the dispute. Both parties to the dispute undertake to enforce the award.

58 Dupuy, *supra* note 43, at 235.

7.4.2.2 Model B

Under this model, if an investor submits an investment dispute to a domestic court in the host state, international arbitration cannot be sought until the investor has withdrawn the lawsuit. At this point, if the investor first sues in the domestic court, they can resort to arbitration only after they have withdrawn the domestic case. On the face of it, it seems that investors can choose only one dispute resolution method. However, as a matter of fact, investors have obtained both domestic and international remedies provided that investors feel at any time that domestic litigation is unfavorable. International arbitration can be initiated on the condition that local remedy has been ruled out. As a result, foreign investors are better treated than domestic investors since they have more exposure to international arbitration. In light of this favoritism toward foreign investors, this model is not widely adopted in Chinese BITs.

The China–Germany Protocol actually adopts a deviated form of this Model B. Compared to Model B, the provisions of the Protocol are more favorable to investors but more detrimental to the host state.

The China–Iran BIT 2000 formulates an advanced version of Model B, fully taking into account the possibility of parallel proceedings in BIT practice. The most relevant and distinctive subclause is Article 12(3) which states:

> 3. A dispute primarily referred to the competent court of the host Contracting Party, as long as it is pending, cannot be referred to arbitration save with the parties' agreement; and in the event that a final judgment is rendered, it cannot be referred to arbitration.[59]

This subsection is similar to Model B in that both allow investors to sue in the host state's court before the investors can submit the dispute to arbitration. However, the major difference between these two is that Model B requires investors to voluntarily withdraw their lawsuit before they can submit to arbitration while Article 12 here allows the dispute to be submitted to arbitration only after the investor and the host state have given their "consent" and the local court has not granted its ruling. If the court has already made a final judgment, the dispute cannot be submitted to arbitration. The "consent" required here is a creative condition posed in the BIT. It effectively avoids the excessive right that investors may enjoy in choosing the forum for dispute settlement under both Models B and C, and fully takes into account the host state's interest. However, this model still allows the parties to agree to conduct arbitration after litigation is initiated, thereby leaving the parallel proceedings unsolved in BIT practice.

7.4.2.3 Model C: Fork-in-the-Road Clauses

Model C, the fork-in-the-road clauses, appears more desirable in terms of avoiding parallel proceedings in BIT practice as foreign investors can choose between only two dispute resolution methods: either domestic litigation or international arbitration. Choosing one of these options means abandoning the other option.

The major purpose of a fork-in-the-road provision associated with the waiver provisions in a BIT is to preclude an investor from commencing other dispute resolution proceedings if it has already made a choice among various dispute settlement options. Therefore, once a party has chosen a particular dispute resolution forum, such a forum selection should be final and no other options can be used later on. By having this provision in the BIT, the finality and

59 China–Iran BIT 2000, Art. 12(3).

certainty can be strengthened for the state party. The host state can avoid ending up in a multiple-proceeding scenario by defending the same claim in different dispute settlement processes. In the same vein, attempts are also made to ensure the exclusivity of proceedings with waiver clauses, whereby a choice in favor of a particular forum may be connected with a written waiver of the jurisdiction of any other forum. In essence, the fork-in-the-road and waiver provisions constitute the other side of the coin of the exhaustion of local remedies principle.

In order for a fork-in-the-road provision to apply, the subsequent proceedings must concern the same legal and factual issues[60] and take place between the same parties.[61] Due to this "triple identity" requirement, very few cases have taken heed of the fork-in-the-road provisions in respect of barring claims. For instance, in both the *LG&E* and *Enron* cases, the fork-in-the-road provision of the US–Argentina BIT 1991 was held not to prevent minority shareholders from bringing arbitral claims in spite of the fact that the company they invested in had already brought ongoing proceedings in its own capacity before the Argentine courts.[62]

Not all Chinese BITs have a fork-in-the-road provision. The China–Norway BIT 1984 does not have this provision as the investor can only have a dispute over the amount of compensation reviewed by the national court or an international tribunal. As dual or multiple choices of forum are not offered to the investor, there is no need to have a fork-in-the-road provision. The investor under the China–Philippines BIT 1992 is entitled to choose to have a quantum dispute arbitrated along with "other matters related thereto" and any other disputes under the BIT that the parties agree to submit to arbitration. Agreement between the disputing parties is required if the dispute to be arbitrated is not a quantum dispute or another related matter. As agreement between the disputing parties is a precondition to arbitration, the aim of the fork-in-the-road provision of avoiding a multiplicity of claims is thus achieved.

A fork-in-the-road clause may insert an exclusion mechanism into a BIT – domestic litigation and international arbitration are exclusive to each other. Due to this exclusiveness, more BITs signed in the 1990s adopted the fork-in-the-road clauses. Similarly, China also incorporated more fork-in-the-road clauses into its BITs.

The China–Jordan BIT 2001 retains a full fork-in-the-road provision under which the provision relating to international arbitration does not apply if the investor has already submitted the dispute to a competent court.[63] The China–Argentina BIT 1992 contains a provision making the choice of either a competent court or ad hoc arbitration "final."[64]

Despite the fork-in-the-road provision, modern BITs may not prevent the investor from submitting a dispute to ICSID or *ad hoc* arbitration even if the investor has resorted to the local administrative review process as a preliminary procedure.[65] The China–Russia BIT 2006 has this qualified fork-in-the-road provision.[66] Most recent BITs are closer to adopting a qualified fork-in-the-road provision so that the investor is allowed to commence arbitration

60 *Azurix Corp* v. *The Argentine Republic*, ICSID Case No. ARB/01/12, Decision on Jurisdiction of December 8, 2003, para 90.

61 *Gami Investments* v. *The Government of the United Mexican States*, UNCITRAL Final Award of November 15, 2004, para 37.

62 *LG&E Energy Corp., LG&E Capital Corp. and LG&E International, Inc.* v. *Argentine Republic*, ICSID Case No. ARB/01/1, Decision on Jurisdiction of April 30, 2004, para 76; *Enron Corporation and Ponderosa Assets, L.P.* v. *The Argentine Republic*, ICSID Case No. ARB/01/3, Decision on Jurisdiction of January 14, 2004, para 95.

63 Jordan–China BIT, Art. 10(2), Botswana–China BIT, Art. 9(3); Guyana–China BIT, Art. 10(4).

64 Argentina–China BIT 1992, Art. 8(3).

65 China–Australia BIT 1988, Art. XII:2.

66 Russia–China BIT 2006 Protocol Ad Article 9.

after the three-month domestic review.[67] The latest example is the China–New Zealand FTA 2008 which allows a dispute to be referred to arbitration even if it has already been referred to a competent domestic court "on the condition that the investor concerned has withdrawn its case from the domestic courts before a final judgment has been reached in the case."[68] This carve-out is similar to a waiver obligation under the NAFTA that an investor must sign a written waiver of any right to commence or continue local court proceedings before resorting to arbitration. The China–Mexico BIT 2008 is odd in the sense that it does not have a fork-in-the-road provision but it does have a waiver requirement, according to which an investor can submit to arbitration only if a specific waiver on behalf of the investment enterprise has been given.[69] This waiver requirement must be interpreted as a mandatory obligation imposed on the investor to go through the local administrative review procedure of the host state prior to its pursuit of international arbitration.

The Agreement on Investment of the Framework Agreement on Comprehensive Economic Cooperation entered into by ASEAN and China on August 15, 2009 divides ASEAN member states and China into two groups and arranges two separate rules to be applied to them. First, this Agreement applies a more conventional approach, in line with general practice, by stipulating: "In the case of Indonesia, Philippines, Thailand, and Viet Nam, once the investor has submitted the dispute to their respective competent courts or administrative tribunals or to one of the arbitration procedures [regarding any of ICSID, ICSID Additional Facility Rules, UNCITRAL or *ad hoc* arbitration], the choice of the procedure is final."[70] This fork-in-the-road provision obviously only has legal effect on Indonesia, the Philippines, Thailand and Viet Nam but not China. A "qualified" fork-in-the-road provision is applicable to China and the rest of the ASEAN member states. The investor is still able to submit the dispute to international arbitration even if the dispute has been submitted to a competent domestic court, provided that the investor concerned has withdrawn its case from the domestic court before a final judgment has been reached in the case.[71]

However, the fork-in-the-road clause is not defect free. There are two reasons why a fork-in-the-road clause may not avoid parallel proceedings as a whole.

The fork-in-the-road clauses in some BITs are too simplistic to be comprehensive, leaving too much space for the tribunal's interpretation. For instance, the fork-in-the-road clause incorporated in earlier Chinese BITs applies only to disputes over the amount of compensation resulting from expropriation, meaning that disputes over compensation amount can be submitted for arbitration whereas other disputes must be left to be litigated in domestic courts. This is a restrictive fork-in-the-road clause as the term "dispute over the amount of compensation resulting from expropriation" has been heavily debated in Chinese BIT-related cases.

The new generation of Chinese BITs has extended the scope of dispute from disputes over the amount of compensation resulting from expropriation to all the disputes or investment disputes. However, this does not mean that there is no dispute over the concept of dispute; such a wide-brushing term triggers heavy debate. For instance, the Chinese BITs with some countries state: "Once the investor submits the dispute to the court of competent jurisdiction

67 Czech Republic–China BIT 2005, Art. 9(4).
68 China–New Zealand FTA 2008, Art. 153(3).
69 Mexico–China BIT 2008, Art. 13(4).
70 The China–ASEAN Agreement, Art. 14(5).
71 The China–ASEAN Agreement, Art. 14(5), the first sentence.

of the party to the dispute, or the ICSID, or the *ad hoc* arbitral tribunal established in accordance with the UNCITRAL Arbitration Rules, the choice will be the final." The question remains unsolved as to how to determine "final" here. Is it the time when the investor submits the dispute to the relevant institution?

In ICSID arbitration practice, some arbitral tribunals often misinterpret the meaning of the fork-in-the-road clause with the aim of expanding the scope of jurisdiction so that a dispute that has been accepted or adjudicated by domestic courts can still be submitted to and accepted by the arbitral tribunal. A typical approach is to interpret the "dispute" involved in domestic litigation and the "dispute" accepted by the arbitral tribunal as two different disputes, thereby avoiding the application of the fork-in-the-road clause.

7.5 MFN TREATMENT AND PARALLEL PROCEEDINGS

In order to avoid parallel proceedings between domestic litigation and international investment arbitration, Article 6(3) of the China–Germany Protocol imposes certain restrictions on the right of German investors to submit disputes to arbitration. Accordingly, as the Chinese court has already administered the Hela case and rendered a second-instance judgment, Hela is unable to withdraw its case from the Chinese court, thereby possessing no legal right to submit the same dispute to the ICSID for arbitration. In other words, the ICSID has no jurisdiction over the dispute under such circumstances.

The China–Germany BIT provides for an MFN treatment clause, that is, "the contracting party's treatment of investors in the territory of the contracting party and its investment-related activities shall not be low. It gives the investment of any third country investor and the treatment of investment-related activities."[72] Is Hela entitled to rely on any more favorable dispute resolution clause in other Chinese BITs according to this MFN treatment clause, and waive the restriction posed by Article 6(3) of the China–Germany Protocol?[73]

Most of the Chinese BITs signed in the 1980s with Western European states provide only for international arbitration; for example, see Article 7 of the China–UK BIT 1986. According to this clause, a dispute between a UK investor and China regarding the amount of compensation resulting from expropriation may be submitted to international arbitration or to a domestic court for resolution. Even if the investor first submits the dispute to a Chinese court, it does not rule out the investor's subsequent submission of the dispute to international arbitration. Compared with the China–Germany BIT 2003 and its Protocol, the dispute resolution clause in the China–UK BIT is broader. Hela may resort to the MFN clause in the China–Germany BIT to piggyback on the more favorable dispute settlement clause in the China–UK BIT. By doing so, Hela may have a chance to enjoy more favorable treatment under the China–UK BIT. How should ICSID decide so?

When ICSID tribunals interpret MFN clauses in BITs, there is indeed a tendency to expand the scope of application of the MFN clause, especially moving from the expansion of substantive rights to procedural rights. In a number of cases filed against Argentina, the claimants argued the possibility of extending the MFN clauses to the settlement of disputes, thereby bypassing the jurisdictional precondition of requiring investors to first present their dispute to domestic courts before international arbitration.[74] The *Maffezini* v. *Spain* case

72 China–Germany BIT 2003, Art. 3(4).

73 The application of the MFN clause can be a supranational advantageous treatment which would discriminate against domestic litigants.

74 Dupuy, *supra* note 43, at 220–221.

heard by the ICSID in 2000 was the earliest case to touch on this procedural right under the MFN clause. The case is a dispute between an Argentine investor and the Spanish government, but the Argentine investor made an attempt to rely on a more favorable dispute resolution clause in the Spain–Chile BIT 1991 according to the MFN clause in the Argentina–Spain BIT 1991. The arbitral tribunal supported the claim made by the Argentine investor. The case sparked widespread controversy over the interpretation and use of the MFN clause in BIT law and practice.[75] In the subsequent *Plama* v. *Bulgaria* case, the ICSID arbitral tribunal made a contrary ruling to the effect that the MFN clause in the basic treaty could not be applied to the procedural rights under the dispute settlement clause in another BIT unless the basic BIT clearly provides for this application.[76] *Maffezini* and *Plama* basically represent a jurisprudential split on the identical doctrinal issue, that is, whether MFN clauses can serve as titles of jurisdiction independently of the basic treaty's dispute settlement provision.

There has been significant controversy over the extent to which MFN clauses should apply to substantive rights or procedural rights, or both. As the MFN treatment clauses in BITs usually grant investors, as regards "management, maintenance, use, enjoyment or disposal of their investment," no less favorable treatment, it is always controversial whether the investor can invoke the MFN obligation to enjoy the more favorable dispute resolution provisions in other BITs, which may include consent to ICSID arbitration as an option for all disputes. Arbitration practice indicates that the broader the language used, the more likely it is that the tribunal will extend the MFN standard to cover procedural rights. For instance, the investors may make use of the MFN treatment in some cases to bypass procedural impediments, that is, the requirement to resolve the dispute in the local courts first.[77] It has been confirmed in other cases that MFN treatment may be relied on to broaden the tribunal's jurisdiction,[78] from disputes relating to the amount or payment of compensation as under the basic treaty, to all disputes including the existence of expropriation under a third-party BIT.[79] As the fork-in-the-road provisions "abound in BITs,"[80] a number of arbitration tribunals have confirmed the intended function of such provision and disallowed its circumvention by the disputing party's invoking the MFN clause.[81] The case law in this respect, however, is divergent.[82]

Given the absence of dispute resolution in some early Chinese BITs and the limitation over the scope of dispute applied to ICSID arbitration, the prevalence of the *Maffezini* approach in ICSID arbitration may be essential for investors to protect their investments under these BITs. An expansive approach may be adopted to grant such investors more favorable rights.

75 *Emilio Agustin Maffezini* v. *The Kingdom of Spain*, ICSID Case No. ARB/97/7, Decision on the Tribunal on Objections of Jurisdiction (January 25, 2000).

76 *Plama Consortium Limited* v. *Republic of Bulgaria*, ICSID Case No. ARB/03/24, Decision on Jurisdiction (February 8, 2005).

77 *Maffezini* v. *Spain*, *supra* note 75.

78 The case law evinces a growing inclination on the part of tribunals to formulate the exhaustion of local remedies clauses as conditions to be satisfied before jurisdiction can be established. In some cases, the tribunals applied a more deferential arbitral treatment of local remedy first provisions. Matthew C. Porterfield, "Exhaustion of Local Remedies in Investor-State Dispute Settlement: An Idea Whose Time Has Come?" (2015) 14 *Yale Journal of International Law Online*, https://ssrn.com/abstract=2735036 (accessed March 8, 2021).

79 *RosInvestCo. UK Ltd* v. *Russian Federation*, SCC Case No. Arb. V079/2005.

80 McLachlan, Shore and Weiniger, *supra* note 27, at para 4.75.

81 *Maffezini* v. *Spain*, ICSID Case No. ARB/97/7 Jurisdiction Award.

82 *Kilic Insaat Ithalat Ihracat Sanayi ve Ticaret Anonim Sirketi* v. *Turkmenistan*, ICSID Case No. ARB/10/1; *Joseph C. Lemire* v. *Ukraine*, ICSID Case No. ARB/06/18; *Amboiente Ufficio S.p.A. and others* v. *Argentine Republic*, ICSID Case No. ARB/08/9.

The China–Germany BIT covers "indirect" investments, which protects "holding constructions where the investment is not directly held by the mother company but effectuated via one or several subsidiaries."[83] According to the Protocol, "[i]nvested indirectly" means "invested by an investor of one Contracting Party through a company which is fully or partially owned by the investor and having its seat in the territory of the other Contracting Party."[84] This allows "corporate structuring via third-country subsidiaries in order to bring an investment under the protection of international law in case no BIT exists between the investor's home State and the PRC."[85] By its explicit consent to this indirect investment provision, which arguably allows investors to benefit from BIT protection without having a BIT or an MFN clause, China implicitly consents to a broad interpretation of its MFN clauses with respect to dispute settlement procedures.

Unlike other earlier cases[86] which have seen a substantial contradiction in the reasoning of the tribunals adjudicating the extension of MFN treatment to procedural rights in BIT cases, the tribunals in China-BIT-related cases have indicated some consistency not only in rejections but also in interpretative techniques.

In *Tza Yap Shum* v. *Peru*, the tribunal was faced with the claimant's concerned attempts to extend the scope of jurisdiction to issues not covered by the arbitration clauses in the disputed China–Peru BIT according to the Peru–Columbia BIT[87] without limited jurisdiction *ratione materiae*. The MFN clause in the China–Peru BIT provides: "The treatment and protection referred to in Paragraph 1 of this Article [fair and equitable treatment] shall not be less favourable than that accorded to investments and activities associated with such investments of investors of a third State." It is clear from the language that the MFN clause merely applies to FET and constant protection but not to all matters under the BIT. Further, the MFN clause in Article 3 of the BIT applies only to investment but not to dispute settlement rights accruing to investors as arbitration is a procedural right of an investor and a right to invoke arbitration is a personal right that must be held by an investor but not an investment.

The tribunal found that the submission to ISA in Article 8(3) reflected the parties' agreement on two fundamental issues – agreement to submit expropriation disputes to ICSID arbitration and that specific agreement would be needed to submit other types of dispute to ICSID arbitration.[88] The tribunal therefore determined that the "specific wording of Article 8(3) should prevail over the general wording of the MFN clause in Article 3."[89] The tribunal was self-disciplined, largely sticking to the "best indicator" of the "intention of the parties expressed in the text,"[90] not to overexaggeratedly broaden its discretion without having any clear indications in the disputed BIT.[91]

83 Stephan W. Schill, "Tearing Down the Great Wall: The New Generation Investment Treaties of the People's Republic of China" (2007) 15 *Cardozo Journal of International and Comparative Law* 73, 85.

84 China–Germany Protocol, Art. 1(2).

85 Schill, *supra* note 83, at 86.

86 *Plama* v. *Bulgaria*, *supra* note 76; *Maffezini* v. *Spain*, ICSID Case No. ARB/97/7, Award on Jurisdiction, January 25, 2000; *Salini et al.* v. *Morocco*, ICSID Case No. ARB/00/4, Decision on Jurisdiction, July 23, 2001 (2003) 42 ILM 609.

87 *Tza Yap Shum* v. *Republic of Peru*, ICSID Case No. ARB/07/6, Decision on Jurisdiction and Competence of June 19, 2009, paras. 189–190.

88 Under Article 8(3) of the BIT, the tribunal's jurisdiction is limited to expropriation. Jurisdiction over all other matters is subject to specific agreement. Those "other matters" include the interpretation of the MFN clause in the first place. This means that the tribunal actually lacks the subject-matter jurisdiction to consider whether MFN can be applied to expand subject-matter jurisdiction.

89 *Tza Yap Shum* v. *Peru*, para. 216.

90 Ibid., para. 206.

91 However, the tribunal appeared to be mistaken in its reasoning. The tribunal took an *effet utile* approach by differentiating between the applications of the MFN clause based on an a priori categorization of general and

In the case of *Beijing Urban Construction Group Co Ltd.* v. *Republic of Yemen*, one defense raised by the respondent was that the 1998 Yemen–China BIT's MFN clause could not be used to circumvent the limited jurisdiction of its dispute resolution clause.[92] The tribunal dismissed most of the respondent's jurisdictional objections but agreed that the wording of the MFN clause tied it to activities that took place "in the territory" associated geographically with the investment. Thus, the MFN clause could not be used by the tribunal to import a broader dispute resolution clause from the Yemen–UK BIT to expand the scope of jurisdiction (which itself is not an activity inherently linked to the respondent's territory) over non-expropriation BIT claims, which are beyond Article 10 of the Yemen–China BIT.[93] The tribunal's focus was unique when it came to the issue of applying MFN provisions to dispute resolution provisions. Instead of addressing this jurisprudential issue in the abstract or relying on other investment tribunal decisions extending to the terms of access to international arbitration based on MFN provision, the tribunal focused on the issue of whether the text of the BIT lends itself to such an application.[94] More precisely, the territorial limits imposed on the treatment in Article 3.1 of the Yemen–China BIT restrained the tribunal from extending more favorable procedural rights (in the form of international arbitration) to the claimant.[95] The tribunal's approach demonstrates its tendency to interpret BIT clauses in line with the object, context and purpose of the dispute resolution clauses and the BIT as a whole.

In *Ansung Housing Co., Ltd.* v. *China*, Ansung sought to invoke the MFN clause in Article 3(3) of the China–South Korea BIT 2007 to save its claim from being time-barred as other Chinese BITs do not prescribe a three-year limitation period within which an investor is required to initiate an arbitration claim against the host state.[96] Relying on a plain reading of the MFN clause,[97] the tribunal held that the MFN clause did not extend to a state's consent to arbitrate with investors or to the temporal limitation period for ISA in Article 9(7).[98] Further, the tribunal pointed out that the BIT offers specific MFN protection in relation to an investor's "access to courts of justice, administrative tribunals and authorities," without making any reference to international dispute resolution such as arbitration.[99] Accordingly, the tribunal dismissed the case due to the application of the limitation period in Article 9(7).[100] The instant case appears to suggest that MFN provisions are not to provide a way to escape limitation periods even though this may turn on the precise wording of the MFN provisions in question.

In response to the debate on MFN clauses and procedural rights, recent Chinese BITs have tried to eliminate all potential controversies by making clear that MFN treatment does not cover procedural rights. The relevant provision in the New Zealand–China FTA 2008 reads: "For greater certainty, the obligation in this Article does not encompass a requirement to extend to investors of the other Party dispute resolution procedures other than those set out in

specific provisions. This is unsound as the purpose of the MFN clause is to establish and maintain at all times fundamental equality without discrimination among all the countries concerned.

92 *Tza Yap Shum* v. *Peru*, para. 110.

93 *BUCG* v. *Yemen*, ICSID Case No. ARB/14/30, Decision on Jurisdiction, para. 120, www.italaw.com/cases/5904 (accessed April 6, 2021).

94 Ibid., para. 114.

95 Ibid., para. 117.

96 *Ansung Housing Co., Ltd.* v. *China*, Award, paras. 125–126.

97 China–Korea BIT 2007, Art. 3(3).

98 *Ansung Housing Co., Ltd.* v. *China*, Award, paras. 140–141.

99 China–Korea BIT 2007, Art. 3(5).

100 *Ansung Housing Co. Ltd.* v. *China*, Award, paras. 136–141.

this Chapter."[101] There is a clarification, too, in the EU–Canada CETA 2016 that MFN treatment does not extend to dispute settlement provisions,[102] which effectively avoids any *Maffezini*-like interpretations of the MFN clause.[103]

From the recent jurisprudence of ICSID cases, the application of the MFN clause to procedural matters is gradually becoming more limited. Even in the case of *Maffezini* v. *Spain*, though the arbitral tribunal supported the application of the MFN clause to procedural matters, it also considered that the MFN clause is subject to public policy consideration, especially as it is not supposed to damage clauses such as exhaustion of local remedies and fork-in-the-road. In the case of Hela, Article 6 of the China–Germany Protocol can be categorized as a restrictive exhaustion of local remedies clause and shall not be replaced by the MFN clause.

7.6 TRANSCENDING CONFLICTS OF JURISDICTION: THE WAY FORWARD

Through analysis of the Hela case and categorization of more than 100 Chinese BITs, it appears that, under each model, parallel proceedings may occur in Chinese BIT practice.

For historical reasons, the vast majority of Chinese BITs concluded in the early days were not well crafted so as to fundamentally resolve the issue of parallel proceedings between domestic litigation and international arbitration in BIT cases. In recent years, China has started negotiations with more than a dozen countries for a number of FTAs. In these FTAs, ISDS clauses are also included, and some new solutions are adopted to address concurrent proceedings between domestic litigation and international arbitration.

China signed its first FTA with Chile in 2005. The Supplementary Agreement on Investments of the FTA between China and Chile states:

> 2. The claimant may submit a claim:
>
> (a) before any court under the law of the respondent; or
> (b) to international arbitration referred to in Article 14.3 accompanied by the claimant's:
>   (i) consent in writing to arbitration in accordance with the procedures set out in this Agreement; and
>   (ii) a written waiver of any right to initiate proceedings before any administrative tribunal or court under the law of the respondent.
>
> For greater certainty, the claimant's choice of one forum shall be definitive and exclusive.[104]

Compared to the BIT, there have been some improvements made, largely in two perspectives. First, the claimant is asked to give up the right to resort to local remedies. Second, it is clearly stipulated that domestic litigation and international arbitration mutually exclusive.

101 New Zealand–China FTA 2008, Art. 139(2).

102 Art. X.8(4).

103 *Maffezini* v. *Spain*, ICSID Case No ARB/97/7, Decision on Jurisdiction, January 25, 2000, paras. 38–64. See, among others, Martins Paparinskis, "MFN Clauses and International Dispute Settlement: Moving Beyond Maffezini and Plama?" (2011) *ICSID Review – Foreign Investment Law Journal* 14–58; Yannick Radi, "The Application of the Most-Favoured-Nation Clause to the Dispute Settlement Provisions of Bilateral Investment Treaties: Domesticating the 'Trojan Horse'" (2007) 18 *European Journal of International Law* 757–774.

104 The Supplementary Agreement on Investments of the FTA between China and Chile, Art. 16, para. 2.

The ChAFTA 2015 contains an MFN treatment clause which stipulates: "For greater certainty, the treatment referred to in this Article does not encompass ISDS procedures or mechanisms."[105] This excludes the likelihood that the parties rely on the MFN clause to resort to international arbitration outside of local litigation. This position is reflected in the China–New Zealand FTA[106] and the CKJ TIT, too.[107]

As far as the relationship between domestic litigation and international arbitration is concerned, competition between the two fora should be avoided as the highest policy orientation for the sake of consistency and legitimacy. The interests of the host country and the interests of investors therefore should be balanced, and not too biased toward either party.

In recent years, ISDS is facing a legitimacy crisis due to the contradiction between the autonomous nature of the arbitration system and the nature of the investment dispute. The use of arbitration, a highly commercialized and decentralized dispute resolution method, to resolve investment disputes that fundamentally involve the public interest of the host state may cause ISDS to lose its impartiality. Taking Hela as an example, the case concerns an unusually complex urban old district reconstruction project and house demolition in China. It is a very special social phenomenon in China's special development stage, involving the redistribution of economic interests of China's entire society. To hand such a dispute to some foreign scholars or commercial lawyers who have little knowledge of Chinese society to conduct arbitration is a risk. How to ensure that their rulings fully consider a fair evaluation of the demolition problem and the fair treatment of the interests of all parties is of great concern to the Chinese government in terms of the public interest. Viewed from this angle, the proposal of having an appeal mechanism with the authority to review the merits of investment arbitral awards[108] to a certain degree guarantees the quality of the ISDS system and maintains the balance across the public interests of host states and the private interests of foreign investors.[109]

105 China–Australia FTA 2015, Art. 9.4.

106 The China–New Zealand FTA 2008 has a broad clause (Art. 139(1)) granting MFN treatment to "investors, investments and activities associated with such investments by investors of the other Party … in like circumstances … with respect to admission, expansion, management, conduct, operation, maintenance, use, enjoyment and disposal." Article 139(2) continues to provide: "For greater certainty, the obligation in this Article does not encompass a requirement to extend to investors of the other Party dispute resolution procedures other than those set out in this Chapter."

107 The Agreement among the Government of the People's Republic of China, the Government of the Republic of Korea and the Government of Japan for the Promotion, Facilitation and Protection of Investment signed on May 13, 2012, Article 14(1) states: "Each Contracting Party shall … accord to investors of another Contracting Party and to their investments treatment no less favourable than that it accords … to investors of the third Contracting Party or of a non-Contracting Party and to their investment …." Article 4(3) further states: "It is understood that the treatment accorded to investors of the third Contracting Party or any non-Contracting Party and to their investments as referred to in paragraph 1 does not include treatment accorded to investors of the third Contracting Party or any non-Contracting Party and to their investments by provisions concerning the settlement of investment disputes between a Contracting Party and investors of the third Contracting Party or between a Contracting Party and investors of any non-Contracting Party that are provided for in other international agreements."

108 David Gantz, "An Appellate Mechanism for Review of Arbitral Decisions in Investor-State Disputes: Prospects and Challenges" (2006) 39 *Vanderbilt Journal of International Law* 39–76.

109 A toll provision may preserve the host state's sovereignty as it encourages the pursuit of settlement and/or local remedies without a claimant's forfeiting the international claim. This approach encourages local dispute settlement while honoring the goal of preventing duplicative proceedings. Andrea K. Bjorklund, "Waiver of Local Remedies and Limitation Periods" in Meg Kinnear, Geraldine R. Fisher et al. (eds.), *Building International Investment Law: The First 50 Years of ICSID* (Kluwer Law International 2016) 250.

8

Transitional Clauses in Transition and the Black Hole in Chinese BIT Law

8.1 THE TRANSITIONAL ISSUE AND TRANSITIONAL CLAUSES

As an important capital-exporting and importing state in the global economy, China has witnessed a rapid increase in the number of BITs signed with other states. By the end of 2015, China had signed 145 BITs.[1] Among them, 24 were signed in the 1980s, 68 in the 1990s and the rest in the 2000s. Scholars are accustomed to roughly dividing Chinese BITs into two categories according to the ISDS clauses and the scope of consent in these BITs – BITs signed prior to 1998 and those signed afterwards.[2]

The first phase of Chinese BITs was more concerned with attracting foreign investors' capital into the territory as a developing country, and therefore adopted a more conservative approach toward the ISDS mechanism. Although the BITs signed in this phase do allow for ISDS through the ICSID or *ad hoc* arbitration, merely a limited consent was given by China in the BITs, and consequently ICSID tribunals have only limited jurisdiction over quantum disputes. In other words, ICSID tribunals do not possess any jurisdiction over disputes caused by the host state's breach of any substantive standard in the BITs.[3]

The second phase of Chinese BITs makes a switch with an attempt to strike a balance between promoting capital importing and protecting capital exporting, thereby applying a more open attitude toward the ISDS mechanism. Chinese BITs signed in this phase allow foreign investors to submit investment disputes with the host state to the ICSID for arbitration. China, as the host state, gives unrestricted consent to arbitration in its BITs. As a result, foreign investors exercise the option whether to choose international arbitration or domestic litigation. This change in China's BIT policy is in line with China's "go globally" strategy put forward in 1998 by the Chinese Communist Party, China's ruling party, with the grand objective of promoting national success in the global market. Since then, the Chinese government has encouraged more outbound investment in order to reduce external surpluses

[1] Data from UNCTAD database, http://unctad.org/en/Pages/DIAE/World%20Investment%20Report/Annex-Tables.aspx (accessed November 14, 2016).

[2] Tong Qi, "How Exactly Does China Consent to Investor-State Arbitration: On the First ICSID Case Against China" (2012) 5(2) *Contemporary Asia Arbitration Journal* 265, 270.

[3] Ibid.

and secure access to other countries' natural resources and, more recently, high technologies. As China's outbound FDI increases, China needs more BITs that include higher investment protection standards to protect Chinese outbound investment. Almost along with China's go globally strategy, China has been actively renegotiating and concluding new-generation BITs to replace old ones, and has become one of the major states to replace its old BITs or bilateral treaties with newer FTAs known as treaties with investment provisions (TIPs).[4]

The transitional issue of Chinese BITs stems from China's BIT policy change and the coexistence of both old-generation and new-generation BITs signed by China with the same country. From a jurisprudential point of view, any change in law, including international treaties, inevitably raises the following question: Which law applies to the established legal facts that were formed under the old law when the provisions of the old and new laws are inconsistent? The VCLT sets out the basic principle of non-retroactivity of treaties.[5] Some of Chinese BITs such as the China–ASEAN Treaty and the China–Switzerland BIT 2009 restate the principle that the provisions in question do not bind either party in relation to any act or fact that took place or any situation that ceased to exist before the BIT entered into force.

This shows that, in the absence of different provisions of the treaty, the changed norms of international law can only be effective against current and future facts or matters and cannot be applied to facts that have ended before the changes to the norms of international law. However, the principle of non-retroactivity of treaties is not an *ius cogens*, and the contracting parties to the treaty may endow the retroactivity of treaties by express or implied means. Whether a treaty can be retroactively applied to past facts or matters depends largely on the shared meaning of the parties to the treaty. The case law also shows that international courts usually adjudicate the facts by reference to valid rules. However, when it comes to human rights, environmental protection and other legal issues, international courts may step beyond the principle of non-retroactivity of treaties and apply the rules developed afterwards to evaluate the facts that have occurred.[6] In addition, the transition between old and new Chinese BITs also involves the issue of public policy for the sake of certainty and stability of China's BIT regime. The stability of the treaty should be a basic principle shared by the parties to the BIT and the dispute resolution body. Investors investing in the territory of the host state rely heavily on the BIT regime for rights protection. The transition between the old and new BITs is not supposed to undermine the stability of the treaty norms or the foreign investor's confidence in the host state's creditability in its legal infrastructure.[7]

The transitional clauses contained in new BITs then become a realistic solution to avoid potential confusion arising out of the inconsistency or conflict between old and new BITs. In the newly signed BITs, the contracting parties delineate clearly the respective treaties' scope of temporal application to guarantee the effective convergence and smooth transition of the

4 UNCTAD, UNCTAD's Reform Package: For the International Investment Regime, 2018, p. 83, https://investmentpolicy.unctad.org/publications/1190/unctad-s-reform-package-for-the-international-investment-regime-2018-edition- (accessed March 6, 2021) (reporting that Germany, China, Egypt, Romania and Morocco are the major states replacing their BITs and TIPs).

5 VCLT, Art. 28.

6 Gabckovo-Nagymaros Project (*Hungary* v. *Slovakia*), ICJ Reports 1997, p. 7, paras. 145, 180, 227–228. Neils Petersen, "The International Court of Justice and the Judicial Politics of Identifying Customary International Law" (2017) 28(2) *European Journal of International Law* 357–385. José E. Alvarez, "Limits of Change by Way of Subsequent Agreements and Practice" in Georg Nolte (ed.), *Treaties and Subsequent Practice* (Oxford University Press 2013) 123.

7 See N. Stephan Kinsella and Noah D. Rubins, *International Investment, Political Risk and Dispute Resolution* (Oceana Publications 2005) at 1–6.

two BITs. By having transitional clauses in the new BIT, which clarify in which situations and for how long after an old BIT's termination (usually within three years)[8] an investor may invoke the old BIT to bring an ISDS case, the tribunal interpreting the treaty terms may have an indication of whether a new or an old norm is applicable to the case. Among Chinese BITs, six BITs signed by China with Germany, France, BLEU, Finland, the Netherlands and Spain contain transitional clauses.[9] Correct understanding and application of these transitional clauses is key to solving transitional issues such as the legal gap or vacuum resulting from the coexistence of both new and old BITs.

8.1.1 *Transitional Issues in Chinese BITs*

From an underdeveloped country that mainly attracts and relies on FDI for economic development, China has grown into an emerging economy with huge simultaneous capital import and export, which has naturally led to the need for new BITs to replace old BITs.[10] In 1978, China established the basic national policy of reform and opening up and began to invite foreign capital into the country on a large scale. For a long period of time, foreign investment in China increased sharply, while outbound FDI by Chinese investors remained comparatively limited. On March 29, 1982, China and Sweden signed China's first BIT, which scholars have called the starting point of China's first-generation BIT.[11] China adopted a mixed – cautiously welcoming – attitude toward FDI, which formed the basic policy in shaping the first-generation BITs.

Although substantive clauses such as MFN treatment, national treatment, and fair and equitable treatment have been absorbed into the first-generation BITs, the ISDS mechanisms codified in these BITs have hardly been cited or relied on by foreign investors for international arbitration. Under the first-generation BITs, for example the China–Singapore BIT 1985,[12] foreign investors may submit a dispute with the Chinese government to the ICSID only if the dispute concerns the amount of compensation arising out of expropriation and nationalization, instead of being about whether the government's act constitutes expropriation and nationalization or the government bears state liability for expropriation and nationalization.[13] Some first-generation BITs allow investors and the host state to "send a dispute over any other matter to an *ad hoc* arbitral tribunal" through a mutual agreement.[14]

Several first-generation BITs restrict investors to only being able to initiate international arbitration after exhausting local remedies.[15] For instance, after the consultation between the investor and the host state government in the first six months, the investor may choose to appeal or litigate the dispute. Where the dispute cannot be resolved within one year, the investor may initiate the arbitration procedure.[16] Such narrowly defined ISDS clauses make most disputes fall within the jurisdiction of the host state's court, effectively avoiding possible

8 UNCTAD, UNCTAD's Reform Package, p. 83.

9 Data from UNCTAD database, http://unctad.org/en/Pages/DIAE/World%20Investment%20Report/Annex-Tables.aspx (accessed November 14, 2016).

10 World Investment Report 2019.

11 Lars Markert, "Arbitration under China's Investment Treaties: Does It Really Work?" (2012) 5(2) *Contemporary Asia Arbitration Journal* 205, 212.

12 China-Singapore BIT 1985, Art. 13(3).

13 Jane Y. Willems, "The Settlement of Investor State Disputes and China New Developments on ICSID Jurisdiction" (2011) 8(1) *South Carolina Journal of International Law and Business* 21–27.

14 E.g., Article 12(1) of the China–Switzerland BIT 1986.

15 Article 8 of the China–France BIT 1984.

16 Ibid.

damages caused by international tribunals' unfavorable awards against the host state. Meanwhile, the narrow scope of dispute and the additional consent required for international arbitration substantially reduce the effectiveness of the ISDS clauses in resolving investment disputes and make the BIT more symbolic rather than a binding commitment. The restrictive ISDS clauses are widely included in the first-generation BITs signed between China and many Eurasian countries: Norway (1984),[17] Denmark (1985)[18] the UK (1986),[19] Singapore (1985),[20] Indonesia (1994)[21] and Cambodia (1995).[22]

China's investment policy has undergone significant changes, which began in the late twentieth century. With the increasing willingness and capability of Chinese investors to invest overseas, the Chinese government in 1998 put forward the so-called go globally strategy. The Chinese government advocates that Chinese enterprises should fully utilize domestic and foreign markets and resources, and actively participate in international competition and cooperation through foreign direct investment, foreign engineering contracting and foreign labor cooperation.[23] The hybrid policy of Chinese BITs being tools to attract foreign investment while restricting foreign investors' capability to bring investment disputes to international arbitration has also been transformed to a more liberal approach of welcoming inbound FDI and encouraging outbound FDI at the same time. Along with this liberal approach is the removal of previous restrictions on the ISDS mechanisms in the first-generation BITs, reflecting a more pragmatic philosophy toward the ISDS mechanisms so that investors are equipped with an easier tool for initiating international arbitration for their disputes with the host state under these new-generation BITs.

China's new-generation BITs started with the China–Barbados BIT signed in 1998.[24] The new-generation BITs are different from the older ones with some breakthroughs in procedural protection standards such as a wider scope of arbitrable matters, a fork-in-the-road clause and an umbrella clause. In the new-generation BITs, the scope of arbitrable disputes is extended from disputes involving the amount of compensation for expropriation to any dispute related to investment. The fork-in-the-road clause is also more flexible. After resorting to the domestic court, the investor can bring the dispute to international arbitration. A foreign investor can also rely on an umbrella clause to upgrade a contractual claim between the host state and the investor to a treaty claim. These breakthroughs are in line with China's ever-increasing investment protection standards.

In terms of arbitrable matters, China's new-generation BITs allow investors to submit any investment dispute, instead of merely disputes involving "the amount of compensation from expropriation," to the ICSID or an ad hoc tribunal. This more liberal ISDS clause appears in

17 China–Norway BIT 1984, Art. 2.
18 China–Denmark BIT 1985, Art. 8.
19 China–UK BIT 1986, Art. 7.
20 China–Singapore BIT 1985, Art. 13(3).
21 China–Indonesia BIT 1994, Art. 9(3).
22 China–Cambodia BIT 1995, Art. 9(3).
23 "The Formation of Jiang Zemin's 'Going Out' Strategy and Its Significance," People.com.cn, November 10, 2008, http://finance.people.com.cn/GB/8215/126457/8313172.html (accessed March 22, 2021). See also "China's 'Going Out' Strategy," *The Economist*, July 21, 2009, www.economist.com/free-exchange/2009/07/21/chinas-going-out-strategy (accessed March 22, 2021); "Decision on Several Issues of Perfecting the Socialist Market Economic System," *Xinhuanet*, October 20, 2003, http://news.xinhuanet.com/newscenter/2003-10/21/content_1135402.htm (accessed March 22, 2021).
24 Tong Qi, "How Exactly Does China Consent to Investor-State Arbitration," 265, 269.

Chinese BITs with the Netherlands (2001),[25] Germany (2003),[26] Canada (2012)[27] and South Korea (2012).[28]

In addition to removing restrictions on arbitrable disputes, the new-generation BITs have adopted more flexible provisions such as fork-in-the-road clauses. Under the first-generation BITs, once an investor has chosen a dispute resolution method, that choice is considered final; the investor can no longer choose a different mechanism. This suggests that once they submit a claim to the domestic court of the host state, the investor loses the opportunity to submit the dispute to international arbitration. The fork-in-the-road clause embodies and reflects the principle of *non bis in idem* in international law, avoiding the host state government defending the same dispute in different dispute resolution bodies for the same reasons. This enhances the stability and predictability of international arbitration as a dispute settlement mechanism.

In the new-generation BITs, the fork-in-the-road clause has turned out to be more flexible. Accordingly, investors can appeal to an international arbitration tribunal even after submitting the dispute to a suitable domestic court. For example, Article 10(2) of the China–Netherlands BIT 2001 states: "An investor may decide to submit a dispute to a competent domestic court. In case a legal dispute concerning an investment in the territory of the People's Republic of China has been submitted to a competent domestic court, this dispute may be submitted to international dispute settlement, on the condition that the investor concerned has withdrawn its case from the domestic court. If a dispute concerns an investment in the territory of the Kingdom of the Netherlands[,] an investor may choose to submit a dispute to international dispute settlement at any time."[29] This shows that the dispute resolution method selected by an investor is no longer final. Under certain conditions (i.e., withdrawing the lawsuit from the domestic court), the investor could still appeal the dispute to international arbitration.

China's new-generation BITs also extend the jurisdiction of international arbitration to the contractual obligations of the host state. Investors may rely on the umbrella clause to escalate the contractual claim between them and the host state to a treaty claim. Therefore, the act of the host state violating its obligation under the investment contract also triggers a treaty obligation under the BIT.[30] On the one hand, an investor can initiate domestic judicial procedures against the host state according to the host state's domestic law on the basis of the host state's breach of its contractual obligation. On the other hand, the investor can resort to international arbitration in accordance with the BIT due to the host state's violation of its treaty obligations.

China's new-generation BITs generally distinguish umbrella clauses from other substantive rules and place an umbrella clause in "Other Obligations" clauses, which often contain the MFN treatment clause.[31] For example, Article 10(2) of the China–Germany BIT 2003 states: "Each Contracting Party shall observe any other obligation it has entered into with regard to investments in its territory by investors of the other Contracting Party." The same or a similar umbrella clause also appears in China's BITs with certain EU countries: the

25 China–Netherlands BIT 2001, Art. 10(3).
26 China–Germany BIT 2003, Art. 9(3).
27 China–Canada BIT 2012, Art. 22.
28 China–Korea BIT 2012, Art. 9(3).
29 China–Netherlands BIT 2001, Art. 10(2).
30 James Crawford, "Treaty and Contract in Investment Arbitration" (2008) 24 *Arbitration International* 351, 351–361.
31 Article 10 of the China–Spain BIT 2005.

Netherlands,[32] Finland[33] and Belgium.[34] Although the effectiveness of the umbrella clause in "elevat[ing] contract breach to the international plane" is a controversial issue,[35] the umbrella clauses in China's new-generation BITs at least provide foreign investors with a route to make a treaty claim.

Some of China's new-generation BITs have also set out the precondition of administrative review for international arbitration. For example, Article 9 of the China–Germany Protocol 2003 states: "With respect to investments in the People's Republic of China[,] an investor of the Federal Republic of Germany may submit a dispute for arbitration under the following conditions only: (a) the investor has referred the issue to an administrative review procedure according to Chinese law; (b) the dispute still exists three months after he has brought the issue to the review procedure, and (c) in case the issue has been brought to a Chinese court, it can be withdrawn by the investor according to Chinese law."[36] The precondition of administrative review increases the burden on foreign investors returning disputes to international arbitration, forcing investors to face the cumbersome administrative review procedure and corresponding substantive law in the host state. However, compared to some old-generation BITs, this is still a step forward as it offers foreign investors international arbitration fora apart from domestic litigation.

The comparison indicates that the differences between the old and the new generations of Chinese BITs are mainly reflected in the ISDS clauses. The new BITs have broader "dispute" terms, a more flexible fork-in-the-road clause and an umbrella clause. Some Chinese BITs set out a precondition of administrative review for international arbitration.

8.1.2 *Application of Law to the Transitional Issue*

Since 1998, China has started to enter into new-generation BITs, and has re-signed new BITs with some countries that once entered into the first-generation BITs. As shown in Table 8.1, as of the end of 2015, China had signed two BITs with twelve countries. Among these new BITs, six – those signed with Germany, France, BLEU, Finland, the Netherlands and Spain – include transitional clauses, which are similar in structure and content. Structurally, the transitional clauses include two provisions: the first paragraph stipulates that the new BIT replaces the old one, and the second paragraph limits the scope of application of the new BIT. In terms of content, the transitional clause includes some basic components. The new BIT applies to all investments made by the investor of one contracting party before and after the new BIT enters into force. The old BIT continues to apply to any disputes that entered judicial or arbitral proceedings before the new BIT came into effect.

In the event that both old and new BITs are in coexistence and effective at the same time, how to interpret and apply the transitional clauses and deal with the relationship between the two successive BITs, in particular where the new BIT has a retroactive effect on investment made under the old BIT, is often a key issue in specific disputes between the host state and the investor.

32 China–Netherlands BIT 2001, Art. 3(4).

33 China–Finland BIT 2004, Art. 11(2).

34 China–BLEU BIT 2005, Art. 7(2).

35 Yuval Shany, "Contract Claims vs. Treaty Claims: Mapping Conflicts Between ICSID Decisions on Multi-sourced Investment Claims" (2005) 99 *American Journal of International Law* 835, 838.

36 The China–Germany Protocol is an integral part of the China–Germany BIT 2003.

TABLE 8.1 *Existence of two successive BITs between China and its counterparties*[37] *(by the end of 2015)*

No.	BIT	Signing date of the old BIT	Signing date of the new BIT	Transitional clauses
1	China–Germany BIT	October 7, 1983	December 1, 2003	Art. 16
2	China–France BIT	May 30, 1984	November 26, 2007	Art. 11
3	China–BLEU BIT	June 4, 1984	June 6, 2005	Art. 10
4	China–Finland BIT	September 4, 1984	November 15, 2004	Art. 13
5	China–Netherlands BIT	June 17, 1985	November 26, 2001	Art. 13
6	China–Switzerland BIT	November 12, 1986	January 27, 2009	The old BIT terminates. No transitional clauses.
7	China–Portugal BIT	February 3, 1992	December 9, 2005	The old BIT terminates. No transitional clauses.
8	China–Spain BIT	February 6, 1992	November 24, 2005	Art. 12
9	China–Nigeria BIT (not come into effect yet)	May 12, 1997	August 27, 2001	No transitional clauses.
10	China–Uzbekistan BIT	March 13, 1992	April 19, 2011	The old BIT terminates. No transitional clauses.
11	China–Korea BIT	September 30, 1992	September 7, 2007	No transitional clauses.
12	China–Cuba BIT	April 24, 1995	April 20, 2007	The old BIT terminates. No transitional clauses.

*Prepared by the author.

Ping An v. *Belgium* is the second investment arbitration case involving a Chinese BIT. As the respondent is an industrialized country, the case, among others, triggered noticeable public opposition to ISDS.[38] It is the first China-related investment arbitration case touching on transitional clauses in Chinese BITs. The case concerns the retroactive effect that a new BIT may have on ICSID jurisdiction in relation to investment that occurred before the new BIT came into force. China and BLEU signed the first BIT on June 4, 1984 and this BIT came into effect on October 5, 1986. China and BLEU then signed the second BIT on June 6, 2005; it came into effect on December 1, 2009.

Ping An argued that the acquisition of Fortis Group's banking sector executed by the Belgian government during the 2008 financial crisis constitutes indirect expropriation.[39] The Belgian government implemented two rounds of intervention into Fortis Group's banking sector on the grounds of the liquidity crisis in the Fortis Group's banking business. Ping An believed that the nationalization by the Belgian government then constituted a violation of the China–BLEU BIT 1986. The Belgian government, as Ping An claimed, should give Ping An reasonable compensation.[40]

On October 14, 2008, Ping An wrote to the Belgian government through the Belgian Embassy in China. It believed that the Belgian government's nationalization of Fortis

37 Data from UNCTAD database, http://unctad.org/en/Pages/DIAE/World%20Investment%20Report/Annex-Tables.aspx (accessed November 14, 2016).

38 Steffen Hindelang and Markus Krajewski, "Towards a More Comprehensive Approach in International Investment Law" in Steffen Hindelang and Markus Krajewski (eds.), *Shifting Paradigms in International Investment Law: More Balanced, Less Isolated, Increasingly Diversified* (Oxford University Press 2016) 1, at 2.

39 See *Ping An Life Insurance Co. of China, Limited and Ping An Insurance (Group) Co. of China, Ltd.* v. *Kingdom of Belgium*, ICSID case No. ARB/12/29, Award of April 30, 2015, at para. 66.

40 Ibid., paras. 66–78.

Group constituted an expropriation of Ping An's investment and required the Belgian government to compensate for its economic loss.[41] On October 14, 2009, Ping An sent a letter to the Belgian ambassador to China, stating that the letter dated October 14, 2008 constituted a notice under Article 10(1) of the China–BLEU BIT 1986. The Belgian government did not give Ping An full compensation and there was a lack of due process,[42] which violated the fair and equitable treatment provisions and the transparency provisions under the China–BLEU BIT 1986.[43] On July 3, 2012, Ping An again wrote to the Belgian ambassador to China, stating that Ping An's letter of October 14, 2009 also constituted a notice of dispute settlement under Article 8(1) of the China–BLEU BIT 2009.[44] Subsequently, Ping An, based on the substantive provisions of the 1986 BIT (e.g., Article 3 equitable treatment clause and Article 4 expropriation and nationalization clause) and the ISDS clauses under the 2009 BIT (e.g., Article 8 dispute settlement clause), brought the Belgian government to the ICSID for arbitration.[45]

The Belgian government's defense focused on the ICSID tribunal's lack of jurisdiction over the case. Belgium questioned Ping An's application of the 2009 BIT to the established facts that had occurred before the BIT 2009 came into effect. However, Belgium's consent to ICSID arbitration in the 2009 BIT only applies to such disputes that occur after the 2009 BIT came into effect.[46] According to the 1986 BIT, the jurisdiction of an ICSID tribunal is limited to the amount of compensation for expropriation.[47] Belgium also pointed out that the 1986 BIT was replaced by the 2009 BIT and so the expired 1986 BIT could not be the basis of substantive law relied on by the ICSID tribunal in this case.[48]

Ping An made a counterargument that the transitional clauses in the 2009 BIT made it applicable to the investment that had occurred before its entry into force.[49] The transitional clauses provide that the 2009 BIT may apply to all investments by investors of either contracting party in the territory of the other contracting party, no matter whether such investments were made before or after the 2009 BIT entered into force.[50] The transitional clauses only exclude the application of the 2009 BIT to disputes that entered judicial or arbitral proceedings before the 2009 BIT took effect. Belgium's understanding of the ISDS clauses in the 2009 BIT was too narrow.[51]

With two BITs in place signed by the two countries, *Ping An* v. *Belgium* presents a series of difficult issues in the application of new and old BITs. Understanding how to apply the transitional clauses guided the concerned tribunals to resolve the normative conflict caused by the old and new BITs.

There are other ICSID cases dealing with the same legal issue. *Jan de Nul* v. *Egypt* involves the Egypt–BLEU BITs 1977 and 2002 respectively.[52] The claimant in this case requested the tribunal to apply the 2002 BIT to a dispute that occurred prior to its entry into force and that

41 Ibid., paras. 106–107.

42 The due process argument may be technically hard to make as the nationalization measure was taken overnight. This point was made by Matthias Vanhullebusch.

43 Ibid., paras. 108–110.

44 Ibid., para. 111.

45 Ibid., para. 38.

46 Para. 113.

47 Para. 115.

48 Paras. 117, 122 and 127.

49 Para. 114.

50 Para. 116.

51 Paras. 118–121, 123–125 and 128.

52 *Jan de Nul N.V. and Dredging International* N.V. v. *Arab Republic of Egypt*, ICSID Case No. ARB/04/13, Award of November 6, 2008.

was supposed to be governed by the 1977 BIT. *Walter Bau* v. *Thailand* also involved the interpretation of two successive BITs. Thailand and Germany signed BITs in 1961 and 2002 respectively. The focus of this case is whether the 2002 BIT should be retrospectively applied to a dispute that occurred prior to the coming into force of the 2002 BIT. If the 2002 BIT should be retrospectively applied, the investor will be able to submit the dispute to the ICSID tribunal.[53] In addition, both *Nordzucker AG* v. *Poland*[54] and *ABCI Investment Company* v. *Tunisia*[55] involve the interpretation and application of two BITs. Therefore, the problems associated with the application of old and new BITs are somewhat universal in the investment arbitration circle.

China's BIT law and practice is at a crossroads. In the future, investment disputes similar to those in the case of *Ping An* v. *Belgium* are likely to arise. The award of *Ping An* v. *Belgium* will have a demonstrative, if not persuasive, effect on the resolution of similar investment disputes in the future. Therefore, an in-depth analysis of the award in the case of *Ping An* v. *Belgium*, and analysis of the applicable principles of the transitional clauses in investment arbitration practice are of great significance for resolving similar investment disputes in the future.

8.2 TREATY INTERPRETATION AND INTERTEMPORAL RULE IN RELATION TO TRANSITIONAL CLAUSES

The transitional clauses in BITs often stipulate the temporal scope of the BIT. The core issue to be resolved by the transitional clauses is the applicability of the particular BIT to the relevant acts, facts or circumstances of the state party before the entry into force of the BIT, that is, whether the validity of the BIT can be traced retrospectively back to the acts, facts or circumstances that occurred prior to the entry into force of the BIT. Application of the transitional clauses needs to conform to the general methods of treaty interpretation and the rules of intertemporal law applicable to the treaties.

8.2.1 *Interpreting Transitional Clauses and Articles 31 and 32 of the VCLT*

Treaty interpretation refers to interpretation of the correct meaning of the specific provisions in the treaty. The correct meaning of the treaty is the basis for the parties' performance of the treaty obligations in good faith. The VCLT compiles the rules of customary law for treaty interpretation and formalizes and corroborates the rules of treaty interpretation. The provisions relating to treaty interpretation are contained in Articles 31 to 33 of the VCLT. Among them, Article 31 provides the general rules for treaty interpretation while Article 32 provides for the use of supplementary materials in treaty interpretation. Articles 31 and 32 are the cornerstones on treaty interpretation in the VCLT. The rules of treaty interpretation in the VCLT adopt three of the most common treaty interpretative methods in modern international law jurisprudence – the textual, the teleological (underlying objective) and the seeking intentions (party intent) approaches[56] – with textual interpretation the foundational

53 *Walter Bau AG (in liquidation)* v. *Thailand* (UNCITRAL), Award of July 1, 2009 (Barker, Lalonde, Bunnag).

54 *Nordzucker AG* v. *Poland* (UNCITRAL), Partial Award of December 10, 2008 (Vera Van Houtte, Bucher, Tomaszewskia).

55 *ABCI Investments N.V.* v. *Republic of Tunisia*, ICSID Case No. ARB/04/12, Award of February 18, 2011.

56 Joost Pauwely and Manfred Elsig, "The Politics of Treaty Interpretation: Variations and Explanations across International Tribunals" in Jeffrey L. Dunoff and Mark A. Pollack (eds.), *Interdisciplinary Perspectives on International Law and International Relations: The State of the Art* (Cambridge University Press 2012) 450.

means of treaty interpretation.[57] The transitional clauses in any BIT need to be interpreted according to the basic principles set out in the VCLT.

8.2.1.1 Textual Interpretation

Article 31 of the VCLT sets out the basic rules to be followed in interpreting a treaty, which are consistent with customary international law.[58] First, the treaty needs to be interpreted in accordance with the principle of good faith. Second, it should be presumed that the treaty terms have an ordinary meaning. Third, the general meaning of treaty terms should be determined in accordance with the context of those terms and by reference to the object and purpose of the treaty. The principle of good faith comes from *pacta sunt servanda*, which was confirmed by the Permanent Court of International Justice in a series of judgments such as the Chorzow Factory Cases (1925–1929).[59] The principle of good faith in treaty interpretation reflects such virtues and adjudicative criteria as honesty, justice and reasonableness, which help to preserve the legal order constructed by the treaty, ensure the realization of the purpose and object of the treaty, and meet the legitimate needs and expectations of the parties.[60]

The term textual is described by the United Nations International Law Commission (ILC) as an indication that the text should be taken as an authentic expression of the intention of the parties. In the *Eritrea–Ethiopia Boundary* case, the arbitral tribunal further pointed out that Article 31, paragraph 1 of the VCLT is a guide to the true agreement of the parties, and the doctrine of contemporaneity requires the tribunal to interpret a treaty by reference to the circumstances prevailing when the treaty was concluded.[61]

An understanding of the natural and ordinary meaning of a treaty term should also examine the context as well as the object and purpose of the treaty.[62] Article 31 of the VCLT clarifies that not only the textual content of the treaty should be given priority in treaty interpretation; the extrinsic evidence related to the text should also be properly considered. The ILC believes that the text of the treaty is the most authoritative expression of the contracting parties' intention in reaching a treaty. Therefore, treaty interpretation should not only refer to external evidence such as legal documents made by the parties to the treaty but also rely on the textual meaning of the treaty terms.[63]

The principles and methods of textual interpretation established by Article 31 of the VCLT are widely used in investment arbitration. The tribunal in the case of *Fraport* v. *The Philippines* pointed out that speculation as to the contracting parties' intention could not exceed the terms stipulated in the BIT. A deduction on the part of the interpretation to nullify explicit BIT clauses, in the tribunal's view, constituted a violation of all the canons of interpretation.[64] The tribunal in the case of *Daimler Financial Services* v. *Argentina* believed that the BIT text is the definitive guide to exploring the contracting parties' meaning as to how

57 See Myres S. McDougal, "The International Law Commission's Draft Articles upon Interpretation: Textuality Redivius" (1967) 61(4) *American Journal of International Law* 992.

58 See, e.g., the *Indonesia* v. *Malaysia* Case, ICJ Reports, 2002, at para. 37; the *Libya* v. *Chad* Case, (1995) ICJ Reports6, 21–2; 100 ILR, 1, 20–1, and the *Qatar* v. *Bahrain* case, (1995) ICJ Reports 6; 102 ILR 47, 59.

59 See *Factory at Chorzow (Germ.* v. *Pol.)*, 1928 P.C.I.J., Series A, No. 13, Order of December 15, pp. 10–11.

60 See *Year Book of the International Law Commission*, Vol. 2, 1966, p. 221.

61 *Eritrea–Ethiopia Boundary* case, award, para. 3.5.

62 See Lord McNair in the *Argentina* v. *Chile Frontier* Case, 38 ILR, pp. 10, 89.

63 International Law Commission, (1996) Vol II Yb ILC, 1996 218, 220.

64 See *Fraport AG Frankfurt Airport Services Worldwide* v. *The Republic of the Philippines*, ICSID Case No. ARB/03/25, Award of December 10, 2014, at paras. 340.

best to protect and promote investment.[65] The tribunal in *Siemens* v. *Argentina* stressed the importance of adhering to treaty interpretation "in good faith in accordance with the ordinary meaning to be given to the terms of the treaty in their context and in the light of its object and purpose."[66]

In practice, the textual approach often turns out to be the starting point of interpretation instead of an investigation *ab initio* into the intention of the parties. In other words, a textual approach often excludes extratextual elements or arguments in treaty interpretation.[67] Only when there is direct evidence that the relevant terms should be understood in other meanings than natural and ordinary ones, or when natural or ordinary meanings will lead to unreasonable or absurd results, can those terms be interpreted in other meanings than natural and usual ones.[68] This turns out to be the most mainstream view for treaty interpretation.[69] Article 31 of the VCLT is considered to lay down a foundation for textual interpretation mixed with a teleological approach. The contracting parties' intentions are used only to be a complementary and supporting method.[70] Therefore, interpreting transitional clauses should start with textual interpretation.

8.2.1.2 Teleological Interpretation

The teleological approach corresponds to the purpose school in treaty interpretation, whose emphasis is the object and purpose, or the goals, of the treaty as the most important factor to be considered in determining the meaning of a particular treaty term.[71] In the 1935 Harvard Draft Convention on the Law of Treaties prepared as part of the Research in International Law undertaken under the auspices of Harvard Law School, the teleological approach was described as the methodology to use to interpret a treaty term in accordance with the general purpose intended to be achieved by the treaty. The historical background, the preparatory materials, the circumstances of the treaty parties at the time of its conclusion, any attempts to change the situation, the actions of the parties to the treaty after the treaty's application, and the prevailing circumstances in treaty interpretation should all be considered in connection with the general purpose that the treaty is intended to achieve.

Among the various interpretative methods, the method of teleological interpretation has its own unique advantages. As the international community is constantly undergoing new changes but treaties cannot be revised frequently enough to keep up with these, the teleological interpretation method can to a certain extent help maintain stability. This interpretative method can allow the treaty to adapt to the changing social reality without changing its rules. The ICJ often uses this interpretative method in the trial of cases.

In international investment arbitration, tribunals often interpret BIT terms based on the object and purpose of the treaty established in its foreword. In the case of *Lauder* v. *Czech*

65 See *Daimler Financial Services AG* v. *Argentine Republic*, ICSID Case No. ARB/05/1, Award of August 22, 2012, at paras. 164.

66 See *Siemens* v. *Argentina*, ICSID Case No. ARB/02/8, Decision on Jurisdiction, August 3, 2004, at paras. 80.

67 George Lestsas, "Internationalism and the Interpretation of the ECHR" in Panos Merkouris, Malgosia Fitzmaurice and Olufemi Elias (eds.), *Treaty Interpretation and the Vienna Convention on the Law of Treaties: 30 Years On* (Martinus Nijhoff/Brill 2010) 266.

68 McDougal, "The International Law Commission's Draft Articles upon Interpretation," 992.

69 David S. Jonas and Thomas N. Saunders, "The Object and Purpose of a Treaty: Three Interpretive Methods" (2010) 43(3) *Vanderbilt Journal of Transnational Law* 565, 578.

70 Ibid.

71 See Malcolm N. Shaw, *International Law* (5th edition, Cambridge University Press 2003) 839; *See also* Ian Sinclair, *The Vienna Convention on the Law of Treaties* (2nd edition, Manchester University Press 1984) 115.

Republic, the tribunal stated that the treaty should be interpreted by reference to its object and purpose as well as by the circumstances of its conclusion. The preamble of the BIT stipulates that either party to the BIT agrees to grant the fair and equitable treatment of investment to the investor of the other contracting party as a framework for investment and maximum effective utilization of economic resources. Accordingly, despite the lack of the notion of fair and equitable treatment in the BIT text, the investors are still entitled to fair and equitable treatment depending on a factual context.[72] In the case of *Siemens* v. *Argentina*, the tribunal stated that the interpretation of the BIT needed to be guided by the object and purpose of the BIT, which is expressed in its preamble and title as aiming to protect and promote investments. The BIT's preamble recognizes the purpose of the BIT as being to create favorable conditions for the investment of nationals or companies of the other contracting party. The interpretation of the BIT therefore cannot deviate from this object and purpose.[73] Apparently, use of teleological interpretation is more beneficial to investors. But such practices have also been criticized. Since the purpose of the treaty itself is a more abstract concept, a treaty interpretation based on the purpose of the treaty may easily lead to deviation, arbitrariness and uncertainty. In the case of *Plama* v. *Bulgaria*, the tribunal warned that the treaty interpretation should not be overly dictated by the object and purpose of the treaty, and that a treaty interpretation based on teleology would constitute a modification of the treaty.[74] The teleological approach, we are reminded, is not a compendious substitute for or an exhaustion of the other interpretative methods. Rather, it is just one of the methods that are relevant to the identification of the ordinary meaning of treaty terms.

Closely related to teleological interpretation is a restrictive interpretation of the treaty. This issue is particularly evident when the treaty interpretation touches on the jurisdiction of the tribunal (e.g., regarding transitional clauses) and the interpretation of these clauses by different tribunals is not always consistent. Some tribunals tend to restrict the jurisdictional provisions of the BIT while other tribunals are inclined to apply the method of teleological interpretation that most fully reflects the rights and interests of investors,[75] leading to restrictions on national sovereignty.[76] There is no consistent approach toward transitional clauses in international investment arbitration.

8.2.1.3 Intentionalist Interpretation

The VCLT identifies the treaty interpretation by reference to the intention of the contracting parties as a supplementary approach. The task of seeking the true intention of the contracting parties can be achieved through an examination of the natural and ordinary meanings of the treaty terms. If this is not sufficient, Article 32 of the VCLT allows reliance on explanatory information including "preparatory materials of the treaty and other circumstances of the treaty" for a determination of the true meaning of the treaty terms, albeit the secondary nature

72 See *Lauder* v. *Czech Republic*, UNCITRAL, Final Award, September 3, 2001, at para. 292.

73 See *Siemens* v. *Argentina*, ICSID Case No. ARB/02/8, Decision on Jurisdiction, August 3, 2004, at para. 81.

74 See *Plama* v. *Bulgaria*, ICSID Case No. ARB/03/24, Decision on Jurisdiction, February 8, 2005, at para. 193.

75 See *Methanex* v. *US*, UNCITRAL, Preliminary Award on Jurisdiction, August 7, 2002, at paras. 103–105; *See also Aguas del Tunari, SA* v. *Bolivia*, ICSID Case No. ARB/02/3, Decision on Jurisdiction, October 21, 2005, at para. 91.

76 See SGS v. *Pakistan*, ICSID Case No. ARB/01/13, Decision on Jurisdiction, August 6, 2003, at para 171; *See also Noble Venture* v. *Romania*, ICSID Case No. ARB/01/11, Award, October 12, 2005, at para. 55.

of *travaux préparatoires* in determining the presumed intention of the parties.[77] The "School of Intentionalist" or intention-based approach therefore stresses the role of the contracting parties' intention in treaty interpretation.[78] The main tenets of this school are: (a) the main purpose of treaty interpretation is to explore the intention of the contracting parties; (b) in order to seek the true intention of the parties to the treaty, the preparatory materials (*travaux préparatoires*) should be studied;[79] and (c) intention is not a separately identifiable factor but is derived from articulation of the "means of interpretation admissible" in the process of interpretation.[80] However, a pure intentionalist approach is not popular in international law and practice even though the ICJ in the Namibia case was "mindful as it is of the primary necessity of interpreting an instrument in accordance with the intentions of the parties at the time of its conclusion."[81] The International Law Commission pointed out that the historical data on which the intention of the treaty was based and the speculation about the intention of the contracting parties were in many cases "incomplete and misleading."[82] Therefore, the ICJ often places this intentionalist method of treaty interpretation after the textual and other interpretative methods so as to avoid an overly expansive interpretation of the contracting parties' intention. At the technical level, ascertaining the meaning of the text matters more than the intention of the parties.[83] The tribunal may search for the contracting parties' true intention only when a textual interpretation is apparently ambiguous or obscure[84] or when the interpretation of the treaty terms points to a "manifestly absurd or unreasonable" result.[85]

In the practice of treaty interpretation, the intentionalist method, however, is often used. In the practice of international investment arbitration, the intentionalist interpretive method is considered by some tribunals probably due to the close nexus between textuality and intentionality.[86] The tribunal in *Noble Ventures* v. *Romania* further pointed out that recourse to supplementary means of interpretation (including the preparatory work and the circumstances of the treaty's conclusion) is to confirm the meaning resulting from the application of the methods of interpretation in Article 31 of the VCLT.[87] However, tribunals have repeatedly pointed out the shortcomings of the intentionalist approach, and tend not to use this method to interpret treaties. In *Wintershall* v. *Argentina*, the tribunal emphasized that there is no room for any presumed intention of the contracting parties to a treaty as an independent basis

77 Report of the ILC on the Work of Its Sixty-Fifth Session A/68/1027; *see* James Crawford, *State Responsibility: The General Part* (Cambridge University Press 2013) 247.

78 See General Principles of International Law, Treaty Interpretation (September 2006) 1(4) American Society of International Law and International Judicial Academy, www.judicialmonitor.org/archive_0906/generalprinciples.html (accessed November 14, 2016).

79 Ibid.

80 1966 ILC Yearbook II 218–219.

81 *Legal Consequences for States of the Continued Presence of South Africa in Namibia (South West Africa) notwithstanding Security Council Resolution 276* (Advisory Opinion) [1970] ICJ Rep 1971 16 [53]. As a matter of fact, the Namibia opinion was the first explicit endorsement of evolutive interpretation, which moves along an assumed intention approach. Christian Djeffal, *Static and Evolutive Treaty Interpretation: A Functional Reconstruction* (Cambridge University Press 2016) 251.

82 *Draft Article on the Law of Treaties with Commentaries*, United Nations Conference on the Law of Treaties, Official Records, Vol. 3, English Version (William S. Hein 2001) 40.

83 Jean-Marc Sorel and Valerie Bore Eveno, "Article 31" in Olivier Corten and Pierre Klein (eds.), *The Vienna Convention on the Law of the Treaties: A Commentary* (Oxford University Press 2011) 804.

84 David J. Bederman, *International Law Frameworks* (2nd edition, Foundation Press 2006) 36.

85 Ibid.

86 Paul Reuter, *Introduction to the Law of Treaties* (Paul Kegan International 1995) 96–97; Martin Dawidowicz, "The Effect of the Passage of Time on the Interpretation of Treaties: Some Reflections on Costa Rica v. Nicaragua" (2011) 24 *Leiden Journal of International Law* 201, 206–207.

87 See *Noble Ventures* v. *Romania*, ICSID Case No. ARB/01/11, Award, October 12, 2005, at para. 50.

of interpretation, which may open up the possibility of treaty interpretation altering the text of the treaty due to the interpreter's purpose of conforming to the presumed best intention of the contracting parties.[88]

The advantage of the intention-based approach is that it maintains the stability and consistency of the treaty, which is a key virtue in law and the legal system.[89] This approach does seem to have inherent limitations, though it allows for expansive interpretation by interpreters amid implicit recognition of the element of intentions in Article 31 of the VCLT as the very aim of the whole treaty interpretation process.[90] Therefore, according to the VCLT, the intentionalist method is an auxiliary means of interpretation that can be used when other treaty interpretive methods are unable to reach a satisfactory result.

8.2.2 *Use of Supplementary Information*

The preparatory work of a treaty, as Article 32 of the VCLT clarifies, is a complementary part of treaty interpretation. The use of supplementary materials in treaty interpretation reflects the position of the "Intentionalist School," which is to discover the true intention of the contracting parties in concluding the treaty and the common understanding of the contracting parties over the treaty terms.[91] Therefore, when any flaws in the treaty text are insufficient to affect the outcome of the interpretation of the text and the reasonable determination of the relevant rights and obligations, the interpreter can identify the minutes of the proceedings, the draft records, the historical background of the contract, the arguments of the negotiators and any other correspondence or information such as correspondence to correct the absurdity and irrationality of treaty interpretation.

In international investment arbitration, invocation of supplementary information to the treaty depends on the availability of the preparatory work materials for the treaty. In *Malaysian Historical Salvors* v. *Malaysia*, the tribunal held that tribunals usually review the treaty preparatory work when interpreting the treaty; tribunals do not use preparatory work materials only when the terms of the treaty are ambiguous and unexplained.[92]

The drafting process of the ICSID Convention was thoroughly documented. Contrary to this, many BIT negotiation processes were not recorded.[93] Therefore, even if the tribunal intends to invoke the preparatory work for treaty interpretation, it will not be realistic because it cannot be obtained. In *Aguas del Tunari, SA* v. *Bolivia*, the tribunal considered that the treaty preparatory materials provided by the parties to the dispute were too insufficient to be

88 See *Wintershall Aktiengesellschaft* v. *Argentine Republic*, ICSID Case No. ARB/04/14, Award December 8, 2008, at para. 88.

89 Constance J. Schwindt, "Interpreting the United Nation Charter: From Treaty to World Constitution" (2000) *UC Davis Journal of International Law and Policy* 198.

90 Separate Opinion of Judge Fitzmaurice, Case of *National Union of Belgian Police* v. *Belgium* (1979–80) 1 EHRR 578, [9].

91 Mark E. Villiger, *Commentary on the 1969 Vienna Convention on the Law of Treaties* (Martinus Nijhoff 2012) 446.

92 See *Malaysian Historical Salvors* v. *Malaysia*, ICSID Case No. ARB/05/10, Decision on Annulment, April 16, 2009, at para. 57.

93 History of the ICSID Convention: Documents Concerning the Origin and the Formulation of the Convention on the Settlement of Investment Disputes between States and Nationals of Other States, Washington, DC, 1968, reprinted 2001.

analyzed in depth.[94] In *Perenco* v. *Ecuador*, the tribunal asked the parties to make an effort to obtain the preparatory work for the BIT.[95]

Meanwhile, tribunals may tend to apply a restrictive approach when invoking the preparatory work for the treaty. In *Methanex* v. *United States*, the tribunal noted that, in accordance with Article 32 of the VCLT, the supplementary means of interpretation may be necessary only under very limited circumstances. Further, as the text of treaty is deemed to be the authentic expression of the intentions of the parties, elucidation of the treaty text, other than the wide-ranging searches for the supposed intention of the parties, should be the proper object of interpretation.[96]

The use of supplementary information is only an auxiliary method of treaty interpretation that can be invoked under Article 32 of the VCLT. The secondary nature of the preparatory work and the circumstances of its conclusion suggest that the use of such information is bound by the principle of treaty interpretation in good faith in accordance with the ordinary meanings of the terms and text of the treaty in their context and in light of the treaty's object and purpose.[97] Supplementary information can only be used with caution if the treaty terms interpreted in accordance with Article 31 are unclear or inexplicable, or if there is a clear irrationality or absurdity. In BIT cases, preparatory work is only occasionally available and rarely of great assistance to the treaty interpretation.[98]

Related to temporality, the reference to analysis of the relevant préparatoires and jurisprudence made in Article 31(3)(c) arguably implicitly incorporates intertemporal law considerations.[99] However, Article 31(3)(c) has been criticized as being too vague. In the *Gabčikovo-Nagymaros Project* case, Judge Weeramantry demonstrated the vagueness of Article 31(3)(c) by pointing out the provision's scarcity in "cover[ing] the aspect of intertemporal law with the degree of clarity requisite to so important a matter."[100]

8.2.3 *Intertemporal Law and Transitional Clauses: Article 28 of the VCLT*

Intertemporal law refers to the scope of application of the treaty in time, including the time when the treaty enters into force for the state party, the applicability of the treaty to relevant acts, facts or circumstances before the entry into force of the treaty, and the validity of an expired treaty. The core issue to be resolved in relation to transitional clauses in BITs is the retroactivity of the BIT. Therefore, application of the transitional clauses,[101] given its connection with contemporality, is subject to intertemporal law.

8.2.3.1 Intertemporal Rules under Treaty Law

The issue of temporality concerns the retroactive effect of the treaty on the established juridical facts that were formed before the treaty came into effect, and the fundamental

94 See *Aguas del Tunari, S.A.* v. *Republic of Bolivia*, ICSID Case No. ARB/02/3, Decision on Jurisdiction, October 21, 2005, at para. 274.
95 See *Perenco* v. *Ecuador*, ICSID Case No. ARB/08/6, Decision on Jurisdiction, June 30, 2011, at paras. 92–95.
96 See *Methanex* v. *United States*, UNCITRAL, Award, August 3, 2005, at para. 22.
97 Pauwely and Elsig, "The Politics of Treaty Interpretation," 448.
98 Tarcisio Gazzini, *Interpretation on Investment Treaties* (Hart 2016) 256.
99 Panos Merkouris, *Article 31(3)(c) VCLT and the Principle of Systemic Integration: Normative Shadows in Plato's Cave* (Brill Nijhoff 2015) 7.
100 Gabčíkovo-Nagymaros Project (Hungary/Slovakia), Judgment of September 25, 1997, [1997] ICJ Rep. 7, Separate Opinion of Vice-President Weeramantry, at 114.
101 *Island of Palmas* case (Permanent Court of Arbitration) (1928) 2 RIAA 829, at 845.

principle is non-retroactivity of treaties in international law. In the *Island of Palmas* case, Judge Huber made an incisive statement on the principle of non-retroactivity of treaties: "A juridical fact must be appreciated in the light of the law contemporary with it, and not of the law in force at the time when a dispute in regard to it arises or falls to be settled."[102] Therefore, the treaty in principle does not apply to relevant acts, facts or circumstances of the state party before the entry into force of the treaty unless there is an explicit exception made in the treaty.[103]

Article 28 has three dimensions: (a) In the absence of an exceptional circumstance, the treaty does not retroactively apply to the past acts, facts or circumstances that occurred before the treaty entered into force for a State. In the event that legal events and acts may occur multiple times or that the circumstances may persist, whether any acts, facts or circumstances related to the state party occurred, completed or terminated when the treaty entered into force is a criterion to determine whether the principle of non-retroactivity of treaties can be applied. The ILC also believes that although acts, facts or circumstances occurred before the treaty entered into force, if they continue to exist after the treaty entered into force, they should be governed by the treaty.[104] (b) A mandatory obligation is not created for the parties to the treaty, meaning that, unless the treaty provides for retroactive effect, or the other party agrees that the treaty can be retroactively applied, the state cannot be forced to accept the principle of non-retroactivity of treaties. (c) Application of the principle of non-retroactivity of treaties should be based on the premise that the treaty is in force for a party. This suggests that this principle does not apply to a treaty that is not in force.[105] In fact, according to the ILC's comments on the final draft of the VCLT, whether the treaty is retroactive or not is essentially a question of whether the contracting parties have a common understanding at the time of signing the treaty. If the contracting parties consider it appropriate, the tribunal is free to decide whether to apply the entire or part of the treaty to past acts, facts or circumstances.[106] The retroactivity of treaties is not *ius cogens*. The parties can give the treaty retroactive effect based on the common meaning, express or implied.[107] The terms "unless the treaty expresses different meanings" and "as otherwise determined" in Article 28 of the VCLT reflect respect for the free will of the state parties to the treaty. Identification of common meaning requires treaty interpretation. According to Article 31 of the VCLT, the common meaning of the retrospective effect of the treaty can be obtained either from the text of the treaty or from the negotiation of the treaty. The search for information in the negotiations can be determined even from the object and purpose of the treaty. The specific object and purpose of the treaty is said to be the root criterion for assessing whether and how a treaty may be susceptible to change over time.[108] As rightly pointed out, different understandings of the temporality in law are attributed to different philosophical standpoints on language, either pragmatist or intentionalist.[109]

102 See *Island of Palmas* case, 2 UNRIAA 829, at para. 845.
103 For instance, the China–Israel BIT 1995 (Art. 12), which applies to both preexisting and post-BIT investments, without any limitation on submission of claims.
104 See Sadie Blanchard, "State Consent, Temporal Jurisdiction, and the Importation of Continuing Circumstances Analysis into International Investment Arbitration" (2011) 10 *Washington University Global Studies Law Review* 419, 458.
105 See Shaw, *International Law*, 834.
106 See ILC Yb 1966, II, pp. 211–212.
107 Ibid.
108 Rosalyn Higgins, "Time and the Law: International Perspectives on an Old Problem" (1997) 46 *International & Comparative Law Quarterly* 501, 519.
109 Djeffal, *Static and Evolutive Treaty Interpretation*, 357.

The terms "except for the treaty's different meanings" and "or otherwise determined" in the provisions of Article 28 of the VCLT show respect for the free will of the contracting parties. "Unless the treaty expresses different meanings" refers to two situations: (a) the treaty clearly states that it can be applied retroactively; and (b) the interpretation of the treaty indicates that it can be applied retroactively. "Or otherwise determined" refers to the inference of the intention of a party from the nature and purpose of the treaty.[110] The ILC particularly emphasized that Article 28 did not adopt the phrase "unless otherwise provided by the treaty" in order to "allow the treaty to express its intention to have some retroactive effect through its nature (not expressly)."[111] This means that the treaty should also be interpreted as having retroactive effect if the contracting parties express such an intention through the text of the treaty even without an explicit indication in the treaty.

8.2.3.2 Temporality of Jurisdictional and Substantive Rules

In international investment arbitration, jurisdictional and substantive issues are often subject to different intertemporal laws. Professor Schreuer pointed out that legal applications of jurisdictional and substantive issues are independent of each other.[112] The fact of the dispute settlement provisions being extended to events that occurred prior to the entry into force of the treaty does not imply that the substantive rules of the treaty can be retrospectively applied to such events as well.

International investment arbitral tribunals often distinguish between jurisdictional and substantive clauses in BITs and apply different rules of intertemporal law to them. In SGS v. *the Philippines*, the tribunal distinguished the intertemporal legal effects of procedural or jurisdictional provisions from those of substantive obligations.[113] In *Impregilo* v. *Pakistan* and *Salini* v. *Jordan*, the tribunals observed a distinction between the jurisdiction *ratione temporis* of an ICSID tribunal and the applicability *ratione temporis* of the substantive obligations contained in a BIT.[114] This means that the tribunal needs to apply different legal rules depending on the different claims.

The applicable rules of substantive terms in a BIT may have implications for its procedural terms.[115] A BIT may stipulate that the scope of consent to arbitration is limited to requests for arbitration for claims under the new BIT. In other words, the date of entry into force of the new BIT is also the date on which the acts are bound by consent. According to the consent clause, the entry into force of substantive rules also determines the time for the tribunal's jurisdiction to be effective, since the tribunal has jurisdiction only over claims arising from any violation under the current BIT. For example, NAFTA clarifies that the scope of consent to arbitration is limited to claims over the violation of NAFTA.[116] Therefore, the retroactivity

110 See Oliver Dorr and Kirsten Schmalenbach (eds.), *Vienna Convention on the Law of Treaties: A Commentary* (Springer Press 2012) 480–481.

111 See *Year Book of the International Law Commission*, Vol. 2, 1966, pp. 212–213.

112 Christoph Schreuer, "Jurisdiction and Applicable Law in Investment Treaty Application" (2014) 1(1) *McGill Journal of Dispute Resolution* 1.

113 See SGS v. *Pakistan*, ICSID Case No. ARB/01/13, Decision on the Tribunal on Objections to Jurisdiction, August 6, 2003, at para. 176.

114 See *Impregilo S.p.A.* v. *Islamic Republic of Pakistan*, ICSID Case No. ARB/03/3, Decision on Jurisdiction of April 22, 2005, at paras. 309. See *Salini* v. *Hashemite Kingdom of Jordan*, ICSID Case No. ARB/02/13, Decision on Jurisdiction, November 29, 2004, at para. 176.

115 See Rudolf Dolzer and Christoph Schreuer, *Principles of International Investment Law* (2nd edition, Oxford University Press 2012) 37.

116 See NAFTA, Art. 1116.

of the ISDS clause to the pre-entry-into-force acts, facts or circumstances under the transitional clauses depends on whether the BIT extends a retroactive effect to the jurisdictional clauses.

8.3 INTERPRETATION AND APPLICATION OF TRANSITIONAL CLAUSES IN *PING AN* V. *BELGIUM*

Ping An v. *Belgium* was registered by the ICSID on September 19, 2012. After nearly three years, the ICSID tribunal issued an arbitral award on April 30, 2015, dismissing the arbitration application filed by Ping An on the grounds of lack of jurisdiction. The focus of the *Ping An* v. *Belgium* case was on whether disputes that occurred before the 2009 BIT came into effect and were filed with a completed notice in accordance with the 1986 BIT but had not yet entered judicial or arbitral proceedings fall under the scope of jurisdiction of the 2009 BIT.[117] The tribunal in *Ping An* v. *Belgium* discussed the "arbitration gap" caused by the transition between the new and old BITs, the scope of the dispute and its retroactivity in the transitional clauses, and the real intention of the contracting parties to the BIT.

The case involved the dispute settlement clauses in both the 1986 BIT and the 2009 BIT as well as the transitional clauses in the 2009 BIT. Article 10 of the 1986 BIT outlines an investment dispute resolution mechanism in which the jurisdiction of domestic courts prevails over that of international arbitration. According to Article 10 of the 1986 BIT, an investor can submit the case to international tribunal only if the dispute involves the amount of compensation for expropriation, nationalization or other similar measures. The transitional clauses state that the 2009 BIT applies to investments made by investors before and after the entry into force of the 2009 BIT. However, the 2009 BIT does not apply to such investment disputes that entered judicial or arbitral proceedings prior to its entry into force. The 2009 BIT is silent on the applicability of the 2009 BIT to such investment disputes that occurred before the 2009 BIT's entry into effect and had completed the notification process in accordance with the 1986 BIT but had not yet entered arbitral or judicial proceedings.

8.3.1 *Arbitration Gap Caused by Transitional Clauses*

The tribunal in *Ping An* v. *Belgium* realized that there was a "black hole" or "arbitration gap" in the form of "silence on the disposition" of disputes that were notified under the 1986 BIT but not yet under the judicial or arbitral process,[118] if the 2009 BIT could not be applied to the case according to the transitional clauses in the 2009 BIT. As Ping An cannot file an international arbitration request based on the 2009 BIT, it may not be able to obtain any relief through other means.[119]

The awkward reality that Ping An had to face was a linguistic interpretation of the transitional clauses in Article 10 of the 2009 BIT. The 1986 BIT was replaced by the 2009 BIT. The 1986 BIT thus applies only to disputes that occurred and entered judicial or arbitral proceedings before the 2009 BIT came into effect. The dispute between Ping An and Belgium did not enter judicial or arbitral proceedings before the 2009 BIT came into effect, therefore

117 Para. 206.
118 Paras. 227, 228.
119 Para. 207.

the 1986 BIT was no longer applicable;[120] Ping An's only remedy was to arbitrate the dispute according to the 2009 BIT.

The Belgian government, however, argued for the non-applicability of the 2009 BIT since Ping An initiated the dispute settlement procedure and completed the notification procedure in accordance with the 1986 BIT, and the dispute consequently should continue to be resolved in accordance with the 1986 BIT.[121]

The tribunal failed to express any meaningful views on the grounds that the parties did not file an arbitration request for this issue.[122] Rather, the tribunal merely provided some "observations" as follows: (a) based on the 1986 BIT, the dispute may be submitted to the domestic court of the host country or to an international arbitral tribunal when the dispute concerns the amount of compensation from expropriation; (b) the sunset clause in the 1986 BIT makes the 1986 BIT still apply ten years after its expiration to investment made by the investor before the 1986 BIT expired; (c) the 1986 BIT was substituted and replaced by the 2009 BIT.[123] Apparently, these observations are not conducive to closing the arbitration gap caused by the old and new BITs.[124]

8.3.2 *Scope of Dispute and Retroactivity in Transitional Clauses*

In *Ping An* v. *Belgium*, determining the scope of "dispute" and the retroactivity of transitional clauses was key to resolving any controversy over the tribunal's jurisdiction. The tribunal first concluded that Article 8 of the 2009 BIT did not lead to the tribunal's *ratione temporis* in this case.[125] The tribunal considered that the interpretation of Article 8 of the 2009 BIT was the key to determining the meaning of the dispute in Article 10 (Transitional Clauses). Based on the textual, good faith and contextual interpretations in accordance with Articles 31 and 32 of the VCLT, the dispute in the Transitional Clauses (Article 10(2)) and the Dispute Settlement Clauses (Article 8(2)) of the 2009 BIT stemmed from "a legal dispute" provided for in Article 8(1) of the "Dispute Settlement Clauses."[126] In order to prove that "a legal dispute" stipulated in Article 8(1) of the 2009 BIT does not cover a dispute that occurred before the 2009 BIT came into effect, the tribunal quoted the cases of *Impregilo* v. *Pakistan*, *ABCI Investment Company* v. *Tunisia* and *Salini* v. *Jordan*.

In *Impregilo* v. *Pakistan*, the tribunal conducted a textual analysis to interpret the term "any dispute arising from the contracting parties" in the ISDS clause, and opined that, in the absence of the treaty's retroactive provisions, the term does not cover such disputes that arose before the entry into force of the concerned BIT.[127] The case of *ABCI Investment Company* v. *Tunisia* is similar to *Ping An* v. *Belgium*. There is a pair of BITs signed by the Netherlands and Tunisia in 1998 and 1963 respectively. Under the 1998 BIT, each contracting party consents to submit any legal dispute arising between that contracting party and a national of the other contracting party to the ICSID for settlement by conciliation or arbitration under the ICSID Convention.[128] The 1998 BIT further states: "Disputes arisen before the entry into force of the

[120] Para. 208.
[121] Para. 208.
[122] Para. 240.
[123] Para. 208.
[124] Para. 209.
[125] Para. 211.
[126] Para. 212.
[127] Para. 214.
[128] Netherlands–Tunisia BIT 1998, Art. 8.

present Agreement shall continue to be ruled by the Agreement of May 23, 1963."[129] The tribunal concluded that if the parties hope that disputes that occurred in the past will be dealt with by the newly formulated BIT, the new BIT will have a term "arisen."[130] In the case of *Salini* v. *Jordan*, the tribunal stated that the term "may arise" in the BIT does not lead to the conclusion that the provisions of the BITs can be applied retroactively to a "dispute" that occurred before the BIT entered into force.[131]

Table 8.2 compares the four ICSID cases, analyzed by the tribunal in *Ping An* v. *Belgium*, relating to the interpretation of the terms of the "Dispute Settlement Clauses." These ICSID cases show that if one of the three terms "arising," "may arise" or "arises" appears in the BIT, only disputes that occurred after entry into force of the BIT would be covered. By contrast, the BIT may be retroactively applied to a dispute that occurred prior to the entry into force of the BIT when the term "arisen" appears in the BIT.[132]

In *Ping An* v. *Belgium*, the first sentence of Article 8 of the 2009 BIT adopts the term "arises." In the tribunal's opinion, in accordance with the semantic interpretation, the phrase "arises" rather than "arisen" indicates that the ISDS clauses are applied only to disputes arising after the entry into force of the BIT and have no retroactive effect.[133]

The tribunal in *Ping An* v. *Belgium* also pointed out that the conclusion can be drawn by relying on the textual approach in treaty interpretation without the need to investigate the retroactivity effect of the BIT. This suggests that the tribunal had no intention to review the (non-)retroactivity of the BIT. The tribunal held that the application of the ISDS clauses in the new BIT to the effectiveness of the illegality under the substantive provisions in the old BIT did not constitute a retroactive application of the law.[134]

8.3.3 *"True Intention" in Transitional Clauses*

The transitional clauses in the 2009 BIT do not provide for any guidance to dealing with a dispute that occurred before the BIT took effect but had not entered any proceedings. It is critically important to investigate the purpose of the transitional clauses.

As shown in Table 8.3, the tribunal pointed out four possibilities of interpreting the true intention of the contracting parties: (a) Although the 1986 BIT was replaced by the 2009 BIT, the contracting parties believe that such disputes should fall within the jurisdiction of the 1986 BIT; (b) The contracting parties consider that the terminology of Article 8 "Dispute Settlement Clause" and Article 10 "Transitional Clause" of the 2009 BIT is sufficient to include such disputes in the jurisdictional scope of the 2009 BIT; (c) The contracting parties forgot at the time of contracting the BIT to deal with such disputes; (d) The contracting parties deliberately choose not to deal with such disputes.[135]

The tribunal first ruled out the possibility of (c). The tribunal held that it is impossible for the contracting parties to forget to deal with such disputes. The contracting parties have already stipulated in the transitional clauses that the 2009 BIT does not apply to investment

129 Netherlands–Tunisia BIT 1998, Art. 12(5).

130 Para. 215.

131 Para. 216. *Tradex Hellas S.A.* v. *Republic of Albania*, ICSID Case No. ARB/94/2, Decision on Jurisdiction, December 24, 1996, at paras. 189–190.

132 *Quiborax S.A., Non Metallic Minerals S.A. and Allan Fosk Kaplun* v. *Plurinational State of Bolivia*, ICSID Case No. ARB/06/2, Decision on Jurisdiction (September 27, 2012), para. 266.

133 *Salini* v. *Hashemite Kingdom of Jordan*, ICSID Case No. ARB/02/13, Award of January 31, 2006, at para. 170.

134 Para. 218.

135 Para. 220.

TABLE 8.2 *The scope of "dispute" in some ICSID cases**

	Impregilo v. *Pakistan*	*ABCI Investments* v. *Tunisia*	*Salini* v. *Jordan*	*Ping An* v. *Belgium*
Dispute Settlement Clause	"Any disputes arising between a Contracting Party and the investors of the other, including disputes relating to compensation for expropriation, nationalization, requisition or similar measures, and disputes relating to the amount of the relevant payments, shall be settled amicably, as far as possible."[136]	"Each Contracting Party consents to submit any legal dispute arising between that Contracting Party and a national of the other Contracting Party concerning an investment of that national in the territory of the former Contracting Party to the ICSID for settlement by conciliation or arbitration under the ICSID Convention opened for signature at Washington on 18 March 1965."[137]	"Disputes concerning investments between a Contracting Party and an investor of the other Contracting Party should as far as possible be settled amicably between the parties in dispute."[138]	"[W]hen a legal dispute arises between an investor of one Contracting Party and the other Contracting Party, either party to the dispute shall notify the other party to the dispute in writing."[139]
Award	"Such language – and the absence of specific provision for retroactivity – implies that disputes that may have arisen before the entry into force of the BIT are not covered (i.e., disputes arising before 22 June 2001)."[140]	The wording "arising" refers only to disputes that occurred after the entry into force of the BIT. If the contracting parties intended to cover disputes that occurred before the entry into force of the BIT, the BIT should have used the wording "arisen."	The wording "may arise" in the BIT means that the BIT does not have jurisdiction over disputes that occurred before the entry into force of the BIT.	The wording "arises" suggests that the disputes covered are only those that occur in the future. The wording "when" suggests only timing. The term "dispute" in the dispute settlement clause does not cover disputes that occurred before the entry into force of the BIT.

*Prepared by the author.

[136] Italy–Pakistan BIT 1997, Art. 9(1).
[137] Netherlands–Tunisia BIT 1998, Art. 8.
[138] Germany–Jordan BIT 2009, Art. 11(1).
[139] China–BLEU BIT 2009, Art. 8(1).
[140] Award, para. 300.

TABLE 8.3 *Four possibilities for contracting parties' intention**

Possibility	Opinion in the award	Reasoning
The dispute arose before the 2009 BIT came into force, but the dispute did not enter arbitral or judicial proceedings. Such dispute shall fall in the jurisdiction of the 1986 BIT.	The 1986 BIT has jurisdiction over it.	(1) The new BIT applies only to such disputes that occurred before its entry into force if there is a term "arisen" in the BIT. (2) The language concerning mutual encouragement, promotion and protection of investment in the preamble of the BIT does not suggest an expansive interpretation of the treaty term. (3) The fact that the BIT applies to investments that occurred before its entry into force does not suggest that it also applies to disputes that occurred before its entry into force. (4) The fact that the BIT does not apply to such disputes that entered arbitral or judicial proceedings does not suggest that it does not apply to disputes that occurred before its entry into force. (5) The existence of two successive BITs does not suggest that the new BIT applies to disputes that occurred before the entry into force of the new BIT. (6) Applying the new BIT to disputes that occurred before its entry into force is to expand the scope of the old BIT.
Article 8 (Dispute Settlement Clause) and Article 10 (Transitional Clause) in the 2009 BIT are wide enough to cover the dispute.	The 1986 BIT may have jurisdiction over it.	Same as above.
The contracting parties forgot to deal with the dispute.	The contracting parties are unlikely to forget to deal with it.	Retroactivity of the treaty is a common issue with successive treaties. It is unlikely that the contracting parties forgot to deal with it. Besides, Belgium's other BITs dealt with it when Belgium signed the new BIT with China.
The contracting parties intended not to deal with the issue.	If this is a possibility, the 2009 BIT does not apply to disputes that arose before the entry into force of the new BIT.	It is illogical to apply a more favorable dispute settlement clause to a dispute that is supposed to be governed by the old BIT simply because a new BIT comes into force.

*Prepared by the author.

disputes that completed the notification procedure and entered judicial or arbitral proceedings in accordance with the 1986 BIT before the entry into force of the 2009 BIT. Given that the question of whether the treaty is retroactive is very common in the application of successive treaties, the contracting parties would be unlikely not to consider this issue during negotiations.[141] In addition, the BLEU–Egypt BIT 2002 explicitly excludes the application of the BIT to investment disputes that occurred prior to the entry into force of the BIT but had not yet entered judicial or arbitral proceedings. When Belgium negotiated a BIT with China, it would have considered the content of the BIT that it had reached with Egypt.[142]

Thereafter, the tribunal considered that (a) is closer to the true meaning of the contracting parties than (b). This conclusion is based on several factors. First, from a textual perspective, the contracting parties expressed their intention in Articles 8(1)(2) and 10(2) of the 2009 BIT that the BIT has jurisdiction only over disputes that arise after the BIT's entry into force. Only in the case where the past tense of "[w]hen a legal dispute arises or has arisen . . . either party to the dispute shall notify, or shall have notified, the other party to the dispute" is adopted in the 2009 BIT may it apply to disputes arising before the BIT's entry into force. Second, the preamble in the 2009 BIT on the mutual encouragement, promotion and protection of investment by the contracting parties cannot lead to the conclusion that the BIT should adopt an expansive interpretive approach when a dispute was raised before the BIT came into effect in 2009. Third, although Article 10(2) of the 2009 BIT states that "the 2009 BIT applies to the investment that is made before and after the entry into force of the BIT," it does not suggest that the 2009 BIT applies to disputes that arose before the BIT took effect. Fourth, in the case that the transitional clauses are silent, the phrase that "the 2009 BIT does not apply to investment disputes that have entered judicial or arbitral proceedings" cannot support that "the 2009 BIT applies to the dispute that has completed the notification proceeding but has not entered the judicial or arbitral proceedings." Fifth, the fact that the 1986 BIT was replaced by the 2009 BIT does not mean that the 2009 BIT has jurisdiction over disputes arising before its entry into force. Sixth, the scope of "dispute" stipulated in the 1986 BIT is very narrow, and the parties allow only disputes over the amount of compensation for expropriation to be submitted to international arbitration. If the broadly defined "dispute" in the 2009 BIT can be extended to disputes that completed the notification proceeding according to the 1986 BIT, the scope of dispute under the 1986 BIT is then expanded.[143]

Finally, in the case of (d), the tribunal drew the conclusion that the 2009 BIT does not apply to disputes that occurred before the BIT took effect. In accordance with the expansive interpretive approach advocated by Ping An, the investors can submit disputes under the 1986 BIT not only to the domestic courts of the host state but also to international arbitration. The tribunal viewed it illogical if a more favorable treatment can be obtained by the investors simply because of the 2009 BIT.[144]

8.4 DEFECTS IN INTERPRETING TRANSITIONAL CLAUSES IN *PING AN* V. *BELGIUM*

The transitional clauses involved in *Ping An* v. *Belgium* and the arbitration gap they left behind may be subject to three applicable principles: the textual interpretation, the

[141] Para. 221.
[142] Para. 222.
[143] Paras. 224–239.
[144] Para. 230.

application of customary international law of "non-retroactivity of treaties" and the "common meaning" of the contracting parties. However, none of them well suits the instant case.

8.4.1 *Two Possible Textual Interpretations of Transitional Clauses*

The real meaning of the specific provisions in the treaty is the premise and basis for the correct application of the treaty. To perform the treaty in good faith, the first step is to seek the real meaning of the treaty terms. The tribunal of *Ping An* v. *Belgium* made it clear from the outset that interpretation of the BIT terms requires compliance with the principles of treaty interpretation as defined in the VCLT and consistency with investment arbitration practice.[145] The tribunal emphasized that textual interpretation is the priority approach among various treaty interpretive methods. The treaty interpretation should start with the original meaning of the term, interpreted by the tribunal in good faith, in a straightforward manner and consistent with the context.[146]

In *Ping An* v. *Belgium*, the tribunal did not deviate from the text of the transitional clauses while interpreting and applying the transitional clauses in the 2009 BIT. The tribunal held that the "disputes" stipulated in the transitional clauses in the 2009 BIT are the same as the "disputes" stipulated in paragraphs 1 and 2 of the dispute settlement clauses. Therefore, from a contextual interpretation perspective, the interpretation of "disputes" in the transitional clauses should be limited to the scope of "disputes" stipulated in the dispute settlement clause. Since the dispute settlement clause covers only disputes arising after the 2009 BIT came into effect, and the term "arises" is grammatically pointed to future disputes, the transitional clauses in the 2009 BIT should not be applied to disputes that occurred before the entry into effect of the 2009 BIT, and that had completed the notification process but had not entered arbitral or judicial proceedings according to the 1986 BIT.

The tribunal's interpretation of the transitional clauses is strictly made in accordance with the context of the 2009 BIT and is not divorced from the treaty text. However, a close reading of the tribunal's award reveals a lack of discussion of the transitional clauses in an integrated framework. As a matter of fact, a holistic examination of the three treaty terms in paragraph 2 of the transitional clauses may reveal another possible interpretation of the transitional clauses, which does not necessarily deviate from the scope covered by the treaty.[147] The first sentence of paragraph 2 of the transitional clauses says: "This BIT shall apply to all investments by investors of either Contracting Party in the territory of the other Contracting Party, whether or not [they were] made before or after the entry into force of this BIT." This indicates that the 2009 BIT will be extended to investments made by the investors of either contracting party prior to the effective date of the BIT. The sentence also indicates the contracting parties' willingness to grant the 2009 BIT certain retroactive effect on the legal facts that occurred prior to the BIT's entry into force. The second sentence of paragraph 2 states: "However, this BIT shall not apply to any dispute or claim relating to investment that has entered the judicial or arbitral proceedings prior to the entry into force of this BIT." This excludes the possibility of applying the 2009 BIT to investment disputes that have entered judicial or arbitral proceedings. According to the third sentence of paragraph 2, investment disputes that have entered judicial or arbitral proceedings prior to the entry into force of the

145 Paras. 164–166.
146 Ibid.
147 See Humphrey Waldock, Sixth Report on the Law of Treaties, *Yearbook of International Law Commission* (1966) Vol. I (Part Two), p. 199.

2009 BIT "should continue to be resolved in accordance with the provisions of the BIT of June 4, 1984 referred to in paragraph 1 of this Article."

Overall, paragraph 2 of the transitional clauses has a logical inference from general to exceptional. The first sentence of paragraph 2 is the general rule: the investments made by investors of either contracting party prior to the entry into force of the 2009 BIT fall in the jurisdiction of the 2009 BIT. Since the 2009 BIT is retroactively applied to investments made prior to its entry into force, naturally, the disputes arising from these investments should also be within the jurisdiction of the 2009 BIT. Investment and investment disputes are the two sides of the same coin. Investment disputes rely on investments, and no investment disputes can occur without investments. The second and third sentences of paragraph 2 constitute an exception to the first sentence: the 1986 BIT should continue to apply to investment disputes that have entered judicial or arbitral proceedings prior to the entry into force of the 2009 BIT. This means that a dispute that occurred before the 2009 BIT's entry into force but has not yet entered judicial or arbitral proceedings will fall within the scope of the first sentence, and accordingly will be subject to the 2009 BIT.

This line of interpretation is also consistent with the principles of good faith, common meaning, and contextual and purposive interpretations established by Article 31 of the VCLT. In compiling the VCLT, the ILC confirmed that the interpretation of the treaty terms should be fully considered to be effective in order to conform to the natural and usual meaning of the terms, in accordance with the other terms of the treaty as well as the object and purpose of the treaty.[148] The principle of effective interpretation is contained in the general principles of treaty interpretation established by Article 31 of the VCLT.[149] In *Noble Ventures* v. *Romania*, the tribunal explicitly indicated that reference should be made to the principle of effectiveness, which plays an important role in interpreting treaties.[150] This line of interpretation places paragraph 2 of the transitional clauses in the same logic system. Compared to the tribunal's interpretation, this alternative interpretation appears more logical and consistent, leaving no arbitration gap. The tribunal could have come up with this conclusion by relying on this interpretive method.

8.4.2 *Comparison of Two Textual Interpretations*

The main difference between the alternative interpretation and the interpretation adopted by the tribunal is the different understanding of the terms "investment" and "investment disputes" and their interrelationship. In the tribunal's view, "investment" is different from "investment dispute" and there is no correlation between the two in interpreting transitional clauses. By contrast, the alternative interpretation may connect "investment" and "investment disputes" in interpreting the transitional clauses. The second sentence uses the wording "any dispute or any claim concerning an investment" while the first sentence says: "The present Agreement shall apply to all investments made by investors of either Contracting Party in the territory of the other Contracting Party." The phrase "all investments" in the first sentence semantically covers the term "an investment" in the second sentence. Thus, the term "any dispute" in the second sentence is literally associated with the phrase "all investments" in the first sentence. In addition, the cases of *Impregilo* v. *Pakistan* and *Salini* v. *Jordan* referred to by the tribunal did not touch on transactional clauses, which are not included in

148 Isabelle Van Damme, *Treaty Interpretation by the WTO Appellate Body* (Oxford University Press 2009) 48.

149 Ibid., p. 50.

150 See *Noble Ventures* v. *Romania*, ICSID Case No. ARB/01/11, Award, October 12, 2005, at para. 50.

the concerned BITs. The transitional clauses interpreted in *ABCI Investment Company* v. *Tunisia* are clear enough to address how to deal with disputes that occurred prior to the entry into force of the new BIT. Apparently, these cited cases are not necessarily relevant to *Ping An* v. *Belgium*.[151]

Table 8.4 compares the interpretation adopted by the tribunal (the first interpretation) with the alternative interpretation described here from three aspects: interpretive logic, interpretive method, and interpretive conclusion. In terms of interpretive logic, the tribunal's interpretation separates the components in the transitional clauses and puts the "dispute" stipulated in the "Transitional Clause" into the "Dispute Settlement Clause"; the alternative interpretation opposes this separatist approach and applies a more integrated approach. The alternative interpretation considers that the three treaty terms in paragraph 2 of the "Transitional Clause" have a logic from the general to the exceptional. In terms of the interpretive method, the tribunal's interpretation first equates "the dispute" in paragraph 2 of the "Transitional Clause" with "a legal dispute" stipulated in paragraph 1 of the "Dispute Settlement Clause." Then, according to case law, the term "arises" stipulated in the "Dispute Settlement Clause" refers only to disputes arising after the entry into force of the BIT and is not retroactive. The second interpretation is that the first sentence of paragraph 2 constitutes a general rule: investment made by any investor in the contracting party before the 2009 BIT came into effect is within the jurisdiction of the BIT, and paragraphs 2 and 3 in the second sentence are exceptional rules to the first sentence. The 1986 BIT shall still apply to an investment dispute that entered judicial or arbitral proceedings before the 2009 BIT took effect. According to the tribunal's interpretation, the "Transitional Clause" cannot be applied to text that was not specified in the treaty. Therefore, the 2009 BIT shall not apply to disputes that completed the notification procedure in accordance with the 1986 BIT but have not yet entered judicial or arbitral proceedings. According to the alternative interpretation, a dispute that occurred before the 2009 BIT's entry into effect but has not yet entered judicial or arbitral proceedings will fall within the general provisions of the first sentence of paragraph 2 of the Transitional Clause. As a result, the 2009 BIT applies to such disputes.

8.4.3 *The Principle of "Non-retroactivity of Treaties" and Transitional Clauses*

Whether the transitional clauses grant any retrospective effect to the 2009 BIT was another contentious issue between the two parties in *Ping An* v. *Belgium*. However, the tribunal did not express much opinion on this. The tribunal stated that the conclusion can be drawn in accordance with the pure textual interpretative approach, and then there is no need to touch on the issue of the non-retroactivity of treaties. Despite this, the tribunal gave its biased opinion: applying the new dispute settlement mechanism to the fact that was adjudicated to be illegal under the old substantive rules does not constitute a retroactive application of the law.

8.4.3.1 Non-retroactivity of Procedural Rules in the Treaty

As far as investment arbitration practice is concerned, the tribunals have repeatedly confirmed the basic principle that substantive rules in BITs cannot be retrospectively applied. In

[151] See *Impregilo S.p.A.* v. *Islamic Republic of Pakistan*, ICSID Case No. ARB/03/3, Decision on Jurisdiction of April 22, 2005, at paras. 162–163, 169–170; *Salini* v. *Hashemite Kingdom of Jordan*, ICSID Case No. ARB/02/13, Award of January 31, 2006, at para. 170; and *ABCI Investments N.V.* v. *Republic of Tunisia*, ICSID Case No. ARB/04/12, Award of February 18, 2011, at paras. 189–190.

TABLE 8.4 *Comparison between the tribunal's interpretation and an alternative interpretation of the transitional clauses in the China–BLEU BIT*

Key perspective	Tribunal's interpretation	Alternative interpretation
Logic	To separate the first sentence in paragraph 2 and the second and third sentences in paragraph 2 of the transitional clauses; to interpret the term "dispute" in the context of the dispute settlement clause.	Not to separate the first sentence in paragraph 2 and the second and third sentences in paragraph 2 of the transitional clauses; the treaty terms in paragraph 2 of the transitional clauses are interpreted in a form general to exceptional logic.
Steps	• Both the term "dispute" in the second sentence in the second paragraph of the transitional clauses and the term "dispute" in the first paragraph in the dispute settlement clause stem from "a legal dispute" in the first paragraph in the dispute settlement clause. • The first sentence in the first paragraph of the dispute settlement clause only uses the term "arises." According to case law, the term "arises," instead of "arisen," indicates that the dispute covered by the dispute settlement clause in the BIT refers only to disputes that happened after the BIT came into force, and the dispute settlement clause is not retroactive.	• The first sentence in the second paragraph of the transitional clauses is a general rule: any investments made by the investor before the entry into force of the 2009 BIT fall in the jurisdiction of the 2009 BIT. • The term "investment" in the first sentence in the second paragraph includes investment dispute. "Any dispute or any claim concerning **an investment**" in the second sentence in the second paragraph and "**all investments**" in the first sentence in the second paragraph are interconnected. Without investment, there is no investment dispute. In this sense, these two terms are the two sides of the same coin. • The third sentence in the second paragraph is an exceptional rule. Any dispute that has entered arbitral or judicial proceedings shall be governed by the 1986 BIT.
Conclusion	Transitional clauses are not applicable to such disputes as are not mentioned in the treaty text, that arose before the entry into force of the 2009 BIT, that have completed the notification process but have not entered arbitral or judicial proceedings.	Any dispute that arose before the entry into force of the 2009 BIT but has not entered arbitral or judicial proceedings falls in the jurisdiction outlined in the first sentence of paragraph 2 of the transitional clauses in the 2009 BIT.

*Prepared by the author.

the case of *Impregilo* v. *Pakistan*, the tribunal stated that the legality of the alleged violations committed against Impregilo by Pakistan should be assessed according to the law effective at the time of these acts.[152] In the cases of *SGS* v. *the Philippines* and *Salini* v. *Jordan*, the tribunals stated that although the BIT applies to investments that occurred prior to its entry

[152] See *Impregilo S.p.A.* v. *Islamic Republic of Pakistan*, ICSID Case No. ARB/03/3, Decision on Jurisdiction of April 22, 2005, at para. 311.

into force, this provision does not confer any retrospective effect on the substantive terms in the BITs.[153] According to international investment arbitration jurisprudence, unless there is an exception stipulated in the treaty, the substantive clauses in the BIT cannot be retroactively applied simply because the BIT stipulates that it applies to investments before its entry into force or the dispute arises after the BIT came into effect.[154]

The basic facts involved in *Ping An* v. *Belgium* are different from these cited cases. First, the *Ping An* v. *Belgium* case does not involve any substantive rules that need to be retroactively applied. On the contrary, Ping An's claim was made on the basis of the 1986 BIT's substantive rules while the arbitration proceeding was initiated on the basis of the 2009 BIT's procedural rules. Second, these cited cases did not involve any transitional clauses in the concerned BITs. Instead, these BITs contain only the wording that "the BIT applies to the investment that occurs before the BIT takes into effect" in the "Definition of Terms" clauses. The contracting parties of these BITs did not enter two successive BITs, thus there is no arbitration gap or vacuum that needs to be resolved by the tribunals. The uniqueness of the *Ping An* v. *Belgium* case, compared to these cited cases, is the retroactivity of procedural rules in the 2009 BIT to the dispute that occurred prior to its entry into force.

The retroactivity of procedural and substantive rules is not the same legal issue. In *Salini* v. *Jordan*, the tribunal stated that "... one must distinguish carefully between jurisdiction *ratione temporis* of an ICSID Tribunal and applicability *ratione temporis* of the substantive obligations contained in a BIT."[155] Jurisprudentially, the substantive rules of the BIT relate to the legality of legal facts governed by the BIT. Any change to the substantive terms has an impact on the reliance interests of the parties. The principle of reliance interest is also termed a principle of reasonable expectation, embodying *pacta sunt servanda*, the rule of customary international law.[156] According to the principle of reliance interest, the parties trust the treaty-maker's treaty-making behavior, and rely on the protection offered by the treaty. In particular, when the treaty-makers change and discard the original agreement, they must take into account the rights that the parties have acquired or the protection of their upcoming rights.[157] Unlike the substantive rules in the treaty, the procedural rules provide only a set of dispute resolution rules and do not involve the evaluation of the legality of relevant legal facts. Therefore, compared with substantive rules, procedural clauses are less detrimental to the reliance interest of the parties, and any change to the procedural rules brings less damage to the parties.

The impact analysis of any treaty change on reliance interest corresponds with the vested rights theory in intertemporal law. According to Savigny, respect for vested rights and the principle of non-retroactivity in law are the two sides of the same coin – when a law damages vested rights, it is retroactive, and in order to make it non-retroactive, it must not damage the vested rights.

Although the phrase at the beginning of Article 28 of the VCLT indicates an interconnection between the retroactivity of the treaty and the contracting parties' agreement, a textual interpretation of transitional clauses alone may not unveil the retroactivity of the 2009 BIT.

153 See *SGS* v. *Republic of the Philippines*, ICSID Case No. ARB/02/6, Award of January 29, 2004, at para. 166. *See Salini* v. *Hashemite Kingdom of Jordan*, ICSID Case No. ARB/02/13, Award of January 31, 2006, at para. 177.

154 *MCI Power* v. *Ecuador*, ICSID Case No. ARB/03/6, Award of July 31, 2007, at para. 62; *Pey Casado* v. *Chile*, ICSID Case No. ARB/98/2, Award of September 25, 2001, at paras. 579–582.

155 See *Salini* v. *Hashemite Kingdom of Jordan*, ICSID Case No. ARB/02/13, Award of January 31, 2006, at para. 176.

156 See Shaw, *International Law*, 832–837.

157 See Paul P. Craig, "The Stability, Coordination and Governance Treaty: Principle, Politics and Pragmatism" (2012) 37 *European Law Review* 231–251.

The contracting states did not expressly or implicitly stipulate this issue in other terms of the 2009 BIT. In the case of a "silent" treaty on retroactivity, international law scholars have varying views on whether the procedural rules of the treaty can be retrospectively applied or not. In addition to the "common agreement" exception to the retroactivity of law, another exception is related to the scenario that the later treaty can be retrospectively applied to disputes arising from the substantive rules of the earlier treaty if the two successive treaties contain similar substantive rules.[158] The tribunal in the case of *Tradex* v. *Albania* disagreed with the presumption in international arbitration that the dispute settlement clause in the treaty can only be applied to disputes that occurred after the treaty came into effect.[159] Instead, the tribunal was convinced that submissions both regarding disputes that have already arisen and regarding future disputes to arbitration can be found in arbitration practice. The tribunal in *Ping An* v. *Belgium* also tended to believe that simply applying the procedural rules of the 2009 BIT to the legal facts already evaluated by the early BIT does not constitute a retroactivity of the treaty.

The ICJ, however, expressed different opinions. In *Ambatielos* v. *the UK*, the ICJ held that the retroactive effect of the procedural rules in the treaty, without exceptions otherwise clearly stipulated, would run counter to the principle that "the treaty comes into force after ratification by the contracting parties." This principle suggests that the legal effect of all the provisions of the treaty, including substantive and procedural provisions, is determined by the contracting parties and will be effective only after the parties have ratified the treaty. This rule of non-retroactivity of treaties can only be rebutted by a special clause or a special object necessitating retroactive interpretation of the treaty.[160] The ICJ also emphasized that, at least as far as English law is concerned, the procedural provisions of the treaty are less inclined to be retroactively applied.[161]

8.4.3.2 "Continuous Circumstances" Exception to the Principle of "Non-retroactivity of Treaties"

In international law, there is still a "continuous circumstance" exception to the "non-retroactivity of treaties" principle. If the acts or facts occurred before the effective date of the treaty but persist after the effective date of the treaty, and have a sufficiently sustainable existence, the later treaty can be applied retroactively to these persistent acts or facts.[162] The non-retroactivity of treaties principle in Article 28 of the VCLT is premised on the criterion that the acts or facts that occurred before the date of entry into force of the treaty have ceased to exist in determining whether the treaty is retroactively applied or not. Therefore, if acts, facts or circumstances occurred before the effective date of a treaty but continue to exist after the date of entry into force of the treaty, the application of the treaty to those acts, facts or circumstances is not considered to be a violation of Article 28. Rather, it should fall within the temporal scope of application of the treaty.[163]

158 Shabtai Rosenne and Yaël Ronen, *The Law and Practice of the International Court, 1920–2005* (Martinus Nijhoff 2005) 918.

159 See *Tradex Hellas S.A.* v. *Republic of Albania*, ICSID Case No. ARB/94/2, Decision on Jurisdiction, December 24, 1996, at p. 194.

160 See Ambatielos, *Greece* v. *United Kingdom*, Judgment, Preliminary Objection, [1952] ICJ Rep 28, p. 40, www.icj-cij.org/docket/files/15/1965.pdf (accessed March 22, 2021).

161 Ibid., at p. 41.

162 See Antoine Buyse, "A Lifeline in Time – Non-retroactivity and Continuing Violations under the ECHR" (2006) 75 *Nordic Journal of International Law* 63–88.

163 Blanchard, "State Consent, Temporal Jurisdiction," 419, 458.

As far as the "continuous circumstances" exception is concerned, the tribunal referred to the *Mavromatis* case. Ping An argued that the ICJ in the *Mavromatis* case applied the treaty provisions to the facts that occurred before the treaty came into effect, indicating that the term "arises" itself does not mean that the "disputes" governed by the treaty refer only to those that occurred after the treaty came into effect. The *Mavromatis* case also shows that the procedural provisions of the treaty have a retroactive effect.[164] The tribunal quoted Mr. Humphrey Waldock's report to the Drafting Committee of the VCLT, arguing that the legal application of the *Mavromatis* case did not imply a retroactive effect of the procedural provisions of the treaty. The *Mavromatis* case involved a continuing dispute that arose before the entry into force of the treaty and persisted after the entry into force of the treaty. Therefore, the dispute in the *Mavromatis* case was not a strictly pre-feudal dispute. Nor did the *Mavromatis* case establish the rule that the procedural provisions of the treaty have a retroactive effect. Humphrey Waldock's views were accepted by the ILC. In commenting on Article 28 of the VCLT, the ILC stated that the term "disputes" in a treaty should be understood to refer to disputes that arise after the treaty's entry into force without any textual limitation or supplementary interpretation.[165]

The facts involved in the *Mavromatis* case may be different from or even irrelevant to *Ping An* v. *Belgium*. In *Mavromatis*, the illegal facts alleged by the plaintiff were continuous and what the defendant committed were continuous breaches. In *Ping An* v. *Belgium*, however, the Belgian government's expropriation as claimed by Ping An was completed and did not persist after 2009.

8.4.4 *"True Intention" in Transitional Clauses*

According to the principle of "non-retroactivity of treaties" in Article 28 of the VCTL, whether the state party has express or implied law-making intention to make the treaty retroactive is an important basis in determining the retroactivity of the BIT. *Ping An* v. *Belgium* involved two BITs with successive relationships, and the 2009 BIT succeeded and replaced the 1986 BIT. Since the parties to the dispute had no objection to the timing of the investment dispute (which could have taken place before the 2009 BIT came into effect), the focus of the controversy in this case was the contractual intention of the parties to the BIT in 2009.

The tribunal categorized the disputes before the entry into force of the 2009 BIT into three types: (i) disputes that occurred before the 2009 BIT came into effect but had not completed the notification procedure and entered judicial and arbitral proceedings according to the 1986 BIT; (ii) disputes that occurred prior to the entry into effect of the 2009 BIT and completed the notification procedure but did not enter judicial and arbitral proceedings in accordance with the 1986 BIT; and (iii) disputes that are explicitly excluded from the scope of the 2009 BIT according to the transitional clauses. For the first two types of dispute, in each case the tribunal held that the parties hoped to resolve it according to the 1986 BIT. This is because the wording "arises," instead of "have arisen," appears in the 2009 BIT "Dispute Settlement Clause," indicating the parties' intention not to apply the 2009 BIT to such disputes as occurred prior to its entry into force.

164 Para. 181.
165 See Yb ILC, 1966, II, p. 212.

The first and second types of dispute categorized by the tribunal do not share substantial differences in this case. Although Ping An completed the notification procedure in accordance with the 1986 BIT on October 14, 2009, Ping An notified the Belgian government of its violation of the substantive rules under the 1986 BIT. This does not suggest that Ping An intended to apply the 1986 BIT's "Dispute Settlement Clause." Ping An subsequently completed the notification procedure in accordance with the 2009 BIT. Ping An's letter of October 14, 2009 constituted a notification under the 2009 BIT's "Dispute Settlement Clause." Ping An completed the notification procedure twice in accordance with the 1986 BIT and the 2009 BIT with the hope that the tribunal would be able to handle its dispute with Belgium in accordance with the substantive rules in the 1986 BIT under the jurisdiction according to the 2009 BIT.

8.4.4.1 Searching for "True Intention"

In investment arbitration, tribunals repeatedly encounter the scenario where two successive treaties are reviewed to explore the "common agreement" between the contracting parties on the transitional clauses. In the case of *Jan de Nul* v. *Egypt*, there were two BITs between the Belgian–Luxembourg Economic Union and Egypt in 1977 and 2002 respectively. The 2002 BIT not only replaced the 1977 BIT but also states that the 2002 BIT will apply to investments made by the investors from one of the contracting parties prior to its entry into force.[166] The 2002 BIT further stipulates that it will not apply to disputes that occurred prior to its entry into force. In the jurisdictional award, the tribunal held that, according to the "common agreement" of the parties in the 2002 BIT, the substantive rules in the 2002 BIT would apply to acts that take place after the 2002 BIT came into effect, and the 1977 BIT applies only to acts that occurred before the 2002 BIT took effect. Meanwhile, the tribunal realized that the distinction may be minimal as the 2002 BIT and the 1977 BIT were almost identical in terms of substantive rules. In terms of procedural rules, only the 2002 BIT is valid and applicable.[167] The case of *Jan de Nul* v. *Egypt* confirms that a request for arbitration based on the substantive terms of the previous BIT can be filed on the basis of the procedural terms of the later BIT, provided that the dispute arises after the later BIT takes effect.

In the case of *Walter Bau* v. *Thailand*, there were two BITs of 1961 and 2002 between Thailand and Germany. The 1961 BIT did not give investors the right to appeal disputes to international arbitration, but the 2002 BIT did.[168] In this case, the tribunal held that the 2002 BIT could not be retroactively applied to disputes that occurred prior to its entry into force. This is because the contracting parties wanted to give the investors more substantial protection in the 2002 BIT including the investors' right to bring disputes to international arbitration. Therefore, the procedural rules in the 2002 BIT cannot be considered as procedural rights only as these procedural rules also give the investors substantial safeguards.

In addition, both the *Nordzucker AG* v. *Poland* case[169] and the *ABCI Investment Company* v. *Tunisia* case[170] involved the tribunals' interpretation of two BITs. However, neither of these

166 See *Jan de Nul N.V. and Dredging International N.V.* v. *Arab Republic of Egypt*, ICSID Case No. ARB/04/13, at paras. 131–141.

167 Ibid.

168 See *Walter Bau AG (in Liquidation)* v. *Thailand* (UNCITRAL), Award, July 1, 2009 (Barker, Lalonde, Bunnag), at para. 9.5.

169 See *Nordzucker AG* v. *Poland* (UNCITRAL), Partial Award, December 10, 2008 (Vera Van Houtte, Bucher, Tomaszewskia).

170 See *ABCI Investments N.V.* v. *Republic of Tunisia*, ICSID Case No. ARB/04/12, Award of February 18, 2011, at paras. 169–170.

two tribunals concluded in the jurisdictional awards that the contracting parties had a "common agreement" to give retroactive effect to the procedural rules in the BITs.

Summarizing the arbitration practice, at least two lines of thought can be drawn in exploring the "common agreement" between the contracting parties. First, the BIT text is the most authoritative expression of the true agreement of the contracting parties. If the BIT text expressly excludes disputes that occurred before the BIT came into effect (i.e., *Jan de Nul* v. *Egypt*), or contains no implied term "the disputes have arisen" before the BIT came into effect (e.g., *ABCI Investment Company* v. *Tunisia*), then there is no "common agreement" between the contracting parties to apply the procedural rules in the BIT to their pre-entry disputes. Second, if the dispute settlement clauses in the two BITs are too different (e.g., *Walter Bau* v. *Thailand*), then the "Dispute Settlement Clause" may be considered to hold substantive terms that would be retrospectively applied under international law even though there is no "common agreement" between the contracting parties.

The 2009 BIT in the case of *Ping An* v. *Belgium* did not expressly exclude the provisions from being applied to pre-entry disputes. On the other hand, there is no such expression as "have arisen," implying a retroactive effect on pre-entry-into-force disputes. Meanwhile, there is a huge difference between the "Dispute Settlement Clause" in the 1986 BIT and that in the 2009 BIT. According to the 2009 BIT, investors can bring all investment-related disputes to international arbitration. However, according to the 1986 BIT, investors can submit to international arbitration only disputes related to the amount of compensation for expropriation. There appears no "common agreement" between China and Belgium to apply the procedural rules in the 2009 BIT to pre-entry-into-force disputes.

The case of *Ping An* v. *Belgium* is not the same as the other cases mentioned here. First, the BIT covered by the *Ping An* v. *Belgium* case provides transitional clauses that indicate the contracting parties' intention to deal with the transitional issues arising from the new and old BITs. Second, the transitional clauses partially, though not fully, address the transitional issues. The 2009 BIT does not apply to disputes that occurred before its entry into force and that entered judicial or arbitral proceedings. However, the transitional clauses are silent on their application to two types of dispute, that is, (a) disputes that occurred before the BIT came into effect but had not completed the notification procedure or entered judicial or arbitral proceedings, and (b) disputes that occurred before the BIT came into effect and had completed the notification procedure but not entered judicial and arbitral proceedings.

8.4.4.2 Teleological Interpretation and "True Intention"

Apart from the textual interpretation, the purposive interpretation can also be relied on to explore the "true agreement" between the contracting parties. The purposive interpretation can identify the intention of the contracting parties, clarify the meaning of the treaty and determine the object and purpose of the treaty itself.[171] The ILC pointed out that there would be no satisfactory interpretation of the treaty if the emphasis were placed too much on the words but not on the intention of the parties; or on the intention of the parties but not on the text of the treaty; or only on the object and purpose in order to make the treaty interpretation more "effective" regardless of the intention of the parties.[172] The purposive interpretation fits the VCLT's requirement that the treaty be interpreted in accordance with the "object and

171 Ian M. Sinclair, *The Vienna Convention on the Law of Treaties* (Manchester University Press 1973) 70.

172 Hugh Thirlway, "The Law and Procedure of International Court of Justice 1960–1989" (1991) *British Yearbook of International Law* 16–17.

purpose" of the treaty and "in view of relevant rules of international law."[173] To explore the purpose of the contracting parties, it is necessary to examine the treaty texts such as the preamble and the preparatory documents, and to analyze the external factors of the treaty, such as its background and environment. In the case of *Ping An* v. *Belgium*, the 2009 BIT preamble states that the purpose of the BIT is "reciprocal encouragement, promotion and protection [of] investments ... [which] will have the effect of stimulating the commercial initiatives of investors and increase[ing] the prosperity of both Contracting Parties."[174] The 2009 BIT's "Dispute Settlement Clause" expands the scope of arbitrable matters and reflects the purpose of the new BIT. According to the 2009 BIT, Ping An can appeal to international arbitration not only disputes on the amount of compensation but also other investment disputes. Compared with the 1986 BIT, the 2009 BIT gives investors more choices regarding dispute settlement, which is in line with the purpose of the 2009 BIT to reciprocally encourage, promote and protect the mutual investment of the contracting parties.

From the contextual perspective, the contracting parties included in the 2009 BIT the Dispute Settlement Clause that appears in other BITs. Since 1998, China has been working on new-generation BITs. Unlike the old-generation BITs before 1998 (that were reluctant to apply higher investment protection standards or to adopt a more liberal ISDS[175]), China's new-generation BITs allow "any dispute" to be submitted to the ICSID or an *ad hoc* arbitral tribunal. The BITs between China and Switzerland (2009),[176] France (2007),[177] Finland (2004),[178] Germany (2003)[179] and the Netherlands (2001),[180] which were concluded at the same time as the 2009 BIT, have all abandoned the restrictive ISDS and allowed investors to freely choose between international arbitration and domestic courts for dispute settlement. As far as Belgium is concerned, Belgium was allowing investors to submit "any dispute" to international arbitration in the same period and even in some earlier BITs (such as the Belgium–Singapore BIT 1978,[181] the Belgium–Bangladesh BIT 1981,[182] the Belgium–Sri Lanka BIT 1982[183] and the Belgium–Rwanda BIT 1983[184]). Applying the 2009 BIT to disputes that occurred prior to its entry into force would not increase any burden to Belgium.

When China negotiated with Belgium and concluded the 2009 BIT in 2005, it also signed new BITs with other countries to replace old BITs. For investment disputes that occurred before the entry into force of these new BITs, China has adopted two different approaches. One is to explicitly stipulate that the new BIT does not apply to such disputes while the other is to exclude from the new BIT only disputes that entered judicial and arbitral proceedings prior to its entry into force.[185] Based on this dichotomy, if China and Belgium had the intention to exclude all investment disputes that occurred before the effective date of the new

173 Bederman, *International Law Frameworks*, 36.
174 BLEU–China BIT (2009), Preamble.
175 See Congyan Cai, "Outward Foreign Direct Investment Protection and the Effectiveness of Chinese BIT Practice" (2006) 7(5) *Journal of World Investment and Trade* 621.
176 China–Switzerland BIT and Protocol 2009, Art. 12.
177 China–France BIT 2007, Art. 10.
178 China–Finland BIT 2004, Art. 8.
179 China–Germany BIT 2003, Art. 9.
180 China–Finland BIT 2001, Art. 10.
181 BLEU–Singapore BIT 1978, Art. 10.
182 BLEU–Bangladesh BIT 1981, Art. 6.
183 BLEU–Sri Lanka BIT 1982, Art. 10.
184 BLEU–Rwanda BIT 1983, Art. 10.
185 The China–Finland BIT 2004 and the China–Germany BIT 2003 explicitly exclude disputes that occurred before their entry into force. The China–Korea BIT 2005 excludes only disputes that had already entered judicial or arbitral proceedings before it came into effect.

BIT, that is, January 1, 2009, the 2009 BIT would have adopted the first approach to addressing a broadly defined "dispute."

Therefore, the teleological interpretation may affirm the "true agreement" under the 2009 BIT as being to offer more substantive protection to foreign investors and to remove hurdles inhibiting foreign investors from submitting disputes to international arbitration so as to encourage and promote mutual investment. Applying the 2009 BIT, based on the transitional clauses, to two unspecified types of dispute is consistent with the "true agreement" of the contracting parties to the 2009 BIT.

As a matter of fact, investment tribunals are supportive of the use of the purposive interpretive method. In *Tradex* v. *Albania*, the tribunal stated that international investment arbitration practice should not make any presupposition on the issue regardless of whether disputes submitted to international arbitration are existing or future ones. Due to Albania's commitment to investor protection, in case of any ambiguity, the textual interpretation of the BIT should be made in favor of investor protection and ICSID jurisdiction.[186]

In this instant case, it may be more appropriate for the tribunal to go through the preparatory work for the BIT and the circumstances at the time of the treaty-making in order to discover the true intention of the contracting parties in concluding the BIT and their common understanding of the treaty terms. When there is greater uncertainty or significant irrationality, the treaty interpreter, that is, the tribunal, can identify the minutes of the contracting process, the drafts of the treaty, the historical background of the treaty-making, the statements of the contracting parties, and further information such as correspondence and information to verify the results of the textual interpretation and to correct errors and irrationalities in it.[187] Judging from the arbitration procedure described by the tribunal, none of the parties to the dispute submitted any preparatory work for the 2009 BIT. The tribunal could have relied on Article 32 of the VCLT relating to the "Supplementary Means of Interpretation" and required the disputing parties to provide information on the history and background of the 2009 BIT in order to seek more certainty and a more persuasive interpretation.

8.4.4.3 Sovereign Transfer and "True Intention"

However, neither the "clue" provided by international investment arbitration jurisprudence nor the method of teleological interpretation discussed herein goes beyond the scope of treaty interpretation. Apart from the "true agreement" that the tribunal needs to explore, the interpretation itself also involves the transfer of sovereignty to international institutions. The contracting parties transfer their judicial sovereignty from domestic courts to international arbitration institutions, relying on the latter to adjudicate disputes.[188] When signing a BIT, though the contracting parties may have different intentions, as evidenced by their policy preferences, it may be fair to say that the host state wishes to give jurisdictional sovereignty to international arbitration tribunals as little as possible while the home state may prefer to authorize international arbitration tribunals to resolve disputes as much as

186 See *Tradex Hellas S.A.* v. *Republic of Albania*, ICSID Case No. ARB/94/2, Decision on Jurisdiction, December 24, 1996, at para. 194.

187 See Dorr and Schmalenbach (eds.), *Vienna Convention on the Law of Treaties: A Commentary*, 480–481.

188 See Todd Allee and Clint Peinhardt, "Delegating Differences: Bilateral Investment Treaties and Bargaining over Dispute Resolution Provisions" (2010) 54(1) *International Studies Quarterly* 1, 15.

possible, thereby reducing investment risks.[189] However, it should be pointed out that the treaty behavior of the host and the home states is not absolute as the bargaining power of the contracting parties varies from one case to another. For instance, a host state may be willing to accept the ICSID as an arbitration venue in order to attract more investment from the home state while the home state may be less welcoming of ICSID arbitration in order to enable investors to enter the host state's market as early as possible. In addition, the degree of propensity or "commitment" of the contracting parties to use ICSID arbitration is also affected by such factors as the rule of law in the host state, the stability of the host state's regime, and the friendliness of relations between the host and the home states.[190] In *Ping An* v. *Belgium*, a fair guess that the Belgian government was willing to reach a restrictive ICSID arbitration clause with China in the 1986 BIT was largely attributed to the attractiveness of China's huge market. China's inclusion of a more comprehensive ISDS clause in the 2009 BIT is in line with China's increasing focus on protecting its outbound investment.

Based on this line of analysis, it is hard to conclude that China had a specific intention to apply the 2009 BIT to its pre-entry-into-effect dispute when it concluded the 2009 BIT due to its hybrid nature as a major capital-importing and simultaneously capital-exporting state. Consequently, the Chinese government needs to serve a dual objective – it needs to provide more comprehensive investment protection to Chinese investors for outbound investment, and to safeguard its own interest by not being sued too often by foreign investors. This suggests that Chinese BITs cannot be "one-sided," serving a sole objective only.[191] China's evolving role from a pure capital-importing state to a hybrid state both importing and exporting capital may justify an evolutive approach. International courts and tribunals are sometimes forced to apply a method of evolutive interpretation under Article 31(3)(c) of the VCLT, which stresses the position of a treaty in the progressive development of international law, and implies treaty interpretation in the broader context of other legal instruments, general international law and international law practices.[192] The intertemporal issue, given its contemporaneous nature, may also be better off being dealt with in both a static and an evolutive manner.

"Concluding a BIT is to transfer sovereignty to the international arbitration mechanism" also indicates a need to interpret treaty terms in favor of the weaker party. Apart from the VCLT, there are no legally binding rules for treaty interpretation.[193] Before the entry into force of the VCLT, treaty interpretation traditionally relied on the "rules of logic" and "the general principle of the treaty text that could be inferred from the nature and character of the [international] legal order" as well as other international customs.[194] The negative effect of the variability and the uncertainty of treaty interpretation is obvious: the end result of treaty interpretation is often favorable to the stronger party. In order to eliminate the shortcomings of treaty interpretation, it needs to limit the free will of the contracting parties to some extent: if there is doubt and controversy over the treaty interpretation, the interpreter should choose an interpretation method that obliges the contracting party to bear less burden. That is to say, the parties will not become more powerful because of their bargaining power, which makes the other contracting party bear more obligations than what the treaty is supposed to

189 See Beth A. Simmons, "Bargaining Over BITs, Arbitrating Awards: The Regime for Protection and Promote of International Investment" (2014) 66(1) *World Politics* 12, 19.

190 Ibid.

191 *See* Congyan Cai, "China-US BIT Negotiations and the Future of Investment Treaty Regime: A Grand Bilateral Bargain with Multilateral Implications" (2009) 12(2) *Journal of International Economic Law* 457, 461–462.

192 Pauwely and Elsig, "The Politics of Treaty Interpretation," 460–462.

193 *See* Antonio Cassese, *International Law* (2nd edition, Oxford University Press 2005) 178.

194 Ibid.

impose.[195] This is the principle of *in dubio mitius* as *Oppenheim's International Law* describes.[196] It means that a defendant may not be convicted by the court when doubts about his guilt remain. Put another way, it is a doctrine stating that ambiguity should be resolved in favor of the more lenient punishment. For this reason, it is also viewed as a principle of restrictive interpretation in deference to the sovereignty of states. In its advisory opinion on the "Border issue between Turkey and Iraq" (1925), the Permanent Court of International Justice (PCIJ) acknowledged its preference for the interpretation imposing the least obligation on the contracting state being chosen among several possible interpretations if the treaty terms are not clear.[197] In *SGS* v. *Pakistan*, the ICSID tribunal held that, in the absence of a clear rule in the BIT that the host state should bear the treaty obligation due to the contract signed with the investor, the principle of *in dubio mitius* may disallow the investor to invoke the umbrella clause to make the host state liable for a contractual claim.[198]

The principle of *in dubio mitius* embodies the idea of sovereignty supremacy. The contracting parties can only subject a particular type of dispute to international arbitration with an express declaration of their intention in the treaty. This express declaration is reflective of the contracting parties' sovereignty to authorize the international arbitration tribunal to administer certain types of dispute. However, when this interpretation rule is applied, the parties must be presumed to have made the treaty effective. The principle of effective interpretation requires the treaty interpretation to be effective and useful and to produce an appropriate effect.

As far as *Ping An* v. *Belgium* is concerned, applying the principle of *in dubio mitius* suggests that the interpretation of the retroactivity of the 2009 BIT is not to increase the parties' obligation under the transitional clauses of the 2009 BIT. If it is presumed that the contracting parties have a "common agreement" to retroactively apply the 2009 BIT to an "investment dispute" that occurred before the entry into force of the 2009 BIT, it is likely to create more burden on the parties under the transitional clauses (this is so because if the 2009 BIT applies to disputes that occurred prior to its entry into force, neither of the contracting parties will be able to refuse the other party's investors submitting such disputes to international arbitration).

8.5 TRANSITIONAL CLAUSES IN TRANSITION: FILLING THE BLACK HOLE

The jurisdictional award in the *Ping An* v. *Belgium* case has far-reaching significance in some respects. First, this is the first ICSID award that interprets and applies the transitional clauses in China's new-generation BITs. Although this award may have some defects, as mentioned in this chapter, its interpretative methodology over the transitional clauses may have a great impact on similar cases in the future. Compared with the expansive interpretative methodology applied by the tribunal in *Yza Yap Shum* v. *Peru*, the restrictive interpretative approach taken by the *Ping An* v. *Belgium* tribunal is undoubtedly a detrimental move to foreign

195 Ibid.

196 See L. Oppenheim, *Oppenheim's International Law*, Vol. 1 Peace, eds. Sir Robert Jennings QC and Sir Arthur Watts KCMG QC (9th edition, Oxford University Press 2008) 666.

197 See Interpretation of Article 3, Paragraph 2, of the Treaty of Lausanne, Advisory Opinion of November 21, 1925, www.icj-cij.org/pcij/serie_B/B_12/01_Article_3_du_traite_de_Lausanne_Avis_consultatif.pdf (accessed November 14, 2016).

198 See *SGS Société Générale de Surveillance* S.A. v. *Islamic Republic of Pakistan*, ICSID Case No. ARB/01/13, Decision on the Tribunal on Objections to Jurisdiction, August 6, 2003, at para. 171.

investors.[199] According to the award, investors can rely on neither the new BIT nor the old BIT for arbitrating disputes that occurred before the entry into force of the new BIT but completed the notification procedure under the old BIT. Such disputes may continue to be governed by the old BIT and may then be adjudicated by the domestic courts in the host state. Alternatively, such disputes may not be governed by the old BIT, falling into the arbitration gap where no remedy is available (depending on whether the tribunal considers the old BIT still valid within the scope of the new BIT).

Second, the award will be of importance to the Chinese government for improving the transitional clauses in BITs, making up for the treaty gap caused by defective transitional clauses. It also has far-reaching effects in terms of China's future BITs. At present, China has a large number of BITs in an automatic renewal status.[200] Some BITs have been in force for more than thirty years and need to be replaced by new ones. Of the twelve pairs of new and old BITs between China and its counterparties, six pairs – between China and Germany, France, BLEU, Finland, the Netherlands and Spain – have successive relations. The transitional clauses are specifically defined in these BITs with similar structure and content. Application of these transitional clauses is likely to result in an award either similar or contradictory to that in the case of *Ping An* v. *Belgium*.

This means that we cannot ignore the side effects or danger that may arise from the *Ping An* v. *Belgium* case. China needs more refined transitional clauses in its future BITs with the aim of offering investors more comprehensive rights protection.

8.5.1 *Rethinking the Transitional Clauses in Chinese BITs*

Table 8.5 lists the specific content of the transitional clauses in Chinese BITs. From a structural analysis, the transitional clauses include two provisions: the first paragraph stipulates that the new BIT replaces the old one, and the second paragraph limits the scope of application of the new BIT. In terms of the substance, the transitional clauses contain at least four meanings: (a) the new BIT replaces the old one; (b) the new BIT applies to all investments made by the investor from either contracting party to the territory of the other contracting party, regardless of whether the investment is made before or after the entry into force of the new BIT; (c) the new BIT does not apply to any investment-related dispute or claim that entered judicial or arbitral proceedings before the entry into force of the new BIT; (d) any dispute or claim relating to investment that entered judicial or arbitral proceedings before the entry into force of the new BIT should continue to be governed by the old BIT. In addition, the transitional clauses in the BITs signed by China with Germany and Spain clarify that the old BIT ceases to apply upon entry into force of the new BIT.

Judging from the actual application of the transitional clauses by the tribunal in *Ping An* v. *Belgium*, the structure and the semantics of the wording at least have created two legal issues:

199 Shen Wei, "Beyond the Scope of 'Investor' and 'Investment': Who Can Make an Arbitration Claim under a Chinese BIT? – Some Implications from a Recent ICSID Case" (2010) 6(2) *Asian International Arbitration Journal* 164–185.

200 "Automatic renewal" means that the validity period of the BIT has expired but neither party to the contract has notified the other party to the contract that the agreement has lapsed and the agreement continues to enter into force. Article 11(2) of the China–Denmark BIT 1985.

TABLE 8.5 *Transitional clauses in Chinese BITs* (by the end of 2015)*

No.	BIT	Signing year	Transitional clauses
1	China–Germany BIT	2003	Article 16: Upon entry into force of this Agreement the Agreement of 7 October 1983 between the Federal Republic of Germany and the People's Republic of China on the Encouragement and Reciprocal Protection of Investments shall terminate. The present Agreement shall apply to all investments made by investors of either Contracting Party in the territory of the other Contracting Party, whether made before or after the entry into force of this Agreement, but shall not apply to any dispute or any claim concerning an investment which was already under judicial or arbitral process before its entry into force. Such disputes and claims shall continue to be settled according to the provisions of the Agreement of 7 October 1983 mentioned in paragraph 1 of this Article.
2	China–France BIT	2007	Article 11:[201] Le présent Accord abroge et remplace l'Accord sur l'encouragement et la protection réciproques des investissements entre le Gouvernement de la République française et le Gouvernement de la République populaire de Chine signé à Paris le 30 mai 1984. Le présent Accord s'applique à tous les investissements réalisés par des investisseurs de l'une des Parties contractantes sur le territoire de l'autre Partie contractante, qu'ils aient été réalisés avant ou après son entrée en vigueur mais ne s'applique pas aux différends ou réclamations portant sur un investissement qui auront déjà été soumis à une procédure judiciaire ou arbitrale avant son entrée en vigueur. Les dits différends et réclamations continueront d'être réglés conformément aux dispositions de l'Accord de 1984 mentionne au premier alinéa du présent article.
3	China–BLEU BIT	2005	Article 10: This Agreement substitutes and replaces the Agreement between the Government of the People's Republic of China and the Belgium–Luxembourg Economic Union on the Reciprocal Promotion and Protection of Investments, signed on 4 June 1984, in Brussels. The present Agreement shall apply to all investments made by investors of either Contracting Party in the territory of the other Contracting Party, whether made before or after the entry into force of this Agreement, but shall not apply to any dispute or any claim concerning an investment which was already under judicial or arbitral process before its entry into force. Such disputes and claims shall continue to be settled according to the provisions of the Agreement of 1984 mentioned in paragraph 1 of this Article.

(*Continued*)

201 Author's translation: This Agreement substitutes and replaces the Agreement on reciprocal encouragement and protection of investments between the Government of the French Republic and the Government of the People's Republic of China signed in Paris on May 30, 1984.

This Agreement shall apply to all investments made by investors of either Contracting Party in the territory of the other Contracting Party, whether they were made before or after the entry into force of this Agreement, but shall not apply to any dispute or any claim concerning an investment which was already under judicial or arbitral process before its entry into force. Such disputes and claims shall continue to be settled according to the provisions of the Agreement of 1984 mentioned in paragraph 1 of this Article.

TABLE 8.5 *(Continued)*

No.	BIT	Signing year	Transitional clauses
4	China–Finland BIT	2004	Article 13: This Agreement substitutes and replaces the Agreement between the Government of the Republic of Finland and the Government of the People's Republic of China for the Protection of Investments, done at Beijing on 4 September 1984. This Agreement shall apply to all investments made by investors of either Contracting Party in the territory of the other Contracting Party, whether made before or after the entry into force of this Agreement, but shall not apply to any dispute or any claim concerning an investment which was already under judicial or arbitral process before its entry into force. Such disputes and claims shall continue to be settled according to the provisions of the Agreement done in 1984, mentioned in paragraph 1 of this Article.
5	China–Netherlands BIT	2001	Article 13: This Agreement substitutes and replaces the Agreement on reciprocal encouragement and protection of investments between the Government of the People's Republic of China and the Government of the Kingdom of the Netherlands, signed June 17, 1985, in the Hague. This present Agreement shall apply to all investments made by investors of either Contracting Party in the territory of the other Contracting party, whether made before or after the entry into force of this Agreement, but shall not apply to any dispute or any claim concerning an investment which was already under judicial or arbitral process before its entry into force. Such disputes and claims shall continue to be settled according to the provisions of the Agreement of 1985 mentioned in paragraph 1 of this Article.
6	China–Spain BIT	2005	Article 12: This Agreement substitutes and abrogates the Agreement on reciprocal encouragement and protection of investments between the Kingdom of Spain and the People's Republic of China, signed in Madrid on 6 February 1992. The present Agreement shall apply to all investments made by investors of either Contracting Party in the territory of the other Contracting Party, whether made before or after its entry into force, but shall not apply to any dispute or any claim concerning an investment which was already under judicial or arbitral process before its entry into force. Such disputes and claims shall continue to be settled according to the provisions of the Agreement of 1992 mentioned in paragraph 1 of this Article.

*Prepared by the author.

8.5.1.1 Treaty Gap

The transitional clauses only stipulate that the new BIT does not apply to investment disputes that entered judicial or arbitral proceedings prior to the entry into force of the new BIT. However, the transitional clauses are silent on whether the new BIT applies to those investment disputes that occurred but did not enter judicial or arbitral proceedings before the entry into force of the new BIT. The treaty gap is likely to continue to trigger similar disputes that were adjudicated in *Ping An* v. *Belgium* – the host state's damage to investment occurred before the new BIT came into force, and the investor's claim was made on the basis of the old BIT but was brought to international arbitration according to the new BIT. The tribunal ultimately made a no-jurisdiction award.

In fact, many countries have already noticed the damages that a defective transitional clause may bring to BIT practice. For example, the Germany–Iran BIT reached in 2002 makes clear that the new BIT does not apply to investment disputes that occurred or were settled before its entry into force.[202] Similar transitional clauses have also appeared in the Germany–Ethiopian BIT 2004,[203] the Czech–Turkey BIT 2009[204] and the Canada–Uruguay BIT 1997.[205]

The treaty gap that stems from the transitional clauses in the Chinese BITs objectively causes randomness and inconsistency in the application of new BITs. The tribunal may rely on its own understanding rather than the contracting parties' true intention in interpreting the true meaning of transitional clauses, which creates confusion in treaty interpretation and brings uncertainty to investors seeking international remedies.

8.5.1.2 Arbitration Gap

No matter whether it is clearly stipulated in the BIT that "the old BIT is terminated after the new BIT comes into effect" or that the legal effect of the old BIT is not extended to disputes that occur after the new BIT comes into effect, the current transitional clauses will trigger the arbitration gap as illustrated in the case of *Ping An* v. *Belgium*. According to the current transitional clauses, the old BIT has been replaced or terminated by the new one. This means that the old BIT can only be applied if the dispute entered judicial or arbitral proceedings before the new BIT comes into effect. Where the dispute between the investor and the host state did not enter judicial or arbitral proceedings before the new BIT came into effect, the investor is unable to rely on the old BIT and seek relief in the domestic courts as the new BIT cannot be applied and the old BIT has expired.

There is no effective solution under international law for dealing with the arbitration gap. The arbitration gap is usually not regarded as a treaty loophole in international law. Rather, it is regarded as an omission to be filled through treaty interpretations. In the view of some international law scholars, the arbitration gap merely reflects the contracting parties' attitudes toward some unregulated matters instead of a treaty loophole. As a result, this gap requires the tribunal to interpret the treaty text.[206] This means that when the transitional clauses have an arbitration gap, investors are likely to lose the possibility of seeking relief under international law, which may not be in line with the principle of international law that legitimate interests deserve legal protection.[207]

202 Germany–Iran BIT 2002, Art. 9.

203 Germany–Ethiopia BIT 2004, Art. 9.

204 Czech–Turkey BIT 2009, Art. 11.

205 Canada–Uruguay BIT 1997, Art. 15.

206 W. Michael Reinman, "The Regime for Lacunae in the ICSID: Choice of Law Provision and the Question of Its Threshold" (2000) 15 *Foreign Investment Law Journal* 362, 371.

207 See Ian Brownlie, *Principles of Public International Law* (8th edition, Oxford University Press 2012) 17.

8.5.2 *Comparing Transitional Clauses in BIT Law*

Regrettably, neither the US 2012 Model BIT nor other countries' Model BITs offer clear guidance for dealing with the arbitration gap left by the transitional clauses. Some other countries' BITs do have transitional clauses, which, however, also have the same or similar issues as the transitional clauses that the Chinese BITs have encountered, and all face the arbitration gap issue. For example, the Czech–Turkey BIT 2009 replaced the Czechoslovak–Turkey BIT 1992. Although the 2009 BIT provides for the application of the new BIT to disputes that occurred prior to its entry into force, it does not clarify whether the old BIT can be applied to disputes that do not fall in the jurisdiction of the new BIT.

Article 11 does not clarify whether the 1992 BIT applies to disputes that are clearly not in the jurisdictional scope of the 2009 BIT. According to the termination clause in the 1992 BIT, the old BIT continues to be valid for a period of ten years after its termination to investments made before the termination.[208] However, the termination clause provides only for "investments" made before the termination, and does not make any mention of "investment disputes" that occurred before the termination. Therefore, investment disputes arising before the entry into force of the 2009 BIT face the risk of being governed by neither the 2009 BIT nor the 1992 BIT.

The Germany–Egypt BIT signed in 2005 is similar to the China–BLEU BIT 2009, and only partially stipulates whether the new BIT can be applied to disputes that occurred before its entry into force. This clause, however, is silent on the application of the 2005 BIT to disputes that were resolved before its entry into force.

Table 8.6 lists some transitional clauses in the BITs signed by Germany, which has the largest number of BITs (155 by the end of 2015). These transitional clauses can be divided into two categories. Merely a small portion of BITs stipulate that the new BIT does not apply to pre-entry-into-effect disputes, whereas the other group of BITs does not specify or only partially specifies whether the new BIT applies to pre-entry-into-force disputes. The latter appears a mainstream approach.

8.5.3 *Filling the Arbitration Gap in Chinese BITs*

Although the award of *Ping An* v. *Belgium* has no precedential effect on subsequent ICSID cases[209] that may involve the same legal issue, the tribunal has sent a signal to potential disputing parties that tribunals are less willing to apply an expansive interpretative approach toward transitional clauses.[210] In other words, the award may have a far-reaching impact on future cases involving the same or similar legal issues. On the question of whether the transitional clauses grant retroactive effect to the procedural provisions in the BIT, it is more appropriate for the contracting parties to expressly clarify their true intentions in making the BIT even though the state parties may frequently fail to include intertemporal rules in the new BIT and it is the arbitral tribunal that often fills the gap out of necessity in the course of interpreting BIT terms. It is likely that we will see more transitional clauses in Chinese BITs arbitrated in the future as China is in the process of signing more new-generation BITs with

208 Czech Republic–Turkey BIT 1992, Art. 10.4.

209 See *Hussein Nuaman Soufraki* v. *The United Arab Emirates*, Decision of the Ad Hoc Committee on the Application for Annulment of Mr. Soufraki, ICSID Case No. ARB/02/7, para. 128.

210 See Willems, "The Settlement of Investor State Disputes," 57.

TABLE 8.6 *Transitional clauses in German BITs*[211] *(selected)*

Types	Type 1	Type 2
BIT	Germany–Iran BIT	Germany–Egypt BIT
Signing date	2002	2005
Transitional clause	"This Agreement shall apply to investments approved by the competent authority of the host Contracting Party, if so required by its laws and regulations, made prior to or after the entry into force of this Agreement . . . However, this Agreement shall not apply to disputes which have been raised or settled prior to its entry into force."[212]	"From the date of its entry into force, this Agreement shall apply to all investments, also those made prior to its entry into force, by the investors of either Contracting States in the territory of the other Contracting State. However, it shall not apply to any dispute concerning an investment which arose or any claim which was settled before its entry into force."[213]
Similar transitional clauses in other BITs	Germany–Ethiopia BIT 2004, Article 9	Germany–Indonesia BIT 2003, Article 7; Germany–Sri Lanka BIT 2000, Article 9; Germany–Thailand BIT 2002, Article 8; Germany–Jordan BIT 2007, Article 9; Germany–China BIT 2003, Article 16.

*Prepared by the author.[214]

other states. Improving the ambiguity that transitional clauses may possess is a realistic quest for China and its counterparties.

Before discussing the issue of what should be specified in the transitional clauses, it is necessary to clarify whether China should give the new BITs' procedural rules retroactive effect. China has entered into new-generation BITs with several countries since 1998, and these BITs often incorporate some unrestrictive ISDS clauses. In theory, applying these unrestrictive ISDS clauses in the new BITs to disputes that occurred before their entry into force will not increase China's substantive or procedural burden. This general observation is evidenced by some empirical figures. Although China has already concluded a considerable number of new BITs, China and Chinese investors still rarely become the parties, either claimant or respondent, in BIT cases. According to the ICSID case database, up to now, China has only been involved in three BIT cases as a respondent. At least three theories have been offered in academic circles justifying such a small number of BIT cases involving China or Chinese BITs. First, the Chinese government still retains enormous power to regulate and monitor foreign investment. Foreign investors do not want to damage their relationship with Chinese authorities. Second, the Chinese legal infrastructure and legal system are in a process of improvement and are in a better position to offer protections to foreign investors. Third, most of China's new-generation BITs require foreign investors to complete the

211 Data from UNCTAD database, http://unctad.org/en/Pages/DIAE/World%20Investment%20Report/Annex-Tables.aspx (accessed November 14, 2016).

212 Germany–Iran BIT 2002, Art. 9.

213 Germany–Egypt BIT 2005 Art. 10(1).

214 Data from UNCTAD database, http://unctad.org/en/Pages/DIAE/World%20Investment%20Report/Annex-Tables.aspx (accessed November 14, 2016).

administrative review procedures in the domestic courts before submitting the dispute to international arbitration. The pre-existing administrative review procedures increase the burden on investors to choose international arbitration, thereby effectively screening and filtering the disputes submitted to international arbitration.

Applying the nonrestrictive ISDS clauses to pre-entry-into-force disputes is also in line with China's underlying logic of concluding new BITs with certain counterparties. This is a liberal trend that China is following.[215] Since 1998, China has concluded a number of new-generation BITs, giving foreign investors less-restricted rights to resort to international arbitration for their disputes with the Chinese government. After 1998, China's BITs gradually shifted focus from attracting and promoting inbound FDI to encouraging and protecting more outbound FDI. This shift not only fits the development of neoliberal expansionism and pragmatism that is beneficial to rights protection in international investment but also coincides with China's status as a growingly open power and a key capital-exporting state. If the nonrestrictive ISDS clauses are limited to post-entry-into-force-of-new-BITs disputes, it will run counter to the rising trend of granting more favorable treatment for foreign investment protection as demonstrated by the new-generation Chinese BITs regardless of the spillover effect on the Chinese companies investing overseas.[216] Figure 9.1 of Chapter 9 shows the leap-forward growth of China's outbound FDI.

The second tier of the issue is finding a way to refine the transitional clauses in BITs so as to avoid ambiguity and difficulty in treaty interpretation and application. China has upgraded 28 percent of its BITs, but ambiguity has already caused some confusion. Two investment arbitration tribunals and one highest court in the seat of arbitration have rendered decisions favoring the application of old BITs over upgraded ones.[217] This has made the formulation of an appropriate model for upgrading existing BITs highly relevant and important. There are at least two different approaches. First, the contracting parties could clarify the terminology of the transitional clauses in the current (new) BITs. Second, the specific wording of the transitional clauses in the BITs could be revised through negotiation, with the contracting parties adding a protocol or amendment. Alternatively, a new-new BIT could be signed to clarify or even replace the vaguely worded transitional clauses in the new BIT.[218]

8.5.3.1 Contracting States' Interpretation of Transitional Clauses

According to the general theory of treaty interpretation, a state party is the subject of a treaty that has the power to interpret it. The interpretation made by the state party helps to clarify the purpose and content of the treaty and plays an important role in removing any vagueness surrounding the BIT. The state party's interpretation can be achieved through a number of ways: States parties can make *ex ante* detailed provisions on specific terms directly in the treaty or make *ex post* interpretations. In the worst scenario, the parties to the BIT may supplement the BIT terms after the tribunal renders its award.

As to the interpretation of transitional clauses involved in the case of *Ping An* v. *Belgium*, China may choose to further improve and clarify the content of the BIT through subsequent

215 Willems, "The Settlement of Investor State Disputes."

216 See "China's Outbound Direct Investment Surges to Over $134 Billion," *The Economic Times* (October 18, 2016), http://economictimes.indiatimes.com/news/international/business/chinas-outbound-direct-investment-surges-to-over-134-billion/articleshow/54915388.cms (accessed November 19, 2016).

217 Jie (Jeanne) Huang, "Procedural Models to Upgrade BITs: China's Experience" (2018) 31(1) *Leiden Journal of International Law* 93–115.

218 Ibid.

negotiations with Belgium. For example, it would be possible to initiate a consultation process between the Chinese and Belgian governments so that the two sides could discuss the solution to the problem and the path for improvement. Article 9 of the China–BLEU BIT outlines the dispute settlement mechanism (either diplomatic channel or joint committee) for disputes over the BIT arising between the two states.[219]

China and Belgium could also make joint statements or memoranda, or exchange letters or other communiqués to express their true intention on the specific meaning of the transitional clauses in the BIT. In fact, at the time of signing the BIT in 2009, China and Belgium had further clarified the definition of investment, treatment standards and foreign exchange transfers in the BIT through the protocol.[220] In *CME* v. *Czech Republic*, after the tribunal made a partial award, the Netherlands and the Czech Republic, the parties to the BIT, published agreed minutes to clarify their common position on the interpretation of the BIT terms.[221] Therefore, China and Belgium could have fully demonstrated their positions on the interpretation of the treaty by means of a joint statement after the *Ping An* v. *Belgium* award was made with the purpose of correcting or supplementing the interpretation of the transitional clauses made by the ICSID tribunal.

The state parties' interpretation has more significance than any revision of the treaty. Treaty interpretation is a clarification of the treaty and therefore is retroactive in its application. On the contrary, revision of the treaty changes its original meaning and is therefore not retroactive in nature.[222] Treaty interpretation can improve the BIT terms applied to the investment and any investment disputes before the interpretation is made.

8.5.3.2 Amending or Concluding Transitional Clauses

The general way by which the contracting parties modify a treaty is to enter into an amendment to the original treaty or a protocol (proposal). Entering into a new treaty, however, requires the parties to renegotiate and conclude a new treaty. Regardless of the fact that the contracting parties are to amend the old treaty or conclude a new one, the legal instrument needs to be approved by the authorized representatives of both contracting parties and approved by the domestic authorities of the contracting parties.

The first paragraph of the transitional clauses in the Chinese BITs addresses the effectiveness of the old BIT after the entry into force of the new one. In order to avoid the arbitration gap in the case of *Ping An* v. *Belgium*, the transitional clauses need to clarify the applicability of the old BIT to such disputes as are not covered by the new BIT after the new BIT becomes effective. If there is a case where a dispute cannot be governed by the new BIT, the parties to the dispute should have the means to seek relief in accordance with the old BIT.

The second paragraph of the transitional clause concerns the retroactive effect of the new BIT on disputes that occurred before the entry into force of the new BIT, and the scope of this retroactive effect. Most BITs of other countries refuse to grant such a retroactive effect. The US 2012 Model BIT clarifies: "For greater certainty, this Treaty does not bind either Party in relation to any act or fact that took place or any situation that ceased to exist before the date of

219 China–BLEU BIT 2005, Arts. 2, 3 and 4.

220 China–BLEU BIT 2005.

221 *CME* v. *Czech Republic*, UNCITRAL, Final Award, March 14, 2003, at para. 89.

222 Charles H. Brower II, "Why the FTC Notes of Interpretation Constitute a Partial Amendment of NAFTA Article 1105" (2006) 46(2) *Virginia Journal of International Law* 347–363.

entry into force of this Treaty."[223] Canada's 2007 Model BIT has a similar clause.[224] However, as discussed earlier, the retroactive effect of a new BIT on disputes that occurred before its entry into force will not increase China's obligation apart from entitling both Chinese and foreign investors to a more comprehensive ISDS as stipulated in the new BIT. Therefore, in order to avoid such an arbitration gap as in the case of *Ping An* v. *Belgium*, transitional clauses in future BITs could be clarified through the means of offering more favorable treatment to investors except relative to investment disputes that entered judicial or arbitral proceedings prior to the entry into force of the new BIT.

8.6 CONCLUSION

The transitional issue of China's BITs stems from the existence of two successive BITs between the same contracting parties. Compared with the old-generation BITs, the new-generation BITs have rid themselves of restrictive provisions on arbitrable disputes, adopted more flexible fork-in-the-road clauses, and extended the jurisdiction to contractual claims made by foreign investors against the host state. The existence of new and old BITs between the same contracting parties brings out a problem in the application of law: which BIT applies to the legal facts that were already formed before the new BIT was signed.

The case of *Ping An* v. *Belgium* shows how the ICSID tribunal dealt with this transitional issue by applying the transitional clauses in the new BIT. Under international law, the interpretation and the application of transitional clauses need to follow the general treaty interpretation methods and conform to intertemporal law. The tribunal used semantic interpretation methods such as "ordinary meaning," "literal interpretation" and contextual analysis to limit the scope of the "Dispute Settlement Clause" in the new BIT to disputes arising before the new BIT came into effect. The tribunal further explored the true agreement between the contracting parties on the transitional clauses in the new BIT. The tribunal concluded that the parties did not intend to extend the nonrestrictive "dispute resolution clause" provided by the new BIT to disputes that occurred before its entry into force. However, the tribunal ignored the other possible interpretation of transitional clauses and avoided the international law issue of jurisdiction *ratione temporis*. Nor did the tribunal fully discuss the "common agreement" of the contracting parties.

Transitional clauses often ensure that investors do not fall between the cracks but remain protected throughout the transition from the old to the new BIT.[225] As an important case of a Chinese investor defending its rights under the ICSID, the outcome of the *Ping An* v. *Belgium* case is criticized as being "not reliable"[226] and is undoubtedly a great disappointment. The abovementioned flaws in the interpretation and application of transitional clauses by the tribunal made the award in this case less convincing.[227] The ruling made in the award,

223 US 2012 Model BIT, Art. 2(3).

224 Canada 2007 Model BIT; Canada–Uruguay BIT 1997; Turkey–Bangladesh BIT 2012.

225 UNCTAD, UNCTAD's Reform Package: For the International Investment Regime, 2018, p. 83.

226 Claire Wilson, "Protecting Chinese Investment under the Investor-State Dispute Settlement Regime: A Review in Light of Ping An v. Belgium" in Julien Chaisse (ed.), *China's International Investment Strategies: Bilateral, Regional and Global Law and Policy* (Oxford University Press 2019) 474–475.

227 One possible reason why the tribunal rejected the jurisdiction is that the tribunal was displeased about the basis of the case, which was to allege expropriation because of a 2008 financial crisis effort to forestall consequences of a liquidity crisis at the financial firm in which Ping An had invested. While Ping An nominally might have had grounds to prevail, the tribunal saw that as being unjust since, without the infusion of government funds, the firm might have failed. The tribunal's decision to find the arbitration gap was a good way to avoid this thorny issue.

as criticized, is reflective of the tribunal's value orientation rather than its textual basis.[228] A solution to resolving the ambiguity of transitional clauses as well as conflict and inconsistency in interpreting transitional clauses is to have more clearly defined transitional clauses in future BITs.

At present, the transitional clauses in Chinese BITs are structurally and textually similar and would create a similar "arbitration gap" to that in *Ping An* v. *Belgium* were they to be interpreted in the same manner in the future. To refine and improve the existing text of transitional clauses, in particular the temporal scope of jurisdiction, in its future negotiations of new BITs, China may adopt a relatively liberal or expansive approach by applying the nonrestrictive dispute settlement clause in the new BIT to disputes arising before the new BIT comes into effect, and clarifying the scope of the old BIT which still has jurisdiction over disputes that do not fall under the jurisdiction of the new BIT. With a more elaborate transitional clause, there could be an effective connection between the old and new BITs as well as a smooth transition of transitional clauses.

This justification is merely a speculation. Technically, the tribunal was not supposed to reject the jurisdiction based on the merit-related concerns. The author thanks Thomas Stanton for this finance-related consideration.

228 Qing Ren, "Ping An v. Belgium: Temporal Jurisdiction of Successive BITs" (2016) 31(1) *ICSID Review* 129, 145.

9

Evolutionary Path of China's BIT Law in the Return of the State Paradigm: A Statistical and Textual Approach

In more recent years, a new movement in international investment law has surfaced along with transformative changes in global economic growth.[1] After Professor José E. Alvarez published his seminal article "The Return of the State," the idea of the "return of the state" became an important paradigm for conceptualizing new changes in international investment law. In his article, Alvarez argues that some states that have concluded a wide range of liberal BITs seem to attempt to claw back on the rather enthusiastic liberalization efforts of the 1990s and to go back to a less liberal position, hence return to the old age of greater sovereignty. The states that created and deeply used the ISDS scheme are now back to the realm of investment disputes through either withdrawal from the ISDS or innovations in treaty-making that provide for a more dominant role for the home state in excluding the resort to or blocking the initiation of the ISDS mechanism. At the same time, there has been a revival of diplomatic protection in the forms of national security review and local adjudication.[2]

The dynamic and changing matrix of economic liberalization and limitation of state sovereignty is the hallmark in the arena of international investment law.[3] The "return of the state" therefore is a metaphor meaning more protection of a host state's sovereignty (in the form of its sovereign right or power to regulate foreign investment activities) in the context of reshaping the modern international investment law regime.[4] For instance, new constitutional arrangements that protect property in South Africa represent a deviation from the norms expressed in the transnational investment-rules regime.[5] Opposite to this movement has been "the leaving (or retreat) of the state," a shorthand for liberalization where the host state imposes various constraints on its sovereignty in exchange for better investor protection with the aim of attracting more foreign investment and promoting economic development.[6] The

[1] M. Sornarajah, *Resistance and Change in the International Law on Foreign Investment* (Cambridge University Press 2015) 4–10.

[2] Rodrigo Polanco, *The Return of the Home State to Investor-State Disputes: Bringing Back Diplomatic Protection?* (Cambridge University Press 2019) 4.

[3] Cynthia Day Wallace, *The Multinational Enterprise and Legal Control: Host State Sovereignty in an Era of Economic Globalization* (Kluwer Law 2002) 1071–1073.

[4] See José E. Alvarez, "The Return of the State" (2011) 20 *Minnesota Journal of International Law* 223, 230–231.

[5] David Schneiderman, "Investment Rules and the New Constitutionalism" (2000) 25(3) *Law & Social Inquiry* 757–787.

[6] See generally Susan Strange, *The Retreat of the State: The Diffusion of Power in the World Economy* (Cambridge University Press 1996) 16.

"leaving of the state", premised on neoliberalism and liberal institutions,[7] made the first-generation BITs possible instruments[8] to be utilized by dominant powers to protect their overseas investment and more importantly exert influence over other countries.[9]

In the "return of the state" paradigm, the USA and China naturally are the focal nations that are reshaping international investment law since the former is the main promoter and builder of the modern international investment law regime and the leader of developed states advocating stronger investor rights protection in the past, while the latter is viewed as the leader of emerging and developing economies representing the interests of developing or transitional states taking advantage of the international investment law regime for economic growth and social development.[10] The article "The Return of the State" may lay more emphasis on the phenomenon of the "return" of states but does not offer more in-depth study on this occurrence in China. Alvarez's original focus was mainly on developed countries' new model BITs in which a host state's regulatory space expanded, departing from the previous pro-investor bias. Thus, the purpose of this chapter is to fill this gap by focusing its analysis on China's basic orientation and development record in the "leaving (return) of the state" paradigm.[11]

The rest of the chapter proceeds as follows. Section 9.1 discusses the trend and "operation" of the "return of the state" paradigm. Well prior to the return of the state, international investment law was largely shaped by states' departure from their sovereign powers to regulate foreign investment, which is labeled "the leaving of the state." Therefore, while the "return of the state" represents more protectionist and conservative measures taken by the host state toward foreign investment, the "leaving (or retreat) of the state" showcases the host state's desire to give away more sovereign or regulatory powers in exchange for more protections to foreign investors. Section 9.2, through statistical and textual investigation of international investment agreements (IIAs) that China has concluded in the past forty years, demonstrates China's past and present BIT law and practice, placing it in a "leaving (or return) of the state" spectrum. The general claim is that Chinese BITs are moving toward a balanced and liberal stance.[12] Section 9.3 makes a preliminary assessment of whether China and the rest of the world are converging or diverging in terms of the development of international investment law. While it warns against the universalized, Western paradigm of law, it also recognizes that the Chinese rule of law on economic matters is still in flux. In summary, it throws the Chinese economic governance into sharp relief against the Western system, thereby helping readers identify convergences and divergences between the two systems.

7 Marc D. Froese, *Sovereign Rules and the Politics of International Economic Law* (Routledge 2018) 8.

8 M. Sornarajah, "The Case Against a Regime on International Investment Law" in Leion Trakman and Nicola Ranieri (eds.), *Regionalism in International Investment Law* (Oxford University Press 2013) 496.

9 Lucas Bento, "From Anarchy to Rational Design: Direction and Perception in International Investment Law" in Andrea K. Bjorklund, *Yearbook on International Investment Law & Policy 2014–2015* (Oxford University Press 2016) 246.

10 See Karl P. Sauvant, "Emerging Markets and the International Investment Law and Policy Regime" in Robert Grosse and Klaus E. Meyer (eds.), *The Oxford Handbook of Management in Emerging Markets* (Oxford University Press 2019) 151.

11 Although Chinese realities have challenged and influenced the formation of sovereignty and the progress of international law in history, the concept of sovereignty was largely Western and Eurocentric and is now a universal order. See, generally, Maria Adele Carrai, *Sovereignty in China: A Genealogy of a Concept Since 1840* (Cambridge University Press 2019).

12 Yu-Ting Ye, "Towards a Balanced and Liberal Chinese Bilateral Investment Treaty Regime in the Context of One Belt One Road" (2018) 41 *Houston Journal of International Law* 107.

9.1 THE "RETURN OF THE STATE" AND THE PATH OF IIL

The modern international investment law regime contributed to and shaped by the "leaving" of the state essentially reflects the overall pattern of international investment in a specific historical period. As a result of the continuous development of the world economy and the change of the international investment pattern, the defects and drawbacks of this regime have gradually emerged, which has led to calls for reform of the modern international investment law regime.[13] The gradual "return" of the state, in a close match with the retreat of neoliberalism,[14] has turned out to be a new trend, and may herald long-term shifting paradigms in international investment law.[15]

9.1.1 *Imbalanced Interests and the Host States' Dissatisfaction with ICSID Arbitration*

The ICSID arbitration regime based on the ICSID Convention is a vital component for maintaining the operation of the modern international investment law regime. The mode of resolving investment disputes by urging the host state to transfer and delegate part of its judicial sovereignty is the central aspect and a powerful illustration of the "leaving" of the states in the field of international investment law.

9.1.1.1 The ICSID's Efficient Operations

The ICSID has become operationally inefficient, triggering a wide range of criticisms and suspicions. Judging from the recent development of ICSID arbitration, a large number of cases illustrate that arbitration tribunals restrict the power of the host state and protect investors excessively when called on to interpret and apply treaty terms. As pointed out by commentators, investment arbitration awards have accorded greater protection to foreign investment than many realized was possible.[16] For instance, with regard to the application of the host state's law by an arbitration tribunal, paragraph 1 of Article 42 of the ICSID Convention stipulates: "The Tribunal **shall** decide a dispute in accordance with such rules of law as **may be agreed** by the parties. In the absence of such agreement, the Tribunal **shall** apply the law of the Contracting State party to the dispute (including its rules on the conflict of laws) and such rules of international law as **may be applicable**" [emphasis added]. In accordance with this provision, the applicable law can be determined in two scenarios. First, in the case that the parties have chosen the applicable law, the arbitration tribunal shall apply the law as chosen by the parties. Second, when the parties do not choose the applicable law, the arbitration tribunal shall apply the laws of one of the contracting states and the rules of international law to the dispute. On closer examination, the following points are worth discussing in the interpretation and application of this provision. In the first case, the so-called "possible consent" essentially gives the arbitration tribunal a greater presumption right. Since the "legal rules" are too abstract, they provide the arbitration tribunal with more discretion in exercising the presumption right, and the arbitration tribunal can infer the

[13] See David Schneiderman, *Constitutionalizing Economic Globalization: Investment Rules and Democracy's Promise* (Cambridge University Press 2008) 25.

[14] M. Sornarajah, *The International Law on Foreign Investment* (3rd edition, Cambridge University Press 2010) 35.

[15] Steffen Hindelang and Markus Krajewski, "Towards a More Comprehensive Approach in International Investment Law" in Steffen Hindelang and Markus Krajewski, *Shifting Paradigms in International Investment Law: More Balanced, Less Isolated, Increasingly Diversified* (Oxford University Press 2016) 1, at 3.

[16] Vaughan Lowe, "Regulation or Expropriation?" (2002) 55 *Current Legal Problems* 447, 456.

implied agreement from various events and specific cases associated with the parties.[17] In the second case, since the ICSID Convention does not prioritize the choices of applicable law, the arbitration tribunal can choose the applicable law at will. This article does not require the compulsory application of the host state's law, thereby creating possibilities for the alternative application of law by arbitration tribunals.[18]

The legal norms in favor of foreign investment protection advanced by ICSID, largely pushed by the USA's endeavor to deny the Calvo Doctrine and to uphold its rights to protect its citizens abroad,[19] encountered some defects resulting from a series of controversial cases. These defects showcase how the regulatory spaces of states were overlooked, affected and even diminished by arbitral practices in ICSID proceedings, and, more importantly, how democratic or public choices available to the host state government were compromised by these arbitration cases.

The application of the host state's law in ICSID arbitration depends entirely on the interpretation of the arbitration tribunals. More often, arbitration tribunals prefer to apply an expansive approach to interpreting vaguely defined substantive terms in the BITs. By doing so, the host state's sovereign acts are reviewed by a tribunal against standards that do not have definite content.[20] The ICSID arbitration tribunal has also defined its position of restricting the application of the host state's law in real practice.

The main methods adopted are as follows. First, international law is used to exclude the application of the host state's domestic law. In the case of *Wena Hotels* v. *Egypt*, the arbitration tribunal pointed out that the ICSID Convention does not limit the scope of application of the host state's law and international law (including BITs) so that the arbitration tribunal is entitled to decide on the specific applicable law.[21] In the case of *ADC Affiliate* v. *Hungary*, facing the BIT's explicit agreement to apply the host state's law to the calculation of compensation for expropriation, the arbitration tribunal directly excluded the application of the host state's law to other disputed matters, emphasizing its position that international law shall be applied preferentially except for special agreements in the BIT.[22] Second, the influence of the host state's law is diluted by its combination with international law. In the case of *Antoine* v. *Burundi*, the arbitration tribunal recognized that excessive restrictions on the host state's law will lead to an imbalance of interests in the investment arbitration regime.[23] Therefore, when settling disputes, the host state's law and international law are often used in combination. In this process, in applying the host state's law at the parties' choice, the arbitration tribunal emphasized the supplementary, corrective and even restrictive function of international law.

This tendency to exclude and restrict the application of the host state's law has occurred frequently in ICSID arbitration practices in recent years. In *Kim and others* v. *Uzbekistan*, even though the host state, following perceived violation by the investors, interpreted the BIT in accordance with the VCLT, the arbitration tribunal, while demonstrating the applicability

17 ICSID, *Documents Concerning the Origin and Formulation of the Convention*, 1968, para. 39.

18 See Emmanuel Gaillard and Yas Banifatemi, "The Meaning of 'and' in Article 42(1), Second Sentence of the ICSID Convention: The Role of International Law in the ICSID Choice of Law Process" (2003) 18 *ICSID Review-Foreign Investment Law Journal* 375, 399–411.

19 Jarrod Hepburn, *Domestic Law in International Investment Arbitration* (Oxford University Press 2017) 193.

20 M. Sornarajah, *The International Law on Foreign Investment* (2nd edition, Cambridge University Press 2004) 233.

21 *Wena Hotels Ltd.* v. *Arab Republic of Egypt*, ICSID Case No. ARB/98/4, Ad Hoc Committee Decision on Application for Annulment, 2002, *ICSID Report*, Vol. 6, 2004, p. 933.

22 *ADC Affiliate Limited and ADC & ADMC Management Limited* v. *The Republic of Hungary*, ICSID Case No. ARB/03/16, Award, paras. 288–293 (2006).

23 *Antoine Goetz and others* v. *Republic of Burundi*, ICSID Case No. ARB/95/3, Award, para. 98 (1999).

of the VCLT,[24] still rejected the host state's defense on the vague ground that investors had conducted investment activities in accordance with the host state's law and had not seriously damaged the interests of the host state, deliberately avoiding the application of the host state's law.[25] Although Philippe Sands, the arbitrator in this case, held in a dissenting opinion that the host state's law should be considered and applied in combination with relevant international laws[26] based on the opinions of the arbitration tribunal in the case of *Urbaser* v. *Argentina*,[27] this view was not supported or adopted by other arbitrators. In the case of *Bear Creek Mining* v. *Peru*, the host state proposed that the host state's local law should be treated differently from international law. However, the arbitration tribunal rejected this view.[28] Therefore, in ICSID arbitration, even if the ICSID Convention and the BIT both stipulate that the host state's law can be applied, the arbitration tribunal often evades the application of the host state's law. Even if the host state's law has to be applied, other methods have often been employed to control the influence of the host state's law to a minimum level.

Apart from the application of the host state's law in ICSID arbitration, relevant cases also show an ICSID arbitration tribunal's inclination toward investors in the interpretation and application of umbrella clauses and MFN treatment clauses.[29] Investment arbitration tribunals' expansive but conflicting interpretations have technically turned substantive standards in the BITs such as the fair and equitable treatment standard into a "black box full of surprises,"[30] which has made the sovereignty of host states more vulnerable while potentially creating a safer investment environment for foreign investors. The discrepancies between varying interpretative approaches have turned into sheer chaos,[31] which has been labeled a legitimacy crisis of the ISDS system, calling for the taking of urgent and effective measures to end the possible manipulation of these substantive standards offering stability and predictability conducive to the host state's regulation over health, environment and other economic, regulatory and social issues.[32]

As a result of the vagueness of substantive terms in a large number of BITs, the inconsistent interpretative techniques applied by a large number of arbitration tribunals probably with the preset objective of offering better rights protection to foreign investors as well as the lack of independence of ISDS owing to a close-knit community of party-appointed international arbitrators,[33] the ISDS system has left varying negative impressions on users and commentators.

24 The Vienna Convention on the Law of Treaties, adopted and opened for signature on May 23, 1969, entered into force January 27, 1980 (1155 United Nations Treaty Series 331) was acceded to by Kazakhstan on January 5, 1994 and by Uzbekistan on July 12, 1995.

25 *Pavel Borissov, Aibar Burkitbayev, Almas Chukin and others* v. *Republic of Uzbekistan*, ICSID Case No. ARB/13/6, Decision on Jurisdiction, para. 413, 541(2017).

26 See *Pavel Borissov, Aibar Burkitbayev, Almas Chukin and others* v. *Republic of Uzbekistan*, ICSID Case No. ARB/13/6, Partial Dissenting Opinion Professor Philippe Sands QC, para. 10 (2017).

27 See *Urbaser S.A. and Consorcio de Aguas Bilbao Bizkaia, Bilbao Biskaia Ur Partuergoa* v. *The Argentine Republic*, ICSID Case No. ARB/07/26, Award, para. 1199 (2016).

28 See *Bear Creek Mining Corporation* v. *Republic of Peru*, ICSID Case No. ARB/14/21, Award, paras. 267–269 (2017).

29 See Gabriel Egli, "Don't Get Bit: Addressing ICSID's Inconsistent Application of Most-Favored-Nation Clauses to Dispute Resolution Provisions" (2007) 34 *Pepperdine Law Review* 1045, 1084.

30 Roland Kläger, "Revising Treatment Standards: Fair and Equitable Treatment in Light of Sustainable Development" in Steffen Hindelang and Markus Krajewski (eds.) *Shifting Paradigms in International Investment Law* (Oxford University Press 2016) 67.

31 Sébastien Manciaux, "The Notion of Investment: New Controversies" (2008) 9 *Journal World Investment and Trade* 443, 444.

32 Clara Picasso Achaval, "Tipping the Balance Towards Investors" (2008) 9 *Journal World Investment and Trade* 147, 162.

33 Susan Karamanian, "International Decision, Compania de Aguas del Aconquija S.A. & Vivendi Universal S.A. v Argentine Republic" (2011) 105 *American Journal of International Law* 553, 555.

Some cases may have indicated a tendency that investors from wealthy states were equipped with more power over the governments of less wealthy host states while other cases may have justified the existence and utility of ISDS as a tool for protecting foreign investors from opportunistic actions like expropriations in host states without strong rule of law and legal institutions. Consequently, both accusations may be in existence simultaneously – weak or poor host states are fighting large multinational companies while private entities are fighting arbitrary actions taken by developing states. Increasing public disapproval has shaken public confidence over ISDS and caused public outcry.

9.1.1.2 Developing States' Withdrawal from the ICSID

It is precisely the excessive investor protection in ICSID arbitration that causes more states' dissatisfaction with this regime. In light of relevant statistics, over the past thirty years, Latin American states, represented by Argentina and Bolivia, have been among the top respondent states in ICSID arbitration cases. The large amount of compensation arising from investment arbitration cases became a vital factor affecting these countries' economic development. Since 2007, Bolivia, Ecuador, Venezuela and other states have announced their decisions to withdraw from the ICSID Convention. Argentina was to reconsider its participation in the ICSID regime because more than sixty arbitration cases have dragged down its economic development.[34]

There has been a domino effect in Latin America. After having entered into twenty-three BITs, Bolivia denounced the ICSID Convention in 2007. After the new Constitution of Bolivia was enacted, the government announced its plan to denounce and renegotiate the existing BITs as they were deemed to be contrary to the new Constitution. Ecuador's denunciation was notified in July 2009 and came into effect in January 2010.[35]

Venezuela announced its withdrawal in late January 2012; it became effective in July 2012. The Foreign Ministry's 2012 press-release points out that the country acceded to the ICSID Convention in 1993 by "a decision of a provisional and weak government, devoid of popular legitimacy, and under the pressure of transnational economic sectors involved in the dismantling of Venezuela's national sovereignty."[36]

The increasing importance of Latin American states before ICSID proceedings and, more importantly, the unfavorable decisions rendered toward them probably justify the denunciation of the ICSID Convention by these countries and explain the regional discussions around having an alternative regional framework to deal with the ISDS system under the auspices of the World Bank. As of May 2013, Latin American countries were parties in 81 out of 262 cases concluded (approximately 31 percent). Of the 167 cases still pending, 73 of them were against Latin American countries (approximately 44 percent).[37] Argentina alone had 25 of the 167 pending cases, and it had already drafted a bill, dated March 21, 2012, indicating its

[34] See Charity L. Goodman, "Uncharted Waters: Financial Crisis and Enforcement of ICSID Awards in Argentina" (2007) 28 *University of Pennsylvania Journal of International Economic Law* 449, 483.

[35] Silvia Karina Fiezzoni, "The Challenge of UNASUR Member Countries to Replace ICSID Arbitration" (2011) 2 *Beijing Law Review* 134, 135–136.

[36] *Gobierno Bolivariano denuncia convenio con Ciadi*, January 25, 2012, www.cadtm.org/Gobierno-Bolivariano-denuncia (accessed February 12, 2019).

[37] Nicolas Beoglin, *ICSID and Latin America: Criticisms, Withdrawals and Regional Alternatives*, Comm for the Abolition of Third World Debt, July 4, 2013.

plan to exit.[38] Since 2001 when the Argentine economy collapsed, Argentina has faced forty-three claims that amount to approximately USD 65 billion in damages. The ICSID has awarded claimants over USD 400 million.[39] Many states of the American hemisphere remain distant from the ICSID – Canada, Cuba, Mexico and the Dominican Republic have not ratified the ICSID Convention, while Costa Rica signed the ICSID Convention in 1982 but ratified it twelve years later.

The withdrawals from the ICSID by Bolivia, Ecuador, Venezuela and Argentina and their termination of BITs[40] are not only a radical expression of these countries' dissatisfaction with the ICSID Convention-centered regime but also a dramatic portrayal of a broader trend to revisit key aspects of international investment law. The exit from the ICSID Convention and the global forum for the settlement of investment disputes signals these countries' loss of faith in the ISDS system. Although their withdrawal from the ICSID Convention does not entirely block future international investment arbitration against these countries, their denouncing the ICSID Convention does send a political message to show their refusal to cooperate in the ICSID-centered regime in the future and, more realistically, that, in situations where these countries are host states, foreign investors will not be able to claim damages against them in ICSID tribunals.

Some scholars have therefore pointed out that the Calvo Doctrine, which was the root foundation against an international minimum standard of treatment for aliens,[41] and was once popular in Latin American states, has not died out and is possible to revive and resist in a mildly radical way.[42] In this sense, the Calvo Doctrine still has value in contemporary international law even though the ICSID or the BIT is said to be a superior solution.[43] Amid the inherent tension, the BIT network and the Calvo Doctrine manage to strike a balance in the framework of international investment. The Calvo Doctrine, conforming with every tenet of conventional international law,[44] pushes for stronger hosting governments with sovereign control over foreign investment, but the BIT law and practice counteract sovereign states[45] and constitute obstacles to sovereign regulation.[46] While the ICSID in its operation has indicated its mechanical or even institutional defects as an arbitration machinery and an instrument of international public policy,[47] the Calvo Doctrine has emerged as a vital institutional source and theoretical basis for the "return" of developing states in the field of international investment.

[38] Bill of Argentina Congress dates April 21, 2012. Text of the draft of that bill available at www1.hcdn.gov.ar/proyxml/expediente.asp?fundamentos=si&numexp=1311-D-2012 (accessed February 29, 2019).

[39] "Come and Get Me," *The Economist*, February 18, 2012.

[40] In 2008, Ecuador terminated nine BITs – with Cuba, the Dominican Republic, El Salvador, Guatemala, Honduras, Nicaragua, Paraguay, Romania and Uruguay.

[41] Hepburn, *Domestic Law in International Investment Arbitration*, 193.

[42] Wenhua Shan, "Is Calvo Dead?" (2007) 55 *American Journal of Comparative Law* 123, 163 (2007).

[43] See Ibrahim F. I. Shihata, "Towards a Greater Depoliticization of Investment Disputes: The Roles of ICSID and MIGA" (1986) 1 *ICSID Review-Foreign Investment Law Journal* 1, 24–25.

[44] John Linarelli, Margot E. Salomon, and M. Sornarajah, *The Misery of International Law: Confrontations with Injustice in the Global Economy* (Oxford University Press 2018) 156.

[45] Jorge A. Huerta Goldman, "Domestic, Regional and Multilateral Investment Liberalization" in Zdenek Drabek and Petros C. Mavroidis, *Regulations of Foreign Investment: Challenges to International Harmonization* (World Scientific 2013) 87.

[46] Federico Ortino, "Public Services, Investment Liberalization and Protection" in Zdenek Drabek and Petros C. Mavroidis, *Regulations of Foreign Investment: Challenges to International Harmonization* (World Scientific 2013) 415.

[47] ICSID, Annual Report (1984) 5.

Apart from the revival of the Calvo Doctrine and the withdrawal of many Latin American states from the ICSID regime, emerging economies as non-parties to the ICSID such as India, Brazil and South Africa,[48] which have become increasingly crucial in the field of international investment in recent years, have also restricted or even excluded the use of the ISDS regime by updating their model BITs and amending their domestic laws. The decline or rise of the Calvo Doctrine suggests the leaving (or retreat) or return of the state when it comes to settling its disputes with foreign investors. The changing role of the Calvo Doctrine indicates the uncertainty of its application, which is likely related to the host state's view on sovereignty. Nevertheless, the principle of diplomatic protection remains part of the realities of international law.[49]

For example, India's model BIT published in 2016 contains full restrictions on the ISDS mechanism. On the one hand, the model BIT strongly emphasizes local remedies such as administrative and judicial tribunals that foreign investors have to rely on in resolving investment disputes with the Indian government after their rights are damaged.[50] Meanwhile, India believes that the international arbitration tribunal has no right to review the judicial decisions of sovereign states, thus denying international agencies the right to review the decisions of their own courts.[51] Although the model BIT allows the ICSID to intervene in disputes "on the premise that both parties are members of ICSID,"[52] the fact that India is not a member of the ICSID and has no intention of joining in the years to come makes this provision meaningless. India embarked on a policy of terminating its BITs in 2017, and has terminated more than sixty BITs.[53]

As another example, Brazil signed a number of BITs as early as the 1990s. However, its congress did not approve these BITs in order to safeguard its right to regulate foreign capital. Brazil showed no interest in ratifying the ICSID or any BIT despite having signed some BITs and even though Brazil named the ICSID Secretary-General the "appointing authority" of arbitrators in some guarantee agreements executed by Brazil in favor of foreign lenders to Brazilian public entities.[54] Since the new century, Brazil also has a cooperation and investment facilitation agreements (CIFA) regime for its own interests in addition to the ICSID regime, continuing its consistent position of safeguarding its right to regulate foreign capital and restricting foreign investors' right to sue. Therefore, some scholars believe that Brazil's investment dispute settlement mechanism (IDSM) intends to return to the international customary law of diplomatic protection.[55] Take one example. The bilateral investment agreement between India and Brazil does not use investor–state arbitration but requires an ombudsman to conduct state-to-state arbitration.[56]

48 By the end of January 2019, India, Brazil and South Africa had not joined ICSID. See ICSID, https://icsid.worldbank.org/en/Pages/about/Member-States.aspx (accessed January 31, 2019).

49 Shihata, "Towards a Greater Depoliticization of Investment Disputes," 1, 3.

50 2016 Model Text for the Indian Bilateral Investment Treaty, Arts. 15.1, 15.2, 15.4, 15.5.

51 Ibid., at Art. 13.5.

52 Ibid., at Art. 16.1.

53 Nish Shetty, "Treaty Protection for Indian Investments Abroad: The Changed Landscape," May 29, 2019, www.cliffordchance.com/briefings/2019/05/treaty_protectionforindianinvestmentsabroad.html (accessed April 5, 2021) at 2.

54 Georges R. Delaume, "ICSID and the Banker" (1983) 2 *International Financial Law Review* 9, 13.

55 Sonia E. Rolland, "The Return of State Remedies in Investor-State Dispute Settlement: Trends in Developing Countries" (2017) 49 *Loyola University Chicago Law Journal* 387, 395-399.

56 See Rohit Bhat, "Will India Do Away with Investor State Arbitration?," August 23, 2017, http://arbitrationblog.kluwerarbitration.com/2017/08/23/will-india-away-investor-state-arbitration/ (accessed January 30, 2019).

In the meantime, South Africa has also conducted in recent years a large number of reviews over those BITs signed in the last century and found that quite a number of BITs are inconsistent with its own investment policies and Constitution.[57] Therefore, after 2010, South Africa terminated BITs with Germany, Switzerland, the Netherlands and other states, and explicitly excluded ISDS in the Investment Protection Act promulgated in 2015,[58] further strengthening its right to regulate foreign capital, in a bid to protect South Africa from the legal risks of being sued by foreign investors. South Africa has decided to modernize its investment protection regime in a manner that balances strong protection for investors with constitutional requirements to safeguard the public interest and promote sustainable development and inclusive growth. This has involved developing a new investment bill that strengthens and clarifies protection provided to all investors in South Africa as well as terminating BITs that pose unacceptable risks to democratic policy-making in South Africa, without delivering any discernible economic benefit. The EU views such a move as hostile and symptomatic of "emerging protectionism" in South Africa, which, however, argues that the Constitution is the supreme law of the law and is sufficient to offer protection to foreign investors. The host state government can either screen foreign investment by relying on a national security review or designate some sectors of the economy as strategic so as to keep them off-limits to foreign investors.

More countries have been and are in the process of reviewing their model BITs and renegotiating existing BITs for the purpose of striking a new balance between foreign investors and home states.

Latin American countries had a strong tradition of keeping a distance from the World Bank and the ICSID in the 1960s and 1970s when almost all of these countries voted against the idea of having the ICSID. Terminating BITs itself is an exercise of a host state's sovereign power. On March 11, 2011, Bolivia, Colombia, Ecuador, Peru, Argentina, Brazil, Paraguay, Uruguay, Chile, Guyana, Suriname and Venezuela formed the Union of South American Nations (UNASUR), one of whose future goals is to establish an international investment arbitration forum that recognizes the distinct nature of these emerging economies.[59] The proposed framework includes various Latin America-favoring components such as hearings being held in an official South American language, the forum being used after the exhaustion of local remedies, transparency with documents and hearings being made available, and an appeal system.[60]

9.1.1.3 Developed States' Rising Opposition to ISDS

Apart from the challenges raised by developing states toward ISDS, developed states represented by the USA and the member states of the EU have also joined the ranks opposing the current ISDS regime. As the world's major capital-exporting state, the USA has long played the role of the largest home state of claimants in ICSID arbitration.[61] Nevertheless, the USA

57 See Jonathan Lang and Bowman Gilfillan, "Bilateral Investment Treaties – A Shield or A Sword?," pp. 2–3, November 8, 2013, www.bowmanslaw.com/wp-content/uploads/2016/09/PPI-article_mailshot_08112013_1038389_1-1.pdf (accessed January 9, 2019).

58 Protection of Investment Act (Act No. 22/2015) (S. Afr.).

59 Katia Fach Gomez, "Latin American Approach to International Dispute Resolution, American Society of International Law Meeting in Washington," March 25, 2011, www.academia.edu/830249/latin_American_Approaches-to_International_Dispute_Resolution (accessed January 9, 2019).

60 Ibid.

61 UNCTAD, *World Investment Report 2018*, p. 93, June 6, 2018, https://unctad.org/en/PublicationsLibrary/wir2018_en.pdf (accessed December 11, 2019).

has also come to recognize the legal risks of ISDS. In March 2018, US Trade Representative Robert Lighthizer testified before Congress that the reason why the US government opposes the inclusion of the mandatory ISDS clauses in the NAFTA renegotiation is that it severely damages US national sovereignty and will put the US at great legal risk. In the meantime, at present, ISDS has also been criticized by many parties, and the USA does not have to continue to cheer for the regime.[62]

As early as 2004, Australia rejected the inclusion of ISDS in the Australia–US Free Trade Agreement (AUSFTA).[63] The ISDS was excluded by Australia and New Zealand in a side letter to the Australia–New Zealand–Association of South East Asian Nations (ASEAN) FTA 2009 and a bilateral protocol in 2011. Australia stated in its trade policy statement in 2011 that it would not include the ISDS clauses in new BITs and regional FTAs. One of the important reasons given was that Australia spent the counsel fee of USD 39 million in the case of *Philip Morris* v. *Australia*, which greatly wasted public funds and aroused public resentment and government vigilance. The official reason for omitting ISA from Australia's FTAs with the USA and New Zealand was the adequate remedies available under local laws through courts in the counterparty states.[64]

However, the rejection of ISDS by Australia was short-lived, and Australia gave consent to ISDS in the treaty after 2013 on a case-by-case basis. It adopted an ISDS mechanism in the Japan–Australia Economic Partnership Agreement 2014[65] and the CPTPP.[66] No mention was made of investor–state arbitration in the Investment Protocol to Australia and New Zealand's Comprehensive Economic Relation and Trade Agreement.

In the past, Australian governments have sought the inclusion of ISDS procedures in trade agreements with developing countries at the behest of Australian businesses. The Australian government has discontinued this practice. The Australian government does not support provisions that would confer greater legal rights on foreign businesses than those available to domestic businesses. Nor will the government support provisions that would constrain the ability of Australian governments to make laws on social, environmental and economic matters in circumstances where those laws do not discriminate between domestic and foreign businesses. The government has not and will not accept provisions that limit its capacity to put health warnings or plain packaging requirements on tobacco products or its ability to continue the Pharmaceutical Benefits Scheme.[67] If Australian businesses are concerned about sovereign risk in Australian trading partner countries, they will need to make their own assessments about whether they want to commit to investing in those countries.[68]

62 See *Brady-Lighthizer ISDS Exchange*, International Economic Law and Policy Blog, March 21, 2018, https://worldtradelaw.typepad.com/ielpblog/2018/03/brady-lighthizer-isds-exchange.html (accessed January 23, 2019).

63 Although no consent to ISDS is given by either party, it is stated that the treaty parties will consult on the possible creation of ISDS procedures. AUSFTAC, Art. 11.16.

64 Luke Nottage and Kate Miles, "'Back to the Future' for Investor-State Arbitrations: Revising Rules in Australia and Japan for Public Interests" (2009) 26(1) *Journal of International Arbitration* 25.

65 Japan–Australia Economic Partnership Agreement 2014, Art. 14.19.1.

66 CPTPP, chapter 9. New Zealand, Canada and Chile explicitly excluded the settlement of investment disputes with investors from specific states through ISDS by way of having explicit appendices.

67 Australia Government, *Department of Foreign Aff. & Trade, Gillard Government Trade Policy Statement: Trading Our Way to More Jobs and Prosperity*, April 14, 2011, www.dfat.gov.au/publications/trade/trading-our-way-to-more-jobs-and-prosperity.html (accessed February 15, 2019).

68 Department of Foreign Affairs and Trade, *Gillard Government Trade Policy Statement: Trading Our Way to More Jobs and Prosperity*, April 2011, p. 14, www.acci.asn.au/getattachment/b9d3cfae-fc0c-4c2a-a3df-3f58228daf6d/Gillard-Government-Trade-Policy-Statement.aspx (accessed December 19, 2018).

Accordingly, Australia excluded certain categories of measure from ISDS claims including denial of benefits provisions for tobacco control measures[69] and public health measures.[70]

Canada's non-participation in the ongoing ISDS mechanisms established by Annexes 14-D and 14-E in the United States–Mexico–Canada Agreement (USMCA) broke it from its previous IIAs that have included ISDS clauses. Opting out of ISDS under the USMCA also means that Canada no longer has to face claims from US investors once the period for legacy claims expires three years after the termination of NAFTA.[71] Accordingly, only the USA and Mexico are subject to the ISDS mechanism under the USMCA, though the Mexican investor may bring a claim against Canada under the CPTPP. However, only the USA and Mexico give consent to a narrow scope of claims only with respect to expropriations (but excluding indirect expropriations), or for breach of the obligations to accord NT or MFN treatment (but excluding claims relating to the establishment or acquisition of investments).

After the Treaty of Lisbon was passed, the power of EU member states to sign BITs was exclusively possessed and controlled by the European Commission, which also began to reassess the ISDS system and responded to the reform of the modern international investment law regime. The EU has been calling for reform of ISDS in recent years, especially in the relevant discussions organized by UNCITRAL, and has clearly pointed out the main problems of the ISDS regime. First, there is a lack of consistency in the interpretation and application of a series of provisions such as the MFN clause and the umbrella clause by investment arbitration tribunals, making investment arbitration less predictable. Second, IIAs are supposed to be not merely concerned with the private interests of investors but linked with the sovereign acts of the host states.[72] However, the investment arbitration tribunals have consistently shown a selective contempt for the sovereign matters of the host states in their long-term investment arbitration practice and have failed to effectively grasp the scale of protection. Third, the lack of a necessary appeal regime makes ISDS lose its ability to self-correct. Even with the annulment mechanism under the ICSID Convention, its practical functionality is rather limited. Fourth, arbitrators play a key role in ISDS. However, the appointment of arbitrators under this regime is often made *ex post* the dispute. When appointing arbitrators, the host state also takes its own interests into account and ignores its public law functions as a sovereign state, which makes the arbitration tribunal lack impartiality in interpreting and applying treaties. Fifth, as the investment arbitration tribunal is not a permanent international organization, huge costs have been involved in maintaining the operation of the whole system.[73] Sixth, the current ISDS is derived from commercial arbitration which mainly deals with commercial disputes. As a result, the ISDS system does not have appropriate institutional arrangements for the checks and balances of public power so as to ensure transparency and fairness. However, the parties to ISDS are sovereign states, and relevant states are obliged to disclose details of their participation in judicial activities, which is the obligation of public organs to their nationals. Despite the fact that relevant international organizations have made great efforts to this end in the past few years, most

69 CPTPP, Art. 29.5

70 The Indonesia–Australia Comprehensive Economic Partnership Agreement, Art. 14.21.1(b).

71 USMCA, Annex 14-C paragraph 3.

72 Anthea Roberts, "Clash of Paradigms: Actors and Analogies Shaping the Investment Treaty System" (2013) 107 *American Journal of International Law* 45, 45–47.

73 See David Gaukrodger and Kathryn Gordon, "Investor-State Dispute Settlement: A Scoping Paper for the Investment Policy Community," OECD Working Papers on International Investment (OECD Publishing 2012) 19.

investors do not wish to make excessive disclosure of arbitration proceedings for commercial concerns, which makes ISDS lack transparency.[74]

In January 2018, the EU further put forward the hope of establishing an effective dispute avoidance regime in its proposal for multilateral reform of ISDS submitted to UNCITRAL,[75] and also came up with new proposals on the relationship between the permanent investment dispute settlement institution and the parties.[76] Meanwhile, the EU also attempts to follow the multilateral discussion and multi-track approach in promoting the reform in an orderly manner, so as to promote the reform of ISDS regime to reach a consensus among all the parties. Apart from voicing support for the reform of ISDS, the EU has been committed to establishing a new international IDSM in recent years. The draft investment chapter of the Transatlantic Trade and Investment Partnership (TTIP) published by the European Commission in 2015 represents the main position of the EU on the current modern international investment law regime. The EU believes that the defects exposed by ISDS are no longer suitable for the twenty-first century.[77] It then proposes to establish an investment court premised on sovereign states as a feasible regime for settling investment disputes. The EU's idea of an investment court directly points to the disadvantages of the current ISDS. First of all, in the scope of actionable disputes, the EU hopes to grant the contracting parties comprehensive rights to regulate in the fields of public safety, environmental protection and consumer rights protection, among others, emphasizing that disputes in these fields can only be resolved through the contracting parties' own judicial channels. Moreover, the EU wishes to prevent the arbitration tribunal from interpreting the treaty arbitrarily under the ISDS regime by establishing a political body authorized by the contracting parties to interpret the investment treaties in a uniform manner. Further, the EU hopes to change the regime of appointing arbitrators by both disputing parties to disputes under the ISDS to tenured judges publicly appointed by the investment court so as to strengthen the legitimacy of the dispute settlement mechanism and the effectiveness and consistency of the rulings thereof.[78] Finally, the EU proposes to change the status quo of the finality of arbitral awards under the ISDS system and to enhance the self-corrective capability of the IDSM by setting up a feasible appeal regime.

9.1.1.4 South–North Divide in ISDS Reform

The contrasting versions of the ISDS and its operations in reality confirm a plurality of conflicting interests of multiple stakeholders using ISDS and, more importantly, a power

74 See UNCITRAL, *Possible Reform of Investor-State Dispute Settlement (ISDS) Submission from the EU*, A/CN.9/WG.III/WP.145, pp. 7–12, December 12, 2017, https://documents-dds-ny.un.org/doc/UNDOC/LTD/V17/088/32/PDF/V1708832.pdf?OpenElement (accessed November 12, 2018).

75 See EU, *Submission of the European Union and Its Member States to UNCITRAL Working Group III: Establishing a Standing Mechanism for the Settlement of International Investment Disputes*, pp. 4–9, January 18, 2019, http://trade.ec.europa.eu/doclib/docs/2019/january/tradoc_157631.pdf (accessed January 20, 2019).

76 See EU, *Submission of the European Union and Its Member States to UNCITRAL Working Group III: Possible Work Plan for Working Group III*, p. 2, January 18, 2019, http://trade.ec.europa.eu/doclib/docs/2019/january/tradoc_157632.pdf (accessed January 20, 2019).

77 Cecilia Malmstrom, "Investments in TTIP and Beyond: Towards an International Investment Court," May 5, 2015, http://trade.ec.europa.eu/doclib/docs/2015/may/tradoc_153408.PDF (accessed December 23, 2018).

78 See EU Parliament, *TTIP: Ease Access to US Market, Protect EU Standards, Reform Dispute Settlement*, July 8, 2015, http://documents.nam.org/IEA/EU%20Parliament%20Press%20release%20July%202015.pdf (accessed December 18, 2018).

imbalance underlying the ISDS system in the form of legal battles. The tribunals' pro-claimant or pro-respondent attitudes are the dominant determinant reviving power politics in international investment and consequently shaping the direction of reconstructing or improving the workings of the ICSID system or international investment law more generally.[79] The core design features of BITs and international investment arbitration that the ICSID attempted to achieve were to mitigate imbalances between foreign investors and host states, the typical South–North divide, which can destabilize power balances between capital-importing and exporting states.[80] ICSID arbitration nevertheless maintains a restrictive policy toward the diplomatic espousal of investment claims by more powerful states, the unexpected consequence of which is to empower foreign investors and create new power imbalances between foreign investors and host states.

The side effect of the ISDS system is over-privatization of ISDS, which can be corrected and rebalanced toward a constructive relationship between foreign investors and host states. Given this private–public divide in nature,[81] this rebalancing trend is mainly reflected and evidenced by the return of the state movement in which host states, either developed or developing ones, are trying to liberate or restore their autonomy, authority or state sovereignty by taking these back from the private parties in ISDS proceedings at least in the field of regulating foreign investment in conformity with their internal police power and public interests. Influenced by this public–private tension, a pragmatic shift from the ICSID system to domestic courts may be an alternative solution or technical response to the public's dissatisfaction with the ISDS including the ICSID, which was seen as a sacrifice for more corporate sovereignty. The rebalancing or repoliticization in the spectrum of sovereignty in the ISDS system appears to be for the general good of the world even though it may be labeled as conservative or nationalistic in nature.[82]

In short, facing the restrictions on the host state's power exposed in ICSID arbitration in recent years, whether developing economies withdraw from and evade the ISDS regime or developed economies attempt to reshape the IDSM, they all emphasize due respect for national sovereignty. This series of measures is rooted in the sovereignty of all states while nurturing and strengthening sovereignty simultaneously. The trend of the "return" of states at the procedural level of international investment law has already taken shape. In contrast to the depoliticization process in which the states were leaving their sovereignty with the aim of mitigating the tensions between the North and the South,[83] the repoliticization movement is an effort to address the distorted tensions between the private and public spheres in the international investment arena. Despite these resistance or withdrawals, it is also asserted that investment claims do not lead to systematic treaty design or institutional changes largely, from an institutional perspective, because of the nonstate constituency with a deep interest in the ISDS mechanism.[84]

79 Sergio Puig and Anton Strezhnev, "The David Effect and ISDS" (2017) 28 *European Journal of International Law* 731, 739.

80 See Arseni Matveev, "Investor-State Dispute Settlement: The Evolving Balance between Investor Protection and State Sovereignty" (2015–2016) 40 *University of Western Australia Law Review* 348, 386.

81 Leon E. Trakman, "The ICSID under Siege" (2013) 45 *Cornell International Law Journal* 603, 649.

82 Wenhua Shan, "From North-South Divide to Private-Public Debate: Revival of the Calvo Doctrine and the Changing Landscape in International Investment Law" (2006–2007) 27 *Northwestern Journal of International Law and Business* 631, 632.

83 Ibironke T. Odumosu, "The Law and Politics of Engaging Resistance in Investment Dispute Settlement" (2007) 26 *Penn State International Law Review* 251, 257.

84 Taylor St John, *The Rise of Investor-State Arbitration: Politics, Law, and Unintended Consequences* (Oxford University Press 2018) 234–235.

9.1.2 *Anti-liberalization Transformation of FIL in the Post-Financial Crisis Era*

The state's "return" to the international investment law regime is superficially a rebound of its practice through the ISDS system of attaching more importance to the protection of foreign investors' rights and interests than the host state's sovereignty in the past several decades. Deeper down, it is a reflection and transformation of the regulatory framework of cross-border capital flows and investment activities in various states after the global financial crisis of 2008. The return of the state in international investment law apparently is a revival of the Calvo Doctrine (in any guise),[85] as a result of investment arbitration being seen as a divestment of judicial powers from national courts to unaccountable but overreached tribunals.

9.1.2.1 Changing Patterns of FDI and FDI Regulation

The international investment law regime formed on the basis of the "leaving" (or retreat) of states effectively facilitated the liberalization of global investment and stimulated the economic takeoff of developing states in the 1980s and 1990s. The assumption of the neoliberal vision is that global and national benefits accrue through the package of legal reform measures (or international law of liberalization) because of the demand for liberalized markets[86] and liberalized flows of assets and investments around the world.[87] However, as shown in Figure 9.1, along with the in-depth development of international investment in recent years, especially the economic recession in developed states since the latest global financial crisis, the economic gap between the North and the South has been continuously narrowing. Especially, the developing states represented by emerging states are catching up or even competing with the developed states in FDI, making developed states begin to be on guard.

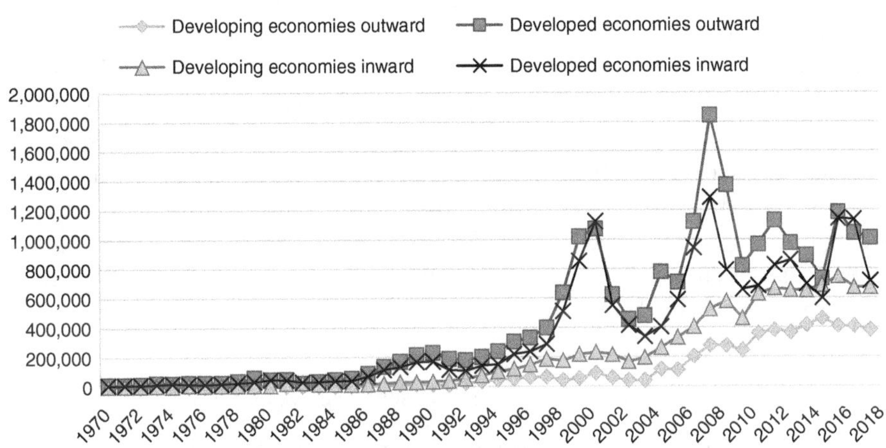

FIGURE 9.1 Developed/developing countries' annual FDI flows (1970–2018)[88]

[85] Rodrigo Polanco Lazo, "The No of Tokyo Revisited: Or How Developed Countries Learned to Start Worrying and Love the Calvo Doctrine" (2015) 30 *ICSID Review-Foreign Investment Law Journal* 172, 173–174.

[86] Froese, *Sovereign Rules and the Politics of International Economic Law*, 41.

[87] Linarelli, Salomon and Sornarajah, *The Misery of International Law*, 151, 159.

[88] Based on data available at UNCTAD, available at UNCTAD Data Center, http://unctadstat.unctad.org/wds/TableViewer/tableView.aspx?ReportId=96740 (accessed January 17, 2019).

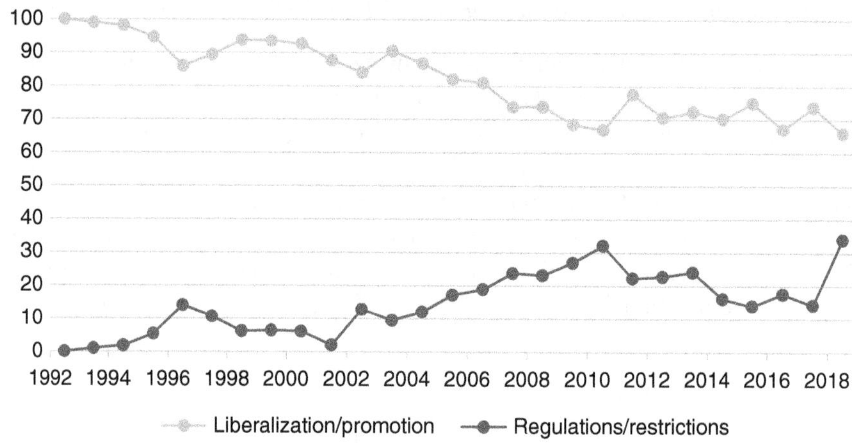

FIGURE 9.2 Changes in national investment policies (1992–2019)[89]

From a global point of view, the rise of developing or emerging states in the field of international investment has deprived developed states of their original dominant position, which is leading to a policy transformation of various states tightening up their regulation of foreign capital or investment.[90] As shown in Figure 9.2, the global financial crisis and the emerging states' rise to become more important players in FDI have resulted in a sweeping change to investment-related policies and measures, gradually shifting from the liberalization stance of the 1990s evidenced by deregulation over investment with less protectionist measures in the context of major liberalization processes to a restrictive or nationalistic position connecting the dispute settlement back to politics instead of law.

The arguments against liberalization have been made on the basis of various concerns including weak domestic industries being crowded out, negative impacts on social welfare and equality, and detriments to sovereign regulation over foreign investment, among others.[91] Especially before and after the 2008 financial crisis, the (populist) ideology and policy arguments underpinning anti-liberalization surfaced again. Consequently, a policy-tightening trend became more obvious, and the policy was not relaxed until 2014. Nevertheless, the position of intervention and restriction of foreign investment has not yet returned to the level of the 1990s. The general trend of anti-liberalization in the field of international investment is embodied in the specific changes in the domestic laws of various states regarding foreign investment supervision policies and the turn of IIAs in the direction of treaties. The mode of interaction among stakeholders in investment dispute settlement faces new challenges.

9.1.2.2 Developed States' Conservative Policy Shift

Developed states have played a vital role in tightening up international investment law in this new anti-globalization or anti-liberalization movement due to the increased regulatory

[89] The figure is the author's, based on data from *World Investment Report 2010* and *World Investment Report 2019*. See UNCTAD, World Investment Report 2010, p. 76, July 22, 2010, https://unctad.org/en/docs/wir2010_en.pdf (accessed October 11, 2018); UNCTAD, World Investment Report 2019, p. 84, https://unctad.org/en/PublicationsLibrary/wir2019_en.pdf (accessed July 11, 2019).

[90] Karl P. Sauvant, Wolfgang A. Maschek and Geraldine McAllister, Foreign Direct Investment by Emerging Market Multinational Enterprises, the Impact of the Financial Crisis and Recession and Challenges Ahead, p. 18, December 8, 2009, www.oecd.org/investment/globalforum/44246197.pdf (accessed January 11, 2019).

[91] Rudolf Dolzer and Christoph Schreuer, *Principles of International Investment Law* (2nd edition, Oxford University Press 2012) ch. V.

restrictions they have imposed on foreign investment. Structural changes in the international investment pattern have made developed states more aware of or even cautious about potential risks that foreign investors may bring into their countries in the fields of science and technology, information, finance and others. These risks and potential regulatory failures, to a certain extent, forced these states to tackle and resolve the corresponding risks by raising the market access threshold and strengthening regulation and monitoring of foreign investment activities.

In the specific field of strengthening supervision of foreign capital, relevant states mainly focus on the impact of foreign investment on national security, resources and economic order. For instance, France, Germany and Italy proposed to establish a review regime for FDI within the EU in 2017, mainly to prevent foreign investment from posing a threat to public safety or order. In October 2017, the British government released the "National Security and Infrastructure Investment Review" to comment on its proposed new structure for reviewing foreign investment.

Judging from these regulatory movements, relevant states are paying more attention to the supervision of mergers and acquisitions involving foreign investment. In light of UNCTAD's observation, in the past few years, quite a number of host governments have opposed sales of key or strategic domestic assets by domestic enterprises to foreign investors on the grounds of national security, which has become a new "protectionist drift."[92] In 2017 alone, at least ten transactions in high-tech manufacturing, financial services or telecommunications industries were canceled for regulatory or political reasons. The USA and New Zealand are the top two host states of investment, while China is the main home state of investment. According to the data in the first four months of 2018, seven mergers and acquisitions transactions were put off for national security concerns, primarily in the USA.[93] Sovereign states, including hegemonic states per se, are prioritizing "national interests."[94]

Various government reports have highlighted a number of CFIUS-related concerns. A January report by the President's Council of Advisors on Science and Technology advocated using CFIUS and export control laws to limit Chinese advances in semiconductor technology, to help the USA maintain its leader in semiconductor technology position. In November 2016, the US–China Economic and Security Review Commission issued a report to Congress recommending that Congress amend the CFIUS statute to empower CFIUS to block Chinese state-owned enterprises (SOEs) from acquiring US companies.[95]

When the Trump administration came into power, it took stricter regulatory measures against emerging economies represented by China. The Trump administration modernized the CFIUS review process by passing the Foreign Investment Risk Review Modernization Act (FIRRMA), which was the first update to the CFIUS statute in more than a decade. The FIRRMA, which came into effect in 2018, comprehensively strengthens the state's right to regulate in the field of foreign investment by expanding the review scope of national security and controlling the sharing of key technologies with emerging economies. For instance, the CFIUS is allowed to review a wider range of transactions including any "non-passive"

92 Theodore H. Moran, "Foreign Acquisitions and National Security: What Are Genuine Threats? What Are Implausible Worries? A Framework for OECD Countries, and Beyond" in Zdenek Drabek and Petros C. Mavroidis, *Regulations of Foreign Investment: Challenges to International Harmonization* (World Scientific 2013) 371.

93 See UNCTAD, *World Investment Report 2018*, pp. 83–85, June 6, 2018, https://unctad.org/en/PublicationsLibrary/wir2018_en.pdf (accessed November 12, 2018).

94 Ernst Ulrich Petersmann, *Multilevel Constitutionalism for Multilevel Governance of Public Goods: Methodology Problems in International Law* (Hart 2017) 9.

95 Patrick Griffin, "CFIUS in the Age of Chinese Investment" (2017) 85 *Fordham Law Review* 1757, 1787.

investment in the US firms involved in critical technology or other sensitive sectors. The effect of FIRRMA includes potentially longer timelines, the disclosure of more material agreements related to the transaction under review in the notice, and mandatory declarations of whether a transaction is covered or foreign government controlled. Although FIRRMA does not name China per se, likely additional types of Chinese investment would be subject to CFIUS review.[96] FIRRMA impacts both investments directly by Chinese entities and investments by non-Chinese entities that might have significant ties to China. FIRRMA's key concerns include proximity to sensitive US government facilities, sensitive personal data, critical infrastructure, critical technology, and technology transfer to China.[97] State-directed and state-funded investment in these areas will be particularly highly scrutinized.

FIRRMA does allow for greater information sharing with US state and local governments and foreign allied governments. CFIUS's formal process for information sharing reflects a broader US government initiative to assist and incentivize partner countries to strengthen their own investment review mechanisms and pursue reviews of transactions of interest to the US government. Reforms have recently been enacted, or are being actively considered, in the EU, the UK, Canada, Australia and Japan, among others, and there is growing awareness and interest in investment-security issues worldwide. The USA, the EU and Japan have already formally agreed to engage in investment security with the aims of cooperation, information exchange and potential coordination.[98] With respect to specific transactions, the increasingly close collaboration on investment-security matters among governments means that in the future certain transactions could face (somewhat) coordinated review across multiple jurisdictions. The potential harmonization of investment-security review processes is an area to watch.

The EU has also stressed the importance of foreign investment monitoring in recent years. Specifically, the EU emphasizes effective implementation of existing investment laws in Europe. For example, in the field of energy such as electricity and natural gas, it should strengthen the maintenance of the safety of relevant infrastructure and attach great importance to the integrity of property rights, so as to prevent possible operational risks. For another example, in the aviation sector, it has always stressed the absolute control possessed by EU citizens over the equity of such enterprises (more than 50 percent); the EU is entitled to terminate this transaction when investment activities lead to the control of aviation enterprises falling into the hands of non-EU citizens and the home state of the investor has not reached an agreement with the EU in this transaction.[99] Similarly, in the exploration and production of hydroxides, the EU allows member states to refuse citizens of a third state to control related enterprises for reasons of national security.[100] Moreover, while strengthening law enforcement, the EU also did establish effective foreign direct investment screening mechanisms (FDISM).

96 Shawn Donnan, "Trump Drops New Restrictions on China Investment," *Financial Times*, June 12, 2018, www.ft.com/content/a819ec8a-79f4-11e8-8e67-1e1a0846c475.

97 See Justin Shields, "Smart Machines and Smarter Policy: Foreign Investment Regulation, National Security, and Technology Transfer in the Age of Artificial Intelligence" (2018) 51 *John Marshall Law Review* 279, 286–287.

98 Dafna H. Rand and Stephen Tankel, *Security Cooperation & Assistance: Rethinking the Return on Investment*, p. 6, August 5, 2015, www.files.ethz.ch/isn/192879/CNAS%20Report_Security%20Cooperation_FINAL.pdf (accessed February 14, 2019).

99 Directive (EU) 2016/1148 of the European Parliament and of the Council of July 6, 2016 Concerning Measures for a High Common Level of Security of Network and Information Systems across the Union.

100 Directive 94/22/EC of May 30, 1994 on the conditions for granting and using authorization for the prospection, exploration and production of hydrocarbons.

From a policy-oriented perspective, the mechanism will examine direct investment into the EU while taking public safety into consideration, and provide a non-exhaustive list to determine which direct investments will affect the EU's public security. This will emphatically prevent foreign SOEs, that are playing an increasingly vital role in current international investment,[101] from interfering in the EU's key technologies and information security. From the perspective of follow-up measures, on the one hand, the EU will formulate more detailed foreign investment supervision rules under FDISM for important strategic areas (such as energy, space, transportation) or assets (technologies and inputs linked with strategic departments, key infrastructure across departments, sensitive data) that may cause problems in areas such as safety and public order, and strengthen data analysis and case screening in evaluation. On the other hand, the EU will also set up an investment policy coordination group composed of the president of the European Commission and representatives of member states to discuss and formulate policies on issues such as public safety, environmental protection and fair competition, to ensure the effective operation of FDISM.[102]

The new legal framework includes an EU-wide framework through a combination of data collection, information exchange and peer pressure for screening of FDI by member states on grounds of security of public order, including transparency obligations, the rule of equal treatment among foreign investment of different origin and the obligation to ensure adequate redress possibilities with regard to decisions adopted under these review mechanisms. The concern over security and public order includes activities related to the operation or provision of critical technologies (such as semiconductors, robotics and artificial intelligence), infrastructure (in the energy, transport, communications, data, space and financial industries), inputs or sensitive information.

The EU also encourages international cooperation on investment screening, including sharing experience, best practices and information on issues of common concern. The move is a policy response to various concerns from some EU governments, notably France and Germany, over investment from China, giving Chinese companies access to key technologies through takeovers of European companies while at the same time protecting local firms.

9.1.3 *Shifting Focus from Investor Protection to the Right to Regulate*

Apart from the trend of anti-liberalization evidenced by the legislative and administrative measures of various states, IIAs, as legal instruments directly regulating and promoting foreign investment, have also taken on some new features in the changes of recent years. Compared with IIAs signed in the 1990s, IIAs signed or revised in recent years placed more emphasis on the host state's right to regulate, and weakened the constraints of ISDS on the host state's sovereignty. For example, in terms of the definition of investment, certain specific assets are excluded so as to limit the scope of application of the treaty; the procedural rules and obligations of the host state government are further clarified concerning expropriation and compensation clauses; and investors' rights boundaries are further clarified with respect to exchange and other issues.[103] With respect to specific direction, IIAs in recent years have

101 See UNCTAD, *World Investment Report 2017*, p. 30, June 7, 2017, https://unctad.org/en/PublicationsLibrary/wir2017_en.pdf (accessed December 15, 2018).

102 See EU Commission, *Welcoming Foreign Direct Investment while Protecting Essential Interests*, COM (2017) 494 final, p. 5.

103 UNCTAD, *World Investment Report 2018*, pp. 95–96, June 6, 2018, https://unctad.org/en/PublicationsLibrary/wir2018_en.pdf (accessed November 12, 2018).

changed the past mode of focusing solely on the protection of private interests of investors to pay more attention to nontraditional government's right to regulate such as labor treatment, environmental protection, and public safety, highlighting the interests of sovereign states.[104]

The ISDS system has been heading down a trajectory of repoliticization.[105] This is the case due to a variety of inherent features of the ISDS system. Although a dispute submitted to the ICSID for arbitration is supposed to be an investment dispute, the tribunal is often called upon to examine the legality of the host state's policies and regulation, which by their nature are political. The adjudication of investment disputes has a great "regulatory chill" impact on future policy-making and legislative activities involving the host state's public interest.

As the representative nation taking the lead in making the "leaving (of the state)" gesture and pushing forward the liberalization of international investment, the USA is showing a conceptual transformation in drafting treaties, faced with the changes in foreign investment patterns since the turn of the new century. As early as 2004, the US model BIT underwent a shift from emphasizing the protection of investors to more respect for the right to regulate of sovereign states in terms of public safety and labor treatment. Generally speaking, the model includes the protection of the right to regulate of contracting parties in terms of public safety, social policy and economic development in the BIT's objectives, while in specific provisions, it emphasizes the power of the host state with regard to environment and labor treatment,[106] allowing the host state to levy taxes due to the above factors and limiting the scope of application of NT and MFN treatment. At the same time, it values the role of local relief measures in the host state in settling investment disputes and further restricts the discretion of the investment arbitration tribunal in legal interpretation linked to the above factors.[107]

When a financial crisis or security interest is at stake, the host state is likely to interfere with so-called internal affairs, and protection takes precedence over investment obligations. As a result, these countries also have deep suspicion about global investment rules that are increasingly stacked against their interests. Their skepticism is further complicated by the growing strategic competition for economic dominance by some emerging states, typically China and some BRICS (Brazil, Russia, India and South Africa) states. Along with the economic recession in developed states due to the latest global financial crisis, the rapid economic growth in emerging states has narrowed the economic gap between the North and the South once again, thereby arousing the vigilance of developed states and intensifying their supervision of foreign investment, typically investment from emerging economies. Conventional capital-exporting states such as the USA and Canada are changing their status from capital-exporting to capital-importing states, leading to their policy shift when they are in negotiations with emerging states. Historically, their BITs with developing states were formulated to protect their own investors in foreign jurisdictions with little focus on promoting inbound investment.[108] But they are now more concerned with regulating inbound investment. Canada's Comprehensive Economic and Trade Agreement is an exemplary of

104 UNCTAD, *World Investment Report 2018*, pp. 107–115, June 6, 2018, https://unctad.org/en/PublicationsLibrary/wir2018_en.pdf (accessed November 12, 2018).

105 Catharine Titi, "Are Investment Tribunals Adjudicating Political Disputes? Some Reflections on the Repoliticization of Investment Disputes and (New) Forms of Diplomatic Protection" (2015) 32 *Journal of International Arbitration* 261, 262.

106 US Model BIT 2004, Arts. 12 and 13.

107 Gilbert Gagné and Jean-Frédéric Morin, "The Evolving American Policy on Investment Protection: Evidence from Recent FTAs and the 2004 Model BIT" (2006) 9 *Journal of International Economics Law* 357, 381–382.

108 Justin Carter, "The Protracted Bargain: Negotiating the Canada-China Foreign Investment Promotion and Protection Agreement" (2009) 47 *Canadian Yearbook of International Law* 197, 206.

Canada's trajectory shift of altering its BIT negotiation position from a capital exporter to a capital importer.[109]

Although Trump announced the USA's withdrawal from the TPP (now CPTPP) after taking office, the consensus reached by Pacific Rim states under the TPP framework still exerts an impact on the reshaping of the current international economic governance regime. For instance, the CPTPP lays emphasis on stipulating the nontraditional right to regulate of the contracting parties while inheriting TPP. On the one hand, the investment chapter of the CPTPP emphasizes that the investment activities carried out by investors in contracting parties shall conform to the laws and regulations of the host state in the fields of public health, safety and environment, allowing the host state to exercise its right to regulate, such as applying expropriation for the just-mentioned reasons.[110] On the other hand, the CPTPP also provides for investment-related matters in the status of SOEs, labor treatment, environmental protection, non-market economy and competition policies through special chapters, further ensuring the consistency of the protection standards of contracting parties in the abovementioned fields, and thereby facilitating the upgrade to higher standards in relevant international economic activities including investment.

Viewed from the development of investment supervision policies in states represented by the USA and the EU in the new century, the protection of investors' rights in developed economies is increasingly giving way to the expansion of the host state's right to regulate, and the government has taken increasing initiative in investment supervision. To take the USA as an example, a growing number of US foreign and security measures in the past two decades have directly targeted private parties. These individualized measures have largely been designed and carried out by administrative agencies. The occasional application of economic sanctions, security watchlists and no fly lists, detentions, targeted killings, and action against hackers responsible for cyber-attacks have all become significant elements of US foreign and security policy.

Those developed states who used to rely on the "leaving (of the state)" to push forward the shaping of the modern international investment law regime have "rebelled" and further affected the formulation of investment policies of developing states, and the "return" of the state has turned into a reality in the neo-international investment law. In this round of "return" of states, the governments of various states have also paid more attention to the protection of the right to regulate in the fields of labor treatment, environmental and health protection, the status of SOEs, industrial policies, among others. As a matter of fact, the scope of the modern international investment law regime focusing on the protection of investors' interests has been expanded further, highlighting the status of the overall interests of states in the entire governance regime. There has emerged a new trend of repoliticization, a novel movement in international investment law when disputes come to some sensitive public policy issues.

The repoliticization movement is harder to define or characterize than the old-generation politicization in the sense that the state is engaged in diplomatic protection through some legal means but clearly with political intentions or agendas. The "return" of the state in ISDS and international investment law reintroduces politics, if not nationalistic centralism, and re-expands regulatory space in a politically charged legal order. Along with this trend of the

[109] David Gantz, "Challenges for the United States in Negotiating a BIT with China: Reconciling Reciprocal Investment Protection with Policy Concerns" (2015) Arizona Legal Studies Discussion Paper No. 14-03, https://papers.ssrn.com/sol3/papers.cf,?abstract_id=2383919, 240.

[110] See CPTPP Arts. 9.2, 9.10, 9.16, Annex 9-B.

"return" of the state, the protection of aliens may be witnessing a resurgence. This is in large part because a number of Global South powers, reconnecting with old patterns, are increasingly wrestling with ideas about how to best protect their diasporas, in a context where territorial human rights remedies may not always be available or adequate. It is also a reflection of the old Arendtian intuition that having the backing of a sovereign is key to protecting one's rights. Finally, it is a result of the influence of human rights themselves, which increasingly encourage citizens to expect a certain level of protection from the state if in harm's way aboard. International investment law ultimately is still about how to protect one's nationals abroad.[111]

9.2 CHINA'S "LEAVING OF THE STATE" IN THE INTERNATIONAL INVESTMENT GOVERNANCE REGIME

9.2.1 *Landscape and the Evolutionary Trend of China's IIAs in the Past Four Decades*

In light of relevant UNCTAD statistics, by the end of 2019, there were 145 BITs signed by China,[112] of which 108 had entered into force (as shown in Table 9.1, 5 BITs were modified through protocols), 21 had been signed but not come into force, and 16 BITs had expired (as shown in Table 9.2). Since 2019, twenty-three TIPs have been entered into.[113]

Based on the signing time, the 163 IIAs can be divided into four stages for statistics: 1980s, 1990s, 2000s and 2010s. As can be seen from Figure 9.3, twenty-six were concluded in the 1980s, sixty-nine in the 1990s, fifty-three in the 2000s and fifteen in the 2010s. The peak period for China to conclude IIAs was the 1990s with sixty-nine IIAs in total. The main reasons for the sharp increase in the number of IIAs at this stage roughly lie in two aspects. On the one hand, after the disintegration of the Soviet Union in the late 1980s, China and twelve of the fifteen former Soviet republics signed BITs successively in the early 1990s (as shown in Figure 9.4).[114] On the other hand, the rapid development of the world economy in

TABLE 9.1 *Chinese BITs modified through protocols*

No.	BITs	Protocols
1	China–Sweden BIT 1982	sign date: September 27, 2004
2	China–Bulgaria BIT 1989	sign date: June 26, 2007
3	China–Slovakia BIT 1991	sign date: December 7, 2005
4	China–Romania BIT 1994	sign date: April 16, 2007
5	China–Cuba BIT 1995	sign date: April 20, 2007

* Compiled by the author.

[111] Surya P. Subedi, *International Investment Law: Reconciling Policy and Principle* (Hart 2008) 158.

[112] See UNCTAD, https://investmentpolicyhub.unctad.org/IIA/CountryBits/42#iiaInnerMenu (accessed June 6, 2020).

[113] See UNCTAD, https://investmentpolicyhub.unctad.org/IIA/CountryOtherIias/42#iiaInnerMenu (accessed June 6, 2020).

[114] In 1992, China signed BITs with Uzbekistan, Kyrgyzstan, Armenia, Kazakhstan, Ukraine and Turkmenistan. In 1993, China signed BITs with Belarus, Tajikistan, Georgia, Estonia, Lithuania and Azerbaijani.

TABLE 9.2 *Expired Chinese BITs*

No.	BITs	Type of Termination
1	China–Germany BIT 1983	Replaced by China–Germany BIT 2003
2	China–France BIT 1984	Replaced by China–France BIT 2007
3	China–BLEU BIT 1984	Replaced by China–BLEU BIT 2005
4	China–Finland BIT 1984	Replaced by China–Finland BIT 2004
5	China–Netherlands BIT 1985	Replaced by China–Netherlands BIT 2001
6	China–Switzerland BIT 1986	Replaced by China–Switzerland BIT 2009
7	China–Russian Federation BIT 1990	Replaced by China–Russian Federation BIT 2006
8	China–Czech Republic BIT 1991	Replaced by China–Czech Republic BIT 2005
9	China–Portugal BIT 1992	Replaced by China–Portugal BIT 2005
10	China–Spain BIT 1992	Replaced by China–Spain BIT 2005
11	China–Uzbekistan BIT 1992	Replaced by China–Uzbekistan BIT 2011
12	China–Korea, Republic of BIT 1992	Replaced by China–Korea BIT 2007
13	China–Ecuador BIT 1994	Unilaterally denounced
14	Chile–China BIT 1994	Replaced by Chile–China FTA 2012
15	China–Indonesia BIT 1994	Unilaterally denounced
16	China–Nigeria BIT 1997	Replaced by China–Nigeria BIT 2001
17	China–India BIT 2006	Unilaterally denounced

*Compiled by the author.

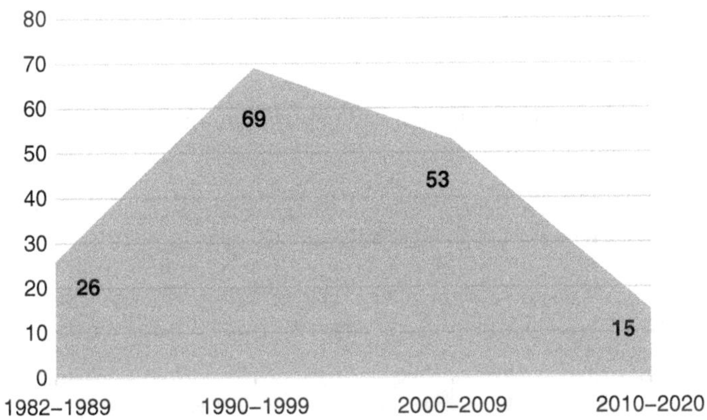

FIGURE 9.3 Number of Chinese BITs (1982–2020)[115]

the 1990s prompted all parties to attach importance to shaping the governance regime in the field of investment. Since the implementation of the economic reform and open door policy in 1979, China's economic restructuring has deepened and the pace of opening-up to the outside world has accelerated as well. In the 1990s, China successively established a socialist market economic system and initiated negotiations on its accession to the WTO, thus accelerating the process of concluding international treaties with other states to drive its economic development.

[115] Based on UNCTAD data, https://investmentpolicyhub.unctad.org/IIA/CountryBits/42#iiaInnerMenu (accessed January 29, 2020).

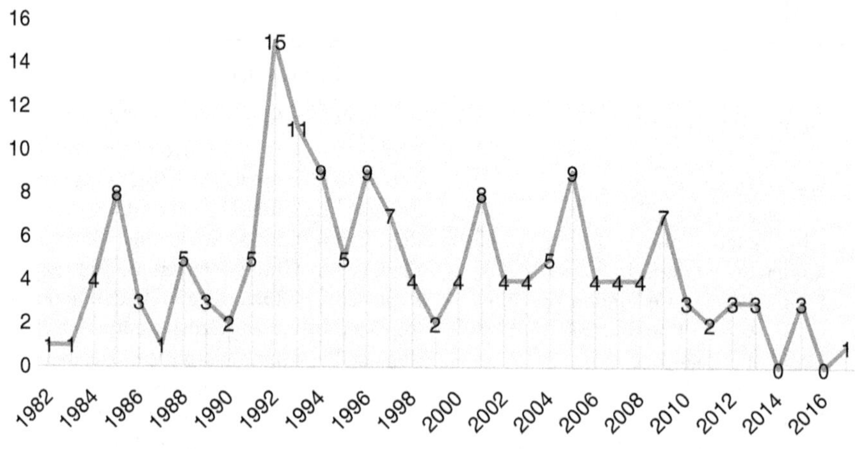

FIGURE 9.4 Chinese BITs signed in each year (1982–2018)[116]

Judging from the overall trend, China has built up the IIA network in the past forty years and is an active practitioner and participant of BIT laws and practices.[117] What is worth mentioning is that China's conclusion of IIAs reached its peak in the period of 1990s–2000s. Given China's massive foreign currency reserves and its continuous efforts to liberalize its foreign exchange controls,[118] Chinese companies desire to grow globally. In addition, the Chinese government has provided crucial support by providing linkages with the investment absorption countries,[119] and BITs are the bonding mechanisms the Chinese government created in the interest of its own investors investing overseas. Under these circumstances, this wave of outbound investment from China will continue to increase.[120]

116 Based on UNCTAD data, https://investmentpolicyhub.unctad.org/IIA/CountryBits/42#iiaInnerMenu (accessed January 29, 2020). There is no new BIT China signed after 2018.

117 Over the past thirty years, China has signed a significant number of BITs. With over 120 BITs, it ranks only second to Germany in the numbers of BITs concluded. See UNCTAD, Recent Developments in International Investment Agreement, IIA Monitor No. 3 (2007), UNCTAD/WEB/ITE/IIA/2007/6; UNCTAD's Investment Instruments Online Database, www.unctadxi.org/templates/DocSearch_779.aspx (accessed January 29, 2020).

118 See Editorial, "China's Renminbi Goes Slowly Global," *Financial Times*, August 27, 2010, at 8 (claiming that China is taking steps to broaden the use of renminbi among international investors and taking measures to internationalize renminbi).

119 Peter J. Buckley et al., "Explaining China's Outward FDI: An Institutional Perspective" in Karl P. Sauvant (ed.), with Kristin Mendoza and Irmak Ince, *The Rise of Transnational Corporations from Emerging Markets: Threat or Opportunity?* (Edward Elgar 2008) 104–157; Jamil Anderlini, "Siemens Boards Chinese Rail Bid," *Financial Times*, March 17, 2010, at 13 (revealing that China's Railway Ministry provided coordinated efforts to a series of bids by state-owned Chinese rail companies in Saudi Arabia and elsewhere).

120 See Editorial, "China's Outbound Investment Totals $183.97B," *China Daily*, September 8, 2009, www.chinadaily.com.cn/china/2009-09/08/content_8668835.htm (explaining that China's outbound FDI added up to USD 183.97 billion by 2008, and will invest USD 150 billion in 2009, which eclipses China's inbound FDI for the first time in history); see also Daniel H. Rosen and Thilo Hanemann, China's Changing Outbound Foreign Direct Investment Profile: Drivers and Policy Implication, Peterson Institute for International Economics, Policy Brief No. PB09-14 (2009), www.ciaonet.org/pbei/iie/0017250/f_0017250_14753.pdf; see UNCTAD, World Investment Report 2009 – Overview, p. 7, www.unctad.org/en/docs/wir2010overview_en.pdf; and World Investment Report 2006 – FDI from Developing and Transition Economies: Implications for Development, pp. 107, 112 and 115, www.unctad.org/en/docs/wir2006_en.pdf (stating that the developing and transition countries' share of outbound FDI in 2009 accounts for 31 percent of world outward flows, compared to 17 percent in 2005 and China rose to the second place after the United States, compared to its sixth ranking in 2005) (accessed April 29, 2010).

During the 1990s, Africa, Latin America and Central Asia replaced the Western European states in becoming the most important commercial and investment partner regions for China. It is also during this decade that over half of China's BITs were signed and China acceded to the ICSID. This changing pattern, as shown in Figure 9.5, is attributable to the growing importance of developing countries as countries absorbing Chinese outbound FDI. An example of this trend is the recent growth of the FDI flows to southern Africa.[121]

Prior to 1998, the old-generation Soviet-style Chinese BITs were marked by a reluctance to apply strong investment protection standards and included a comprehensive ISDS mechanism.[122] Starting with the Barbados–China BIT of 1998, China departed from this model.

After the new millennium, China gave more emphasis on using BITs as legal instruments for the protection of Chinese investments overseas by signing new BITs with developing countries and updating old BITs with developed countries. China adopted a more liberal approach providing foreign investors with stronger and more comprehensive substantive and procedural protections, largely comparable to those of capital-exporting states.[123] China's stance in BIT practice was evolving from a restrictive to a liberal stance. It is no coincidence that the change in Chinese BIT policy actually overlapped in time with the launch of the "go globally" strategy.

Since the global financial crisis, Chinese players have yet to slow down their expanding pace. Rather, more Chinese companies are finding their way to a heightened profile in a growing number of industries.[124] It appears inevitable that Chinese companies will become a major force in FDI in the global sphere. Oddly, China appears to have ceased its practice of signing more BITs after 2008. Theoretically, China should have been more active in negotiating and signing BITs after 2008 given Chinese companies' proactive participation in the global market. Nevertheless, in the next decade subsequent to the financial crisis, China signed only three BITs. One explanation or speculation may be that China changed its

121 United Nations Conference on Trade and Development – UNCTAD, *World Investment Report 2008* (hereinafter "WIR 2008"), www.unctad.org/en/docs/wir2008_en.pdf, at 41 (accessed April 29, 2010); William Wallis, "*Chinese Investment Has Put Africans in the Driving Seat,*" *Financial Times*, January 27, 2010, at 6 (reporting that trade between China and Africa rose to USD 107 billion in 2008, ten times that one decade ago, and Chinese funding of infrastructure and development in Africa grew to rival lending by the World Bank and the IMF).

122 Congyan Cai, "Outward Foreign Direct Investment Protection and the Effectiveness of Chinese BIT Practice" (2006) 7 *Journal of World Investment & Trade* 621 (listing a limited scope of national treatment to treatment based on domestic laws and regulations, transfer rights, and recourse to investor–state arbitration to the determination of compensation for expropriation).

123 Stephan W. Schill, "Tearing Down the Great Wall: The New Generation Investment Treaties of the People's Republic of China" (2007) 15 *Cardozo Journal of International and Comparative Law* 73, 73–118 (revealing that it was China that took the initiative in having a comprehensive dispute settlement provision in the new German–China BIT); Yuqing Zhang, "The Case of China" in Michael Moser (ed.), *Investor-State Arbitration: Lessons for Asia* (2008) 156 (indicating that it was Western countries that wanted China to adopt the modern dispute resolution clause when updating their old BITs with China).

124 See Roel Landingin and Patti Waldmeir, "China's Zijin Eyes Indophil Gold Stake," *Financial Times*, December 2, 2009, at 19 (explaining the recent business expansion of Zijin Mining, the largest gold producer and third largest copper producer in China, by the AUD 545 million purchase of Australia-listed Indophil Resources); see also Tom Mitchell, "Egypt Courts Chinese over Suez Zone," *Financial Times*, March 3, 2010, at 4 (explaining that the Tianjin Economic Technological Development Area is taking up to a 49 percent stake in the USD 1.5 billion investment in Egypt's Suez Economic Zone); see *Hong Kong Economic Journal*, March 17, 2010, at 27 (reporting on CNOOC's USD 3.1 billion acquisition of 50 percent equity in Bridas Energy's Bridas Corp. in Argentina); Louise Nordstrom, "Chinese Automaker Buying Volvo from Ford," MSNBC, March 29, 2010, www.msnbc.msn.com/id/36071933/ns/business-autos (reporting on China's Geely USD 1.8 billion acquisition of Volvo from Ford); Editorial, "Nasdaq Aims for More Listings from Mainland," *South China Morning Post*, December 15, 2009, at B4 (reporting on Nasdaq OMX Group's desires to host more new listings from China this year in its competition with stock exchanges around the world for new listings).

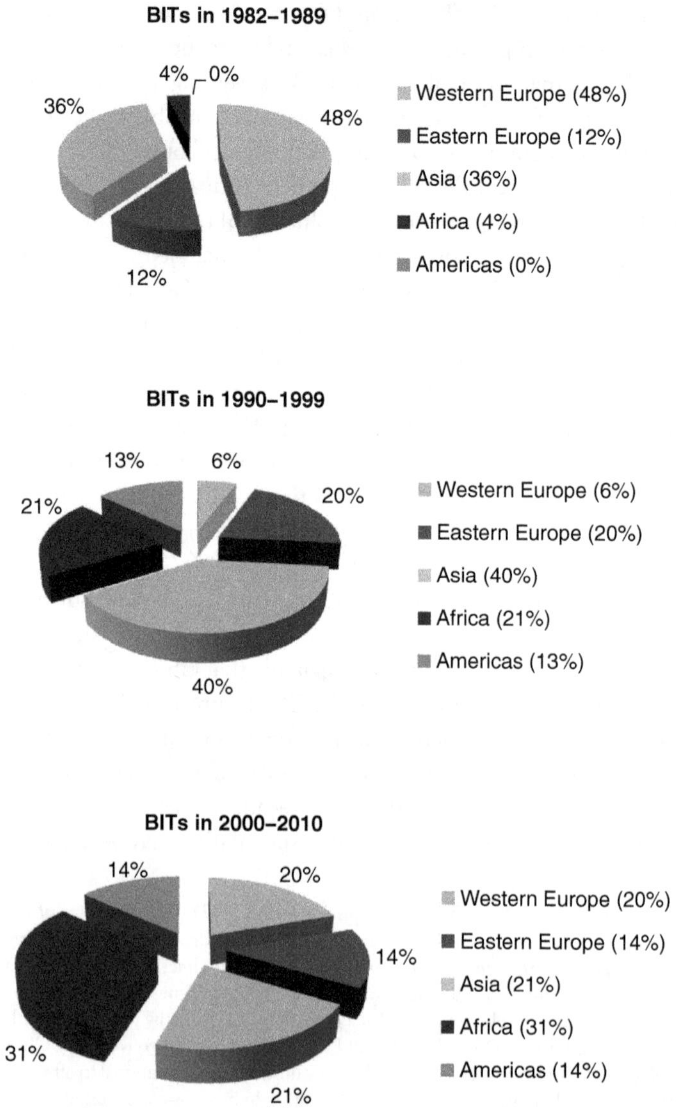

FIGURE 9.5 Growth of Chinese BITs with trading partners[125]

strategy to focus more on FTAs instead of BITs. As seen in Table 9.3, there were more FTAs signed in the same period than BITs.

Scholars prefer to categorize Chinese BITs into several generations. Figure 9.6 shows the generational evolution of Chinese BITs. There are various ways of dividing Chinese BITs, and scholars may have different criteria in grouping them.[126] The China–Barbados BIT 1998

[125] This diagram is produced based on BIT data available at UNCTAD IIO (including China's old BITS and new BITs concluded with developed countries, such as the China–Pakistan FTA, the China–New Zealand FTA, the China–Singapore FTA, the China–Peru FTA, and the Agreement on Investment of the Framework Agreement on Comprehensive Economic Cooperation). In this figure, Asia includes Australia, New Zealand and Pacific countries such as Papua New Guinea and Vanuatu. Americas include both North American and South American countries. In terms of North America, neither Canada nor the USA signed a BIT with China. Eastern Europe mainly covers Russia, other former Soviet Union states and former socialist countries in that region.

[126] Guang Hong, "Scope of Arbitration in Chinese BITs: Policies and Implications" (2009) University of Miami, https://works.bepress.com/guang_hong/1/.

TABLE 9.3 *China's IIAs (2011–2019)*

Date of Signature	IIAs
April 19, 2011	China–Uzbekistan BIT 2011
August 11, 2011	China–Congo, Democratic Republic of the BIT 2011
May 13, 2012	China–Japan–Korea, Republic of Trilateral Investment Agreement 2012
September 9, 2012	Canada–China BIT 2012
March 24, 2013	China–United Republic of Tanzania BIT 2013
April 15, 2013	China–Iceland FTA 2013
August 6, 2013	China–Switzerland FTA 2013
June 1, 2015	China–Korea, Republic of FTA 2015
June 17, 2015	Australia–China FTA 2015
July 29, 2015	China–Turkey BIT 2015
May 13, 2017	China–Georgia FTA 2017
October 17, 2019	China–Mauritius FTA 2019

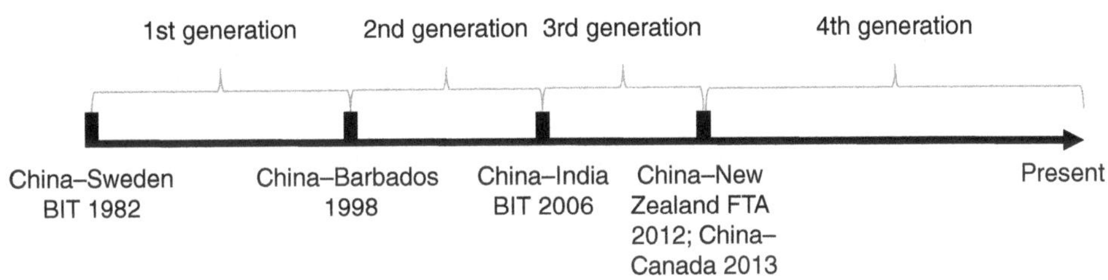

FIGURE 9.6 Generations of Chinese BITs

is taken as the cut-off point to separate old- and new-generations of BITs as, for the first time, it no longer attached quantum to the concept of "dispute," allowing a wider scope of jurisdiction for arbitral tribunals. Accordingly, the very first generation of BITs contained conservative ISDS clauses. By contrast, the later generations of BITs contain more liberal ISDS clauses.[127] The first-generation BITs were made in a less globalized time with the economic premise of financial independence instead of interdependence. China's BITs signed at that time with developed countries were illustrative of an economic construction or asymmetry between industrialized and non-industrialized states (China). The negotiation dynamic was in favor of capital-exporting/industrialized states.[128]

Others may distinguish a "new generation" of Chinese BITs beginning in the early 2000s, particularly the China–Netherlands BIT 2001 and the China–Germany BIT 2003, breaking from China's past BIT practice with more limited provisions. These two new BITs, with some exceptions allowing China to maintain investment restrictions, conform to most BITs with standard guarantees of both substantive and procedural rights to foreign investors.[129] The new BIT practice coincided with China's accession to the WTO, which not only made extensive trade liberalization concessions but also increased transparency and predictability in China's legal system. While disagreement may exist on the time of dividing the old and the new generations of BITs, the general consensus is that the new-generation BITs contain expansive

[127] Yu-ting Ye, "Towards a Balanced and Liberal Chinese Bilateral Investment Treaty Regime," 107–146.

[128] Pedro J. Martinez-Fraga and C. Ryan Reetz, *Public Purpose in International Law: Rethinking Regulatory Sovereignty in the Global Era* (Cambridge University Press 2015) 277.

[129] Schill, "Tearing Down the Great Wall," 73–118.

provisions and higher standards of protection, manifested by more liberal definitions of "dispute" and "investment" and less reliance on state laws in defining substantive and procedural rights (i.e., ISDS clauses).[130]

The China–India BIT 2006 was of symbolic significance in the sense that it recognized the concept of indirect expropriation. Recognizing the norm of indirect expropriation eventually offers more protections to investors due to its constraining of government discretion and regulatory autonomy with an alleged negative effect on foreign investment.[131] Its jurisdictional value should not be overrated as China's later FTAs, for example the China–Korea FTA, limit the scope for frivolous claims by investors that challenge state regulations. The provision says that "non-discriminatory regulatory actions adopted by the Party for the purpose of legitimate public welfare do not constitute indirect expropriation."[132] The investment chapter of the China–New Zealand FTA (signed in 2008) and the China–Canada BIT (signed in 2012) present a new generation of BITs modeled on the model Canada BIT (which quite resembles the model US BIT), showing China's flexibility to lean closer toward Western standards. In particular, the investment chapter of the China–New Zealand FTA was acknowledged to advance China's liberalization commitments. The China–Canada BIT and the China–Japan–Korea investment pact (signed in 2012 and entered into force in 2014) are viewed as a follow-up of China–New Zealand's incremental approach toward more investment liberalization.[133]

Some Western European countries chose to renegotiate BITs with China in order to eliminate some of the gaps and reservations that reduced the practical value of their older BITs with China. This reveals China's growing acceptance of modern BIT jurisprudence and related international investment law, as well as its confidence in providing sufficient protections to foreign investors. Currently, China is proactively negotiating BITs with countries with which it does not have BITs, such as the USA[134] and the EU,[135] after China managed to sign the BIT with Canada in 2012.[136] In negotiating these new BITs, China is indicating its liberal and balanced approach.[137]

130 Mahdev Mohan, "Asian Perspective on Investment Agreements and Arbitration: An Evolving Marcottage" in Andrea K. Bjorklund (ed.), *Yearbook on International Investment Law & Policy 2014-2015* (Oxford University Press 2016) 338.

131 Lukas Stifter and August Reinisch, "Expropriation in the Light of the UNCTAD Investment Policy Framework for Sustainable Development" in Steffen Hindelang and Markus Krajewski (eds.), *Shifting Paradigms in International Investment Law: More Balanced, Less Isolated, Increasingly Diversified* (Oxford University Press 2016) 86.

132 Jeffrey J. Schott, Euijin Jung and Cathleen Cimino-Isaacs, "An Assessment of the Korea-China Free Trade Agreement," Peterson Institute for International Economics Policy Brief Number PB15-24, December 2015, 12.

133 Ibid., 10–11.

134 See, e.g., Pat K. Chew, "Political Risk and U.S. Investment in China: Chimera of Protection and Predictability" (1994) 34 *Virginia Journal of International Law* 615, 660 (describing China and the USA's intense negotiations to enter into a BIT in the 1980s. However, the efforts failed partly due to the Tiananmen Square accident and partly because of the staunch position of the USA on its domestic law requirements for the timely, adequate and sufficient compensation for expropriation and nationalization. The two countries recently resumed their negotiations and included this in the Strategic Economic Dialogue launched in September 2006); see also Zhang, *supra* note 124, at 155–156.

135 See Chapter 4 of this book.

136 See United Nations Conference on Trade and Development, World Investment Report: Transnational Corporations and the Infrastructure Challenge (2008), at 15 (explaining that Canada is a relatively new entrant into the BIT practice. In its BIT negotiations with China, it even included environmental considerations.). Timothy S. McNamara, "The China–Canada BIT, Its Shortcomings, and the Risks for Chinese Investors" (2019) 10(2) *Beijing Law Review* 287–301.

137 Yu-ting Ye, "Towards a Balanced and Liberal Chinese Bilateral Investment Treaty Regime," 107–146.

Through the investigation mentioned earlier of the "leaving" and "return" trends of states in shaping the entire modern international investment law regime, the trend of these IIAs basically conforms to the trend in the world. Therefore, China has always been actively involved in shaping the modern international investment law regime.[138] However, what role China has played in the "leaving" and "return" of the state paradigm still needs further investigation and analysis.

The detachment of investment arbitration from domestic law is a means of limiting the host state's control over an investment dispute. And in this investigation, the appearance of the factor of the "host state's law" in relevant provisions of IIAs is the focus of statistics and analysis. Among the 163 samples mentioned, the factor of the "host state's law" mainly appears in terms of "definition of investment," "investor–host state dispute settlement," "definition of investor," "expropriation" and "currency exchange and transfer." The following is an investigation of this host state's law factor in these five clauses.

Among these 163 samples, the exceptions are the China–Guinea BIT 2005, the China–Turkey BIT 2015 and the China–Congo BIT 2011, which cannot be acquired from official public channels, and four IIAs – the China–EC Trade and Economic Cooperation Agreement 1985, the China–ASEAN Economic Cooperation Framework Agreement 2002, the China–Australia Trade and Economic Cooperation Framework Agreement 2003 and the China–Switzerland FTA 2013 – do not include ISDS provisions. The remaining 156 IIAs stipulate that investors must comply with the "host state's law," that expropriation can be carried out premised on the public interests of the host state, and that investors must exchange and transfer currencies in accordance with the host state's law. Therefore, states have never been "leaving" in the clauses of "definition of investors," "expropriation" and "currency exchange and transfer."

Apart from the above three clauses, the factor of the "host state's law" in the "definition of investment" clause and the "investor–host state dispute settlement" clause has different configurations, and the following sections emphatically investigate and analyze these two clauses.

9.2.2 *The "Host State's Law" Factor in the "Definition of Investment" Clause*

As to the "definition of investment" clause, of the 156 IIAs, 144 stipulate that investments should comply with the "host state's law" accounting for 92 percent of the total, as indicated in Figure 9.7. Judging from this proportion,[139] from the first BIT concluded between China and Sweden in 1982 to the latest BIT concluded between China and Tanzania in 2013, the "host state's law" has always been the main element of China's definition of investment in BITs. In other words, in the past forty years, China has always stressed the importance of the host state's sovereignty over foreign investment by reference to the "host state's law." It appears that China has never been "leaving" sovereignty behind in the BIT context.

Certainly, along with the strengthening and influence of the collective "leaving" trend of developed states in shaping the international investment law regime, China has not

138 Shaun Breslin, "How China Changed the Global Economy and the Global Economy Changed China: Thirty Years of Investment and Trade," pp. 33–34, https://warwick.ac.uk/fac/soc/pais/people/breslin/research/30years.pdf (accessed May 29, 2020).

139 For details, see UNCTAD data, https://investmentpolicyhub.unctad.org/IIA/CountryBits/42#iiaInnerMenu (accessed January 29, 2020).

TABLE 9.4 *IIAs without the requirement of compliance with the "host state's law"*

No.	BIT	No.	BIT
1	China–Singapore–Malaysia–Thailand–Indonesia–Philippines–Brunei Trilateral Investment Agreement 1987	7	China–France BIT 2007
2	China–Netherlands BIT 2001	8	China–Switzerland BIT 2009
3	China–Germany BIT 2003	9	Canada–China BIT 2012
4	China–Uganda BIT 2004	10	China–New Zealand FTA 2008
5	China–Portugal BIT 2005	11	China–Japan–Korea Trilateral Investment Agreement 2012
6	China–Seychelles BIT 2007	12	China–Korea FTA 2015

*Compiled by the author.

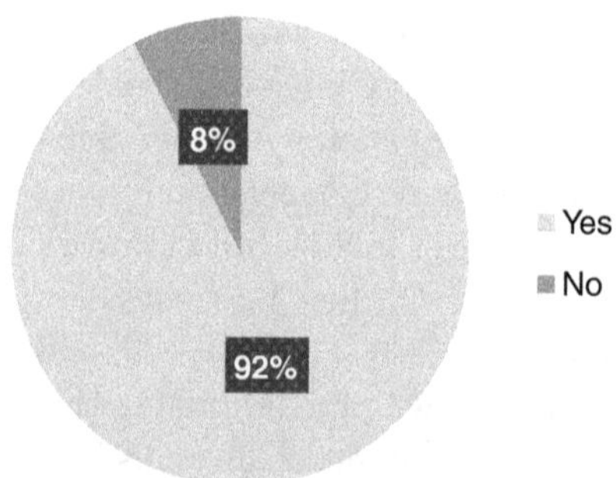

FIGURE 9.7 Should investment comply with the requirement of "host state's law"?

completely refused to restrict its own sovereignty. Of 167 IIAs, 12 (8 percent) do not stipulate that investments need to conform to the "host state's law," as shown in Table 9.4.

Over time, except for the investment protection agreement concluded between China and Singapore and another six Southeast Asian states in 1987, the remaining IIAs were concluded after 2000. Apart from the BIT concluded between China and Uganda in 2004[140] and the BIT concluded between China and Seychelles in 2007,[141] the new BITs concluded between China and five developed states in Western Europe – the Netherlands, Germany, Portugal, France and Switzerland – after the new century have all deleted the reference to "host state's law." Meanwhile, the FTA concluded between China and New Zealand in 2008 also deleted the requirement of investment to conform to the "host state's law" which appeared in the 1988 BIT between the two states, instead changing it to only require relevant investments to be within the territory of the contracting counterparties.

On the one hand, the definition of "investment" as "property" has long been adopted by developed economies such as the USA and the EU, and is also followed by the BITs concluded by China.[142] On the other hand, it appears that the BIT concluded by China and Canada in 2012 was influenced by the 2012 US model BIT.[143] Although the definition of investment in the

[140] China–Uganda BIT 2004, Art. 1.1

[141] China–Seychelles BIT 2007, Art. 1.1

[142] US Model BIT 1983, Art. 1.3.

[143] US Model BIT 2012, Art. 1.

China–Canadian BIT was not adopted by the IIAs concluded by China later, the impact of the China–Canada BIT can be seen in the BIT concluded between China and Tanzania, which can be regarded as China's attempt to reach a higher standard of investment.

From the point of view of contracting counterparties, most BITs without a reference to the host state's law are signed by China with developed states. The renewal of BITs by China and developed states shows both sides' intention to restrict their own sovereignty.[144] This consensus may not only come from the requirements of developed states but also reflects China's change in IIAs position. As far as the "host state's law" clause is concerned, China has never been "leaving" its sovereignty. However, from the text of the IIAs forged since the new century, China has already shown its willingness to restrict its own sovereignty by not requiring compliance with the host state's law, especially in those newer BITs signed with developed economies. The notable change is an elimination of the "host state's law" in the definition of investment. However, this "leaving" stance has not been that obvious, showing China's tendency to preserve its sovereignty.

9.2.3 *The "Host State's Law" Factor in Substantive Standards*

9.2.3.1 Fair and Equitable Treatment

Fair and equitable treatment (FET), basically being included in all existing IIAs and invoked in the majority of investment arbitration cases,[145] mainly refers to the principle under which the contracting party ensures that the investments made by the investor from the counterparty are treated fairly and equally in the host state. There are 149 (96 percent) IIAs with FET clauses, leaving 6 (4 percent) IIAs without FET clauses; instead, these merely emphasize fair and reciprocal treatment of investors. The China–Australia FTA 2015 may be a special case as its investment chapter does not have FET clauses[146] but leaves minimum treatment (possibly including FET)[147] for future negotiation and only mentions NT and MFN treatment clauses in its main body. In terms of timeline, except for the China–Slovak BIT Additional Protocol 2005, which retained the relevant provisions in the 1991 BIT, other BITs were signed in the late 1980s and early 1990s,[148] showing a trend of offering better protection to foreign investors.

The FET provisions often make compliance with the host state's law or public order a condition of exceptional measures. These FET clauses are more conservative than others. For example, the China–BLEU BIT 1984 states: "Protection and equitable treatment shall be accorded as regards management, operation, use or liquidation of the above said investment unless necessary measures should be taken for the maintenance of public order and in defense of the State law."[149] This is a typical qualified FET standard, opposite to an

144 Tingliang Wang, "Western Misperceptions and China's Approach to International Investment Law" (2019) 17 *Santa Clara Journal of International Law* 1, 34.

145 Yulia Levashova, *The Right of States to Regulate in International Investment Law: The Search for Balance Between Public Interest and Fair and Equitable Treatment* (Wolters Kluwer 2019) 1.

146 Jean Ho, *State Responsibility for Breaches of Investment Contracts* (Cambridge University Press 2018) 227.

147 FET and the minimum standard of treatment are sometimes interchangeable, but their relationship is disputed for two reasons. First, the FET standard is a stand-alone term mentioned in many BITs, thereby constituting an autonomous rule. Second, there has been no consensus on the content of the minimum standard of treatment either in BIT law or in BIT jurisprudence. Amaud de Nanteull, *International Investment Law* (Edward Elgar 2020) 285.

148 China–Japan BIT 1988, China–Czechoslovakia BIT 1991, China–Korea BIT 1992, China–Belarus BIT 1993 and China–Romania BIT 1994.

149 China-BLEU BIT 1984, Art. 3.2.

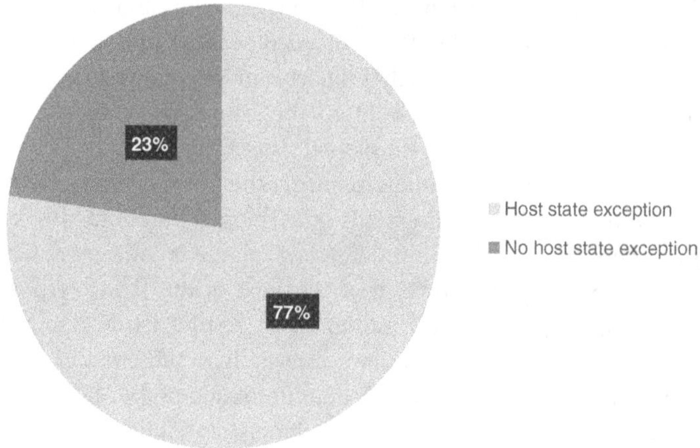

FIGURE 9.8 FET provisions with or without exceptions for host states

unqualified one which usually makes a reference to the minimum standard of treatment of aliens under customary international law,[150] and which is said to be minimalist, autonomous and self-standing.[151]

Of the 149 IIAs with FET provisions, as shown in Figure 9.8, 34 (23 percent) of them provide for exceptions (qualified FET standard) while 115 (77 percent) make no exceptions to the FET provisions (unqualified FET standard), showing China's willingness not to place considerable constraint on the state's sovereignty while granting FET to foreign investors.

Figure 9.9 indicates that, in the 1980s, the numbers of IIAs with and without exceptions were roughly the same. Moving to the 1990s, the proportion of IIAs without exceptions for the host states increased significantly, and this trend continued. A clear contrast surfaced between China and others. More recently, the EU expressed its favoritism toward complex FET clauses as a basis to negotiate the EU–Canada Comprehensive Economic Trade Agreement (CETA) and the EU–US Transatlantic Trade and Investment Partnership (TTIP)[152] while China seemed to have abandoned reservations against unqualified FET. This contrast highlighted China's intention to take a more liberal approach in terms of granting the FET to foreign investors without reserving some exceptional measures for the host states in the IIAs.

9.2.3.2 MFN Treatment

The MFN treatment clause mainly refers to commitments made by the contracting state to treat the investors of the counterparty no less favorably than investors of a third country. Of the 156 IIAs, except for the China–Syria BIT Protocol 1996, which stipulates that only China

150 China–Argentine Republic BIT 1994, Art. 3(1); China–India BIT 2007, Art. 3(2) (both having the concisely formulated language stating that "each Contracting Party shall at all times ensure fair and equitable treatment to investments"); China–Trinidad and Tobago BIT 2004, Art. 3(2) and China–Egypt BIT 1996, Art. 3(1) (both providing that foreign investments "shall be accorded fair and equitable treatment").

151 UNCTAD, "Fair and Equitable Treatment: UNCTAD Series on International Investment Agreements II" (New York 2012), http://unctad/org/en/Docs/unctaddiaeia2011d5_en.pdf (accessed June 12, 2020); OECD, "Fair and Equitable Treatment in International Investment Law" [2004] Working Papers on International Investment 2003/2004, www.oecd.org/daf/inv/investment-policy/WP-2004_3.pdf (accessed June 15, 2020).

152 Kläger, "Revising Treatment Standards," 66.

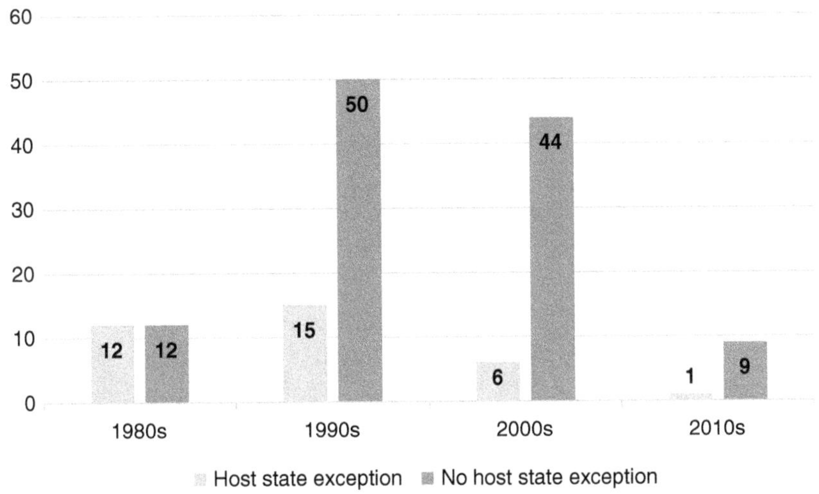

FIGURE 9.9 Time distribution of FET clauses with or without host state exceptions

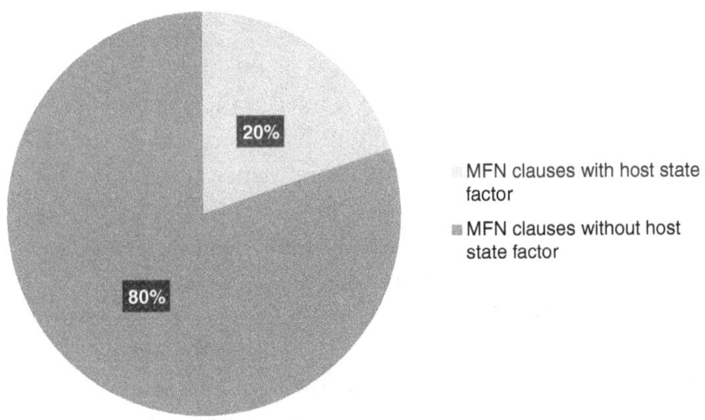

FIGURE 9.10 MFN clauses with or without the host state factor

abides by this requirement,[153] 155 apply the MFN clause reciprocally to the contracting states. The MFN treatment is often applied on the condition that the host state's domestic law, administration or taxation is satisfied. For example, the China–New Zealand BIT 1988 allows the contracting party to take measures inconsistent with MFN treatment while "in accordance with the provisions of this Agreement."[154]

As shown in Figure 9.10, 31 of the 156 IIAs (20 percent) include a host state factor clause that affects the MFN clause, and the remaining 125 IIAs (80 percent) do not include this type of clause, showing a liberal tendency in the MFN clauses.

As shown in Figure 9.11, we see slightly more IIAs in the 1980s with MFN exceptions than those without such exceptions. This reversed in the 1990s and continued to the 2010s, reflecting a liberal trend.

[153] China–Syria BIT Protocol 1996, Art. 1.

[154] China–New Zealand BIT 1988, Art. 4.2.

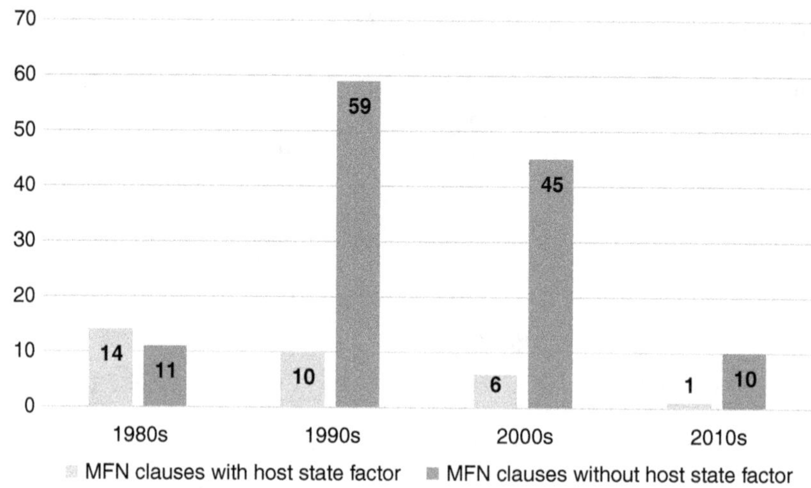

FIGURE 9.11 IIAs with or without MFN exceptions

9.2.3.3 National Treatment

The NT clause mainly refers to treatment granted by the host state to the investor from the counterparty being no less favorable than that granted to the domestic investor. The 156 IIAs can be divided into two groups: with or without NT clauses. Of the 154 IIAs, 76 have NT provisions and 78 do not. It appears that the liberal stance is not that clear. Except for the China–Syrian BIT Protocol 1996[155] and the China–South Africa BIT 1997,[156] which only provide for NT granted by the counterparty to Chinese investors, other NT clauses are reciprocal and are applicable to investors from both contracting states.

As shown in Figure 9.12, the majority of Chinese IIAs signed in the 1980s and 1990s did not contain an NT clause. The early BITs with NT clauses were those signed with the UK, Japan, Spain and other developed countries, which highlights the importance these countries attached to NT and China's compromise when it came to negotiating BIT terms with capital-exporting states. However, since the beginning of the new century, in addition to the China–Georgia FTA 2017 which adopted the old BIT signed by the two countries in 1993,[157] the newly concluded IIAs have all stipulated NT clauses. The liberal trend is quite clear.

The seventy-six IIAs with NT provisions can be divided into two groups according to the host state's law factor, that is, whether NT granted by the contracting party is required to be based on the law of the host state. The China–Iceland BIT 1994 is one of these IIAs; its Article 3.3 stipulates: "In addition to the provision of paragraphs 1 and 2 of this Article[,] either Contracting Party shall, to the extent possible, accord treatment in accordance with the stipulations of its laws and regulations to the investments of investors of the other Contracting Party the same as that accorded to its own investors." As shown in Figure 9.13, fifty-one of these seventy-six IIAs (67 percent) require NT not to breach the host state's law[158] while twenty-five (33 percent) have no such requirement, showing a weak attitude toward a complete departure from sovereignty.

[155] China–Syrian BIT Protocol 1996, Art. 1.
[156] China–South Africa BIT 1997, Art. 3.3.
[157] China–Georgia FTA 2017, Art. 12.2.
[158] China–Brunei BIT Protocol 2000, Art. 1.

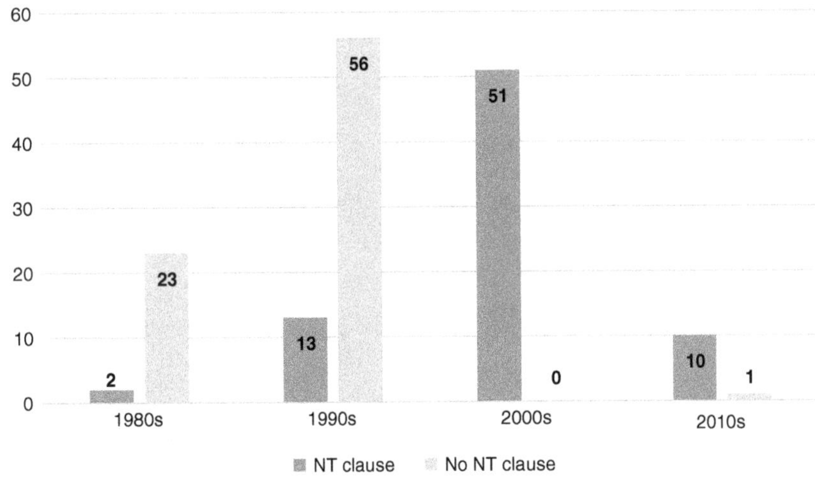

FIGURE 9.12 Time spread of BITs with NT clauses

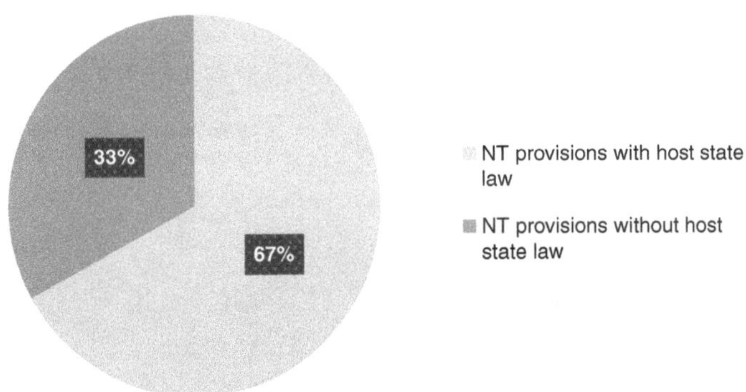

FIGURE 9.13 NT provisions with or without the "host state's law" factor

As shown in Figure 9.14, the majority of the NT provisions in Chinese IIAs contain a host state's law factor, requiring NT to be granted on the basis of the host state's law. Chinese IIAs signed in the new century have more NT provisions without such a host state's law factor, indicating a more liberal trend. These liberal NT provisions appear in Chinese BITs with Germany, the Netherlands, Spain and other European states as well as some FTAs that China signed. It is quite clear that China adopted a more liberal attitude toward investor protection standards.

In terms of the NT standard, though more liberal than before, China's overall stance is a gradualist approach moving toward liberty. This movement was made clear only after the new century.

9.2.3.4 Expropriation and Compensation

Under the expropriation and compensation clause, except for the China–Singapore BIT 1985, the China–Sri Lanka BIT 1986 and the China–New Zealand BIT 1988, all of which stipulate that expropriation can be carried out for "the purpose [that] is permitted by law" and "according to legal procedures," the remaining 153 IIAs concluded by China identify "public

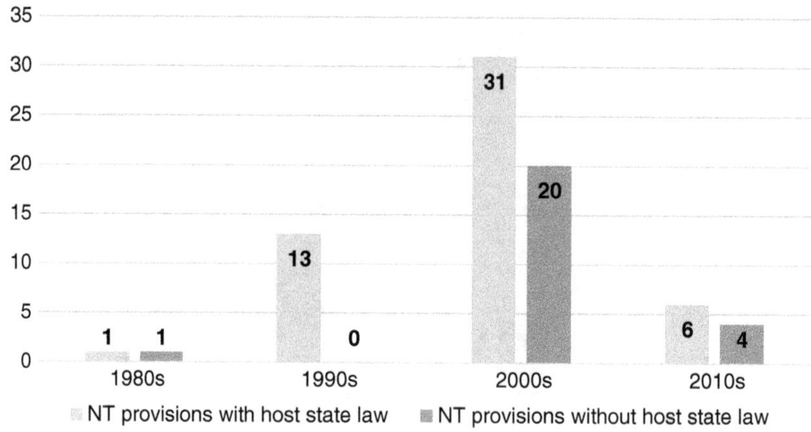

FIGURE 9.14 Time spread of NT provisions with or without the "host state's law" factor

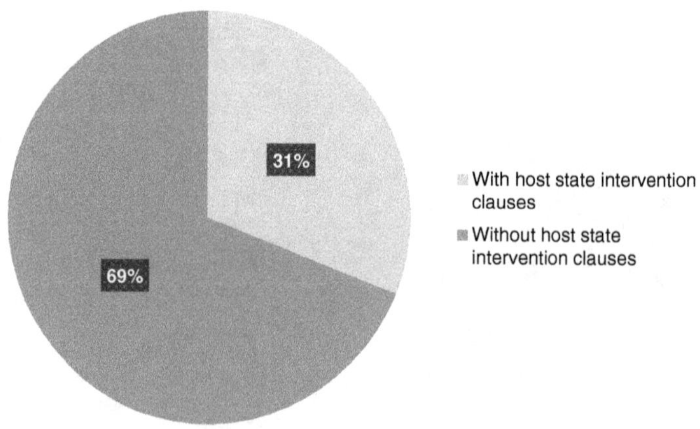

FIGURE 9.15 IIAs allowing the host state's intervention into expropriation

interest of the host country" and "compl[iance] with relevant legal procedures" as preconditions to valid expropriation. Public interest is an essential element of lawful expropriation. This reflects China's consistent and firm stance on sovereignty and expropriation. Examples include Article 5.5 of the China–Korea BIT 1992 and Article 4.3 of the China–Portuguese BIT 2005.

Of the 156 IIAs, except for the China–Australia FTA 2015,[159] which made no mention of it, the other 155 IIAs include the expropriation clauses. As shown in Figure 9.15, 48 (31 percent) of the IIAs allow the host state to intervene in expropriation while 107 (69 percent) changed its conservative stance.

As shown in Figure 9.16, most IIAs that China signed in the 1980s allowed the host state to intervene in expropriation matters. The trend rose to a peak in the 1990s then weakened thereafter, although the general trend remains the same.

9.2.3.5 Umbrella Clauses

The umbrella clause essentially elevates the commitment undertaken by the host state toward the investment of the investor of the other contracting party in its territory to an international

159 China–Australia FTA 2015, Art. 9.9.

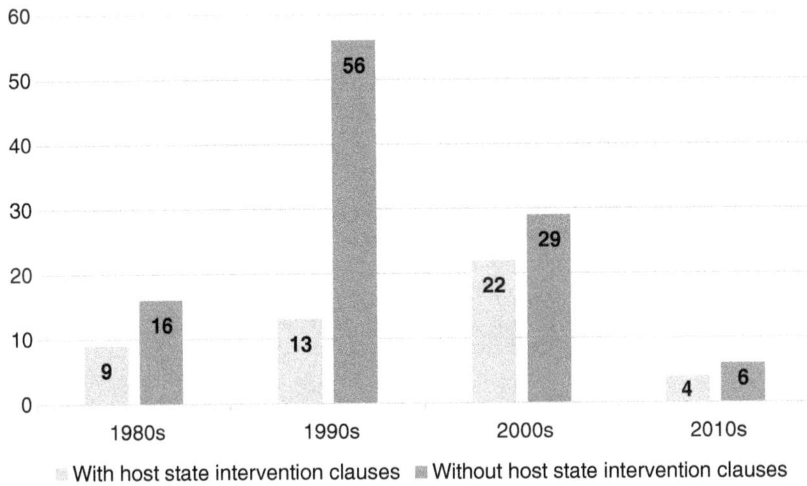

FIGURE 9.16 Time spread of IIAs with or without host state intervention clauses

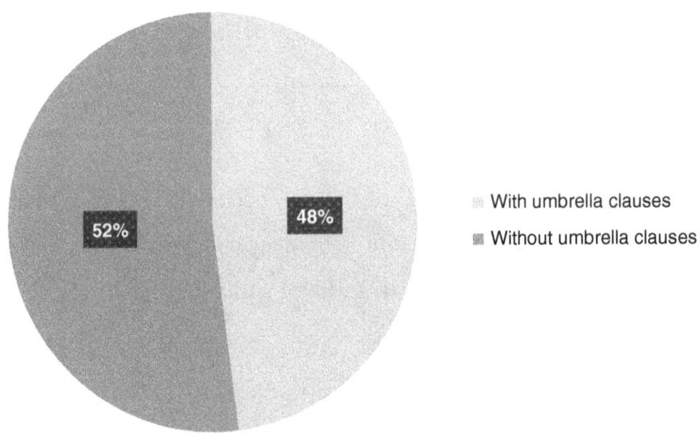

FIGURE 9.17 IIAs with or without umbrella clauses

obligation[160] under the BIT. Having an umbrella clause in the BIT shows the host state's willingness to subject governmental behaviors to international law,[161] and its desire for rule of law and better rights protection. Among the 156 IIAs, 75 (48 percent) have umbrella clauses while 81 (52 percent) do not. Figure 9.17 shows China's less willingness to take state liability for foreign investment.

As shown in Figure 9.18, there were slightly more IIAs with umbrella clauses in the 1980s and the counterparties of these IIAs were Western European countries including Germany, France and Finland. There were fewer IIAs with umbrella clauses in the 1990s. The trend

160 Monique Sasson, *Substantive Law in Investment Treaty Arbitration: The Unsettled Relationship between International Law and Municipal Law* (2nd edition, Kluwer Law International 2017) 183.

161 Martina Magnarelli, *Privity of Contract in International Investment Arbitration: Original Sin or Useful Tool?* (Wolters Kluwer 2020) 153.

TABLE 9.5 *IIAs with exception clauses*

BIT	Time of signing
China–Singapore BIT	21/11/1985
China–Sri Lanka BIT	13/03/1986
China–New Zealand BIT	22/11/1988
China–Mauritius BIT	04/05/1996
China–Columbia BIT	22/11/2008
China–Canada BIT	09/09/2012
China–Singapore FTA	23/10/2008
China–ASEAN FTA	15/08/2009

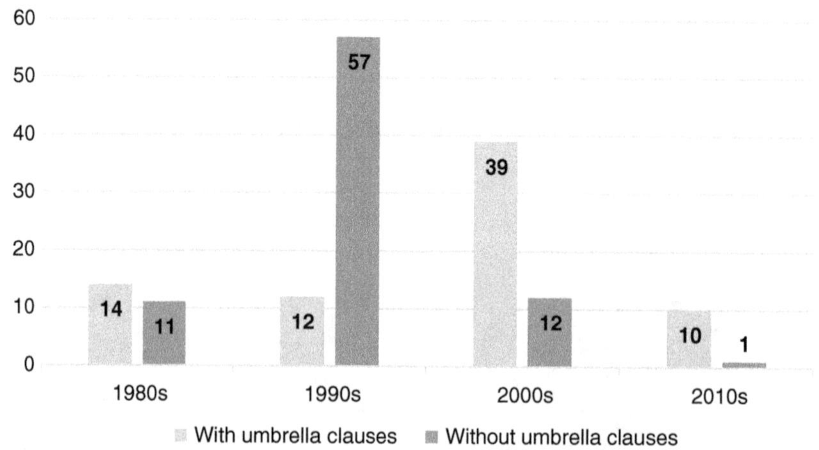

FIGURE 9.18 Time spread of IIAs with or without umbrella clauses

reversed in the twenty-first century with more IIAs having umbrella clauses, indicating China's desire to take a more liberal approach towards foreign investment.

9.2.3.6 Exceptional Clauses

As shown in Table 9.5, of the 156 IIAs, 8 provide for exceptions to the IIA's application, which allows the contracting party to apply any restriction or take other measures based on the host state's national security, public health and other reasons. A closer look at these eight IIAs shows that they were signed in the late 1980s and after the turn of the new millennium, and most counterparties to them were countries along the Indian Ocean. To a certain extent, this trend highlights the importance these contracting states attach to the exceptional clauses in IIAs. Some of China's more recent FTAs simply refer to Article XX of the GATT as general conditions for the lawfulness of exceptions.[162] Under the GATT, the measure must be neither an "arbitrary or unjustifiable discrimination" nor a "disguised restriction", and must include lists of the objectives considered "legitimate." These clauses help prevent the foreign investor's interests from overriding the host state's interests.

[162] China–New Zealand FTA 2012, Art. 200.

9.2.4 *The "Host State's Law" Factor in ISDS Clauses*

9.2.4.1 Arbitrable Scope of Investment Disputes

Among the 156 IIAs already mentioned, the China–Thailand BIT 1985, the China–Turkmenistan BIT 1992, the APTA National Promotion and Protection Investment Treaty 2009, the China–Iceland FTA 2013 and the China–Georgia FTA 2017 do not provide ISDS clauses.[163] Further, in the China–Argentina BIT 1992, due to its nonreciprocal application in terms of the scope of arbitrability, China allows Argentine investors to submit arbitrations only for "disputes on compensation amount," but Argentina allows Chinese investors' "arbitrable disputes" to be submitted to arbitration.[164]

The remaining 150 IIAs can be divided into two categories for the settlement of disputes between investors and the host state: one is that any dispute associated with investment can be settled through the IDSM and the other is that the contracting party allows only investment disputes arising from expropriation to be settled through the IDSM, with the remaining disputes settled in accordance with the domestic laws of the host state.

The different configuration of these components in the ISDS is closely related to a state's "leaving" or "return" (of the state) status. The greater the scope of dispute for investment arbitration, the lower the degree of intervention by the state in ISDS,[165] and the more obviously the state can be seen to "leave (the state)".

Of the 150 IIAs, as shown in Figure 9.19, only 87 (58 percent) allow "dispute over the amount of compensation from expropriation" to be arbitrated, and 63 (42 percent) allow "any dispute" to be arbitrated. In general, the contracting states have imposed strong restrictions on the IDSM, and China's "leaving (of the state)" trend is not obvious.

As far as concerns the scope of a "dispute" for the purposes of arbitration, as shown in Figure 9.20, in the 1980s and 1990s, the Agreement between China and Singapore, Thailand

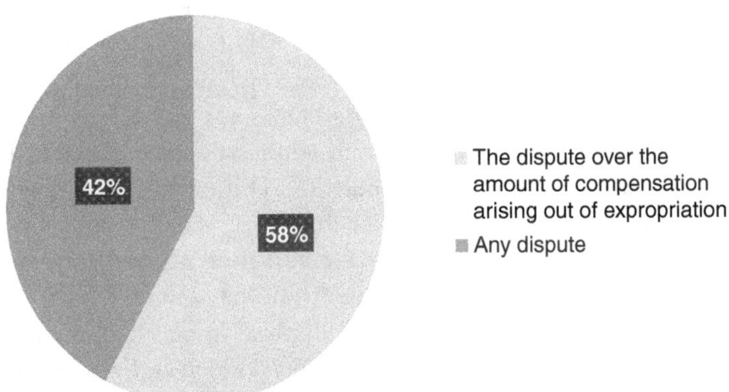

FIGURE 9.19 Dispute clauses in Chinese IIAs

163 Although the China–Sweden BIT 1982 did not provide for an ISDS clause, the Protocol signed between China and Sweden in 2004 added the relevant provisions.

164 China–Argentina BIT 1992, Art. 8.

165 See August Reinisch, "The Scope of Investor-State Dispute Settlement in International Investment Agreements" (2013) 21 *Asia Pacific Law Review* 3, 24–25.

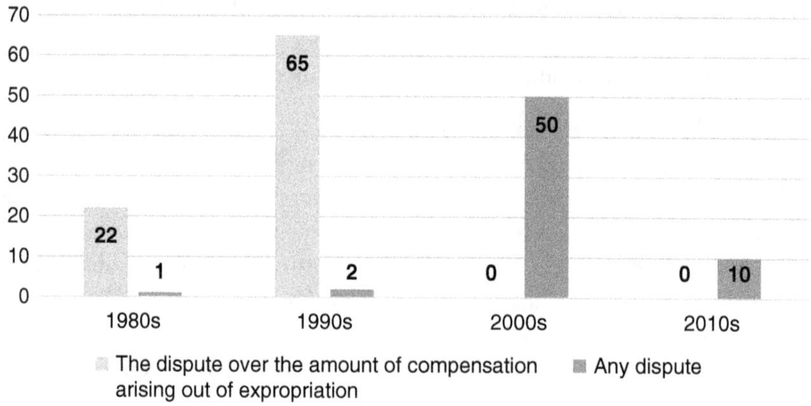

FIGURE 9.20 Scope of dispute in Chinese IIAs (1982–2020)

and six other governments on the Promotion and Protection of Investment 1987, the China–Romania BIT 1994 and the China–Barbados BIT 1998 allow "any dispute" to be submitted to arbitration.[166] The rest of the BITs allow only disputes over the amount of compensation from expropriation to be arbitrated, showing strong restrictions on the IDSM. In particular, the positions of China and Argentina on ISDS in the China–Argentina BIT 1992 further highlight China's stronger restrictions on the scope of investment dispute resolution.[167] After entering the twenty-first century, this phenomenon has undergone a fundamental change. The IIAs concluded by China in the twenty years since the new century have relaxed restrictions on the scope of dispute and demonstrate the liberalization of China's stance on its sovereignty.[168] China's sovereignty has been impacted greatly by a much more integrated global market. As a result, China has increasingly delegated more authority to international organizations or the ISDS regimes.

There are two important points in time that are worthy of attention. First, on February 6, 1993, China formally ratified its accession to the ICSID Convention. Article 25(4) of the Convention allows a contracting state to limit the scope of dispute resolution when it agrees to submit an investment dispute to the ICSID for arbitration. When China joined the ICSID Convention, it made a clear statement that it only allowed disputes related to the amount of compensation from expropriation to be arbitrated.[169] This reflects China's position on the IDSM in the 1990s, and China's "leaving (of the state)" stance is not obvious. Second, although the China–Romania BIT 1994 for the first time allowed "any dispute" to be arbitrated, this clause was only a short-lived one. Until the signing of the China–Barbados BIT in 1998,[170] China completely allowed "any dispute" to be submitted to international arbitration, and then embarked on the liberalization position in the scope of dispute for arbitration.

166 Agreement between China and Singapore, Thailand and six other governments on the Promotion and Protection of Investment (1987), Art. 10; China–Romania BIT 1994, Art. 8; China–Barbados BIT 1998, Art. 9.
167 China–Argentina BIT 1992, Art. 8.
168 See Axel Berger, "The Politics of China's Investment Treaty-Making Program" in Tomer Broude, Marc L. Busch and Amelia Porges (eds.), *The Politics of International Economic Law* (Cambridge University Press 2011) 174–176.
169 See News from ICSID, Vol. 10 No. 1, Winter 1993 p. 1, https://icsid.worldbank.org/en/Documents/resources/vol%2010%20winter%201993.pdf (accessed April 19, 2019).
170 China–Barbados BIT 1998, Art. 9.

As far as the scope of dispute is concerned, in general, the IIAs signed by China over the past forty years still present a strong pattern of state intervention, and the degree of "leaving (of the state)" is generally limited.[171] China has undergone an evolutionary process from early restrictions on the scope of dispute to "any dispute," showing a gradual "leaving (of the state)" status. This evolutionary process matches a globalizing process of economic integration across national borders,[172] as well as its evolving economic liberalization evidenced by the reduction of barriers to trade and investment.

9.2.4.2 Exhaustion of Local Remedies

In terms of the "exhaustion of local remedies" clause, prior to the China–Barbados BIT 1998 only disputes over the amount of compensation from expropriation were allowed to be submitted to arbitration. This suggests that China possessed a restrictive stance toward international investment arbitration, and maintained its sovereignty by not giving up its judicial sovereignty over investment disputes.[173] Here the focus is on the sixty BITs that China has signed since 2000.

Throughout these sixty IIAs, the contracting states allow foreign investors to choose to rely on local remedies (either administrative and/or court proceedings) or international investment arbitration. This has been a huge shift from China's previous position on the "exhaustion of local remedies" clauses where foreign investors could not opt for arbitration without exhausting local remedies.[174] These sixty BITs can be further divided into three groups depending on the use of administrative review – no administrative review, optional administrative review, and administrative review – the difference of which indicates a varying degree of "leaving," surrendering sovereignty to arbitration or the ISDS mechanism.

In general, the sixty IIAs can be classified into two categories: reciprocal and nonreciprocal application of administrative review between the contracting parties of the BITs. The administrative review in forty-four IIAs is reciprocally applied to investors from the contracting states of the BITs while sixteen IIAs include nonreciprocal clauses.

In forty-four IIAs with reciprocity clauses, as shown in Figure 9.21, four (9 percent) stipulate that the parties may directly arbitrate without administrative review, and 37 (84 percent) stipulate that the contracting state may require the investors to conduct administrative review in the host state before opt-in arbitration. Three IIAs (7 percent) subject foreign investors to administrative review. Of these three types of IIA, four require no administrative review, twenty-eight opt for administrative review, and three specify compulsory administrative review. In the 2010s, the proportions changed to 0:9:0, meaning that China's stance on administrative review softened, reflecting its growing recognition of the influence, universality and de-territorial effect of the ISDS regime in the field of international investment.

Among the sixteen IIAs that are not applicable reciprocally to investors from contracting states to the BITs, except for the 2009 China–ASEAN FTA, which allows investors who are ICSID members to submit disputes directly to international arbitration without

[171] The China–Sweden BIT 1982 and the China–Thailand BIT 1985 did not include any ISDS provisions, reflecting to some extent the conservative position in the early days of reform and opening up.

[172] David Held et al., *Global Transformations: Politics, Economics, and Culture* (Stanford University Press 1999) 2.

[173] See Matthew C. Porterfield, "Exhaustion of Local Remedies in Investor-State Dispute Settlement" (2015) 41 *Yale Journal of International Law Online* 1, 5.

[174] See Manjiao Chi and Xi Wang, "The Evolution of ISA Clauses in Chinese IIAs and Its Practical Implications" (2015) 16 *Journal of World Investment and Trade* 869, 890–891.

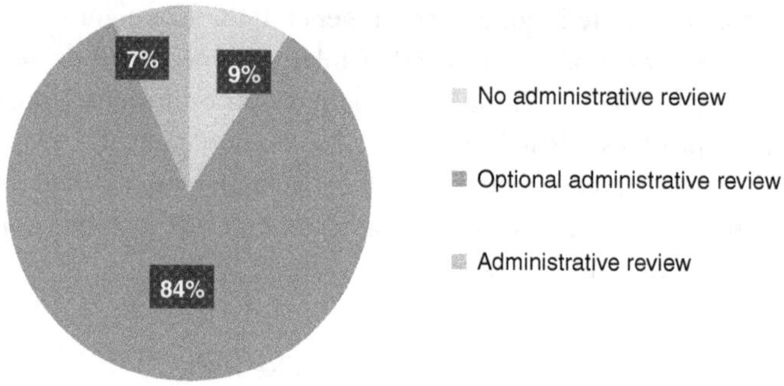

FIGURE 9.21 Administrative review clauses in reciprocal Chinese IIAs (2000–2020)

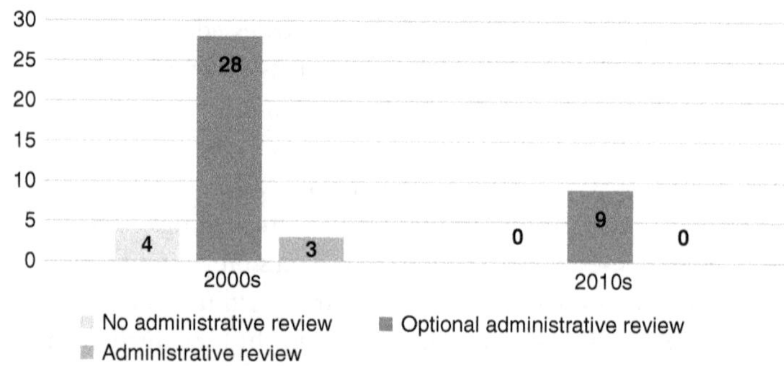

FIGURE 9.22 Extent of administrative review clauses in reciprocal Chinese IIAs (2000–2020)

administrative review[175] and is thus leaning toward a liberal stance,[176] China in the remaining fifteen IIAs requires foreign investors to rely on administrative review first before arbitration. From the standpoint of the contracting states, in addition to the China–Cyprus BIT 2001 where Cyprus can require Chinese investors to conduct administrative review in the host country before arbitration[177] and the China–Malta BIT 2009 which requires Chinese investors to first exhaust local remedies (court, arbitration or administrative proceedings),[178] Chinese investors are not subject to administrative review in the other thirteen IIAs.

It appears that China's leaving (of its sovereignty) stance in the new century is still not strong, which is in line with China's conventional position on sovereignty as well as the nation-state as a meaningful unit of sovereign institution.[179]

9.2.4.3 Fork-in-the-Road Clauses

With a fork-in-the-road clause, a foreign investor has an alternative choice of either applying to a local court or an arbitral tribunal or else before resorting to investment arbitration.[180] A fork-in-

175 China–ASEAN FTA 2009, Art. 14.4.

176 See Shen Wei, "Is This a Great Leap Forward? A Comparative Review of the Investor-State Arbitration Clause in the ASEAN-China Investment Treaty: From BIT Jurisprudential and Practical Perspectives" (2010) 27 *Journal of International Arbitration* 379, 417–418.

177 China–Cyprus BIT 2001, Art. 9 and the Protocols.

178 China–Malta BIT 2009, Art. 9.

179 The opposite view is that the nation-state is no longer a meaningful unit of social organization. See generally Kenichi Ohmae, *The End of the Nation State: The Rise of Regional Economies* (Free Press 1995).

180 Zachary Douglas, *The International Law of Investment Claims* (Cambridge University Press 2009) 152; Martina Magnarelli, "The Unresolved Conundrum of Contract-Based and Treaty-Based Claims: An Extra Element of

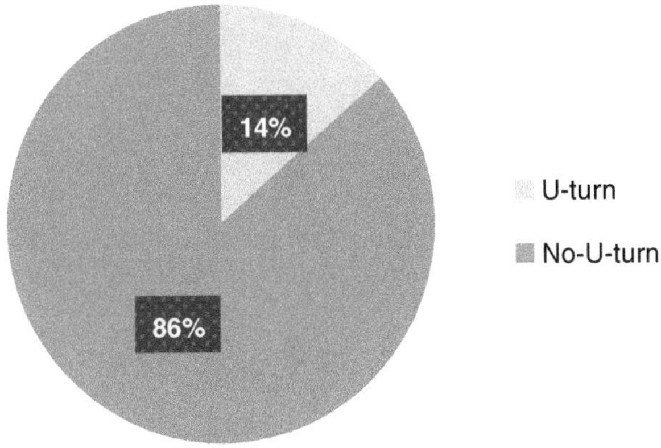

FIGURE 9.23 Fork-in-the-road clauses in Chinese IIAs (2000–2020)

the-road clause is devised in a BIT to avoid multiplication of proceedings with regard to the same investment dispute. Therefore, it acts not only as an additional safeguard of the host state's sovereign rights against the tribunals' expansionistic trend in defining the scope of jurisdiction[181] but also as a limitation imposed onto the exhaustion of local remedies clauses.[182]

In the sixty BITs, the fork-in-the-road clauses can be divided into two groups: no-U-turn and U-turn. The former refers to a scenario where the investor cannot switch to arbitration if it first chooses to rely on local remedy as long as there is no final decision in the proceeding made already, and vice versa. The latter gives the investor more flexibility by allowing the investor to switch to arbitration even if it first chooses local remedy. Clearly a varying level of flexibility is offered to investors by these two types of fork-in-the-road clauses.[183]

There is one multilateral investment agreement entered into between China and ASEAN which applies a no-U-turn fork-in-the-road clause to Indonesia, the Philippines, Thailand and Vietnam while a U-turn fork-in-the-road clause applies to China and other ASEAN member states.[184] In the remaining fifty-nine BITs, as shown in Figure 9.23, fifty-one (86 percent) include a no-U-turn fork-in-the-road clause while eight (14 percent) have U-turn ones. As shown in Figure 9.24, eight BITs with a U-turn fork-in-the-road clause were signed after 2000 but switched back to no-U-turn after 2010.

The composition of the fork-in-the-road clauses and the switch between U-turn and no-U-turn fork-in-the-road clauses indicate a contracting state's open attitudes toward the ISDS, especially the reliance upon either local remedy or international arbitration.[185] China's changing stance on the fork-in-the-road clause matches its gradual "leaving (of the state)" status in

Contention: Privity of Contract and Forum Selection Clauses in Investment Contracts" (2016) 1 *European Investment Law and Arbitration Review* 85.

181 Magnarelli, *supra* note 180, at 90.

182 International Institute for Sustainable Development, *Exhaustion of Local Remedies in International Investment Law: IISD Best Practices Series*, p. 2, January 2017, www.iisd.org/sites/default/files/publications/best-practices-exhaustion-local-remedies-law-investment-en.pdf (accessed May 29, 2019).

183 Markus A. Petsche, "The Fork in the Road Revisited: An Attempt to Overcome the Clash between Formalistic and Pragmatic Approaches" (2019) 18 *Washington University Global Studies Law Review* 391.

184 China–ASEAN FTA 2009, Art. 14.5.

185 Shu Zhang, "Developing China's Investor-State Arbitration Clause Discussions in the Context of the 'Belt and Road' Initiative" in Wenhua Shan, Kimmo Nuotio and Kangle Zhang (eds.), *Normative Readings of the Belt and Road Initiative: Road to New Paradigms* (Springer International 2018) 160–161.

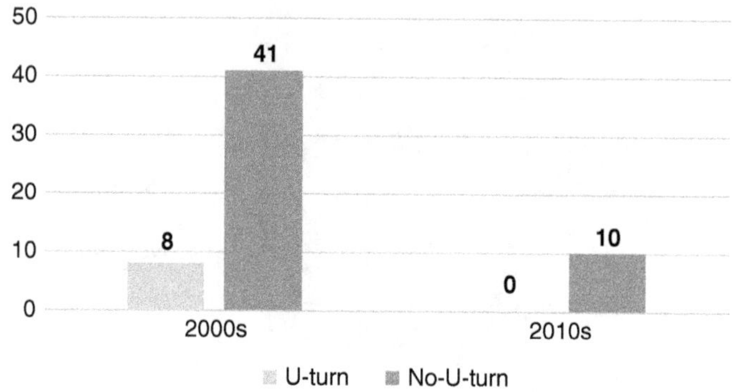

FIGURE 9.24 Time spread of fork-in-the-road clauses

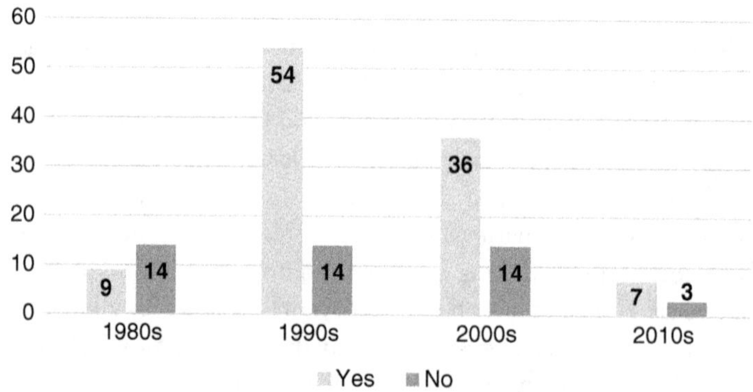

FIGURE 9.25 Time spread of "host state's law" clauses in Chinese IIAs (1982–2020)

BIT patterns along with a fundamental shift in the nature and scope of international investment law, which in turn imposes limitations on the conduct of a nation-state's domestic policies.

9.2.4.4 Host State's Law as Applicable Law

Of the 151 IIAs that contain investor dispute settlement clauses, 106 (70 percent) require the arbitration tribunal to settle investment disputes "in accordance with the laws of the state where the investment is located, including its conflict of laws rules" while 45 (30 percent) have no such requirement. In general, the vast majority of IIAs concluded by China require the arbitration tribunal to apply the host state's law in the settlement of investment disputes. Clearly, sovereignty is a major concern when China enters into IIAs with its counterparties.[186]

From the point of time distribution, as shown in Figure 9.25, the proportion of IIAs requiring the arbitration tribunal to "apply the host state's law" is greater than the proportion of IIAs "not applying the host state's law" in the remaining three decades except for the close balance between the two in the 1980s. Evidently, China has all along emphasized the application of the host state's law by the investment arbitration tribunal and has never been "leaving" its sovereignty behind.

186 See Kim M. Rooney, "ICSID and BIT Arbitrations and China" (2007) 24 *Journal of International Arbitration* 689, 692.

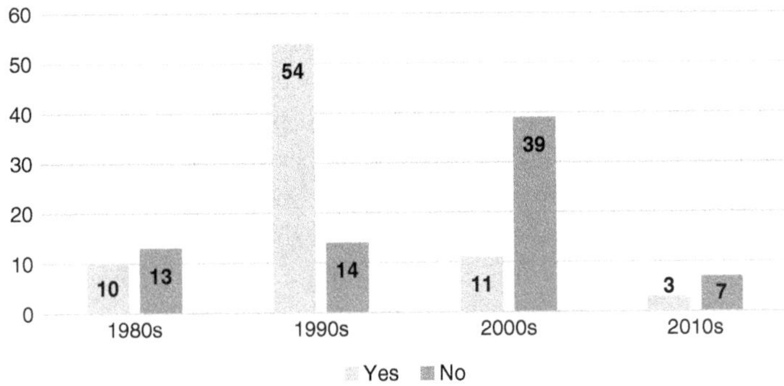

FIGURE 9.26 Chinese IIAs where award enforcement must comply with the "host state's law" clauses

Of 151 IIAs, 78 IIAs (51 percent) require investment arbitration awards to be executed in accordance with the host state's law while 73 (49 percent) do not contain such a provision. Thus, the proportions of whether this clause is based on the host state's law are basically the same. Figure 9.26 reveals that from the time distribution point of view, except where the relevant IIAs in the 1980s and 1990s put more emphasis on enforcement of investment arbitration awards pursuant to the host state's law, IIAs in recent years no longer place as much emphasis.

To sum up, in the analytical framework of the "leaving" and "return" of the state, the factor of the "host state's law" has always dominated the IIAs concluded by China. Apparently, China has not indicated an obvious "leaving (of the state)" trend in the past four decades when it came to negotiate and sign BITs. China seems to opt for the old-style ISDS with special arrangements for politically sensitive disputes[187] such as national security review, approval of an investment,[188] intellectual property and prudential measures.[189] Under the China–Australia FTA 2015, a public welfare measure (i.e., a nondiscriminatory measure for the legitimate public welfare objectives of public health, safety, the environment, public morals or public interest) alleged to be in breach of an obligation that allows the use of ISDS is not the subject of an ISDS claim.[190]

To find out the reasons, on the one hand, from the perspective of path dependence, China's participation in shaping the modern international investment law regime goes hand in hand with its gradual opening-up to the rest of the world. In this process, China has applied a piecemeal approach moving from the early strict regulation of foreign investment to the gradual admission of foreign investment and then to the freer introduction of foreign investment.[191] Therefore, every step forward in this process requires a huge reform price,[192] and the state's attitude, posture and pace of "leaving (of the state)" are relatively cautious. On the other hand, IIAs concluded by China with foreign states have been mainly concentrated in the 1990s and early 2000s. Just as shown in Figure 9.1, at this stage, China, as

187 Wenhua Shan and Peng Wang, "A Matrix Analytical Framework for Investment Disputes and Their Settlement" (2018) *ICSID Review – Foreign Investment Law Journal* 22.

188 China–Canada BIT 2012, Art. 3.

189 China–Japan–Korea TIT 2012, Art. 15.12.

190 China–Australia FTA 2015, Art. 9.11.4-5.

191 See An Chen, "To Open Wider or to Close Again: China's Foreign Investment Policies and Laws" in *The Voice from China: An CHEN on International Economic Law* (Springer 2013) 451–452.

192 See Kerry Brown, *The Rise of the Dragon: Inward and Outward Investment in China in the Reform Period 1978–2007* (Chandos 2008) preface xxiii.

a developing, transitional or emerging economy, still participated in the modern international investment law regime as a capital-importing state. Therefore, at this stage, IIAs are more focused on the sovereignty of the host state, which is essentially closely linked with the restrictions of its own legislation and its role and position in the overall international investment pattern.[193] Moving into the twenty-first century, in response to a much more integrated global market and deeper domestic economic reform, China is more willing to detach legal, economic and political decisions from the government. Effectively, China's evolving IIA regime, as a legal institution, becomes a realistic consent to undermine its sovereignty. These newer IIAs diminish the Chinese government's autonomy to regulate foreign investment, though doing so itself is an exercise of China's sovereign powers.

9.3 FAREWELL OR REUNION? CHINA AND THE WORLD IN THE TRANSFORMATIVE ERA

In the past four decades, China's foreign investment law has experienced an evolutionary process starting from a closed-ended self-reliant economy to a gradually opened-up export-oriented economy. In this process, China has continuously stressed the role of sovereignty and the importance of the state in policy-making, market-building and resource allocation. Different from other states, China did not seem to depart from its firm position on sovereignty or sovereign control on the regulation of foreign investment. State control is a strong feature of the Chinese economy, its economic growth model and even its economic governance regime, which may somehow explain China's economic success in a short period of time.[194]

The side effect of this economic model is excessive state intervention. Consequently, the rule of law, legal institutions and the legal infrastructure lag behind. Meanwhile, in recognition of its self-interest, China also participates in a rule-based and multi-layered global governance regime as well as the judicial enforcement system, submitting itself to "economic constitutionalism premised on transnational rule of law and judicial protection."[195] As far as IIAs are concerned, conservativism was a clear feature attached to China's old-generation IIAs and BITs. References to the law of the host state can often be seen in Chinese BITs, demonstrating China's sincerity over sovereignty and state power, which matches its ideological faith in collective rights and the public interests of the state, the key source of its ruling legitimacy. Driven by its transformation from a pure capital-importing state to a capital-importing and exporting state, China is in a process of rendering its sovereign power in a limited scale and reaching a new equilibrium by not only attracting foreign investment into the country but also protecting its outbound investment. This new equilibrium serves China's more recent "go globally" strategy and the Belt and Road Initiative, whose objectives are to encourage Chinese investors to invest more in the global markets.[196] Likely, China will move toward a more liberal stance in negotiating future BITs so as to engage more actively with the rest of the world in shaping a deeper level of multilateralism.

In the analytical paradigm of the leaving or return of the state, China has been mainly a capital-importing state for a long time. Consequently, the domestic judicial system as well

193 See Alan Bevan, Saul Estrin and Klaus Meyer, "Foreign Investment Location and Institutional Development in Transition Economies" (2004) 13 *International Business Review* 43, 61–62.

194 See Pitman B. Potter, "Foreign Investment Law in the People's Republic of China: Dilemmas of State Control" (1995) *China Quarterly* 155, 185.

195 Petersmann, *Multilevel Constitutionalism for Multilevel Governance of Public Goods*, 50.

196 Yu-Ting Ye, "Towards a Balanced and Liberal Chinese Bilateral Investment Treaty Regime," 107, 145.

as IIAs and their related ISDS system, which can be viewed as public goods, are also shaped by China's capital-importing status and its keen policy to attract foreign investment. Essentially, it is fair to say that China has probably never been leaving away its position of stressing and protecting its sovereignty while participating in the global IIA network. Seen from this angle, China's policy toward foreign investment is one of only limited[197] or incremental liberalization.[198] China and most developed states tend to diverge in terms of their approach to being engaged in the international investment law regime. Put differently, as far as rights protection in IIAs is concerned, China is still distant from other developed states and lags behind more liberal substantive and procedural standards.[199] This makes sense as Chinese BITs with developing countries primarily serve political, rather than economic, purposes.[200]

Given China's go globally strategy and Belt and Road Initiative, having higher rights protection standards in its IIAs would be in China's own best interests due to its shifting role from a pure capital-importing state to a capital-importing and exporting state. It therefore makes sense to see China's switch from its conservative position in entering into IIAs to a more liberal stance embracing better rights protection standards. Meanwhile, the USA and other conventional developed states are taking an opposing trajectory by having more restrictive BITs offering less favorable investment protections than those in earlier versions.[201] At this juncture, China and the USA and other developed states are in a collision course of two distinct and opposing approaches in spite of converging on some standards in IIAs.[202] Having said this, it is not to say that leaving its sovereignty would prevent the host states from encountering any risks. Emerging states should be cautious about this strategy or approach toward IIAs. The return of developed states and the leaving of developing states may offer a great opportunity for a convergence of state policies in IIAs, leading to a smooth and healthy transformation of international investment law in the years to come.

197 Janina Witkowska, "The Attitude of the European Union and China towards Foreign Direct Investment: Implications for Bilateral Relations" (2019) 22(3) *Comparative Economic Research* 83–98.

198 Jeffrey J. Schott and Cathleen Cimino, "The China-Japan-Korea Trilateral Investment Agreement: Implications for US Policy and the US-China Bilateral Investment Treaty" in Peterson Institute for International Economics, *Toward a US-China Investment Treaty* (PIIE Briefing 15-1, February 2015) 14.

199 See Berger, "The Politics of China's Investment Treaty-Making Program," 176–178.

200 Kate Hadley, "Do China's BITs Matter? Assessing the Effect of China's Investment Agreements on Foreign Direct Investment Flows, Investors' Rights and the Rule of Law" (2013) 45 *Georgetown Journal of International Law* 255.

201 Carter, "The Protracted Bargain," 213.

202 Kyle Dylan Dickson-Smith, "Lessons Learned from the Canada-China FIPA for the US-China BIT and Beyond: Chinese Whispers or Chinese Chequers?" in Julien Chaisse (ed.), *China's International Investment Strategy: Bilateral, Regional, and Global Law and Policy* (Oxford University Press 2019) 119.

10

Who Makes Chinese BITs? An Empirical Investigation

A related but unsettled question is – what is the real driving force shaping China's BIT regime and its evolution? The general consensus is that China's shifting role from a pure capital-importing state to a capital-importing and exporting state[1] is the key driving force pushing for the liberalization of the Chinese BIT regime.

This question essentially concerns China's treaty behavior or treaty pattern. China is not merely applying (or copying) these liberal model BITs mechanically.[2] China has adapted itself to various model BITs and trading partners according to different treaty partners. During negotiation, it is necessary to promote mutual understanding.[3] For example, while Japan joins these agreements to secure nondiscriminatory investment liberation, China holds a more cautious (or conservative) attitude against investment liberalization, for instance by applying NT, "as it may crimp industrial policy."[4] When negotiating BITs with developed countries such as the USA, China takes into account the following issues: S&D treatment, conduct of investors, and sustainable development.[5] Negotiating a BIT with China presents distinct challenges due to the radical differences that exist between these countries' and China's legal frameworks, their differing values, varying levels of development, and economic structures.[6] Negotiation may go quite differently between China and developing countries

1 Shen Wei, "Expropriation in Transition: Evolving Chinese Investment Treaty Practices in Local and Global Contexts" (2015) 28 *Leiden Journal of International Law* 579 (clarifying China's switching stance of being a pure capital-importing state to a capital-importing and exporting state).

2 This idea is also demonstrated in Xiuli Han, "The China–South Africa Bilateral Investment Treaty: National Rule of Law versus International Rule of Law" (2017) 24 *South African Journal of International Affairs* 269, where the author holds that China's treaty partner should also take differential policies toward China, considering China's future.

3 Wei Yin, "Challenges, Issues in China-EU Investment Agreement and the Implication on China's Domestic Reform" (2018) 26 *Asia Pacific Law Review* 170.

4 Shintaro Hamanaka, "China-Japan-Korea Trilateral Investment Treaty: Implications for Future Investment Negotiations in Asia" in Julien Chaisse, Tomoko Ishikawa and Sufian Jusoh (eds.), *Asia's Changing International Investment Regime: Sustainability, Regionalization, and Arbitration* (Springer, Singapore 2017) 121–139.

5 Congyan Cai, "China-US BIT Negotiations and the Future of Investment Treaty Regime: A Grand Bilateral Bargain with Multilateral Implications" (2009) 12 *Journal of International Economic Law* 457.

6 David Hallinan, "The EU–China Bilateral Investment Treaty: A Challenging First Test of the EU's Evolving BIT Model" (2016) 5 *China-EU Law Journal* 31.

given the various concerns ranging from environmental concerns to human rights aspects, labor issues, and economic development.[7] What's more, some scholars hold that it is necessary to take into consideration "shifts in CCP leadership and the party's perception of what is required to guarantee its stability and continued dominance."[8]

While China adapts the model BITs with different treaty partners, it finds that some treaty partners adopt the US or Canadian model BIT with only moderate modifications, in which some critical provisions regarding dispute settlement not only deviate from relevant international conventions but also harm the national interests of China and other developing countries.[9] Therefore, some scholars support the view that China should insist on protecting its rights authorized by international conventions[10] and embracing disciplines commonly found elsewhere[11] throughout the process of negotiating and drafting BITs. After all, neither the US nor the Canadian model BIT should be treated and used as a well-established and widely accepted BIT model.[12]

China is not satisfied only by entering into BITs. Investigation of China's BITs and FTA investment chapters shows that it has adopted the "from BIT to FTA" approach. The pace of China's FTA-making has been even quicker in recent years.[13] In general, those BITs and FTAs help promote property rights and rule of law in China[14] and improve China's global trade governance.[15] The traditional global investment strategy does not fit in the current world while BITs continue to lack breadth and efficiency. The best investment governance strategy for China should be more flexible, with a focus on the bilateral, regional and multilateral levels, making a suitable adaption when facing different treaty partners, and contributing to the architecture governing global investment.[16] Nor does China content to be just a rule-follower. In the long term, China is likely to become a rule-maker "evolve[ing] from selective adaption to selective innovation."[17]

One task of this chapter is to investigate the correlation between China's liberalization of its BIT regime and all the variables in relation to the evolution of BIT norms, especially the counterparty which has been in negotiation with China for the BIT. Some empirical studies are conducted to see how the landscape of China's BIT regime has been shaped in the past four decades. This question is also associated with China's treaty behavior when it comes to negotiating and signing BITs. The conventional consensus is that China has not been an inexperienced rule-maker particularly in the international law arena. In terms of

7 Catherine Elkemann and Oliver C. Ruppel, "Chinese Foreign Direct Investment into Africa in the Context of BRICS and Sino-African Bilateral Investment Treaties" (2015) 13 *Richmond Journal of Global Law and Business* 593.

8 Tyler Cohen and David Schneiderman, "The Political Economy of Chinese Bilateral Investment Treaty Policy" (2017) 5(1) *Chinese Journal of Comparative Law* 110–128.

9 An Chen, "Should the Four 'Great Safeguards' in Sino-foreign BITs Be Hastily Dismantled? Comments on Critical Provisions Concerning Dispute Settlement in Model US and Canadian BITs" (2006) 7 *Journal of World Investment & Trade* 899.

10 Ibid.

11 Cohen and Schneiderman, *supra* note 8, 110–128.

12 Tingliang Wang, "Western Misperceptions and China's Approach to International Investment Law" (2019) 17 *Santa Clara Journal of International Law* 1.

13 Manjaio Chi, "The China-EU BIT as a Stepping Stone towards a China-EU FTA: A Policy Analysis" in Marc Bungenburg et al., *European Yearbook of International Economic Law 2017* (Springer 2017) 476–489.

14 Kate Hadley, "Do China's Bits Matter – Assessing the Effect of China's Investment Agreements on Foreign Direct Investment Flows, Investors Rights, and the Rule of Law" (2013) 45 *Georgetown Journal of International Law* 255.

15 Chi, *supra* note 13.

16 Heng Wang, "The RCEP and Its Investment Rules: Learning from Past Chinese FTAs" (2017) 3 *Chinese Journal of Global Governance* 160.

17 Ibid.

BITs, nevertheless, China has appeared to follow in the footprints of the EU, the USA and other major trading partners. These indicate China's own logic of signing BITs instead of following a uniform approach.[18] The other perspective this chapter is trying to offer is an investigation of China's treaty behavior, or at least some factors affecting the shaping of Chinese BITs. Most of the existing research into China's BITs uses comparative study, case study and treaty interpretation methodologies. However, empirical study is rare when it comes to China and its BIT law and practice.

10.1 EMPIRICAL STUDIES IN IIL: ATTEMPTS AND FINDINGS

The world is complex and international law is the product of specific forces and factors. International law has attracted the interest of not only law professionals but experts in other fields, too. In addition to their areas of expertise, international law scholars are also interested in the methods used by other disciplines.[19] The new wave of empirical scholarship by experts from legal and other disciplines should lead, and may have led, to a better understanding of how, and the conditions under which, international law works, ultimately informing normative projects or shaping normative rules. For instance, it is difficult to investigate more than 3,200 IIAs and their 24,000 articles in unprecedented detail by treating treaty text as data through either doctrinal methodology or other theoretical methodologies. Yet, this grand project can be efficiently conducted – indeed, it has already been conducted in *Mapping the Universe of International Investment Agreements*[20] and others – through empirical methodology. This point is also demonstrated by Shaffer and Ginsburg; as they noted in their article, "[t]he increased empirical attention given to international law is also supported by technical developments and funding opportunities that facilitate data gathering and analysis, such as the rapid increase in the power of statistical packages." While some authors use only empirical research to test their hypotheses[21] so as to understand how the law actually functions, Shaffer and Ginsburg argue that empirical research does more than confirm or refute hypotheses; "it initiates, it reformulates, it deflects, and it clarifies theories."

Although the trend toward empirical study has expanded through the efforts of scholars in multiple disciplines, legal scholars still play central roles independently and as collaborators in generating new empirical work. In other words, empirical methodology is (and should be) led by legal scholars who "help social scientists inexpert in the law build and test models that reflect a more persuasive understanding of law."[22] Empirical methodology has expanded to

18 An Chen, *supra* note 9 (arguing against the idea of China going to copy other countries' model BITs).

19 Gregory C. Shaffer and Tom Ginsburg, "The Empirical Turn in International Legal Scholarship" (2012) 106(1) *American Journal of International Law* 1.

20 Wolfgang Alschner and Dmitriy Skougarevskiy, "Mapping the Universe of International Investment Agreements" (2016) 19(3) *Journal of International Economic Law* 561–588.

21 Empirical research is used for testing hypotheses in Emilie M. Hafner-Burton and Alexander H. Montgomery, "The Hegemon's Purse: No Economic Peace between Democracies" (2008) 45 *Journal of Peace Research* 111.

22 Legal scholar-centric mode is reinforced in Jason Webb Yackee's 2013 article "Incorporating Legal Expertise into Political Science Studies of International Law, with Special Reference to Bilateral Investment Treaties," http://law.scu.edu/wp-content/uploads/investment/Yackee-Santa-Clara-paper.pdf (accessed April 6, 2021) (arguing that legal research can contribute meaningfully to truly interdisciplinary research projects without turning them into quants while the academic trend is to conduct increasingly empirical and interdisciplinary research into BITs and other social phenomena, and more and more lawyers are becoming quantitatively minded social scientists). This mode can also be found in Catherine M. Amirfar, "Dispute Settlement Clauses in Investor-State

several fields, including international human rights law,[23] international environment law[24] and IIL, among others. Empirical methodology is conventionally divided into quantitative methods – again, for an example, see *Mapping the Universe of International Investment Agreements* – and qualitative methods, which "offers the advantage of paying closer attention to dynamic social contexts, as it often involves field work and interviews."[25] Besides, other scholars suggest that when designing and carrying out studies, researchers should also consider "subjects–objects," "purposes–factors," "normative, sociological and political legitimacy," "elements of legitimacy" and "balancing elements of legitimacy."[26]

In brief, there are two main empirical topics in IIL. The first divides into two questions: whether the signing of BITs can increase the flow of investment between host and home states, and how this works in reality. In dealing with the first question, it has been argued that issues related to BITs are of great significance because "investment law remains subject to a complex array of bilateral investment treaties."[27] However, there has been conflicting literature on the positive relationship between the strength of investor protection in BITs and investment flows.[28] While some support a positive correlation, a negative correlation between the number of BITs and the size of FDI inflows (FDII) has been confirmed by other empirical studies.[29] That said, "BITs provide 'credible commitments' when foreign investors have grounds to believe that a state's domestic legal system is inadequate and thus cannot be trusted to uphold a contractual bargain." In other words, in the eyes of foreign investors, BITs work as a kind of guarantee for countries that are without an adequate legal system; they show those countries' commitment to contractual enforcement and to not arbitrarily expropriating foreign companies. Thus, BITs help to "improve all investment flows into the host states regardless of the source, and not simply the flows between the BIT parties."

However, other scholars disagree with the importance of BITs in attracting FDI flows or "competing for capital."[30] From an international political perspective, the quality of political

Arbitration: An Informed Approach to Empirical Studies about Law: A Response to Professor Yackee" (2014) 52 *Columbia Journal of Transnational Law* 506.

23 Emilie M. Hafner-Burton, "Trading Human Rights: How Preferential Trade Agreements Influence Government Repression" (2005) 59 *International Organization* 593.

24 Kal Raustiala and Robert O. Keohane, "Toward a Post-Kyoto Climate Change Architecture: A Political Analysis" (2008) 5 *Journal of Scholarly Perspectives* 50.

25 Shaffer and Ginsburg, *supra* note 19. Quantitative method is also deployed in Jason Webb Yackee, "Conceptual Difficulties in the Empirical Study of Bilateral Investment Treaties" (2008) 33(2) *Brooklyn Journal of International Law* 405–462 (examining dispute settlement provisions in nearly 1,000 BITs). Examples of the qualitative method can be found in Jonathan Bonnitcha, "Assessing the Impacts of Investment Treaties: Overview of the Evidence" (2017) International Institute for Sustainable Development Report, www.iisd.org/sites/default/files/publications/assessing-impacts-investment-treaties.pdf (accessed December 27, 2019) where the author suggests that in order to figure out investment treaties' impact on domestic governance and their potential chilling effect on policy-making, it is necessary to interview government decision-makers "who are actually involved in negotiating, implementing and ensuring compliance with investment treaties."

26 Daniel Behn, Ole Kristian Fauchald and Malcolm Langford, "Empirical Perspectives on the Legitimacy of International Investment Tribunals" (2015) PluriCourts Investment, Internal Working Paper, www.jus.uio.no/pluricourts/english/topics/investment/documents/1-2015-legitimacy-book-project.pdf (accessed December 27, 2019).

27 Shaffer and Ginsburg, *supra* note 19.

28 Deborah L. Swenson, "Why Do Developing Countries Sign BITs?" (2005) 12 *UC Davis Law Review* 131.

29 Jason Webb Yackee, "Sacrificing Sovereignty: Bilateral Investment Treaties, International Arbitration, and the Quest for Capital" (2007) https://core.ac.uk/reader/210602180 (accessed March 18, 2021).

30 Ibid.

relations between the signatory countries is more potent in promoting FDI.[31] Besides, some of the most effective legal institutions are those whose formal levels of compliance are very low.[32] What's more, BITs without dispute settlement mechanisms are not credible options for developing countries.[33] There are no obvious disparities on credible commitment functions between municipal law and investment contracts and BITs.

The other question relates to why BITs adopt various rational design propositions. For example, different BITs allow different dispute settlement mechanism options. Through quantitative research, some point out (even while failing to find any empirical support) that "states possess systematic preferences regarding the degree to which an international institution should have centralized functions and flexible arrangements."[34] These preferences derive from domestic political conditions within each signatory country. Caution must be given to the surrounding features of a particular BIT such as the scope of coverage, the generosity of substantive rights, and the dispute settlement mechanisms which affect the costs and benefits of signing that BIT even though all the BITs may have a set of generic elements of relevance.[35]

The second main topic is on the quality or functionality of investment treaty arbitration, which involves several interrelated questions. Since the use of investment arbitration is unique in settling international investment disputes, people believe that ensuring fair and just arbitration can provide a better environment for attracting investment inflows into host countries. Fairness and independence are of great concern.[36] Thus, some empirical research has been directed toward the quality of adjudicators, which are arbitrators in BIT arbitration. For instance, one may ask whether an arbitrator's nationality will influence the outcome of an investment arbitration case since an arbitrator's nationality is generally deemed an appropriate proxy for bias in the investment law context. On this question, Susan Franck concludes through empirical study that the nationality of the presiding arbitrator does not lead to outcomes favoring developed states.[37] However, while the arbitrator's nationality does not make any difference to the outcomes, issues of cost will create challenges for using ITA in the most fair and efficient manner possible. Therefore, to avoid the outcomes of ITA becoming just words on paper and having no actual effects, the arbitrators "are encouraged to consider specific factors when making cost-related (including the costs of lawyers for both sides, as well as administrative and tribunal expenses) decisions, obligate investors to particularize their claimed damages at an early stage."[38]

31 Rodolphe Desbordes and Vincent Vicard, "Foreign Direct Investment and Bilateral Investment Treaties: An International Political Perspective" (2009) 37 *Journal of Comparative Economics* 372.

32 Emilie M. Hafner-Burton, David G. Victor and Yonatan Lupu, "Political Science Research on International Law: The State of the Field" (2012) 106 *American Journal of International Law* 47.

33 Yackee, "Conceptual Difficulties," *supra* note 25.

34 See Todd Allee and Clint Peinhardt, "Not the Least BIT Rational: An Empirical Test of the 'Rational Design' of Investment Treaties" (paper prepared for submission to the first Conference on the Political Economy of International Organizations Monte Verità, Switzerland 2008) www.peio.me/wp-content/uploads/2014/04/Conf1_Allee.Peinhardt_BITs.Rational.Design.pdf (accessed December 27, 2019).

35 Lauge N. Skovgaard Poulsen, Jonathan Bonnitcha and Jason Webb Yackee, "Analytical Framework for Assessing Costs and Benefits of Investment Protection Treaties" (2013) www.international-arbitration-attorney.com/wp-content/uploads/2014/08/85arbitrationlawAnalytical-framework-for-assessment-costs-and-benefits-of-investment-protection.pdf (accessed March 18, 20201).

36 Gus Van Harten, "Contributions and Limitations of Empirical Research on Independence and Impartiality in International Investment Arbitration" (2011) 1(4) *Oñati Socio-Legal Series* 1, 3.

37 Susan D. Franck, "Development and Outcomes of Investment Treaty Arbitration" (2009) 50 *Harvard International Law Journal* 435.

38 Susan D. Franck, "Rationalizing Costs in Investment Treaty Arbitration" (2011) 88(4) *Washington University Law Review* 769.

On the contrary, through examining the trend in legal interpretations instead of case outcomes, other research proves that arbitrators still have some kind of preferences.[39] ITA is also criticized for a lack of transparency compared with other peer institutions.[40] Reforms aimed at promoting transparency therefore become a heated issue. But in some cases where contract violations resulted from strong political incentives, the parties to disputes favor less transparent outcomes.[41] Thus, in order to improve ITA and equip IIL with meaningful dispute solutions, it is necessary to take into account all reliable variables; viewing variables in isolation, such as focusing on the transparency of the ITA system but ignoring the political incentives underlying violations or a state's internal political infrastructure, fails to attract "high-quality" investment.[42]

A sideline question in relation to the functionality of the IIL regime is to explore its rule of law nature. The general consensus is that the IIL regime does not encourage the investor and the host state to cooperate as foreign investors use arbitration as a last resort. Empirical studies, however, show that claimant investors reinvest in the host state 31 percent of the time.[43] This may suggest the policy relevance of the ISDS regime and its ongoing reform as the probability of reinvestment can reinforce the host state's commitments to the ISDS regime.

Other research investigates secrecy and transparency in international investment arbitration, a very strong variable to test the legitimacy and accountability of ISDS. Empirical studies show that the enduring pressure of secrecy has been a central element of the public backlash against investment law and arbitration due to the lack of legal consistency and perceptions of bias and incompetence. The policy implication of this tension between the two effects of secrecy, however, is quite disturbing due to the lack of apparent negative correlation between the adoption of transparency-oriented reforms and the actual practice of keeping awards and settlements secret.[44]

The availability of "big data" now presents new ways of analyzing, phrasing and presenting legal issues and phenomena.[45] Above all, sound empirical work facilitates analysis of legal terms and invents reasonable laws and rules, but it will be a long time before this empirically oriented goal is achieved. As criticized, empirical studies so far have failed to ensure their internal validity, accuracy and completeness in capturing the underlying theoretical concepts or logics.[46] The prerequisite is to ensure legal experts' predominance in collaborations with scholars in other disciplines during the entire research process and to use empirical methodology at the right spot.

BITs are usually used to attract FDI. The general empirical approach thus aims to quantify the impact of BITs on FDI at aggregated levels. Some research focuses on a micro level, for

39 Gus Van Harten, "Arbitrator Behaviour in Asymmetrical Adjudication: An Empirical Study of Investment Treaty Arbitration" (2012) 50 *Osgoode Hall Law Journal* 211.

40 Samuel Levander, "Resolving 'Dynamic Interpretation': An Empirical Analysis of the UNCITRAL Rules on Transparency" (2014) 52 *Columbia Journal of Transnational Law* 506.

41 Emilie M. Hafner-Burton and David G. Victor, "Secrecy in International Investment Arbitration: An Empirical Analysis" (2016) 7 *Journal of International Dispute Settlement* 161.

42 Susan D. Franck et al., "The Diversity Challenge: Exploring the 'Invisible College' of International Arbitration" (2015) 53 *Columbia Journal of Transnational Law* 429.

43 Rachel L. Wellhausen, "International Investment Law and Foreign Direct Reinvestment" (2019) 73 *International Organization* 839–858.

44 Emilie M. Hafner-Burton, Zachary C. Steinert-Threlkeld and David G. Victor, "Predictability versus Flexibility: Secrecy in International Investment Arbitration" (2016) *World Politics* 1–41.

45 Wolfgang Alschner, Joost Pauwelyn and Sergio Puig, "The Data-Driven Future of International Economic Law" (2017) 20 *Journal of International Economic Law* 217–231.

46 Yackee, "Conceptual Difficulties," *supra* note 25, at 406, 407.

example the foreign activity of the universe of German multinationals. Evidence confirms that there have been changes in multinational firms' investment activity due to the effects that BITs have on intensive and extensive investment margins. The conclusion is that BITs raise the number of multinational firms that are active in a particular host country and have a positive effect on the number of plants per firm as well as on FDI stocks and fixed assets per firm.[47]

Some empirical research appears to confirm the correlation between the number of BITs and FDI stock at the aggregated level. For instance, it was confirmed that the BITs that South Korea signed with developing countries have positive and statistically significant effects on Korea's FDI into those countries while those it signed with developed countries do not.[48]

10.2 METHODOLOGY

10.2.1 *Data Description*

Indexes used for empirical study of the key question listed at the beginning of this chapter are listed in Table 10.1.

Let's now look into the "quality" of the counterparties to Chinese BITs, with quality here including number of BITs, number of TIPs, GDP, FDI inflows and outflows, personal remittances (payments and receipts), the World Bank's Doing Business Index (DBI) ranking, economic freedom, rule of law, property rights protection, political risk, and transparency.

A BIT is an agreement between two countries regarding promotion and protection of investments made by investors from respective countries in each other's territory. The great majority of IIAs are BITs. Currently, the total number of BITs is 2,932 worldwide and 2,343 are in force. The number of BITs is a very relevant quality of a counterparty, indicating the country's positive attitude toward BITs as means for foreign investors' rights protection. The more BITs a country has, the more likely it is that it will prefer to sign a BIT with its counterparty and to subject itself to international rule of law.

The category of treaties with investment provisions (TIPs) brings together various types of treaties that are not BITs but may serve the same purpose as BITs. Three main types of TIPs can be distinguished: broad economic treaties that include obligations commonly found in BITs (e.g., an FTA with an investment chapter); treaties with limited investment-related provisions (e.g., those concerning only establishment of investments or free transfer of investment-related funds); and treaties that contain only "framework" clauses such as those on cooperation in the area of investment and/or those mandating for future negotiations on investment issues. The number of TIPs worldwide is 386 and 313 of them are in force.

The GDP at purchasers' prices is the sum of the gross value added by all resident producers in the economy plus any product taxes and minus any subsidies not included in the value of the products. It is calculated without making deductions for depreciation of fabricated assets or for depletion and degradation of natural resources. Data are in current US dollars. Dollar figures for GDP are converted from domestic currencies using single year official exchange

47 Peter Egger and Valeria Merlo, "BITs Bite: An Anatomy of the Impact of Bilateral Investment Treaties on Multinational Firms" (2012) 114(3) *Scandinavian Journal of Economics* 1240–1266.

48 Heon Joo Jung and Eun Mi Kim, "International Treaties and Foreign Direct Investment: An Empirical Analysis of Effects of Bilateral Investment Treaties on South Korea's FDI" (2020) 25(3) *Journal of the Asia Pacific Economy* 402–417.

TABLE 10.1 *Indexes*

Category	No.	Index	Organization	Data source (website)
Counterparty IIAs	1	Numbers of BITs (BITs)	UNCTAD	https://investmentpolicyhub.unctad.org/IIA
	2	Numbers of TIPs (TIPs)	UNCTAD	https://investmentpolicyhub.unctad.org/IIA
Economic index	3	GDP	UNCTAD	World Bank, National accounts data and OECD, National accounts data https://databank.shihang.org/data/reports.aspx?source=2&type=metadata&series=NY.GDP.MKTP.CD#
	4	FDII	UNCTAD	- UNCTAD, Division on Investment and Enterprise, *World Investment Report*, Statistical Annex (http://unctad.org/en/Pages/DIAE/World%20Investment%20Report/World_Investment_Report.aspx) - UNCTAD, *UNCTADstat*, Total trade in goods and services - UNCTAD, *UNCTADstat*, Gross domestic product
	5	FDIO	UNCTAD	- UNCTAD, *UNCTADstat*, Total population https://unctadstat.unctad.org/wds/TableViewer/summary.aspx?ReportId=96740
	6	Personal remittances: payments (PRP)	UNCTAD	- World Bank, Migration and remittances data - IMF, Balance of payments statistics - EIU, online database - *UNCTADstat* (series on GDP and total trade)
	7	Personal remittances: receipts (PRR)	UNCTAD	- UNCTAD secretariat calculations[49] https://unctadstat.unctad.org/wds/TableViewer/summary.aspx
	8	Doing Business Index (DBI)	World Bank	www.doingbusiness.org/en/data
	9	Economic Freedom Index (EFI)	Heritage Foundation	www.heritage.org/index/about
Law index	10	World Justice Program's Rule of Law Index (WJPRLI)	World Justice Project	https://worldjusticeproject.org/sites/default/files/documents/WJP_RuleofLawIndex_2019_Website_reduced.pdf
	11	Worldwide Governance Indicators: Rule of Law (WGIRL)	World Bank	https://databank.worldbank.org/data/metadataglossary/worldwide-governance-indicators/series

(Continued)

49 The main source of personal remittances data is the World Bank. In cases of missing data, data from the IMF or the Economic Intelligence Unit have been used instead. Capital transfers data have been taken from the IMF.

TABLE 10.1 *(Continued)*

Category	No.	Index	Organization	Data source (website)
	12	International Property Rights Index (IPRI)	Property Rights Alliance	www.internationalpropertyrightsindex.org/about
Politics index	13	Political Risk Services International Country Risk Guide (PRS)	PRS Group	www.prsgroup.com/explore-our-products/political-risk-services/
	14	Corruption Perceptions Index (CPI)	Transparency International	www.transparency.org/research/cpi

rates. For a few countries where the official exchange rate does not reflect the rate effectively applied to actual foreign exchange transactions, an alternative conversion factor is used.[50]

FDI flows are an important factor shaping a particular country's BIT law and practice. Conventional wisdom affirms a correlation between a host state's attitudes toward levels of foreign investment protection and its status as a capital-importing or exporting state. FDI flows mainly comprise three components: acquisition or disposal of equity capital (FDI includes the initial equity transaction that meets the 10 percent threshold and all subsequent financial transactions and positions between the direct investor and the direct investment enterprise); reinvestment of earnings which are not distributed as dividends; and inter-company debt. Here, FDII and FDIO are the key statistical factors. China's accumulated FDI exceeded USD 2.1 trillion by the end of 2018, ranked second in the world according to the UN Conference on Trade and Development.

Remittance is a key factor in foreign investment protection guaranteeing a foreign investor's freedom to remit money in and out of the host state's border. Personal remittances are the sum of two items:[51] (a) compensation of employees, defined as the income of workers employed in an economy where they are not resident and of residents employed by non-resident employers; and (b) personal (current) transfers, defined as current transfers in kind or in cash, between resident and non-resident households.[52]

A country's business-friendly environment is the key to the attractiveness of foreign investment. The DBI offers economic data from 2003 to the present. The data present a variety of factors that have an impact on business such as business form, business law and ease of doing business. A business-friendly (legal) environment usually entails a well-perceived rights protection regime, which is the fundamental objective of the BIT, and an ISDS mechanism

[50] GDP represents the sum of value added by all its producers. Value added is the value of the gross output of producers less the value of intermediate goods and services consumed in production, before accounting for consumption of fixed capital in production. The United States System of National Accounts calls for value added to be valued at either basic prices (excluding net taxes on products) or producer prices (including net taxes on products paid by producers but excluding sales or value added taxes). Both valuations exclude transport charges that are invoiced separately by producers. Total GDP is measured at purchaser prices. Value added by industry is normally measured at basic prices.

[51] This is in line with the guidelines of the Balance of Payments and International Investment Position Manual, Sixth Edition (BPM6).

[52] A broader definition of personal remittances would include capital transfers between resident and nonresident households. Capital transfers between resident and nonresident households are not included herein.

therein. According to the DBI, China's ease of doing business score ranked 31st in the world in 2020, behind countries such as the USA, Germany and even Russia and Malaysia.

Countries' levels of economic freedom, that is, their progress toward reducing poverty, are measured in the Economic Freedom Index (EFI).[53] The EFI measures twelve freedoms – property rights, government integrity, judicial effectiveness, government spending, tax burden, fiscal health, business freedom, labor freedom, monetary freedom, trade freedom, investment freedom and financial freedom – across 186 countries.

The ultimate purpose of ISDS and BITs is to ensure rule of law in the host state, which is a safeguard of foreign investment. There are two rule of law indexes – the World Justice Project's Rule of Law Index (WJPRLI) and the World Bank's Worldwide Governance Indicators: Rule of Law Index (WGIRL) – that capture perceptions of the extent to which agents have confidence in and abide by the rules of society, and in particular the quality of contract enforcement, property rights, police, courts, as well as the likelihood of crime and violence. The general consensus is that a country with a better rule of law regime is more able and potentially more willing to offer higher rights protection standards to foreign investors. By contrast, a country without a strong rule of law regime may be less willing to offer the same level of rights protection as international standards. Likely, any BITs signed by countries with a weak rule of law regime will be drafted in such a way as to signal to the foreign investment community those countries' intention to rely on an independent dispute settlement mechanism for rights protection.

Property rights exist essentially to create a prosperous economy and a just society. There is a robust relationship between property rights and other economic and social indicators of well-being including entrepreneurship, research and development, human development, civic activism, and internet-related factors. The International Property Rights Index (IPRI), the world's only index entirely dedicated to the measurement of intellectual and physical property rights and covering 125 countries, scores the underlying institutions of a strong property rights regime: the legal and political environment, physical property rights, and IPR.

Political risk is the key risk that foreign investors must tackle when they invest into a foreign country. The uncertainty of political risk undermines foreign investors' willingness to invest and increases the transaction costs to foreign investors. The PRS model forecasts and quantifies political and country risks by examining and rating the risk to foreign assets for each regime including general turmoil, restrictions on transfers (e.g., exchange controls), direct investment risk (e.g., regulatory constraints) and export barriers (e.g., tariffs).

Transparency is a related factor that foreign investors have to encounter in shaping their investment decisions. Transparency is also related to corruption. A transparent regime usually sees less corruption. Transparency International captures corruption perceptions of examined countries.

This chapter carries out statistical analyses of the above fourteen indexes of 2017 (China did not signed any BITs from 2017 to 2020). The index names, statistical institutions and sources of relevant data are shown in Table 10.1.

10.2.2 *Indicator Processing*

Due to the objective reasons of the collective indicators themselves, the indicators are incommensurable. In this chapter are mainly problems of different magnitudes of the basic indicators. Since many indicators are derived from the internationally renowned evaluation

53 An annual guide published by The Heritage Foundation, a Thinktank in Washington, DC.

system when the basic indicators is being selected, there are no dimensions in themselves, and many indicators are derived from the indexes (on an annual basis). The dimensions of the indicators are not completely the same. Therefore, this chapter will perform the dimensionless processing of the basic indicators. In the process of dimensionless processing, in order to better measure the trend of individual indicators, each individual indicator is scored. The scoring is based on the following principles: each indicator scores between 0 and 10 points, and the score for the individual indicator is as follows:

$$\text{The } i\text{-th indicator } t\text{-year score} = \frac{X_{i(t)} - X(min)}{X(max) - X(min)} \times 10$$

According to the above score formula, the basic indicators are scored separately, as shown in Table 10.2.

Based on these data, this chapter uses the principal component analysis method, as shown in Table 10.3, to conduct an empirical analysis of the level of "leaving (of the state)", first calculating the weight of each basic indicator and then calculating the comprehensive evaluation index of "leaving (of the state)".

Table 10.3 shows that the relevant data have passed the test and can be analyzed by principal component analysis.

Looking at the total variance shows that there are three principal components in the basic refinement development index. The cumulative variance contribution rate of these three principal components' analysis is 77.23 percent, as shown in Table 10.4.

Combined with the component matrix results, the first two principal components are selected to construct a comprehensive evaluation index of "leaving (of the state)".

The component matrix results and the initial eigenvalues of each principal component are used to calculate the weight of the different principal component base indicators, as shown in Table 10.5.

According to the statistical method used in this chapter, in the calculation of the whole "leaving (of the state)" and "return (of the state)" index, the coefficient of principal component 1 accounts for 79.86 percent and the coefficient of principal component 2 accounts for 20.14 percent. Principal component 1 has the most impact on the "leaving (of the state)" and "return (of the state)" index.

In the composition of principal component 1, as shown in Table 10.6, the WGIRL (0.294) and PRR (0.128) indices are ranked first and last in descending order, respectively. First, the five indexes – that is, WGIRL, CPI, WJPRLI, IPRI and PRS – belong to the legal and political indexes. What this means is that the higher the rule of law in a country, the cleaner the government, the higher the investor protection standards and the lower the political risk, then the higher is the country's "leaving (of the state)" index in the field of international investment; the host country's intervention reflected in IIA terms is therefore weaker. In addition, among the six sub-indexes of PRS, the four indexes related to law and politics accounted for the highest proportion. The lower the risk of corruption in a country, the higher the administrative efficiency, the stronger the predictability of the law and the higher the quality of administrative regulations, especially investment-related ones, then the higher is the country's "leaving (of the state)" index in the field of international investment.

Second, although DBI and EFI are economic in nature, the rule of law and the political level of a country also have a strong influence in determining the index. At the same time, PRS-VA and PRS-PV are related to the politics of a country, to democratic stability and political stability, respectively. Therefore, the better the business environment of a country

TABLE 10.2 *Indicators and scores*

	BITs	TIPs	GDP	FDII	FDIO	PRP	PRR	DBI	EFI	WJPRLI	WGIRL	IPRI	PRS						CPI
													VA	PV	GE	RQ	RL	CC	
Sweden	5.00	9.81	1.09	2.50	1.53	0.00	1.35	9.19	6.62	9.87	9.68	9.97	10.00	10.00	10.00	8.47	9.38	7.73	9.82
Germany	10.00	9.81	7.54	5.61	5.14	10.00	8.71	8.70	6.35	9.31	8.52	8.79	10.00	3.88	10.00	8.33	7.50	8.75	9.30
France	7.38	9.81	5.29	8.03	3.64	0.69	0.26	8.09	3.75	7.38	7.91	7.66	8.75	3.56	6.67	5.00	7.50	6.25	7.37
Belgium	5.63	9.81	1.00	0.14	1.32	0.00	0.38	7.09	4.86	8.10	7.58	8.57	10.00	4.39	10.00	5.00	7.50	7.50	8.25
Finland	5.16	9.81	0.50	0.23	0.13	0.00	0.66	9.00	6.40	10.00	10.00	10.00	10.00	6.55	10.00	7.50	10.00	10.00	10.00
Italy	5.40	9.63	3.96	2.77	0.30	0.35	0.01	7.00	3.56	5.64	3.96	5.20	9.38	4.93	5.00	5.83	5.00	3.75	3.86
Netherlands	6.98	9.81	1.68	9.35	1.47	1.70	3.25	7.90	6.84	9.69	9.30	9.40	10.00	6.01	10.00	8.33	10.00	8.75	9.47
Austria	4.44	9.81	0.84	1.57	0.70	0.00	0.01	8.61	5.98	8.90	9.24	8.89	10.00	5.40	10.00	5.83	10.00	7.50	8.25
Sri Lanka	1.75	0.37	0.16	0.24	0.03	0.08	0.16	4.24	2.30	3.19	3.01	4.13	3.75	3.31	3.33	1.67	3.75	1.25	1.75
United Kingdom	7.30	9.81	5.37	2.45	6.22	0.00	10.00	9.46	6.99	8.78	8.77	9.10	10.00	3.45	10.00	9.17	7.50	8.75	9.47
Poland	4.60	9.81	1.07	1.06	0.24	0.00	0.00	8.26	4.99	6.08	4.49	5.69	9.38	6.33	6.67	5.83	3.75	5.00	5.61
Australia	1.27	2.59	2.70	7.48	0.32	0.00	0.00	8.94	8.12	8.79	8.78	9.31	10.00	3.92	10.00	10.00	8.75	7.50	8.60
Japan	2.06	2.78	10.00	1.70	10.00	3.82	0.78	7.90	5.31	8.35	8.37	9.46	7.50	6.80	10.00	8.33	7.50	7.50	7.89
Bulgaria	4.52	9.81	0.10	0.19	0.04	0.02	0.05	6.88	4.89	3.35	2.67	3.08	8.13	4.71	3.33	7.50	2.50	3.75	2.63
Turkey	5.87	2.59	1.73	1.77	0.18	0.00	0.00	6.30	4.22	1.08	1.93	3.28	1.25	0.79	3.33	0.00	2.50	2.50	2.11
Hungary	4.13	9.81	0.27	0.42	0.04	0.02	7.47	6.92	4.37	3.62	4.69	5.22	9.38	5.61	6.67	7.50	5.00	3.75	2.98
Czech Republic	5.87	9.81	0.43	1.21	0.12	0.04	0.90	8.01	6.22	7.40	6.77	6.79	8.75	5.40	6.67	7.50	7.50	3.75	5.09
Greece	3.17	9.81	0.40	0.67	0.06	0.22	0.37	6.24	1.70	4.73	3.11	4.12	8.75	5.11	6.67	5.83	6.25	2.50	3.51
Philippines	2.38	1.85	0.63	1.55	0.12	0.01	0.04	3.51	4.32	2.11	1.34	4.02	3.75	3.67	6.67	5.83	1.25	2.50	1.05
Kazakhstan	3.25	1.30	0.32	0.77	0.07	0.01	2.22	7.80	5.16	3.00	1.35	2.39	3.13	4.75	3.33	3.33	3.75	0.00	0.53
Ukraine	4.37	0.37	0.21	0.37	0.02	0.00	0.03	5.46	0.00	2.67	0.29	0.56	7.50	1.94	0.00	3.33	5.00	1.25	0.35
Argentina	3.81	1.67	1.29	1.93	0.09	0.03	0.42	3.91	0.57	4.33	1.94	2.63	5.63	6.12	6.67	3.33	0.00	1.25	1.93
Moldova	2.94	0.19	0.00	0.05	0.02	0.24	0.32	7.32	2.44	2.53	1.34	0.11	5.00	2.09	0.00	1.67	5.00	1.25	0.53
Albania	2.78	0.74	0.01	0.20	0.02	0.44	1.96	6.00	4.02	2.88	1.39	1.28	7.50	5.36	3.33	3.33	1.25	2.50	1.75

(*Continued*)

TABLE 10.2 *(Continued)*

	BITs	TIPs	GDP	FDII	FDIO	PRP	PRR	DBI	EFI	WJPRLI	WGIRL	IPRI	PRS						CPI
													VA	PV	GE	RQ	RL	CC	
Croatia	3.65	9.81	0.10	0.36	0.06	0.00	1.01	6.86	2.79	4.91	4.00	2.97	8.13	4.32	6.67	2.50	6.25	3.75	3.68
Estonia	1.98	10.00	0.04	0.15	0.02	0.00	1.06	9.01	7.65	8.55	7.36	7.41	8.13	4.42	5.00	5.83	5.00	6.25	7.54
Slovenia	2.62	9.81	0.08	0.13	0.03	2.30	2.94	7.69	2.74	6.08	6.44	5.22	8.13	3.92	8.33	1.67	6.25	5.00	5.79
Uruguay	2.22	2.04	0.10	0.00	0.03	0.00	0.00	4.83	5.33	6.85	4.89	5.98	5.63	5.90	3.33	6.67	1.25	7.50	7.37
Ecuador	0.08	0.74	0.20	0.12	0.04	0.00	0.00	3.91	0.30	2.14	0.33	2.74	0.63	2.63	3.33	0.00	1.25	1.25	0.70
Egypt	5.56	1.48	0.47	1.21	0.03	0.47	0.11	3.39	1.11	0.00	0.92	2.39	0.00	4.46	3.33	3.33	2.50	1.25	0.70
Jamaica	0.71	1.11	0.01	0.16	0.02	0.00	0.00	5.86	5.28	4.22	2.26	5.25	7.50	6.40	6.67	5.00	0.00	2.50	2.81
Morocco	3.89	0.74	0.21	0.45	0.08	0.00	0.00	6.33	3.31	2.89	2.19	4.33	5.63	3.42	3.33	2.50	5.00	3.75	2.11
Bangladesh	1.75	0.00	0.50	0.37	0.03	0.00	0.00	0.00	1.70	0.93	0.43	0.00	3.13	1.62	3.33	1.67	0.00	2.50	0.00
South Africa	0.87	1.11	0.70	0.23	0.48	0.03	0.24	5.46	3.51	4.46	2.77	7.05	7.50	4.35	3.33	3.33	0.00	2.50	2.63
Botswana	0.00	0.74	0.02	0.08	0.00	0.00	0.00	5.49	5.43	4.35	4.64	5.46	5.63	6.01	3.33	5.83	3.75	5.00	5.79
Kenya	0.71	0.56	0.15	0.13	0.03	0.00	0.00	4.95	1.33	1.68	1.35	3.16	5.63	2.48	3.33	4.17	2.50	0.00	0.00
Trinidad and Tobago	0.79	1.11	0.03	0.05	0.03	0.00	0.00	4.65	3.23	3.85	2.43	4.33	6.25	3.92	6.67	3.33	0.00	1.25	2.28
Russian Federation	4.84	0.56	3.23	4.09	2.26	0.31	3.76	7.88	2.22	2.09	0.00	1.68	2.50	2.01	0.00	3.33	2.50	0.00	0.18
India	3.81	1.11	5.33	6.44	0.72	0.54	1.63	3.44	1.11	3.07	2.83	4.44	7.50	1.62	6.67	4.17	6.25	2.50	2.11
Colombia	0.40	2.22	0.63	2.36	0.25	0.00	0.00	6.46	5.33	2.79	1.54	4.06	3.75	4.68	3.33	3.33	0.00	2.50	1.58
Pakistan	2.38	0.56	0.61	0.47	0.02	0.00	0.02	2.65	1.16	0.59	0.25	0.65	2.50	0.00	3.33	3.33	2.50	1.25	0.70
Singapore	2.78	5.00	0.65	10.00	1.56	0.00	0.00	10.00	10.00	8.54	9.28	9.51	3.75	7.19	10.00	8.33	7.50	8.75	9.82
Peru	2.14	3.52	0.42	1.11	0.04	0.00	0.08	6.26	5.14	3.16	1.04	3.81	6.88	2.45	3.33	3.33	2.50	2.50	1.58
Costa Rica	0.95	2.04	0.10	0.50	0.03	0.01	0.26	6.23	4.17	6.34	4.43	5.34	9.38	5.47	3.33	2.50	1.25	3.75	5.44

TABLE 10.3 *Principal component analysis using SPSS, first tested by Kaiser Meyer Olkin (KMO) and Bartlett*

KMO and Bartlett Test		
Sampling enough KMO metrics		.852
Bartlett's sphericity test	Approximate chi square	1348.962
	df	171
	Sig.	.000

TABLE 10.4 *Total variance of interpretation*

Ingredients	Initial eigenvalue			Extract square sum loading		
	Total	Variance %	Accumulation %	Total	Variance %	Accumulation %
1	10.767	56.668	56.668	10.767	56.668	56.668
2	2.715	14.287	70.955	2.715	14.287	70.955
3	1.192	6.275	77.230	1.192	6.275	77.230
4	.883	4.647	81.878			
5	.696	3.662	85.539			
6	.508	2.674	88.213			
7	.443	2.332	90.545			
8	.415	2.184	92.729			
9	.344	1.811	94.540			
10	.247	1.302	95.842			
11	.233	1.228	97.070			
12	.196	1.034	98.104			
13	.119	.624	98.728			
14	.074	.387	99.115			
15	.053	.278	99.393			
16	.052	.276	99.669			
17	.037	.195	99.864			
18	.018	.093	99.957			
19	.008	.043	100.000			

Extraction method: principal component analysis

and the higher its degree of economic freedom, the higher is that country's degree of "leaving (of the state)" in the field of international investment.

Finally, indexes related to a country's economy, such as FDII, FDIO, GDP and other objective conditions, have less impact on a country's level of "leaving (of the state)" or "return (of the state)."

Using all these indexes, therefore, we can draw preliminary conclusions as to countries' economic strength and their degrees of "leaving (of the state)" and "return (of the state)" in the field of international investment.

As shown in Table 10.7, the coefficients of principal component 2 are arranged in descending order. The economic indexes of the sample countries, namely GDP, PRP, FDIO, PRR and FDII, and the number of BITs signed by each have a positive correlation with their level of "leaving (of the state)" or "return (of the state)" in the field of international investment. The higher the economic index, the higher is that country's level of "leaving (of the state)" in the field of international investment. Indexes related to law and politics, such as

TABLE 10.5 *Component matrix results*

	BITs	TIPs	GDP	FDII	FDIO	PRP	PRR	DBI	EFI	WJPRLI	WGIRL	IPRI	PRS						CPI
													VA	PV	GE	RQ	RL	CC	
Coefficient of principal component 1	0.16	0.23	0.15	0.17	0.17	0.13	0.13	0.24	0.23	0.29	0.29	0.28	0.22	0.18	0.26	0.25	0.26	0.28	0.29
Coefficient of principal component 2	0.32	−0.03	0.46	0.14	0.39	0.42	0.38	−0.05	−0.18	−0.11	−0.10	−0.11	−0.09	−0.30	−0.06	−0.05	−0.01	−0.08	−0.10

TABLE 10.6 *Weight and coefficient of principal component 1*

Weight of principal component 1 0.798642277	Coefficient of principal component 1
WGIRL	0.294
CPI	0.290
WJPRLI	0.290
IPRI	0.284
PRS-CC	0.283
PRS-GE	0.265
PRS-RL	0.256
PRS-RQ	0.253
DBI	0.241
EFI	0.234
TIPs	0.229
PRS-VA	0.220
PRS-PV	0.181
FDII	0.168
FDIO	0.166
BITs	0.164
GDP	0.146
PRP	0.132
PRR	0.128

TABLE 10.7 *Weight and coefficient of principal component 2*

Weight of principal component 2 0.201357723	Coefficient of principal component 2
GDP	0.458
PRP	0.421
FDIO	0.390
PRR	0.384
BITs	0.324
FDII	0.135
PRS-RL	−0.014
TIPs	−0.030
DBI	−0.047
PRS-RQ	−0.054
PRS-GE	−0.063
PRS-CC	−0.076
PRS-VA	−0.094
WGIRL	−0.098
CPI	−0.098
WJPRLI	−0.111
IPRI	−0.112
EFI	−0.184
PRS-PV	−0.297

WGIRL, WJPRLI and CPI, as well as economic and economically relevant indicators such as DBI and EFI, have a negative correlation with the degree of "leaving (of the state)" and "return (of the state)" in the international investment field. The higher the index value, the lower is the country's degree of "leaving (of the state)" in the field of international investment. In addition, because there are six sub-items under PRS, a country with an overall negative impact on the degree of "leaving (of the state)" and "return (of the state)" in the field of international investment can have a different degree of negative impact for each sub-item. The sub-items – legal predictability, quality of administrative regulations, efficiency of government work, level of corruption, political democracy and stability of political power – have gradually increased the negative impact of countries' "leaving (of the state)" and "return (of the state)" levels in the field of international investment.

Therefore, seen from the internal structure of principal component 1 and principal component 2, the effects of the legal, political and economic indexes are different. In general, it shows an inverted data pattern.

Based on these scores and weight calculations, the "leaving (of the state)" indexes of different countries can be calculated and ranked, as shown in Table 10.8.

At the same time, an empirical analysis of the current effective BITs signed between China and the above countries is conducted, dividing the legal factors of the "host country" in the relevant BIT. There are eight indicators, and each indicator has a perfect score of 1. The more that emphasis is placed on the laws of the host country, the higher is the factor indicator and the lower is the liberalization index. In detail:

1. Investment definition: 1 is required to comply with the laws of the host country, and 0 is not required;
2. Whether the investor is required to rely on the laws of the host country: there is 1 and no 0;
3. Allowing for the public interest of the host country: 1 for, no for 0;
4. Exchange currency according to the host country law: Yes 1, not 0;
5. Any dispute over the use of host country relief: 0.25, no 0; pre-position 0.25, no 0. Bilateral equivalent application*2, not applicable*1;
6. Expropriation of compensation disputes The use of local remedies is an option or a pre-emptive, unilateral or bilateral: 0.25, no 0; pre-position 0.25, no 0. Bilateral equivalent application*2, not applicable*1;
7. The applicable law exists in the host country law: there is 1 and no 0;
8. The arbitral award is enforced on the basis of the host country law: there is 1 and no 0.

According to the method used here, Table 10.9 scores and ranks the departure and regression indexes of relevant BITs.

Accordingly, Table 10.10 indicates the correlation between the qualitied BIT and the level of "leaving (of the state)".

The statistical meaning of each variable is indicated in Table 10.11.

It is possible to construct an empirical equation to find the linear relationship between the explained variable and all the other variables, to be expressed in the sum of the explained variables.

$$y = \sum \alpha_i x_i$$

In order to enhance the stability of the data, this chapter takes the logarithm of the dependent variable and the economic basic indicator. The empirical results are outlined in Table 10.12.

The empirical equation is as follows:

TABLE 10.8 *Leaving (of the state) index*

Country	Leaving Index	Ranking
Germany	29.66303	1
United Kingdom	27.12436	2
Netherlands	26.13228	3
Sweden	24.39783	4
Japan	24.06078	5
Finland	23.71669	6
Singapore	22.78166	7
Australia	21.99587	8
Austria	21.79587	9
France	21.73484	10
Belgium	20.24762	11
Czech Republic	18.12976	12
Estonia	17.75031	13
Poland	16.19285	14
Slovenia	15.92655	15
Hungary	15.91804	16
Italy	15.69283	17
Greece	13.34943	18
Croatia	13.16832	19
Uruguay	12.92659	20
India	12.26994	21
Bulgaria	12.21777	22
Botswana	11.19802	23
Costa Rica	11.10838	24
Jamaica	9.799571	25
Morocco	9.198558	26
South Africa	9.126126	27
Peru	8.860384	28
Argentina	8.423569	29
Philippines	8.394936	30
Kazakhstan	8.141239	31
Albania	8.09502	32
Trinidad and Tobago	7.939891	33
Colombia	7.909245	34
Russian Federation	7.893605	35
Turkey	7.799573	36
Sri Lanka	7.048782	37
Ukraine	6.093885	38
Moldova	5.933027	39
Egypt	5.832776	40
Kenya	5.743058	41
Pakistan	4.354822	42
Ecuador	3.700234	43
Bangladesh	3.191254	44

$$\text{Lny} = \alpha_1 \text{dtips} + \alpha_2 l\text{ndgdp} + \alpha_3 \text{lnusd} + \alpha_4 \text{ lnfdi} + \alpha_5 \text{ prspv} + \alpha_6 \text{ prsge} + \alpha_7 \text{ prsrq} + \alpha_8 \text{ prsrl} + \alpha_9 \text{prscc}$$

Table 10.13 explains each variable and its "legal significance" in this empirical research.

TABLE 10.9 *Leaving and return (of the state) index*

Country	Effective BITs
Germany	3.625
United Kingdom	4
Sweden	4
France	4
Philippines	4
Poland	5
Hungary	5
India	5
Pakistan	5
Netherlands	5.25
Japan	5.5
Austria	5.5
Italy	5.5
Greece	5.5
Turkey	5.5
Belgium	6
Bulgaria	6
Botswana	6
Kazakhstan	6
Trinidad and Tobago	6
Colombia	6
Russian Federation	6
Ukraine	6
Kenya	6
Singapore	6.5
Australia	6.5
Singapore	6.5
Argentina	6.5
Sri Lanka	6.5
Uruguay	7
Uruguay	7
Finland	7.25
Czech Republic	7.25
Estonia	7.5
Peru	7.5
Croatia	7.5
Jamaica	7.5
Albania	7.5
Moldova	7.5
Egypt	7.5
Ecuador	7.5
Bangladesh	7.5
South Africa	8

According to the empirical results, the most significant is the political risk-related index, the most significant of which are prspv, prsge and prscc.

Prsge has positive impact while prspv has negative impact.

TABLE 10.10 *BITs, the leaving (of the state) index and correlation*

BITs name	Date of signature	Parties	OECD	BITs	TIPs	GDP (USD/ million)	FDII (USD/ million)	FDIO (USD/ million)	WGI	PRS						CPI	EF
										VA	PV	GE	RQ	RL	CC		
BLEU–China BIT (2005)	Jun 6, 2005	Belgium	1	94 (73 in force)	70 (56 in force)	387365750528.54	378156.4353	478170.2378	1.27	1.00	0.77	1.00	0.95	0.83	0.67	7.4	69
		Luxembourg	1	96 (73 in force)	70 (56 in force)	37347394602.66	64729.34946	60795.7657	1.83	1.00	0.90	1.00	1.00	1.00	0.83	8.5	76.3
China–Spain BIT (2005)	Nov 14, 2005	Spain	1	79 (72 in force)	70 (56 in force)	1157276458151.97	384538.478	305426.6055	1.13	0.92	0.72	0.75	1.00	0.83	0.67	7	67
China–Namibia BIT (2005)	Nov 17, 2005	Namibia	0	15 (9 in force)	8 (7 in force)	7121391945.38	2453.440243	25.61264822	−0.07	0.83	0.85	0.50	0.82	0.83	0.25	4.3	61.4
China–Madagascar BIT (2005)	Nov 21, 2005	Madagascar	0	9 (8 in force)	5 (4 in force)	5039293030.82	250.298636	12.455	−0.35	0.50	0.70	0.25	0.64	0.42	0.67	3.1	63.1
China–Czech Republic BIT (2005)	Dec 8, 2005	Czech Republic	1	79 (76 in force)	70 (56 in force)	136280689891.22	60662.27428	3610.407516	0.87	0.96	0.77	0.75	0.95	0.83	0.42	4.3	64.6
China–Portugal BIT (2005)	Dec 9, 2005	Portugal	1	55 (45 in force)	70 (56 in force)	197304513120.26	66696.6401	40926.51412	1.23	1.00	0.83	0.75	1.00	0.83	0.67	6.5	62.4
China–Russian Federation BIT (2006)	Nov 9, 2006	Russian Federation	0	79 (63 in force)	6 (6 in force)	989930542278.68	263903	232881	−0.95	0.63	0.68	1.00	0.95	0.83	0.58	2.4	52.4
China–India BIT (2006)	Nov 21, 2006	India	0	60 (50 in force)	13 (9 in force)	920316529729.61	70870.28365	27035.63567	0.18	0.83	0.60	1.00	1.00	1.00	0.83	3.3	52.2
China–Korea, Republic of BIT (2007)	Sep 7, 2007	South Korea	0	94 (90 in force)	20 (17 in force)	1122679154632.41	121956.5	74776.5	1.03	0.83	0.76	1.00	0.95	0.83	0.58	5.1	67.8
China–Costa Rica BIT (2007)	Oct 24, 2007	Costa Rica	0	22 (14 in force)	18 (14 in force)	26743874205.85	10819.53124	856.4908413	0.38	0.96	0.80	1.00	1.00	1.00	0.83	5	64
China–France BIT (2007)	Nov 26, 2007	France	1	103 (95 in force)	70 (56 in force)	2657213249384.07	623625.4273	1010033.829	1.47	0.96	0.68	0.75	1.00	0.83	0.67	7.3	62.1

(Continued)

TABLE 10.10 *(Continued)*

BITs name	Date of signature	Parties	OECD	BITs	TIPs	GDP (USD/ million)	FDII (USD/ million)	FDIO (USD/ million)	WGI	PRS						CPI	EF
										VA	PV	GE	RQ	RL	CC		
China–Mexico BIT (2008)	Jul 11, 2008	Mexico	1	32 (29 in force)	17 (15 in force)	1109989063586.62	280679.5625	63170.24143	−0.67	0.88	0.70	1.00	0.86	0.83	0.58	3.6	66.2
China–Colombia BIT (2008)	Nov 22, 2008	Colombia	0	16 (7 in force)	20 (15 in force)	241710969502.89	67266.725	14730.002	−0.40	0.54	0.67	1.00	0.91	1.00	0.83	3.8	62.2
China–Switzerland BIT (2009)	Jan 27, 2009	Switzerland	1	113 (111 in force)	35 (32 in force)	541506500413.57	532404.9914	866484.1737	1.75	1.00	0.80	1.00	0.86	0.83	0.83	9	79.4
China–Mali BIT (2009)	Feb 12, 2009	Mali	0	22 (8 in force)	9 (7 in force)	10181021770.43	1882.763498	10.5570392	−0.37	0.54	0.73	1.00	0.91	1.00	0.83	3.1	55.6
China–Malta BIT (2009)	Feb 22, 2009	Malta	0	22 (20 in force)	71 (57 in force)	8528202278.41	125192.471	65071.22775	1.48	1.00	0.88	0.75	0.91	0.83	0.67	5.2	66.1
China–Libya BIT (2010)	Aug 4, 2010	Libya	0	37 (23 in force)	10 (7 in force)	74773444900.54	16334.497	16614.867	−0.99	0.33	0.88	1.00	0.77	0.83	0.83	2.2	40.2
Canada–China BIT (2012)	Sep 9, 2012	Canada	1	31 (34 in force)	22 (18 in force)	1824288757447.57	953502.8135	972041.8006	1.76	1.00	0.78	1.00	0.64	0.83	0.83	84	79.9
China–Turkey BIT (2015)	Jul 29, 2015	Turkey	1	108 (76 in force)	21 (17 in force)	859796691176.47	158108	35673	−0.11	0.50	0.49	1.00	0.91	1.00	0.83	42	63.2

TABLE 10.11 *Statistical description of variables*

Variable	Obs	Mean	Std. Dev.	Min	Max
Y	20	5.75325	.8569328	4	7.25
Oecd	20	.5	.5129892	0	1
dbits	20	48.8	33.31287	7	111
dtips	20	29.5	24.1214	4	70
dgdp	20	6.16e+11	7.17e+11	5.04e+09	2.66e+12
usd	20	209201.7	253743.2	250.2986	953502.8
fdi	20	213417.3	340491.3	10.55704	1010034
dgi	20	.5238124	.9615647	−.9934169	1.83068
prsva	20	.8104167	.2173383	.3333333	1
prspv	20	.7506629	.0992359	.4924242	.9015151
prsge	20	.875	.2067925	.25	1
prsrq	20	.9022727	.1116087	.6363636	1
prsrl	20	.8625	.1304373	.4166667	1
prscc	20	.6958333	.1605796	.25	.8333333
cpi	20	10.855	19.19302	2.2	84
efi	20	63.755	9.252395	40.2	79.9

TABLE 10.12 *Empirical results of the equation model*

Source	SS	df	MS			
				Number of obs	=	20
				F(9, 10)	=	4.40
Model	.377795117	9	.041977235	Prob > F	=	0.0150
Residual	.095298877	10	.009529888	R-squared	=	0.7986
				Adj R-squared	=	0.6173
Total	.473093995	19	.024899684	Root MSE	=	.09762

lny	Coef.	Std. Err.	t	P>ItI	[95% Conf. Interval]	
dtips	.0022049	.002217	0.99	0.343	−.0027348	.0071447
lndgdp	−.1135924	.031797	−3.57	0.005	−.1844406	−.0427443
lnusd	−.0525018	.0721973	−0.73	0.484	−.2133674	.1083638
lnfdi	.0359241	.0396981	0.90	0.387	−.0525287	.1243769
prspv	−1.091886	.4601508	−2.37	0.039	−2.117165	−.0666057
prsge	1.15834	.3195242	3.63	0.005	.446396	1.870285
prsrq	−.5289573	.4336181	−1.22	0.251	−1.495119	.437204
prsrl	−.6601155	.4303523	−1.53	0.156	−1.619	.2987692
prscc	−.8099863	.2966467	−2.73	0.021	−1.470956	−.1490163
_cons	6.263493	1.159834	5.40	0.000	3.679221	8.847764

Table 10.9 indicates the degree of "leaving (of the state)" and "return (of the state)" of BITs signed between China and the sample countries. The higher the value, the lower the degree of "liberty" of the BIT signed between China and that country. The trend of return (of the state) is more obvious. As shown in Table 10.13, among all the variables, the index of $|t|>2$ is PRS-GE (3.63), GDP (−3.57), PRS-CC (−2.73) and PRS-PV (−2.37), so these variables are highly correlated with the "leaving (of the state)" and "return (of the state)" of the countries. From the coefficient of the four indices (Coef), the degree of influence on the change of the "leaving (of the state)" and "return (of the state)" degrees of the BIT is PRS-GE (1.16), PRS-PV

TABLE 10.13 *Meaning of each basic indicator*

Indicator	Meaning
OECD	Is it an OECD member state?
BITs	Number of BITs
TIPs	Number of TIPs
GDP	GDP (USD/million)
FDII	FDI inward flows (USD/million)
FDIO	FDI outward flows (USD/million)
WGI	Worldwide Governance Indicators: Regulatory Quality and the Rule of Law
PRS	Political risk services international country risk guide • Voice and accountability (VA) • Political stability and absence of violence (PV) • Government effectiveness (GE) • Regulatory quality (RQ) • Rule of law (RL) • Control of corruption (CC)
CPI	Corruption Perceptions Index
EFI	Economic Freedom Index

(−1.09), PRS-CC(−0.81), GDP(−0.11), which means: on the one hand, when the government's administrative efficiency is higher, the lower are likely to be the degrees of "leaving (of the state)" and "liberty" in the BIT signed between China and that country; on the other hand, the higher the political stability of a counterpart country, the better the democratic political system, the lower the degree of corruption and the higher the total GDP, then the higher are the degrees of BIT "leaving (of the state)" and "liberty" that the Chinese BIT may indicate.

GDP may have less impact on the degree of leaving (of the state), although it may be reflective of a counterpart country's economic and political strength.

10.3 CONCLUSION

Treaty behavior is a critical issue in IIAs as states may be influenced by various factors when entering into them. Although ISDS is at a crossroads, facing great challenges and calling for deep reforms, new IIAs appear every year. What is the driving force or key determinant shaping these new IIAs or the new terms in these IIAs? It was affirmed by empirical research that legalization in IIL via the changing content of IIAs is driven by capital-exporting states and evidenced by increasing legal precision in IIAs. The content of new IIAs is improved by states having less ambiguity and more precision to reflect the host state's preference accumulated in investment arbitration cases.

Scholars do not sufficiently understand what determines Chinese BITs' content, although they offer various explanations. The general consensus is to attribute Chinese IIAs' evolution to China's changing status from being a major capital-importing state to a capital-importing and exporting state. This changing status triggers China's changing stance in its IIAs' objective and content, switching from a conservative and state-centric one to a more liberal and investor-friendly one. This, however, was not evidenced either by China's explicit policy or by empirical investigation. The contribution made by this chapter, through its empirical study, is to confirm that at least part of the driving force rests with China's counterparties who sign the IIAs with the Chinese government. It appears, at least through the policy lens, that developed countries have a more influential role in upgrading China's IIAs in terms of their level of liberalism (i.e., investor rights protection standards). This is somehow manifested by the fact that China's FTAs with non-Western counterparts may be far from the best in terms of the depth of liberalization and the scope of obligation on investment policies.[54] The China–Korea FTA is a recent example in which the pace and scope of liberalization are less ambitious, partly because neither side wanted to use the FTA to push domestic reform except to reinforce existing trade relations.[55] Although Korea applied a KORUS-minus approach to the China–Korea FTA, it tried to piggyback on the China–US BIT to narrow the gap between the Chinese commitments in FTAs and international best practice.[56]

This is the first piece of empirical study investigating the driving force behind the upgrading and evolution of China's IIAs. Although the finding of this chapter overlaps with and supports the general consensus that Chinese IIAs evolve toward more liberal ones, it is more important to supplement the general view that the Chinese legal regime is shaped by external forces. The policy implication is at least twofold. First, future Chinese IIAs are more likely to be influenced by counterparties. Second, given the fact that the developed states are retreating from globalization and returning to sovereignty, there is a likelihood that we will see China's IIAs converging toward the developed states' approach or closing the gap with these states.

This is in line with some of the existing literature that argues that the pro-investor and pro-rule of law elements actually appeared in Chinese BITs with developed and liberal partners. This means that the BIT programs initiated by developed states or developed country groups have been effective policy instruments for increasing investment flows and improving rule of law standards in developing countries such as China.[57] A tentative conclusion may be drawn from this chapter that China may have not been a rule-maker at least in the international investment arena or a leader in the global rule-making process as it claimed. Rather, China is a rule-follower following other developed states' footprints to further raise its investor rights protection standards and liberalize its BIT regime.

54 Jeffrey J. Schott, Euijin Jung and Cathleen Cimino-Isaacs, "An Assessment of the Korea-China Free Trade Agreement" (December 2015), Peterson Institute for International Economics Policy Brief Number PB15-24, at 1.

55 Ibid., at 4.

56 Ibid., at 14.

57 Hadley, *supra* note 14.

11

By Way of Conclusion: Chinese BIT Law and Practice in the Jungle

The flows of international investment – the cross-border movement of capital – have been a major element of the world economy for decades. Foreign investment has significant impacts on economic development in developed and developing countries. BITs and BIT-related investment arbitration cases have proliferated particularly in the past two decades and drawn great attention from policy-makers, regulators, international organizations, multinational corporations and the like. IIL has been investigated and analyzed as a subject in many fields with very diversified views and reform proposals, and it has not gone untouched as a subject of philosophical inquiry.[1] The current IIL regime is in a "state of transition," with the possible emergence of a more complex and heterogeneous system.[2] New developments have led to a change of the predominant paradigm of IIL from investor protection to a more comprehensive, balanced and diversified but less isolated regime,[3] with more focus on the host state's right to regulate in public interests.

China's rise and America's global retreat have made China's role in global governance more important than ever. The 2008 global financial crisis was a turning point of Chinese discourse. China has since taken a faster pace in its outbound investment while the USA's and other Western countries' outbound investment has shrunk not only in volume but also in scale. As an increasingly vital economy in the field of international investment, China deserves special attention to be paid to its critical but underscrutinized role associated with the development of a modern international investment regime.

China's investment is often observed through the Western lens and a conclusion has been drawn that China's investment in other developing countries is a reflection of its attempt and ambition to replicate the similar state of affairs that Western powers have developed historically with the South states. The investing state's rule is labeled "the law of greed" as the investor rights protection is disguised to cover the multinational corporations' interests in maximizing profits. At least in international trade, a very polarizing area, poverty has turned out to be a

[1] Steven R. Ratner, "Global Investment Rules as a Site for Moral Inquiry" (2019) 27(1) *Journal of Political Philosophy* 107–135.

[2] Steffen Hindelang and Markus Krajewski, "Towards a More Comprehensive Approach in International Investment Law" in Steffen Hindelang and Markus Krajewski (eds.), *Shifting Paradigms in International Investment Law: More Balanced, Less Isolated, Increasingly Diversified* (Oxford University Press 2016) 3.

[3] Ibid., at 5.

paradoxical narrative which has been relied upon by the poor and the weak states to transform their powerlessness into a source of power, an effective political tool and negotiation strategy.[4] WTO, as a result, also changed its image from a Rich Man's Club to one of the most equitable organizations.[5] This somehow has blocked the Doha Round negotiation and stalled trade liberalization progress. Is the rule of the game still a reflection of power imbalance, especially when China is ascending in global leadership at the same time that the USA is descending?[6] Will China develop a more balanced framework to satisfy all the stakeholders' needs? In the arena of cross-border investment, China, among others, has become one source of investment, and, in a larger context, has greater clout to back the cause of development.[7]

As the global economic and power hierarchy shows notable variability and the flow of investment has increasingly defied traditional patterns, the variability and change may set in motion a shift in the normative milieus. The shift in the ground rules and the implications for contemporary world economic order require a new configuration of the previous North–South relations to match the South–South relations, thanks to a more integrated global economy that favors interdependence over independence.[8] For instance, the pressing question is whether the existing global economic governance system mainly tackling North–South relations serves the investment relations between China and other emerging states in any meaningful way. The existing rules and institutions are a reflection of power relationships dominated by the USA and its Western allies. The question is whether China can maximize its own interests by relying on such rules and institutions when it pursues outbound investment through either the "go globally" strategy or the BRI, under which Chinese investors are competing with or even replacing the South's traditional investors from the North.[9]

When China moves to the upper end of the hierarchy, it may itself turn out to be a beneficiary of the current global investment governance system, and, more importantly, a coalition or Third World cohesion led by China and other emerging economies,[10] if not a China-based pole in the future global investment governance.[11] However, it is still on the defensive side vis-à-vis its Northern partners.[12] US policy-makers are growing increasingly wary of China's tactics and policy agenda. China has been viewed by the USA, an incumbent economic power, as a rising challenger. The ongoing commercial and diplomatic relations threaten to worsen bilateral ties. China's challenge to the prevailing Western-designed norms of global governance is a possible systematic alternative to the existing liberal order, and the BRI is the core of such a concern.[13] The challenge for China, in the USA–China rivalry

4 Amrita Narlikar, *Poverty Narratives and Power Paradoxes in International Trade Negotiations and Beyond* (Cambridge University Press 2020) 1.

5 Ibid., at 22.

6 Ronald C. Brown, "A New Leader in Asian Free Trade Agreements: Chinese Style Global Trade: New Rules, No Labor Protections" (2017) 35(1) *UCLA Pacific Basin Law Journal* 1–32.

7 Narlikar, *supra* note 4, at 14.

8 Pedro J. Martinez-Fraga and C. Ryan Reetz, *Public Purpose in International Law: Rethinking Regulatory Sovereignty in the Global Era* (Cambridge University Press 2015) 261.

9 Won Kidane, "China and India's Differing Investment Treaty and Dispute Settlement Experiences and Implications for Africa" (2017) 49 *Loyola University Chicago Law Journal* 405–477.

10 M. Sornarajah, *The International Law on Foreign Investment* (3rd edition, Cambridge University Press 2010) 241.

11 Dilini Pathirana, "Rising China and Global Investment Governance: An Overview of Prospects and Challenges" (2018) 4(2) *Chinese Journal of Global Governance* 122–153.

12 Won Kidane, *supra* note 9.

13 Lee Jones, "Does China's Belt and Road Initiative Challenge the Liberal, Rules-Based Order?" (2019) *Fudan Journal of the Humanities and Social Sciences*, DOI: 10.1007/s40647-019-00252-8.

paradigm,[14] is to create a China-friendly global governance framework while it is being identified as a rival and adversary.[15]

Malleability is claimed to be the primary feature of China's BIT (FTA) regime,[16] or even other countries' FTAs.[17] Others use flexibility and divergence to describe this feature,[18] as in the à la carte approach used by countries such as Canada[19] and Australia.[20] Although flexibility is based on limited state autonomy to regulate and is often tautological,[21] malleability (or flexibility) applies a varying level of investment liberalization with selected partners. The selection serves China's self-interest to benefit Chinese companies investing overseas (by way of reciprocity), boost foreign investors' confidence in the Chinese market and, more importantly, facilitate domestic legal reforms. This selection is also seen in the varying scope of regulatory freedom enjoyed by the host state in BITs. More regulatory autonomy allows the host government to regulate foreign investment in the public interest such as for environment protection and public health. For instance, the ChAFTA preserves much stronger regulatory autonomy than the China–Australia BIT[22] and other Chinese FTAs. This regulatory autonomy is reflected in the parties' greater control over ISDS, for instance in the scope of claims,[23] in selecting and regulating arbitrators and in providing interpretation and guidance, as well as in the omission of some typical IIA provisions such as FET and expropriation.[24] But the China–Korea FTA 2015 is quite different.[25]

China's more recent BITs manifest certain key features: (i) they are premised on the fact that outflows of capital from China need to be protected; (ii) they resemble BITs that Western

14 Barbara Lippert and Volker Perthes (eds.), "Strategic Rivalry between United State and China: Causes, Trajectories, and Implications for Europe," German Institute for International and Security Affairs, SWP Research Paper, April 2020, www.swp-berlin.org/fileadmin/contents/products/research_papers/2020RP04_China_USA.pdf (accessed September 13, 2020).

15 Peter Goettler and Daniel Ikenson, "Averting Conflict by Promoting Commerce: The Case for a US-China Investment Treaty" in Tim Wenniges and Walter Lohman (eds.), *Chinese FDI in the EU and the US: Simple Rules for Turbulent Times* (Palgrave MacMillan 2019) 41–49.

16 Heng Wang, "Paradigm Shift in Investment Rules of China's Free Trade Agreements? The Present and Future," LKI, August 14, 2018, https://lki.lk/blog/paradigm-shift-in-investment-rules-of-chinas-free-trade-agreements-the-present-and-future/ (accessed September 13, 2020).

17 Amokura Kawharu and Luke Nottage, "Models for Investment Treaties in the Asia-Pacific Region: An Underview" (2017) 34(3) *Arizona Journal of International & Comparative Law* 525.

18 Shu Zhang, "Developing China's Investor-State Arbitration Clause Discussions in the Context of the 'Belt and Road' Initiative" in Wenhua Shan, Kimmo Nuotio and Kangle Zhang (eds.), *Normative Readings of the Belt and Road Initiative* (Springer 2018) 147–181.

19 Nikos Lavranos, "Beyond USMCA: ISDS a la carte," Kluwer Arbitration Blog, October 8, 2018, http://arbitrationblog.kluwerarbitration.com/2018/10/08/beyond-usmca-isds-la-carte/?doing_wp_cron=1591771908.0552899837493896484375 (accessed September 11, 2020).

20 Jürgen Kurtz and Luke Nottage, "Investment Treaty Arbitration 'Down Under': Policy and Politics in Australia" (2015) 30(2) *ICSID Review* 465, 465 (stating that the Australian government took a case-by-case policy by rejecting the ISID clauses in some BITs but including them in others).

21 Leila Choukroune, "Indian and Chinese FDI in Developing Asia: The Standards Battle Beyond Trade" (2015) 7 *Indian Journal of International Economic Law* 89.

22 Elizabeth Sheargold, "The USMCA/CUSMA/T-MEC's Entry into Force: USMCA as Part of a Global Trend Away from ISDS – An Australian Perspective," Kluwer Arbitration Blog, June 27, 2020, http://arbitrationblog.kluwerarbitration.com/2020/06/27/the-usmca-cusma-t-mecs-entry-into-force-usmca-as-part-of-a-global-trend-away-from-isds-an-australian-perspective/ (accessed September 11, 2020).

23 The notable exception in the ChAFTA is Article 9.12.2, which states that ISDS claims can be brought only for breach of the NT obligation.

24 Australian Government Department of Foreign Affairs and Trade, China–Australia Free Trade Agreement, 2015, http://dfat.gov.au/trade/agreements/in-force/chafta/Pages/australia-china-fta.aspx (accessed March 18, 2021).

25 Asia Regional Integration Center, People's Republic of China-Republic of Korea Free Trade Agreement, 2015, https://aric.adb.org/fta/peoples-republic-of-china-korea-free-trade-agreement (accessed March 18, 2021).

industrialized states have signed;[26] and (iii) they vary at different times with different motivations and considerations as circumstances change,[27] depending on which counterparties China is negotiating with.[28] Although scholars suggest that China should take a more convergent approach to making its BITs through using its own model BIT,[29] given China's transition from a pure capital-importing state to a hybrid capital-importing and exporting state, China's BIT policy may still be in flux, creating *lex specialis* with its counterparties instead of customary principles of international law,[30] and its coherent and convergent approach may take time to form even though there has been some manifestation that China is embracing a more liberal and balanced approach toward new BITs.[31] As a matter of fact, China, as observed, has diverged quite extensively from its own model BIT in negotiating individual BITs such as the China–Canada BIT 2012.[32] Its approach provides a pragmatic path for countries with strong outbound and inbound investment perspectives[33] to follow in the negotiation of new BITs – maintaining the status quo by using the existing models – which is helping to send an image of continuity while China gradually remodels its BIT commitments.

More recently, in light of anti-globalization[34] and populism, regionalism (in the form of FTAs)[35] has appeared to prevail over multilateralism, largely represented and driven by the WTO, which has made little progress in solidifying deeper integration at the multilateral level. IIL has been increasingly regionalized, and rules and norms have been tailored to meet regional interests and needs.[36] Consequently, FTAs are gaining importance[37] and have enhanced regionalism.[38] Along with this trend, in tandem with its BIT-making, China has also expended energy in FTA (including mini-regional FTAs like the CKJ TIT) negotiations and is using FTAs as strategic tools to counter the challenges posed by megaregional trade deals, in particular TPP and RCEP.[39] At the technical level, China has appeared to rely on

26 Sornarajah, *supra* note 10, at 174.

27 Sornarajah, *supra* note 10, at 177.

28 Kyle Dylan Dickson-Smith, "Lessons Learned from the Canada-China FIPA for the US-China BIT and Beyond: Chinese Whispers or Chinese Chequers?" in Julien Chaisse (ed.), *China's International Investment Strategy: Bilateral, Regional, and Global Law and Policy* (Oxford University Press 2019) 118 (different from others, expecting that China will maintain its negotiating of liberal/legalized BITs with developing states but negotiate more restricted BITs with developed countries).

29 Shu Zhang, *supra* note 18.

30 Sornarajah, *supra* note 10, at 177.

31 Yu-ting Ye, "Towards a Balanced and Liberal Chinese Bilateral Investment Treaty Regime in the Context of One Belt One Road" (2018) 41(1) *Houston Journal of International Law* 107–146.

32 Leon E. Trakman and Kunal Sharma, "Jumping Back and Forth between Domestic Courts and ISDS: Mixed Signals from the Asia-Pacific Region" in Steffen Hindelang and Markus Krajewski (eds.), *Shifting Paradigms in International Investment Law: More Balanced, Less Isolated, Increasingly Diversified* (Oxford University Press 2016) 336.

33 UNCTAD, IIA Issue Note No. 3: Reform of the IIA Regime: Four Paths of Action and a Way Forward (2014).

34 Ray Kiely, *The Clash of Globalisations: Neo-Liberalism, the Third Way and Anti-Globalization* (Brill 2005) ch. 7.

35 Notwithstanding the bilateral nature, FTAs are usually referred to as regional arrangements as WTO members are obliged to report FTAs to the WTO for review by the Committee on Regional Trade Agreements. Guiguo Wang, "China's FTAs: Legal Characteristics and Implications" (2011) 105(3) *Chinese Journal of International Law* 493–516.

36 Leon E. Trakman and Nicola W. Ranieri (eds.), *Regionalism in International Investment Law* (Oxford University Press 2013) xvii.

37 World Investment Report 2012.

38 The counterargument is that FTAs like TPP may rip apart economic integration in East Asia. Guoyou Song and Wen Jin Yuan, "China's Free Trade Agreement Strategies" (2012) 35(4) *Washington Quarterly* 107–119.

39 Xiaoming Pan, "China's FTA Strategy," *The Diplomat*, June 1, 2014, https://thediplomat.com/2014/06/chinas-fta-strategy/ (accessed September 13, 2020).

the FTAs proposed by the counterparties, especially those developed economies, in FTA-making.[40] This may explain the greater malleability depending on the counterparties. Given the fact that it is the contemporary US practice that has inspired other countries such as Australia and New Zealand in their FTA-making,[41] the USA ultimately dominates the discourse and is influencing the future trajectory of treaty negotiations amid some deviations toward the EU-style of drafting which is more deferential to host state interests. The Australia–USA FTA 2004 is a good example, as its investment chapter incorporates substantive rights largely based on the 2004 US model BIT, including an annex that restates US case law on indirect expropriation.[42] This suggests that the USA and the EU are leading the course of IIL.[43]

The malleability, however, does not cover such intrusive clauses as SOEs, labor and the environment in Chinese BITs or FTAs.[44] Further, because of the difficulty in satisfying all the parties' interests, multi-party investment agreements such as the CKJ TIT, entered into in May 2012,[45] though a small leap forward in regional integration, fall short of having protections as rigorous and comprehensive as those in the US model BIT.[46]

It appears that China, as a capital exporter, possesses the capability to influence the shape of BITs and FTAs even for other developed states. This is changing the dynamics between the two sides, which used to be one-way with the focus on protection of EU investors investing into China. The change from one-way to two-way interaction complicates the legal and policy analysis.[47] The latest ChAFTA is an example of such influence. Accordingly, China's FTAs and BITs are likely to be influenced by China's investment policies and needs.[48] Even the future China–EU BIT may be shaped by the surge of China FDI through its centripetal and centrifugal pressures.[49] Meanwhile, Chinese outbound FDI is heavily influenced by the host state's policy. The return of the state movement in the EU and the USA, for example, may undermine Chinese investors' confidence amid the recent national security review system put forward by the USA and the EU over Chinese investment in certain sensitive or strategic industries.[50] The EU's screening of foreign investment reflects the EU's concerns over Chinese investment, but that concern may be overrated.[51] The screening mechanism

40 Heng Wang, *supra* note 16.

41 Amokura Kawharu and Nottage, *supra* note 17, at 525.

42 Luke Nottage, "Investor-State Arbitration Policy and Practice in Australia," CIGI Investor-State Arbitration Series Paper No. 6, June 2016, 6.

43 Ibid., at 36.

44 Heng Wang, *supra* note 16.

45 Agreement among the Government of Japan, the Government of the Republic of Korea and the Government of the People's Republic of China for the Promotion, Facilitation and Protection of Investment, May 2012, www.mofa.go.jp/announce/announce/2012/5/pdfs/0513_01_01.pdf (accessed March 18, 2021).

46 Jeffrey J. Schott and Cathleen Cimino, "The China-Japan-Korea Trilateral Investment Agreement: Implications for US Policy and the US-China Bilateral Investment Treaty" in Peterson Institute for International Economics, *Toward a US-China Investment Treaty*, PIIE Briefing 15-1, February 2015, at 6, 13.

47 Jeremy Clegg and Hinrich Voss, "The New Two-Way Street of Chinese Direct Investment in the European Union" (2016) 5(2) *China-EU Law Journal* 79–100.

48 Weihuan Zhou, "Chinese Investment in Australia: A Critical Analysis of the China-Australia Free Trade Agreement" (2017) 18 *Melbourne Journal of International Law* 407.

49 Sophie Meunier, "Divide and Conquer? China and the Cacophony of Foreign Investment Rules in the EU" (2014) 21(7) *Journal of European Public Policy* 996–1016.

50 Lawrence Eaker and Sun Tao, "Chinese Investment in the European Union & National Security Review: Is the EU Legal Regime about to Follow the US Model?" (2014) 9(1) *Frontiers of Law in China* 42.

51 Monkey Cage, "The EU Will Start Screening Foreign Investment. Here Is the Full Story," *Washington Post*, April 10, 2019, www.washingtonpost.com/politics/2019/04/10/eu-will-start-screening-foreign-investment-heres-full-story/ (accessed September 5, 2020).

reflects the EU's national security fear over Chinese investors' intention and tactics in achieving a flow of knowledge from the subsidiary abroad to the parent company at home. There has been a call for a new international investment regime to secure stability and certainty.[52]

China's influence in rule-making is also evidenced in its FTAs in the Asia-Pacific region. Its growing network of regional FTAs has crucial economic and strategic implications not only for China but also for its partners. China's regional FTA network in the region also involves regional power dynamics, presenting a new framework to maximize China's growing bargaining leverage and influence, given its strengthened economic position vis-à-vis its regional counterparts and the economic dependence of these partners.[53]

However, caution must be paid to the fact that China and its developed counterparties may not have reciprocal arrangements in their BITs or FTAs. The China–Canada BIT 2012, as a good example, in key respects is nonreciprocal in favor of China. Examples include a general right of market access by Chinese investors to Canada but not by Canadian investors to China, and a wider scope for investment screening by China than by Canada.[54] These more favorable terms being exclusively applicable to China indicates the imbalance between China and Canada in terms of their economic status in the bilateral relationship. In other words, China may be viewed as a less economically advanced state and thus deserves more preferential treatment compared to Canada and Canadian investors. If this is the case, China should not be unduly tasked to advance investment protection standards in BIT rule-making. Certainly, this one-way favorable arrangement is not free, and China, probably in exchange for such favors, places virtually no restrictions on Canada's ability to reject Chinese investor-initiated deals or on the conditions that Canada may impose for approving such deals.[55] Canada, in the BIT, managed to reserve for itself the freedom to review and approve new investments and takeovers under the Investment Canada Act 1985, including those by SOEs. Further, these decisions are not subject to any sort of dispute settlement claims by aggrieved investors, giving back more rights to regulate to Canada.[56]

China is also following the trend toward FTAs (equivalent to preferential trade and investment agreements (PTIAs)) which often include more terms than BITs have. Comparing the content of China's BITs with that in its FTAs and its counterparties' FTAs, Chinese BITs showcase an "Americanized" evolutionary path,[57] or a partially NAFTA-ized PTIA policy, which is an encroachment of Western BIT standards into Chinese BITs and BIT policy. There is a diffusion of certain minimum international standards such as transparency, rights protection, prohibition of performance of requirements, and environmental provisions from China's counterparties to China's PTIAs.[58] However, the PTIA terms are not used to

52 Brigid Gavin, "Europe Needs a Dynamic International Investment Regime with China" (2012) 47(2) *Intereconomics* 248–256.

53 Michael Sampson, "The Evolution of China's Regional Trade Agreements: Power Dynamics and the Future of the Asia-Pacific" (2019) *Pacific Review* 1–31, DOI: 10.1080/09512748.2019.1660397.

54 Gus van Harten, "The Canada-China FIPPA: Its Uniqueness and Non-reciprocity" (2014) 51 *Canadian Yearbook of International Law* 3–55.

55 Matthew Kronby, "Canada-China Investment Treaty: Evidence Doesn't Support Doomsayers," *The Globe and Mail*, October 26, 2012, www.theglobeandmail.com/opinion/canada-china-investment-treaty-evidence-doesnt-support-doomsayers/article4665002/ (accessed September 9, 2020).

56 Ibid.

57 Dickson-Smith, *supra* note 28, at 119.

58 Axel Berger, "Investment Rules in Chinese Preferential Trade and Investment Agreements – Is China Following the Global Trend towards Comprehensive Agreements?" German Development Institute Discussion Paper 7/2013, www.files.ethz.ch/isn/163216/DP%207.2013.pdf (accessed September 8, 2020).

experiment with higher protection standards as the BIT terms pose limitations on PTIAs. In a broader picture, China's FTAs reconfirm its deliberate and incremental approach to trade and investment liberalization.[59] This approach is justified by the costs of complete liberalization and possible market failures.[60] As two leading capital exporters and importers, China and the USA are now concluding their separate BITs with similar terms.[61] However, China's investment liberalization progress has not been as great as expected; it has not narrowed the gap between China's commitments and international best practice, and may have even fallen short of China's own lofty aim.[62]

China seems to have taken over the flag of globalization since the USA indicated its intention to withdraw from globalization. However, a distinction needs to be drawn between the ambition to exercise such leadership and the capacity to do so.[63] China's effective leadership is facing some institutional difficulties. Domestically, its state-managed economy and state-controlled market hinder its capability to promote rule of law and market openness. Globally, the US-led governance regime prevents China from relying on an effective network for standard-setting and rule-making. Its energetic FTA strategy, BIT network, WTO negotiations and regional efforts are part of its institutional framework underpinning its pluralist strategy to have a China-friendly framework,[64] and to use the law as a tool for mastering international legal regimes.[65]

China's efficacy and success at being the leader in globalism[66] and global economic governance largely rest on its ability to reform its domestic market, which requires economic openness. Without domestic economic reform, its economy will remain semi-closed, which cuts it off from the global market and global supply chain. It may even need deeper political reform[67] to enhance rule of law and restrain arbitrary state actions.[68]

The most challenging BIT terms relate primarily to China's domestic reform agenda. For instance, pre-establishment NT is related to the approval system applied to foreign investment and the negative list closes the link to market access for foreign investment. Adopting these so-called international (almost Western) standards compromises the authoritarian

59 This is also in line with the institutional investment hypothesis that the government, by signing the regional trade agreements, invests in governance and collaborative market regulation endeavors so as to gain the benefits of multilateral (including regional and megaregional) liberalization and global value chains. Marc D. Froese, *Sovereign Rules and the Politics of International Economic Law* (Routledge 2018) 112.

60 Leon E. Trakman, "Bilateral Trade and Investment Agreements" in Leon E. Trakman and Nicola W. Ranieri (eds.), *Regionalism in International Investment Law* (Oxford University Press 2013) 85–86.

61 José Alvarez et al. (eds.), *The Evolving International Investment Regime: Expectations, Realities, Options* (Oxford University Press 2011) xl.

62 Jeffrey J. Schott, Euijin Jung and Cathleen Cimino-Isaacs, "An Assessment of the Korea-China Free Trade Agreement," Peterson Institute for International Economics Policy Brief PB15-24, December 2015, 15.

63 Weinian Hu and Jacques Pelkmans, "China-EU Leadership in Globalization: Ambition and Capacity," CEPS Policy Insights No. 2017/18, May 2017, 1–20.

64 Ibid.

65 Guillermo J. Garcia Sanchez, "The Footprint of the Chinese Petro-Dragon: The Future of Investment Law in Transboundary Resources" (2020) 94 *Tulane Law Review* 313–364.

66 Ronald C. Brown, "China-EU BIT and FTA: Building a Bridge on the Silk Road Not Detoured by Labor Standard Provisions" (2019) 29(1) *Washington International Law Journal* 61–116.

67 Investment treaty claims against host states framed by foreign investors are often related to state conduct that is politically motivated even though arbitral tribunals lack a coherent conception and consistent understanding of politically motivated state conduct. This lack is a reflection of the tension between the IIL's objective of protecting foreign investment and the host state's legitimate scope of democratic decision-making and responsive politics. Jonathan Bonnitcha and Zoe Phillips Williams, "State Liability for 'Politically' Motivated Conduct in the Investment Treaty Regime" (2020) 33(1) *Leiden Journal of International Law* 77–100.

68 Stephan W. Schill, "In Defense of International Investment Law" (2016) 7 *European Journal of International Economic Law* 309–341.

function of the government and the interlinked nature of the domestic state–society model. Therefore, the scale and speed of domestic economic and governance reform have an impact on China's international economic policies and its determination and capability to make more concessions in BIT negotiations. China's accession to the WTO is an example of this two-way movement. China's entry into the WTO provided major impetus to China's use of extensive trade liberalization to solidify its economic reform and open up discourse. Meanwhile, China's internal reforms allow China to fulfill its international commitments under the WTO. This two-way movement complicates the orthodox binary scenarios of adaptation and conflict.[69] Therefore, China's desire and ability to engage in bilateral, regional and global integration are strong indicators of the government's interest in a path of market-oriented reform. Local perspectives such as economic and social structures as well as domestic power relations must be brought into the context to conceptualize China's incorporation of international standards into its international economic rule-making.

Several examples may be self-illustrative. First, seventy-four countries have domestic investment laws that include ISA, forty-two of which provide consent to it. However, no developed state consents to arbitration in its domestic law. Those countries which do give such consent in their domestic laws do so largely due to the World Bank's "asymmetric diffusion" through its technical assistance.[70] This means that the US-centric governance system still heavily influences the rule of law in developing states.[71] Second, as indicated in some research, China's BITs with its African partners fail to show a planned strategy, which, as a capital-exporting state, China is supposed to have no matter how large its investment into Africa. Rather, these BITs are simple and benign, and appear to be a replication of its existing BIT text.[72]

China's domestic governance system also presents a challenge to global governance. The BRI is viewed by Western countries as a grand strategic program to undermine and challenge the incumbent superpowers and the US-centric international economic structure. Nevertheless, thorough study of BRI policy statements reveals that they do not contain any normative content that threatens global governance norms relating to trade, investment and finance. The (mis)perception of BRI as an authoritarian, against-market, singular and China-centric global order with the aim of expanding China's spheres of influence and strategic space[73] is probably a (un)reasonable assumption of China's fragmented governance inside China. Even with its great policy orientation, BRI is tainted as a program that may erode established international norms without offering any coherent alternative.[74]

China's unique ideology may have deprived it of the opportunity to deliberate on options, refine theory, and pursue a systematic BIT program[75] as the USA has done in building up a US-centric global economic governance system. Chinese views of global economic

69 Nana de Graaff, Tobias ten Brink and Inderjeet Parmar, "China's Rise in a Liberal World Order in Transition – Introduction to the Forum" (2020) 27(2) *Review of International Political Review* 191–207.

70 Tarald Laudal Berge and Taylor St John, "Asymmetric Diffusion: World Bank 'Best Practice' and the Spread of Arbitration in National Investment Laws" (2020) *Review of International Political Economy*, https://ssrn.com/abstract=3447365 or http://dx.doi.org/10.2139/ssrn.3447365 (accessed September 8, 2020).

71 This is also the case in finance. The Structural Adjustment Program of the 1980s, advocated by the IMF and the World Bank, was modeled on neoliberal ideology. John Linarelli, Margot E. Salomon and M. Sornarajah, *The Misery of International Law: Confrontations with Injustice in the Global Economy* (Cambridge University Press 2018) 9.

72 Won Kidane, "China's Bilateral Investment Treaties with African States in Comparative Context" (2016) 49(1) *Cornell International Law Journal* 176.

73 Nadège Rolland, "China's Belt and Road Initiative: Underwhelming or Game-Changer?" (2017) 40(1) *Washington Quarterly* 133.

74 Jones, *supra* note 13.

75 Won Kidane, *supra* note 72.

governance highly value the role of the state but pay less attention to civil society.[76] Political-economic analysis supports a differentiated approach to explain China's engagement and contestation with the current US-dominated global economic governance model,[77] which is a liberal one and mismatches China's political system and ideological underpinnings. While China actively interplays with the WTO and other major liberal mechanisms in global governance, it often contests the validity and application of liberal norms and rules. The contestation is much more prevalent in state-dominated and/or heavily regulated sectors. This selective contestation may also rationalize and suggest the way of China's participation in the BIT network or FTA regime. The liberal ordering and constitutionalism on which the BIT network and the ISDS mechanism are premised[78] undermine China's authoritarian ideology and clash with its political or regulatory regime. Likely, China may neither abandon the BIT system nor proactively engage with it. China has been placed in a third category – a group of developed but not optimally industrialized nations, and a new category of sovereign-ties.[79] Against the backdrop of greater balance and less disparity between industrialized and less industrialized states,[80] it is still reasonable to roll out a mixed picture (hybrid scenario[81] or duality narrative) of China's future interaction with the BIT regime – it may adapt and even strengthen liberal institutions and rules of the game, confront some of them, or even develop alternative paths, all of which primarily depends on China's own economic or even ideological interests. This probably explains China's overall attitudes toward ISDS reform. It largely supports the policy choice to refine and improve the existing system as it lacks willingness and ability to invest in a better alternative which may depart from the liberal value that other stakeholders would support.

Rising protectionism is challenging both the global economy and global economic governance. There has been a wider trend moving away from investment liberalization and ISDS in which states are approaching investor-friendly policy and ISA with great caution amid policy fluctuations on ISDS. Major capital-exporting states, especially the USA, are revisiting their investment liberalization strategy and sending confusing and uncertain signals. While the USA is trying to open China's market access wider within the investment protection rhetoric, it is using CFIUS to block Chinese investments on national security grounds. These investment policies are hard to reconcile in the narrative of investment liberalization.[82] A number of developing and developed countries are practicing "ISDS à la carte" through their recent BIT-making.[83] China appears to be taking a pragmatic approach to this global trend away from ISDS. China's position on globalization will determine the direction of the global economy and its own economic development in the years to come.

76 Jianghan Zeng, "Chinese Views of Global Economic Governance" (2019) 40(3) *Journal of Third World Quarterly* 578–594.

77 Clara Weinhardt and Tobias ten Brink, "Varieties of Contestation: China's Rise and the Liberal Trade Order" (2020) 27(2) *Review of International Political Economy* 258–280.

78 José Alvarez, *The Public International Law Regime Governing International Investment* (Martinus Nijhoff 2011) (arguing that the legal regime that governs trans-border capital flows consists principally of a network of more than 3,000 BITs as well as a large body of arbitral awards, and should be characterized as "global administrative law" as a form of "constitutionalization").

79 Pedro J. Martinez-Fraga and C. Ryan Reetz, *Public Purpose in Customary International Law* (Cambridge University Press 2015) 130.

80 Martinez-Fraga and Reetz, *supra* note 8, at 261.

81 De Graaff, ten Brink and Parmar, *supra* note 69.

82 Jonathan Bonnitcha, "Investment Wars: Contestation and Confusion Debate about Investment Liberalization" (2019) 22 *Journal of International Economic Law* 652.

83 Lavranos, *supra* note 19.

Bibliography

Achaval, Clara Picasso, "Tipping the Balance towards Investors" (2008) 9 *Journal of World Investment & Trade* 147.

Adda, Marco, "Consolidation of Arbitral and Court Proceedings in Investment Disputes" in Bernardo M. Cremades Sanz-Pastor and Julian D. M. Lew (eds.), *Parallel State and Arbitral Procedures in International Arbitration* (Kluwer Law International 2005) 100.

Adede, A. O., "A Fresh Look at the Meaning of the Doctrine of Denial of Justice under International Law" (1976) 14 *Canadian Yearbook of International Law* 73.

Adlung, Rudolf, and Martin Molinuevo, "Bilateralism in Services Trade: Is There Fire Behind the (BIT)–Smoke?" (2008) WTO Staff Working Papers ERSD-2008-01, World Trade Organization (WTO), Economic Research and Statistics Division.

Allee, Todd, and Clint Peinhardt, "Delegating Differences: Bilateral Investment Treaties and Bargaining over Dispute Resolution Provisions" (2010) 54(1) *International Studies Quarterly* 1.

Alschner, Wolfgang, and Dmitriy Skougarevskiy, "Mapping the Universe of International Investment Agreements" (2016) 19(3) *Journal of International Economic Law* 561.

Alschner, Wolfgang, Joost Pauwelyn and Sergio Puig, "The Data-Driven Future of International Economic Law" (2017) 20 *Journal of International Economic Law* 217.

Alvarez, Guillermo Aguilar, "The New Face of Investment Arbitration: NAFTA Chapter 11" (2003) 28 *Yale Journal of International Law* 365.

Alvarez, José E., "Limits of Change by Way of Subsequent Agreements and Practice" in Georg Nolte (ed.), *Treaties and Subsequent Practice* (Oxford University Press 2013) 123.

Alvarez, José E., "The Once and Future Foreign Investment Regime" in Mahnoush H. Arsanjani, Jacob Katz Cogan, Robert D. Sloane and Siegfried Wiessner (eds.), *Looking to the Future: Essays on International Law in Honor of W. Michael Reisman* (Brill 2010) 607.

Alvarez, José E., *The Public International Law Regime Governing International Investment* (Martinus Nijhoff 2011).

Alvarez, José E., "The Return of the State" (2011) 20 *Minnesota Journal of International Law* 223.

Alvarez, José E., and Karl P. Sauvant with Kamil Gérard Ahmed and Gabriela P. Vizcaíno (eds.), *The Evolving International Investment Regime: Expectations, Realities, Options* (Oxford University Press 2011).

Amerasinghe, C. F., *Local Remedies in International Law* (2nd edition, Cambridge University Press 2004).

Amirfar, Catherine M., "Dispute Settlement Clauses in Investor-State Arbitration: An Informed Approach to Empirical Studies about Law: A Response to Professor Yackee" (2014) 52 *Columbia Journal of Transnational Law* 506.

Arsen, Matveev, "Investor-State Dispute Settlement: The Evolving Balance between Investor Protection and State Sovereignty" (2015–2016) 40 *University of Western Australia Law Review* 348.

Ayangbah, Shirley, and Liu Sun, "Comparative Study of Foreign Investment Law: The Case of China and Ghana" (2017) 3 *Cogent Social Sciences* 1.

Baetens, Freya, "Discrimination on the Basis of Nationality: Determining Likeness in Human Rights and Investment Law" in Stephen Schill (ed.), *International Investment Law and Comparative Public Law* (Oxford University Press 2010) 279.

Balkanyi-Nordmann, Nadine, "The Perils of Parallel Proceedings: Is an Arbitration Award Enforceable If the Same Case Is Pending Elsewhere?" in Thomas E. Carbonneau and Jeanette A. Jaeggi (eds.), *Handbook on International Arbitration and ADR* (American Arbitration Association 2006) 185.

Barber, Nigel, *Evolution in the Here and Now: How Adaptation and Social Learning Explain Humanity* (Prometheus Books 2020).

Barry, Donald, and Ronald Keith (eds.), *Regionalism, Multilateralism and the Politics of Global Trade* (UBC Press 1999).

Basedow, Robert, "A Legal History of the EU's Investment Policy" (2016) 17(5) *Journal of World Investment & Trade* 743.

Bath, Vivienne, "'One Belt, One Road' and Chinese Investment" in Lutz-Christian Wolff, Chao Xi and Jenny Chan (eds.), *Legal Dimensions of China's Belt and Road Initiative* (Wolters Kluwer 2016) 8.

Bath, Vivienne, "Substantive Provisions in ChAFTA's Investment Chapter" in Colin Picker, Heng Wang and Weihuan Zhou, *The China-Australia Free Trade Agreement: A 21st-Century Model* (Hart Publishing 2018) 195.

Bederman, David J., *International Law Frameworks* (2nd edition, Foundation Press 2006).

Behn, Daniel, Ole Kristian Fauchald and Malcolm Langford, "Empirical Perspectives on the Legitimacy of International Investment Tribunals" (2015) PluriCourts Investment, Internal Working Paper, www.jus.uio.no/pluricourts/english/topics/investment/documents/1-2015-legitimacy-book-project.pdf.

Bento, Lucas, "From Anarchy to Rational Design: Direction and Perception in International Investment Law" in Andrea K. Bjorklund (ed.), *Yearbook on International Investment Law & Policy 2014–2015* (Oxford University Press 2016) 246.

Berge, Tarald Laudal, and Taylor St. John, "Asymmetric Diffusion: World Bank 'Best Practice' and the Spread of Arbitration in National Investment Laws" (2020) *Review of International Political Economy*, https://ssrn.com/abstract=3447365 or http://dx.doi.org/10.2139/ssrn.3447365.

Berger, Axel, "Investment Rules in Chinese Preferential Trade and Investment Agreements – Is China Following the Global Trend towards Comprehensive Agreements?" (2013) German Development Institute Discussion Paper 7/2013, www.files.ethz.ch/isn/163216/DP%207.2013.pdf.

Berger, Axel, "The Politics of China's Investment Treaty-Making Program" in Tomer Broude, Marc L. Busch and Amelia Porges (eds.), *The Politics of International Economic Law* (Cambridge University Press 2011) 174.

Bergsten, C. Fred, Gary Clyde Hufbauer and Sean Miner, *Bridging the Pacific: Toward Free Trade and Investment between China and the United States* (Peterson Institute for International Economics 2014).

Bevan, Alan, Saul Estrin and Klaus Meyer, "Foreign Investment Location and Institutional Development in Transition Economies" (2004) 13 *International Business Review* 43.

Binder, Christina, Ursula Kriebaum, August Reinisch and Stephan Wittich (eds.), *International Investment Law for the 21st Century: Essays in Honour of Christoph Schreuer* (Oxford University Press 2009).

Bird, Robert, and Daniel R. Cohay, "The Impact of Compulsory Licensing on Foreign Direct Investment: A Collective Bargaining Approach" (2008) 45 *American Business Law Journal* 283.

Bishop, R. Doak, James Crawford and W. Michael Reisman, *Foreign Investment Disputes: Cases, Materials and Commentary* (Kluwer International Law 2005).

Bjorklund, Andrea K., "Waiver of Local Remedies and Limitation Periods" in Meg Kinnear, Geraldine R. Fischer, Jara Mínguez Almeida, Luisa Fernanda Torres and Mairée Uran Bidegain (eds.), *Building International Investment Law: The First 50 Years of ICSID* (Kluwer Law International 2016) 250.

Blanchard, Sadie, "State Consent, Temporal Jurisdiction, and the Importation of Continuing Circumstances Analysis into International Investment Arbitration" (2011) 10 *Washington University Global Studies Law Review* 419.

Bonnitcha, Jonathan, "Assessing the Impacts of Investment Treaties: Overview of the Evidence" (2017) International Institute for Sustainable Development Report, www.iisd.org/sites/default/files/publications/assessing-impacts-investment-treaties.pdf.

Bonnitcha, Jonathan, "Investment Wars: Contestation and Confusion Debate about Investment Liberalization" (2019) 22 *Journal of International Economic Law* 652.

Bonnitcha, Jonathan, and Zoe Phillips Williams, "State Liability for 'Politically' Motivated Conduct in the Investment Treaty Regime" (2020) 33(1) *Leiden Journal of International Law* 77.

Bonnitcha, Jonathan, Lauge N. Skovgaard Poulsen and Michael Waibel, *The Political Economy of the Investment Treaty Regime* (Oxford University Press 2017) 57.

Brower, Charles. H., II, "Why the FTC Notes of Interpretation Constitute a Partial Amendment of NAFTA Article 1105" (2006) 46(2) *Virginia Journal of International Law* 347.

Brower, Charles N., and Paula F. Henin, "Res Judicata" in Meg N. Kinnear et al. (eds.), *Building International Investment Law: The First 50 Years of ICSID* (Kluwer Law International 2015) 55.

Brower, Charles N., Micael Ottolenghi and Peter Prows, "The Saga of CMS: Res Judicata, Precedent and the Legitimacy of ICSID Arbitration" in Christina Binder et al. (eds.), *International Investment Law for the 21st Century: Essays in Honour of Christoph Schreuer* (Oxford University Press 2009) 846.

Brown, Kerry, *The Rise of the Dragon: Inward and Outward Investment in China in the Reform Period 1978–2007* (Chandos Publishing 2008) Preface xxiii.

Brown, Ronald C., "A New Leader in Asian Free Trade Agreements: Chinese Style Global Trade: New Rules, No Labor Protections" (2017) 35(1) *UCLA Pacific Basin Law Journal* 1.

Brown, Ronald C., "China-EU BIT and FTA: Building a Bridge on the Silk Road Not Detoured by Labor Standard Provisions" (2019) 29(1) *Washington International Law Journal* 61.

Brown, Ronald C., "China-U.S. Implementation of ILO Standards by BITs and Pieces (FTAs)" in Ulla Liukkunen and Yifeng Chen (eds.), *Fundamental Labour Rights in China – Legal Implementation and Cultural Logic* (Springer 2016) 169.

Brownlie, Ian, *Principles of Public International Law* (8th edition, Oxford University Press 2012).

Brownlie, Ian, *System of the Law of Nations* (Clarendon Press 1983).

Brummer, Chris, *Minilateralism: How Trade Alliances, Soft Law, and Financial Engineering Are Redefining Economic Statecraft* (Cambridge University Press 2014).

Bruner, Philip I., "Dual Track Proceedings in Arbitration and Litigation: Reducing the Peril of 'Double Jeopardy' by Consolidation, Joinder and Appellate Arbitration" (2014) (31) 4 *International Construction Law Review* 537.

Buckley, Peter J., et al., "Explaining China's Outward FDI: An Institutional Perspective" in Karl P. Sauvant et al. (eds.), *The Rise of Transnational Corporations from Emerging Markets: Threat or Opportunity?* (Edward Elgar 2008) 104.

Bunn, Isabella D., *The Right to Development and International Economic Law: Legal and Moral Dimensions* (Hart 2012).

Buser, Andeas, "Recalibrating Policy Space in Bilateral Investment Treaties: Is There a Common B(R) ICS Approach?" in Congyan Cai and Huiping Chen (eds.), *The BRICS in the New International Legal Order on Investment* (Brill 2020) 163.

Buyse, Antoine, A., "Lifeline in Time – Non-retroactivity and Continuing Violations under the ECHR" (2006) 75 *Nordic Journal of International Law* 63.

Cage, Monkey, "The EU Will Start Screening Foreign Investment. Here Is the Full Story," *Washington Post*, April 10, 2019, www.washingtonpost.com/politics/2019/04/10/eu-will-start-screening-foreign-investment-heres-full-story/.

Cai, Congyan, "China-US BIT Negotiations and the Future of Investment Treaty Regime: A Grand Bilateral Bargain with Multilateral Implications" (2009) 12(2) *Journal of International Economic Law* 457.

Cai, Congyan, "Outward Foreign Direct Investment Protection and the Effectiveness of Chinese BIT Practice" (2006) 7(5) *Journal of World Investment & Trade* 621.

Cai, Congyan, "Trans-Pacific Partnership and the Multilateralization of International Investment Law" (2013) 6 *Journal of East Asia and International Law* 385.

Carrai, Maria Adele, *Sovereignty in China: A genealogy of a Concept Since 1840* (Cambridge University Press 2019).

Carter, Justin, "The Protracted Bargain: Negotiating the Canada-China Foreign Investment Promotion and Protection Agreement" (2009) 47 *Canadian Yearbook of International Law* 197.

Carver, Jeremy, "How to Avoid Conflicting Awards: The Lauder and CME Cases" (2004) 5 *Journal of World Investment & Trade* 23.

Cass, Ronald A., "Compulsory Licensing of Intellectual Property: The Exception that Ate the Rule?" (2007) Washington Legal Foundation Working Paper Series No. 150.

Chai, Joseph C. H., and Kartik C. Roy, *Economic Reform in China and India: Development Experience in a Comparative Perspective* (Edward Elgar 2006) 51.

Che, Luyao, *China's State-Directed Economy and the International Order* (Springer 2019).

Chen, An, "Queries to the Recent ICSID Decision on Jurisdiction upon the Case of Tza Yap Shum v. Republic of Peru: Should China-Peru BIT 1994 Be Applied to Hong Kong SAR under the 'One Country Two Systems' Policy?" (2009) 10 *Journal of World Investment & Trade* 829.

Chen, An, "Should the Four 'Great Safeguards' in Sino-foreign BITs Be Hastily Dismantled? Comments on Critical Provisions Concerning Dispute Settlement in Model US and Canadian BITs" (2006) 7 *Journal of World Investment & Trade* 899.

Chen, An, "To Open Wider or to Close Again: China's Foreign Investment Policies and Laws in The Voice from China" in *AN CHEN on International Economic Law* (Springer-Verlag 2013) 451.

Chen, Chunlai, "The Liberalisation of FDI Policies and the Impacts of FDI on China's Economic Development" in Ross Garnaut, Ligang Song and Cai Fang (eds.), *China's 40 Years of Reform and Development* (ANU Press 2018) 612.

Chen, Huiping, "China's 'One Belt, One Road' Initiative and Its implications for Sino-African Investment Relations" (2016) 8(3) *Journal of Transnational Corporations Review* 178.

Chen, Huiping, "China's Innovative ISDS Mechanisms and Their Implications" (2018) 112 *American Journal of International Law* 207.

Chen, Richard C., "Bilateral Investment Treaties and Domestic Institutional Reform" (2017) 55 *Columbia Journal of Transnational Law* 547.

Chew, Pat K. "Political Risk and U.S. Investment in China: Chimera of Protection and Predictability" (1994) *Virginia Journal of International Law* 34, 615.

Chi, Manjaio, "The China-EU BIT as a Stepping Stone towards a China-EU FTA: A Policy Analysis" in Marc Bungenburg et al. (eds.), *European Yearbook of International Economic Law* (Springer 2017) 475.

Chi, Manjiao, "The 'Greenization' of Chinese BITs: An Empirical Study of the Environmental Provisions in Chinese Bits and Its Implications for China's Future BIT-Making" (2015) 18(3) *Journal of International Economic Law* 511.

Chi, Manjiao, and Xi Wang, "The Evolution of ISA Clauses in Chinese IIAs and Its Practical Implications: The Admissibility of Disputes for Investor-State Arbitration" (2015) 16(5–6) *Journal of World Investment & Trade* 869.

Choudhury, Barnali, "Evolution or Devolution? Defining Fair and Equitable Treatment in International Investment Law" (2005) 6 *Journal of World Investment & Trade* 297.

Choukroune, Leila, "Indian and Chinese FDI in Developing Asia: The Standards Battle Beyond Trade" (2015) 7 *Indian Journal of International Economic Law* 89.

Chow, Daniel C. K., "Why China Wants a Bilateral Investment Treaty with the United States" (2015) 33 *Boston University International Law Journal* 101.

Christie, George C., "What Constitutes a Taking of Property under International Law?" (1962) 28 *British Yearbook of International Law* 207.

Claxton, James, Luke Nottage and Ana Ubilava, "Pioneering Mandatory Investor-State Conciliation Before Arbitration in Asia-Pacific Treaties: IA-CEPA and HK-UAE BIT," Kluwer Arbitration Blog, September 5, 2020, http://arbitrationblog.kluwerarbitration.com/2020/09/05/pioneering-mandatory-investor-state-conciliation-before-arbitration-in-asia-pacific-treaties-ia-cepa-and-hk-uae-bit/?print=pdf.

Clegg, Jeremy, and Hinrich Voss, "The New Two-Way Street of Chinese Direct Investment in the European Union" (2016) 5(2) *China-EU Law Journal* 79.

Coe, Jack, Jr., and Noah Rubins, "Regulatory Expropriations and the TECMED Case: Context and Contributions" in Todd Weiler (ed.), *International Investment Law and Arbitration: Leading Cases from the ICSID, NAFTA, Bilateral Investment Treaties and Customary International Law* (Cameron May 2005) 601.

Cohen, Tyler, and David Schneiderman, "The Political Economy of Chinese Bilateral Investment Treaty Policy" (2017) 5(1) *Chinese Journal of Comparative Law* 110.

Correa, Carlos M., "Investment Protection in Bilateral and Free Trade Agreements: Implications for the Granting of Compulsory Licenses" (2004) 26 *Michigan Journal of International Law* 346.

Craig, Paul P., "The Stability, Coordination and Governance Treaty: Principle, Politics and Pragmatism" (2012) 37 *European Law Review* 231.
Crawford, James, *Brownlie's Principles of Public International Law* (Oxford University Press 2012).
Crawford, James, "Treaty and Contract in Investment Arbitration" (2008) 24 *Arbitration International* 351.
Dawidowicz, Martin, "The Effect of the Passage of Time on the Interpretation of Treaties: Some Reflections on Costa Rica v. Nicaragua" (2011) 24 *Leiden Journal of International Law* 201.
De Graaff, Nana, "China Inc. Goes Global: Transnational and National Networks of China's Globalizing Business Elite" (2020) 27(2) *Review of International Political Economy* 208.
De Graaff, Nana, Tobias ten Brink and Inderjeet Parmar, "China's Rise in a Liberal World Order in Transition – Introduction to the Forum" (2020) 27(2) *International Political Review* 191.
Delaume, Georges R., "ICSID and the Banker" (1983) 2 *International Financial Law Review* 9.
Delaume, Georges, "ICSID Arbitration in Practice" (1984) 2 *International Tax and Business Lawyer* 58.
De Luca, Anna, and Angelica Bonfanti, "Investment and Human Rights: Is There an Elephant in the Room?" Columbia FDI Perspectives No. 282, July 23, 2020, http://ccsi.columbia.edu/files/2018/10/No-282-de-Luca-and-Bonfanti-FINAl.pdf.
De Nanteull, Amaud, *International Investment Law* (Edward Elgar 2020).
Deng, Xiaoping, "Emancipating the Mind, Seeking Truth from Facts, Looking Forward Together" in *Selected Works of Deng Xiaoping*, Vol. 2 (Foreign Language Press 1994) 146.
Deng, Xiaoping, "Make a Success of Special Economic Zones and Open More Cities to the Outside World" in *Selected Works of Deng Xiaoping*, Vol. 3 (Foreign Language Press 1994) 61.
Desbordes, Rodolphe, and Vincent Vicard, "Foreign Direct Investment and Bilateral Investment Treaties: An International Political Perspective" (2009) 37 *Journal of Comparative Economics* 372.
Dickie, Mure, "Chinese Takeover Fears Grow," *Financial Times*, August 4, 2006, 6.
Dickson-Smith, Kyle Dylan, "Lessons Learned from the Canada-China FIPA for the US-China BIT and Beyond – Chinese Whispers or Chinese Chequers?" in Julien Chaisse (ed.), *China's International Investment Strategy: Bilateral, Regional, and Global Law and Policy* (Oxford University Press 2019) 138.
Dimopoulos, Angelos, *EU Foreign Investment Law* (Oxford University Press 2011).
Djeffal, Christian, *Static and Evolutive Treaty Interpretation: A Functional Reconstruction* (Cambridge University Press 2016).
Dolzer, Rudolf, "Fair and Equitable Treatment: A Key Standard in Investment Treaties" (2005) 39 *International Law* 87.
Dolzer, Rudolf, "Indirect Expropriation of Alien Property" (1986) 1 *ICSID Review – Foreign Investment Law Journal* 41.
Dolzer, Rudolf, "Indirect Expropriations: New Developments?" (2002) 11 *New York University Environmental Law Journal* 79.
Dolzer, Rudolf, and Christoph Schreuer, *Principles of International Investment Law* (Oxford University Press 2008).
Dolzer, Rudolf, and Christoph Schreuer, *Principles of International Investment Law* (2nd edition, Oxford University Press 2012).
Dolzer, Rudolf, and Margrete Stevens, *Bilateral Investment Treaties* (Martinus Nijhoff 1995).
Donnan, Shawn, "Trump Drops New Restrictions on China Investment," *Financial Times*, June 12, 2018, www.ft.com/content/a819ec8a-79f4-11e8-8e67-1e1a0846c475.
Dorr, Oliver, and Kirsten Schmalenbach (eds.), *Vienna Convention on the Law of Treaties: A Commentary* (Springer 2012).
Douglas, Zachary, *The International Law of Investment Claims* (Cambridge University Press 2009).
Dupuy, Pierre-Marie, "Preconditions to Arbitration and Consent of States to ICSID Jurisdiction" in Meg Kinnear et al. (eds.), *Building International Investment Law: The First 50 Years of ICSID* (Kluwer Law International 2016) 235.
Dyer, Geoff, Sundeep Tucker and Tom Mitchell, "Forbidden Country? How Foreign Deals in China Are Hitting Renewed Resistance," *Financial Times*, August 8, 2006, 11.
Eaker, Lawrence, and Sun Tao, "Chinese Investment in the European Union & National Security Review: Is the EU Legal Regime About to Follow the US Model?" (2014) 9(1) *Frontiers of Law in China* 42.

Egger, Peter, and Valeria Merlo, "BITs Bite: An Anatomy of the Impact of Bilateral Investment Treaties on Multinational Firms" (2012) 114(3) *Scandinavian Journal of Economics* 1240.
Egli, Gabriel, "Don't Get Bit: Addressing ICSID's Inconsistent Application of Most-Favored-Nation Clauses to Dispute Resolution Provisions" (2007) 34 *Pepperdine Law Review* 1045.
El-Hosseny, Farouk, *Civil Society in Investment Treaty Arbitration: Status and Prospects* (Brill Nijhoff 2019) 22.
Elkemann, Catherine, and Oliver C. Ruppel, "Chinese Foreign Direct Investment into Africa in the Context of BRICS and Sino-African Bilateral Investment Treaties" (2015) 13(4) *Richmond Journal of Global Law & Business* 593.
Endicott, Martin, "China and International Investment Law: An Evolving Relationship" in Wenhua Shan (ed.), *China and International Investment Law: Twenty Years of ICSID Membership* (Brill-Nijhoff 2014) 220.
Enright, Michael J., "China's Inward Investment: Approach and Impact" in Julien Chaisse (ed.), *China's International Investment Strategy: Bilateral, Regional, and Global Law and Policy* (Oxford University Press 2019) 28.
European Commission, "Investment in TTIP and Beyond – The Path for Reform," May 6, 2015, http://trade.ec.europa.eu/doclib/docs/2015/may/tradoc_153408.PDF.
Ewert, Insa, "The EU-China Bilateral Investment Agreement: Between High Hopes and Real Challenges" (2016) Security Policy Brief No. 68, www.egmontinstitute.be.
Fauchald, Ole Kristian, "The Legal Reasoning of ICSID Tribunals: An Empirical Analysis" (2008) 19(2) *European Journal of International Law* 301.
Fiezzoni, Silvia Karina, "The Challenge of UNASUR Member Countries to Replace ICSID Arbitration" (2011) 2 *Beijing Law Review* 134.
Finnemore, Martha, and Kathryn Sikkink, "International Norm Dynamics and Political Change" (1998) 52 *International Organization* 887.
Franck, Susan D., "Development and Outcomes of Investment Treaty Arbitration" (2009) 50(2) *Harvard International Law Journal* 435.
Franck, Susan D., "Foreign Direct Investment, Investment Treaty Arbitration, and the Rule of Law" (2007) 19 *Global Business & Development Law Journal* 348.
Franck, Susan D., "Rationalizing Costs in Investment Treaty Arbitration" (2011) 88(4) *Washington University Law Review* 769.
Franck, Susan D., "The Legitimacy Crisis in Investment Treaty Arbitration: Privatizing Public International Law through Inconsistent Decisions" (2005) 73 *Fordham Law Review* 1521.
Franck, Susan D., et al., "The Diversity Challenge: Exploring the 'Invisible College' of International Arbitration" (2015) 53 *Columbia Journal of Transnational Law* 429.
Frankenberg, Gunter, "Critical Comparisons: Re-thinking Comparative Law" (1985) 26 *Harvard International Law Journal* 411.
Friedman, Steven, "Changes to the Constitution May Boost, Not Weaken, South African Property Rights," *The Conversation*, August 3, 2018, https://theconversation.com/changes-to-the-constitution-may-boost-not-weaken-south-african-property-rights-100979.
Froese, Marc D., *Sovereign Rules and the Politics of International Economic Law* (Routledge 2018).
Fu, Hongyu, and Meng Wan, "Convergences and Divergences in the China-EU and the China-US BIT Negotiations" in Yuwen Li, Tong Qi and Cheng Bian (eds.), *China, the EU and International Investment Law: Reforming Investor-State Dispute Settlement* (Routledge 2019) ch. 3.
Gaillard, Emmanuel, and Yas Banifatemi, "The Meaning of 'and' in Article 42 (1), Second Sentence of the ICSID Convention: The Role of International Law in the ICSID Choice of Law Process" (2003) 18 *ICSID Review – Foreign Investment Law Journal* 375.
Gallagher, Norah, "Parallel Proceedings, Res Judicata and Lis Pendens, Problems and Possible Solutions" in Loukas A. Mistelis and Julian D. M. Lew (eds.), *Pervasive Problems in International Arbitration* (Kluwer Law International 2006) 334.
Gallagher, Norah, and Wenhua Shan, *Chinese Investment Treaties: Policies and Practice* (Oxford University Press 2009).
Gann, Pamela B., "The US Bilateral Investment Treaty Program" (1985) 21 *Stanford Journal of International Law* 373.

Gantz, David, "An Appellate Mechanism for Review of Arbitral Decisions in Investor-State Disputes: Prospects and Challenges" (2006) 39 *Vanderbilt Journal of International Law* 39.

Gantz, David, "Challenges for the United States in Negotiating a BIT with China: Reconciling Reciprocal Investment Protection with Policy Concerns" (2015) Arizona Legal Studies Discussion Paper No. 14-03, https://papers.ssrn.com/sol3/papers.cf,?abstract_id=2383919.

Gantz, David A., "Challenges for the United States in Negotiating a BIT with China: Reconciling Reciprocal Investment Protection with Policy Concerns" (2014) 31(2) *Arizona Journal of International & Comparative Law* 204.

Gardiner, Richard K., *Treaty Interpretation* (Oxford University Press 2008).

Garnaut, Joh, "Australia Scores 'Most Favoured Nation' Provisions. in FTA with China," *Sydney Morning Herald*, March 13, 2015.

Gaukrodger, David, and Kathryn Gordon, "Investor-State Dispute Settlement: A Scoping Paper for the Investment Policy Community," OECD Working Papers on International Investment (OECD 2012).

Gavin, Brigid, "Europe Needs a Dynamic International Investment Regime with China," (2012) 47(2) *Intereconomics* 248.

Gazzini, Tarcisio, *Interpretation of International Investment Treaties* (Hart 2016).

George, James P., "Parallel Litigation" (1999) 51(4) *Baylor Law Review* 774.

Gilbert, Gagné, and Jean-Frédéric, Morin, "The Evolving American Policy on Investment Protection: Evidence from Recent FTAs and the 2004 Model BIT" (2006) 9 *Journal of International Economics Law* 357.

Ginsburg, Robert, "Legitimizing Expectations in Arbitration through Political Risk Analysis" in Andrea K. Bjorklund (ed.), *Yearbook on International Investment Law & Policy 2014–2015* (Oxford University Press 2016) 224.

Goettler, Peter, and Daniel Ikenson, "Averting Conflict by Promoting Commerce: The Case for a US-China Investment Treaty" in Tim Wenniges and Walter Lohman (eds.), *Chinese FDI in the EU and the US: Simple Rules for Turbulent Times* (Palgrave MacMillan 2019) 41.

Goldman, Jorge A. Huerta, "Domestic, Regional and Multilateral Investment Liberalization" in Zdenek Drabek and Petros C. Mavroidis (eds.), *Regulations of Foreign Investment: Challenges to International Harmonization* (World Scientific 2013) 87.

Gomez, Katia Fach, "Latin American Approach to International Dispute Resolution," American Society of International Law Meeting in Washington, March 25, 2011, www.academia.edu/830249/latin_American_Approaches-to_International_Dispute_Resolution.

Gómez-Palacio, Ignacio, and Peter Muchlinski, "Admission and Establishment" in Peter Muchlinski, Federico Ortino and Christoph Schreuer (eds.), *The Oxford Handbook of International Investment Law* (Oxford University Press 2008) 229.

Gong, Baihua, "The Change of the Perspective of Rule of Law from China's Free Trade Pilot Zone to Free Trade Port" (2019) 190 *Journal of Political Science and Law* 109.

Goodman, Charity L., "Uncharted Waters: Financial Crisis and Enforcement of ICSID Awards in Argentina" (2007) 28 *University of Pennsylvania Journal of International Economic Law* 449.

Gradziuk, Artur, and Damian Wnukowski, "Rocky Road to a Level Playing Field in EU-China Investment and Trade Relations" (2014) 8(91) Polish Institute of International Affairs Policy Paper.

Griffith, Spencer S., "US-China BIT Negotiations March On: The Road Ahead Is Challenging but Worthwhile" (2009) China Brief 13.

Gupta, Sayantan, "Changing Faces of International Trade: Multilateralism to Regionalism" (2008) 3(4) *Journal of International Commercial Law and Technology* 260.

Hadley, Kate, "Do China's BITs Matter – Assessing the Effect of China's Investment Agreements on Foreign Direct Investment Flows, Investors Rights, and the Rule of Law" (2013) 45(1) *Georgetown Journal of International Law* 255.

Hafner-Burton, Emilie M., "Trading Human Rights: How Preferential Trade Agreements Influence Government Repression" (2005) 59 *International Organization* 593.

Hafner-Burton, Emilie M., and Alexander H. Montgomery, "The Hegemon's Purse: No Economic Peace Between Democracies" (2008) 45 *Journal of Peace Research* 111.

Hafner-Burton, Emilie M., and David G. Victor, "Secrecy in International Investment Arbitration: An Empirical Analysis" (2016) 7 *Journal of International Dispute Settlement* 161.

Hafner-Burton, Emilie M., Zachary C. Steinert-Threlkeld and David G. Victor, "Predictability Versus Flexibility: Secrecy in International Investment Arbitration" (2016) 68(3) *World Politics* 413. doi:10.1017/S004388711600006X.

Hafner-Burton, Emilie M., David G. Victor and Yonatan Lupu, "Political Science Research on International Law: The State of the Field" (2012) 106 *American Journal of International Law* 47.

Hallinan, David, "The EU-China Bilateral Investment Treaty: A Challenging First Test of the EU's Evolving BIT Model" (2016) 5(1–2) *China-EU Law Journal* 31.

Hamanaka, Shintaro, "China-Japan-Korea Trilateral Investment Treaty: Implications for Future Investment Negotiations in Asia" in Julien Chaisse, Tomoko Ishikawa and Sufian Jusoh (eds.), *Asia's Changing International Investment Regime: Sustainability, Regionalization, and Arbitration* (Springer 2017) 121.

Hamanaka, Shintaro, "Dynamics of Investment Negotiations between China and Japan: The China-Japan-Korea Trilateral Investment Treaty and Beyond" (August 2016), Institute of Developing Economics Discussion Paper No. 613, www.ide.go.jp/library/English/Publish/Download/Dp/pdf/613.pdf.

Han, Xiuli, "The China–South Africa Bilateral Investment Treaty: National Rule of Law Versus International Rule of Law" (2017) 24(3) *South African Journal of International Affairs* 269.

Hanotiau, Bernard, "Foreword" in Albert Badia, *Piercing the Veil of State Enterprises in International Arbitration* (Wolters Kluwer 2014) xxi.

Harpaz, Marcia Don, "China's Coherence in International Economic Governance" (2016) 21 *Journal of Chinese Political Science* 123.

He, Fan, and Bijun Wang, "Chinese Interests in the Global Investment Regime" (2014) 7(1) *China Economic Journal* 4.

Hepburn, Jarrod, *Domestic Law in International Investment Arbitration* (Oxford University Press 2017).

Higgins, Rosalyn, "The Taking of Property by the State: Recent Developments in International Law" in *Academie de Droit International, 176 Recueil des Cours. Collected Courses of the Hague Academy of International Law, 1982-III* (M. Nijhoff 1983) 271.

Higgins, Rosalyn, "Time and the Law: International Perspectives on an Old Problem" 46 *International & Comparative Law Quarterly* (1997) 501.

Hindelang, Steffen, and Markus Krajewski, "Towards a More Comprehensive Approach in International Investment Law" in Steffen Hindelang and Markus Krajewski (eds.), *Shifting Paradigms in International Investment Law: More Balanced, Less Isolated, Increasingly Diversified* (Oxford University Press 2016) 2.

Hirsch, Moshe, "International Tribunals as Agents of Harmonization" in Zdenek Drabek and Petros C. Mavroidis (eds.), *Regulations of Foreign Investment: Challenges to International Harmonization* (World Scientific 2013) 342.

Hobér, Kai, "Res Judicata and Lis Pendens in International Arbitration" (2013) 366 *Recueil de courses* 311.

Hoffmann, Anne K., "Indirect Expropriation" in August Reinisch (ed.), *Standards of Investment Protection* (Oxford University Press 2008) 156.

Hofmann, Rainer, Stephan W. Schill and Christian J. Tams (eds.), *Preferential Trade and Investment Agreements: From Recalibration to Reintegration* (Nomos 2013).

Hong, Guang, "Scope of Arbitration in Chinese BITs: Policies & Implications" (2009) University of Miami, https://works.bepress.com/guanghong/1/.

Horn, Norbert, "Arbitration and the Protection of Foreign Investment: Concepts and Means" in Norbert Horn and Stefan Kroll (eds.), *Arbitrating Foreign Disputes* (Kluwer Law International 2004) 1.

Hsieh, Pasha L., "The China-Australia Free Trade Agreement: A 21st-Century Model by Colin B. Picker, Heng Wang, and Weihuan Zhou (eds), Oxford: Hart Publishing, 2018. ISBN 978 1 509 91538, 363pp." (2018) 21(4) *Journal of International Economic Law* 923.

Hu, Jiaxiang, "FTZs, Can They Initiate a New Round of Reforms in China?" (2016) 59 *Boletim Ciencias Economicas* 9.

Hu, Weinian, and Jacques Pelkmans, "China-EU Leadership in Globalization: Ambition and Capacity," CEPS Policy Insights No. 2017/18, May 2017.

Huang, Jie (Jeanne), "Procedural Models to Upgrade BITs: China's Experience" (2018) 31(1) *Leiden Journal of International Law* 93.

Huang, Jie, "Challenges and Solutions for the China-US BIT Negotiations: Insights from the Recent Development of FTZs in China" (2015) 18 *Journal of International Economic Law* 307.

ICSID, Documents Concerning the Origin and Formulation of the Convention (1968).

International Law Commission, Yearbook of the ILC, Vol. II (1996).

Jadhav, Pravin, "Determinants of Foreign Direct Investment in BRICS Economies: Analysis of Economic, Institutional and Political Factor" (2012) 37 *Procedia-Social and Behavioral Sciences* 5.

Jansen, Marion, Joost Pauwelyn and Theresa Carpenter, *The Use of Economics in International Trade and Investment Disputes* (Cambridge University Press 2017).

Jean, Ho, *State Responsibility for Breaches of Investment Contracts* (Cambridge University Press 2018).

Jemielniak, Joanna, Laura Nielsen and Henrik Palmer Olsen, *Establishing Judicial Authority in International Economic Law* (Cambridge University Press 2016).

Jennings, Robert and Arthur Watts KCMG QC (eds.), *Oppenheim's International Law* (9th edition, Longman 1992).

Jiang, Zemin, "Highly Holding the Great Banner of Deng Xiaoping Theory and Pushing the Construction of Socialism with Chinese Characteristics into the 21st Century" in *Selected Works of Jiang Zemin*, Vol. 2 (Foreign Language Press 2006) 27.

Jiang, Zemin, "Open Strategy for the Implementation of 'Introduction' and 'Going Global'" in *Selected Works of Jiang Zemin*, Vol. 2 (Foreign Language Press 2006) 91.

John, Shijian Mo, "The Dilemma of Applying Bilateral Investment Treaties of China to Hong Kong and Macao: Challenge Raised by Sanum Investments to China" (2018) 33(1) *ICSID Review – Foreign Investment Law Journal* 125.

John, Taylor St., *The Rise of Investor-State Arbitration: Politics, Law, and Unintended Consequences* (Oxford University Press 2018).

Jonas, David S., and Thomas N. Saunders, "The Object and Purpose of a Treaty: Three Interpretive Methods" (2010) 43(3) *Vanderbilt Journal of Transnational Law* 565.

Jones, Lee, "Does China's Belt and Road Initiative Challenge the Liberal, Rules-Based Order?" (2019) *Fudan Journal of the Humanities and Social Sciences*, DOI: 10.1007/s40647-019-00252-8.

Jung, Heon Joo, and Eun Mi Kim, "International Treaties and Foreign Direct Investment: An Empirical Analysis of Effects of Bilateral Investment Treaties on South Korea's FDI" (2020) 25(3) *Journal of the Asia Pacific Economy* 402.

Kao, Chi-Chung, "Alternative Access to Investor-State Arbitration for Taiwanese Corporate Investors against China via Treaty Shopping" (2015) 23(2) *Asia Pacific Law Review* 121.

Karamanian, Susan, "International Decision, Compania de Aguas del Aconquija S.A. & Vivendi Universal S.A. v Argentine Republic" (2011) 105 *American Journal of International Law* 553.

Karton, Joshua, "Beyond the 'Harmonious Confucian': International Commercial Arbitration and the Impact of Chinese Cultural Values" in Chang-fa Lo et al. (eds.), *Legal Thoughts between the East and the West in the Multilevel Legal Order: Liber Amicorum in Honour of Professor Herbert Han-pao Ma* (Springer 2016) 519.

Kaufmann, Daniel, Aart Kraay and Massimo Mastruzzi, "Governance Matters VIII: Aggregate and Individual Governance Indicators 1996-2008" (June 2009) World Bank Policy Research Working Paper WPS 4978.

Kaufmann-Kohler, Gabriella, "Interpretive Powers of the Free Trade Commission and the Rule of Law" in Emmanuel Gaillard and Frédéric Bachand, *Fifteen Years of NAFTA Chapter 11 Arbitration* (JurisNet LLC 2011) 190.

Kawashima, Shin, "Japan's Painful Choice on RCEP," *The Diplomat*, August 3, 2020, https://thediplomat.com/2020/08/japans-painful-choice-on-rcep/.

Kawharu, Amokura, and Luke Nottage, "Models for Investment Treaties in the Asia-Pacific Region: An Underview" (2017) 34(3) *Arizona Journal of International & Comparative Law* 525.

Kelley, Judith, "Assessing the Complex Evolution of Norms: The Rise of International Election Monitoring" (2008) 62 *International Organization* 221.

Kidane, Won, "China and India's Differing Investment Treaty and Dispute Settlement Experiences and Implications for Africa" (2017) 49 *Loyola University Chicago Law Journal* 405.

Kidane, Won, "China's Bilateral Investment Treaties with African States in Comparative Context" (2016) 49(1) *Cornell International Law Journal* 141.

Kiely, Ray, *The Clash of Globalisations: Neo-liberalism, the Third Way and Anti-Globalization* (Brill 2005).

Kinsella, N. Stephan, and Noah D. Rubins, *International Investment, Political Risk and Dispute Resolution* (Oceana 2005).

Kläger, Roland, "Revising Treatment Standards – Fair and Equitable Treatment in Light of Sustainable Development" in Steffen Hindelang and Markus Krajewski (eds.), *Shifting Paradigms in International Investment Law* (Oxford University Press 2016) 67.

Koh, Harold Hongju, "Internationalization through Socialization" (2005) 54 *Duke Law Journal* 975.

Kohl, Tristan, "The Belt and Road Initiative's Effect on Supply-Chain Trade: Evidence from Structural Gravity Equations" (2019) 12 *Cambridge Journal of Regions, Economy and Society* 77.

Kong, Qingjiang, "Bilateral Investment Treaties: The Chinese Approach and Practice" in K. Sik, Miyoshi Masahiro, M. Pinto and S. Subedi (eds.), *Asian Yearbook of International Law 1998/1999* (Martinus Nijhoff 2003).

Kong, Qingjiang, "Towards WTO Compliance: China's Foreign Investment Regime in Transition" (2002) 3 *Journal of World Investment* 859.

Kong, Qingjiang, and Yilin Wang, "Transparency Standards in International Investment Agreement Negotiations: A Chinese Lawyer's Perspective on the UNCITRAL Rules" (2015) 1(1) *China and WTO Review* 7.

Kotera, Akira, "Regulatory Transparency" in Peter Muchlinski et al. (eds.), *The Oxford Handbook of International Investment Law* (Oxford University Press 2008) 617.

Koven, Vance R., "Expropriation and the 'Jurisprudence' of OPIC" (1981) 22 *Harvard International Law Journal* 269.

Kronby, Matthew, "Canada-China Investment Treaty: Evidence Doesn't Support Doomsayers," *The Globe and Mail*, October 26, 2012, www.theglobeandmail.com/opinion/canada-china-investment-treaty-evidence-doesnt-support-doomsayers/article4665002/.

Ku, Julian, "The Enforcement of ICSID Awards in the People's Republic of China" (2013) 6 *Contemporary Asia Arbitration Journal* 31.

Kueh, Y. Y., "Foreign Investment and Economic Change in China" (1992) 131 *China Quarterly* 637.

Kurkela, Matti, "Due Process in Arbitration: A Finnish Perspective" (2004) 21(2) *Journal of International Arbitration* 221.

Kurtz, Jürgen, and Luke Nottage, "Investment Treaty Arbitration 'Down Under': Policy and Politics in Australia" (2015) 30(2) *ICSID Review* 465.

Lauterpacht, Elihuand, and Daniel Bethlehem, "The Scope and Content of the Principle of Non-refoulement: Opinion" in Erika Feller, Volker Türk and Frances Nicholson (eds.), *Refugee Protection in International Law: UNHCR's Global Consultations on International Protection* (Cambridge University Press 2003) 104.

Lavranos, Nikos, "Beyond USMCA: ISDS à la carte," Kluwer Arbitration Blog, October 8, 2018, http://arbitrationblog.kluwerarbitration.com/2018/10/08/beyond-usmca-isds-la-carte/?doing_wp_cron=1591771908.0552899837493896484375.

Lawder, David, and Karen Freifeld, "Exclusive: U.S. Commerce's Ross Eyes Anti-China 'Poison Pill' for New Trade Deals," Reuters, October 6, 2018, www.reuters.com/article/us-usa-trade-ross-exclusive/exclusive-u-s-commerces-ross-eyes-anti-china-poison-pill-for-new-trade-deals-idUSKCN1MF2HJ.

Lazo, Rodrigo Polanco, "The No of Tokyo Revisited: Or How Developed Countries Learned to Start Worrying and Love the Calvo Doctrine" (2015) 30 *ICSID Review – Foreign Investment Law Journal* 172.

Lestsas, George, "Internationalism and the Interpretation of the ECHR" in Panos Merkouris, Malgosia Fitzmaurice and Olufemi Elias (eds.), *Treaty Interpretation and the Vienna Convention on the Law of Treaties: 30 Years On* (Martinus Nijhoff/Brill 2010) 266.

Levander, Samuel, "Resolving 'Dynamic Interpretation': An Empirical Analysis of the UNCITRAL Rules on Transparency" (2014) 52 *Columbia Journal of Transnational Law* 506.

Levashova, Yulia, *The Right of States to Regulate in International Investment Law: The Search for Balance between Public Interest and Fair and Equitable Treatment* (Wolters Kluwer 2019).

Li, Wangqiang, "Chinese Foreign Investment Laws: A Review from the Perspective of Policy-Oriented Jurisprudence" (2011) 19(1) *Asia Pacific Law Review* 35.

Li, Yuwen, and Cheng Bian, "A New Dimension of Foreign Investment Law in China: Evolution and Impacts of the National Security Review System" (2016) 24 *Asia Pacific Law Review* 149.

Lieberthal, Kenneth, and Michael Oksenberg, *Policy Making in China: Leaders, Structures, and Processes* (Princeton University Press 1988).

Lillich, Richard B., and Burns H. Weston, "Lump Sum Agreements: Their Contribution to the Law of International Claims" (1988) 82 *American Journal of International Law* 69.

Lin, Tsai-Yu, "Compulsory Licenses for Access to Medicines, Expropriation and Investor-State Arbitration under Bilateral Investment Agreements – Are There Issues Beyond the TRIPS Agreement?" (2009) 40 *International Review of Intellectual Property Law* 152.

Linarelli, John, Margot E. Salomon and M. Sornarajah, *The Misery of International Law: Confrontations with Injustice in the Global Economy* (Oxford University Press 2018).

Lippert, Barbara, and Volker Perthes (eds.), "Strategic Rivalry between United States and China: Causes, Trajectories, and Implications for Europe," German Institute for International and Security Affairs, SWP Research Paper, April 2020, www.swp-berlin.org/fileadmin/contents/products/research_papers/2020RP04_China_USA.pdf.

Liu, Meichen, "The New Chinese Foreign Investment Law and Its Implication on Foreign Investors" (2018) 38 *Northwestern Journal of International Law and Business* 285.

Lo, Chang-fa, Nigel Li and Tsai-Yu Lin (eds.), *Legal Thoughts between the East and the West in the Multilevel Legal Order – A Liber Amicorum in Honour of Professor Herbert Han-Pao Ma* (Springer 2016).

Lowe, Vaughan, "Regulation or Expropriation?" (2002) 55 *Current Legal Problems* 447.

Lui, Gladie, "Shanghai Pilot Free Trade Zone: Shaping of China's Future Foreign Investment Environment" (2014) 40 *Journal of International Taxation* 31.

Magnarelli, Martina, *Privity of Contract in International Investment Arbitration: Original Sin or Useful Tool?* (Wolters Kluwer 2020).

Magnarelli, Martina, "The Unresolved Conundrum of Contract-Based and Treaty-Based Claims: An Extra Element of Contention: Privity of Contract and Forum Selection Clauses in Investment Contracts" (2016) 1 *European Investment Law and Arbitration Review* 85.

Mahdev, Mohan, "Asian Perspective on Investment Agreements and Arbitration: An Evolving Marcottage" in Andrea K. Bjorklund (ed.), *Yearbook on International Investment Law & Policy 2014–2015* (Oxford University Press 2016) 338.

Malmstrom, Cecilia, "Investments in TTIP and Beyond – Towards an International Investment Court," May 5, 2015, http://trade.ec.europa.eu/doclib/docs/2015/may/tradoc_153408.PDF.

Manciaux, Sébastien, "The Notion of Investment: New Controversies" (2008) 9 *Journal of World Investment & Trade* 443.

Marisi, Flavia, *Environmental Interests in Investment Arbitration: Challenges and Directions* (Wolters Kluwer 2020).

Markert, Lars, "Arbitration under China's Investment Treaties: Does It Really Work?" (2012) 5(2) *Contemporary Asia Arbitration Journal* 205.

Martinez, Sebastian Green, "Case Comment: Ping An Life Insurance Company of China, Limited and Ping An Insurance (Group) Company of China, Limited v. Kingdom of Belgium – A Jurisdictional Black Hole Between Two BITs?" (2015) *Transnational Dispute Management*.

Martinez-Fraga, Pedro J., and C. Ryan Reetz, *Public Purpose in International Law: Rethinking Regulatory Sovereignty in the Global Era* (Cambridge University Press 2015).

McDougal, Myres S., "The International Law Commission's Draft Articles upon Interpretation: Textuality Reviews" (1967) 43(3) *American Journal of Translational Law* 992.

McLachlan, Campbell, Laurence Shore and Matthew Weiniger, *International Investment Arbitration: Substantive Principles* (Oxford University Press 2007).

McNamara, Timothy S., "The China-Canada BIT, Its Shortcomings, and the Risks for Chinese Investors" (2019) 10 *Beijing Law Review* 287.

McRae, Donald, "The World Trade Organization and International Investment Law: Converging Systems – Can the Case for Convergence Be Made?" (2014) 9 *Jerusalem Review of Legal Studies* 13.

Merkouris, Panos, *Article 31(3)(c) VCLT and the Principle of Systemic Integration: Normative Shadows in Plato's Cave* (Brill Nijhoff 2015).

Mertha, Andrew, "'Fragmented Authoritarianism 2.0': Political Pluralization in the Chinese Policy Process" (2009) 200 *China Quarterly* 995.

Meunier, Sophie, "Divide and Conquer? China and the Cacophony of Foreign Investment Rules in the EU" (2014) 21(7) *Journal of European Public Policy* 996.

Milner, Helen V., "Introduction: The Global Economy, FDI, and the Regime for Investment" (2014) 66 *World Politics* 1.

Mitchell, Andrew D., and Tania Voon, "Senior Editor's Preface" in Jarrod Hepburn (ed.), *Domestic Law in International Investment Arbitration* (Oxford University Press 2017) vii.

Mitchell, Andrew D., David Heaton and Caroline Henckels, *Non-discrimination and the Role of Regulatory Purpose in International Trade and Investment Law* (Edward Elgar 2016).

Mitrovic, Dragana, "The Belt and Road: China's Ambitious Initiative" (2016) 59 *China International Studies* 76.

Monique, Sasson, *Substantive Law in Investment Treaty Arbitration: The Unsettled Relationship between International Law and Municipal Law* (2nd edition, Kluwer Law International 2017).

Moran, Theodore H., "Foreign Acquisitions and National Security: What Are Genuine Threats? What Are Implausible Worries? A Framework for OECD Countries, and Beyond" in Zdenek Drabek and Petros C. Mavroidis (eds.), *Regulations of Foreign Investment: Challenges to International Harmonization* (World Scientific 2013) 371.

Mouyal, Lone Wandahl, *International Investment Law and the Right to Regulate* (Routledge 2016).

Mwanza, Rosemary, "Chinese Foreign Direct Investment and Human Rights in Kenya: A Mutually Affirming Relationship" (2016) 2 *Strathmore Law Journal* 133.

Narlikar, Amrita, *Poverty Narratives and Power Paradoxes in International Trade Negotiations and Beyond* (Cambridge University Press 2020).

Naughton, Barry, *State Capitalism, Institutional Adaption, and the Chinese Miracle* (Cambridge University Press 2015).

Newcombe, Andrew, "The Boundaries of Regulatory Expropriation in International Law" (2005) *ICSID Review – Foreign Investment Law Journal* 8.

Newcombe, Andrew, "The Use of General Exceptions in IIAs: Increasing Legitimacy or Uncertainty" in Armand De Mestral and C. Lévesque (eds.), *Improving International Investment Agreements* (Routledge 2012) ch. 15.

Newcombe, Andrew, and Lluis Paradell, *Law and Practice of Investment Treaties* (Kluwer Law International 2009).

Ning, Hongling, and Qi Tong, "A Chinese Perspective on the Investment Court System in the Context of Negotiating EU-China BIT" (2018) 11 *Tsinghua China Law Review* 91.

Nottage, Luke, "Investor-State Arbitration Policy and Practice in Australia," CIGI Investor-State Arbitration Series Paper No. 6, June 2016.

Nottage, Luke, and Miles, Kate, "'Back to the Future' for Investor-State Arbitrations: Revising Rules in Australia and Japan for Public Interests" (2009) 26(1) *Journal of International Arbitration* 25.

Odumosu, Ibironke T., "The Law and Politics of Engaging Resistance in Investment Dispute Settlement" (2007) 26 *Penn State International Law Review* 251.

Ofodile, Uche Ewelukwa, "Africa-China Bilateral Investment Treaties: A Critique" (2013) 35 *Michigan Journal of International Law* 131.

Ohmae, Kenichi, *The End of the Nation State: The Rise of Regional Economies* (The Free Press 1995).

Oppenheim, L., *Oppenheim's International Law, Volume 1 Peace*, edited by Sir Robert Jennings QC and Sir Arthur Watts KCMG QC (9th edition, Oxford University Press 2008).

Ortino, Federico, "Public Services, Investment Liberalization and Protection" in Zdenek Drabek and Petros C. Mavroidis (eds.), *Regulations of Foreign Investment: Challenges to International Harmonization* (World Scientific 2013) 415.

Pan, Xiaoming, "China's FTA Strategy," *The Diplomat*, June 1, 2014, https://thediplomat.com/2014/06/chinas-fta-strategy/.

Paparinskis, Martins, "MFN Clauses and International Dispute Settlement: Moving Beyond Maffezini and Plama?" (2011) *ICSID Review – Foreign Investment Law Journal* 14.

Parra, Antonio R., "Provisions on the Settlement of Investment Disputes in Modern Investment Laws, Bilateral Investment Treaties and Multilateral Instruments on Investment" (1997) 12 *ICSID Review – Foreign Investment Law Journal* 334.

Pathirana, Dilini, "Rising China and Global Investment Governance: An Overview of Prospects and Challenges" (2018) 4(2) *Chinese Journal of Global Governance* 122.

Patrick, Griffin, "CFIUS in the Age of Chinese Investment" (2017) 85 *Fordham Law Review* 1757.

Paulsson, Jan, *Denial of Justice in International Law* (Cambridge University Press 2005).

Pauwely, Joost, and Manfred Elsig, "The Politics of Treaty Interpretation: Variations and Explanations across International Tribunals" in Jeffrey L. Dunoff and Mark A. Pollack (eds.), *Interdisciplinary Perspectives on International Law and International Relations: The State of the Art* (Cambridge University Press 2012) 450.

Peat, Daniel, *Comparative Reasoning in International Courts and Tribunals* (Cambridge University Press 2019).

Peerenboom, Randall, *China's Long March Toward Rule of Law* (Cambridge University Press 2002).

Peled, Hadas, and Marcia don Harpaz, "Innovation as a Catalyst in the China-Israel Investment Relationship: The China-Israel Bit (2009) and the Prospective FTA" in Julie Chaisse (ed.), *China's International Investment Strategy: Bilateral, Regional, and Global Law and Policy* (Oxford University Press 2019) 142.

Petersen, Neils, "The International Court of Justice and the Judicial Politics of Identifying Customary International Law" (2017) 28(2) *European Journal of International Law* 357.

Petersmann, Ernst Ulrich, *Multilevel Constitutionalism for Multilevel Governance of Public Goods: Methodology Problems in International Law* (Hart 2017).

Petsche, Markus A., "The Fork in the Road Revisited: An Attempt to Overcome the Clash between Formalistic and Pragmatic Approaches" (2019) 18 *Washington University Global Studies Law Review* 391.

Picker, Colin B., Heng Wang and Weihuan Zhou (eds.), *The China-Australia Free Trade Agreement: A 21st-Century Model* (Hart 2018).

Pietrowski, Robert, "Evidence in International Arbitration" (2006) 22(3) *Arbitration International* 373.

Pinard, Laurie A., "United States Policy Regarding Nationalization of American Investments: The People's Republic of China's Nationalization Decree of 1950" (1984) 14 *California Western International Law Journal* 148.

Polanco, Rodrigo, *The Return of the Home State to Investor-State Disputes: Bringing Back Diplomatic Protection?* (Cambridge University Press 2019).

Porterfield, Matthew C., "Exhaustion of Local Remedies in Investor-State Dispute Settlement: An Idea Whose Time Has Come?" (2015) 41 *Yale Journal of International Law Online*, https://ssrn.com/abstract=2735036.

Potter, Pitman B., "Foreign Investment Law in the People's Republic of China: Dilemmas of State Control" (1995) *China Quarterly* 155.

Poulsen, Lauge N. Skovgaard, Jonathan Bonnitcha and Jason Webb Yackee, "Analytical Framework for Assessing Costs and Benefits of Investment Protection Treaties" (LSE Enterprise 2013) www.italaw.com/sites/default/files/archive/Analytical-framework-for-assessment-costs-and-benefits-of-investment-protection.pdf.

Prislan, Vid, "Non-investment Obligations in Investment Treaty Arbitration: Towards a Greater Role for States?" in Freya Baetens (ed.), *Investment Law within International Law: Integrationist Perspectives* (Cambridge University Press 2016) 450.

Puig, Sergio, and Gregory Shaffer, "Imperfect Alternatives: Institutional Choice and the Reform of Investment Law" (2018) 112(3) *American Journal of International Law* 361.

Puig, Sergio, and Anton Strezhnev, "The David Effect and ISDS" (2017) 28 *European Journal of International Law* 731.

Pye, Lucian, *The Mandarin and the Cadre* (University of Michigan Press 1988).

Qi, Tong, "How Exactly Does China Consent to Investor-State Arbitration: On the First ICSID Case Against China" (2012) 5(2) *Contemporary Asia Arbitration Journal* 265.

Qian, Hongdao, Sonia Azam and Hamid Mukhtar, "China Pakistan Economic Corridor: Legal Injunctions and Protection of Chinese Investment in Pakistan Under OBOR Initiative" (2018) 6(2) *European Journal Research in Social Sciences* 29.

Radi, Yannick, "The Application of the Most-Favoured-Nation Clause to the Dispute Settlement Provisions of Bilateral Investment Treaties: Domesticating the 'Trojan Horse'" (2007) 18 *European Journal of International Law* 757.

Rajput, Aniruddha, "Safeguarding India's Regulatory Autonomy: Analysis of the New Model Bilateral Investment Treaty" (2017) 14(3) *Manchester Journal of International Economic Law* 279.

Ratner, Steven R., "Global Investment Rules as a Site for Moral Inquiry" (2019) 27(1) *Journal of Political Philosophy* 107.

Raustiala, Kal, and Robert O. Keohane, "Toward a Post-Kyoto Climate Change Architecture: A Political Analysis" (2008) 5 *Journal of Scholarly Perspectives* 50.

Reinisch, August, "The Issues Raised by Parallel Proceedings and Possible Solution" in Michael Waibel, Asha Kaushal, Kyo-Liz Chung and Claire Balchin (eds.), *The Backlash Against Investment Arbitration: Perceptions and Reality* (Kluwer Law International 2010) 115.

Reinisch, August, "The Scope of Investor-State Dispute Settlement in International Investment Agreements" (2013) 21 *Asia Pacific Law Review* 3.

Reinman, W. Michael, "The Regime for Lacunae in the ICSID: Choice of Law Provision and the Question of Its Threshold" (2000) 15 *Foreign Investment Law Journal* 362.

Reisman, W. Michael, and Robert D. Sloane, "Indirect Expropriation and Its Valuation in the BIT Generation" (2004) 74 *British Year Book of International Law* 115.

Ren, Qing, "Ping An v. Belgium: Temporal Jurisdiction of Successive BITs" (2016) 31(1) *ICSID Review* 129.

Repousis, Odysseas G., "On Territoriality and International Investment Law: Applying China's Investment Treaties to Hong Kong and Macao" (2015) 37(1) *Michigan Journal of International Law* 113.

Reuter, Paul, *Introduction to the Law of Treaties* (Kegan Paul International 1995).

Ripinsky, Sergey, "Global Economic Crisis and the Danger of Protectionism: Does International Law Help?" (2009) 1 *Amsterdam Law Forum* 3.

Roberts, Anthea, "Clash of Paradigms: Actors and Analogies Shaping the Investment Treaty System" (2013) 107 *American Journal of International Law* 45.

Roberts, Anthea, "Incremental, Systemic and Paradigmatic Reform of Investor-State Arbitration" (2018) 113(2) *American Journal of International Law* 410.

Roberts, Anthea, "Power and Persuasion in Investment Treaty Interpretation: The Dual Role of States" (2010) 104 *American Journal of International Law* 179.

Robin, Patricia M., "The BIT Won't Bite: The American Bilateral Investment Treaty Program" (1984) 33 *American University Law Review* 941.

Roland, Kläger, "Revising Treatment Standards – Fair and Equitable Treatment in Light of Sustainable Development" in Steffen Hindelang and Markus Krajewski (eds.), *Shifting Paradigms in International Investment Law: More Balanced, Less Isolated, Increasingly Diversified* (Oxford University Press 2016) 66.

Rolland, Nadège, "China's Belt and Road Initiative: Underwhelming or Game-Changer?" (2017) 40(1) *Washington Quarterly* 133.

Rolland, Sonia E., "The Return of State Remedies in Investor-State Dispute Settlement: Trends in Developing Countries" (2017) 49 *Loyola University Chicago Law Journal* 387.

Rooney, Kim M., "ICSID and BIT Arbitrations and China" (2007) 24 *Journal of International Arbitration* 689.

Rosenne, Shabtai, and Yaël Ronen, *The Law and Practice of the International Court, 1920–2005* (4th edition, Martinus Nijhoff 2006).

Sacerdoti, Giorgio, "Is USMCA Really 'the New Gold Standard' of Investment Protection?" Columbia FDI Perspectives No. 281, June 29, 2020, http://ccsi.columbia.edu/files/2018/No-281-FINAL-Sacerdoti.pdf.

Salacuse, Jeswald W., *The Law of Investment Treaties* (Oxford University Press 2010).

Sampson, Michael, "The Evolution of China's Regional Trade Agreements: Power Dynamics and the Future of the Asia-Pacific" (2019) *Pacific Review* 1. DOI: 10.1080/09512748.2019.1660397.

Sanchez, Guillermo J. Garcia, "The Footprint of the Chinese Petro-dragon: The Future of Investment Law in Transboundary Resources" (2020) 94 *Tulane Law Review* 313.

Saunders, Matthew, "Bilateral Investment Treaties Oil the Wheels of Commerce: An Increase in BITs Is Helping to Encourage and Protect International Business," IBA in the News, June 23, 2004.

Sauvant, Karl P., *Appeals Mechanism in International Investment Disputes* (Oxford University Press 2008).

Sauvant, Karl P., "Emerging Markets and the International Investment Law and Policy Regime" in Robert Grosse and Klaus E. Meyer (eds.), *The Oxford Handbook of Management in Emerging Markets* (Oxford University Press 2019) 151.

Sauvant, Karl P., "Introduction, International Investment Law and Policy 2008–2009: Overview" in Karl P. Sauvant (ed.), *Yearbook on International Investment Law & Policy 2008–2009* (Oxford University Press 2009) 6.

Sauvant, Karl P., and Huiping Chen, "A China-US Bilateral Investment Treaty: A Template for a Multilateral Framework for Investment?" (2013) 5(1) *Transnational Corporations Review* 1.

Sauvant, Karl P., and Victor Zitian Chen, "China's Regulatory Framework for Outbound Foreign Direct Investment" (2014) 7(1) *China Economic Journal* 141.

Schemers, Henry G., and Niels M. Blokker, *International Institutional Law* (3rd revised edition, Martinus Nijhoff 1995).

Schill, Stephan W., "Fair and Equitable Treatment under Investment Treaties as an Embodiment of the Rule of Law" (2006) IILJ Working Paper 06.

Schill, Stephan W., "In Defense of International Investment Law" (2016) 7 *European Journal of International Economic Law* 309.

Schill, Stephen W., "Multilateralizing Investment Treaties through Most-Favored-Nation Clauses" (2009) 27(2) *Berkeley Journal of International Law* 496.

Schill, Stephan W., "Tearing Down the Great Wall: The New Generation Investment Treaties of the People's Republic of China" (2007) 15(1) *Cardozo Journal of International and Comparative Law* 73.

Schill, Stephan W., *The Multilateralization of International Investment Law* (Cambridge University Press 2009).

Schill, Stephan W., Christian J. Tams and Rainer Hofmann, *International Investment Law and History* (Edward Elgar 2018).

Schneiderman, David, *Constitutionalizing Economic Globalization: Investment Rules and Democracy's Promise* (Cambridge University Press 2008).

Schneiderman, David, "Investment Rules and the New Constitutionalism" (2000) 25(3) *Law & Social Inquiry* 757.

Schott, Jeffrey J., and Cathleen Cimino, "The China-Japan-Korea Trilateral Investment Agreement: Implications for US Policy and the US-China Bilateral Investment Treaty" in Peterson Institute for International Economics, *Toward a US-China Investment Treaty* (PIIE Briefing 15-1, February 2015).

Schott, Jeffrey J., Euijin Jung and Cathleen Cimino-Isaacs, "An Assessment of the Korea-China Free Trade Agreement," Peterson Institute for International Economics Policy Brief Number PB15-24, December 2015.

Schreuer, Christoph, "Fair and Equitable Treatment in Arbitral Practice" (2005) 6 *Journal of World Investment & Trade* 357.

Schreuer, Christoph, "Jurisdiction and Applicable Law in Investment Treaty Application" (2014) 1(1) *McGill Journal of Dispute Resolution* 1.

Schreuer, Christoph H., "The Concept of Expropriation under the ETC and Other Investment Protection Treaties" (2005) 5(2) *Transnational Dispute Management* 28.

Schwindt, Constance J., "Interpreting the United Nation Charter: From Treaty to World Constitution" (2000) *UC Davis Journal of International Law and Policy* 198.

Seid, Sherif H., *Global Regulation of Foreign Direct Investment* (Routledge 2017).

Shaffer, Gregory C., and Tom Ginsburg, "The Empirical Turn in International Legal Scholarship" (2012) 106(1) *American Journal of International Law* 1.

Shan, Wenhua, "From North-South Divide to Private-Public Debate: Revival of the Calvo Doctrine and the Changing Landscape in International Investment Law" (2006–2007) 27 *Northwestern Journal of International Law and Business* 631.

Shan, Wenhua, "Is Calvo Dead?" (2007) 55 *American Journal of Comparative Law* 123.

Shan, Wenhua, and Jinyuan Su (eds.), *China and International Investment Law: Twenty Years of ICSID Membership* (Brill Nijhoff 2015).

Shan, Wenhua, and Lu Wang, "The China-EU BIT: The Emerging 'Global BIT 2.0'" (2014) Columbia FDI Perspectives No. 128.

Shan, Wenhua, and Nora Gallagher, *Chinese Investment Treaties, Policies and Practice* (Oxford University Press 2009).

Shan, Wenhua, and Peng Wang, "A Matrix Analytical Framework for Investment Disputes and Their Settlement" (2018) *Foreign Investment Law – ICSID Review* 1.

Shan, Wenhua, Norah Gallagher and Sheng Zhang, "National Treatment for Foreign Investment in China: A Changing Landscape" (2012) 27 *ICSID Review* 120.

Shany, Yuval, "Contract Claims vs. Treaty Claims: Mapping Conflicts Between ICSID Decisions on Multi-sourced Investment Claims" (2005) 99 *American Journal of International Law* 835.

Shany, Yuval, *The Competing Jurisdictions of International Courts and Tribunals* (Oxford University Press 2003).

Sharma, Ajay, "A Comparative Analysis of the Chinese and Indian FDI Regimes" (2015) 15(1) *Chicago-Kent Journal of International and Comparative Law* 1.

Shaun, Breslin, "How China Changed the Global Economy and the Global Economy Changed China: Thirty Years of Investment and Trade" (n.d.), https://warwick.ac.uk/fac/soc/pais/people/breslin/research/30years.pdf.

Shaw, Malcolm N., *International Law* (5th edition, Cambridge University Press 2003).

Sheargold, Elizabeth, "The USMCA/CUSMA/T-MEC's Entry Into Force: USMCA as Part of a Global Trend Away from ISDS – An Australian Perspective," Kluwer Arbitration Blog, June 27, 2020, http://arbitrationblog.kluwerarbitration.com/2020/06/27/the-usmca-cusma-t-mecs-entry-into-force-usmca-as-part-of-a-global-trend-away-from-isds-an-australian-perspective/.

Shen Wei, "'A Tale of Three Zones' – Promises and Pitfalls of Three Financial Experimental Zones in China" (2014) *Banking Law Journal* 399.

Shen Wei, "Beyond the Scope of 'Investor' and 'Investment': Who Can Make an Arbitration Claim Under a Chinese BIT? – Some Implications from a Recent ICSID Case" (2010) 6(2) *Asian International Arbitration Journal* 164.

Shen Wei, "Expropriation in Transition: Evolving Chinese Investment Treaty Practices in Local and Global Contexts" (2015) 28 *Leiden Journal of International Law* 579.

Shen Wei, "Is SAFE Safe Now? – Foreign Exchange Regulatory Control over Chinese Outbound and Inbound Investments and a Political Economy Interpretation of Policies" (2010) 11(2) *Journal of World Investment & Trade*.

Shen Wei, "Is This a Great Leap Forward? A Comparative Review of the Investor-State Arbitration Clause in the ASEAN-China Investment Treaty: From BIT Jurisprudential and Practical Perspectives" (2010) 27 *Journal of International Arbitration* 379.

Shen Wei, "The Good, the Bad, or the Ugly? A Critique of the Decision on Jurisdiction and Competence in Tza Yap Shum v. The Republic of Peru" (2011) 10(1) *Chinese Journal of International Law* 55.

Shen Wei, and Matthias Vanhullebusch, "Where Is the Alchemy? The Experiment of the Shanghai Free Trade Zone in Freeing the Foreign Investment Regime in China" (2015) 16(2) *European Business Organization Law Review* 321.

Shetty, Nish, "Treaty Protection for Indian Investments Abroad: The Changed Landscape," May 29, 2019, www.cliffordchance.com/briefings/2019/05/treaty_protectionforindianinvestmentsabroad.html (accessed April 5, 2021).

Shields, Justin, "Smart Machines and Smarter Policy: Foreign Investment Regulation, National Security, and Technology Transfer in the Age of Artificial Intelligence" (2018) 51 *John Marshall Law Review* 279.

Shihata, Ibrahim F. I., "Towards a Greater Depoliticization of Investment Disputes: The Roles of ICSID and MIGA" (1986) 1 *ICSID Review – Foreign Investment Law Journal* 1.

Shirk, Susan L., *The Political Logic of Economic Reform in China* (University of California Press 1993).

Simmons, Beth A., "Bargaining over BITs, Arbitrating Awards: The Regime for Protection and Promote of International Investment" (2014) 66(1) *World Politics* 12.

Sinclair, Ian M., *The Vienna Convention on the Law of Treaties* (Manchester University Press 1973).

Sinclair, Ian, *The Vienna Convention on the Law of Treaties* (2nd edition, Manchester University Press 1984).

Song, Guoyou, and Wen Jin Yuan, "China's Free Trade Agreement Strategies" (2012) 35(4) *Washington Quarterly* 107.

Sorel, Jean-Marc, and Valerie Boré Eveno, "Article 31" in Olivier Corten and Pierre Klein (eds.), *The Vienna Convention on the Law of Treaties: A Commentary* (Oxford University Press 2011) 804.

Sornarajah, M., *Resistance and Change in the International Law on Foreign Investment* (Cambridge University Press 2015).

Sornarajah, M., "The Case Against a Regime on International Investment Law" in Leion Trakman and Nicola Ranieri (eds.), *Regionalism in International Investment Law* (Oxford University Press 2013) 496.

Sornarajah, M., *The International Law on Foreign Investment* (2nd edition, Cambridge University Press 2004).

Sornarajah, M., *The International Law on Foreign Investment* (3rd edition, Cambridge University Press 2010).

Sornarajah, M., *The Settlement of Foreign Investment Disputes* (Kluwer Law International 2000).

Stifter, Lukas, and August Reinisch, "Expropriation in the Light of the UNCTAD Investment Policy Framework for Sustainable Development" in Steffen Hindelang and Markus Krajewski (eds.), *Shifting Paradigms in International Investment Law: More Balanced, Less Isolated, Increasingly Diversified* (Oxford University Press 2016) 86.

Strange, Susan, *The Retreat of the State: The Diffusion of Power in the World Economy* (Cambridge University Press 1996).

Suda, Ryan, "The Effect of Bilateral Investment Treaties on Human Rights Enforcement and Realization" in Oliver de Schutter (ed.), *Transnational Corporations and Human Rights* (Hart 2006) 80.

Surya, P. Subedi, *International Investment Law: Reconciling Policy and Principle* (Hart 2008).

Swenson, Deborah L., "Why Do Developing Countries Sign BITs?" (2005) 12 *UC Davis Law Review* 131.

Taylor, St. John, *The Rise of Investor-State Arbitration: Politics, Law, and Unintended Consequences* (Oxford University Press 2018).

Thirlway, Hugh, "The Law and Procedure of International Court of Justice 1960–1989" (1991) *British Yearbook of International Law* 16.

Titi, Catharine, "Are Investment Tribunals Adjudicating Political Disputes? Some Reflections on the Repoliticization of Investment Disputes and (New) Forms of Diplomatic Protection" (2015) 32 *Journal of International Arbitration* 261.

Tobin, Jennifer, and Marc L. Busch, "A BIT Is Better than a Lot: Bilateral Investment Treaties and Preferential Trade Agreements" (2010) 62(1) *World Politics* 1.

Trakman, Leon E., "Bilateral Trade and Investment Agreements" in Leon E. Trakman and Nicola W. Ranieri (eds.), *Regionalism in International Investment Law* (Oxford University Press 2013) 85.

Trakman, Leon E., "China's Regulation of Foreign Direct Investment" in Julien Chaisse, Tomoko Ishikawa and Sufian Jusoh (eds.), *Asia's Changing International Investment Regime: Sustainability, Regionalization and Arbitration* (Springer 2017).

Trakman, Leon, "Geopolitics, China and Investor–State Arbitration" in Lisa Toohey, Colin B. Picker and Jonathan Greenacre (eds.), *China in the International Economic Order: New Directions and Changing Paradigms* (Cambridge University Press 2015).

Trakman, Leon E., "The ICSID under Siege" (2013) 45 *Cornell International Law Journal* 603.

Trakman, Leon E., and Nicola W. Ranieri (eds.), *Regionalism in International Investment Law* (Oxford University Press 2013).

Trakman, Leon E., and Kunal Sharma, "Jumping Back and Forth between Domestic Courts and ISDS: Mixed Signals from the Asia-Pacific Region" in Steffen Hindelang and Markus Krajewski (eds.), *Shifting Paradigms in International Investment Law: More Balanced, Less Isolated, Increasingly Diversified* (Oxford University Press 2016) 336.

UNCTAD, IIA Issue Note No. 3: Reform of the IIA Regime: Four Paths of Action and a Way Forward (2014).

UNCTAD, World Investment Report 2016 – Investor Nationality: Policy Challenges (2016).

Vadi, Valentina, *Analogies in International Investment Law and Arbitration* (Cambridge University Press 2016).

Van Damme, Isabelle, *Treaty Interpretation by the WTO Appellate Body* (Oxford University Press 2009).

Vandevelde, Kenneth J., "A Brief History of International Investment Agreements" (2005) 12 *UC Davis Journal of International Law and Policy* 157.

Vandevelde, Kenneth J., "US Bilateral Investment Treaties: The Second Wave" (1993) 14 *Michigan Journal of International Law* 621.

Vandevelde, Kenneth J., *United States Investment Treaties: Policy and Practice* (Kluwer 1992).

Vandevelde, Kenneth J., *U.S. International Investment Agreements* (Oxford University Press 2009).

Van Harten, Gus, "Arbitrator Behaviour in Asymmetrical Adjudication: An Empirical Study of Investment Treaty Arbitration" (2012) 50 *Osgoode Hall Law Journal* 211.

Van Harten, Gus, "Contributions and Limitations of Empirical Research on Independence and Impartiality in International Investment Arbitration" (2011) 1(4) *Oñati Socio-Legal Series* 1.

Van Harten, Gus, *Investment Treaty Arbitration and Public Law* (Oxford University Press 2007).

Van Harten, Gus, "The Canada-China FIPPA: Its Uniqueness and Non-reciprocity" (2014) 51 *Canadian Yearbook of International Law* 3055.

Van Harten, Gus, and Martin Loughlin, "Investment Treaty Arbitration as a Species of Global Administrative Law" (2006) 17(1) *European Journal of International Law* 121.

Van Harten, Gus, and Pavel Malysheuski, "Who Has Benefited Financially from Investment Treaty Arbitration? An Evaluation of the Size and Wealth of Claimants" (2016) 12 Osgoode Legal Studies Research Paper No. 14.

Vanhonnaeker, Lukas, *Shareholders' Claims for Reflective Loss in International Investment Law* (Cambridge University Press 2020).

Van Houtte, H., *The Law of International Trade* (2nd edition, Sweet & Maxwell 2002).

Villiger, Mark E., *Commentary on the 1969 Vienna Convention on the Law of Treaties* (Martinus Nijhoff 2012).

Wälde, Thomas, and Abba Kolo, "Environmental Regulation, Investment Protection and 'Regulatory Taking' in International Law" (2001) 50 *International and Comparative Law Quarterly* 811.

Wälde, Thomas W., "Interpreting Investment Treaties: Experiences and Examples" in Christina Binder, Ursula Kriebaum, August Reinisch and Stephan Wittich (eds.), *International Investment Law for the 21st Century: Essays in Honour of Christoph Schreuer* (Oxford University Press 2009) 724.

Waldock, Humphrey, Sixth Report on the Law of Treaties, *Yearbook of International Law Commission* (1996) Vol. I (Part Two).

Wallace, Cynthia Day, *The Multinational Enterprise and Legal Control: Host State Sovereignty in an Era of Economic Globalization* (Kluwer Law 2002).

Wang, Guiguo, "China's FTAs: Legal Characteristics and Implications" (2011) 105(3) *Chinese Journal of International Law* 493.

Wang, Guiguo, "China's Practice in International Investment Law: From Participation to Leadership in the World Economy" (2009) 34 *Yale Journal of International Law* 575.

Wang, Guiguo, "Chinese Mechanisms for Resolving Investor-State Disputes" (2011) 1(1) *Jindal Journal of International Affairs* 204.

Wang, Guiguo, "International Investment Law: An Appraisal from the Perspective of the New Haven School of International Law" (2016) 18(1) *Asia Pacific Law Review* 19.

Wang, Guiguo, *International Investment Law: A Chinese Perspective* (Routledge 2014).

Wang, Guiguo, and He Xiaoli, "Mediation and International Investment: A Chinese Perspective" (2012) 65(1) *Maine Law Review* 216.

Wang, Heng, "Paradigm Shift in Investment Rules of China's Free Trade Agreements? The Present and Future," August 14, 2018, https://lki.lk/blog/paradigm-shift-in-investment-rules-of-chinas-free-trade-agreements-the-present-and-future/.

Wang, Heng, "The Differences between China's Recent FTA and the TPP: A Case Study of the China-Korea FTA" in Julien Chaisse, Henry Gao and Chang-fa Lo (eds.), *Paradigm Shift in International Economic Law Rule-Making* (Springer 2017) 299.

Wang, Heng, "The RCEP and Its Investment Rules: Learning from Past Chinese FTAs" (2017) 3(2) *Chinese Journal of Global Governance* 160.

Wang, Huiyao, and Lu Miao, "China's Outbound Investment: Trends and Challenges in the Globalization of Chinese Enterprises" in Julien Chaisse (ed.), *China's International Investment Strategy: Bilateral, Regional, and Global Law and Policy* (Oxford University Press 2019) 47.

Wang, Orange, "China, Japan, South Korea Agree to Continue Push for Free-Trade Deal Despite Ongoing Tensions Across Region," *South China Morning Post*, December 22, 2019, www.scmp.com/economy/china-economy/article/3043166/china-japan-and-south-korea-agree-continue-push-free-trade.

Wang, Tingliang, "Western Misperceptions and China's Approach to International Investment Law" (2019) 17(1) *Santa Clara Journal of International Law* 1.

Wang, Wei, "Super-National Treatment: A Misconception or a Creation with Chinese Characteristics?" (2010) 5 *Frontiers of Law in China* 376.

Wang, Yong, "China's Domestic WTO Debate" (2000) 27 *China Business Review* 54.

Weeramenatry, J. Romesh, *Treaty Interpretation in Investment Arbitration* (Oxford University Press 2012).

Wei, Dan, "Bilateral Investment Treaties: An Empirical Analysis of the Practices of Brazil and China" (2010) 33(3) *European Journal of Law and Economics* 663.

Weinhardt, Clara, and Tobias ten Brink, "Varieties of Contestation: China's Rise and the Liberal Trade Order" (2020) 27(2) *Review of International Political Economy* 258.

Wellhausen, Rachel L., "International Investment Law and Foreign Direct Reinvestment" (2019) 73 *International Organization* 839.

Willems, Jane Y., "The Settlement of Investor State Disputes and China New Developments on ICSID Jurisdiction" (2011) 8(1) *South Carolina Journal of International Law and Business* 21.

Wilson, Claire, "Protecting Chinese Investment under the Investor-State Dispute Settlement Regime: A Review in Light of Ping An v. Belgium" in Julien Chaisse (ed.), *China's International Investment Strategies: Bilateral, Regional and Global Law and Policy* (Oxford University Press 2019) 474.

Witkowska, Janina, "The Attitude of the European Union and China towards Foreign Direct Investment: Implications for Bilateral Relations" (2019) 22(3) *Comparative Economic Research* 83.

Wu, Kane, "Investment Deal Expected to Bolster European Dealmaking in China," Reuters, January 7, 2021, www.reuters.com/article/us-china-eu-investments/investment-deal-expected-to-bolster-european-dealmaking-in-china-idUSKBN29C0LE (accessed March 24, 2021).

Xi, Jinping, "Decisive Victory to Build a Well-Off Society in an All-Round Way to Win a Great Victory in Socialism with Chinese Characteristics in the New Era – Report at the 19th National Congress of the Communist Party of China," *People's Daily*, October 28, 2017.

Xi, Jinping, "Opening, Creating, Prospering, Innovating, Leading the Future – Keynote Speech at the Opening Ceremony of the 2018 Annual Meeting of the Boao Forum for Asia," *People's Daily*, April 11, 2018.

Xiao, Jun, "How Can a Prospective China-EU BIT Contribute to Sustainable Investment: In Light of the UNCTAD Investment Policy Framework for Sustainable Development" (2015) 8(6) *Journal of World Energy Law & Business* 521.

Xiao, Lin, *National Test: System Design of China (Shanghai) Pilot Free Trade Zone* (Springer 2016).

Yackee, Jason Webb, "Conceptual Difficulties in the Empirical Study of Bilateral Investment Treaties" (2008) 33(2) *Brooklyn Journal of International Law* 405.

Yackee, Jason Webb, "Sacrificing Sovereignty: Bilateral Investment Treaties, International Arbitration, and the Quest for Capital," http://ssrn.com/abstract=950567.

Yang, Songling, "China's Administrative Mode for Foreign Investment: From Positive List to Negative List" (2015) 33 *Singapore Law Review* 93.

Yannaca-Small, Katia, "Practical Proceedings" in Peter Muchlinski, Federico Ortino and Christoph Schreuer (eds.), *The Oxford Handbook of International Investment Law* (Oxford University Press 2008) 1026.

Ye, Yu-ting, "Towards a Balanced and Liberal Chinese Bilateral Investment Treaty Regime in the Context of One Belt One Road" (2018) 41(1) *Houston Journal of International Law* 107.

Yin, Wei, "Challenges, Issues in China-EU Investment Agreement and the Implication on China's Domestic Reform" (2018) 26(2) *Asia Pacific Law Review* 170.

Yu, Peter K., "The Incremental Development of the ASEAN-China Strategic Partnership for Intellectual Property" in Christoph Antons and Michael Blakeney (eds.), *Intellectual Property in Southeast Asia* (Edward Elgar 2020).

Zarra, Giovanni, "The Issue of Incoherence in Investment Arbitration: Is There Need for a Systemic Reform?" (2018) 17(2) *Chinese Journal of International Law* 127.

Zeitler, Helge Elisabeth, "The Guarantee of 'Full Protection and Security' in Investment Treaties Regarding Harm Caused by Private Actors" (2006) *Stockholm International Arbitration Review*.

Zeng, Jianghan, "Chinese Views of Global Economic Governance" (2019) 40(3) *Journal of Third World Quarterly* 578.

Zhang, Anran, "Letter to the Journal: The Standing of Chinese State-Owned Enterprises in Investor-State Arbitration: The First Two Cases" (2018) 17 *Chinese Journal of International Law* 1147.

Zhang, Guangliang, "China's Stance on Free Trade-Related Intellectual Property: A View in the Context of the China-Japan-Korea FTA Negotiations" (2016) 24(1) *Asia Pacific Law Review* 36.

Zhang, Jianhong, and He Xinming, "Economic Nationalism and Foreign Acquisition Completion: The Case of China" (2014) 23 *International Business Review* 212.

Zhang, Sheng, "The Status of State-Owned Enterprises in ISDS from a Chinese Perspective" in Yuwen Li et al. (eds.), *China, the EU and International Investment Law: Reforming Investor-State Dispute Settlement* (Routledge 2019) 198.

Zhang, Shu, "Developing China's Investor-State Arbitration Clause Discussions in the Context of the 'Belt and Road' Initiative" in Wenhua Shan, Kimmo Nuotio and Kangle Zhang (eds.), *Normative Readings of the Belt and Road Initiative* (Springer 2018) 147.

Zhang, Yuqing, "The Case of China" in Michael Moser (ed.), *Investor-State Arbitration – Lessons for Asia* (Juris 2008) 156.

Zhao, Chunlei, "Investor-State Mediation in a China-EU Bilateral Investment Treaty: Talking about Being in the Right Place at the Right Time" (2018) 17(1) *Chinese Journal of International Law* 111.

Zheng, Xinli, *China's 40 Years of Economic Reform and Development: How the Miracle Was Created* (The Commercial Press/Springer Nature 2018).

Zhou, Weihuan, "Chinese Investment in Australia: A Critical Analysis of the China-Australia Free Trade Agreement" (2017) 18 *Melbourne Journal of International Law* 407.

Zhu, Keliang, and Roy Prosterman, "Land Reform Efforts in China," *China Business Review*, October 1, 2012, www.chinabusinessreview.com/land-reform-efforts-in-china/.

Zhu, Wenlong, "The National Treatment Clause in Chinese Bilateral Investment Treaties" (2014) 4 *WTO & China* 72.

Index

For EU product safety concerns, contact us at Calle de José Abascal, 56–1°,
28003 Madrid, Spain or eugpsr@cambridge.org.

www.ingramcontent.com/pod-product-compliance
Lightning Source LLC
LaVergne TN
LVHW081939200926
848484LV00009B/2472

* 9 7 8 1 1 0 8 4 9 0 9 8 6 *